Windows® 95

UNLEASHED

Ed Tiley, et al.

SAMS
PUBLISHING

201 West 103rd Street
Indianapolis, IN 46290

For Maurice L'Heureaux who convinced me I could write for a living. Someday I'll get even with him for that.

Copyright © 1995 by Sams Publishing

FIRST EDITION

All rights reserved. No part of this book shall be reproduced, stored in a retrieval system, or transmitted by any means, electronic, mechanical, photocopying, recording, or otherwise, without written permission from the publisher. No patent liability is assumed with respect to the use of the information contained herein. Although every precaution has been taken in the preparation of this book, the publisher and author assume no responsibility for errors or omissions. Neither is any liability assumed for damages resulting from the use of the information contained herein. For information, address Sams Publishing, 201 W. 103rd St., Indianapolis, IN 46290.

International Standard Book Number: 0-672-30474-0

Library of Congress Catalog Card Number: 94-061093

98 97 96 95   4   3   2   1

Interpretation of the printing code: the rightmost double-digit number is the year of the book's printing; the rightmost single-digit, the number of the book's printing. For example, a printing code of 95-1 shows that the first printing of the book occurred in 1995.

Composed in AGaramond and MCPdigital by Macmillan Computer Publishing

Printed in the United States of America

All terms mentioned in this book that are known to be trademarks or service marks have been appropriately capitalized. Sams Publishing cannot attest to the accuracy of this information. Use of a term in this book should not be regarded as affecting the validity of any trademark or service mark.

Publisher and President:	*Richard K. Swadley*
Acquisitions Manager:	*Greg Wiegand*
Development Manager:	*Dean Miller*
Managing Editor:	*Cindy Morrow*
Marketing Manager:	*Gregg Bushyeager*
Assistant Marketing Manager:	*Michelle Milner*

Acquisitions Editors
Grace Buechlein, Greg Croy

Development Editors
L. Angelique Brittingham, Phillip W. Paxton

Software Development Specialist
Steve Flatt, Timothy Wilson

Production Editor
Mary Inderstrodt

Copy Editors
Susan Christophersen, Ryan Rader, Marla Reece, Tonya Simpson

Technical Reviewers
Robert Bogue, David Geller, Ewan Grantham, Greg Guntle, John Mueller

Editorial Coordinator
Bill Whitmer

Technical Edit Coordinator
Lynette Quinn

Formatter
Frank Sinclair

Editorial Assistant
Sharon Cox

Cover Designer
Tim Amrhein

Book Designer
Alyssa Yesh

Production Team Supervisor
Brad Chinn

Page Layout
Charlotte Clapp, Mary Ann Cosby, Terrie Deemer, Ayanna Lacey, Steph Mineart, Casey Price, Tina Trettin, Susan Van Ness, Mark Walchle, Angelina Ward, Dennis Wesner, Michelle Worthington

Proofreading
Georgiana Briggs, Michael Brumitt, Michael Dietsch, Mike Henry, Brian-Kent Proffitt, Kevin Laseau, Paula Lowell, Donna Martin, SA Springer

Indexer
Gregg Eldred

Part III Exploiting Windows 95

Part VII Overview of Windows Programming Issues

Acknowledgments

Thanks to Melva Webb for her support these long months.

Thanks to Benita Kenn and Theresa Pulido of Creative Labs (408) 428-6600 for supplying multimedia support.

Thanks to Andy Thomas and all the other hardworking folks at Microsoft for information and support, and for putting up with me.

Thanks to the folks, especially Richard Roccanti, at Tallahassee SuperNet (904) 671-5929 for Internet guidance.

There were a hundred and one other folks who helped bring this book to you in one way or another, notably all the folks behind the scenes at Sams, the folks at Waterside Productions, Al Wimberly, Midge Watson, Greg Croy, Jet Halligan, Nino Violante, George Sommer, Ken Harley, Ian Butterworth, Melanie Rose, Shirley Jones, and everyone else.

About the Authors

Ed Tiley

Ed Tiley lives and teaches in Tallahassee, FL. He is the author of more than a dozen books, all published by Que and Sams. His books include *Windows Stuff Microsoft Forgot, Windows After Hours, Tricks of the Windows 3.1 Masters, Using MS-DOS 6.22, Special Edition,* and *Using Clipper.* He also makes limited appearances on the lecture circuit, writes freelance magazine articles, develops custom software for business and government, and plays a mean game of 8-ball.

John Mueller

John Mueller is a freelance author and technical editor. He has writing in his blood, having produced 25 books and almost 200 articles to date. The topics range from networking to artificial intelligence, and from database management to heads-down programming. Some of his current books include *CA-Clipper Programmers Guide* and a Windows 95 advanced user tutorial. His technical editing skills have helped more than 22 authors refine the content of their manuscripts. In addition to book projects, John has provided technical editing services to both *Data Based Advisor* and *Coast Compute* magazines.

When John isn't working at the computer, you can find him in his workshop. He's an avid woodworker and candle maker. On any given afternoon you can find him working at a lathe or putting the finishing touches on a bookcase. One of his favorite projects is making candle sticks and the candles to go with them. You can reach John on CompuServe at 71570,641.

Paul Cassel

Paul Cassel has been designing and programming database systems on a wide range of computers for more than 15 years. His clients have included Intel Corp., Los Alamos National Laboratory, Pacific Gas & Electric, federal and state governments, the Navajo Nation, and many small to medium-sized companies. He currently travels nationally giving lectures, teaching seminars, and consulting about numerous small computer topics. He's also co-host of the weekly Egghead Software Hour radio show.

He lives in the high desert of New Mexico with his wife, whom he exasperates, and his two children, whom he confuses.

David Geller

David Geller is a principal engineer at Traveling Software, Inc. Located just outside of Seattle, WA, David designs and develops software for Windows 95 and Traveling Software's award-winning product LapLink for Windows. David is also an avid fan of the Internet and the author of the popular HTML authoring tool WEB Wizard: The Duke of URL. He is also developing a WEB server for the Windows 95 and NT platforms. David can be reached by e-mail at davidg@arta.com or through his Web page at http://www.halcyon.com/geller/.

Ewan Grantham

Ewan Grantham has been involved with microcomputers since the days of the Apple II and the TRS-80. He now runs an independent consulting firm that specializes in the design and creation of electronic documentation and multimedia presentations. In addition to his programming and writing, he teaches classes on related subjects and publishes an "almost monthly" electronic magazine, *RADIUS*. Ewan can be reached on CompuServe at 74123,2232.

Robert Griswold

Robert M. Griswold, Jr. received his BS in Electrical and Electronic Engineering from California State University, Sacramento, in December 1990. Robert worked as a SCSI hardware and software design engineer following graduation, joining Adaptec, of Milpitas, CA, in September 1992. As a Product Support Specialist for Adaptec, Robert led the Hardware Team in the diagnosis of end-user issues involving SCSI, RLL, and ESDI controllers. As an Applications Engineer for Adaptec's SPO and PI units, Robert supported Adaptec's engineering role in Plug and Play, and Windows 95, while supporting important customer designs with Adaptec's low-cost SCSI solutions. Currently, as Customer Engineering Manager, Robert directs Applications Engineers in the solution of large and small customer design needs with Adaptec's high-performance SCSI and RAID products.

Bill Montemer

Bill Montemer is a multimedia producer and programmer. He specializes in new media in all its forms, and is currently developing software engines and children's educational content to drive them.

Timothy Parker

Timothy Parker, Ph.D., is an internationally recognized writer, programmer, and systems analyst who has published more than 500 articles in various computer industry magazines. He is a contributing author to *The Internet Unleashed* (published by Sams) and has written two highly successful books on UNIX. Currently he is the president of Timothy Parker Consulting, Inc. (TPCI), a consulting company with a wide range of services, including technical writing, programming, systems analysis, and training.

Judy Petersen

Judy Petersen provides software training and support through a retail facility for the more popular word processing and spreadsheet programs. In her own business, Judy is a computer software consultant and trainer for businesses and individuals in the Tallahassee area and provides abstracts of title for firms performing environmental audits of real property throughout the Southeastern U. S. She has been a coauthor of Que's *Using WordPerfect 6, Using WordPerfect 6 for Windows, Using WordPerfect 6.1 for Windows, Using PC Tools 8.0* and *Using PC Tools for Windows, Killer WordPerfect 6 Utilities, Killer Windows Utilities,* and *Upgrading to Windows 3.1,* as well as revision author for *Que's Computer User's Dictionary,* 5th Edition.

Before she discovered what she wanted to do with her life, she practiced law (and still does when sufficiently tempted), managed a restaurant, was secretary to a university department chairman, and drafted soil profile illustrations for an engineering firm. She would rather spend her time cheering on the FSU Seminoles and puttering in the garden.

Wilfred Smith

Wilfred Smith is co-founder of Smith, Kenner Consulting, specializing in Windows NT and Windows 95 software development, with an emphasis on device drivers. He is based in New Orleans, LA. He can be contacted on CompuServe at 71732,2571.

Ned Snell

Ned Snell is an award-winning computer journalist and author. After a brief career as a teacher, Snell entered the software industry as a documentation and training specialist for several of the world's largest software companies. He then moved into the computer trade magazine business, where he served as staff writer and eventually as editor for several national publications. In 1991, he became a freelancer so he could pursue his dual professions: computer journalist and actor. In the last several years, he has written for international publications such as *Datamation* and *Software Magazine,* and has developed documentation and training materials for diabetes management software. At the same time, he has also acted in regional professional theatres, commercials, and industrial films. Snell is the author of *Souping Up Windows, Curious About the Internet,* and *Navigating the Internet with Windows 95,* all published by Sams. He lives with his wife Nancy Gonzalez, a writer and translator, and their two children in New Jersey.

Van Thurston, Jr.

Van Thurston, Jr. has been a Windows power user since 1986. First drawn to Windows programming by his interest in computer animation, Van began programming in Visual Basic at its release with Version 1.0.

He is the creator of Media BlastOFF!, a shareware multimedia audio, video, and graphics file player for Windows, with registered users all around the world.

Van is an International Check-Caption for a major airline and lives near Atlanta with his wife, Teresa, and sons, Ike and Zachary. His hobbies include playing Chicago-style Blues guitar. Van can be reached on CompuServe at 70774,1232.

Introduction

> **NOTE**
>
> The Microsoft Network information in this book is based on information on Windows 95 made public by Microsoft as of July 1995. Because this information was made public before the release of the product, there might be some differences between the information in this book and the final packaging of Windows 95 as it relates to the Microsoft Network.

When I began to help assemble expert co-authors to write Windows 95 Unleashed, my goal was a book specifically designed for the experienced Windows 3.x user so he or she could get Windows 95 up and humming along in the shortest possible time. You, the reader, will be the ultimate judge of our success when you either tuck this book under your arm and head for the cash register, or put it back on the shelf. Will that be cash or charge?

Who Do We Think You Are?

When you put together a book that has the wide scope of *Windows 95 Unleashed*, you have to remember who you are writing for and make some assumptions about the reader.

Here's who we think you are. You are the office guru, the one everyone comes to with their computer questions because you once had the poor judgment to reveal that you actually know what you're doing with computers and software.

You might be a support person working the company help desk, or a system administrator responsible for your workgroup. You might even be a computer repair technician who needs to fix user's software installation about as often as the hardware needs tending. You're someone who makes above average demands on your system, someone who is always looking for just the right way to smooth some little irritating wrinkle on the system.

In other words, you might have come to town on the turnip truck just yesterday, but you were driving. Each of us authors has tried very hard not to bore experienced users with beginner explanations, while at the same time providing readers the background information needed to understand complex issues.

Between the Covers

Here's a quick peek at what you'll find between the covers of this book. The information in Windows 95 Unleashed is divided into nine parts. Each part contains several chapters that deal with a specific aspect of the overall topic.

Prologue: The prologue provides you with a brief overview of the new features in Windows 95, and how they relate to the evolution of Windows.

Part I. Welcome to Windows 95: Windows 95 is very different from its ancestors. It might take a while to get used to it, but once you do, you'll wonder how you ever got along in any other fashion. In Part I you will learn about the new user interface in Windows 95, the small utility programs, called *applets*, that are included with Windows 95, and about the Plug and Play specification that makes installing add-on hardware in your system easier than ever.

Part II. Installing, Customizing, and Tuning Windows 95: Few things are as frustrating as something that just doesn't work up to its potential. Part II concerns itself with installing Windows 95, customizing Windows 95 to work the way you want to work, and in fine-tuning Windows 95 for the best performance. You'll soon have the beast under control.

Part III. Exploiting Windows 95: This part of the book provides you with a glimpse into the inner workings of Windows 95's architecture so you can reap all the benefits of upgrading to Windows 95. You will learn how applications and hardware are supported, how the Windows 95 Registry tracks your system configuration, how to take Windows 95 on the road with the Mobile Computing components, how to share data between applications, and what to do with that computer you have at home.

Part IV. Windows 95 and Multimedia: Few other innovations have sparked as much interest in the last few years as multimedia. The addition of sound and full motion video to the data stream has presented a whole new computing environment. In Part IV, you will see how to take control of the multimedia capabilities of your system, and put them to work. In this section, you also get your first look at Microsoft Plus!, the add-on package for those Windows 95 users with high-end machines. Plus! wasn't quite finished when we had to go to press, but this chapter gives you a good overview of what Plus! contains.

Part V. Connecting to the Outside World: Communications is the next hot area of computing, and is poised to make the multimedia excitement look tame. In Part V you will see just what all the fuss is about, and why everybody is talking about, and logging onto, commercial online services like CompuServe and Prodigy.

Part VI. Networking with Windows 95: Windows 95's networking features turn the old ideas about what it means to be networked. There is, of course, an entire peer-to-peer network environment included in the box. In addition, there are new network client drivers that let you be connected to more than one network, even more than one kind of network, all at the same time. Part VI gives you the essential information you need to install, optimize, and maintain your network connections.

Part VII. The Consumer's Guide to Windows 95 Programming: *Windows 95 Unleashed* is not a programming book, but experienced users are often confronted with the need to develop or acquire custom software. This section of the book begins by giving you the information you need to know when hiring someone to produce a program for your organization. Other chapters show you how you can automate tasks using the macro languages built into most full-featured software, and show you what some of the most-used programming products look like just in case you want to take a stab at it yourself.

Part VIII. Troubleshooting: Not everything goes right every time. Windows 95 is incredibly reliable, but sometimes hardware and software collide. It is still a computer after all. This part of the book breaks down Windows 95 into its main areas of installation and hardware, application support, multimedia, communications, and networking to provide you with specific examples of what to do when things go wrong.

Epilogue. The Future of Windows: The last part of *Windows 95 Unleashed* is a special section interview with Brad Silverberg, Microsoft's Senior Vice President for the Personal Systems Division. Brad and I have a far-ranging conversation on the future of Windows, Microsoft's plans for the coming years, and the future of computing in general.

In Conclusion

A lot of work, by a lot of people, went into bringing you this book. On behalf of my co-authors and all the folks at Sams, I'd like to say that we hope you find this book to be your most valuable Windows 95 reference. This is your book, so let us know what you think. To report any errors or omissions, or just to send cheers and jeers, please drop me a message on CompuServe at `72007,3455` or `edtiley@supernet.net` if you're on the Internet.

Ed Tiley
August 24, 1995

How Did We Get Here? And What Have We Got?

by Ed Tiley

IN THIS CHAPTER

Just about everything related to computers is moving at breakneck speed. About the only thing that hasn't changed in the last 10 years is the generic printer cable. Printer cables might be the same as they were 10 years ago, but everything they plug into has changed radically—especially the software that we use to make our computers work and play.

To fully appreciate the value of Windows 95, it is perhaps helpful to reflect briefly on that which has come before. Windows 95 wasn't designed in a vacuum, and in this day of increased competition in the operating system market, quick review of the history of the graphical user interface (GUI) may be in order.

Big Brother and the Holding Company

Viewers of the 1984 Super Bowl Game were treated to the premiere showing of the famous commercial that introduced the Macintosh computer. In this commercial a stark portrayal of the world according to Orwell is disrupted by a lone individual who runs into a theater where Big Brother is addressing the masses and shatters the TV screen.

The hero, or terrorist, depending on your viewpoint, became the embodiment of the rugged individualist who would buck the system and opt out of DOS text-based, command-line world in favor of a graphical method of using a computer.

Of course the Macintosh wasn't the world's first graphical interface. Apple's unsuccessful Lisa computer line takes that honor. The folks at Apple Computer relied heavily on research that had been conducted by Xerox Corporation's Palo Alto Research Center.

Bill Gates and the Microsoft folks took many of the same tours as did Jobs, Wozniak, and the Apple corps. Within a year of the Macintosh launch, Microsoft introduced the first version of Windows. It was largely ignored as a poorly conceived "me too" effort mostly because the DOS compatible processors made by Intel lacked the horsepower to perform intense graphical computations efficiently.

Still, Gates and company believed in the future of the graphical user interface, and Windows development kept pace with the available hardware. Finally in 1990 the convergence of the 80386 processor, fast VGA video systems, and other hardware advances helped people sit up and take notice when Windows 3.0 was released.

By the time Windows 3.1 was released in the Spring of 1992, Windows had reached critical mass. In 1994, sales of Windows software outpaced sales of DOS software for the first time. That trend isn't likely to be reversed.

Say what you like about Microsoft, but give them credit for persistence. They continued to fund Windows development even when the future of Windows looked bleak. The future of Windows looks very different 10 years on. Microsoft's newest offering is called Windows 95, and is one of the most anticipated and thoroughly tested pieces of software in history.

Windows 95 is not the first full-blown, 32-bit operating system in history, but by the time 60 million plus users of Windows 3.1 upgrade, it will be the most successful. Microsoft has done a masterful job of giving users just the right blend of what they want, what they need, and what their employers want, too. Windows 95 is both evolution and revolution in the same box, and a touch of controversy, too.

The controversy concerns Windows 95's DOS support. Some folks, even some who should know better, are under the impression that Windows 95 is nothing more than a slick repackaging of DOS and Windows, and that Microsoft's claim that Windows 95 is an operating system is just hype. Yes, there is a copy of DOS that gets loaded at startup. No, Windows 95 doesn't use the services of that copy of DOS when running Windows applications.

When you flip the power button on your computer, the processor, even a Pentium processor, comes to life in real mode—an emulation of the original IBM PC. Since the processor is in real mode anyway, doesn't it make sense to load a copy of real mode DOS before kicking into protected mode—a mode of operation enabled by the architecture of the Intel 80386 and above? Once Windows 95 is loaded, that copy of DOS is used in support of any DOS applications you might run, and when Windows 95 needs information from your real mode CMOS (setup) chip.

Windows is a full-blown operating system, not just a layer over DOS. Still, you can run all your old DOS software, including some things that wouldn't previously run under Windows. And, yes, if you really want one, you can get an honest-to-goodness DOS prompt that has more functionality than DOS 6.22, as well as a special DOS mode that all but removes Windows 95 from memory for those DOS programs that simply refuse to cooperate.

The rest of Windows 95 is the same story. Everything you used to do is supported, but Windows is bigger. The horizon is much farther away, and there is much more room in Windows 95 for communications, networking, managing data, and getting useful things done.

So What is Windows 95?

With the release of Windows 95, Windows becomes a full-fledged operating system. Previous versions of Windows gradually replaced more and more of the DOS operating system until finally Windows 3.1 used DOS only to manage files.

Windows 95 is an advanced operating system that offers support for 32-bit application software, yet still runs 16-bit Windows 3.x applications and old DOS apps. The list of changes and new features in Windows 95 is long. Here is the top-ten list of hot new stuff, direct from the home office in Indianapolis, Indiana:

- **32-bit Operating System:** The first personal computers used 8-bit processors, meaning that the processor could operate on only a byte at a time. The first IBM PC introduced 16-bit processing, which more than doubled the speed because twice the amount of data is moved to the processor in half the number of operations. Since the introduction of the 80386 chip, hardware has been capable of running 32-bit programs, but DOS and Windows have remained 16-bit. OS/2 and some flavors of UNIX offer 32-bit capability but have never been embraced by the masses. Windows 95 is destined to become the first 32-bit operating system to gain near universal commercial acceptance.

■ **Preemptive Multitasking:** Multitasking is the apparent capability of the computer to run more than one program at a time. In truth, a computer that contains only a single processor cannot run more than one program at a time. Multitasking is an optical illusion of sorts. Windows 95 provides a new and more efficient multitasking subsystem that enables 32-bit applications to more effectively work together.

■ **Multithreading:** When you launch an application, the application's programming code is loaded into memory and memory is allocated for the data that application uses. Multithreading is an ingenious technique that enables an application to split the tasks it needs to perform into threads. Each thread is like an independent program in the way it is scheduled for processor time. Also, threads share the same global memory, so the overhead they require is small. The effect is that programs can more efficiently perform both background and foreground activities by delegating tasks to threads.

■ **Built-in Networking:** Every copy of Windows 95 is fully capable of becoming part of a peer-to-peer network, a workgroup. Computers belonging to the workgroup can exchange e-mail, share printers and modems, share disk drives, and share other computer resources. Each copy of Windows 95 is capable of being a *client* (a user of another's resources), a *server* (a giver of resources to others), or a combination of the two.

■ **Multiple Network Connection Support:** The concept behind the Windows 95 networking model is that network resources should be no different to the user than resources within their computer system. In Windows 95 it is possible to be logged onto more than one network server at a time, even if the two networks are totally different. For example, using Windows 95, you might be part of a peer-to-peer workgroup while simultaneously logged into a Novell NetWare server, a Banyan Vines network server, a Windows NT Server domain, and be connected to a dial-in network such as CompuServe or the MS Network, all at the same time.

■ **Plug and Play:** One of the most frustrating things computer users do is to install, or attempt to install, new cards or devices in their systems. Some equipment can quickly become a major hassle to install because of conflict with some other device in the system. A committee of major hardware and software manufacturers has created a new standard called Plug and Play. Windows 95 uses the Plug and Play standard to support automatic installation of new hardware devices by actually doing most of the work for the user.

■ **PCMCIA Support:** Windows 95 supports warm and hot docking of PCMCIA devices. PCMCIA devices can be plugged into and removed from the computer (usually a notebook or laptop computer), and Windows 95 will automatically load and unload drivers as necessary.

■ **Long Filenames:** One of the things that users have always hated about computers is the requirement to truncate filenames into an eight-character name followed by a three-character extension. Under Windows 95, however, the old 8.3 filename system becomes obsolete, as long as your applications can support this new feature. Instead of having to name a letter to your grandmother LTRGRANY.DOC, you can now, under most circumstances use a filename like "A letter to Granny on her 95th birthday." In addition, adherence to Universal Naming Conventions (UNC for short) makes it possible to use network resources more easily and efficiently.

■ **Better Device Support:** In Windows 3.1, Microsoft applied the concept of the Unidriver architecture to printing. Under Windows 95, Unidrivers are also used for video displays and serial communications. In addition, most of the Windows subsystems have been replaced with new 32-bit versions. The new file, printing, video, multimedia, and NetWare connectivity subsystems provide the highest level of performance and standardization of support.

■ **A New User Interface:** Microsoft has done extensive testing to determine what features in a user interface make new users productive quickly while enabling power users to unlock even more of their computing potential. Not since Windows 3.0, when the text-ish MS-DOS Executive gave way to Program Manager, has the Windows GUI undergone such a transformation.

So there you have it, the top ten things about Windows 95 that make it such an improvement over Windows 3.1. The next few pages are dedicated to giving you more details about each of these ten items and how they make your work easier, faster, and more productive. You will also see how the new features form the foundation for all the other new features that didn't make it into the top ten list.

Not Just Another Pretty Face

The first thing you are likely to notice about Windows 95 is that it doesn't look much like Windows 3.1, so perhaps it is best to start here. Of course, every version of Windows has altered and refined the user interface of the previous version. This time around, the changes are both striking and welcome. Of course, if you are one of those people who hates the idea of giving up familiar friends, File Manager and Program Manager are still available in the Windows directory so you can use the new Windows power while retaining the Windows 3.1 look and feel.

6

Windows 95 Unleashed

Windows 95's revamped user interface (See Figure P.1) is the result of a great deal of usability testing and talking to folks who train users for a living. What Microsoft found out was that Windows 3.1 just isn't intuitive enough for new users and not powerful enough for old hands.

FIGURE P.1.

The new Windows interface provides a clean, uncluttered data-centric way of working with a computer.

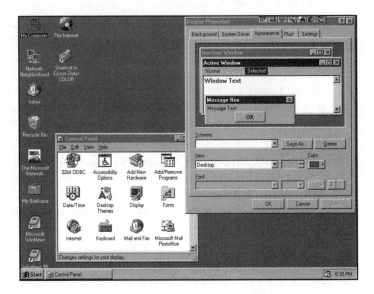

According to the results of their usability testing, Microsoft learned that newcomers to Windows were intimidated. When presented with a myriad of windows and icons, as they were in Windows 3.1, the typical new user had a hard time figuring out where to start.

More than one Windows 3.1 user is going to be reluctant to adjust to the new interface. The knee-jerk reaction is to install the Windows 95 versions of Program Manager and File Manager during Setup. You will do well to resist that temptation.

Almost universally, users who worked with pre-release copies of Windows 95 report how strange it seems to go back to Windows 3.1 when they are forced to work with someone else's machine. Once you catch on to the new user interface, you too will find the Windows 3.1 user interface awkward and limiting when compared to the Windows 95 interface. In two or three days, you will be a convert.

The new Windows 95 user interface is built around an entirely redesigned shell that uses various objects to give you a real working desktop, a taskbar that serves both as program launcher and tray where minimized applications reside, and that supports folders and shortcuts. The sections that follow introduce you to the new features of the Windows 95 Shell.

The New Windows Shell

In Windows, the program that provides the user an interface with the operating system is called the shell. The Windows 2.x shell was called the Executive. The Windows 3.x shell was the Program Manager. In Windows 95, it is just called the Windows Shell, launched using code in SHELL32.DLL. It is the shell that provides the Windows 95 user interface. In other words, it is the shell that launches programs and lets you manage your computer resources.

The conduit that enables users to access the power of the Windows 95 engine is a real working desktop. Under Windows 3.x, the desktop served as a place where minimized applications resided, a place to hang wallpaper, and a place to double-click to bring up the Task Manager. No more.

In Windows 95 the desktop is a real work surface where you can store data files, folders (containers of files), and shortcuts, as well as run programs, create new documents, and more.

Programs, files, folders, and shortcuts (see the section below) all use icons to represent themselves to users. In Windows 95, all of these objects can reside on the desktop where they are instantly accessible. Add the taskbar and you have a self-contained working environment that is easy enough for beginners to use immediately, and powerful enough to satisfy experienced users.

The Taskbar

The taskbar. The Windows 95 taskbar is a tray that has a button marked Start. To launch programs, click the Start button and select an entry in the menus that appear. Many of the entries in the Start menu are controlled by the content of the Start menu folder. You can customize the Start menu to fit the way you want to work.

Applications that are minimized don't get lost the way they sometimes did in Windows 3.x. Instead, they reside on the taskbar, where a single click will restore them to window form, ready to be used.

Microsoft's usability testing discovered that new users find Windows 3.1 intimidating, and often don't know how to begin working with all the icons and windows of Program Manager. Microsoft also knows there are still a lot of new users out there; after all, 60 million out of 5 billion is just a beginning really.

Many of the features of the Windows 95 interface are designed to make new users feel comfortable quickly. For this reason, Windows 95 is very unambiguous about how to begin using the computer. When you first start Windows 95, the taskbar appears with a big button labeled Start. In case that doesn't give you a big enough clue, an arrow labeled "Click Start to Begin" drifts across the taskbar and bounces off the Start button a few times.

When you click the Start button, you get a cascading menu of choices similar to the one shown in Figure P.2. The black arrow to the right of some choices in the Start Menu indicates that there are subchoices to be viewed. Windows 95 uses sticky menus—so all you have to do is move the mouse pointer over an item and its submenu will automatically open. To launch a program or open a document, you only need to click one time on the Start button, and once again to select an item from the cascading menus.

When you select an item from the Start menu, the menu closes, leaving behind only the taskbar. Unlike Program Manager that laid about on the desktop cluttering things up, the Start Menu closes back up. If you like, you can even hide the taskbar from view.

FIGURE P.2.

The Start Menu provides a quick and easy way to get to the documents and programs you use all the time.

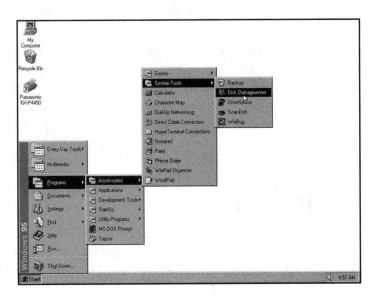

The remainder of the taskbar is occupied by minimized applications. As a visual hint to new users, a simple animation is used to show where the window goes when you minimize, and where it comes from when you restore the window. Experienced users can appreciate the way windows spring to and from the taskbar as "a neat effect."

Folders and Files

At the most technically accurate level, coupled with a DOS view of the world, a folder is a subdirectory on a disk. Philosophically, however, a folder is simply a container that can contain folders, files, and shortcuts. Folders can be placed on the desktop. They can be moved into other folders. They can be cut, copied, and pasted just like blocks of text in a text editor. In short, folders are powerful things.

As you will see in chapters to come, there is a tremendous emphasis on freeing users from the intricacies of file management in Windows 95. The best news is the way Windows 95 expands the old DOS file system. Instead, Windows 95 uses a group of installable file systems (IFS) that make data sources such as hard disks, CD-ROM disks, network server disks, and even online services appear to be just another disk drive full of folders.

One of the tricks to becoming proficient with Windows 95 is to fall in with the concept that any hierarchical data source can be rendered as a collection of folders containing shortcuts, files, or other folders.

Shortcuts

A shortcut is a link file that enables you to place an icon in a folder or on the desktop to point to a program or a document, even a folder. Shortcuts are easily identified visually by the small black arrow added to the bottom left corner of the icon.

One imaginative user has likened a shortcut to a Windows 3.x Program Group icon on steroids. A shortcut can be placed anywhere that a program or document can reside. Shortcuts can be placed on the desktop or in a folder. If you are familiar with Windows 3.1, think of a shortcut as an icon in a Program Manager group. When you double-click the icon, the specified action takes place. The main difference between a shortcut and a PM icon is that shortcuts are individually maintained as link (.LNK) files instead of being grouped together in .GRP files.

Shortcuts can exist for both applications and documents (files) created by those applications. For example, if you have a database file that you work with all the time, you can drag the file's icon onto the desktop or into a folder as a shortcut. From that time on, all you need do is double-click on the shortcut to open the file with the proper application for that type of data. When you no longer need the shortcut, simply delete it without worrying that you are damaging the underlying program or data file.

My Computer and Explorer

By default, the old warhorses File Manager and Program Manager are not part of the Windows 95 user interface. They have been replaced by a single application that has two names and two appearances. EXPLORER.EXE replaces both File Manager and Program Manager for many tasks.

Explorer is capable of producing both a single pane (one window), or a dual pane view of your computer and its resources. Microsoft's usability testing revealed that new users were put off by the complexity of the dual pane File Manager. Apparently they don't understand the relationship between the file tree in the left pane and the contents pane on the right. On the other hand, experienced users find the dual pane File Manager a convenient way of navigating around their hard disk resources.

Microsoft's answer is to expand the view of system resources beyond simple representations of disks, and to create a single browser to replace File Manager that can present the entire computer and its resources to the user. That browser is called both My Computer and the Explorer.

Explorer is a single applet (EXPLORER.EXE) that produces two views of your system and its resources. The My Computer view uses a single pane window that shows you system resources, folders, programs, and documents and can be made to act a lot like a Windows 3.x Program Manager group.

The Explorer view simply adds to the single pane view a second pane containing a hierarchical tree of your system's resources. You use it in much the same way you used File Manager. When you select an item in the tree, its contents are shown in the right-hand pane. You can view resources and folders as groups of icons or as content lists, and double-clicking an item has the expected result of launching a program, opening a document, or moving to another folder.

Figure P.3 shows a side-by-side comparison of Explorer and My Computer. As you can see, they are very similar. Their menu choices are nearly identical, and their toolbars are identical.

FIGURE P.3.

My Computer is easier to use, but the Explorer view is more powerful.

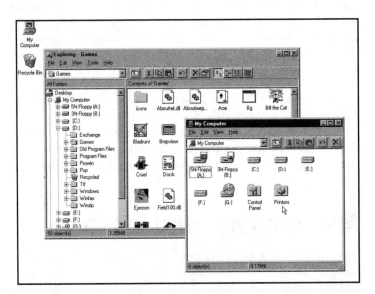

FYI

The four buttons on the right side of the toolbar enable you to choose from four views of your system's resources. From left to right they are large icons, small icons, list, and detail. Large and small icons represent files and folders in a manner similar to Windows 3.1's Program Manager. List and Detail show folder contents in a manner similar to the Windows 3.1 File Manager.

Usability testing convinced Microsoft designers that many users, especially new users, found the double-paned window format of File Manager to be confusing. They simply didn't understand the hierarchical tree depicted in the left pane, or its relationship with the information in the right pane. For these users, Microsoft created My Computer and nailed it to the desktop.

The Explorer, as its name suggests, is intended for more adventurous users who are not intimidated by double pane views of their system. Explorer's interface is very similar to the Windows 3.1 File Manager in that the left pane shows a hierarchical view of your system resources down to the folder level. Clicking a folder in the left pane causes Explorer to display the contents of that folder in the right-hand pane of the Explorer window. Presumably more advanced users will prefer Explorer over My Computer.

Details about the new user interface, My Computer, Explorer, and more can be found in Chapter 1, "The Windows 95 User Interface."

Where is DOS?

With the release of Windows 95, Microsoft enters a new era. Windows 95 is their first full 32-bit operating system intended for mainstream computer systems. Although the Windows 3.1 disk set had the words *operating system* printed on them, purists and pundits would always give you a sarcastic chuckle and a snort. Over the years and the versions, however, Windows has steadily replaced DOS functionality with code of its own. Windows 3.1 essentially uses DOS only as a platform to launch its own files, and as a manager for the file system. To the true computer puritan, this reliance on DOS leaves you one fry short of a Happy Meal when it comes to calling yourself an operating system.

Windows 95 changes that forever. The only time you will ever need DOS is when you need to install Windows 95. After that, your DOS disks can go into the disk box for good. Windows 95 uses only the copy of DOS it loads at startup to support old, real-mode program code. Windows 95 itself is a 32-bit, multitasking, multithreading, protected-mode, long filename-supporting juggernaut of an operating system. Some of the core features of the Windows 95 architecture are good enough to make the top-ten list. The enabling technology is the 32-bit nature of Windows 95.

32-Bit Application Software Support

The core of the Windows operating system has been rewritten and recompiled using Microsoft C (interestingly, not C++) and assembly language code. This new Windows core uses the capabilities of the Intel 386/486/Pentium family of processors to run programs using the full 32-bit data path that has yet to be exploited on all but a few computer systems. According to Microsoft, if your system is a 386 with four or more megs of memory, Windows 95 will give you performance equal to or better than Windows 3.1.

Any software that has been written using the Win32 API (Application Programming Interface) will take full advantage of Windows new core. To be precise, there are still some parts of Windows 95 that are written in 16-bit code, but they are there mostly to provide backward compatibility with Windows 3.x applications. There are also some 16-bit functions still used because moving them to 32-bit code would not have provided any increase in performance as a trade-off to the larger size of 32-bit code.

A perhaps unexpected advantage of the 32-bit architecture is that adding memory to the system provides even better performance gains than adding the same amount of memory to a 16-bit system. For more information on the 32-bit aspects of Windows 95, see Chapter 9, "The Architecture of Windows 95."

Because Windows 95's 32-bit installable file system architecture replaces the protected-mode file systems inherited from DOS by earlier versions of Windows, there is a perceptible boost in performance because the processor no longer has to return to real mode and the constraints of conventional memory whenever a file needs to be read or written.

Preemptive Multitasking? What's That?

Multitasking is the apparent capability of a computer to run multiple programs as the same time. Of course, multitasking is an optical illusion because a computer with only one processor can be running only one process at a time.

What you are actually seeing is the single processor switching rapidly between programs, doing a bit of work, and then passing the processing resources on to the next program. Usually the processor can keep up with the workload, and you seem to see more than one program running.

Previous versions of Windows used a technique called cooperative multitasking in which programs would yield processor time to each other. Unfortunately an ill-behaved application can easily bring down a communication program running in the background by refusing to yield processor time.

Windows 95 supports preemptive multitasking for 32-bit applications. In this technique, the operating system allocates fixed time slices to each application that is running. When time expires, the processor turns back to another application. A tasking manager constantly adjusts the percentage of processor resources each running application receives based on need. If a communications program is sending a long document to another system and a word processor is also running, their priorities will be adjusted according to their activities.

Your old Windows 3.x applications will still cooperatively multitask under Windows 95, but newer 32-bit software will use the new scheduler in the Windows core to preemptively schedule the processor to provide smoother, better multitasking. At last you can format a floppy disk while a print job is running and your comm program is downloading long files from another computer.

Multithreading?

Multithreading is a brand-new concept to many experienced computer users. It is even quite likely that if nobody ever mentioned it to you, you wouldn't even notice multithreading since it is all but invisible to users. That doesn't mean that it isn't important.

To understand multithreading conceptually, imagine you are putting together a report for the boss. You and several assistants are standing in the library. As you put together the report, you delegate some of the subtasks to your assistants. "Phil, please find anything you can on the Chinese tariffs and get back to me as soon as you can. And Sue, would you please get me the GATT statistics on trade for 1992." As you assemble your report, the assistants do small chores for you. You are multithreading.

In Windows 3.1, it is possible to open the same program multiple times. For example, you might have two or more copies of Sound Recorder running, each having a different sound file loaded. To accomplish this, Windows 3.1 loads multiple copies of the application in memory.

Multithreading enables a program to break itself up into multiple small running programs that share the same memory space with other threads. Only a small amount of overhead is used per thread over and above shared memory and resources.

Multithreading opens up a whole new horizon of computing possibilities. Say, for example, a spreadsheet program needs to make a long complex calculation. By breaking the calculation into three or four threads, and then combining the results, a small miracle can occur. Each of those threads, from the perspective of Windows 95, is a process, a self-contained running program. That means that each of the threads is treated equally by the multitasking manager. Instead of a single spreadsheet application vying for processor time, you now have three or four threads queuing up for processor time.

The effect is that the spreadsheet program effectively gets bumped up in multitasking priority compared to a single thread of an application running elsewhere. The three or four spreadsheet threads appear to the multitasking manager as separate programs and thus get the attention they "deserve." Viola! To the user, the calculation seems to get done quicker.

Plug and Play

Anyone who has worked with computers for very long has at least one horror story about trying to add equipment to his or her system. It doesn't seem to matter whether the equipment is a simple serial port, replacement video card, sound card, network card, or tape backup system; somewhere along the way something will be in conflict with the card you are installing and you get to learn about great new things like device addressing, jumper pins, and cute new acronyms like DMA and IRQ. What the guy at the store said should take 15 minutes to install turns into hours and days, terminating finally with a service call from the nice guy at the store. Grrr.

The Plug and Play standard aims to end the wasted time, the frustration, and the wasted money that has traditionally been a part of the joy of computer ownership. While the Plug and Play standard was not specifically developed for Windows 95, Microsoft is the first operating system developer to deploy the standard for mainstream usage.

The idea behind Plug and Play is simple. Hardware manufacturers can, for only a few cents, add a chip to their board that enables the board to register with the operating system and respond to setup instructions. You add a card and turn on the system. Windows scans your system and notices the new card. They negotiate a bit and settle on settings. If a driver is needed, Windows 95 prompts you to insert the proper disk, and off you go.

At least that's the way things are supposed to work. The problem is that there is so much hardware out in the field, and at present almost none of it is compatible with Plug and Play. To compensate for this, Microsoft has assembled data on legions of legacy cards that are currently in use. During installation, Windows 95 looks over the installed cards, tries to determine what they are, and makes installation decisions accordingly. Even this small advance, however, is a big help. As Plug and Play compatible devices come onto the market, they will already be supported by your computer system through Windows 95. More information on Plug and Play can be found in Chapter 3, "Plug and Play."

Built-In Networking

Windows for Workgroups was a separate product sold by Microsoft to enable small offices to link their machines together and share resources. With the release of Windows 95, that capability is now built right into the operating system. All you have to do to create workgroups is to install network interface cards in the machines, hook them up with a cable and have a short, friendly visit with Windows Setup.

The effect is startling. From that point on, each of the users in the workgroup can specify system resources on his or her computer as shareable, and other users in the workgroup can tap into those resources. A single fax modem can serve three or four users, important data can be placed in a single location on someone's hard disk where everybody can get to the latest information, all the printers in the workgroup become available to anyone who has permission, and so on.

Microsoft even includes a limited feature version of Post Office, an application that handles the exchange of electronic mail. Suddenly, everyone in the office is interconnected, and fewer budget dollars go to buying unnecessary, duplicate equipment. Instead of buying eight modems, you can deploy two or three that can be shared on an as-needed basis. OLE-capable applications can now share links between systems, and whole new opportunities for working together become possible.

Multiple Network Connection Support

Networking is one of the hottest areas inside Windows 95. One of the design goals for Windows 95 was to make it the most connected version of Windows ever. They have succeeded. In addition to a new 32-bit NetWare Manager that uses zero bytes of conventional (640 KB) memory, Windows 95 is also capable of connecting to multiple network operating systems at the same time.

That means you can be part of a workgroup, be connected to the Novell NetWare server in the building, and connect to a Banyan Vines or DEC Pathworks network all at the same time. And unlike previous versions of Windows, you no longer have to map a network resource like a file server onto your system as a disk drive. Connected resources are simply listed as belonging to your Network Neighborhood. More information on Windows 95's networking support can be found in Part IV, which is a group of chapters that detail Windows 95's support for networking.

PCMCIA Support

The Personal Computer Memory Card International Association was the moving force behind the development of small credit-card-sized cards that can be plugged into computers to provide just about anything from an extra serial port, to modems, to network interface cards. Not surprisingly, these cards have come to be known by the initial letters of the association that created the standard, PCMCIA.

PCMCIA devices are usually used in mobile computers, notebooks, laptops, and handhelds. They provide the opportunity to configure the hardware of a system on the fly. Need a scanner? Plug it in. How about connecting with the home office? Plug in a modem or a network card.

Windows 95 supports PCMCIA devices dynamically, meaning that you can simply plug them in and take them out. Windows 95 senses the event and automatically loads or unloads drivers as needed. More information on PCMCIA support in Windows 95 is found in Chapter 11, "Mobile Computing."

Long Filenames

How many times have you worked with new computer users who just can't seem to figure out the 8.3 filename scheme used by DOS and previous versions of Windows. Trying to model data names using only eight characters plus a three-character extension is incredibly foreign to the way humans think. Finally Windows 95 puts the old DOS filenaming requirements to sleep, instead allowing you to name a file just about anything that comes to mind.

Not only can you now name files just about anything you want, but other possibilities exist too. For instance, because Windows 95 supports the Universal Naming Convention (UNC), you no longer have to fool your system into thinking a file server is a discrete disk drive on your system. More information about long filenames is available in Chapter 1.

Better Device Support

The way Windows 95 supports devices in your system is radically improved from previous versions. Virtual Device Drivers (VxDs) are dynamic in Windows 95. That means that device drivers can be loaded and unloaded from memory as needed. If, for example, you have a scanner connected to your system that only gets occasional use, you can still install it without worrying that the driver is wasting memory resources by occupying space even when it isn't being used. Typically, Windows 95 will not load a driver until the first time it is needed, thus conserving memory resources.

In addition, new 32-bit device drivers have been released to replace the old DOS device drivers. The major benefit to using these drivers is that they run in protected mode full-time. In previous versions of Windows running in 386 Enhanced mode, every time a device driver was requested to perform an action, the processor in the computer had to be talked into leaving protected mode to pop into real mode.

Windows 3.1 introduced the Unidriver concept, where a single monolithic driver takes care of most of the work of controlling a device. The Windows 3.1 Unidriver for printing greatly simplified things for both the user and for printer manufacturers. Instead of having to produce a driver that performed every possible printing task, a printer manufacturer has only to produce a short driver that handles the specialized functions of the printer only.

In Windows 95, the Unidriver concept has been extended to video display and to modem control. As a result, communications are smoother, and video display is much easier to control. You can even change color schemes and video resolutions on the fly without restarting Windows. For more information on device drivers, see Chapter 5.

The Last Word

In these pages, you have been introduced to the major new features of Windows 95. Of course, in these few pages there is only room to scratch the surface. The net effect of all the new features incorporated into Windows 95 is to create a working environment that is both friendly for new users and powerful enough to let advanced users feel there are few limits to what they can make their computer do.

As you go through the chapters in this book, you will begin to see how all these changes mesh and entwine to produce what many people believe is the most workable version of Windows ever. Several months ago, a pre-release version of Windows 95 was shown to a man who had just bought his first computer loaded with Windows 3.1. After getting the guided tour and trying a few things on his own, he said, "I didn't think they could make it much easier, but they have haven't they?" Substitute the words more powerful for easier, and the statement is still true.

Welcome to
Windows 95

Welcome to Windows 95

If Windows 95 were a luxury automobile, you might hear some smooth-voiced announcer in a TV commercial extol Windows 95 with phrases such as "completely new," "restyled for 95," or "classic performance with a whole new look." Windows 95 *is* completely new and restyled for the 1995 model year. The following figure shows you what your display will look like just after Setup finishes installing Windows 95 on your system. Looks a bit different than previous versions, doesn't it?

FIGURE P1.1.

The new look of Windows is clean, spare, and uncluttered.

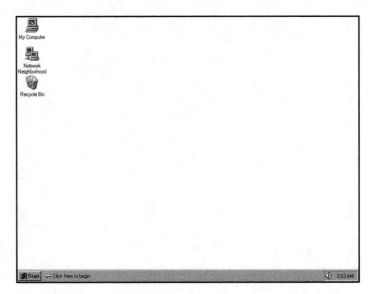

Gone (sort of) is Program Manager with its bewildering array of boxes full of icons. Gone is the File Manager and the Task Manager. In their place is a whole new object-oriented shell that uses a refinement of the Desktop metaphor, the Explorer, the Recycle bin, and the taskbar.

If you are one of those folks who doesn't like too much change, the File Manager and Program Manager have been reworked as Windows 95 applets—so you don't have to completely give them up if you don't want to. In fact, you are asked if you want them installed during setup. You would be well advised, however, to give the new Windows 95 tools a fair chance before deciding to stay with old tried and true. Once you get used to the new tools—a process that should take less than three working days—you will rebel at the idea of going back.

If It Ain't Broke, Don't Fix It

Microsoft's Visual Design Group, which was originally formed to design consistent application interfaces, steps into the spotlight in a big way with the release of Windows 95. This release is the first major reworking of the Windows user interface since the introduction of Windows 3.0 replaced the text-ish MS-DOS Executive with Program Manager. Windows 95 extends some concepts that have been lurking just below the surface for years and incorporates a wide range of new ideas.

The Windows 3.x user interface is colorful and appealing. Compared to learning to use DOS and DOS-based applications, the Windows 3.x interface is a snap to learn and use— so much so that Windows has become the standard operating environment around the world. By the end of 1994, Microsoft had sold more than 60 million copies of Windows, and that's only the legal user base. Obviously, they had done something right. Certainly, you don't change something that's successful just for the sake of change.

So, as the saying goes, why fix it if it ain't broke? The answer to that question is, as much as anything else, because the way people use computers is changing. In case you haven't noticed, computers are simply everywhere.

The pioneers—the early adopters of personal computers—were willing to undergo some rigors to bring the benefits of computing to their work. Unfortunately, the pioneer spirit infects relatively few individuals. As the number of computers has multiplied, the world has shaken out into three camps: people who would rather die than use a computer, people who use computers because they have to, and people who really like computers. In case you haven't figured it out, those of us who really like computers are still outnumbered by a wide margin.

How many people have you met that work all day long with a word processor and can't copy files from a hard disk to a floppy if you held a gun to their head? For those who are curious and want to know everything there is to know about computers, it seems crazy; but the majority of computer users are uninterested in computers. All they want to do is get a job done; some are actually hostile to the idea of learning anything about the tool used to get the job done.

By conducting hundreds of hours of usability testing and consulting with trainers of Windows users, Microsoft learned something that many of us have known for a long time. Double-clicking icons isn't intuitive. It's a whole lot easier than learning DOS commands, but there are still vast numbers of people out there who find Windows 3.x intimidating. Clearly, something is broken.

The aim of the changes in the user interface for Windows 95 is to make it easier for new computer users to get going and give old hands even more powerful tools. The new Windows 95 user interface largely succeeds in accomplishing both goals.

An Overview of the Windows 95 Landscape

Our lead chapter, "The Windows 95 Interface," takes you on a tour of the new user interface. You will learn how a single program, EXPLORER.EXE, provides two different views of your computer's resources. There is a single window view, sometimes referred to as My Computer, that lets you move from folder (directory) to folder by double-clicking objects. The dual pane (two window) view, Explorer, resembles the Windows 3.x File Manager, but there the similarity ends. Both views produced by EXPLORER.EXE enable you to perform file management using the same cut, copy, and paste methods you have used all along to work with blocks of text. Drag and drop, the capability to create shortcuts to programs and documents, and a dozen more thoughtful features, provide both new and experienced users with a whole new way of looking at data.

Apart from the changes in the user interface, many of the traditional Windows applets, such as small applications like Notepad, have been reworked. Paint, for example, has new tools that make editing bitmaps even easier. Other applets, such as Exchange, the all-in-one e-mail inbox, make their appearance in Windows 95 for the first time. In Chapter 2, "The Windows 95 Applets," you will learn what's old and what's new. Because many of the new applets, and even some of the old ones, pertain to a specific area of Windows 95, they are covered in their own chapters. A list in Chapter 2 will direct you to where you can find the information you need.

Many Windows 95 users assume that Microsoft created Plug and Play especially for this new version of Windows. In fact, however, Plug and Play is a specification worked out by a group of hardware and software vendors that promises to end the installation blues. How many times have you popped open the computer's case to install a new card, only to spend hours getting the thing to work right? Plug and Play mercifully puts an end to the nightmare for all but the most uncooperative of legacy devices.

In Chapter 3, "Plug and Play," you will learn about the Plug and Play specifications, how computer systems equipped with a Plug and Play BIOS and cards practically install themselves, and how Windows 95 makes working with non-Plug and Play devices much easier than before.

The Game's Afoot!

All the preliminaries are out of the way. You've met the authors, checked out the contents of this book, and gotten a bit of an idea how Windows 95 came to be. It's time to dig in. If you are like most other new users of Windows 95, you'll soon be wondering how you ever got your work done the old fashioned way. Welcome to Windows 95.

The Windows 95 User Interface

1

by Ed Tiley

IN THIS CHAPTER

A New Way of Looking at Data

Over the years computer users have learned to think of their computer as being a box full of files. Working with a computer is seen as altering the content of files, creating files, discarding files, installing files, and so on. To many users, however, files are abstract things more apt to confuse and confound them than anything else.

The dread of "doing something wrong" and loosing information is an often-stated fear among rank and file computer users. Copying files, deleting files, arranging files in subdirectories, doing backups of files, having to come up with names that fit the DOS imposed 8.3 filename template, and worst of all, remembering the syntax of complex commands is daunting to a new user who just wants to start up WordPerfect and type. Many experienced computer users haven't a clue what it means to efficiently manage the files on their hard disk, and the fact that hard disks are 10 times larger than they used to be only compounds the problem.

To combat this problem, Microsoft has taken the best of the old Windows interface and married it to the best features of other influential GUI user interfaces. The result is a new, object-oriented, document-centric way to look at computing with Windows. To be sure, it is very different from the interface presented by previous versions of Windows. An experienced Windows user frankly has to unlearn concepts that have been around for a long time, concepts that have previously been useful. Once you have become acclimated to the new interface, however, you won't even miss File Manager and Program Manager.

> **NOTE**
>
> Unless you specifically go looking for it, the old Windows 3.x File Manager is gone. Windows 95 versions of File Manager and Program Manager are included in the box as a security blanket for those users who hate to change tools; but you have to go looking for those tools to use them unless you installed them during setup. The functions of the File Manager and Program Manager have been distributed throughout Windows 95 in the Start menu, Explorer, and Find; even the Clipboard has a part in the new scheme of things since you can now perform file management chores using cut, copy and paste just like you would blocks of text in Notepad. If you want to move a file from one folder to another, you can cut it and then paste it into the folder you want.

An Object-Oriented User Interface

The Windows 95 user interface uses the desktop as the platform in which you can interface with running programs. The Windows 95 user interface utilizes the desktop to present everything in your system as an object. Everything that shows up on your desktop, except a running program, is an object associated with an underlying resource such as a disk drive, printer, file, or font.

New users will immediately see the new interface as logical and will take all this talk of objects in stride. Users who are familiar with Windows 3.x and DOS will take a little longer to catch on. It is ironic that experienced users have to unlearn old ways to most efficiently learn the new, but the effort is worth it.

Object-Oriented?

Object-oriented is one of the most misused and overhyped bits of jargon in all of computerese. In this case, it isn't misused at all. Here's a bit of background information that will put it all together for you.

Simply put, an object is an entity in memory that contains data—often expressed as properties—and the code to act on that data. For example, in Windows 95, a *shortcut* is an object that knows about a program, document, or folder. It also has the programming to react to events such as double-clicks, right-clicks, being dragged to another folder, and so on, so it knows how to act.

Each object inherits what it knows and what it can do from its ancestor object class. An object class is like a template that can create a specific type of object—a shortcut, for example. Every shortcut has the same kinds of data stored about the file or folder that it represents. Also, every shortcut inherits the code needed to act on that data.

In this model, Windows itself is event-driven, meaning that it sits in the background doling out system services in response to the events the user causes to be triggered. When a mouse movement, a mouse click, a keystroke, or some other user-initiated event happens, Windows 95 notices it and generates an event message. A message is Windows' way of letting an object know that it should do something.

Modeling the Real World

A lot of folks have a hard time understanding objects and events explained in computer terms. Sometimes it is helpful to use everyday human examples. After all, object orientation at its best is a way of modeling the real world.

You are a human object. There are many variations in the human object, but under all the differences are characteristics that distinguish humans from other living creatures. You cannot be both human and a fish or a car. Like all healthy human objects, you have a brain connected to your spinal column, which in turn connects to your two arms, two legs, and other organs via a nervous system.

Take this human object and make it a shortstop in the sixth game of the World Series; then, see how the *object* will react to events. When the eyes see a batted ball coming its way, for instance, a message is sent to the brain and the arm puts the glove up to catch the ball. An even better example is the reaction of your eyes to smoke. The tear ducts empty, trying to wash off the eyeball, and you blink. No one taught you to tear up from smoke or onions or sad movies. You inherited that characteristic because you are human.

Like humans, all objects are unique, but they all have the same characteristics. Only the data they carry is different. Two shortcuts may be identical in structure, but the data they carry is different.

Windows 95 Objects

When you double-click an object, Windows 95 reacts to the double-click event and sends a message to the appropriate message queue. All objects scan their messages, so when an object (like a shortcut) receives the message that it has been double-clicked, it reacts by sending a message back to Windows 95 saying what needs to happen. The shortcut object contains the information about what it is supposed to act on, and how to act.

Specifically, to double-click a shortcut creates an open event. If the shortcut is to a folder, the folder is opened. If the shortcut is to a program, it is launched. If the shortcut is to a document, the associated program is launched with the document open.

When Windows 95 is launched and opens for business, you are presented with a desktop object. The desktop is a special type of folder called a container that can house other objects. The desktop is the highest-level visible object in Windows 95.

Objects that the desktop knows about and can cooperate with include shortcuts, folders, files, and running applications such as the taskbar, Explorer, or your favorite card game. The desktop represents the services that Windows 95 is ready and able to provide for you to work with your data and programs by communicating with other user interface objects.

The objects in the Windows 95 user interface aren't the files on your disk, or the printers installed on your system. The objects represent those files or printers. When you do something in Windows 95, you create an event that Windows and its objects need to respond to.

Windows 95 Object Properties

Each of the objects on your desktop has a set of properties. Properties are the "knowledge" part of the object. When you right-click most objects, a context menu appears. The items in the context menu represent events the object can respond to. That is the code part of the object. For example, in Figure 1.1, the Network Neighborhood object has been right-clicked to reveal its context menu.

Note that the bottom item in the Network Neighborhood's context menu is Properties. If you click this item, the Properties dialog for the object will be displayed, enabling you to change settings and alter the way the object behaves. Figure 1.2 shows the Properties dialog for Network Neighborhood, Windows 95's way to access network services.

FIGURE 1.1.

One of the best ways to discover the features of the Windows 95 interface is to right-click everything to reveal the context menu associated with objects.

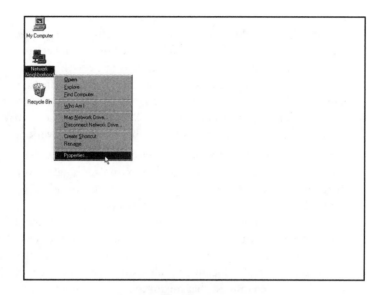

FIGURE 1.2.

Properties dialogs can be complex, as in the example shown here, or they can be relatively simple.

As you can see, the Network Neighborhood Properties dialog has three tabs that enable you to edit three different sets of information. Other Properties dialogs, like the ones for documents, folders, and programs, are much more simple and tell you about the file. The only settable properties are the file attributes archive, hidden, read-only, and system.

NOTE

In case you haven't noticed, the term *personal computer* is falling into disuse. The concept of a personal computer, isolated from the control of the folks in the MIS department, is fading as computers become more and more connected to the outside world.

Windows 95 puts a heavy emphasis on connectivity. Peer-to-peer networking for creating localized workgroups is right in the box when you purchase Windows 95. Backup agents that enable workstation disks to be backed up remotely by system administrators are supplied as well, so users are largely relieved of their responsibility to manage their own storage. MS Exchange, remote access tools, remote administration tools, At Work Fax, and a host of other Windows 95 features make it easy to connect to the outside world via modem communications or networking.

At the same time, Windows applications regularly work with types of data that were unheard of as little as five years ago. For example, a single Word for Windows document can easily contain text, pictures, segments of spreadsheets, data-entry forms, graphs that update information in real time, object packages that let you launch applications, and even shortcuts to full motion video and sound. By the same token, a spreadsheet application can place all of the same data into the confines of a spreadsheet. When dealing with *compound documents,* as they are called, the application launched to create the document is almost immaterial. The type of data embedded into the document determines what mix of tools is to edit and view the document, not the application launched to begin work.

The whole idea of a word processor that only knows how to manage text is blown to pieces. Using DDE (Dynamic Data Exchange) and OLE (Object Linking and Embedding), Word for Windows and other full-featured word processors can contain anything from shortcuts to another document to a fully interactive multimedia presentation coming off a satellite feed. You might have a Save item in the File menu, but what is it you think you are going to get when you tell Word to save to a floppy disk or your local hard drive? Will the printer explode if you try to get this "document" onto paper?

Windows 95 Folders

In the terminology of DOS and previous versions of Windows, disks are divided into directories and subdirectories. The problem is that many users, new and old, are intimidated by directories. Probably not one in ten could tell you the semantic difference between a directory and a subdirectory. Not one in a hundred cares.

Windows 95 instead applies the concept of folders. New users seem to more easily grasp the concept of a folder as a container, and experienced users soon find out that a folder can be more than just another word for directory. Just about any kind of hierarchical data can be packaged to look like a folder to Explorer, including network resources, groups of printers (the Printers system folder), and output from online services such as Microsoft Network. For the moment, however, we will stick to the concept of folders as disk-bound containers of files, shortcuts, and other folders.

When you create a folder on the desktop, it is true that you create a folder within the hidden WINDOWS\DESKTOP folder; but it is much more productive to think of it as a new folder object residing on the desktop. Thinking this way enables you to expand the way you work with folders.

TIP

You cannot normally see the Desktop folder within the Windows 95 shell, but it is there. Try launching a DOS session and looking at your Windows directory. Sure enough it's there. You can also select Show All Files in the Explorer's View | Options dialog.

Folders don't have to be static. Folders can be as temporary as a single session or last until they drag you out the door feet first. That's the point. Folders can contain anything you want them to for as long as you want them to. The primary tool for managing and using folders is Explorer.

WINDOWS' WINDOWS

Those readers familiar with previous versions of Windows will immediately see that the appearance of windows in Windows 95 is a bit different than before. There is a new etched, more three-dimensional look to the display.

The title bar has been completely reworked, as you can see. The control menu button in the upper-left corner is represented by an icon that changes to indicate the type of resource you are looking at and also indicates what system level options are contained within. My Computer will display a computer icon while at the highest level. In the middle of the title bar is a description of what the window contains, and at the far right there are three buttons for minimizing, maximizing, and closing the window.

Just below the title bar are the menubar and toolbar. Menus work pretty much the way they always have, but now exhibit a "sticky" behavior—meaning that you click one time to open the menu, and as you point at various items they become selected. Any menu items that lead to another level (indicated by the dark arrow at the right of the menu item) automatically reveal the next level when pointed to. Thus, the menu becomes a two-click operation. Click once to open the menu and a second time to choose a particular menu item.

Toolbars are extremely common in Windows 95. The toolbar consists of icons that represent actions the application can deliver. There is a redundancy in that actions available from the toolbar are also normally available as menu items.

Not all windows can be resized. Those that can be resized have a special indicator in the lower-right corner of the window's frame. When you put the mouse pointer on the indicator, you can resize the window by holding down the mouse button and dragging the frame to its new size.

A Tour of the Windows 95 User Interface

Before you get the quick tour of the features, you should take note that Windows 95 has a number of interrelated concepts and features. It is hard to talk about any one feature without putting it into the context of related features. In the sections that follow, new concepts are introduced as gently as possible. Each of these new concepts will be covered in more detail later in this chapter.

The Windows 95 interface expands the role of the desktop in your everyday work. It is no longer limited to containing just windows, wallpaper, and icons that represent minimized applications as in Windows 3.x. You can drag and drop just about anything onto the desktop, including shortcuts to files or resources.

NEW CONCEPT—SHORTCUTS

A *shortcut* is a representation of a system resource that enables you to "get to" that resource. For example, if you have a word processing document in a folder on your hard disk, you can create a shortcut to that document that can be placed on the desktop or in a folder.

For readers familiar with Windows 3.x, a shortcut is very similar to an icon in a Program Manager group. A Program Manager icon isn't the program or document itself, but a representation of it. A Windows 95 shortcut is very similar, with the notable exception that a shortcut is stored singly and is not part of a group. You can have multiple shortcuts for the same application or document.

Shortcuts point to an application program or a document. To open the document or launch the program, all you have to do is use the shortcut.

A shortcut is easily identifiable by the arrow in the lower-left corner of the icon. Throughout the rest of this chapter, you will see that working with shortcuts is similar to working with any other object. A shortcut is an object that points to another object.

Unlike Windows 3.x, the desktop in Windows 95 is a functioning part of the user interface. The desktop is the foundation for the Windows 95 user interface. Applications that you use all the time can be placed onto the desktop as shortcut objects. Whole folders of icons can serve as a gateway to a group of programs or documents. Links to network resources are as easy to manage as anything inside your own computer.

Poking Around Your System

When you need lower-level access to files, disks, printers, and so on, the Windows Explorer, an application that replaces File Manager, has two ways to deliver views of your resources. Explorer is to Windows 95 what Program Manager and File Manager were to Windows 3.x, and then some. Because Microsoft's usability testing found that many users were intimidated by File Manager, they tried to come up with another way of presenting files and system resources. In the end, they settled on using a cabinet metaphor. In fact, the Explorer was originally named the Cabinet.

As you will see shortly in this chapter, the Windows Explorer is a very versatile program that can act as either a single pane (My Computer) or double pane (Explorer) browser of your system and its resources. As you will soon learn, almost anything can be explored. If you call up the Microsoft Network, for example, everything is presented as folders that your end of the communication can explore.

One of the icons permanently glued to the desktop is labeled My Computer. When you double-click this object, you see, in a single window, all of the objects contained in the top level of your system. Local disk drives, printers, network resources, and so on, are represented as objects. Using the four buttons on the right side of the toolbar, you can display these objects as Program Manager style icons or as lists. When you double-click an object, the result depends on the type of object it is. Folders open to show you their contents, programs are launched, and documents are opened.

The Explorer provides a window with two panes, where container objects, such as disk drives and folders, are arranged in the left pane as a hierarchical tree. When an object in the left pane is clicked to select it, the right pane of Explorer changes to show you all of the objects contained within whatever object is selected in the left pane. Later sections of this chapter provide detailed information about using Explorer. Figure 1.3 shows you the My Computer and Explorer views side by side.

Any number of computer resources can be represented as a hierarchy of objects. Disks, network resources, folder, and the like all can contain other objects, so Explorer becomes one of the busiest bits of software on your system. The Network Neighborhood, printer drivers, fonts, and other object types are also represented using the Explorer or My Computer views.

It may seem strange, but My Computer and Explorer are the same program. To prove it to yourself, try holding down the Shift key when you double-click My Computer on the desktop. My Computer will open up in the dual pane Explorer view. From this point in the book forward, please keep in mind that when My Computer or Explorer are mentioned, they are one and the same. So the terms My Computer and Explorer refer to the view of resources that is offered, not the application itself. Also keep in mind that, in most cases, the term Explorer outside the context of viewing resources means the cabinet program that can render either a single or dual pane view of those resources.

FIGURE 1.3.
My Computer gives you a single pane view of your system, whereas Explorer provides a dual pane view.

As powerful as Explorer is, it requires too many steps through the layers of your computer's resources to be an all-purpose tool for opening documents and launching applications. That is why Windows 95 has the taskbar. The taskbar is a highly customizable application launcher, which also serves as a tray for minimized applications.

The Taskbar

One of the things that Microsoft's usability testing revealed was that new users confronting the Program Manager for the first time were both dazzled and intimidated by Windows. Often they are unsure of how they should get started. Double-clicking an icon is not intuitive. To a new user, a single click is much more discoverable.

In Windows 95, the place to start is unambiguous. By default, the taskbar appears at the bottom of the screen and has a button marked Start. Before any programs are launched, there is an arrow pointing to the Start button with the legend, "Click here to begin." Even a newly arrived little green man from Mars could figure out how to use the taskbar.

The taskbar is deceptively simple looking. It is, in fact, an indispensable tool for launching programs, opening recently used documents, finding files, and so on. Fortunately, using the taskbar is an art you quickly acquire.

NEW USER INFORMATION

A running Windows application can be represented in three different ways onscreen while you are working. The three representations are minimized, normal, and maximized.

Maximized applications fill the entire screen edge to edge. The normal view uses a window that is sizable, but doesn't fill the entire screen. A minimized application has all of its windows closed and is represented by a single icon on the taskbar. A program in any of these three states continues to run.

Figure 1.4 shows you the taskbar after some programs have been launched and the Start button clicked. As you can see, each of the running applications have their own button in the taskbar's tray. Although all the applications are shown in the figure to be minimized, even applications with open windows have an entry on the taskbar tray.

To switch to an application, all you have to do is click the application's button on the taskbar tray. If the program is minimized, the view is restored to either the normal or maximized view, depending on how it was viewed when minimized, and the application becomes the current window.

FIGURE 1.4.

The taskbar provides easy opening of documents, launching of applications, and control over running applications.

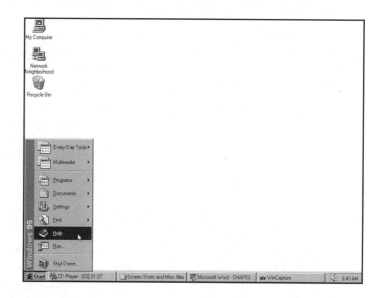

One feature of the taskbar that is sure to get a great deal of use is the capability of applications to place icons into the status area of the taskbar. As you can see in Figure 1.4, Windows 95

shows the time. If you have multimedia devices installed, Windows 95 also automatically provides a handy volume control, as shown, that can be quickly accessed with a single click. When documents are printing, a printer icon is also displayed in this area so you can easily check on your print job in progress.

Moving and Sizing the Taskbar

The taskbar is not a static thing. You have your choice of where you want the taskbar to appear. Using drag and drop, you can position the taskbar along any of the four edges of your display. You can also use drag and drop to change the size of the taskbar. These techniques are described in Chapter 5.

Taskbar Properties

As you will see throughout this book, almost every object can be right-clicked to display its properties. Properties are settings that can be adjusted to change the appearance or behavior of an object. The taskbar has other properties that can be altered using a dialog. To get to the properties dialog, position the mouse pointer on the taskbar and click the right mouse button.

TIP

For years computer users wondered what the right mouse button was for. Windows 95 finally provides a good excuse for the right button of the mouse to exist.

The right button of the mouse has three basic functions in Windows 95. Use the right button to get information, to get a context menu, or to perform a special drag.

When you right-click text entry boxes, checkboxes, and other controls in dialogs, you usually get a small floating button that pops up, bearing the words "What's this?" If you would like a explanation of the control, left-click the button to see a Help window that explains the control.

When you right-click just about any object in Windows 95, you will see what is called a *context menu.* The actions and options available on the menu will depend on what kind of object you right-click—thus the name context menu. Almost every object has an item on its context menu that enables you to edit the properties of the object.

When you right-click an object and keep the button mashed down, you can perform a special drag by pulling the icon to which you were pointing across the desktop and dropping (releasing the right mouse button) the icon into a window or onto the desktop. When you drop the icon, a context menu will appear that enables you to specify what action you want performed, such as moving files, copying files, or creating shortcuts to the file or files you dragged.

You will find that a great way to learn the Windows 95 user interface is to right-click everything. You will soon find out that there is a great deal of power and functionality lurking just below the surface of the new interface.

When you right-click an empty space on the taskbar, you will get a context menu that enables you to cascade or tile all open windows on the desktop, minimize all running applications, undo the minimize operation, and edit the properties of the taskbar. Figure 1.5 shows you the dialog that appears when you select the Properties item from the context menu.

FIGURE 1.5.

The Properties dialog for the taskbar enables you to configure the taskbar and the Start menu.

The Properties dialog shown in Figure 1.6 is similar to every other Property dialog in Windows 95. Within the window are tabs that switch from dialog to dialog so you can edit different groups of settings. The dialog associated with each tab presents you with a group of options. You can click the OK button to close the Properties dialog and make the changes you've selected, or you can click Cancel to close the dialog an discard changes. The Apply button lets you see the effect of your changes without closing the Properties dialog. Any changes you apply, however, cannot be canceled.

The Taskbar's Start Menu

It seems that every other utility, shareware and commercial, for Windows 3.x is a program launcher. Obviously a lot of users found the Program Manager inadequate as a means of easily starting programs. The taskbar is going to put a dent in the quantity of new program launchers available because the taskbar has an integrated Start menu that is quick, easy, and fully customizable.

When you click the Start button with the left mouse button, the Start Menu you see in Figure 1.6 appears as a popup from the taskbar. It doesn't look much like a Windows 3.x menu does it? It isn't. As you will see shortly, the Start Menu is highly customizable for each individual user.

FIGURE 1.6.

The Start Menu is integrated into the taskbar and is your way of quickly performing common tasks.

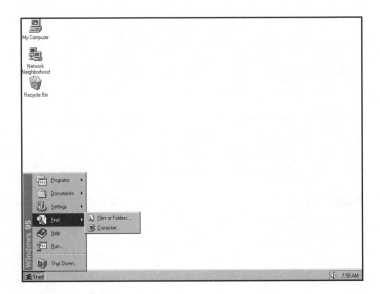

The Start Menu quickly reveals the new "sticky" behavior of menus in Windows 95. Menu items that cascade to another level are marked in Windows 95 with a black arrow icon. As the mouse pointer lingers over an item that leads to another level, that level appears. When you find the application program you want to use, a single click launches it.

As installed by Setup, the Start Menu is three layers deep. Starting a program, even in the third layer, requires only a single mouse click on the Start button and a second click on the program. This is much easier for new users of Windows to learn.

The Programs Section of Start Menu

When you point at the Programs item in the Start Menu, as the arrow indicates, a second level of choices will cascade out to the right. This layer of the Start Menu contains entries that will correspond to the Windows 3.1 Program Manager groups that were on your system when you installed Windows 95, if you performed an upgrade installation. If you installed Windows 95 clean, this menu section will contain just a few default items.

This portion of the Start menu is a direct reflection of your system's hard disk. Contained in the Windows folder is a folder named Start Menu, which in turn contains a folder named Programs. All of the items in the Programs portion of the Start Menu reflect the objects in the Windows\Start Menu\Programs folder. Generally these objects are folders and shortcuts.

When you install Windows 95 over Windows 3.1x, your Program Manager groups are migrated into the Programs folder as a folder filled with Shortcuts. Other folders, such as Accessories, will contain still more folders and Shortcuts to the Windows 95 applets. An *applet* is a small utility application, such as NotePad, WordPad, or Paint, that is supplied as a part of Windows 95.

The Documents Section of the Start Menu

Figure 1.7 shows a typical example of the Documents section of Start menu. When you use My Computer or Explorer to start an application by double-clicking a document object, a shortcut to that file is automatically created and placed in the Recent folder, which is contained in the Windows folder. The last 15 documents opened in this way are remembered. This feature enables you to easily return to work with documents you have opened recently.

FIGURE 1.7.

The Documents section of the Start menu enables you to quickly open a data file you have recently worked with.

The Documents section of Start menu is a reflection of the shortcuts contained in the Recent folder. To launch the application associated with that data file, all you need is a single click. The application that created the data file is launched, and the file is opened.

Right-Clicking the Start Button

When you right-click the Start button, you will get a context menu of three options. Open launches a My Computer view of the Start Menu folder, and Explore launches an Explorer view with the Start Menu selected in the left pane. The third item, Find, enables you to search for files on your system and is the same as choosing the Find item in the Start Menu itself, except that initially the search is limited to the Start Menu folder and the folders contained within.

Right-Clicking the Taskbar Tray

When you right-click any of the entries on the taskbar tray, a context menu will appear that enables you to minimize, maximize, restore, move, and size a normal window, or to close the application. In short, the taskbar is a versatile tool for launching and managing applications.

The Hierarchy of Data

When you double-click the My Computer object on the desktop, Explorer opens a single pane view of your system. If you pull down the listbox in the toolbar, you will see that the Desktop object is the highest level. Everything branches off from that point except the Recycle Bin.

Double-clicking the My Computer object on the desktop launches a single pane Explorer session that begins at the My Computer namespace. A namespace can be a network disk drive or domain attached to your computer, a pathname, or folder name within your system that indicates a particular location. Simply stated, a namespace is a way of specifying a location within your system.

Branching off My Computer are all the disks you have installed in your system, any network drives you may be attached to, system folders, CD-ROM drives, the printers folder, and so on. When you double-click a disk object, it opens to show you the folders it contains. Folders are containers, so a folder can contain other folders, program files, or documents. As you continue to click folders, you drill down through the layers of folders until you reach the end of a branch.

Each different resource is represented by an icon that pictorially indicates the type of resource. Drive types have special icons attached to their desktop objects that identify them as floppy drives, standard hard disks, removable media, and so on. System folders have special icons that differentiate them from standard file folders and also to indicate their purpose. The CD-ROM icon changes depending on the type of disc inserted in the drive so you can easily distinguish between data discs and music discs.

> **NOTE**
>
> The program EXPLORER.EXE produces two ways of browsing data. The My Computer (single pane) view and the dual pane Explorer view are both produced by Explorer. All of the information in the next few pages about My Computer applies equally to the Explorer view. There are a few added capabilities you can take advantage of with the Explorer view, however, and these will be covered later in this chapter.

Working with Explorer

The main tool for browsing your system in Windows 95's new document-centric interface is the Explorer. As has been mentioned before, EXPLORER.EXE is capable of producing both a single pane view and a dual pane view of your system's resources. The single pane view is often referred to as My Computer or the My Computer view.

Explorer provides an object-oriented view of your folders, programs, and documents. Each item presented has the same status as any other object. All objects can be cut, copied, pasted, renamed, deleted, and so on. Of course, there have to be exceptions to prove the rule, so some objects, like system folders, cannot be moved or renamed. Aside from these few exceptions, however, Explorer is quite egalitarian and treats all objects equally.

> **TIP**
>
> If you prefer the dual pane Explorer view to the My Computer view, all you have to do is hold down the Shift key while double-clicking the My Computer icon. In either case, the four buttons along the right side of the toolbar enable you to view the contents of your system as (moving right to left) large icons, small icons, list view, and detail view.

Explorer is used for a number of different situations within Windows 95, including Network Neighborhood, Recycle Bin, and the Control Panel. Microsoft Network even uses Explorer to present online information to you. Just about anything that can be represented using the folder and document object metaphor can be presented using Explorer in either the single pane or dual pane mode.

> **NOTE**
>
> The first time you find it necessary to copy an object from one folder to another, it might occur to you, as it has to many other folks, that the easiest way of copying is to have two Explorer sessions going at once, one session open to the source folder and the other open to the destination folder.
>
> As you will see in the next few pages, it really isn't the most efficient, or even the easiest, way to copy and move objects from one folder to another.
>
> Having multiple sessions of Explorer running simply clutters up your desktop and uses system resources without adding any real value. It is recommended that you use the techniques shown in the examples that follow.

Working with Explorer's My Computer View

Figure 1.8 shows how Explorer looks in the single pane, or My Computer, view. Take a moment to look over the parts of the window.

Across the top of the window is a standard title bar with the icon in the left corner indicating the control menu and the standard minimize, maximize, and close buttons in the right corner. Below the title bar are the menu and toolbar. Within the window frame is a work surface where all of the objects (folders, programs, and documents contained in the current folder) are displayed.

The bottom of the window frame contains a status bar that can be toggled on and off. The status bar gives you information about the contents of the window.

FIGURE 1.8.

Explorer's single pane view is often called the My Computer view because it is the default view when My Computer is double-clicked.

NOTE

Most of the techniques for selecting, copying, moving, and deleting objects work the same in both the single and dual pane views. For the purposes of showing you the fundamentals of working with Explorer, the single pane view is presented first. Later in this chapter, the dual pane view is presented so you can see how it makes things even more powerful.

TIP

If you hold down the Ctrl key when clicking the close button of an open folder window in Explorer, the settings for the window will become the new default settings for any as yet unopened window. Whatever settings you have for the view, arrangement of icons, display of the toolbar, and so on, will become the new default view for windows in Explorer.

The Explorer Toolbar

The toolbar provides most of Explorer's features at the click of a button. The toolbar is the same for both the My Computer view and Explorer view. Take a moment to run down each of the buttons and the actions they provide, moving left to right.

> **Jump to Folder:** This listbox enables you to jump between folders and disks. Just open the list and click where you want to jump to. In the single pane view, you are restricted to jumping to disks and system folders.

> **Up One Level:** This button changes the selected folder by going up one level.

> **Map Network Drive:** If you have any kind of networking installed, use this button to connect to server disk drives.

> **Disconnect Network Drive:** This button disconnects you from a network disk drive.

Cut: Marks selected objects and places them on the Clipboard.

Copy: Copies selected objects on the Clipboard for copying.

Paste: Places objects on the Clipboard into the current window. Objects previously marked as Cut are then removed.

Undo: Reverses the previous action taken.

Delete: Removes the selected objects. You are prompted to place them in the Recycle Bin.

Properties: Shows you the properties dialog for the selected object(s). If more than one object is selected, the Properties dialog summarizes the selected items.

Large Icons: Displays objects using large Program Manager style icons.

Small Icons: Displays objects using smaller icons that conserve screen real estate.

List: Displays objects as a list. This option enables the maximum number of filenames to be displayed in the window.

Details: Displays maximum information about objects, including the name, file type, and date last edited.

Navigating Disks and Folders

In the single pane view, My Computer, double-clicking an object will perform different actions depending on the type of object it is. If the object is a program, the program will be launched without opening a document. If the object is a document, the program that is associated with that document type is launched with the document open for editing.

OPENING FOLDERS

One of the great things about the new Windows 95 interface is that you nearly always have several ways of doing anything. As the old saying goes, "There's more than one way to skin a cat." It's a wonder that there are any cats left in Redmond, because the Windows 95 development team has found so many ways to skin them. Here is a list of ways to open folders and peek inside to see what they contain.

Desktop-Based Folders

Double-click to open a single pane view.

Hold down the Shift key and double-click for a dual pane view.

Right-click to bring up the context menu and select Open for a single pane view.

Right-click to bring up the context menu and select Explore for a dual pane view.

Disk-Based Folders (Explorer single pane view)

Double-click to open the folder; whether the current window is used or a new window opens depends on the Options setting of Explorer.

Right-click and then choose Open for single pane view.

Right-click and then choose Explore for dual pane view.

Disk-Based Folders (Explorer dual pane view)

Click the folder in the left pane to view its contents in the right pane.

Double-click a folder in the right pane to view its contents.

Right-click a folder in either pane and choose Open to launch a single pane view session.

Right-click a folder in either pane and choose Explore to view the folder's contents in the right pane.

From a Command Line

Type `Explorer /e, /root,c:\windows` and press Enter or click OK to open a dual pane (`/e`) Explorer session with the Windows folder as the topmost viewable folder (`/root`).

There you have it, an even dozen ways to look into a folder to see what is there.

Double-clicking folder and disk objects, however, is a little more complex. How Explorer reacts to double-clicking a folder or disk object depends on the setting you make using the View | Options command in the menu. Figure 1.9 shows you the dialog that appears when you use the View | Options command.

FIGURE 1.9.

The Folder tab of the Options dialog appears only when Explorer is in the single pane mode.

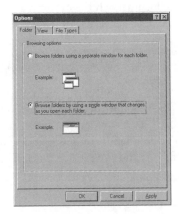

The Options dialog has three tabs when Explorer is in the single pane mode. The Folder tab has two radio buttons that let you decide how you want Explorer to browse when you open a disk or folder. The default setting is one that enables you to open a new window for each disk or folder opened. In some cases this is convenient, but more often it simply leads to screen clutter. As you browse around your system, you leave a trail of open windows behind you as you drill down to the folder you want to view.

> **TIP**
>
> Hold down the Shift key and click the close button on the title bar of one of the subwindows to close that window and all of the windows that were opened before it. This way you can reduce screen clutter as it occurs. Shift-closing the most recently opened window will close all of the windows including the original My Computer window.

The first inclination of most users, new and old, is to have each folder open into its own window. It would seem to make copying and moving objects from folder to folder easier if you just drag from one window and drop into another window. While this technique works, the constant clutter of so many open windows makes most users change the Options property so that Explorer uses just a single window, the contents of which change as you navigate around your system. This setting reduces screen clutter, and as you will soon see, you do not need multiple windows open to easily copy and move objects from one folder to another. In the pages that follow, the single window mode is used.

Copying, Moving, and Deleting Objects

The only difference between copying and moving objects is that copying leaves a duplicate behind in the original folder, while moving the object doesn't. Depending on the settings you have made in the Recycle Bin's Properties dialog, deleted objects are either moved to the Recycle Bin, or are erased outright.

The two preferred methods of copying, moving, and deleting are drag and drop and using the context menu's cut, copy, paste, and delete commands.

Copying an Object

All you have to do to copy an object to the desktop is to point at the object, depress the left mouse button, drag the icon over a spot on the desktop, and let go of the mouse button. That's all there is to it.

Figure 1.10 shows that the context menu for objects in Explorer has cut, copy, and paste commands. Yes, you can manipulate objects just as if they were blocks of text in NotePad or WordPad!

To copy the object, select Copy from the context menu. This places a copy of the object onto the Clipboard. Then navigate to the folder or the desktop where you want the object to be copied to, and right-click. From the context menu that appears, select Paste.

FIGURE 1.10.

The context menu for objects lets you cut, copy, and paste them as if they were blocks of text.

Moving an Object

Moving an object is almost exactly the same as copying an object. If you drag an object and drop it onto another folder in the single pane view of Explorer, the object is moved to that folder, not copied.

Alternately you can right-click the object to be moved, and select Cut from the context menu. The icon for the object is then displayed using grayed text to show that the object is unavailable. Right-click the desktop in a folder where you want the object moved to and select Paste from the context menu. Only when the object has been safely pasted into the new folder does the original icon disappear. If you cut an object to the clipboard without ever pasting it somewhere else, the original is restored to its previous state.

If you want to use the drag and drop method in a context that would by default copy the object, use the right mouse button to drag. When you let go of the button to drop the object, a menu similar to the one shown in Figure 1.11 appears. You have four choices: move the original object to the spot where you dropped it, copy the object to that spot, create a shortcut to the original object at that spot, or cancel the operation without doing anything.

FIGURE 1.11.

Right-dragging an object and dropping it reveals a menu that lets you choose how the object should be handled.

Deleting an Object

There are, of course, several ways to delete an object. To delete an object that is currently selected (highlighted) just press the Del key. You can also right-click the object and select Delete from the context menu. Another method is to drag the object to the Recycle Bin and drop it in.

> **NOTE**
>
> Depending on the way you have set the Properties of Recycle Bin, you will be asked to confirm deletion operations. In this way Windows 95 double checks your intentions, unless you set it not to by editing the properties of Recycle Bin.
>
> Dragging an object and dropping it on the Recycle Bin, however, will delete the object without confirmation regardless of the settings. Of course you have the option of undoing the delete.
>
> If you turn off the recycling feature, and tell Recycle Bin to immediately delete files without storing them for possible recall, you will be prompted to confirm the deletion regardless of the method used to delete or the confirmation setting. In other words, if you do not have the option to recall the object, deletions always need to be confirmed.

Working with Multiple Objects

Once multiple objects are selected, you can copy, move, and delete them using exactly the same techniques as you would to manipulate a single object. As you might expect, there are several ways of selecting multiple objects.

The simplest method is to select one object, then hold down the Shift key and select another object. Not only are the two objects you click selected, but also all the objects in between.

How this method behaves, however, depends on the type of view you are using. If you are using Large Icon or Small Icon view, all of the objects within the rectangle formed by the two clicked objects will be selected. In List and Detail view, all of the objects in the list between the two end objects will be selected.

> **TIP**
>
> If the objects you want to select do not fall into a convenient pattern, select a group of objects using the Shift-click method and then select additional objects by holding down the Control key and clicking each object you want to add to the group.

Perhaps the easiest way of selecting objects in Explorer is to drag a selection frame around them. Figure 1.12 shows how this works. All you have to do is point to a blank spot inside the Explorer window and click the left mouse button; then drag the selection frame around those files you want to select. As they are surrounded by the frame, the objects become highlighted. When you let go of the mouse button, all of the objects within the frame are selected.

FIGURE 1.12.

Dragging a selection frame around a group of objects selects all of the objects within the frame.

TIP

If you right-drag a selection frame around a group of objects, they are selected and a context menu immediately appears when you let off the right mouse button. From the context menu you can select to cut, copy, or delete the objects. Additionally you can also select Open, Quick View, or any other valid context menu command.

Once you have the objects you want to work with selected, follow the same techniques for dragging and dropping, or selecting a command from the context menu, that you would to manipulate a single object.

Working with Explorer's Dual Pane View

In addition to the single pane view, Explorer is capable of creating a dual pane view of your system resources. As with almost everything in Windows 95, there are several different ways of launching a dual pane Explorer view. Here are a few:

- Right-click the My Computer desktop icon and click Explore.
- Hold down the Shift key while double-clicking the My Computer desktop icon.
- Right-click the Start button on the taskbar and choose Explore from the context menu to open Explorer with the Start Menu folder open.

- Right-click any container object and choose Explore from the context menu to open Explorer with the container selected.

- Choose Explorer from the Start Menu.

- Create a shortcut to Explorer on the desktop or in a folder and double-click it.

Figure 1.13 illustrates how Explorer looks when the dual pane view is chosen. In this view, Explorer has a similar appearance to the Windows 3.x File Manager. The similarity, however, is only on the surface.

FIGURE 1.13.

The dual pane Explorer view puts a hierarchy of your system resources in the left pane and contents of folder in the right.

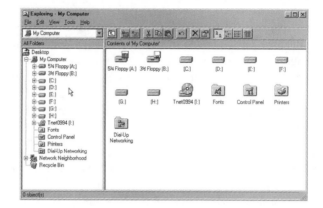

As you might expect from looking at the Explorer session shown in Figure 1.14, the dual pane view has a bit more horsepower than the single pane My Computer view. The single pane view is presented, by default, because Microsoft's usability testing has shown the dual pane view to be less user-friendly for novices. New users have been shown to be intimidated by the amount of information presented. Experienced users, however, tend to prefer the dual pane Explorer view because of the amount information presented. However ironic that is, as users become accustomed to the Windows 95 user interface, they more and more rely on the Explorer, dual pane view because it is more flexible.

The Explorer view, as it is commonly called, is very much the same as the single pane view, with the exception that a window pane has been added on the left side. As you can see, all of the toolbar buttons are the same. So are the menu commands, with the single exception that the View | Options property sheet lacks the Folders tab that determines if multiple windows are opened when you double-click a folder.

You can use the right-hand pane of the Explorer view to drill down to a folder or document by double-clicking, just as you can in the single pane view. You don't actually have to use the left pane. What makes the left pane so valuable, however, is its capability to let you move quickly from one place in your system to another.

The left pane of the Explorer view shows you all of your system resources as a hierarchical tree of container objects that branch out like a family tree. Each disk drive is a branch off the My

Computer branch of the tree, and the drive's folders branch off from there. Using this tree of objects as a road map, you can quickly find the folder, program, or document you want to use quickly, and with a minimum of mouse manipulation or keystrokes.

> **NOTE**
>
> A container object is an object that can contain other objects. Folders, disk drives, Network Neighborhood, and My Computer are all examples of container objects.

When Explorer is first launched, all of the disk drives and other container objects are shown in their collapsed state. A box to the left of container objects shows either a plus or a minus sign, which indicates the status of containers. If the container object contains other container objects (usually folders), a small plus sign indicates that the view of the tree can be expanded to show more details. A small minus sign indicates that the view is expanded, and the tree will show all the container objects at the next level down. Any folders that contain other folders will have their own indicator.

When you click a container object in the left pane, the right pane view changes to show you what is contained within that object. If the hierarchical tree in the left pane is taller than the window, a scrollbar appears enabling you to bring other disks and folders into view. The right-hand pane will not change view until a different container object is actually selected.

Because you can move the view of the tree without changing the view in the right-hand pane, you can much more easily move and copy folders, programs, and documents from one place to another than you can using the single pane view.

Using the Drag and Drop Method

When you drag objects from the right-hand pane to the tree in the left pane, the container object that will receive the dropped object(s) will be highlighted so you can easily tell where the objects will go. Use the same techniques for selecting objects to be copied as were detailed above in the section on the single pane view of Explorer.

Keep in mind that dragging objects and dropping them into another folder will cause a move operation to be done. If your intention is to copy the files, or to create shortcut objects, use the right mouse button to perform the drag. When you drop the objects onto another container a context menu is shown so you can choose whether the objects should be moved, copied, or if shortcuts should be created.

Using the Context Menu Method

To move or copy an object, you can right-click the object and select Cut or Copy in the context menu; the objects are placed on the Clipboard. In a Cut operation, which will translate into a move, the icon and label for the object will be grayed out to indicate that they will be deleted when the operation is complete. To complete the move or copy, right-click the container in the left pane you want to receive the object. In the context menu that appears, click Paste. That's all there is to it.

Figure 1.14 shows how you can easily right-drag a selection frame around a group of objects to be moved or copied. When you release the mouse button, the objects within the frame are highlighted to show they are selected, and a context menu automatically appears. Select Cut or Copy from the menu and then Paste the objects where you want them to go.

FIGURE 1.14.

Right-dragging a selection frame selects multiple objects and reveals the context menu in a single operation.

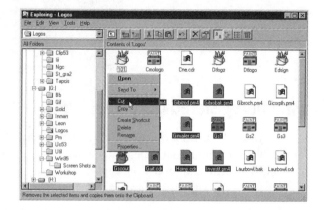

Copying and moving files is much easier using the Explorer view because you can use the scrollbar of the left-hand pane, if necessary, to bring the destination folder into view while still maintaining the view of the objects to be copied in the right-hand pane.

Viewing and Editing Document Objects

When you double-click a document in Explorer you should expect the application it is associated with to be launched with the document open. For example, by default the Registry contains an association between a Windows bitmap (.BMP file) and the Paint applet. When a BMP document is double-clicked, Paint is automatically launched, and the document opened. Many times, however, you can get a peek at the contents of document objects by right-clicking their icons and selecting Quick View from the context menu that appears. (See Figure 1.15.) Windows 95 ships with a number of Quick View applets that display the contents of documents.

Note that the Quick View applet has a button on the toolbar that enables you to launch the associated application in case you want to edit the document. Remember, document doesn't just mean text as in the example above. A document can be any kind of data from spreadsheets and text files to pictures and databases.

Multimedia documents like sounds and video clips when double-clicked launch the appropriate application in play mode. Once the sound or MIDI file, or whatever, is played, the application automatically closes. To open the application, right-click the icon and choose Open from the context menu.

FIGURE 1.15.

*Right-clicking a document
and choosing Quick View
from the context menu
allows you to see the
contents of the document.*

Viewing Unregistered Document Types

Occasionally you will obtain a document that isn't associated in the Registry with an application capable of opening that type of document. You have two choices, you can either right-click the document and specify the application to be used using Open With, or you can associate the document with an application.

If you do not work with a specific type of document very often you may want to just open it and not associate it with an application, or you may just want to make sure an application is compatible with the document before associating it. In this case just right-click the document, and choose Open With from the context menu. The Open With dialog shown in figure 1.16 will open allowing you to select an application to try opening the file with.

FIGURE 1.16.

*The Open With dialog
enables you to open
documents that are not
associated with a particular
application.*

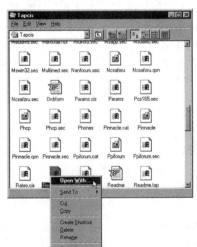

If you know which application on your system is compatible with the document, you can associate the document easily by clicking View in the menu bar and selecting the Options item from the menu. Click the File Types tab of the dialog and click New Type.

Beyond the Basics

Once you get used to working with Explorer and the taskbar, you can really start working with the document-centric user interface of Windows 95. There are nice little touches throughout the new user interface that add power and ease of use to Windows 95. The sections that follow contain a potpourri of useful information about some of these features.

The Explorer Command Line

It can be a real advantage to know the command syntax for Explorer. For example, by altering the command line in a shortcut, you can make Explorer open a specific folder when it launches, or restrict the view Explorer can provide to a single set of resources. You may even want to launch Explorer from the Run dialog of the Start menu, or a DOS prompt. You can easily do any of these if you know the Explorer command line syntax, so, here it is:

```
EXPLORER [/n][/e][,/root,object][[,/select],subobject]
```

It looks a lot more complex than it really is. To understand the syntax, just take each piece one at time. The /n and /e switches determine the view used. If a switch is optional, it is surrounded in flat brackets.

The default view is the single pane (My Computer) view, which means that unless you tell it to launch in Explorer mode with /e, the single pane view is used. The /n switch means to open a new window in the single pane view for each item selected regardless of the properties setting, even if the new window would duplicate one already open.

The simplest command line is

```
EXPLORER
```

since everything except the command is optional. This command line will launch Explorer in the single pane view rooted at the Desktop. Rooted, in this case, means that the Desktop is the highest level that can be browsed.

The /root switch determines the root level of the available view. For example:

```
EXPLORER /e, /root,E:\
```

This command line tells Explorer to open in dual pane view with E:\ (the root folder of the E disk drive) as the root of the view. When Explorer launches, the only thing you can browse is the E disk and its folders because Explorer is rooted to the highest level of E:. Making a folder the root causes anything above the folder in the resource tree to be invisible.

The /select switch tells Explorer which folder to open at launch. For example:

```
EXPLORER /e, /root,E:\, /select, winword
```

This command line tells Explorer to use the dual pane view, root at the highest level of E:, and to open the Winword folder in the right-hand pane.

If you look back at the syntax, you will see that the /select switch itself is optional. See how the flat brackets are different from the /root switch? Because the /select itself is optional, you can use a shorthand form like this

```
EXPLORER /e, C:\windows
```

This command line opens in dual pane view, rooted at the Desktop, with the Windows folder open for viewing. If you don't specify either /root or /select, Explorer understands you to mean /select.

New Common Dialogs

One of the features of Windows that makes it easy to use is that all Windows programs look and act a lot alike, no matter what they are supposed to do. Once you have learned one Windows program, you have a good idea how to run any Windows program. One of the elements in this standardization is a dynamic link library (DLL) that provides common dialogs for programmers. The common dialogs are supplied by Microsoft with every copy of Windows 95.

Because there are standard dialogs for opening files, altering color palettes, printing, and the like, programmers don't have to create their own. Every Windows user has a copy of the common dialogs, so the programmer doesn't have to reinvent the wheel, so to speak. Users already know how they work, so there is no training.

The new common dialogs that come with Windows 95 are quite a bit different than the ones that were distributed with previous versions of Windows. They are easier to use, and have some data-centric features that give you more control over your computer. As you will see in the next sections, the Windows 95 common dialogs are almost miniature versions of the Explorer. The best part is that they are useful as can be.

The Open Dialog

If you check out Figure 1.17, you will see the new Open common dialog in use by WordPad, the applet that replaces Write in Windows 95. In this figure, the user has asked to open a file.

Just like Explorer, the Open dialog has a listbox so you can easily choose from disk drives and other resources. When you select a disk, the folders of that disk are shown in the box labeled Look In. Use the Look In box to double-click folders and drill down to the folder where the document you want opened is contained.

FIGURE 1.17.

The new Open dialog is chock full of useful features that resemble a miniature version of Explorer.

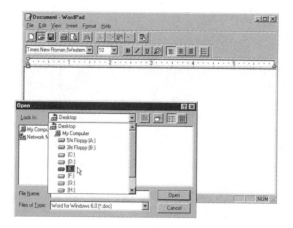

Another feature in common with Explorer is the Up One Level button that lets you go back if you have drilled down too far. A really handy new feature is the button just to the right of the Up One Level button that lets you create a new folder. When you click the icon, a new folder is created with the name label highlighted so you can immediately type in a new name.

But that's not all! If you have a list of document objects in the Look In box, you can right-click a name to bring up a context menu like the one shown in Figure 1.18. You can cut, copy, rename, and even edit the properties of the document. Of course, if you locate the document you want to open, you can just double-click to open it up.

FIGURE 1.18.

The Open dialog lets you manage document objects just like you can in Explorer.

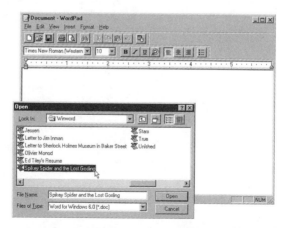

NOTE

If you still don't quite get all this talk about object-oriented features in Windows 95, looking at Figure 1.19 may make a light bulb go on over your head.

Because the representations of files you see onscreen are actually objects instead of the files themselves, they can carry their features almost anywhere. That's why you can do all the things to files that you can do in the Open dialog. The objects are the same as they are in Explorer, or on your desktop. They carry their properties with them wherever they are used.

One of the most frustrating things about working with documents in Windows 3.x is that if you select the File|Open command instead of the File|New, you have to go back to the menu and start all over again. In the object-oriented world of Windows 95, all you have to do is right-click an empty spot in the Look In box to reveal a context menu—and of course, the context menu contains a New command.

The File Save Dialog

Just as the File Open dialog has new features, the File Save common dialog can also do more than just save files. Take a look at Figure 1.19, and you will see the new File Save dialog that can be called by Windows 95 programs.

FIGURE 1.19.

Only the name of the dialog changes when you elect to save a file.

Surprise! The File Save dialog is the same dialog as the Open dialog, only the title bar changes to reflect the name Save As. All of the features listed above work here, too.

Creating New Documents On the Fly

Creating new documents from the desktop is a snap in Windows 95. All you have to do is right-click either a blank spot in an Explorer window, or on the desktop itself. The context menu that appears has an item labeled New. A submenu that cascades from the New command shows you the types of documents you can create. As you begin to upgrade to 32-bit versions of your favorite software, you will find that many of them will register their file type in this menu.

As an example, clicking Word's entry will create a new Word 6 for Windows document. This object is already associated with the program. When you double-click the new object, the program (in this case Word) it is associated with is launched and the file opened.

> **TIP**
>
> Creating new folders is even easier. Just select Folder from the New menu, and then type the name you want the folder to have.

The Quick View Feature

When you view the context menu for many types of objects you will see an option marked Quick View. The Quick View feature enables you to peek inside of many different file formats without having to open the full-blown application that created them. This feature is at its handiest when you are looking through a stack of documents to find the exact one you need, but can't remember the name.

When you find a likely candidate, all you have to do is right-click and choose Quick View from the context menu. Windows 95 then launches a Quick View reader program similar to the one shown in Figure 1.20. The document is opened for viewing, but you cannot edit it.

FIGURE 1.20.

The Quick View feature makes finding the file you want to edit quick and easy.

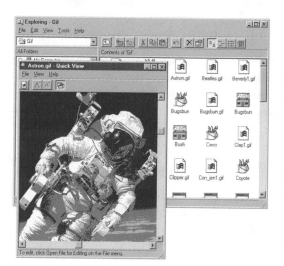

56

There are a number of Quick View readers included with Windows 95. By the time this book finds its way into your hands, there will be other commercially available Quick View readers that give you even more functionality.

The Recycle Bin and the Undo Feature

Windows 95's Recycle Bin takes the worry out of managing files for novice users, and can also come in handy when your favorite power user acts like a rookie. The Recycle Bin is tightly integrated with Explorer. Recalling accidentally deleted files can be as simple as selecting Undo from the Edit menu of My Computer or Explorer. The Undo feature simply keeps a record of your file management activities, deleting, moving, renaming, and so on. You can back up the chain of changes in the reverse order you made them by repeatedly clicking Undo.

Of course there will be times when you don't want to undo a whole chain of deletions just to correct a single mistake. That's why the Recycle Bin object sits on the Desktop. Double-clicking Recycle Bin opens a single pane Explorer session. To restore a file to its previous folder, all you have to do is right-click and choose Restore from the context menu.

Unlike other folders, the Recycle Bin limits what can be done with the objects presented. You are limited to viewing their properties, cutting them to the Clipboard (handy for restoring a file to a different folder than it formerly occupied), deleting the file altogether, and restoring the file. Double-clicking will not open the document. Instead the properties menu will be popped up.

Recycle Bin Properties

How far back the objects in the bin go is limited by the size of the Recycle Bin itself. You have the ability to adjust the percentage of disk space allocated to the Recycle Bin. Figure 1.21 shows you the dialog you get when you right-click the Recycle Bin icon and select Properties from the context menu.

FIGURE 1.21.

You can configure all drives together, or you can adjust each individually.

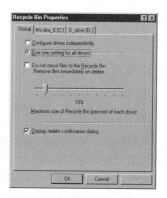

At the top of this dialog are tabs, one for each hard disk volume you have in your computer. Notice that even hidden compressed volume hosts are shown. If you select "Use one setting for all drives" the settings of the Purge checkbox and the slider that regulates the percentage of space allocated to recycling will be system-wide.

If, on the other hand, you select "Configure drives independently," you can click the tab for each drive and set the Purge and percentage options for each drive separately.

Figure 1.22 shows the dialog for setting the options on an individual drive. Checking the Purge checkbox will keep deleted files from being archived in the Recycle Bin. So will setting the slider to 0%. Generally you will want to allow the Recycle Bin to use from 5 to 10 percent of the hard disk. Note that the actual amount of space you are allocating is reflected at the top of the dialog.

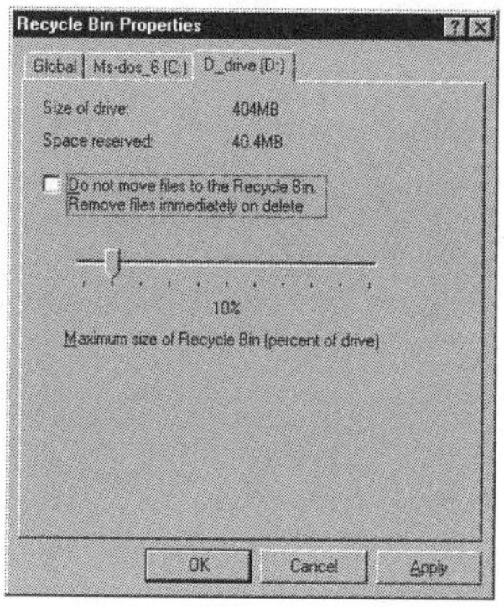

FIGURE 1.22.

Each drive's Recycle Bin can be sized to accommodate the way you use data on that particular drive.

Setting the slider to allow a larger Recycle Bin does not mean that your drive will automatically have a reduced capacity for storing "live" files. Instead it sets an upper limit for how large the Recycle Bin can grow.

As you delete files, the Recycle Bin grows, eventually reaching its maximum allowed size. To make room for further deletions, the oldest files are removed from the bin, and are lost forever. As files in the bin age, they are replaced by newer deletions.

> **TIP**
>
> Whenever you need to free up some space on a drive or know that you will never need the files contained in the Recycle Bin again, you can right-click the Recycle Bin object on the desktop and choose Empty Recycle Bin from the context menu.

Set Up the Desktop Your Way

Between the Start Menu of the taskbar and objects you create on the desktop, you can customize Windows 95 to look and work just the way you want to. In this respect Windows 95 is probably the most personal operating system ever to run personal computers. Using either My Computer or Explorer, you can easily alter the landscape of your desktop to suit the way you want to work.

> **NOTE**
>
> On some highly administered systems, the system administrator may elect to remotely set up the desktop on your system to conform to company standard. This type of installation may limit the changes you can make to your desktop environment. Ask your system administrator what customizations can be done.

With Windows 95 you can create folders that act just like Program Manager groups. Or you can drop shortcuts to disk drives and printers onto the desktop and create an environment similar to the old Norton Desktop or PC Tools. You can arrange your most used programs and documents around the desktop where you can quickly and easily find them. In short, the Windows desktop can be as clean or messy, as organized or as trashed as your real desktop.

Moving a Folder Onto the Desktop

One of the first things many new users of Windows 95 do is to create a shortcut to their printers or fonts on the desktop. It is simple to do, and gives you immediate access to those resources without having to launch My Computer or use the Start Menu.

You may have your choice of several printers, but mostly just use the one directly attached to your system. In that case you may want to place a shortcut to a particular printer on the desktop instead of the whole printers folder.

After you create a desktop icon for your printer, you have an icon on the desktop you can double-click to change printer properties, view the status of print jobs, and effectively monitor the overall status of your printer.

Creating Folders on the Desktop

If you right-click a blank area of the desktop, a context menu appears. One of the options on the menu is New. Pointing to the New option causes a second menu to cascade from the context menu. From this second menu, you can choose to create any number of new objects. One of those choices is to create a new folder. Clicking this option will place a folder called New Folder onto the desktop. Select Rename from its context menu to give it any name you want.

Once you have created the folder you can use it in two basic ways. You can leave it closed on the desktop ready to be brought into use with a double-click, or you can leave the folder open on the desktop to display its icons in a similar fashion to a Windows 3.1 Program Manager group. Figure 1.23 shows how you might create an open folder to house your text editors and word processing applications.

FIGURE 1.23.

An open folder can be used like a Windows 3.1 Program Manager group.

Since the open folder is really an instance of My Computer, you can use the open folder as a way of hopscotching around your system—something a Program Manager group could never do.

When you perform an orderly shutdown of the system using the last item in the Start menu, Windows 95 remembers the configuration of your desktop. The next time you start up your system, the open folders will be restored.

Customizing the Start Menu

Once you are comfortable with using Explorer, you can easily customize your Start Menu. The official way of altering the Start menu is with the property sheet of the taskbar. You will probably want to avoid using the property sheet.

Thus, the most efficient way of editing your Start menu is to launch Explorer and locate the Windows\Start Menu folder. Now all you have to do is create shortcuts and folders in the Start menu folder, or in the folders contained in Start menu. Complete instructions for editing the Start menu are in Chapter 5.

> **TIP**
>
> If you installed Windows 95 over an existing Windows 3.x setup, the icons found in Program Manager groups were converted to shortcuts and placed into folders having the same name as the Program Manager group they originally belonged to. These folders appear in the Programs menu item of the Start Menu.

Shut Down

It may be ironic that the way to turn off your system is found on the Start menu, but when it's time to knock off for the day, the Shut Down button of the Start menu is the place to be. Figure 1.24 shows the dialog that appears when you select this Start menu item. Depending on the way you have Windows 95 installed, the third option in the dialog may vary.

FIGURE 1.24.

An orderly shut down is recommended to maintain the health of your computer's resources.

The reason for requiring an orderly shutdown of the system is basically to prevent a meltdown. Windows 95 uses a write-behind cache that sometimes delays disk activity for a few seconds in favor of providing the user with snappier screen performance. In addition, Windows 95 logs updates to the Registry and severs connections with remote resources before telling you it is safe to turn off your computer.

If, for example, you exit an application and immediately flip the power switch on your system, the disk write cache may not get a chance to save your documents before the power goes off. Connections to network resources are not logged out, and thus left in limbo, and your User portion of the Registry may not be saved. For these reasons, and others, it is recommended that you always perform an orderly shut down of your system at the end of your work session.

Summary

In this chapter you have seen how the redesigned, object-oriented user interface of Windows 95 significantly changes the way users interact with Windows. It may take you a couple of days to get used to working with the taskbar, Explorer, the Start Menu, and an active Desktop. After you get used to the new interface, however, Windows 3.x seems crude by comparison.

In the next chapter you will find out how the Windows 3.x applets have been changed, and what new applets are included in this release.

The Windows 95 Applets

by J

IN THIS CHAPTER

The term *applets* refers to the small applications that are shipped with Windows 95. Windows 95 includes a variety of applets to help you perform routine tasks, work between applications, network better, and fine-tune your disks. A few are carryovers from Windows 3.1, some have been enhanced, and many are newcomers designed especially to improve the overall usefulness of Windows 95.

An Overview

In the typical Windows 95 installation, only a few of the available applets are installed for you. If you perform a custom installation, you have the opportunity to pick the ones you want. After you have logged some time with Windows 95, you might find a use for an applet that isn't installed on your system. Use Windows Setup tab in the Add/Remove Programs dialog in Control Panel to install any that you want to use.

Not all of the applets are described in detail in this chapter. Those applets that pertain to a particular part of Windows 95 are covered in the chapters devoted to that subject. Here's a quick rundown by category of the applets found in Windows 95. If the applet is not covered in this chapter, a reference to its location is provided.

Accessibility Options: Although the options are primarily designed for users who are hearing and sight impaired, they offer ways that anyone can use to add sounds, improve display, and customize keyboard and mouse performance. Options such as controlling the keyboard repeat rate and increasing the keyboard support available in Help are also of interest to anyone who regularly uses the keyboard as an input device. See the Part II overview.

Calculator: The Windows 95 Calculator includes a standard and a scientific calculator, both of which are operated in much the same way as their desktop or pocket counterparts. The Calculator has the added advantage of being able to copy the answer into the document where the data is needed.

Character Map: This applet is used to insert symbols and nonstandard characters into a document. The character map applet can be used for quickly accessing foreign language characters and symbols from extended character sets and is particularly helpful when working with the Symbol and Wingding typefaces.

Clipboard Viewer: This applet provides a window into the contents of the Windows 95 Clipboard by displaying the data that has most recently been cut or copied from a document. The contents of the Clipboard can be saved as .CLP files so you can archive data that can be retrieved later and pasted where needed. (See Chapter 12, "OLE.")

Clipbook: The Clipbook applet extends the usefulness of the Clipboard. The Clipboard is only capable of storing one data item at a time. The Clipbook enables you to store multiple Clipboard entries in local or shared Clipbook pages rather than in dozens of little .CLP files. The contents of the shared pages can be used (and even edited) by others in your network workgroup. Page contents can later be copied back to the Clipboard and pasted into documents.

Screen Savers: In the past, computer screens were subject to *burn in*. Burn in occurs when an image is displayed onscreen for long periods of time. A permanent image of the screen is literally burnt into the phosphors of the monitor. Although modern VGA monitors are not subject to burn in, screen saver applets remain quite popular among Windows users because they hide what you are working on after a few minutes of idle time. By enabling password protection, you can prevent others from accessing your computer when you are called away from your desk. Refer to Chapter 5, "Customizing the Desktop and Integrating Windows 95 Applications."

Games: The games included with Windows 95 provide entertainment as well as mouse practice. The games included with Windows 95 include Minesweeper, Solitaire, Hearts, Rumor, Party Line, and Freecell. Refer to Chapter 13, "Family Computing."

Net Watcher: The Net Watcher applet enables you to check who is using network resources as well as manage folders and user connections.

Object Packager: The Object Packager is used to create OLE (Object Linking and Embedding) links so you can attach data (sounds, portions of documents from other applications, video presentations, and so on) to an icon that can be pasted into documents. When a user double-clicks the icon in the document, the linked data is displayed or played, depending on what the appropriate action is. Refer to Chapter 12, "OLE".

Paint: This applet is a handy tool for creating, modifying, or viewing bitmap format pictures. You can create line drawings that illustrate your documents, crop screen shots, and zoom in to edit images pixel by pixel.

Quick View: Quick View is a series of small applets that enable you to preview documents before opening them.

WordPad: WordPad is a word processor with enough features to create a variety of letters, memos, and other documents that can be saved as text files, Word for Windows documents, or RTF (Rich Text Format) documents.

Dial-Up Networking: This applet makes it possible to share resources with other computers if each has a modem. Dial up your office computer from your computer at home or from a portable while on the road. Refer to Chapter 11, "Mobile Computing."

Direct Cable Connection: Using this applet enables two computers to share data by connecting the computers with a parallel or serial cable. Refer to Chapter 11, "Mobile Computing."

HyperTerminal: If you have a modem installed, you can use HyperTerminal Connections to connect to other computers and log on to computer bulletin boards and other online services.

Microsoft Exchange: Exchange acts as a central service for sending and receiving electronic mail or fax messages. Refer to Chapter 11, "Mobile Computing."

Microsoft Fax: This applet, when coupled with a fax modem, can be added to Microsoft Exchange to enable you to send and receive fax communications directly from your applications. Refer to Chapter 11, "Mobile Computing."

Accessibility

To use Accessibility Options shortcut keys, the shortcut keys must be enabled.

Press	*To*
Shift 5 times	Toggle StickyKeys on and off
Right-Shift for 8 seconds	Toggle Filter Keys on and off
NumLock for 5 seconds	Toggle ToggleKeys on and off
Left Alt+Left Shift+NumLock	Toggle MouseKeys on and off
Left Alt+Left Shift+Print Screen	Toggle High Contrast on and off

Getting Help with Your Math

Calculator offers both a standard view (shown in Figure 2.1) and a scientific view in which you can perform routine or complex calculations, and then copy and paste the answer into a document where the data is needed. You can calculate percentages and square roots, store numbers in memory for later use, and do it all with the mouse!

FIGURE 2.1.

In the standard Calculator, type numbers on your numeric keypad or select them in the Calculator with the mouse.

The Calculator includes a scientific view in which you can perform statistical and trigonometric calculations, use scientific notation, and convert numbers to other numbering systems. Click any of the Calculator features with the right mouse button and then click What's This to see a description of the feature and (sometimes) information on its use.

> **TIP**
>
> Remember to activate NumLock if you want to use the numeric keypad to enter calculations.

Inserting Special Characters

Character Map offers a quick way to insert symbols and other special characters in a document. Although the same symbols can be accessed within applications by changing fonts, the Character Map displays the entire set of characters for the font, making it easier to find the character you want.

All font sets in Windows do not contain the same 256 characters; you might want to check all the available sets to see what they contain. The Symbol and Wingding fonts (see Figure 2.2) are particularly rich sources of icons, symbols, and characters that you can use instead of bullets or other graphics devices in a chart or flyer.

FIGURE 2.2.

Character Map makes it easy to view the graphics included in the Wingdings font set.

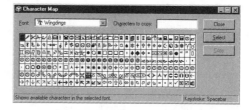

When you find a character you want to use, choose Insert to add it to Characters to copy. When you have selected the characters you need, simply paste them into a document.

Finding the Files You Want

As hard disks become larger and larger, it is often difficult to remember where things are stored. Also, as the number of documents stored on your system increases, it is often difficult to remember what file contains the data you are looking for. Fortunately, the Find applet is automatically installed for you when you install Windows 95. You can use this applet to locate files and folders on your system quickly and easily, no matter how large your disk is or how many folders you have.

When you have difficulty locating a file or folder, Find is the solution. Find is also a handy tool; access to it shows up at every turn. Try looking on

- The Start menu
- The context menu for My Computer on the desktop

68

- The context menu for drives in Explorer
- The context menu for any drive or folder name in Windows Explorer
- The Tools menu in Explorer

When you launch Find from a specific location, that location appears as the default starting place in the Look In list box (see Figure 2.3). If you want to hunt in another location, select the location in the Look In drop-down list of all your drives. To look for a file that seems to have gone astray, type all or part of the filename in the Named text box. If you have searched for this file previously, click the arrow to drop down a list of your last 10 searches. You can narrow the search if you know a word or phrase in the desired document. Using the Advanced tab, you can also specify text to search for.

FIGURE 2.3.

*Use the * and ? wildcards in the file or folder name to look for a group of related files or when you are unsure of the full filename. The Named text box contains a drop-down list of your last 10 entries, so you don't have to remember how you set up a search that you want to repeat.*

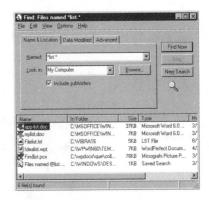

Options in the Advanced dialog box include an extensive list of file types that expands to include all registered file types, so you can easily find documents of a particular type. If you know the approximate file size, enter it in kilobytes and indicate whether you want to search for files of equal to or greater than that size.

Perhaps the most powerful feature of Find is the capability to search files for specific text. Enter a specific word or phrase in the Containing textbox, and choose the Find Now button to search for occurrences of the word or phrase in documents. If you turn on Include subfolders in the Name and Location dialog, you can search for the text in an entire branch or an entire drive of files.

TIP

If you want to find specific text and the search will include several folders, speed things up by choosing a file type, or at least provide a file extension. Otherwise, the search will be slowed while Find looks in unrelated documents.

The search can be narrowed somewhat by choosing Case Sensitive from the Options menu. If you know an approximate date that the file was created or modified, options in the Date Modified dialog can help narrow a search. Maybe the file was modified during the last 30 days or several months, or you can try suggesting a beginning and ending date for the search.

One of the handiest features of Find is that the result window provides a miniature Explorer. To open a document, all you need to do is double-click the document object. Of course, you can also right-click objects to display their context menu, from which you can choose to Quick View or edit properties.

If you find you are performing the same search over and over again, choose Save Search on the File menu to save all your search settings to a file. If you want to save the list of found files, turn on Save Results on the Options menu before choosing Save Search. Either way, the search is saved with a long filename, such as the one at the end of the list in Figure 2.3, and an icon is placed on the desktop that enables you to pull up the results as needed.

TIP

If you save several searches and don't want the desktop cluttered with Find file icons, add a new folder to your hard drive or the desktop and move the Find icons into it.

To perform another search, enter the new information and choose Find Now. If you want to completely start over, choose New Search to clear all the information you have entered in the dialog box. The setting in the View and Options menu are not cleared, however.

Quick View

Quick View enables you to preview documents of various formats without having to open them with the application that created them. Because a full-blown application can take a while to load into memory, it is often much more convenient to use Quick View to make sure that the document contains the data you are looking for. To activate Quick View, just right-click any registered file type and choose Quick View from the context menu.

The font size can be increased if the text is too small to read in the Quick View window (see Figure 2.4), or you can change to a full page display to check the layout of the document. When you find the document you want, it can be opened for editing by clicking the File Open button at the extreme left edge of the Toolbar. When you click the open button, Windows 95 launches the application associated with the file and opens the file in a document window.

FIGURE 2.4.

Buttons are available on the Quick View toolbar to open the document for editing, increasing or decreasing the font size, and replacing the window contents.

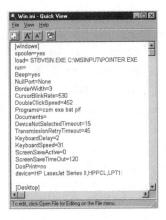

Getting Help

The Help applet has been totally redesigned for Windows 95 to make it easier to use and much more powerful. There are several ways to obtain quick information about applications, onscreen features, and Windows 95 itself. Here is a brief list of the ways you can get help on just about any Windows 95 topic:

- Press F1. If you are in an application, it brings up Help specific to the application. If you are at the desktop, Windows 95 Help is displayed.
- Point to any button on a toolbar, and the task it performs is displayed in a tip box.
- In a dialog box, right-click almost any control. A small button marked What's This? appears. Clicking this button displays an explanation of the option and often offers suggestions for its use.
- When a ? appears in the title bar of a dialog, you can click the ? button and then click a feature or option to see a description of it.

> **NOTE**
>
> Because Windows provides the Help interface for all Windows applications, the Help features described in this section are available everywhere. However, toolbar tips and What's This? descriptions are created by the individual application developers and might not be available in all applications. Check each application's user manual to find what interface assistance is offered.

To look for specific topics in Help, try using Index rather than working your way through Contents topics. You can narrow the available topics by toggling Use the Combined Index for Windows Help topics off. From the list provided in the Current index, you can now choose specific help for topics such as basic tasks, the mouse, or networks, to name a few.

An extremely powerful approach is to use Find to create a word and topic list for the current Help file. Depending upon available disk space and the speed of your computer, choose Express setup to index the entire Help file, or use Custom options to limit what is indexed. When creating a custom index, you can elect to exclude untitled topics, phrase searching, matching phrase display, and similarity searches. Figure 2.5 shows the results of a word list created with the Express option.

FIGURE 2.5.

After generating a word list, Find displays alphabetized lists of the words and the topic titles in the Help file. Type a word or select one from the word list to see the topics in which the word is found.

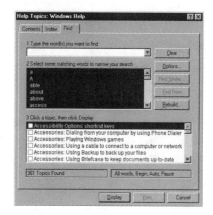

To begin searching in the word list as you type, pause briefly after each character. Otherwise, the search begins if you pause at the end of a word. In the Options dialog box, you can change the behavior of the index to delay searching until you select the Find Now button.

No matter how many words you type, the resulting topics list will include all topics that contain any one of the words. Again, using Options, you can request that the search match all of the words, or you can search for phrases by requiring an exact match of what you type. Broaden the search, if you prefer, by allowing matches that begin with, end with, or just contain the same letters as those you type; or, you can authorize a match if the words share a common root.

If you find that you like working with the word list format, go ahead and index the Help file in the other Windows applications you use regularly. After you have created a word list, it is available each time you reopen the Help file. If you later decide you want to streamline the file, simply click the Rebuild button of the Find dialog and customize the reindexing process by eliminating one or more of the display options.

Jot It Down in NotePad

Not all documents are heavily formatted like word processing documents. Many use a simple text format. Examples include INI files, AUTOEXEC.BAT, CONFIG.SYS, and DOS batch files. The NotePad applet is quite handy for editing and creating text files that contain less than 64 KB of data. Figure 2.6 shows NotePad in action editing AUTOEXEC.BAT.

FIGURE 2.6.

In Windows Explorer, the Shortcut menu for AUTOEXEC.BAT includes Edit rather than Quick View. Choose Edit and the file is opened in a NotePad window.

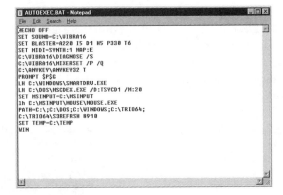

The simplicity of NotePad makes it handy for creating other kinds of short documents as well. Naturally, no text formatting commands are available, but the current date can be inserted; word wrap is available; and pages can be laid out with margins, portrait or landscape orientation, and a header and footer that can display page numbering.

If you want to include formatting in a document, or if the file is too large to edit in NotePad, use WordPad.

Creating Documents in WordPad

WordPad is a simple but effective word processor that you can use as a text file editor or to create routine personal and business documents. Launch WordPad from the Accessories section of the Start Menu to display a blank document ready for you to complete.

For the smoothest performance when creating documents that require word wrap, maximize WordPad so it fills the screen. WordPad can work with documents in text only, Rich Text Format, Word 6, and Windows 3.1 Write formats. The default word wrap behavior depends upon the format you use; each can be customized to suit your work habits. In fact, you can even control the way embedded text wraps in a WordPad document.

> **NOTE**
>
> Word wrap controls only how text appears on the screen. When the document is printed, text wraps to the margins set in Page Setup.

The ruler simplifies setting tabs and paragraph indents, while the addition of a toolbar and format bar puts frequently used commands within easy reach of the mouse. (See Figure 2.7.)

Both the toolbar and format bar can be dragged to other positions on the screen, although the format bar can be displayed only horizontally. Using the Options command, you can also indicate for each document format which, if any, of the various bars or rulers you want displayed.

FIGURE 2.7.

WordPad begins with the ruler, toolbar, and format bar displayed. Point to a button or menu command and a description of the item appears in the status bar at the bottom of the window.

TIP

It's easy to arrange WordPad to maximize the document area. For those familiar with the menu commands, the status bar serves little purpose except to take up space. You can hide it by selecting Status Bar from the View menu. Then drag the toolbar to the right edge of the screen. If you don't need the paragraph align or bullet buttons, try moving the toolbar to the left as far as possible, and then place the format bar at the right end of the toolbar. Also, turn the Ruler off except when actually setting tabs.

WordPad includes the popular control key combinations found in most Windows applications, such as Ctrl+B for Bold, Ctrl+C for Copy, and Ctrl+S for Save, which are also shown on the drop-down menus. You can also click the right mouse button anywhere in the document screen to display a quick menu that provides quick access to commands to edit or format a selection (be it text or an object), or to change the layout of a paragraph.

WordPad is configured to automatically select whole words when you use the mouse to highlight text. You can turn this option off in the Options dialog box. While there, you can also change the units of measurement used on the ruler to picas, centimeters, or points. (See Figure 2.8.)

FIGURE 2.8.

Configure the units of measurement, toggle selection of whole words, and set preferences when working with various file formats in the Options dialog box.

Formatting Paragraphs

Emphasize text by indenting paragraphs from the left, right, or both margins. If you want the first line of paragraphs to be indented but don't like having to press Tab to indent paragraphs, specify a measurement to indent the first line. Set up paragraph indents using the pull-down menu commands or the ruler. In fact, the ruler provides the only way to create a hanging indent, in which all lines of the paragraph except the first line are indented.

Drag the markers at either end of the ruler to set indents. The top and bottom markers, or pointers, can be dragged separately. The top marker sets the amount that you want to indent the first line of the paragraph. The bottom marker controls the left indent for the rest of the paragraph. Use the box to drag both markers to indent the entire paragraph. Move the right indent marker to set a right margin indent.

Organizing ideas into a list and enhancing each item in the list with a bullet is an effective way to communicate with your reader. The bullet feature makes this easy. Select Bullet Style from the Format menu or select the Bullet button on the format bar to add the bullet and a left indent to the paragraph.

> **NOTE**
>
> The format of a paragraph, such as tab settings, indentation, bullets, and text alignment, is stored in the paragraph mark that is added at the end of a paragraph when you press Enter. You can use this paragraph mark to copy the way a paragraph is formatted and apply the formatting to another paragraph. If you delete the paragraph mark, you delete the formatting for that paragraph.

Working with Fonts

A Font and Font size drop-down list are the most prominent features on the format bar of WordPad. The more familiar Font dialog box is accessed from the Format menu.

WordPad accommodates very large font sizes, and you can change the font as often as you wish. You can create a personal letterhead, flyers, or newsletters that do not require columns. Redline and strikeout are available for on-line editing of documents. (See Figure 2.9.)

FIGURE 2.9.

Change the font, font size, and color in the Font dialog box. Several language alternatives are included in the Script drop-down list.

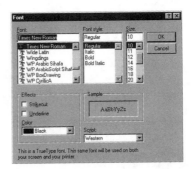

The Turkish, Greek, Cyrillic, and Eastern European font support Windows 95 provides is indicated in parentheses after the font name in the drop-down list. Check your choice carefully; the language may be partially obscured if the font name is long.

Setting Up the Page

Set margins and paper orientation in the Page Setup dialog box, which includes a sample page preview area shown in Figure 2.10. Margins are stated in inches even if you have changed the measurement unit on the ruler.

FIGURE 2.10.

The sample page shows the new margins, paper orientation and size, and other changes you make in the Page Setup dialog box.

If you embed a chart or create a flyer using WordPad, try changing the paper orientation to landscape. A variety of paper sizes such as envelopes and ledgers, and paper sources such as envelope feeders, are also available and are limited only by the capability of your printer.

Previewing and Saving Documents

The preview provided in Page Setup is of a mock page, so use Print Preview to check the layout of your document before printing. (See Figure 2.11.) Use the buttons on the Preview toolbar to move through the document a page at a time or change to a two-page display, if you prefer. Return to the editing window with Close, or choose Print if you are satisfied with what you see.

FIGURE 2.11.

Print Preview displays a document as it will appear when printed. Use the Zoom In button for a closer look at the document if you need to be able to read the text.

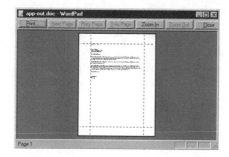

WordPad can save and retrieve Word for Windows 6, text only, and Rich Text Format (.RTF) files. Rich Text Format preserves most or all formatting and can be used by most of the better known word processing applications.

Paint

The Paint applet, shown in Figure 2.12, can be used to edit or create Windows bitmap (.BMP) files. To add text to a drawing, click the Text button in the toolbox and use the crosshair cursor to draw a textbox on the screen. Don't make the textbox too big; you can use the handles to increase the box size but not reduce it. When you release the mouse button, a Fonts toolbar appears from which you can choose a different typeface or size, or change the text to bold, underlined, or italics. Click elsewhere in the drawing to close the text box when you finish entering text. You can also use Paint to copy a bitmap or select just a portion of it, so it can be copied to the Clipboard and pasted into your documents.

FIGURE 2.12.

Paintbrush has a Tool Box of drawing tools and a Color Box to help you create your drawing. The flower petals are drawn with the Curve tool. The position of the pointer is shown in the Status Bar as 177,216.

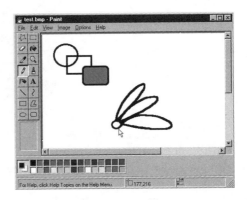

The Paint Tool Box contains tools to select an irregular or regular area, draw various closed shapes, fill an enclosed area with color, and draw lines of varying thickness. Users with a high degree of skill can achieve excellent results with the Airbrush tool. Magnify the size of the drawing by a factor of 2, 6, or 8 to edit a drawing or create interesting shading effects by applying colors one pixel at a time.

> **TIP**
>
> Creating custom colors may not always give you the results you want. If you have the desired color in a .BMP file, you can paint with it. Use Pick Color (the eyedropper) to pick up the color you want to use elsewhere in the drawing.

You must select part, or all, of the picture before copying it. The Paste command automatically places the Clipboard contents in the upper-left corner of the drawing; drag the image where you want it. Or, you can move and copy in one step with the keyboard. Just drag a selection to move it, or press Ctrl while dragging the selection to copy it. You can also stretch, skew, rotate, or flip a selection or the entire picture.

TIP

To sweep (make multiple overlapping copies) of an image, first select it, and then press the Shift key while you drag the selection. The faster you drag the image, the farther apart the overlapping copies in the sweep. Try it by drawing a small oval in a corner of the window, selecting it with the Select tool, and then dragging the selection around the window.

Using Paint to capture screens in Windows 95 is simple. Press the Print Screen key to capture the entire screen or press Alt+PrtScr to capture the active window. Paste the result in Paint and you can edit the image or crop parts of it for use elsewhere.

When you have completed a drawing, save the image as a bitmap (.BMP) file or select part of the drawing and paste it into another application or drawing.

HyperTerminal

If your computer has a modem installed, use HyperTerminal to establish connections to other computers and to log on to computer bulletin boards and other on-line services.

When you launch HyperTerminal from the Accessories menu, the HyperTerminal window contains the connections you have created and the HyperTerminal program. Run Hyper-Terminal to create a new connection. Provide a connection name, choose an icon to represent the connection (see Figure 2.13), and in the next dialog box provide the phone number. If you have more than one modem, specify which you want to use to make the connection.

In the Connect dialog box, choose Dialing Properties if you want to dial out using a credit card, disable call waiting, or need to access an outside line for the phone line you are using. Choose Modify to configure the modem settings, such as to control the volume; set the data bits, parity, and stop bits; and indicate whether the call is operator assisted. You can also provide advanced error- and flow-control settings, if necessary.

After you have set up the numbers you call frequently, you connect to services directly from the HyperTerminal. (See Figure 2.14.)

FIGURE 2.13.

Begin creating a new connection by providing a name for the connection and choosing an icon to use in the HyperTerminal window.

FIGURE 2.14.

When a connection is successfully dialed, the on-line service interface appears in the Hyper-Terminal window. Use the buttons on the Toolbar to download or upload files, or to disconnect when you finish a session.

If you want a transcript of an online session, you can capture text to a file or directly to a printer. However, if all you want is to copy a screen or two, select the text while it is displayed in the window, press Ctrl+C to copy it, paste it in another application, and then continue working online.

Phone Dialer

Phone Dialer is a straightforward little applet that enables you to dial the phone by entering the phone number from your numeric keypad or the on-screen telephone keypad.

As shown in Figure 2.15, up to eight phone numbers can be stored in Phone Dialer. In the Edit Speed Dial dialog box, choose a button and then type the name and phone number for each number you want to add. Return to Speed Dialer and click the appropriate Speed Dial button and Windows dials the number.

FIGURE 2.15.

Use the mouse to dial a number on the Phone Dialer keypad or select one of the Speed Dial buttons.

You can log calls that you make or receive. Use the log menu commands to edit the log, or double-click a name or phone number to dial it directly from the log. In the Options dialog box, choose whether you want to log outgoing or incoming calls, or both.

The Line Properties can be customized. Use this option to control the volume; set the data bits, parity, and stop bits; set a baud rate for the modem; and set how long to let the phone ring. Choose Dialing Properties if you want to use a credit card, set up another location, access an outside line for the phone number you are using, or other properties. Unless you choose otherwise, all voice call requests from any application are handled by Phone Dialer.

The Windows 95 Command Line

Over the years, many users have become accustomed to using DOS commands for everyday computing tasks. If you know these commands well, you might want to continue using the command-line interface to perform some tasks. Although the command line isn't specifically an applet, it is covered here because most experienced Windows 95 users work with the command line as if it were an applet.

NOTE

It is perhaps ironic that in the first version of Windows that doesn't rely on DOS as its foundation, the command line interface has been significantly expanded. There are new commands for network administration and new commands for use with TCP/IP connections. In addition, traditional DOS commands have been enhanced to support long filenames. Other traditional DOS commands have been eliminated entirely.

Several ways to launch the command-line interface are available in Windows 95. You can run COMMAND.COM by selecting Run from the Start Menu or by double-clicking the file in Windows Explorer, or you can launch a MS-DOS session by selecting MS-DOS Prompt from the Programs section of the Start Menu. The sections that follow document the changes in the DOS command-line interface.

The DOS prompt that Windows 95 provides is actually a Win32-based application. A complete virtual computer (running the version of MS-DOS installed by Windows 95) is established in memory whenever you launch MS-DOS–based or Windows 16-bit applications. The commands available are called *native Windows 95 system commands*. They are designed to take advantage of the 32-bit operating system. You will find a listing of the available commands in Appendix C, "Command-Line Reference."

Three very useful features to make your life a little easier deserve some discussion here. You can use lengthy, descriptive names for files. Also, the popular Doskey program is installed automatically by Windows 95. And finally, you can copy and paste information to and from a command prompt.

> **NOTE**
>
> The DOS prompt that is accessed when you use Shut Down to restart the computer in MS-DOS mode, or when you press F4 at startup to boot to DOS instead of Windows 95 uses real-mode and your old version of DOS.

Long Filenames

Using long filenames in Windows 95 is possible because of the 32-bit virtual File Allocation Table (VFAT) file system. On the disk, file allocation is 12-bit (for very small volumes) or 16-bit, the familiar DOS structure for so many years. Windows 95, however, uses VFAT as its main file system to handle all disk drive requests using 32-bit codes for file access.

In a VFAT file system, a file logically has two names. The *filename* can be up to 256 uppercase and lowercase characters and can include spaces. The path for a long filename can be as long as 260 characters. Directories can also have long names. The following characters can be used in long filenames:

```
~ ' ! @ # $ % ^ & ( ) _ - ' + = , ; [ ]
```

Files also have an *alias*, which is an additional filename in the familiar 8.3 format but is all uppercase characters. An alias can include any of the preceding characters except for the last six.

An alias is generated automatically and is usually the first six characters of the long name, followed by ~1, and then the extension used in the long name. The three-character extension is usually mandated by the application that created the file.

> **TIP**
>
> Actually, you can exercise some control over the alias name in two ways. Provide an 8.3 name, and it will be used as both the filename and the alias (in uppercase). The other way is by what you provide as the first eight characters and the extension of the long filename.

When you look at a directory list in a command-prompt window, the alias is listed on the left of the screen and the long filename appears immediately after the time the file was created.

To use MS-DOS commands with long filenames, you enclose the filename in quotation marks. You can also use long names for directories. To make a directory with a long directory name, type the following at a DOS prompt:

```
MD "WordPerfect Files"
```

If you now type DIR at the DOS prompt, the resulting directory will appear in the directory list as

```
WORDPE~1     <DIR>     03-16-95 10:58p WordPerfect Files
```

Although long directory names show up on the command line in their truncated (alias) form, they display normally when using Explorer, Find, and so on. Long filenames can be used with any command that accepts a filename or directory name as a parameter. Review the examples for the MS-DOS commands in Appendix C for several illustrations of how to use long filenames.

Simplify the Command-Line With Doskey

The Doskey interface enables you to edit the current command, replay your recent commands, and create command-line macros for frequently repeated commands. To use Doskey, simply enter doskey at the command prompt. Once installed, you can edit a command using

- Left arrow or Right arrow to move left or right one character at a time.
- Ctrl+Left Arrow or Ctrl+Right Arrow to move left or right one word at a time.
- Home or End to move to the beginning or the end of the command line.

After you enter a command, the F1 through F5 keys are still available to recall all or part of the command. What's new is that instead of a one-line template, previous commands are stored in a buffer from which they can be recalled if you want to run one again. Try these keystrokes:

- F7 for a sequential display of all commands in the memory buffer with a number (beginning with 1) adjacent to each command.
- Alt+F7 to clear all commands in memory.

■ F8, which when pressed after you type the first few characters of a previously entered command, causes Doskey to search memory for the command and display the command. Continue pressing F8 if the first command displayed is not the one you want.

■ F9 to display the prompt line number, where you can enter the number of the command you want redisplayed.

If you repeatedly use a command with a complex syntax or a series of commands that always are in sequence, try creating a macro to run the commands. Creating a macro is simple. The syntax is

```
DOSKEY macroname=command parameters command-parameters
```

For example, if you regularly use xcopy to copy updated files to floppy disks in the A or B drive, you might try

```
DOSKEY XC=xcopy \docs\*.* $1 /m
```

In this example, you enter XC followed by either A: or B:. $1 is a special character that is re-placed by information you provide after the macro name. The macro runs the xcopy command, copies your data files to the drive you specify, and uses the /m switch, which copies only files that have the file archive bit on—and then turns off the archive bit.

The special characters $1 through $9 are available to enable several variables to be added to the macro name when you enter it at the command prompt. Other special characters are also avail-able. For example, to have a Doskey macro run more than one command, type the various commands, one after another, separating the commands with the special character $T.

TIP

If you want to have several macros available, you need to type them all each time. A better solution is to create a batch file with all the Doskey macros you want to create set out in the file. Then just run the batch program.

Sharing Information with MS-DOS

As with Windows 3.1, it is possible to copy and paste information to and from MS-DOS and DOS-based applications. However, Windows 95 has made the process easier, both by provid-ing Copy and Paste buttons on the MS-DOS window toolbar, available when running DOS-based applications in a window, and by the use of QuickEdit.

TIP

To change the command prompt or DOS-based application from full-screen display to running in a window, press Alt+Enter. A title bar and toolbar are available, and the Windows 95 taskbar is visible when DOS-based applications are run in a window. If it is difficult to read the text in the application, change the font.

The toolbar available in a command-prompt window makes copying and pasting data simple. Click the Move button on the toolbar, and a blinking white box appears at the upper-left corner of the editing window. Use the arrow keys to move the box to the beginning of what you want to copy, and then press the Shift key while using the cursor keys to highlight the data you want. The selection is a rectangle, so plan your beginning and ending points with care. Click the Copy button.

You can accomplish copying data more easily using the mouse. The QuickEdit feature enables you to drag with the mouse to highlight text, although you are still limited to the rectangular selection shape. When you have finished marking the data with the mouse, click the right mouse button to copy the data to the Clipboard.

Now you can move to where you want this data to be copied. In the same or another DOS-based application, click the Paste button. In a Windows application, use any of the paste commands available in the application. And if the application is not open, go ahead and launch it. Just don't cut or copy anything else until you have completed the paste operation.

TIP

The Mark, Copy, and Paste buttons work in all DOS-based applications. In fact, this is the only way you can copy data into the Clipboard or paste from the Clipboard in a DOS-based application. Don't bother trying to use a copy or paste command available in a non-Windows application. The data will never get to the Clipboard.

Summary

In this chapter, you have been introduced to the new applets available with Windows 95, and you learned how to use many of them. You have also seen the applets brought forward from previous versions and how they have been improved.

You became acquainted with long filenames and how you can create sensible names to keep track of your important data. Using the Doskey program was described and you also learned how to share information between Windows applications and the command-line window.

Plug and Play

3

by John Mueller

Anyone who has had to spend any time at all installing hardware knows about the difficulties of getting it to work correctly. It always seems that the settings for one piece of hardware interfere with the port address or interrupt settings of another. Of course, there is always the jumper juggle to deal with. Taking a card out to change one jumper setting at a time can consume quite a bit of a technician's time. Fortunately, software configuration has at least reduced the number of times you need to remove and reinstall the hardware. Most of the hardware available today uses a flash ROM or other strategies (such as device driver command line switches) to enable you to configure the device using software in place of a jumper.

Unfortunately, installation doesn't end with a correctly configured device. After you get the hardware installed, there are always the device drivers to contend with. So even if the physical setup doesn't get in the way, some sort of driver incompatibility might. Or, problems can be caused by the conventional or upper memory that these drivers consume.

So what does hardware configuration have to do with a book on Windows 95? This product provides an automated hardware recognition and driver installation capability through Plug and Play. In a way, this capability is simply an extension of the software configuration techniques that most hardware uses. All you do when you run a software configuration program is tell the installation routine what ports and interrupts to use. Plug and Play performs essentially the same task. The only difference is that the computer, not you, provides answers to the setup questions.

Plug and Play starts here, but it goes a lot further. A Plug and Play compatible system also reconfigures itself dynamically. You might have seen advertisements for portables that provide a capability called *hot swapping*. This is really a component of the Plug and Play specification. Hot swapping enables you to remove components from a machine without rebooting it. For example, what if you have a MODEM card in your PCMCIA (Personal Computer Memory Card International Association) slot and need to exchange it for a network card? Currently, you need to turn the machine off, exchange the cards, and then reboot. Of course, you also need to remove any MODEM-specific device drivers or TSRs and add the network card software.

The computer automatically recognizes that it can no longer communicate with your favorite BBS but that the network lines are now open. The Plug and Play component of Windows 95 even installs the required drivers and configures them for you in the background. This means that users no longer need to worry about how a device works; they only need to think about what work they need the device to perform.

> **NOTE**
>
> The only exception to this rule is when Windows 95 cannot find the required drivers on your hard disk; it will ask you to supply a disk containing the required drivers.

Another Plug and Play feature is *hot docking*. This feature enables you to remove a portable computer from its docking station without turning it off. The portable automatically reconfigures itself to reflect the loss of docking station capability. Plug that portable back into the original docking station or a new one somewhere else, and it automatically reconfigures itself to take advantage of the new capabilities that the docking station provides.

By now you're asking where the magician is or where we mounted the hidden camera. The more experience an installer has with DOS, the harder it is to grasp this concept of instant configuration. Plug and Play is a reality, but it is only a partial reality. There are limitations to the current implementation. Fortunately, most users won't even notice the majority of the current Plug and Play limitations. The following paragraphs will help you get a better idea of what Plug and Play really entails and how viable it is for you today.

Updated Systems

Plug and Play is really a combination of three elements: operating system, hardware, and BIOS.

Operating System

The operating system part of the equation is fairly obvious. Even if you have the capability to implement Plug and Play when running Windows 3.1, the operating system lacks the capability to utilize it. Contrast this with Windows 95. When you install a new piece of hardware that it recognizes, it displays a message during the boot process that says it sees the device and has already configured it for you. You don't have to do anything else; the detection process takes care of all the details for you automatically. The same holds true when you take a memory card out of a PCMCIA slot and replace it with a network card. Windows 95 automatically detects the change and makes the appropriate modifications to the system setup.

Hardware

However, an operating system alone can't do the job. It needs hardware that cooperates with it. The hardware must identify itself during the boot process and maintain that contact while active. The boot process, in this context, refers to the startup and testing period required whenever the system applies power to a device, even if the device receives power after the rest of the system is online, as is the case with a PCMCIA bus device. This means that the hardware must provide a certain level of intelligence that the operating system can talk to. In most cases, this intelligence is found in the form of an on-board BIOS and processor combination.

BIOS

The BIOS forms the third part of this group. Your computer performs a Power On Self Test (POST) during the boot process. During the time that the BIOS is testing your system memory, it is also testing all the add-on boards and the motherboard. In some cases, the BIOS also notes the presence of specific devices such as hard drives so that it can configure the system to accept input from them. Both the standard and the Plug and Play BIOS perform these tasks.

Recognizing Hardware

To make Plug and Play work, the system BIOS has to go further. It has to help the operating system recognize which pieces of hardware are present and which are not. It is also responsible for communicating with those devices and finding out about their needs. To accomplish this task, a Plug and Play BIOS includes a dual-mode resource allocation module. This module provides both 16-bit real- and protected-mode services to the operating system. Its purpose is to help the operating system find ports, memory addresses, and interrupts that each device can use without conflicting with other devices in the machine. Another module, the event module, alerts the operating system to changes in system configuration. This proactive communication allows the operating system to maintain contact with each device without wasting the clock cycles required to poll them.

One time at which this three-way communication process is essential is during the initial boot process. Windows 95 finds out what most devices need after it boots. In other words, these devices do not come online until after Windows 95 can talk to them. This is because most devices need some type of device driver to activate them. Windows 95 still uses the system BIOS to talk to these devices, but it takes care of loading and configuring the device drivers that each device needs.

The system BIOS does contain logic that ensures there is a way to boot the machine. This means that it looks for a boot device (hard or floppy disk drive), the keyboard, and a display device. After Windows 95 boots, it obtains the setup information for these devices from the system BIOS and performs any protected mode setups required. In most cases, this means that it must load a device driver for each boot device.

Plug and Play Features

All three of these components have to work together to make Plug and Play a reality. A system that provides all three components provides the following features:

- **Identify installed devices:** Windows 95 automatically detects all of the plug and play components attached to your system. This means that you need to provide a minimum of information during installation and nothing at all during subsequent reboots. Contrast this with the almost continuous flow of information needed under Windows 3.1.

- **Determine device resource needs:** Every device on your computer needs resources in the form of processor cycles, input/output ports, DMA channels, memory, and interrupts. Windows 95 works with the BIOS and peripheral devices to meet these needs without any intervention.

- **Automatic system configuration updates and resource conflict detection:** All of this communication between peripheral devices, the BIOS, and the operating system allows Windows 95 to create a system configuration without any user intervention. The Device Manager configuration blocks are grayed out because the user doesn't need to supply this information any more. The enhanced level of communication also allows Windows 95 to poll the peripherals for alternate port and interrupt settings when a conflict with another device occurs.

- **Device driver loading and unloading:** CONFIG.SYS and AUTOEXCEC.BAT used to contain line after line of device driver and TSR statements. This is because the system had to bring those devices online before it loaded the command processor and Windows 3.1. Windows 95 can actually maintain or even enhance the performance of a Plug and Play compatible system without using an AUTOEXEC.BAT or CONFIG.SYS. Plug and Play compatibility allows Windows 95 to dynamically load and unload any device drivers that your system needs.

- **Configuration change notification:** Plug and Play can make system configuration changes automatic, but that doesn't mean that Windows 95 leaves you in the dark. Every time the system configuration changes, it notifies you by displaying a dialog box onscreen. Essentially, the dialog box tells you what changed. This capability does provide an additional side benefit. Windows 95 also notifies you whenever your equipment experiences some kind of failure. When a piece of equipment fails, Windows 95 notices that it is no longer online. Remember that Plug and Play requires three-way communication and a defective device usually fails to communicate. Instead of finding out that you no longer have access to a drive or other device when you need it most, Windows 95 notifies you of the change immediately after it takes place.

IS YOUR SYSTEM REALLY PLUG AND PLAY?

There are more than a few machines on the market today that claim to possess Plug and Play capability. They do, in fact, have Plug and Play peripheral boards installed. This is a fine first step, but it hardly completes the Plug and Play picture. A Plug and Play system has to have a special BIOS in it as well. Make sure you ask about this additional feature before you buy a system. Some people have purchased what they thought were Plug and Play systems only to find out later that they also needed to buy a BIOS upgrade. You can also download a BIOS test program from the Plug and Play forum (GO PLUGPLAY) on CompuServe. Look in Library 6 (the BIOS library) for BIOTST.ZIP.

In addition to this testing program, the same forum contains a complete copy of the Plug and Play BIOS specification. Intel, Compaq, and Phoenix Technologies worked together to write it. Look for BIO10A.DOC. This specification talks about the capabilities of the Plug and Play BIOS. It also provides some information about the peripheral board setup.

Now that you have some idea of what Plug and Play can do for you, let's look at the hardware involved in implementing it. The following paragraphs describe the major Plug and Play hardware types and how Windows 95 interfaces with them.

Personal Computer Memory Card International Association (PCMCIA) Bus

The portable market spawned a new type of bus. The PCMCIA bus uses credit card-sized cards that connect to external slots on the machine. This makes it very easy for the user to change the hardware configuration of his machine without opening it up. For example, you can take out a memory card to make room for a MODEM card.

This bus also supports solid-state disk drives in the form of flash ROM or SRAM boards. The flash ROM boards are especially interesting because they provide the same access speeds as regular memory, with the permanence of other long-term storage media such as hard drives. Unlike SRAM boards, flash ROM boards do not require battery backup. Many people use solid-state drives to store applications or databases that change infrequently. This frees up precious space on the internal hard disk for data and applications that the user needs to access on a continuous basis.

Unfortunately, the PCMCIA bus also creates a problem for people who use it. Every time they plug in a new card type, they need to reconfigure their system. (Of course, this does not apply to exchanging one hard disk card for another.) Configuration programs make this really neat feature a real pain to implement. Of course, some vendors provide utility programs to make the change easier, but this still can't change the way that Windows itself operates. It also can't make up for deficiencies in DOS. The operating system must provide dynamic loading and unloading of device drivers to make the system as user-friendly as possible.

Plug and Play changes all this. No longer do PCMCIA bus users need to reconfigure their system when a component changes. Windows 95 is designed to detect system changes and make the appropriate modifications to its setup. However, this flexibility comes at a price. The user must disable his PCMCIA-specific utilities and allow Windows to manage the bus. The bus vendor must also provide the 32-bit drivers needed under Windows 95 (unless your bus already appears in the Windows 95 support list). Doing this enables the PCMCIA enhanced mode. So, what does enhanced support buy you? The following paragraphs provide an overview of enhanced support features.

■ **Friendly device names:** This feature provides users with device names that they can recognize (instead of the more familiar *XYZ.VXD*, the user sees something like Flash ROM Driver). It also helps the user determine which devices are actually present and which are disconnected.

■ **Automatic installation:** The automatic installation feature enables the user to hot swap various devices in and out of the PCMCIA slot without worrying about reconfiguring the machine.

■ **Drive change detection:** There are situations in which the user has to unmount and then mount a PCMCIA drive before Windows 95 will recognize the change if enhanced support is disabled.

■ **Other device specific mode and configuration information:** Each PCMCIA card vendor implements special features for its device. Check the documentation that comes with the device for further details.

In most cases, Windows 95 does not automatically enable enhanced mode; it will not do so if you have any real mode PCMCIA drivers loaded. Fortunately, it is very easy to see whether Windows 95 enabled enhanced mode on your machine.

Use the Start | Settings | Control Panel command to display the folder shown in Figure 3.1.

FIGURE 3.1.

The Control Panel provides access to many configuration settings.

Double-click the System icon and then select the Performance tab to display the dialog box shown in Figure 3.2.

If your dialog box looks like the one in Figure 3.2, Windows 95 has not enabled enhanced support. The first method that you should use to try to correct the problem is to click the Details pushbutton. This displays the help dialog shown in Figure 3.3.

FIGURE 3.2.

The Performance tab helps you to optimize system performance. It displays all performance bottlenecks including PCMCIA status.

FIGURE 3.3.

This help dialog provides a button that enables PCMCIA 32-bit support.

Notice the button that enables 32-bit PCMCIA support. Try clicking this button. Windows 95 attempts to help you enable 32-bit support. However, there are situations in which the attempt will fail. The following paragraphs provide some troubleshooting tips.

- The most common problem associated with enabling enhanced support is the presence of PCMCIA device drivers in CONFIG.SYS or TSRs in AUTOEXEC.BAT. Removing these entries should fix the problem.

- Windows 95 normally tells you if there is an I/O port address or interrupt conflict, but you should check the settings under the Resources tab of the PCIC or Compatible PCMCIA dialog to make sure. (See Figure 3.4.) Any conflicting devices appear in the Conflicting Devices field near the bottom of the dialog.

- Always install a card in the slot while booting. Failure to do so might prevent Windows 95 from detecting it.

- Make sure that Windows 95 supports your card by checking for it with the Hardware Installation Wizard in the Control Panel. (You can browse through the list of hardware presented on the second screen, and then press Cancel to exit the utility without installing anything.)

Even if Windows 95 does not support your PCMCIA slot, you can still use it by installing the real mode drivers. Of course, using real mode drivers means that you won't gain any benefit from the Plug and Play features. It always makes sense to contact the bus vendor to see whether there is a 32-bit driver available.

FIGURE 3.4.

The Resources tab for the PCIC or Compatible PCMCIA dialog box alerts you to any conflicting devices.

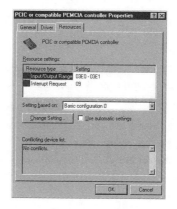

VL and PCI

The VL (VESA local) and PCI (peripheral component interconnect) buses have one thing in common: They are not the primary bus on your system. VESA (Video Electronics Standards Association) originally designed the VL bus to provide 32-bit graphics card capability for the ISA bus. In fact, this is still its primary mission. The VL bus appeared before Plug and Play was an issue. As a result, it is not Plug and Play compliant in its current configuration. However, VESA is working on a VL bus update that will provide Plug and Play capability.

> **NOTE**
>
> You can contact VESA at (408)435-0333 to obtain a copy of the VL bus standard. VESA also publishes a wide variety of other standards for display adapters and other computer-related peripheral devices.

Many people view the PCI bus as the logical successor to the VL bus. It already appears in many Pentium and Macintosh PowerPC machines. The PCI, unlike the VL bus, is Plug and Play compliant. However, if the primary bus is not Plug and Play compliant, Windows 95 will not enable the Plug and Play capabilities of the PCI bus. Both the primary and secondary buses must provide Plug and Play capability or Windows 95 must treat both buses the same way it treats other legacy devices.

> **DETERMINING PCI BUS CAPABILITIES**
>
> There are different implementations of the PCI bus, so it pays to know what features your bus supports. The Plug and Play forum (GO PLUGPLAY) on CompuServe provides a free utility that you can download to test your system. Simply look for PCI.EXE and follow the instructions included in the file description.

Use the procedures described in the PCMCIA section of this chapter to determine whether Windows 95 found the PCI bus (and the VL bus when an updated version becomes available). Many of the same troubleshooting procedures will work as well. Of course, there are no special drivers associated with the PCI bus, so you can eliminate that source of potential problems. The most common reason that Windows 95 does not recognize a PCI bus is that the primary bus doesn't support a Plug and Play capability.

All EISA buses support Plug and Play capability as long as you perform the EISA bus setup. Windows 95 uses a bus enumerator to detect the EISA setup information and make it available to the system for configuration purposes. (This is a software setup that configures each slot for a specific card; see your vendor manual for further details.)

Disk Controllers

There are three categories of Plug and Play compatibility for disk controllers. The vast majority of the IDE, MFM, and ESDI controllers do not provide Plug and Play capabilities. Fortunately, Windows 95 can supply these controllers with a generic device identifier and serial number.

Most SCSI host adapters and devices do not provide Plug and Play information either, and Plug and Play compatible SCSI devices are still somewhat of a rarity. The main reason is that the SCSI-2 standard does not provide the means for the automatic ID assignment required by Plug and Play. It also does not provide any method for configuring the host adapter through software instead of jumpers. The lack of automated configuration means that the user must configure the device and host adapter manually. When the user completes the manual configuration, Windows 95 can read that configuration from the SCSI bus.

A second category of SCSI controllers are those that do provide Plug and Play information. In this case, Windows 95 can perform dynamic configuration of the SCSI devices, which includes the following:

- ■ **SCSI device ID assignment:** Every device on the SCSI bus requires a unique ID. Otherwise, the host adapter cannot access it.

- ■ **Bus termination:** The first and last device on the SCSI bus must provide a terminator. Essentially, the terminator is a stop sign that tells the computer that it is the end of the line.

- ■ **Host adapter configuration:** The host adapter requires port, interrupt, and DMA addresses. Normally, the user manually configures the adapter using jumpers. A Plug and Play adapter allows the system to configure it using software. (Some SCSI devices also provide a manual override for the automated settings.)

Monitors and Display Adapters

The biggest Plug and Play contribution that Windows 95 offers for monitors and display adapters is the capability to detect the maximum number of colors and the resolution that both devices support. A Plug and Play display adapter uses the standard BIOS and processor combination to communicate with Windows 95. The main difference between a standard monitor and a Plug and Play monitor is that the latter usually includes an extra *detection wire*. The detection wire allows Windows 95 to poll the monitor. The combination of a Plug and Play display adapter and a Plug and Play monitor allows Windows 95 to dynamically configure the system. Fortunately, you can still get a partial benefit if only one device is compatible with Plug and Play.

> **NOTE**
>
> Windows 95 does not currently provide hot swapping capability for Plug and Play display adapters. The current set of VXDs do not allow dynamic loading and unloading. The major contributor to this problem is the fact that each display adapter uses different ports and interrupt addresses.
>
> There is no problem with hot swapping monitors. Windows 95 can detect the changes in monitor capability and adjust the resolution settings appropriately.

One of the benefits of on-the-fly resolution and color detection is that you can change these parameters without rebooting the machine. Using legacy equipment means that you must reboot each time the configuration gets changed. (There are some instances in which the user can change display adapter resolution without rebooting even if a legacy device is used; any change in a legacy system's number of colors setting will require a reboot.) There isn't much magic behind this capability. Windows 95 can communicate with the Plug and Play device; it cannot communicate with a standard (or legacy) device.

The Plug and Play benefits for a monitor and display adapter combination don't stop here of course. Windows 95 also detects your monitor and display adapter vendor and installs the correct device drivers. A legacy system installation requires the user to input the monitor type as a minimum.

Pointer Devices

When you consider pointer devices, you need to think about more than just the standard mouse. Windows 95 provides Plug and Play capability for a variety of pointer devices including drawing pads, mice, light pens, and trackballs. In fact, about the only pointer devices missing from the list are touch screens.

The main reason for using a Plug and Play pointer under Windows 95 is to double or even triple the load that one serial port can handle. This capability is especially useful for users who do not need a drawing tool all day. They can unplug their mouse and plug in a drawing pad as needed. It also enables multiple users to use one machine even if they prefer different pointing devices. One user might like a trackball, while another uses a mouse. For that matter, one user might prefer a Microsoft two-button mouse, while another user likes the Logitech three-button version.

Printers

The Plug and Play printer provides two-way communication with the operating system. There are already programming techniques in place for detecting some of the events that occur with a printer. For example, it is possible to detect when the printer is offline or out of paper. A Plug and Play printer provides enhanced capabilities in this regard. It can tell you when it needs additional toner or some type of maintenance action. A Plug and Play printer can also provide unsolicited messages. This means that Windows 95 doesn't need to constantly poll the device to determine its condition. However, these events merely tell you the printer's status and nothing about the printer itself. Plug and Play printers provide more information; they actually describe themselves to the operating system.

> **NOTE**
>
> Windows 95 adheres to the IEEE 1284 standard for Plug and Play printers.

Just how the printer describes itself is with the two-way connection through the printer port. Older ports do not provide this capability; make certain that there is a two-way port attached to the machine. The operating system queries the printer during startup, whenever the user changes the printer port connection, or when the user makes a new network connection. The printer sends back all or part of the information found in Table 3.1. A printer only needs to supply the manufacturer and model information; the other entries help Windows 95 provide a more precise printer configuration without user intervention. Windows 95 interprets the information and decides whether it needs to load additional drivers. Plug and Play printers offer the following capabilities in addition to the standard Plug and Play capabilities.

- **Automatic device identification:** Like all Plug and Play devices, one of the advantages of a Plug and Play printer is that it identifies itself to Windows. However, unlike most devices, printers can provide additional capabilities within a specific model. For example, a laser printer can provide additional memory, while a dot matrix printer can provide additional font cartridges.

- **Device configuration change detection:** Imagine that the user has an A/B switch connected to the parallel port. If there is a Plug and Play printer attached to both outputs, Windows 95 automatically detects the change in printers. In addition, it detects changes to the printer configuration. For example, if the user takes out one font cartridge and inserts another, Windows 95 automatically reflects this fact.

■ **Network printer detection:** Not only will Windows 95 detect the type of network plug and printer that the user attaches to, it will remember that this is a network and not a local printer. Networks do not affect most devices attached to the local machine. One of the big exceptions is the printer.

Table 3.1. Printer configuration data.

Data	Description
Manufacturer	The printer's manufacturer.
Model	This is the specific model number. It provides more than the usual amount of model information. For example, there is an Epson LQ-850 and an Epson LQ-850 Plus. Even though the user might not know the difference, the printer will.
Class	This entry simply differentiates a printer from some other device such as a hard drive.
Description	A vendor can use this entry to provide the user with additional information. It contains a detailed description of the printer and can talk about some of its capabilities. The vendor can even add information such as its technical support number here.
Compatible ID	Installing a printer that does not provide the correct 32-bit driver is frustrating. This field allows the vendor to list some compatible devices in order of preference. Windows 95 detects this list and determines whether any of these alternate drivers are available.

DETERMINING WHETHER YOUR PRINTER IS PLUG AND PLAY

There are a variety of methods to determine whether a printer provides Plug and Play compatibility (other than relying on the vendor documentation). The easiest method is watching Windows 95 during installation. If Windows 95 asks for a printer port, the printer is not Plug and Play compatible.

Another good method of detection is to change the printer's configuration. The printer dialog in the Control Panel should reflect the change if the printer is Plug and Play compatible.

Serial and Parallel Ports

Windows 95 provides Plug and Play capabilities for the serial and parallel ports. The extent of this support depends on two factors: The capabilities of the port itself and the capabilities of the device.

A parallel port provides Plug and Play support for devices that use it. Windows 95 also provides built-in support for enhanced capabilities ports (ECP). Future MODEMs will use this type of port to improve file transfer throughput. Currently there is no way to test for either an ECP or a port compatible with Plug and Play.

> **TIP**
>
> Even though you can't test the Plug and Play parallel port directly, there is a way to test the serial port using the procedure described in the following paragraphs. A machine that includes support for one usually includes support for the other.

A serial port must provide support for a communications rate of 115.2 Kbps or greater. Most Plug and Play compatible serial ports also use the 16550 UART (universal asynchronous receiver/transmitter). Keeping these two criteria in mind, it is fairly easy to determine whether there is a Plug and Play serial port attached to your machine.

> **NOTE**
>
> The following procedure assumes that you have two serial (COM) ports and that one of them has an external MODEM attached to it.

Use the Start | Settings | Control Panel command to display the contents of the Control Panel folder as shown in Figure 3.1.

Turn the MODEM power on. Double-click on the Modems icon, and then select the Diagnostics tab to display the dialog box shown in Figure 3.5.

Highlight the serial port with the MODEM attached as shown in Figure 3.5. Click on the More Info... pushbutton to display the dialog shown in Figure 3.6.

There are quite a few hints here as to the capabilities of the serial ports in the computer and the capabilities of the MODEM as well. The field at the bottom of the dialog shows the result of various interrogations. All the ATI codes ask the MODEM for specific pieces of information. Unfortunately, this information varies by vendor, so you need to consult the MODEM manual to determine the exact meaning of each result. The one constant across all MODEMs is the ATI0 code result. This normally returns the product code, a detailed reference to the particular MODEM installed on the machine. The vendor normally needs this information to provide detailed troubleshooting assistance.

FIGURE 3.5.

The Modem Diagnostics tab displays the current serial port connections for your machine. Note the More Info... pushbutton near the bottom.

FIGURE 3.6.

The More Info... dialog box can tell you a lot about your serial port and your modem. The UART type and maximum communication speed can help you determine whether the port supports Plug and Play.

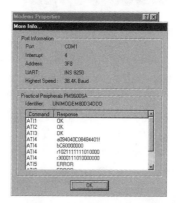

There are two other fields that can help identify the serial port itself. The port information block contains the UART field. If this field contains an INS 16550, the port meets the first criteria for Plug and Play. The Highest Speed field (right below the UART field) tells you the port's highest transmission speed. If this field contains 115.2, the serial port meets the second Plug and Play criteria.

Click the OK pushbutton twice to close the MODEM dialog. You should see the Control Panel (as in Figure 3.1).

After you determine that the port can provide Plug and Play capability, it's time to test for that capability. Loosen the screws holding the MODEM plug to the serial port in the back of the machine. Now, disconnect the connector.

Double-click the MODEM icon to reopen the MODEM dialog. If the connection information changes, you know that the serial ports provide Plug and Play capability. Click OK to close the MODEM dialog.

Reconnect the MODEM connect. Double-click on the MODEM icon to reopen the MODEM dialog. Make sure that you restored the MODEM connection by clicking the More Info pushbutton. If the MODEM responds, click OK twice to close the MODEM dialog.

If the MODEM fails to respond, you'll see the error dialog shown in Figure 3.7. Click OK twice to close the More Info... dialog. Check the connection and click the More Info... pushbutton again to recheck the connection. Repeat this process until you restore the connection.

FIGURE 3.7.

This dialog shows the error message that Windows 95 provides if the MODEM cable fails to make contact after the port test.

Standard Bus Support

The standard or ISA (Industry Standard Architecture) bus requires no changes to make it Plug and Play compatible. (The team that designed the Plug and Play BIOS went to great lengths to make certain it wouldn't require any changes.) It is the responsibility of the system BIOS and the individual peripheral boards to make Plug and Play work in this situation. A Plug and Play computer using ISA bus employs the following procedure to initialize itself.

- **Identify the Plug and Play devices:** The BIOS searches the bus for Plug and Play devices using I/O ports. The search mechanism also activates the Plug and Play circuitry on the peripheral device.

- **Assign the device an ID and serial number:** When the BIOS finds a Plug and Play compatible peripheral, it assigns that device an identification number. The ID provides the operating system with a device type. For example, all serial ports use the same identification number. The BIOS also assigns each Plug and Play device a serial number. The ISA Plug and Play specification calls this serial number a card select number (CSN). The CSN helps the operating system identify each device. This is especially important if there is more than one of each device type.

- **Determine peripheral resource requirements:** The on-board Plug and Play mechanism provides the system BIOS and the operating system with the information they need to configure the system. The BIOS configures devices that the system needs to boot; Windows 95 takes care of configuring all other devices. The device tells the system which ports and interrupts it can use. It is the responsibility of the BIOS to assign each boot peripheral device a set of ports and interrupts that will not conflict with other boards in the system. Windows 95 completes the allocation task using the remaining ports and interrupts.

- **Activate the Plug and Play peripherals:** After the BIOS sets all the boot devices up, it can turn them on. In actuality, Windows 95 performs this task for most of the nonboot devices such as the mouse. Theoretically, the system should run without any user intervention, unless the BIOS or operating system runs out of port or interrupt assignments. In the case of an unresolved conflict, the user still has to step in and make a decision about which peripheral to activate.

The Plug and Play standard allows great flexibility with the ISA bus. Unfortunately, with this added flexibility comes an opportunity for additional conflicts. Windows 95 enables you to mix legacy devices with Plug and Play devices on an ISA bus. Unlike other buses, there is no identification information supplied with an ISA device. Windows 95 must poll the device to determine its type. This can lead to misidentification or a failure to identify the device as any type. See the "Workarounds for Some Types of Hardware Detection Problems" section in this chapter for methods of helping Windows 95 identify legacy devices.

Software Issues

Using Plug and Play does not mean that the user will never again run into a device driver problem. It does mean that if the driver is available, the user will expend a minimum of effort to get that device installed. In fact, if the driver already appears on the local or network drive, the user won't even realize that Windows 95 has loaded a new driver.

The problems begin when the user has a Plug and Play device that does not provide a 32-bit Windows 95 driver. Because Windows 95 is a new operating system, most devices that do not appear in the list of Windows 95 supported devices fall into this category. So, what happens if the device is not on the supported list and there is no 32-bit driver? Windows 95 will still enable you to use the device after installing the real-mode or legacy drivers. It will not, however, provide full Plug and Play support. Obviously then, using devices that appear on the Windows 95 support list or come with a Windows 95 compatible driver is the best way to go. Always check with the vendor as well to see whether it provides updated drivers that do support Windows 95 capabilities.

Legacy Systems

Using Plug and Play to automatically install the hardware it recognizes is a great idea. The computer can figure out a set of port and interrupt settings faster than the average human and with greater accuracy. The reason is simple: The computer has all of the statistics about the hardware handy. It's contained in the on-board BIOS that Plug and Play hardware uses to communicate with the rest of the machine.

> **NOTE**
>
> The setup program may not create an INF folder if your system does not need it. This will only happen if you have a completely Plug and Play compatible system without any legacy (such as non-Plug and Play) hardware attached.

Windows 95 does a fairly good job of detecting hardware that is not Plug and Play, even when it gets mixed with Plug and Play compatible hardware. All the configuration information for the hardware that Windows 95 supports is stored on the hard disk. In fact, if you look in the \WIN95\INF directory, you see some of these files (they all have an INF extension). Besides storing the required configuration information on disk, Windows 95 gives legacy hardware first choice of ports and interrupts. This allows older hardware to work most of the time.

Problems start to arise when the system doesn't or can't recognize one or more components in your system. What usually happens is that the unrecognized hardware refuses to work properly, if at all. Unrecognized hardware falls into two categories. There is the difficult to recognize piece of hardware that emulates something else so well that the computer has a hard time telling exactly what it is. The second category is legacy hardware that lacks Windows 95-specific drivers.

Device Recognition Methods

Windows 95 provides two methods for handling Plug and Play hardware. Both of these methods are in accordance with the Plug and Play specification that the hardware vendors use for development. Devices such as hard drives and MODEMs always provide an online BIOS that interacts with the system BIOS and the operating system. The information that the device exchanges includes a device identifier and any setup parameters. The device identifier usually contains the vendor name and the device model. It can contain other pieces of information depending on the device (see the "Printers" section earlier in this chapter for an example). For the most part, the interaction takes place during startup, any device configuration change, or when the user makes a network connection. However, these devices also notify the operating system if they experience a failure or need some other type of user service during normal use.

Windows 95 can perform a second type of detection. Some interconnection hardware, such as a bus, doesn't really need anything special to make it work properly as a Plug and Play device. For example, there is no such thing as an ISA Plug and Play bus, yet Windows 95 can fully support Plug and Play devices on that bus. This makes an ISA bus Plug and Play compatible (some specifications use *friendly*), even though it does not provide a Plug and Play capability. The operating system handles all the communication needs for the bus and other interconnection elements. Some vendors call interconnection hardware *Plug and Play ready*.

Workarounds for Some Types of Hardware Detection Problems

Now we come to the part where Plug and Play will fail to meet your needs. There are some situations in which Windows 95 fails to recognize a peripheral connected to a legacy system. For example, it might confuse one type of sound board with another (or fail to recognize the board at all). The following troubleshooting tips will help you locate most of the problem boards.

- Avoid interrupt and port address conflict whenever possible. This is probably the number one reason that Windows 95 will fail to recognize the board. If two devices use the same address, there is no way that Windows 95 can test for the presence of the second board.

- Plug all your legacy boards into the slots next to the power supply whenever possible. The BIOS checks the slots in order during POST. Placing the legacy boards first, and then the Plug and Play boards, ensures that the BIOS will see the legacy boards first.

- Try different board configurations to see whether Windows 95 will recognize one of them. There are situations in which the INF files that Windows 95 uses to check for the legacy boards contain only the default board settings. A good rule of thumb is to try the best setting first, and then try the default setting if that doesn't work.

- Check the INF files to see whether they contain all the settings for your boards. There is an INF directory directly below the main Windows 95 directory. It contains ASCII text files that Windows 95 uses to search for legacy boards. Modifying these files is a tricky proposition, but it might help Windows 95 find the peripherals in your machine.

Even these tips won't fix every situation. There are some boards that will not work within Windows 95 Plug and Play guidelines. Fortunately, there are a few things you can do to help Windows 95 along.

Installation with Real-Mode Drivers Intact

Some devices—especially those that rely on software configuration instead of jumpers—do not provide enough information for autodetection until you turn them on. Normally, this means that the user has to install any required real-mode drivers in CONFIG.SYS. These drivers perform the setups required to make the device visible to Windows 95.

After you install these drivers, reboot the machine. When Windows 95 starts, use the Start | Settings | Control Panel command to open the Control Panel. (See Figure 3.1.)

Double-click the Add New Hardware icon. You should see the dialog shown in Figure 3.8.

FIGURE 3.8.

The Hardware Installation Wizard enables you to install new hardware with a minimum of effort.

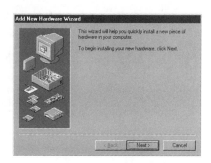

Click the Next pushbutton. You should see the dialog box shown in Figure 3.9. Notice that the Automatically Detect Installed Hardware radio button is selected.

FIGURE 3.9.

Using automatic hardware detection reduces the amount of work the user needs to perform. In addition, it can reduce the possibility of hardware conflicts because Windows 95 performs some additional detection steps.

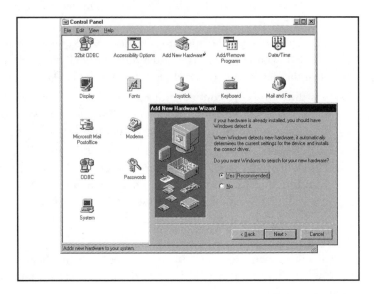

Click the Next pushbutton on this dialog and on the dialog that follows it. Windows 95 displays the dialog shown in Figure 3.10 during the detection process.

> **NOTE**
>
> The detection process takes several minutes and always slows down near the end of the detection cycle. The detection process might even cause the machine to freeze. Wait for at least five minutes between increments on the progress bar before rebooting the machine.

FIGURE 3.10.

Windows 95 displays this detection progress indicator while it searches the machine for new devices.

Click the Details pushbutton to determine whether Windows 95 successfully detected the new hardware (as shown in Figure 3.11).

FIGURE 3.11.

The Detected field of the final Installation Wizard dialog tells you whether Windows 95 detected the new hardware correctly.

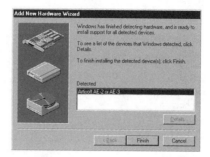

If Windows 95 successfully detected the new hardware, click the Finish pushbutton to complete the installation process. Windows 95 might ask you to supply some setting information if this is not a Plug and Play device. In most cases, it provides default settings that match your current real-mode setup. Windows 95 copies all the required drivers to disk and tells you to reboot. Make sure you remove the real-mode drivers from CONFIG.SYS before you shut down and reboot the machine. If Windows 95 didn't detect the new hardware, remove the real-mode drivers from CONFIG.SYS, shut down and reboot the system, and then perform the manual installation procedure in the next section.

Manual Installation

There are a few situations in which Windows 95 won't detect a legacy device in your machine. It might even configure a Plug and Play device to use the same settings that the missed device does. You can usually get Windows 95 to recognize the legacy device if you use the procedure in the previous section. However, there are times when the hardware picture becomes so complex that the user needs to go a bit further. In these cases, you need to manually install the device. The following example shows how to install a CD-ROM drive; the same principles apply to any manual installation.

Use the Start | Settings | Control Panel command to open the Control Panel (see Figure 3.1). Double-click the Add New Hardware icon (see Figure 3.8). Click the Next pushbutton (see Figure 3.9), highlight the CD-ROM Controller entry of the Install Specific Hardware field, and then click the Next pushbutton. You should see the dialog box shown in Figure 3.12.

This dialog appears every time the user selects one of the devices on the previous dialog. The manufacturer list changes to match the particular device type. A special Unknown hardware device type enables the user to view all the supported devices on one screen. Normally, you select the device connected to your machine. In this case, leave the default device highlighted and click the Next pushbutton. Windows 95 displays a dialog containing the interrupt and address settings for this particular device, as shown in Figure 3.13. Windows 95 chooses a device setting based on all available information; it chooses the best setting that will not interfere with other devices in the system (if possible).

FIGURE 3.12.

The manufacturers and models lists in this dialog enable you to scroll through the list of devices supported by Windows 95 with ease. If the device installed on the current machine does not appear on the list, the dialog also affords the opportunity to use a third-party disk.

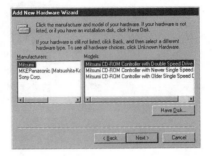

FIGURE 3.13.

Windows 95 always tells the user what interrupts and addresses it uses for the devices it installs.

Clicking the Next pushbutton again installs the device drivers required for this device. Normally, you take this action. Windows 95 might prompt you for a disk, if the driver does not appear on the hard drive and the appropriate disk does not appear in the CD-ROM drive. It displays a dialog showing the progress of the file copy process. However, because we don't want to install this particular device, click the Cancel pushbutton. Windows 95 exits the Hardware Installation Wizard without installing the new device.

Extending Autodetection Through INF File Modification

The INF file is the cornerstone of Windows 95's capability to recognize hardware that is not Plug and Play. These files are enhanced versions of the OEMSETUP.INF files used to install drivers under Windows 3.1. There are two main differences between these INF files and the Windows 3.1 version. First, the Windows 95 version contains a lot more information. It provides detailed configuration and detection information to the system. Second, Windows 95 has constant access to these INF files. It can scan them any time you install new hardware.

As good as these new INF files are, there are times when you might want to modify them. For example, what if you have a piece of hardware that provides interrupt and port address settings in addition to those found in the INF file. Modifying the INF file to reflect these additional capabilities can help you install a piece of hardware in some cases.

> **TIP**
>
> The complete INF file specification appears on the CompuServe Plug and Play forum (GO PLUGPLAY) as INFWHITE1.DOC. A copy also comes with the Windows 95 DDK (driver development kit). This file contains a lot more information than the average user needs; however, it can help a system administrator find a way to incorporate some devices into the Windows 95 environment.

All INF files share several characteristics that you can use to successfully modify their contents. Table 3.2 outlines these basic sections.

Table 3.2. INF file generic sections.

Heading	*Description*
Version	Provides version-specific information such as the operating system, vendor name, and device class supported by the INF file. It also provides the name of the general setup file. Never change the contents of this section.
Manufacturer	Contains a list of all the manufacturers for devices of this class. Not every INF file contains this section. For example, this section appears in the MONITOR.INF file, but not the MSPORTS.INF file. The only time you might need to change this section is if you want to add a new vendor. There is a subsection below this one that provides specifics about each device supported by that vendor. If the vendor already appears in the manufacturer list, adding a new device consists of adding an entry here, in the Install section, and in the Strings section.
Install	This is the most important section of the file. It describes all the characteristics of the hardware and the device drivers needed to activate it. Follow the example of other entries in this section when adding a new device. Change only physical characteristics such as port address and interrupt when modifying an existing entry.

continues

Table 3.2. continued

Heading	Description
Miscellaneous Control	This section indicates how a device interacts with the Windows 95 interface. Most INF files do not contain this section.
Strings	This section contains the user-friendly strings that the user sees when selecting the device from the Add New Hardware dialog in the Control Panel. It identifies the device in a human-readable form.

Simply looking at these sections does not provide much input on how to actually use them. Let's add a monitor to the list of available monitors. The Samsung CQ-4551 VGA monitor does not currently appear in the list.

> **NOTE**
>
> If you have a fully Plug and Play compatible system, you may not have an INF folder below your main Windows 95 folder. In that case, you will not find this file. (For that matter, you won't need this procedure to make your system work.)

Use Wordpad to open MONITOR2.INF. There are four sections in the INF file that you need to change. Use the Find command to locate the first Samsung CT-4581 entry. Add the following boldfaced text:

```
[Samsung]
%CQ-4551%=CQ-4551.Install
%CT-4581%=CT-4581.Install
```

This entry tells Windows 95 that there is a CQ-4551 monitor and that it can find further details about that monitor in the CQ-4551.Install section of the INF file. Now, use the Find command to locate the second CT-4581 entry. Add the following boldfaced text:

```
[KDM-2066.Install]
DelReg=DEL_CURRENT_REG
AddReg=KDM-2066.AddReg, 1280

[CQ-4551.Install]
DelReg=DEL_CURRENT_REG
AddReg=CQ-4551.AddReg, 640

[CT-4581.Install]
DelReg=DEL_CURRENT_REG
AddReg=CT-4581.AddReg, 800
```

There are two entries in the section. The first one tells Windows 95 to delete the current registry entry. This ensures that it will not confuse the new monitor entry with the old one. The second entry tells Windows 95 to add a new registry entry following the instructions located in the `CQ-4551.AddReg` section of the INF file. Note the `640` after the add registry command. This tells Windows 95 to use the 640 display mode as a default. Use the `Find` command to find the third `CT-4581` entry. Add the following boldfaced text:

```
[KDM-2066.AddReg]
HKR,"MODES\1280,1024",Mode1,,"30.0-67.0,40.0-120.0,+,+"

[CQ-4551.AddReg]
HKR,"MODES\640,480",Mode1,,"31.5,60.0-70.0,-,-"

[CT-4581.AddReg]
HKR,"MODES\800,600",Mode1,,"15.0-38.0,47.0-73.0,+,+"
```

Trying to read this entry might prove frustrating until you take the time to analyze its component parts. Any change you make to an INF file ultimately requires this type of detective work. In this case, the first important component is `"MODES\640,480"`. This describes the operational resolution for that monitor mode. The second component, `Mode1`, tells Windows 95 that this is the first mode supported by the monitor. Looking at other entries in this INF file shows that some monitors support multiple modes. The final component, `"31.5,60.0-70.0,-,-"`, looks a bit mysterious until you check a monitor manual. The first number, `31.5`, is the horizontal scanning frequency. You can supply a numeric range here as well. The second numeric range, `60.0-70.0`, is the vertical scanning frequency. The two minus signs tell you that this is not a multiscanning monitor. Use the `Find` command to find the fourth and final `CT-4581` entry. Add the following boldfaced text:

```
CQ-4551="Samsung, Inc. CQ-4551"
CT-4581="Samsung, Inc. CT-4581"
```

The reason for this entry is pretty obvious. It provides the user with a device name that a human can understand. Now it's time to look at the results. Save the MONITOR2.INF file and close WordPad. Use the Start | Settings | Control Panel command to open the Control Panel (see Figure 3.1).

Double-click the Display icon. Click the Settings tab to display the dialog box shown in Figure 3.14.

FIGURE 3.14.

The Change Display Type dialog enables you to change the current monitor settings.

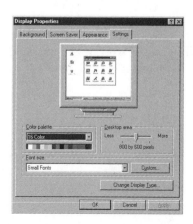

110

Use the Change Display Type | Change command to display the Select Device dialog. Windows 95 displays an updated dialog while it adds the new monitor to the list. Click the Show All Devices radio button. Use the scrollbar to find and then select the Samsung entry. You should see a display similar to the one shown in Figure 3.15.

FIGURE 3.15.

Modifications to the MONITOR2.INF file appear in the Select Device dialog box.

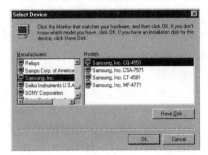

Click Cancel three times to exit the Display Settings dialog without changing the monitor type. Adding a new device to an INF file can prove time-consuming and even frustrating at times. However, the benefits in reduced maintenance time are well worth the effort.

Summary

Plug and Play is probably the best thing to happen to computer users in a long time. It makes hardware setup a breeze and enhances a user's ability to exploit the full potential of his system. This chapter explained what Plug and Play is, what the user needs to activate it, and how Plug and Play can help. It also looked at how you can check your system for Plug and Play compatibility.

It is important to realize that the transition to a fully Plug and Play compatible setup takes time. This chapter also looked at how Plug and Play works with and on legacy systems. Windows 95 provides all of the hooks needed to make this transition simple.

Finally, what happens when Plug and Play fails to work properly with your legacy system? The final section of this chapter looked at some techniques you can use to get around problem areas. Exploring the potential workarounds for conflicts between legacy and Plug and Play components is one way to maintain integrity.

PART

II

Installing, Customizing, and Tuning Windows 95

Why Fix It if It Ain't Supposed to be Broke?

Windows 3.1 was always a handyman's special in real-estate parlance. Getting 3.1 to run, keeping it running, and making it look good was a substantial part-time job for those who had the inclination to tweak CONFIG.SYS and .INI files.

Many more users, however, shied away from pulling up Windows' floorboards and finding the termites; and for them, Windows 3.1 was always a little unreliable in operation, sluggish in performance, boring and cluttered in appearance, and sloppy in use.

Users expect more from Windows 95. After all, Microsoft had a full five years between Windows 3.0 and 95 to work the bugs out. Shouldn't Windows 95 set itself up, look good, run smoothly, and link together applications without forcing the user to perform extensive setup, monitoring, and maintenance?

Well, yes and no. Windows 95 makes great strides forward in reliability, and its revised approach to starting programs—the taskbar and Start menu—are a huge leap forward in both usability and aesthetics. The new automated Wizards also help you do things right the first time—especially setting up Windows—so you don't run into problems down the road. Other new features take some of the guesswork out of performance tuning. Nevertheless, to use Windows 95 comfortably, reliably, and productively, you need to conduct a careful setup and perform a little regular maintenance.

Of course, you can look at the fix-up job as an opportunity rather than a burden. Proper setup and customization means more than just moving in and slapping up wallpaper. This is your chance to tailor your Windows 95 environment to your own tastes and productivity requirements, starting from the choices you make during setup, and continuing through the maintenance and tuning of your environment over time. You'll find that, by making a few smart choices and keeping up with the housework, you'll make your Windows system a responsive, convenient, reliable, and pleasant place to be.

In a well-customized system, for example, the program you need is right at hand when you need it. The screen is never cluttered with icons you don't touch, but any program you might need waits no more than a few clicks away and is easy to find. The taskbar is handy when you want it to be, but inconspicuous (or invisible) when you're focused on a single task. In the well-customized system, data is shared seamlessly among applications, eliminating duplicate effort. Such a system performs efficiently with little regular maintenance and adapts easily to the addition of new software or hardware. Finally, a well-customized system expresses its user's personality. That's more important than it sounds; you are more productive in an environment that feels like home.

The next three chapters show you how to build that well-customized system on a stand-alone computer (though nearly all of what's shown applies on the network, as well). You'll learn how to install Windows 95 and then customize and tune your environment to your exact requirements.

Choices, Choices

One handicap of Windows 95 is also one of its great advantages: You can pretty much fly through setup with your brain on the Bahamas, accept all the defaults for your screen display and menu structure, and get to work. A lot of people do that. If you do that, this part—in fact, this whole book—isn't going to do you much good.

The authors of this part show you how to take charge of your Windows environment, to approach setting up and customizing so that your Windows 95 environment fits your needs (and your computer) like a glove. As you'll see, that doesn't require much effort or much knowledge. It does require making decisions, from before you even begin setup through tuning your system for performance.

Nearly every choice you make in Windows involves some kind of trade-off; for example, if you want access to all of the Windows applets and tools, you'll pay in disk space. If you want the jazziest-looking desktop around, you may pay in performance. That's why making careful, informed choices at every step is so important.

The following is just a sampling of the choices covered in the next three chapters.

Choices Before Setup

- Do I have the right hardware for running Windows 95? Is there anything in my configuration I should upgrade before installing Windows?

- Is my computer properly prepared for Windows installation? Do I have enough disk space? Should I decompress, defragment, or otherwise reconfigure my hard disk before installation?

- Should I update my existing DOS/Windows configuration, or start from scratch with a "clean" Windows 95 installation?

- How much of Windows 95 and its accessories should I install? Everything? The bare essentials?

Choices During Setup

■ Which command and switches should I use to install most effectively for my configuration?

■ Should I let Windows detect and configure my hardware automatically, or should I tell Windows about my hardware?

■ Do I need a boot disk?

Choices Soon After Setup

■ How should I organize my Start menu?

■ Where should I put my taskbar?

■ Should I use desktop icons?

■ What do I want my desktop to look like?

■ Do I need more than one Windows desktop configuration?

Ongoing Choices

■ What practices can I follow to keep my system running smoothly?

■ If I run low on disk space, how do I decide whether to upgrade my system or compress my disk?

■ What types of configuration choices tend to slow my system down or make it unreliable?

■ What do I gain by upgrading to Windows 95 applications?

■ How do I track down the source of an apparent decrease in performance?

■ What do I do when a program locks up or crashes?

You don't have to ask (or answer) all of these, or really, any of them. If you become aware of the possibilities and pitfalls revealed in these questions and others, you'll develop a full command of Windows, which is, after all, just a dumb computer program. Of the people who have complained that Windows didn't work for them, many failed to take charge of Windows and *make* it work for them. That's the secret to successful Windows computing.

> **NOTE**
>
> Before you work through setup and customization, you should be aware of a few special options Windows 95 supplies. These options can be changed in the

During Windows setup, you'll have the chance to choose a language. Windows 95 is not designed to display its menus, help boxes, or other text in languages other than English, but it can adjust the characters produced by the keyboard to make writing and editing text in other languages easier. It can also adjust the way currencies, dates and times, and other types of data are expressed to conform to the standards used in different countries and cultures. You can set these options during setup, or you can change them later through the Control Panel's Keyboard and Regional Settings icons.

Windows 95 features a set of customization tools specially designed to accommodate the needs of disabled users. Grouped in Control Panel under Accessibility Options, these tools can be used to select a high-contrast color scheme or large screen fonts for the visually impaired, use pop-up boxes to indicate sounds for the hearing-impaired, and adjust the way the keyboard and mouse respond to make Windows easier to use for people with motor impairments. The accessibility options also enable you to set up and control alternative input devices used by some disabled people.

Now, although I can climb stairs, I've been known to walk up wheelchair ramps sometimes. The same goes for Windows 95's accessibility options. They're designed for the disabled, and if you're disabled, you may find one or more of them very helpful. However, even if you're not disabled, if you'd like a high-contrast color scheme, big type on title bars, or any of the other variations enabled by these options, knock yourself out. It's your Windows.

You begin taking charge of your Windows environment by turning the page.

Installing Windows 95

It should come as no surprise that each new version of Windows is larger and more complex than its ancestors. What is perhaps surprising is that installing Windows 95 is a thoroughly straightforward process that in most cases requires little or no input from the user. So, as Windows becomes more complex, installing it doesn't. Even installing network drivers can be trusted to a beginner.

Like most other components in Windows 95, Setup has been reworked from top to bottom. Windows 95 Setup is now totally a Windows program; there is no text component as there has been in previous versions. Also, as you might expect from previous versions, Windows 95 Setup is fully configurable, so system administrators can create customized, hands-off installations that can even install key application programs at the same time that Windows 95 is installed.

In fact, about the hardest part of installing Windows 95 is deciding beforehand how you want your system to be configured. There are some issues, mostly network-related, that need to be considered ahead of time.

> **NOTE**
>
> In all likelihood, you have already installed Windows 95 on your system. There may come a time when you need to reinstall, or when you need to install Windows 95 on another machine. The information in this chapter is intended to help you become more knowledgeable about the setup process so that you can more efficiently set up any systems that you must support.

Before you get to the mechanics of installing Windows 95, take a few minutes to go through a short preinstallation checklist. Deciding how you want to handle these issues before you begin the process of installation will save you time and energy because it increases the likelihood that you'll never need to reinstall Windows 95.

Clean Installation Versus Update Installation

The first consideration you'll have to face is whether to install Windows 95 from the ground up, or to let it perform an upgrade to your existing configuration. As always, each method has trade-offs.

NOTE

There are two configurations of Windows 95 installation disks available: the upgrade version and the original installation version. The original installation version does not require that Setup find a previous version of Windows before continuing. The upgrade version checks your system for previously installed versions of Windows. If they are not found, Setup will not continue.

Installing Clean

A *clean installation* means that you don't install Windows 95 over an existing operating system such as DOS or Windows NT. The main advantage to a clean installation is that you get to clean out your Windows directories. Another advantage is that you retain the ability to dual boot with whatever operating system you're currently running on your system.

Most important, perhaps, is the opportunity that a clean installation affords to trim the dead-wood from your hard disk. Ten years ago, the average size of hard disks was ten megabytes, but today the average hard disk is more than ten times that size. There seems to be some strange corollary to Murphy's Law that states that a hard disk more than three months old, no matter the size, is perpetually in danger of overflowing. Install a 2GB hard disk and use DriveSpace to compress it, and you'll still manage to fill it. A whole lot of that filler will be in the Windows directories.

It seems that almost every Windows application comes with its own set of dynamic link librar-ies (DLLs) that get installed in your WINDOWS\SYSTEM directory, even when you install the core of the application in another directory. By the way, *folder* is the preferred term in the language of Windows 95, and we'll switch to that term as soon as you have Windows 95 in-stalled.

If you're one of those people who often tries out new software, whether commercial or shareware, you probably have scores of files in your Windows directories that never get used, and some of them can be quite large. Fortunately, Microsoft has recognized this problem and has taken steps to correct it in this release, but chances are that even if you don't do a lot of software inspec-tion, your current Windows installation contains files that are never used any more.

If you simply delete your WINDOWS directory before installing Windows 95, you get rid of all those files that are no longer in use. Of course, you'll have to reinstall most of your Win-dows software. That's the trade-off. If, however, your Windows installation has been on your system for a couple of years, you'll probably free up quite a bit of space on the disk.

Update Installation

By default, Windows 95 will offer to install on top of your current DOS/Windows 3.1 setup, or over Windows NT. The advantage of allowing this to happen is that Windows 95 converts all of your Program Manager groups to folders of shortcuts in your Start Menu, and preferences and application settings from WIN.INI, SYSTEM.INI, and PROTOCOL.INI are preserved so that old applications will continue to run without having to be reinstalled. Also, any network connections that you have are automatically upgraded to the Windows 95 versions.

The disadvantage of an update installation is that you can't dual boot with your previous installation. Also, Windows 95 Setup won't detect which files that are already on the disk are up to date, so unused files will remain, taking up space on your hard disk.

INSTALLING OVER OTHER OPERATING SYSTEMS

The default method of running Setup is to double-click it from the Windows 3.1 or Windows for Workgroups File Manager. That is the fastest way to get a stand-alone update installation going.

If, however, you don't have Windows 3.1x installed, you'll want to run Setup from a DOS prompt. By running Setup from DOS, you can install over DOS, OS/2, Windows 3.x, and Windows NT.

Scalable Installation

Windows 95 Setup gives you four choices that determine how Windows 95 is installed. There are four types of installation: typical, portable, compact, and custom.

> The *typical* installation is designed to be used by the vast majority of people installing Windows 95. When you choose typical, almost all of the capabilities of Windows 95 are installed on your hard disk.

> The *portable* installation is designed for putting Windows 95 on notebook and laptop computers. The special features of Windows 95 dedicated to mobile computers such as hot docking, power management, and Briefcase are automatically installed.

> The *compact* installation option enables you to put just the bare bones of Windows 95 onto your system. You'll get a fully capable system minus any of the optional features available.

> The *custom* installation option is designed for system administrators and experienced Windows users to allow them to control exactly what parts of Windows 95 are installed and how they are configured. Custom installation enables you to decide exactly what features you want installed.

Setup and Networks

During the setup process, you'll have the opportunity to install networking options. Keep in mind that networking in the Windows 95 scheme of things is a broader concept than just attaching to a file server.

Of course, traditional networking connections via NetWare, Banyan Vines, and others is an option, as is creating workgroups of users who share resources with each other within a localized area such as a single office.

The main difference to a user between attaching to a server and being part of a workgroup is that the server is capable of handling hundreds of user clients, whereas a workgroup is usually made up of ten people or fewer. Network operating systems such as NetWare are capable of providing users links to the outside world via gateways to mainframe resources and the Internet. Workgroups are smaller groups of people who share data, modems, printers, and so forth. And, yes, it's possible to be connected to both a workgroup and to a company-wide network.

If you're going to be connected to a network or be part of a workgroup, the system administrator will give you instructions on how to install Windows 95. There are a number of options available.

Shared Installations Versus Stand-Alone Installations

A computer system that is not connected to the outside world except perhaps via modem communications is a typical stand-alone system. All the files needed to run Windows 95 are installed on the hard disk of the computer. If, however, your computer is a network client, the system administrator for the network may elect to have you create a shared installation.

By creating a directory on the file server from which users can install, the system administrator of the network has a measure of control and flexibility not afforded by connecting computers that have stand-alone installations. For example, by using the network file server as the distribution point for Windows 95, three types of installations can be accomplished:

- Running Windows 95 from diskless workstations connected to a NetWare server where all the files to run Windows 95 and all the user's configuration files reside on the server. With this type of installation, users can be allowed to log onto Windows 95 using their name and password from any machine and retain their individual configuration.

- Running Windows 95 from a workstation that has all but the system start-up files stored on the server. With this type of installation, users also can be allowed to log onto Windows 95 using their name and password from any machine and retain their individual configuration.

■ Running Windows 95 from a workstation that has all the Windows 95 files installed on the workstation's hard disk, yet has connections to servers and workgroups. The advantage of this method is that traffic on the network is minimized, conserving bandwidth. The disadvantage is that individual users' settings also are stored on the hard disk, preventing users from roaming to another machine and retaining their individual configuration.

Before installing Windows 95, consult with your system administrator for instructions on how to install Windows 95. The administrator can give you a command line that will automatically install Windows 95 using a script file. The script file can be edited so that it will automatically provide Setup with configuration options that are normally obtained by asking the person installing Windows 95. For more information on creating hands-off installation scripts, see the section on customizing MSBATCH.INF later in this chapter.

Technical Requirements for Installing Windows 95

The system requirements for installing Windows 95 fall into two categories: hardware and operating system. The hardware requirements specify the type of machine that you need to run Windows 95, whereas the operating system requirements specify the configuration of the hardware that Setup can work with.

Hardware Requirements for a Windows 95-Compatible Computer

Unlike its cousin, Windows NT, which can run on multiple processor types, Windows 95 requires a single Intel 80386 or higher microprocessor to be installed in the system. Windows 95 does not support Symmetric Multiple Processor (SMP). The following list shows you an outline of the hardware required to run Windows 95.

Computer	386/486/ Pentium processor with a high-density floppy disk and hard disk with approximately 40 MB free disk space for typical installation
Memory	4 MB RAM minimum; 8 MB recommended
Display	VGA minimum; SVGA with a video card capable of rendering 16-bit TrueColor recommended
Optional Hardware	Modem
	CD-ROM drive, double speed or higher recommended
	Sound Card and other multimedia devices

Network Interface Card (NIC)

Tape Backup Subsystem

Printer

Disk space requirements vary according to the type of installation. The recommended 40 MB of free space includes approximately 30 MB for a typical Windows 95 installation, plus 8–9 MB for a swap file. You'll want to make sure that the disk drive onto which you install Windows 95 has enough room to accommodate new DLLs, help file indexes, and so on.

Operating System Requirements for Installing Windows 95

The Windows 95 operating system is designed to be installed on computers as an upgrade to some other already running operating system. The following list shows the operating systems that can be upgraded with Windows 95.

MS-DOS Version 3.2 or higher

Windows 3.0

Windows 3.1

Windows for Workgroups 3.11

DR DOS (Digital Research DOS)

Novell DOS

IBM PC-DOS

OS/2 (configured to dual boot with MS-DOS)

Windows NT (configured to dual boot with MS-DOS)

See the following section concerning FAT requirements for installing Windows 95.

In each case, Windows 95 will replace the operating system listed in Table 4.2. When installation is complete, Windows 95 will completely take over as the operating system on systems on which it has been installed.

Windows 95 Requires FAT Disk Structure

Windows 95's Installable File System (IFS) specification is an open doorway that enables vendors and programmers to access files that are stored using systems other than the standard DOS file system. For example, Windows 95 uses an IFS called CDFS (CD-ROM File System) to read data files written on CDs.

During installation Windows 95 installs an IFS called VFAT, which is an advanced version of the standard DOS FAT (file allocation table) specification for hard disk structures. As you might expect, the V in VFAT stands for virtual. The new Virtual File Allocation Table IFS is capable of supporting long file names and the Universal Naming Convention (UNC), while still retaining support for DOS disks.

In the FAT specification, a hard disk is partitioned using the utility FDISK, or a utility supplied by the vendor of the hard disk. Each partition can then be formatted to suit the operating system that will use that part of the disk. For example, it has long been possible to have DOS, UNIX, and DR Concurrent DOS (CP/M) residing on the same hard disk.

To successfully install Windows 95, you must have a sufficiently large partition formatted to the DOS 16-bit File Allocation Table Specification. In this case, *sufficiently large* means that the hard disk must exceed 32 MB. Versions of DOS less than 3.31 may or may not support the creation of partitions on the hard disk that exceed 32 MB. Any version of DOS 3.2 or higher that is capable of creating partitions greater than 32 MB is a suitable platform for launching Windows 95 Setup.

Disk Partition Requirements

All versions of MS-DOS and most OEM (Original Equipment Manufacturers) versions of DOS come with the FDISK utility, which is used to prepare a hard disk for formatting. Each partition created on the hard disk can be formatted according to the needs of DOS or some other operating system. The vast majority of computer systems in use today have a single large DOS partition, but there are some computer systems with the hard disk partitioned so that the computer can be booted by more than one operating system (for example, DOS and UNIX). In these cases, one of the operating systems is assigned as the primary operating system and the secondary OS must be booted from floppy disk.

FDISK

If you have any questions about partitioning your hard disk, you can use FDISK to inspect the partitioning status before installing Windows 95 to make certain that the hard disk is properly and efficiently prepared.

WARNING

FDISK is not a utility to be taken lightly. Altering a partition table for a disk in use will destroy all the data on that disk! For this reason, FDISK should be used only by experienced computer users and system administrators.

Before you run the FDISK utility, check with your system administrator.

Creating a Partition

How to partition the hard disk is a matter of preference. Many people simply create one large partition that contains all the storage space on the disk. This single large partition is then formatted, usually as C. Others, myself included, prefer to create a single DOS partition but then take the second step of dividing that partition into secondary partitions. The primary partition becomes C, whereas the secondary (non-bootable) partitions become D, E, and so on.

> **TIP**
>
> Systems with disk drives larger than 500 MB typically require a disk management program to install correctly. Although Windows 95 can be installed on a system that uses disk managers such as Disk Manager and others, you may want to eliminate the need for the disk manager by partitioning the hard disk into multiple drives that are smaller than 500 MB.

The manner in which your hard disk is partitioned will be reflected in Windows 95 as different hard disk drive letters. The advantage to breaking up a large hard disk in this way is that you can, in effect, more easily break up your disk into smaller, more manageable groups of folders that makes finding files easier when you need them.

Third-Party Disk Partitions

There was a period of time, not too many years ago, when the pressure to make larger hard disks available to users came into conflict with the capability of DOS and the BIOS chips installed in computer systems to handle those larger hard disks. To get around this problem, many drive manufacturers included installation utilities with their hard disks that could be used to fool DOS into thinking that it was dealing with one type of hard disk, when in fact it wasn't.

Although they have become largely unnecessary, except to install very large drives, many computers capable of running Windows 95 were originally installed using one of these utilities. Windows 95 is compatible with the following utilities.

- Disk Manager   (look for DMDRVR.BIN on the boot disk)
- SpeedStor   (look for SSTOR.SYS on the boot disk)
- Golden Bow   Vfeature

If any of these disk partitioning schemes are detected by Setup, they will automatically be converted. If you encounter a problem with Setup, you may wish to repartition your disk into smaller volumes (D, E, and so on).

Setup and Disk Compression

One of the most useful utilities to come along in the last few years is disk compression. By installing a compression utility, users can effectively increase the size of their hard disk to approximately twice the stated capacity.

Typically, a disk compression utility works by taking over a disk drive and renaming it to the next available drive letter. All the files on that disk drive are then written into a single compressed file that is presented to the user as if it were the disk drive itself. So convincing is the illusion that the compressed "disk drive" even has the original name.

If, for example, you have a computer with drives C and D, and have a CD-ROM device plugged in as E, a disk compression utility will rename the C drive as F. F is said to be the host drive for C. A single large file is created on drive F that contains all the files that are supposed to be on C in compressed form. That file's contents are then displayed to the user as drive C.

Windows 95 will automatically install on compressed hard disks. The following disk compression utilities are supported:

- Microsoft DriveSpace
- Microsoft DoubleSpace
- Stacker (versions 3.0 and 4.x)
- SuperStor

Usually, the host drive will retain some of the disk's space in uncompressed form, so you can actually write files to the host drive as well as the compressed volume. Windows 95 takes advantage of this uncompressed area to store parts of the Registry, an internal database of configuration information. Before you install Windows 95, you should make sure that your host drive contains at least 3 MB and preferably 4 MB of free disk space that Windows 95 can use to store Registry.

Last Stop Before Windows 95!

Before running Setup to install Windows 95, you'll want to be certain that you've covered the following four areas.

- Make sure that you have a working DOS bootable floppy disk.

    One of the first things that Windows 95 Setup does is to alter the boot sectors of your hard disk and install a very small-scale version of Windows. Usually, if you encounter problems installing Windows 95, you can get the machine to come up in a fail-safe boot. Just in case Murphy's Law is operating in your vicinity, however, make sure that you have a bootable floppy disk on hand. In addition to any disk compression drivers and utilities (such as DBLSPACE or DRVSPACE) needed, you'll also want to copy

FDISK, FORMAT, SCANDISK, DEFRAG, EDIT, and any other DOS utilities that you think you might need onto the boot disk. Don't forget to include your current versions of AUTOEXEC.BAT and CONFIG.SYS so that any devices (such as the CD-ROM drive) are properly installed when booting from the floppy.

■ Make sure that you have a good backup of the hard disk.

Even though Setup has a Smart Recovery feature to help you get past any troubles you may encounter installing Windows 95, it's a really good idea to make sure that the entire hard disk is backed up just in case you accidentally destroy needed files.

■ Remove unnecessary device drivers and TSR programs from your configuration files.

AUTOEXEC.BAT and CONFIG.SYS serve as the main configuration vehicles for DOS-based computer systems. Entries in these files are responsible for loading device drivers, TSR (terminate and stay ready) programs, environment variables, and so on.

You'll want to edit these files for the purpose of getting rid of TSR programs, unneeded environment variables, and most device drivers. In the case of device drivers, Windows 95 Setup will automatically detect the hardware components of the system and install protected mode versions of the device drivers needed to operate the hardware it finds whenever possible.

You will, however, want to leave entries for device drivers for network connections and for CD-ROM drives (if you're installing from CD).

Remember to reboot the machine after you've edited the configuration files to clear the memory occupied by TSRs and device drivers. Windows 95 Setup requires 471 KB of free conventional memory to run.

■ Defragment and optimize the disk onto which you're installing Windows 95.

Many long-time computer users are surprised to learn that files aren't necessarily written as a single block of disk space. Instead, as files are created and erased, the content of a large file may be spread over the entire surface of the hard disk in small chunks or fragments.

Highly fragmented drives lose performance as the disk heads scour the disk scanning for the various locations where data is written. Loss of performance can easily be remedied by running a defragmenting utility such as the MS-DOS 6.2*x* or later ScanDisk utility. Norton Utilities, PC Tools, and others offer similar utilities for systems that don't have the latest versions of DOS installed. ScanDisk checks out your hard disk to identify bad sectors where data shouldn't be written, identifies file corruption on the disk, and defragments the drive so that files are rewritten as contiguous sectors instead of being scattered over the disk.

If, during installation, Windows 95 Setup reports that the drive is fragmented, you can use the Windows 95 Defrag utility to correct the problem after Setup is finished.

CAUTION

After you have installed Windows 95, many of your favorite disk maintenance tools such as Norton Utilities or PC Tools will become obsolete because they are incompatible with Windows 95's installable file system (IFS). It's time to put them away. Windows 95 comes with a set of system tools that will take care of most of the disk maintenance chores you'll need to do in the future. It's almost certain as well that the major disk tool companies will find some reason to provide tools compatible with the Windows 95 file scheme.

Windows 95 and Dual Booting

In the normal course of events, Windows 95 is set up to replace any other operating system on your system. You can, however, install Windows 95 to dual boot with DOS or with Windows NT if NT is installed to dual boot with DOS.

NOTE

The term *dual boot* means that your computer has the capability to boot up either your old operating system or Windows 95 using the F4 key during the boot process.

Dual boot capability is intended primarily for advanced users who must develop and test software to run under both operating systems, and for those who just don't want to let go of the old ways entirely.

It's the second group of people who, in general, really shouldn't set up with dual boot capability. Maintaining both operating systems uses extra disk resources.

Although some users may be tempted to hang on to their old version of Windows or DOS, there isn't much reason to do so. If you're dead set on keeping the Windows 3.x interface, you can elect to have Setup include 32-bit versions of File Manager and Program Manager. Most people will be best served, however, by avoiding both dual boot capability and using the Windows 3.x interface components. It will only take longer to get used to the new Windows 95 interface. After you get used to Windows 95, you'll almost certainly like it better than the old ways. On the other hand, pressing F4 to boot up your old version of DOS can be handy when you have an old program that is so ill-behaved it won't even run in Windows 95's special MS-DOS mode.

Dual Booting with Windows 3.x and DOS

Dual boot capabilities are restricted to DOS versions 5.0 and higher. Because Windows 3.x is loaded on top of DOS, creating dual boot with DOS automatically enables you to load Windows 3.x.

TIP

To enable dual boot capabilities, you'll need to ensure that the line BootMulti=1 appears in the [Options] section of the file MSDOS.SYS. You can edit this file with Notepad. Before editing, however, you'll need to remove the check in the Read Only checkbox of the file's properties dialog. Details on the use of this file are covered later in this chapter.

To preserve your previous version of DOS and retain the capability of running Windows 3.x, you need only specify that Windows 95 should be installed in a directory other than the one containing Windows 3.x. Setup will preserve your current setup, including your current AUTOEXEC.BAT and CONFIG.SYS files.

CAUTION

By default, Windows 95 installs the new IFS that supports long file names. Although a certain amount of backward compatibility is retained with older versions of the DOS FAT, the new VFAT is not compatible with many old DOS commands and disk utilities. For this reason, Windows 95 Setup deletes a number of DOS' external command files. A list of these files is provided later in this chapter.

Avoid using utilities such as PC Tools and Norton Utilities written for your earlier DOS versions, and don't reinstall the missing DOS files. These programs can severely damage files on your hard disk, effectively corrupting the disk so badly that you'll need to reformat.

The drawback to setting up a dual boot with your old version of DOS is that, in effect, you're choosing a clean install, which means that you'll need to reinstall many of your Windows applications for use with Windows 95. Be sure to install them into the same directories as they currently are in to ensure that the applications can be used both in Windows 95 and Windows 3.x.

If You Have Already Installed Windows 95

If you already installed Windows 95 as an upgrade to DOS by specifying your old Windows 3.x as the directory for Windows 95, you can still restore DOS dual boot capability, but it's a painstaking process that should be performed only by an experienced user. You'll need backup copies of your old AUTOEXEC.BAT and CONFIG.SYS files. Here are the steps:

Find a bootable floppy disk containing version 5.0 or higher of DOS.

Run the command `ATTRIB *.* -r -h -s` on the floppy disk to remove hidden, read-only, and system attributes.

Rename the files IO.SYS and MSDOS.SYS to IO.DOS and MSDOS.DOS, respectively. Don't omit this step or you'll severely damage your Windows 95 installation.

Copy the renamed files to C:\.

Copy the version of COMMAND.COM on the floppy to C:\, changing the name to COMMAND.DOS. Make sure that the name is changed to avoid trashing Windows 95's COMMAND.COM file.

Copy the backup copies of AUTOEXEC.BAT and CONFIG.SYS to C:\ as AUTOEXEC.DOS and CONFIG.DOS, respectively. Again, failing to rename these files will damage your Windows 95 installation.

If you're using disk compression, copy all the files that you placed in C:\ onto the root directory of your host drive as well.

Edit MSDOS.SYS (the Windows 95 version) to include the line `BootMulti=1` in the `[Options]` section.

Cross your fingers and restart the computer, pressing F4 during the reboot to boot to your old version of DOS. If you've done everything correctly, you'll boot into your old configuration.

Dual Booting with Windows NT

To create a dual boot situation between Windows NT and Windows 95, you'll first need to make sure that the system is set up to dual boot between DOS and Windows NT because Windows 95 requires access to a 16-bit, FAT-style disk format. Also, keep in mind that the NTFS file system is incompatible with Windows 95, and files stored in a disk partition formatted for NTFS won't be available during Windows 95 sessions.

To install Windows 95 to dual boot with Windows NT, follow these steps:

1. Boot up the system using F4 to boot to DOS rather than Windows NT.
2. Remove the read-only status of BOOTSECT.DOS and BOOT.INI using the following commands:

```
ATTRIB -r BOOTSECT.DOS
ATTRIB -r BOOT.INI
```

3. Copy the file BOOTSECT.DOS, changing the name to BOOTSECT.SAV or some other name that you will remember as being the old version of the file.

4. Run Windows 95 Setup from the command line and specify any empty directory. Don't install over any Windows NT system files.

5. Rename `BOOTSECT.DOS` to `BOOTSECT.W40` and rename `BOOTSECT.SAV` to `BOOTSECT.DOS`.

6. Use Notepad or some other text editor to add Windows 95 entries into the file `BOOT.INI`. Make sure that `BOOT.INI` contains the following settings in the proper sections:

```
[BOOT LOADER]
TIMEOUT=30
DEFAULT=C:\WINNT

[OPERATING SYSTEMS]
C:\WINNT="Windows NT"
C:\BOOTSECT.DOS="MS-DOS v6.22" /win95dos
C:\BOOTSECT.W40="Windows 95" /win95
```

When you reboot the computer, the Windows NT dual boot menu will include an item that you can select to boot to Windows 95 as an option.

Dual Boot Warp = No Go

Although you can't dual boot with OS/2 Warp, you can install Windows 95 on a system running any version of OS/2 as long as the system contains a portion of the disk formatted for DOS' FAT file structure. Of course, that partition must have enough free space to hold Windows 95. OS/2 uses the HPFS (High Performance File System) file format, and any files written to disks formatted for HPFS are unavailable to Windows 95.

To install a copy of Windows 95 that can be run from OS/2, follow these steps:

1. Boot the computer using a bootable floppy disk containing DOS version 5.0 or higher.

2. Run Windows 95 Setup from the command line.

3. Specify an empty directory for Windows 95.

Windows 95 Setup won't incorporate any desktop or other settings from OS/2, and you may have to reinstall Windows applications to make them work in Windows 95.

NOTE

If your OS/2 installation uses Boot Manager, you'll receive a warning that Windows 95 Setup is about to disable it. Because Windows 95 can't predict what operating system or configuration will be used to reboot, the Boot Manager is disabled so that Windows 95 will restart properly during that portion of Setup when the system is rebooted. No other OS/2 files are affected.

To restore Boot Manager, boot OS/2 from the floppy and run the OS/2 FDISK utility. This will enable both OS/2 and Windows 95 to operate normally.

Running Windows 95 Setup

By far the most common method of installation is to create a stand-alone version of Windows 95 so that all the system files reside on the hard disk of the computer. As I mentioned previously in this chapter, you also can create installations so that some or all of the system files reside on a file server. Whichever method is employed, the overall progression of Setup is similar. The examples shown in the following sections relate to installing on a stand-alone system.

Starting Setup

How you will start Setup depends on whether you have Windows 95 on floppy disk or CD-ROM, and whether you're installing from Windows or DOS. Each variation has at its core the simple act of running the program SETUP.EXE. This file can be found on disk 1 of the floppy set, in the root directory of the CD-ROM version, or in a shared directory on a network file server.

If you're installing from Windows, you can use File Manager to locate SETUP.EXE and double-click it, or you can use the File | Run command from the File Manager or Program Manager menu. If your system administrator or computer support specialist has asked you to include command-line switches, you'll need to use the File | Run method.

If you're installing from a DOS prompt, log onto the floppy, network, or CD-ROM drive where SETUP.EXE is located, type SETUP, and press Enter. If your system administrator or computer support specialist has asked you to include command-line switches, just type them on the command line.

Setup Command-Line Options

Windows 95 Setup has two command-line options that can be specified to control how your installation proceeds. Users familiar with DOS commands are already familiar with using command-line options. Windows 95 Setup uses the following syntax:

```
SETUP [batch][/T:tempdir][/?]
```

Usually, the command-line options are not needed. Each serves a single purpose, however, and Table 4.1 documents these options.

Table 4.3. Setup command-line options.

`batch`	This option specifies the filename of the batch file that is to be used to control the actions of SETUP.EXE. Such batch files often are used to create customized hands-off installations for users. With a batch file, the system administrator can easily make sure that the proper features of Windows 95 are installed.
`/T`	Setup initially copies files onto the hard disk to provide a temporary copy of Windows that is run to support the setup process. The default temporary directory is created on the same disk drive on which you're installing Windows 95. If you're short of disk space, you can specify another directory (folder) to use. This folder can be on a different disk to ensure that there is enough disk space remaining to install Windows 95. **WARNING:** Any files in the temporary folder specified by `/T` will be erased!
`/?`	Displays a list of the available command-line options. Running setup in later versions using the `/?` switch will inform you of any changes to Setup's syntax.

Installing Windows 95

Windows 95 Setup is a complex Wizard that is about the easiest Windows program you'll ever use. Like all other Wizards in Windows 95, various dialogs are presented to you in a window. Each of the windows has three buttons in the lower-right corner. The Back button allows you to return to the last dialog to change an answer. The Next dialog indicates that you have made whatever choices are to be made and want to move to the next phase of installation. The Cancel button enables you to abort the installation process before it has completed.

WHEN PROBLEMS OCCUR

Fortunately, most installations are as smooth as glass. Once in a while, however, a problem may occur that makes it impossible for the Setup Wizard to continue. If this happens, Smart Recovery is available to finish an aborted installation so that you can correct the problem. To use Smart Recovery, just turn the computer off with the power switch. Do *not* use Ctrl+Alt+Del.

When the computer restarts after you turn the power back on, Smart Recovery will kick in and complete the installation if you have successfully cleared the problem.

To begin installation, locate SETUP.EXE. It's on disk 1 if you're installing for floppies, or in the Win95 folder of the CD edition. If you're running Windows 3.x, double-click SETUP.EXE using File Manager. If you're installing to dual boot with Windows NT, OS/2, or if you have only DOS on your system, change directories to the location of SETUP.EXE, type SETUP on the command line, and press Enter.

A Three-Step Process

Installing Windows 95 is a three-step process. The Setup Wizard first collects information about your system. The second step is to copy necessary files to your hard disk. The third step is to reboot your system, launch Windows 95, and configure your system.

The First Step: Gathering Information

First, Setup goes about gathering information about your system and its component parts. In the process, your hard disks are tested for performance and available space, and the system is searched to discover what hardware your system is using. A dialog box will appear during setup asking you whether the Setup Wizard should automatically detect hardware, or whether you should be allowed to specify the hardware manually. Select the manual method only if you are an experienced user and know exactly the model and maker of each of the peripheral devices in your system. You also may need to manually configure hardware if Windows 95 fails to properly detect your devices.

TIP

If there is less space on your hard disk than is required to install Windows 95, a dialog box will appear to show you what condition disk resources are in. If you're reinstalling over a previous version of Windows 95, you can usually ignore this warning safely because the formula used doesn't account for disk space that will not be used when old files are written over. If, however, disk space is really tight, it's better to be cautious and clean up the disk by moving files somewhere else.

When the Setup Wizard is ready to proceed, you're shown the dialog box in Figure 4.1, asking you what kind of installation you want. Typical is the recommended choice for everyday use. Portable provides the features designed for laptop and notebook computers. Compact provides a minimal installation. Custom enables you to exercise every possible option for installing Windows 95.

FIGURE 4.1.

Four radio buttons enable you to choose the type of installation you want.

Next, Setup checks your system for a pre-existing version of Windows. If one is found, a dialog box appears asking whether Setup should upgrade in the current Windows directory or create a new installation. If you click Other Directory to create a new installation, then press the Next button to go to a dialog box that enables you to specify the directory where you want Windows 95 to be installed. If no previous version of Windows is found, the default is C:\WINDOWS.

> **TIP**
>
> Remember that a clean install will require you to reinstall any applications you have that require registration, put files in the Windows or System folders, or use WIN.INI and SYSTEM.INI settings. Simple applications that are fully contained within their own folder will usually not require reinstallation.

Selecting Features to Be Installed

If you've chosen Custom as the installation type, the next dialog box that you'll see is pictured in Figure 4.2. In this dialog you can select exactly which optional components of Windows 95 you want installed. Each component has a check box along the left side of the Components list box. Only when an item is checked will its files be copied to your system.

Each item in the list box, when highlighted, changes the display under the list box to show a description of the item, how much total disk space is needed to install Windows 95, and how much disk space is available.

Some features are dependent on having some other feature installed. If you select a feature that has such a dependency, you'll be asked to confirm that both features should be installed.

The items in the list box represent related applets and accessories. To pick and choose from these, highlight an item and click the Details button, or double-click an item. Doing either of these will cause a dialog to appear, allowing you to choose which applets and features you want installed.

FIGURE 4.2.

During Custom installation, you can select exactly which optional Windows 95 features you want installed.

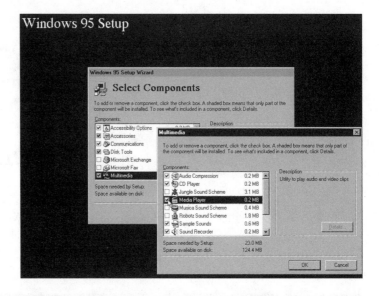

TIP

The choices you make during setup are not etched in stone. The Windows 95 Control Panel has two dialog boxes that enable you to change the hardware and software settings you have installed. The Add/Remove Programs dialog box enables you to install applets that you didn't install with Setup, and the Add/Remove Hardware dialog enables you to change the settings for hardware resources.

Providing User Information to Setup

Like almost all Microsoft software products, Windows 95 requires you to enter user information during setup. You're asked for your name and the name of your company or organization. Enter the required information and click Next. Information provided in the User Information dialog box is used to formulate a network name and to display in the About box of Explorer.

CAUTION

Part of the information-gathering process involves telling Windows 95 what kind of printer is connected to the system. If your printer comes with an installation disk, you can click the Have Disk button in the dialog box to install the driver supplied by the printer manufacturer.

One thing to watch out for, however, is that the manufacturer's driver may not be as up to date as the Microsoft-supplied driver unless the printer's documentation states that the driver is compatible with Windows 95. If your printer is listed in the Add Printer Wizard, you're probably better off using the Microsoft-supplied driver unless the driver disk you have specifically states that it is meant for Windows 95.

Creating a Windows 95 Boot Disk

If you select to do a Typical or Custom installation, a dialog box will appear asking you whether Setup should create a start-up disk. This disk can be used to perform a fail-safe boot up in the event that the Windows 95 files on the hard disk become damaged, or a hardware conflict prevents normal booting.

There is simply no excuse for not taking the time to create an emergency boot disk for your system unless you have a diskless workstation. All you have to do is answer yes and place a floppy disk in your A drive. If for some reason you ever need to boot up your system and the hard disk is damaged, having a boot disk will come in very handy.

TIP

You can make a new emergency boot disk if the old one becomes lost or damaged by opening the Control Panel and running Add/Remove Programs.

Installing Network Features

When you elect to create a Custom installation, you're presented with several dialogs that enable you to select just exactly the networking drivers and features that you want to install. What appears in the network components list is determined by what networking hardware or drivers, if any, were detected in the system.

Figure 4.3 shows you the type of dialogs that need to be filled in when you're installing network components. Check with your system administrator before installing network features.

The Second Step: Copying Files

After you have entered information about the options you want installed, and Setup has gathered information about your computer, Setup begins to copy files to your hard disk or to your directory on a network server.

FIGURE 4.3.

Network components of Windows 95 can easily be installed during setup.

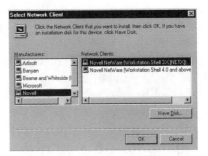

The length of the copying process depends on the source of the Windows 95 files. If you're installing from floppy disk, you'll need to stay close to the system so that you can feed each disk as needed. Installing from floppy usually takes the longest time. If you're installing from CD-ROM, you won't need to remain so close to the system. You have time for a twenty-minute coffee break. If you're installing from a network server's disk, the amount of time it takes to finish copying the files will depend on the speed of the server and the bandwidth of the network connection.

After Setup has finished copying the files for your Windows 95 installation, a dialog box will appear to signal that the final phase of setup is about to begin.

The final phase of setup involves restarting the computer so that the Windows 95 files just copied can be loaded into memory rather than DOS and possibly Windows, which are still loaded in memory during setup. Click Finish to restart the computer.

During the rebooting phase, just before the graphical portions of Windows 95 are loaded, setup creates configuration files. The changes made to your system are discussed in detail later in this chapter.

After your configuration files are created, the graphical parts of Windows 95 are loaded and the final phase of setup is done. During this phase, your Start Menu is created and your desktop is assembled.

If you installed Windows 95 as an upgrade over a previous version of Windows 3.x, Setup migrates your settings from WIN.INI, SYSTEM.INI, and, in the case of Windows for Workgroups, PROTOCOL.INI, and places these settings into the Registry. After the Registry is built, Setup asks you to specify the time zone in which your computer will be used, and to configure your printer. If any devices remain that have not been configured fully, Setup will take you through those steps as well.

Step Three: A Whole New Ball Game

After setup is complete, you'll notice a number of changes that have taken place, most of which show up in C:\. These changes are reflected in how Windows 95 boots up a system.

According to the hype, Windows 95 doesn't need DOS to boot up. According to the skeptics, there's really very little new in how Windows 95 starts up compared to booting DOS and then running Windows 3.x. As usual, the truth lies somewhere between the positions of the zealots on either end of the argument.

The following sections describe how Windows 95 boots up your system in three steps, and also describes the changes made to system files from your previous version of DOS.

Booting Windows 95

Although the core of Windows 95 is a 32-bit, protected-mode operating system, there remains some real mode requirements, especially when dealing with legacy devices that don't yet have protected mode drivers. For this reason, booting Windows 95 is divided into three steps.

> **TIP**
>
> Many of the files discussed in the next few sections are hidden files, and some even have the system attribute. To view and manipulate these files, use the **View | O**ptions menu item in Explorer to display the Options property sheet. Using the View dialog box, click Display All Files and remove the check from the item marked "Hide MS-DOS file extensions for files that are registered."

BIOS Bootstrapping

When you first power on your system, the BIOS chip built into the computer comes to life and begins a short program called the Power On Self Test (POST). This program examines memory, checks to see that the hardware and configuration settings in the CMOS are valid, initializes any peripheral cards that are plugged into the bus, and then searches disks for a bootstrap program provided by the operating system.

Unless you have a system with a Plug and Play BIOS, this part of the boot process isn't changed. Everything about the boot process is exactly the same as before, right up to the point where the boot files on disk are loaded.

In all likelihood, your next computer will contain a Plug and Play compatible BIOS that does a lot more work than the old-style BIOS. Standard ISA cards, like the ones you have been using for years, typically use jumper blocks or DIP switches to provide configuration information. Put two cards in the same system that want to use the same IRQ (Interrupt Request) lines and your system won't function properly.

By contrast, Plug and Play cards are software configurable. A Plug and Play BIOS arbitrates the needs of all the devices in the system, assigning IRQ lines, DMA channels, and memory addresses so that no two cards are in conflict.

Real-Mode Bootstrapping

Keep in mind that an operating system is a program with many of the same characteristics as the applications that you run every day. Files containing programming code are loaded into memory and then executed.

The first code that Windows 95 loads is a replacement for the real-mode core of MS-DOS (MSDOS.SYS and IO.SYS). The old files, if found during setup, are renamed in case they are needed for dual booting. Windows 95 uses its own real-mode code found in a new file that also has the name IO.SYS. This is the part of the boot process that sets off the Windows 95 skeptics who point to this step of the boot process and say that it's just DOS in disguise.

Although this part of Windows 95's boot code is in many ways similar to your old DOS, the way it behaves is very different. The new real-mode code seats itself in memory where it can be accessed if needed, and then processes the AUTOEXEC.BAT and CONFIG.SYS files if they are found.

The only times that you need AUTOEXEC and CONFIG are when you need to load real-mode drivers for hardware devices that don't have protected-mode drivers available, to load DOS environment variables that you want every DOS session launched in Windows 95 to have, to load any TSR software that is necessary to your system, or when you need to override the default settings of IO.SYS, which are listed later in this section. If you have none of these needs, you can eliminate these configuration files altogether.

During this phase of the boot process, IO.SYS also loads any static real-mode virtual drivers (VxDs). Unlike their protected-mode cousins, static VxDs can't be loaded and unloaded from memory as needed. Once loaded, a static VxD remains in memory until you shut down Windows 95.

> **NOTE**
>
> During the real-mode boot step is when Windows 95 spawns a virtual machine to serve as the blueprint for all DOS virtual machines created by running DOS applications in Windows 95. Each new VM will have identical settings for environment variables and memory. Any TSRs loaded during this step will be available in each new DOS VM as well.

The last thing IO.SYS does is to load the Windows 95 versions of traditional DOS drivers. By default, IO.SYS loads the following:

- HIMEM.SYS: The real-mode memory driver that provides access to memory addresses between 640 KB and 1 MB
- IFSHLP.SYS: Installable File System helper, which loads drivers to provide access to the protected-mode IFS

■ SETVER.EXE: A real-mode TSR that enables DOS applications that look for a specific version of DOS to run under later versions

■ DBLSPACE.BIN or DRVSPACE.BIN: File compression drivers

> **TIP**
>
> IO.SYS doesn't load an equivalent of EMM386.EXE. If you have DOS applications that require the use of Expanded (EMS) memory, you'll have to use CONFIG.SYS to load EMM386 just as you have done in the past.

IO.SYS Configuration Settings

Most of the commonly used settings that used to be found in CONFIG.SYS are automatically loaded by IO.SYS. Table 4.2 lists the default settings imposed by IO.SYS. To override these settings, place a line into CONFIG.SYS containing the value that you want set.

Table 4.2. IO.SYS default settings.

```
dos=high,umb

himem.sys

ifshlp.sys

setver.exe

files=60

buffers=30

lastdrive=z

stacks=9,256

shell=command.com /p

fcbs=4
```

Booting the Protected-Mode Components

After the real-mode components are loaded and running, the Windows 95 boot process loads the 32-bit protected-mode core of the operating system. From this point forward, the real-mode stuff is accessed only when a call is made to a real-mode driver, a real-mode DOS app is run, or a TSR driver is required to run.

The remainder of the Windows 95 components are loaded in this step. Up to this point, none of the graphical portions of Windows 95 has been loaded. The real-mode portion of the boot process uses only text mode.

The third and final step of the boot process involves loading the rest of Windows, including core components such as the VxDs that implement the Virtual Machine Manager, the Scheduler, protected-mode drivers for devices, and so on. This part of the process is where initial loading of dynamic VxDs takes place, as well as the loading of GDI, USER, KERNEL, and finally the shell.

> **TIP**
>
> To see the boot process for yourself, examine the file BOOTLOG.TXT, which can be found in the root of C. This file details each step of the process after the system BIOS starts loading disk-based boot files.
>
> Knowing about this file and having an idea of what it contains can be very helpful when trying to troubleshoot a system that doesn't want to finish the boot process.

Shuffling Files

If you install Windows 95 onto a computer with a virgin hard disk, one that doesn't even have an older version of DOS, you won't have to worry about what files are named what. Windows 95 will just use its own boot files. Most users, however, will not opt to perform this type of installation because they will choose instead to update their old system files.

As you've already seen, Windows 95 uses a file called IO.SYS to boot the real-mode stuff. Something has to be done with the old version of IO.SYS that is part of the boot process for your old version of DOS. During setup, these old files, including AUTOEXEC and CONFIG, are renamed, and Windows 95-specific versions of these files are created where necessary. Table 4.3 provides a rundown of the changes made to file names during setup.

Table 4.3. Files changed during setup.

DOS File Name	Windows 95 Name
AUTOEXEC.BAT	AUTOEXEC.DOS
COMMAND.COM	COMMAND.DOS
CONFIG.SYS	CONFIG.DOS
IO.SYS*	IO.DOS
MODE.COM	MODE_DOS.COM
MSDOS.SYS	MSDOS.DOS

* Named IBMIO.SYS in IBM versions of DOS.

> **NOTE**
>
> If it's necessary to have versions of AUTOEXEC.BAT and CONFIG.SYS available during the Windows 95 boot process, these files are created and given their traditional names. Windows 95 also uses a version-specific implementation of COMMAND.COM. As you'll see in the next section, Windows 95 also uses a file named MSDOS.SYS that is very different from the file of the same name used by DOS.
>
> When you dual boot to your previous version of DOS, each of the Windows 95 versions of these files is renamed to have the extension .W40 (for example, COMMAND.W40). The old versions of these files that were renamed to have the .DOS extension are renamed to their traditional names, and the old version of DOS is booted.
>
> In other words, AUTOEXEC.DOS is your old DOS AUTOEXEC. When you want to boot to your old DOS, the AUTOEXEC.BAT file used by Windows 95 is renamed AUTOEXEC.W40, and AUTOEXEC.DOS is renamed AUTOEXEC.BAT before the boot takes place.
>
> The sole exception to this scheme is IO.SYS, which gets renamed WINBOOT.SYS when you boot to your previous version of DOS.

In DOS, the file MSDOS.SYS is a binary file containing program code that provides part of the core of the DOS operating system. Under Windows 95, however, the role of MSDOS.SYS is very different. This time around, it's a text file that has a structure like a Windows INI file. The settings that can be contained in this file determine how Windows 95 boots up. Table 4.4 explains each of the possible settings that MSDOS.SYS can contain. Settings found in MSDOS.SYS are divided between the [Options] section and the [Paths] section.

Table 4.4. MSDOS.SYS option settings.

Setting	Purpose
[Options]	
BootDelay=n	Delays the start of booting by n seconds so that the user can press one of the function keys that alters the boot process. Setting BootKeys to 0 disables the delay entirely.
BootFailSafe=0	When set to 1, specifies that Windows 95 should boot into fail-safe mode. This setting is intended primarily for equipment manufacturers to use during the installation of their products.

continues

Table 4.4. continued

Setting	Purpose
[Options]	
BootGUI=1	Specifies booting into Windows 95's graphical shell. When set to 0, the Windows 95 command prompt is booted.
BootKeys=1	Enables start-up option keys (see the Tip that follows). When set to 0, option keys are disabled.
BootMenu=0	Specifies whether the F8 boot menu should be displayed even when F8 isn't pressed. When set to 0, the menu is suppressed.
BootMenuDefault=n	Specifies which boot menu item should be highlighted. The default is 1.
BootMenuDelay=n	Specifies the number of seconds to delay before the boot menu's default choice is run. The default is 30 seconds.
BootMulti=0	When set to 1, enables the user to dual boot to DOS by pressing F4. Also, a value of 1 includes the dual boot option on the boot menu.
BootWarn=1	When set to 1, the safe mode warning and menu are enabled.
BootWin=1	When set to 1, Windows 95 boots. When set to 0, the previous version of DOS is booted. This is meaningful only when the previous operating system is DOS 5.0 or higher.
DblSpace=1	When set to 1, enables the automatic loading of DBLSPACE.BIN.
DoubleBuffer=0	When set to 1, enables double-buffering for SCSI disk controllers.
DrvSpace=1	When set to 1, enables automatic loading of DRVSPACE.BIN.
LoadTop=1	Specifies where to load COMMAND.COM or disk compression drivers. Set to 0 only if you have problems with software that expects OS files to reside at a specific address.
Logo=1	Displays start-up logo. Set to 0 to suppress logo display, or when conflicts arise with non-Microsoft memory managers.

Setting	Purpose
Network=0	When set to 1, enables networking as a Safe mode menu option.

[Paths]

HostWinBootDrv=C	Specifies the drive letter of the boot disk.
WinBootDir=	Specifies the folder containing start-up files as specified during installation.
WinDir=	Specifies the location of the Windows folder.

TIP

The following keys are active at boot time when BootKeys is set to 1. Network administrators can increase system security by suppressing this feature.

F5 bBoots into Windows 95 Safe mode. Bypasses AUTOEXEC and CONFIG and loads only minimal drivers such as disk compression.

SHIFT+F5 boots into Windows 95 Safe mode command line. This choice also bypasses configuration files.

CTRL+F5 Boots into Windows 95 Safe Mode without loading configuration files or compression drivers.

F4 dual boots system to previous version of DOS.

F6 boots Windows 95 into Safe mode with networking enabled.

F8 presents Windows 95 boot menu, enabling users to choose which option to use in booting the system.

Shift+F8 boots normally but displays line-by-line confirmation for entries found in AUTOEXEC and CONFIG (when Windows 95 boot menu is displayed).

Summary

In this chapter, you have seen how the various choices you make about system configuration affect the installation of Windows 95. You have seen how to install Windows 95 to dual boot with previous versions of DOS and with Windows NT.

You've seen how to control the Setup Wizard to provide just the type of setup that you want a system to have, depending on the type of system (portable) and the Windows 95 features that you want installed (custom).

You've also seen how Windows 95 uses the traditional file names employed by DOS in new ways, and how they are renamed during dual booting. You've seen how the settings in MSDOS.SYS affect the boot process.

In the next chapter, you'll learn how easy it is to customize your running installation of Windows 95.

Customizing the Desktop and Integrating Windows 95 Applications

5

by Ned Snell

IN THIS CHAPTER

After a careful and successful setup, there's really nothing that you *must* do to begin working in Windows 95. You'll find the taskbar and Start Menu button waiting to show you shortcuts to your applications. A few icons already appear on the desktop for important new Windows components such as the Recycle Bin and My Computer. A pleasant, conservatively cool color scheme dresses your desktop. You're ready to go.

Or are you? Your Windows desktop can be adapted, retrofitted, decorated, and retrained in many different ways. Knowing that, ask yourself two questions:

1. Am I exactly like everybody else?
2. Does anybody at Microsoft know exactly how I work?

If you answer "No" to either question, you stand to gain from customizing your Windows desktop and perhaps integrating your applications. You can make a few quick, easy changes, such as picking a new color scheme or moving the taskbar, or you can strip the walls, rip out the cabinets, and really rework the way your Windows environment looks and behaves. It's all up to you. What matters is that, when you're done, your Windows environment should appeal to your senses and respond to your needs.

In this chapter, you'll learn how to create such a system. Before you begin, know that this chapter makes use of Windows 95's Control Panel. It's different from Windows 3.1's Control Panel, but it serves the same basic function. You open the Control Panel using one of the following methods:

- Choosing Settings from the Start Menu and then choosing Control Panel
- Opening My Computer and then opening Control Panel

Organizing Your Desktop

Many of the customizable aspects of Windows 95 are the same as those for Windows 3.1. The most significant change is the elimination of Windows 3.1's Program Manager shell, and the inevitable fiddling with the sizes, positions, and contents of program group windows. You'll also see that, although Microsoft has added some significant new ways to customize, it actually simplified customization by removing some minor options that few people ever used in Windows 3.1.

Customizing the Taskbar

As you know, the Windows 95 taskbar is your starting point for most activities (though not your only one, because you also can place shortcuts on the desktop and start programs from Explorer). It doubles as the staging area for switching among open applications and the point from which you call up your Start Menu.

The taskbar also is the dominant visual element of your desktop; in other words, you'll see it more often than you see any other single element. So, it's important to know that you can change the taskbar's size, position, and behavior.

In certain locations or at certain sizes, the taskbar may cover important areas of an application. Most Windows applications, when maximized to fill the screen, will automatically make room for the taskbar so that nothing is covered. But some screen elements, such as toolbars, can't be adjusted easily because they're built out of bitmapped graphics that can't be scaled down.

If I place the taskbar at the bottom of the screen when I use Microsoft Word, nothing is covered; Windows shortens the document window by a few lines so that the Word status bar sits above the taskbar. If I move the taskbar to the right side of my screen, however, the document squeezes left to make room, but the taskbar still obscures several icons on the Word toolbar.

HIDING THE TASKBAR

To avoid the whole question of fitting your taskbar to your applications, you can use the Auto-Hide option that removes the taskbar from the screen except when you demand it. See taskbar Options later in this chapter.

Moving the Taskbar

After setup, the taskbar automatically rests on the bottom of the screen. You can move it to any other edge—the top or either side. You can do this at any time, even when in the middle of a maximized application.

To move the taskbar:

1. Move the cursor to the taskbar.
2. Click and hold the right mouse button.
3. Drag the pointer to the edge of the screen where you want the taskbar to rest.
4. Release the mouse button.

Unless you manually resize it as described next, the taskbar is automatically sized to be as high as the Start button when on the top or bottom of the screen, and a little narrower than the button when on either side.

Sizing the Taskbar

You size the taskbar just as you size any window. You move the pointer onto the edge of the taskbar, where the arrow pointer turns into a sizing pointer. Click and hold the left mouse button, drag the outline of the taskbar to change the size, and then release the mouse button.

NOTE

The size of the taskbar has no effect on the size of the Start Menu. From a shrunken or expanded taskbar, a click of the Start button calls up standard-sized menus.

Whenever you move the taskbar, it automatically takes on the size it was when it last rested in that spot. For example, suppose that the taskbar is resting on the bottom of the screen and you resize it to double its usual height. When you move it to the side of the screen, the taskbar is resized for its new location. If you then move it back to the bottom, it returns to double height.

Honestly, I can't think of a reason to *increase* the size of the taskbar. I have *decreased* its size, though. One effective arrangement is to position the taskbar on the right side of the screen and then cut it roughly in half so that the program icons show, but not the names. (See Figure 5.1.) I find that this arrangement allows me to keep my taskbar handy but not obtrusive. Clicking the icons alone works just fine for calling up the Start Menu or any open programs staged on the taskbar.

FIGURE 5.1.

The taskbar at right, cut down to its essentials.

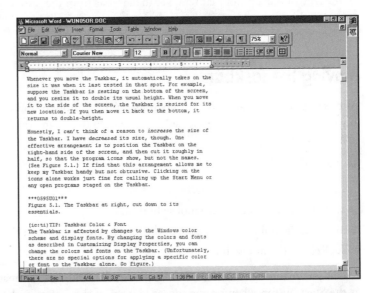

TASKBAR COLOR AND FONT

The taskbar is affected by changes to the Windows color scheme and display fonts. By changing the colors and fonts as described in Customizing Display Properties, you can change the colors and fonts on the taskbar. (Unfortunately, there are no special options for applying a specific color or font to the taskbar alone. Go figure.)

Taskbar Options

The Taskbar Properties sheet (see Figure 5.2) features three options that allow you to customize the behavior of the taskbar. To display this Properties sheet, move the pointer to the taskbar, right-click, and select Properties. The options are as follows:

- Placing a checkmark next to Always on top keeps the taskbar visible at all times, even when another application is maximized. This keeps the Start Menu and other open programs at hand, and also reminds you which other applications are running.

- Placing a checkmark next to Auto hide clears the taskbar from the screen when it isn't needed. When you need it, you easily can display the taskbar by moving the pointer to the edge of the screen where the taskbar last appeared. (It's a great option unless you move your taskbar a lot. Then you might have to try all four screen edges to find the silly thing!)

- Placing a checkmark next to Show clock puts a digital display of the current time on the taskbar, always at the end opposite the Start button. (Sorry, fans of the Windows 3.1 Clock applet—Windows 95 doesn't include an analog clock for the taskbar. You can bet somebody will come up with one, though!)

> **TIP**
>
> If you single-click the taskbar's clock, the day and date pop up. If you double-click the clock, you call up the Date/Time Properties sheet, where you can change the system time and date, and the time zone.

If you place checkmarks in *both* of the top two boxes, you get the best of both worlds: The taskbar hides itself away, but appears on top of anything else when you move the pointer to the edge. Avoid checking Auto-Hide if you don't *also* check Always on top. With that configuration, when an application is maximized or is covering the edge of the screen where the taskbar is hiding, the taskbar still reappears when you move the pointer to the edge—but you can't see it because it remains covered by the application.

FIGURE 5.2.

The Taskbar Properties sheet, which also can be used for some Start Menu customization and to clear the contents of the Documents menu.

NOTE

The Taskbar Properties sheet is a rare example of unintuitive organization in Windows 95. It includes two pages: one for the taskbar and the other for the Start Menu. (Why can't the Start Menu have its own Properties sheet, called by right-clicking the Start Button or menu?)

Worse, one of the three items on the taskbar's own page is actually for the Start Menu (Show small icons, covered later in this chapter) and one item on the Start Menu's page is for clearing the contents of the *Documents menu*! If you wanted to clear the Documents menu and didn't know where to look, would you start by looking at the Properties for the *taskbar*? Somebody at Microsoft is sitting too close to the laser printers and inhaling fumes.

Customizing the Start Menu

Together, the taskbar and the Start Menu effectively replace Windows 3.1's clunky Program Manager shell. Unfortunately, they inherit from Program Manager one flaw: the inability to read your mind.

Without that capability, they can't possibly know how you want your programs arranged—which ones you use often, which you use rarely, and which you use together. Unless you take the time to organize it, your Start Menu will inevitably grow and branch into a messy, cluttered collection of folders and shortcuts. Programs you need often will be tucked two or three menus out of reach, whereas stuff that you never use will clog up the menus that you pass through on the way to what you want. And your Accessories menu will become the kitchen junk drawer, stuffed with everything that Windows can't decide where to store.

When you install Windows 95 over an existing Windows 3.1 configuration, the Setup Wizard organizes your Start Menu in the same basic structure as your old Program Manager setup (see Chapter 4). Each of the Program Manager's old "program groups" becomes a folder (or rather, a menu) in Programs; the top folder on the Start Menu. Each of those folders leads to a menu containing shortcuts for what used to be the "program items" under Program Manager.

If you've always done a good job organizing your programs under Program Manager, your Start Menu may start out pretty well organized. Because the Start Menu is *hierarchical*—allowing you to tuck folders in folders in folders, and so on—and Program Manager wasn't, many people find that their initial Windows 95 Startup Menu has too few menus with too many items. You take better advantage of Windows' hierarchical Start Menu if you really categorize your programs, starting with just a few basic groupings and then moving down through the menu levels to more specific groupings.

For most users, this arrangement makes the most logical sense and also simplifies locating specific programs, simplifies management of the Start Menu, and makes the desktop more attractive during Start Menu operations. Anytime that you see a menu with more than a dozen choices on it, you should ask yourself how those items might be better broken up. (Of course, it's your desktop. If you want everything in one fat menu, be my guest.)

Also, whenever you install a new application in Windows 95, its setup program may deposit the program in a menu where you don't want it, or it may deposit icons for its accessory programs on the same menu with the application, clogging the works.

For example, when I installed Word for Windows 6.0 in Windows 95, it wound up in my Applications menu, which is where I wanted it. Also appearing in that menu after Word installation were a Word Help program, a Word Setup Program, and a Word Dialog Editor program, none of which really belonged in my Applications menu. (I moved Word's accessories to another menu, further out of reach.) The setup routines for Windows 95 applications may also deposit one or more desktop icons, just as many programs used to automatically stick themselves in your Windows 3.1 Startup menu so that they would run automatically every time you started Windows. (Every software company thinks its program is the most important one you own.)

INSTALLING PROGRAMS WHERE YOU WANT 'EM

You can run the setup programs that install Windows applications in the same ways that you can run any program:

- By clicking on the program in My Computer
- By clicking on the program in Explorer
- By choosing Run from the Start Menu and then entering the setup program's drive letter and name (usually SETUP)
- By entering the setup program's drive letter and name from the MS-DOS prompt

The best choice, however, is to open Control Panel, choose Add/Remove Programs, and then choose Install. For one thing, this tool automatically locates any setup programs on a floppy disk or CD-ROM for you. For another, this tool presents a drop-down list that allows you to specify exactly which menu to place the program shortcut in, saving you the trouble of finding and relocating the shortcut later.

Reorganizing Programs

Reorganizing your Start Menu is a straightforward drag-and-drop (or, if you prefer, cut-and-paste) job. You can edit your Start Menu through two vehicles: the taskbar Properties sheet and Explorer.

Of course, the most important step in organizing your Start Menu is analyzing how you work. Your goal is to set up your desktop and Start Menu so that the programs you need are easy to find and to open, and so that your desktop isn't cluttered by shortcuts and folders that you rarely touch. That way, your desktop is both aesthetically pleasing and convenient to use.

Think carefully about how you use Windows. Are there two or three programs you use far more often than any others? Is there a program you almost always use first; for example, do you check your e-mail first thing every session? Are there programs that you tend to use together? After you've thought carefully through these questions, you'll be ready to edit your Start Menu and desktop by moving folders and shortcuts among menus, adding folders, deleting folders, creating shortcuts, and moving shortcuts and folders onto and off of the desktop.

> **NOTE**
>
> Unfortunately, three icons—My Computer, Recycle Bin, and Network Neighborhood (if you're on a network)—can't be removed from the desktop.

As you work, keep the following in mind:

- Place icons on the desktop sparingly. Littering your desktop with icons clutters it, obscuring your wallpaper (if you use one) and possibly distracting and confusing you, like any messy desk. Also, avoid using desktop icons for programs that you tend to open while already working in another program. When an open program is covering the screen, it's more convenient to pull up the Start Menu and select a shortcut than it is to minimize the running application or move it so that you can open a desktop shortcut. In that case, the desktop icon is superfluous desktop clutter.

- Data files and documents can be used to open programs. For example, if there's a particular word processing document that you plan to work on regularly for a period of time, put a shortcut to that document in your Start Menu or even on your desktop. Selecting that icon will open your word processor and the file in one easy step, so you can get straight to work. (Be sure the file type of the document is registered to the correct application.)

- Don't be afraid to delete shortcuts from your Start Menu. Unless you do it in Explorer (and improperly, to boot), you delete only the shortcut; the program itself remains on your hard disk, ready to be run from Explorer or restored to the Start Menu when your needs change.

- All references in this chapter to "adding" programs to your Start Menu refer to creating shortcuts for programs that have already been installed on your system. You can't install a program by adding it to your Start Menu. You must install the program (see Chapter 8), add it to your Start Menu (if it hasn't automatically been added by the Setup program), or relocate it.

■ You can change the contents of the Programs menu, and any menu that follows it, in any way you like. You can't, however, change the initial Start Menu that contains the items Programs, Documents, Settings, Find, Help, Run, and Shut Down. That stuff stays as is.

Editing the Start Menu Through Taskbar Properties

The Taskbar's Properties sheet features—incongruously—a page for adding programs to and deleting programs from the Start Menu. I'm not sure why Microsoft put it there. There's nothing you can do with it that you can't do with Explorer, and Explorer also allows you to easily reorganize programs, whereas the Taskbar Properties sheet is best suited to adding programs or removing them, not moving them around. (To move a program with the Taskbar's Properties sheet, you have to remove the program and then add it back where you want it.)

I think the intention was to offer an automated process for editing the Start Menu, one in which you don't have to know what you're doing. The Taskbar Properties sheet delivers on that promise, but I think that you would serve yourself best by learning how to take complete control of your menu structure through Explorer. Still, for the timid or the impatient, the Properties sheet is a way to go. Here's how it works.

Open the Taskbar Properties sheet by choosing taskbar from the Settings menu or by right-clicking on the taskbar and then choosing Properties.

You'll notice immediately that this Properties sheet has two pages: Taskbar and Start Menu Programs. Choose the Start Menu Programs page by clicking the tab at its top. The box shown in Figure 5.3 appears.

FIGURE 5.3.

The Start Menu Programs page of the Taskbar Properties sheet.

The Start Menu Programs page has a button for clearing the Documents Menu. Click the button to clean the slate.

As for *why* this button (which has nothing to do with taskbar Properties and little to do with the Start Menu) appears in this spot...got me.

On the page shown in Figure 5.3, three buttons pertain to the Start Menu:

Add Programs: Click here and you get a Create Shortcut dialog box in which you can type the name and drive/directory location of the folder, program, or data/document file to add to the Start Menu. If you're not sure of the name or program location, click Browse to bring up a Browse dialog box so that you can hunt down the program you want.

After you enter a program name and drive/directory location in the Create Shortcut box and click Next, Windows presents you with an outline-style map of the folders used in the current Start Menu. The folders within a folder appear indented beneath the folder in which they belong. Double-click any folder to add the program there. (To put the program in a new folder, select the folder in which you want to insert a new folder, then click New Folder. Type a name for the new folder, then double-click it to insert your program there, and continue.) When you're done, click Next.

Windows presents you with a chance to enter a name that will appear next to the program icon on the Start Menu. You can enter a name, or simply click Next to use the default name for that program.

Remove Programs: Click here and Windows presents you with a map of the current Start Menu (see Figure 5.4 that follows), showing each menu and everything that's in it, outline style. It's similar to the outline presented by Add Programs, but different in that you can see shortcuts as well as folders.

At first, the list shows only the Programs folder and any folders or programs within it. Note that some items have a plus sign next to them; the sign indicates that the folder contains more folders or programs. To reveal a folder's contents, double-click it or select it and press the + key. When you see the program shortcut that you want to delete, select it and click Remove. Windows prompts you to confirm that you want to remove the item. Click Yes.

The folders and shortcuts that you remove are listed in the Recycle Bin. (See Chapter 2.) If you change your mind before these files are cleared from the Bin, you easily can restore them to your Start Menu by opening the Recycle Bin, selecting the removed items, and then choosing File and Restore. If you change your mind after the files have been cleared from the Bin, simply follow the steps for adding programs to the Start Menu, and recreate the shortcuts.

If you use a program only occasionally, consider leaving it off your Start Menu and running it from My Computer or Explorer when you need it.

REMOVING FOLDERS

Note that you can remove entire folders, as well as shortcuts, and in doing so delete any folders or program shortcuts they contain. This is one reason that you may want to create small folders with logically related programs in them. When your needs change, you make wholesale revisions to your Start Menu quickly by dumping an entire folder of items related to a need that no longer exists, such as a completed project.

FIGURE 5.4.

Removing programs through the Taskbar Properties sheet.

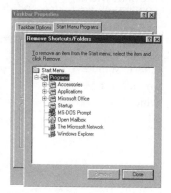

Advanced: Click here and Explorer pops up, showing the location and listings for the Start Menu folders and shortcuts. From here, you can edit your Start Menu as described in the next section. Note that, when you enter Explorer through this Advanced button, Explorer is "rooted" at the Start Menu folders and doesn't allow you beyond them, except when using the Create Shortcut dialog. Rooting protects you from accidentally moving or deleting a program file.

Editing the Start Menu Through Explorer

If you're handy with Explorer (and becoming so should be a top priority), you can easily edit your Start Menu there. You can add programs, move them around, or rename them easily, using basic Explorer techniques. (For more about Explorer, see Chapter 2.)

CAUTION

When editing your Start Menu, you must follow one rule: Edit the shortcuts, but stay away from the programs and data files!

In other words, when using Explorer to remove a program from the Start Menu, a careless user could accidentally delete the program files or the folders that hold them, instead of merely deleting a shortcut or a folder full of shortcuts. Not only would that mistake zap valuable files off of your hard disk (Quick! To the Recycle Bin!), but it would also leave useless shortcuts on the Start Menu.

Remember that each menu is just a folder whose contents are other menus (folders) and/or shortcuts to programs or files. To find the Start Menu folders in Explorer, open your Windows folder. Within the Windows folder, you'll see a folder called Start Menu (as shown in Figure 5.5), which contains all the folders and shortcuts that appear there.

FIGURE 5.5.

Finding the Start Menu folder in Explorer.

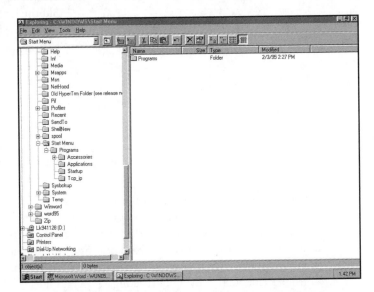

A SHORTCUT TO THE SHORTCUTS

There's another way to arrive at the same spot in Explorer shown in Figure 5.5. Right-click the taskbar, choose Properties, choose the Start Menu Programs page, and then click the Advanced button. Explorer opens, showing the Start Menu folders.

This method of opening Explorer includes a safety valve: When you open Explorer this way, it shows you only the Start Menu stuff and won't let you navigate to other folders and files on your hard disk, so there's no way you could accidentally delete a real program or data file. When you want to add a program here, though, the Create Shortcut dialog box enables you to locate and add a program from anywhere on your hard disk.

Within the Start Menu folder, the folders and shortcuts that make up the Start Menu are organized exactly as they are in the Start Menu itself. Each menu is a folder, and it contains the folders (other menus) and shortcuts that appear on it as menu items.

Moving Programs: To move a folder or shortcut from one folder to another (in effect, from one menu to another), you can use either cut and paste or drag and drop.

- Cut and Paste: Select the item to move, open Edit, and choose Cut. Then select the destination folder, open the Edit menu, and choose Paste.

- Drag and Drop: Arrange your Explorer display so that both the item you want to move and the destination folder are visible on the same screen (see Chapter 2). Move the pointer to the item, click and hold the left mouse button, drag the pointer to the destination folder, and release the mouse button.

Renaming Programs: Select the shortcut or folder to rename. Choose File | Rename (or right-click the file and choose Rename). Type a new name for the shortcut or folder.

Adding Programs: Select the folder in which you want to add the program, then choose File | New | Shortcut. The Create Shortcut dialog box appears. Create a shortcut to the program as described in "Editing the Start Menu through taskbar Properties" earlier in this chapter.

Removing Programs: Select the program or folder to remove and press the Del key or choose Delete from the File menu. The shortcuts are removed from the Start Menu and moved to the Recycle Bin.

Large Icons or Small?

As you know from Chapter 1, Windows 95 is built to use icons in one of two sizes: 32 pixels × 32 pixels, or 16 × 16 (half the size of the regular icon, but with all the flavor!). Windows 95 applications are required to supply all icons in both sizes and to make any necessary aesthetic changes to the smaller icons so that they remain legible. For Windows 3.1 programs, which include only full-size icons, Windows 95 can actually crunch the icons down to the smaller size when necessary.

You can use small icons anywhere. Shrinking the icons cuts the amount of space between menu items or items in any on-screen list.

The disadvantage of small icons is that they can be hard to make out, especially when you use high-resolution display settings. (See "Using the Display Properties Sheet" later in this chapter.) Because small icons still have full-size captions, and I can read, that doesn't worry me much; however, when icons become indecipherable, they serve no aesthetic purpose and therefore constitute unnecessary screen junk. Small icons (and the tighter spacing they impose) also require greater precision in mouse movements and may make you more likely to click the wrong icon.

Windows 95 uses only small icons throughout the Start Menu, except for the opening menu that first appears when you click the Start button. That menu can use large or small icons.

To use small icons in the opening menu:

1. Open the Taskbar Properties sheet by right-clicking the taskbar and then choosing Properties.
2. Click the checkmark box next to Show small icons in Start Menu to place a checkmark there. Note that the sample Start Menu shown on the Properties sheet immediately shows the effect of the change. Note also that the sideways Windows banner on the menu disappears.
3. Click Close.

To use small icons in Explorer, Control Panel, My Computer, and in most other windows that show groups of icons:

1. Select View from the menu bar.
2. Select Small icons.

ICON SCALING

Windows can actually scale icons to any size between 32 × 32 pixels and 16×16 pixels. You can control the scaling (plus icon spacing and other attributes) through the Appearance page of the Desktop Properties sheet, covered later in this chapter. If you choose 16×16 on this page, small icons will be used automatically, everywhere in Windows, and you'll never see a full-size icon.

Because bitmap images scale poorly, you'll find that icons look best at either of the two standard sizes: 32 × 32 (large) or 16 × 16 (small).

Using Desktop Icons

One advantage of Windows 95 over Windows 3.1 is that you can position shortcuts to programs and files, and folders of shortcuts, directly on the desktop for immediate access. Actually, you could have done this with Windows 3.1, too, but it required the type of twiddling that most users never knew how to do, and tended to poke Windows 3.1 right in the spots that made it unreliable and crash-prone. In Windows 3.1, placing icons on the desktop required the use of the Load and Run commands to place programs in memory, reducing the memory available to other programs and decreasing Windows's performance and reliability. Windows 95 handles desktop-based icons as a matter of design; placing an icon on the Windows 95 desktop does not require the loading of the program itself, so it exacts no performance penalty. Windows 95 also makes using desktop icons easy and reliable.

CHANGING STOCK DESKTOP ICONS

You can change the name of the stock desktop icons (the one Windows creates for you) such as My Computer, Recycle Bin, and Network Neighborhood. Just right-click the icon, select Rename, type your new name, and press Enter. You also can click the name once and then again. (Be careful that you click twice, rather than double-click.) Then type your new name and press Enter.

If you create multiple-user profiles (as described later in this chapter, under "Creating Multiple Configurations on the Same PC"), each user can give these icons his or her own set of names.

Putting folders on your desktop can be especially valuable when you tend to use a group of shortcuts together. When you click a desktop folder, a window opens, showing the shortcuts inside (a lot like old Program Manager in Windows 3.1). The window stays open until you close it, so all the shortcuts remain handy. If the same shortcuts shared a group on the Start Menu, you'd have to open the Start Menu all over again, each time you opened one of the shortcuts.

For example, I have a suite of different programs that I use for navigating the Internet. Whenever I log onto the Internet, I use several of these, one right after another. If I group them in a desktop folder, they're all handy until I close the folder. If I group them in the Start Menu, I have to click the Start button and navigate to the group every time I start up a new program. (For more about the Internet, see Chapter 21, "The Internet.")

WHEN NOT TO USE THE DESKTOP

Desktop icons are great, but they're also an invitation to get sloppy. If you're the type of person who never files papers but instead keeps piles lying around so that everything remains handy, you have the basic character flaw that can lead to a sloppy Windows desktop. As with your Start Menu, you must regularly re-evaluate the folders and shortcuts on your desktop and clear away those you don't need. In fact, you might try following this simple formula for keeping your configuration lean and mean:

If you use it

Daily, put it on your desktop and/or in your Start Menu.

Weekly, put in your Start Menu but not on the desktop.

Less than weekly, keep it off the desktop and out of the Start Menu; use Find or Explorer to get it when you need it.

Also, if you tend to use a particular shortcut only when another application is open on the desktop, you may prefer having that shortcut in your Start Menu instead of on the desktop. You can bring the Start Menu up on top of anything on the screen, whereas you'll have to clear things away to locate a desktop icon.

To place an icon on the desktop, simply drag any program or folder from where you find it and drop it on the desktop. (For a refresher on drag-and-drop techniques, see Chapter 1.) You can drag a program to the desktop from Explorer or from a window in My Computer.

Another method is to right-click the desktop, choose New, and then choose Shortcut or Folder. Choosing Shortcut brings up the Create Shortcut dialog box (see "Editing the Start Menu Through Taskbar Properties" earlier in this chapter), which deposits the shortcut on the desktop when you finish. Choosing Folder drops a new folder on the desktop and prompts you to name the folder. After you do, you can open the folder, choose File | New, and Shortcut to open the Create Shortcut dialog box and add shortcuts to the folder. You also can drag program files from Explorer or My Computer and drop them on your new folder to create the shortcuts.

Keep in mind that you can put data files or document files from registered applications on the desktop as well. For example, suppose that you plan to edit the same document daily for a few weeks. Drag the document file from Explorer to the desktop and keep it there as long as you need it. With a quick click, Windows opens both your word processor and the file.

LINING UP DESKTOP ICONS

You can easily "dress up" your desktop icons from the desktop's Context menu. Right-click a bare spot on the desktop. Then, choose Line up icons to quickly snap your icons into basic alignment within an invisible on-screen grid. (If your icons are spread all over the screen, Line up isn't much help; it leaves them spread all over the screen but lined up on the grid.) Or choose Arrange icons and select from among the options listed.

Selecting Auto Arrange will maintain your desktop icons in neat columns on the left side of the screen at all times. The other choices arrange your icons in columns on the left side of the screen, organized by Name, Size, Type, or Date. Unless Auto Arrange is selected, these other options aren't permanent; when you move an icon, it stays moved until you arrange icons again.

Customizing Display Properties

The taskbar, Start Menu, and desktop icons constitute a major change in the way that you customize your Windows desktop. Most of the other ways for you to change the look of Windows haven't changed much since Windows 3.1, however. You still can change your wallpaper and patterns, use screen savers, and change colors.

You also can do a few new things. You can easily change the fonts used in places such as title bars and icon captions. (Actually, you could do that in Windows 3.1, but it was tricky then and it's easy now.) You can control the energy-saving features of Energy Star monitors. And you can dynamically change the display resolution and color palette in several useful ways.

Using the Display Properties Sheet

Display customization begins with the Display Properties sheet, shown in Figure 5.6. You can get to the Display Properties sheet two ways:

- **Easy Way:** Right-click any empty area of the desktop, and then select Properties.
- **Less Easy Way:** Open Control Panel and then open Display.

Either way, you arrive at the Display Properties sheet, which has four tabbed pages:

- **Background:** Enables you to choose a wallpaper and pattern to decorate your Windows desktop when it isn't covered up by something else.
- **Screen Savers:** Enables you to choose one of Windows' screen savers and control the screen-saving and power-saving features of an Energy Star monitor.
- **Appearance:** Enables you to modify the colors, fonts, and sizes used in standard screen elements such as title bars, borders, document windows, scrollbars, icons, and so on.
- **Settings:** Enables you to control the available color palette and resolution of your display adapter.

With these four pages, you can modify most aspects of the look, feel, and behavior of the Windows 95 desktop. Most of what you do here is borrowed directly from the Desktop icon in Windows 3.1's Control Panel—changing wallpaper and screen savers, for example. You'll see a few interesting additions, though, as you work through the choices described in the next several pages.

NOTE

In the top portion of each page of the Display Properties sheet, a sample screen appears. This screen shows the results of any changes you make as you go along.

When making changes to the Display properties, you may discover that sometimes the sample screen is too small to give you an accurate sense of how your display will look when you finish. Click the Apply button to apply your selections to your real desktop immediately, to better judge your choices without leaving the Display Properties sheet.

Customizing the Background

The Background page enables you to choose a background pattern and wallpaper from drop-down lists. To use no pattern or wallpaper, leaving behind a solid desktop in a single color, pick the top choice in each list (None).

FIGURE 5.6.

Changing the desktop background through Display Properties.

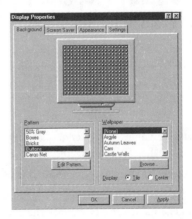

A pattern is a design created by repeating one small graphical element over the entire desktop screen. The basic element used to create a pattern is a simple two-color grid in which some pixels (picture elements) are the pattern color and the others are the color of the desktop. (To learn about choosing the two colors, see "Customizing Appearance" later in this chapter.)

This simple approach can yield interesting designs, including a waffle pattern or a web of little dogs. Patterns lend texture to your desktop, although they can make icon captions and other on-screen text difficult to read when combined with certain color schemes. Trial-and-error attempts as well as frequent use of the Apply button are often necessary to come up with a pattern/color combination that works.

Windows 95 comes with a set of predefined patterns that you can modify by clicking the Edit Pattern button. That button displays a blown-up version of the single element out of which the pattern is created. You edit the element by clicking each pixel to turn the pixel on or off. When you've created a pattern you like, you can save it under its original name or give it a new name.

NOTE

You can use a pattern and wallpaper together, but the wallpaper might cover most of the pattern. Typically, you'll see the pattern only behind icon captions, and that's one place where patterns can be a problem because they tend to make the captions difficult to read. In general, use a wallpaper or a pattern, or neither—but not both.

A Windows *wallpaper* is a graphics image that appears on your desktop behind everything else that appears there, including desktop icons, the taskbar, and any open application. To the extent that you spend much time looking at your bare desktop (uncovered by applications in progress), wallpaper offers a fun way to personalize your display, to make it colorful and inviting. Note that wallpaper images have their own colors; they are unaffected by the color scheme choices that you make on the Appearance page.

Depending on the size of the graphic image used, you'll want to center or tile the wallpaper using the radio buttons below the Wallpaper list. Some images are very small and are designed to be repeated across the screen so that they create some pattern. These must be tiled to fill the screen; otherwise, you'll see a single, postage-stamp-size graphic in the center of your screen. Other wallpaper images are large enough to cover the whole screen; these are centered. Wallpapers built as 256-color graphic files can be used on displays configured to use only 16 colors (see "Customizing Settings") but, of course, they won't look as good as they would in glorious 256-color mode.

Windows includes an interesting selection of wallpapers, but you can buy or make your own. Any graphics file in the Windows bitmap (.BMP) or device-independent bitmap (.DIB—see Chapter 10) format can be used as a wallpaper image and can be tiled or centered as required. Note that a Browse button is offered on this page, so you can search your hard disk for other .BMP or .DIB files.

To acquire new wallpaper images, you can

- Create a new image in the Windows MSPaint applet (see Chapter 2) or in any other graphics program that can save images in .BMP format.

- Use a graphics conversion program or paint program to convert an existing image into .BMP format for use as wallpaper.

- Use a scanner to capture your favorite photo and save it as a .BMP file for use as wallpaper. (A friend of mine uses a scanned snapshot of his daughter for his wallpaper.)

- Use any commercial or shareware Windows wallpaper files, even those created for Windows 3.1, because it, too, used the .BMP format for wallpaper.

> **WALLPAPER OR PAINT?**
>
> Before using wallpaper, consider carefully whether you'll ever see it. For many people, the Windows desktop is always covered by an open, maximized application when they're working, and covered by a screen saver (or switched off) when they're not working. For them, wallpaper is superfluous. Those who use lots of desktop icons also obscure part of the wallpaper area and risk making their displays look too busy by adding a wallpaper to the pile of visual information already presented.
>
> Wallpaper exacts a small performance penalty (see Chapter 6, "Tuning Windows 95 for Optimal Performance and Reliability"), which you may or may not notice, depending on the horsepower of your system. Nevertheless, good performance practice dictates eliminating anything unnecessary. If your work patterns mean that you'll rarely see your wallpaper, consider the elegant alternative: a bare, clean desktop in a nice, solid color.

Choosing and Using a Screen Saver

Remember when everybody thought that milk and eggs were good for you? Now we know that they're not so healthful, but we still have milkshakes, omelets, and eggnog, 'cause we like 'em. Screen savers are like that.

The original purpose of screen savers was to prevent dreaded *burn-in*. When only certain areas of the screen were active, as was the case when MS-DOS systems sat idle for hours with nothing but C:\> displayed, over time that area could get burned-in with those characters, so that a ghost of them appeared all the time, muddying whatever else appeared in that space. Screen savers blanked the screen when the computer was not in use, or displayed animated scenes that didn't allow a static image to sit in one place. Most monitors manufactured in the last five years or so, however, have newer phosphors that are highly resistant to burn-in, and the Windows desktop keeps the whole screen active, anyway, making burn-in more or less impossible.

On most Windows systems today—and on notebooks and laptops, whose LCD screens are immune to it—burn-in isn't a concern, and screen savers have only two purposes:

- Security—Windows' screen savers can refuse to uncover the desktop unless a password is supplied.
- Fun—'Nough said.

Windows 95 comes with a collection of screen savers, which you can pick from a list on the Screen Saver page, shown in Figure 5.7. When you select a screen saver, it goes into action on the sample display. If that doesn't give you a clear view of what to expect, click the Preview button. The screen saver will take over your screen exactly as it would in practice. Press any key or move the mouse to return to the Screen Saver page.

FIGURE 5.7.

Choosing a screen saver through Display Properties.

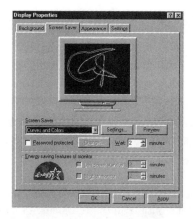

> **TIP**
>
> Some Windows 3.1 screen savers—including Microsoft's—have trouble saving the screen when DOS applications are active, especially when a DOS application is maximized. Because DOS applications under Windows 95 ream in under the full control of Windows (rather than running outside of Windows, as they basically do under Windows 3.1), screen savers work over DOS applications exactly as they do over Windows applications.

The Settings button calls up a dialog box for setting any special options for the screen saver that you selected. The options differ for each saver; you may be able to choose the number of colors or the speed at which things move, for example.

The number in the Wait box is the number of minutes the system will wait before kicking the screen saver into action. If the number shown is 3, anytime Windows detects no keystrokes or mouse movements for three minutes, it will start the screen saver. Raise or lower this number to your liking.

Unless you have checked the Password protected box, an active screen saver automatically disappears and uncovers your desktop at the first keystroke or mouse movement (or earthquake). If you check the Password box, Windows prompts you to enter a password for your screen saver. You type it once (what you type doesn't appear on the screen, in case someone is peering over your shoulder), and then type it again to confirm your choice.

After you've set up your screen saver this way, a keystroke or mouse movement doesn't clear away the saver; instead, a box pops up, prompting you to enter your password. Enter the correct password, and the screen saver goes away. Otherwise, the saver stays put, preventing unauthorized use. Even if you haven't password protected your Windows logon (see Part VI), the screen saver is smart enough to keep your system secure. If a snoop switches it off, or presses your PC's reset button, when a password-protected screen saver is active, the screen saver automatically comes back the moment Windows reappears.

THIRD-PARTY SCREEN SAVERS

You know by now that you can use most of your Windows 3.1 applications with Windows 95. But what about the rich field of third-party screen savers for 3.1? Will they work?

They might, depending on which you try. I installed Berkeley Systems, Inc.'s *Star Trek: The Screen Saver*, which is based on Berkeley's popular After Dark engine, just to see what would happen. It worked fine on my system. Others may work also.

As a rule, though, stick with the built-in Windows screen savers or pick up a new screen saver package designed for Windows 95. By virtue of how they interact with Windows, screen saver engines have always tended to adversely affect system performance and reliability. You can rest assured that the screen saver engine included with Windows 95 has been optimized for Windows 95 and thoroughly tested on it. Screen savers for Windows 3.1 depend on older, 16-bit interface routines and other outdated aspects of Windows, which may tend to slow your system or affect its reliability. To me, that's too high a price for a utility that's unnecessary—albeit fun—in the first place.

If you have a monitor built with Energy Star circuitry, the Screen Saver page enables you to control the energy-saving features of your monitor. (Windows determines whether you have such a monitor during setup, and lets you change these settings only if you do.) For each setting, you can check the checkmark box to enable that feature, then enter the number of minutes to wait (detecting no keystrokes or mouse movements) before activating the feature.

■ Low-power standby keeps the current image on your screen, but shuts down some of the monitor circuitry to save power.

■ Shut-off monitor switches off the monitor to save all the power it consumes—the ultimate screen saver.

Customizing Appearance

The Appearance page of the Display Properties sheet is where you really get down to the business of customizing your display. You can individually select and change the colors for nearly every standard screen element here, as well as change fonts used for text in standard display elements (such as title bars and icon caption), icon spacing, border width, and more.

Most people are not great decorators; I'm sure not. So, I like to rely on the predefined schemes that you can select. These are packaged sets of choices for colors, fonts, and more that go together well.

Some schemes have special purposes; for example, the choices with (large) next to their names use big fonts for clarity, which is helpful on small displays, such as those in notebook and subnotebook PCs, and also helpful to those with vision problems.

Note that there are several choices for displays using a 256-color palette (those with 256 next to them) and a few "hi-color" choices that use colors from the 64,000-color, 16-bit hi-color palette. (See Figure 5.8.) These schemes don't display more colors at once than the rest; they simply exploit the richer variety of colors available in these display modes. (Of course, you'll see the correct colors only if you're using the proper color palette; see "Customizing Settings" later in this chapter.)

Also featured are choices followed by (flat); these remove all of the three-dimensional shading effects from the screen, in effect "flattening" windows and other elements and giving them a very sharp, graphical look. Flat choices aren't pretty but they may improve clarity on small, fuzzy displays, especially older laptops and notebooks, whose 16- and 32-grayscale displays don't handle shading well.

FIGURE 5.8.

Changing screen colors, element sizes, and font sizes and styles through Display Properties.

If no scheme looks just right to you, you can pick a good one as a starting point and then modify what you don't like. For example, you might choose Wheat and leave the nice palette of earth-tone colors alone, but then move down to the Font box and change the letter style used in title bars. When you're done, you can choose Save As and save your customized scheme with a new name. You can also use the Delete button to delete schemes, but I can't think of why you'd want to, unless you were incredibly hard up for disk space.

The Item section enables you to select a screen element to modify; the controls to the right of the list and below it are used to modify the item selected. Depending on the selection, you can change the color and size of the item, and change the font, size, and style (regular, bold, or italic) of any text that appears on or in it. The Size control next to Item describes the size or thickness (as in the case of borders) of the Item selected in pixels, except for the two Icon spacing items, for which Size describes how many pixels apart to automatically space icons appearing on the desktop and in the windows.

Alas, there is no "item" choice for specifically customizing the colors and fonts used for the taskbar. The taskbar takes its color from the selection made for the item 3-D objects, and takes its font style and size from the choice made for the item Active title bar.

When you change the Icon size on the Appearance page, the change affects only large icons (see "Large Icons or Small?" earlier in this chapter), which are 32 pixels high by default, but can be made larger or smaller here. Small icons are always 16 pixels high. Note that, because bitmap graphics aren't inherently scalable, icons tend to look fuzzy and scrambled except in their standard large and small sizes.

Note that you can use a different size, color, and font for active and inactive elements, such as title bars and windows. Typically, Windows tells you what's active by dulling the colors in the inactive elements. On a monochrome display, as on many notebook PCs, that method can make distinguishing between active and inactive elements difficult. By making the active elements larger than the inactive ones, or by making the fonts radically different in each element, you can make finding the active element a snap.

When you drop down the Item list and make a selection, the controls applicable to that item become active. For example, you can change the size, color, and font used in title bars. When you select Active title bar from the Item list, the Size, Color, and Font controls all show the current settings for that item, and allow you to make changes. (See Figure 5.9.) When you choose Scrollbar as the item, only Size is active because there are no fonts or colors to change in a scrollbar.

FIGURE 5.9.

Changing screen colors and fonts through Display Properties.

When changing fonts, you can choose any font in the drop-down list, which includes all your TrueType fonts plus standard Windows system fonts. (Try Brush Script in your title bars for a wild-looking setup!) You can use any available point size for that font. If you choose a font size that is too large for the item, the item is automatically enlarged to accommodate the larger font. Note that you also can control the color of the text through the Color control to the right of the Font control. The buttons to the right of the Color control select the letter style: B for bold, / for italic. (Why didn't they use *I* for italic? Probably a concession to proper typography terminology. A true italic is actually a separate font, not a mere adjustment to an existing font. When you choose /, Windows merely slants the regular font. It looks like italic, but technically, it isn't.)

Customizing Settings

The final page of Display Properties | Settings controls the configuration of your display adapter. Everything you do on this page is limited by the capabilities of the particular display adapter that you use, and its drivers.

In the best of all possible worlds, this page would allow you to dynamically change the color palette that you use (from basic 16-color VGA to 16.7 million-color "true color" in adapters that support it), the screen resolution (from 640 x 480 up to the limits of the adapter), and screen font. Ideally, you should be able to do all of this on the fly without having to restart Windows to make your changes take effect. Sadly, though, some users find that they can use only some of the features available here, owing mainly to limitations in the display drivers for some adapters, incompatibilities between Windows 95 and Windows 3.1 display drivers, or limitations in the adapter hardware.

For example, if Windows 95 has a display driver for your adapter, the Setup Wizard automatically installs it. That's good, because even though Windows 95 supports display drivers written for Windows 3.1, your display will perform better with new drivers that exploit Windows 95's high-performance screen-drawing code. The Windows 95 drivers may not support your adapter's ability to change settings on the fly, however, or the utilities packaged with the adapters for making changes on the fly. What will work—and what won't—is unpredictable. For example, the Settings page can lower my screen resolution (Desktop area) on the fly, but if I *increase* resolution, I have to restart Windows.

Until all the major manufacturers begin supplying stable Windows 95 drivers for their display adapters, many users will share my predicament:

- ■ Use the high-performance Windows 95 drivers and possibly sacrifice some extended features, or
- ■ Use the slower, less reliable Windows 3.1 drivers

For more on display drivers, see Chapter 7.

Assuming that your display adapter and drivers support the works, here's what you can do on the Settings page:

- ■ **Color palette:** Select from the drop-down list to increase or decrease your *color palette*, the number of colors that Windows can display on-screen at once.

- **Desktop area:** Use the controls to increase or decrease the screen resolution. Note that on-screen graphics, such as icons, appear smaller as you increase screen resolution.
- **Fonts:** Use the list to choose Small Fonts or Large Fonts, or click Custom to choose a custom size for your screen fonts.

Recall that you can change the fonts used everywhere on the desktop on the Appearance page. The Font changes that you select on the Settings page don't change your Appearance settings; they simply enlarge or reduce the apparent size of all fonts on-screen equally to help counter the effects of changes in your screen resolution.

For example, suppose that you choose your fonts and sizes in Appearance when working with a 640 × 480 desktop area. If you later switch to 800 × 600 or a higher desktop area, you'll notice that your fonts look much smaller—maybe too small. You could go back to the Appearance page and choose larger font sizes, but that would be inconvenient because you have to select the font size for each screen element individually. And if you switch back to 640 × 480 in the future, you'll have to go back and adjust each font once more. The Fonts control in Settings allows you to avoid all that by automatically changing the size of all text on the desktop by a certain percentage.

When you select a desktop area above 640 × 480, you have a choice of Small fonts (your original font size settings, which may now appear too small) or Large fonts (approximately double the apparent size of the small fonts). If neither of these choices is quite right, click Custom. You'll see a box like the one in Figure 5.10.

FIGURE 5.10.

Choosing a custom enlargement/reduction size for display fonts.

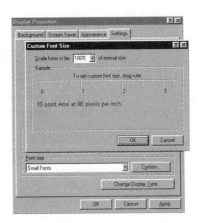

In the Custom Font box, select a percentage from the drop-down list (100 percent leaves the fonts unchanged) to size the fonts. The text below the ruler changes to show the effects of your selection. You also can drag across the ruler to select a custom percentage.

After you make all your Settings changes, Windows may or may not prompt you to restart your system, depending on the capabilities of your display adapter and driver.

DO YOU NEED HIGH RESOLUTION?

SuperVGA display adapters with extended video modes (resolutions above 640×480 and color palettes from 256 to 16.7 million colors) have become the model of choice in recent years, and they're great, especially for performance. Keep in mind, though, that more colors and more resolution place higher demands on your display adapter, your PC, and Windows. So, consider carefully whether you'll see any real benefit before using high resolution and extra color.

Resolutions above 640×480 have a "smoothing" effect on your display, and they can have real practical benefits in graphics editing and page layout software because they allow you to see very small text and manipulate graphics with great precision. But on displays smaller than 17 inches, they can make icons and other images so small that they're hard to work with—Windows' 16×16 small icons can nearly disappear! Video clips, already fairly small in most applications, also squeeze down to an unwatchable size in resolutions above 640×480.

The Windows desktop itself never exploits color palettes beyond 256 colors, except in the case of the few "hi-color" color schemes, which use colors from the 16-bit, hi-color palette (see "Customizing Appearance" earlier in this chapter). You can't even create a wallpaper image that exceeds 256 colors; the .BMP file format doesn't permit it. If you increase your color palette beyond 256 colors, the only difference that you might notice on your Windows desktop is deeper, richer colors—but not *more* colors. The only real reason to go beyond 256 colors is to use applications that exploit high-color modes, such as high-end paint and photo-retouching programs. Few people use those, but nearly everybody uses (or wants to use) multimedia entertainment, education, and reference software. Nearly all such software is designed and optimized for 640×480 resolution and 256 colors (a few exploit hi-color modes). Go beyond that and you'll see no real display improvement, pay a performance penalty, and possibly run into problems with your multimedia software. (See Figure 5.11.)

If you do use applications that benefit from extended video modes, consider using a display adapter supported by Windows capability to change settings on the fly. You then can easily shift into extended video modes when using those applications, but enjoy the improved performance and multimedia compatibility of standard 256-color, 640×480 Windows the rest of the time.

FIGURE 5.11.

Changing your color palette
and screen resolution
through Display Properties.

Changing Pointers

Ah, the lowly pointer. It's our finger in cyberspace, our representative in Windows. And yet, most of us give it little thought and less respect. Why should we not make our pointers pretty (and practical), just as we spiff up the rest of the desktop?

In Windows 95, the pointer finally gets its due. You can choose from among a suite of sizes, types, and styles, and apply any available pointer type to any particular pointer job. Fittingly, the Pointers page can be found in the Mouse Properties sheet, which you'll find in Control Panel. Open Mouse, select the Pointers page, and you'll see a screen like the one in Figure 5.12.

FIGURE 5.12.

Customizing pointers.

You can select any of several schemes from the drop-down list. My favorite is 3-D, which gives you a set of nicely shaded, three-dimensional pointers. (Note: You can select 3-D pointers in any video mode, but you can't see the 3-D shading in 16-color mode.) They go well with the desktop because their apparent light source (the direction of the light shining on them, as indicated by the areas of light and shadow) is the same as that used for all other 3-D screen elements. Other schemes include large pointers for small screens or strained eyes.

You may not have realized how many different pointers Windows uses before looking at the list. My advice is to pick a scheme and to not monkey with the individual pointers; they're all well thought out and designed for their specific jobs. Still, you may find that you like most of the choices in a scheme but that one or more icons doesn't work for you; for example, perhaps a few look too small in certain situations.

To change a pointer, select it from the list and then click Browse. A file selection box appears, from which you can select any file with a .CUR (cursor) or .ANI (animated cursor) extension. Animated cursors, as the name implies, move. For example, there's an hourglass icon that rotates while you wait.

You'll find Windows's cursor files in the Cursors folder. Helpfully, their file icons show what they'll look like. The Preview box also shows you a full-size (and animated, for .ANI pointers) version of any selected pointer file. Select a pointer and click Open to return to the Pointers page, which will reflect the change you have just made. (To return to the default choice for the selected scheme, select the pointer you changed and click Use Default.)

MAKING POINTERS STAND OUT

Another way to change the look of pointers is to add pointer trails. *Pointer trails* are lingering "ghosts" of the pointer that trail behind it for a moment whenever you move the mouse, and then they vanish. They're especially useful on notebook screens, where the small size and lack of contrast can make the pointer hard to see. When you lose the pointer, just move the mouse and the pointer becomes impossible to miss.

To turn pointer trails on, open Mouse Properties in Control Panel, choose the Motion page, and click the Show pointer trails box to put a checkmark in it. Use the slider control to change the length of the trail.

Changing Icons

As in Windows 3.1, you can apply any icon in your system to any program or other file, within certain limitations. All Windows programs have one or more icons built in. (All Windows 95 icons have two—a large and a small. See "Large Icons or Small?" earlier in this chapter.) MS-DOS programs are assigned an icon by Windows, but you can change those, too.

Windows 95 won't allow you to change the basic icon for a Windows program; that is, you can't change the icon that appears with the actual program file in Explorer and in other windows, and on the application's title bar. You can, however, assign *any* icon to a shortcut, which means that you can use whatever icon you want for any item that appears in your Start Menu and for shortcuts you place on the desktop.

Whether you're changing the icon for an MS-DOS program or a shortcut, the process is basically the same. You right-click the icon you want to change, then select Properties. Next, you'll need to find the Change Icon button.

■ For an MS-DOS program, you'll find the button on the Program page of the Properties sheet.

■ For a shortcut, you'll find the button on the Shortcut page of the Properties sheet.

When you click the Change Icon button, the Change Icon dialog box appears, along with a scrolling list of available icons. (See Figure 5.13.)

FIGURE 5.13.

Changing the icon used for an MS-DOS program or Windows shortcut.

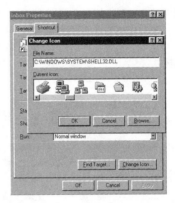

What's on that list varies. DOS programs show a standard list of icons that Windows uses for DOS programs, whereas shortcuts show the icons available in the main program file for the program to which the shortcut points. In either case, you have two choices:

■ Select one of the icons in the list and click OK.

■ Click Browse to bring up a Browse dialog to hunt for other icons.

When you use browse, you can pick any icon from anywhere on the system. Here are a few places to look:

■ **.ICO files:** These are files containing nothing but Windows icons. None comes with Windows 95, but you may find some deposited by other applications or utilities.

■ **.EXE files for Windows programs:** All of these, whether Windows 95 or Windows 3.1, contain one or more icons from which to choose. (Note that MS-DOS programs are .EXE files, too, but they usually contain no Windows icons.)

■ **.DLL files:** Some have many icons, others have none. For example, the file PIFMGR.DLL, in the WINDOWS/SYSTEM directory, contains a collection of icons usually applied to DOS programs. Another file, SHELL32.DLL, also has many icons.

After you select a file and click Open, the Change Icon dialog box shows you any icons embedded in the file. You can select one and click OK, or click Browse again to keep hunting.

Creating Multiple Configurations on the Same PC

Through Windows's User Profiles feature, you can create multiple, customized configurations on the same PC. These enable you to select, at Windows start-up, from among different configurations—including different Display Properties settings, Start Menu arrangements, and Desktop icons—for special purposes, or to keep from getting bored.

For example, suppose that you use your PC for work and for entertainment. You might want different desktop icons, wallpaper, screen resolution, or other environmental settings to accommodate the differences between the two ways you use your PC. Instead of creating one compromise configuration, you can set up two—one arranged for work and the other for play. You could even set up your play configuration so that none of your work programs appear in the Start Menu or on the desktop.

Other applications of User Profiles include:

■ Allowing multiple office workers who share one PC to have their own, customized settings

■ Allowing a PC to be configured at start-up for a particular application or project

■ Allowing multiple family members to have their own configurations on a home computer

To enable User Profiles, open Control Panel and then open Passwords. Choose the User Profiles page. You'll see a box like the one shown in Figure 5.14.

FIGURE 5.14.

*Creating customized
User Profiles.*

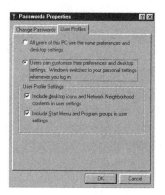

To enable User Profiles, select the second radio button, Users can customize. Using the checkmark boxes in User Profile Settings, choose whether users should be permitted to have their own desktop icons and network neighborhood settings, Start Menu settings, or both. Click OK to finish.

The following paragraphs describe how to use User Profiles.

- **For a PC with multiple users:** Each user must now supply a different username and password (if not already doing so) at Windows start-up. The first time that each user logs on after User Profiles have been enabled, the configuration matches the Default settings established before User Profiles were enabled. Over time, as each user customizes his or her configuration, the new settings are saved by Windows and recalled each time this user signs on.

- **For a PC with a single user who wants multiple configurations:** Pretend that you're multiple users. For each different configuration, sign on with a different name and password (you can use descriptions rather than names to help you remember which profile to use for a given purpose). Any configuration changes that you make while logged on as a given user will be saved and recalled the next time you log on as that user. To change configurations quickly, choose Shut Down from the Start Menu, then choose Close all programs and log on as a different user.

Customizing Through the Registry

A few years back, I wrote a book about Windows 3.1. After reading my chapter about customizing the desktop—changing colors, wallpaper, icon spacing, border width, and so on—my editor was bothered by the fact that I showed how to change these things only with Control Panel. "People also can change these things by editing their .INI files," my editor commented, "Why not show them how to do it that way, too?"

"Because it's easier and safer to do it with Control Panel," I replied. "Why show them a harder and riskier way to do the same thing if doing so doesn't provide any added capability?" My editor then explained to me that there exists a class of Windows users who simply likes tinkering with things, and that they would want to know how to customize their displays by editing .INI files because doing so makes them feel smart and in control.

Now, I'm all for tinkering and tuning when it comes to undocumented features or things that you can't do any other way—as long as you know what you're doing. Nevertheless, I'm a big believer in using the tools provided for a task, unless you have a bloody good reason not to. Windows 95 provides a Display Properties sheet for customizing your display, and that's what you should use, unless you want to change something that can only be changed through the Registry.

The Registry is a much more dense, complex, and tricky animal than the .INI files ever were, especially considering that it can affect the whole network. Most users will find the Registry a difficult, risky, and—most important—*unnecessary* vehicle for customizing the desktop, except for the few unusual changes it allows.

The moral: To adjust the picture on your TV, try turning a knob. Don't open it up and start yanking on the wires.

That said, here's the bottom line on editing the Registry. First, you'll find complete information about editing the Registry in Chapter 8. Don't pass Go and don't do a blessed thing to the Registry until you've read that chapter and observed any Dos, Don'ts, and warnings presented there.

When you understand the basics of Registry editing, all you need to know is where to find the display configuration settings. To find them, open the Registry editor and locate the values for desktop and display attributes under the following headings:

On a single-user machine:

```
Open HKEY_CURRENT_USER, then Control Panel
```

On a multi-user machine (or one on which a single user has set up multiple User Profiles):

```
Open HKEY_USERS, then the desired user name (or .Default, to edit default
settings), then Control Panel.
```

In the Colors folder, you can select colors individually for some of the items that are grouped together under "3D items" or left out altogether in the Display Properties Appearance page. These include the colors of Button shadows, various highlight colors, and more. Edit these according to the general instructions for editing colors described in Chapter 8.

Configuring Files to Open Their Own Applications

Like Windows 3.1, Windows 95 can "associate" all files using a certain extension with a specific application. Because of these associations, when you double-click a data file's icon in Explorer, My Computer, or on the desktop, Windows can automatically open the application required for editing or playing the file. Perhaps because these associations are now recorded in the Registry, Windows 95 has renamed *associating files* to *registering file types*.

Some registrations are predefined (although you can change any of them). For example, Windows automatically opens its media player when you double-click an .AVI (video clip) file or an .RMI or .MID (MIDI music sequence) file. Images in .BMP format are registered to Microsoft Paint. Files with the extension .DOC are registered as Word for Windows files, and any file with the extension .XLS, .XLW, .XLT, or .XLM opens Microsoft Excel.

180

Registering a File Type

The easy way to register a file type (for opening purposes only) that's not registered is to double-click it in Explorer or My Computer. (You also can right-click it and choose Open With.) An Open With dialog appears, as shown in Figure 5.15.

FIGURE 5.15.

Registering an unregistered file type.

Choose a program from the list or click Other and browse for the program that you want to use. Make sure that the box next to Always use this program to open this file is checked. After you click OK, the file opens with the program you selected, and all files with the same extension have been registered to that program.

Editing Registrations

To change registrations for file types (or to create new registrations with actions other than opening the file), choose Options from the View menu of My Computer or Explorer. Click the File Types tab. The screen that appears shows a list of registered file types, including their descriptions and file type icon. When you select a file type, the File type details box shows the extension and the file used to open the file type.

To edit an existing registration, select a file type and click Edit. You'll see a screen like the one shown in Figure 5.16 for HyperTerminal (.HT) files.

NOTE

Note the two checkboxes at the bottom of the screen shown in Figure 5.16.

- ■ The first adds a Quick View item to the context menu so that the files can be viewed through Quick View.

- ■ The second prevents Explorer from hiding the file's extension, which it does by default for all registered file types.

FIGURE 5.16.

Editing a registration.

Each of the Actions listed appears in the context menu for a file of that type. The action shown in bold (Dial, in Figure 5.16) is the default; that's the action taken automatically when you double-click on a file of this type. The other actions are usually selected from the context menu. The Print action can be selected from the Context menu or executed by dropping the file on a printer icon.

TIP

For most file types, you can change the icon by clicking the button at the top of the screen shown in Figure 5.16 and then following the steps described for changing icons earlier in this chapter. The icon that you select will be used to represent all files of the same type.

Behind the scenes, each action listed is performed by a command line, typically an application start-up command. (You may use any command supported under Windows, including application command-line switches.) To see the command, select an action and click Edit. For this example, I'll click the Dial action. I see a screen like the one in Figure 5.17

FIGURE 5.17.

Editing a registered action.

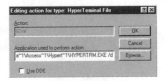

Note that the command shown is the command to open HyperTerminal, plus HyperTerminal's command-line switch to dial (/d). (The Open action is the HYPERTRM.EXE command without switches.) You can create any action for which a command line is available to work on the particular file format selected.

- To edit the command line for an action, click Edit.

- To create a new action for this file type, click New. Enter a name for the action, preceded by an asterisk (for example, *Print). Then enter a command line (and switch, if necessary). After you finish, your new action appears in the context menu for all files of that type.

- To make an action the default (the action taken on double-clicking), select the action and click Set Default.

Integrating Windows 95 Applications

What do I mean when I say that you can *integrate* applications? That's often confusing, because *integration* is one of those buzzwords like *ease of use* that's been tossed around so many different ways, nobody knows what it means anymore.

So I'll redefine it here. *Integration* means *time savings*. After all, your only real investment in the work that you do on your PC is your own time and effort. The only reason to integrate anything is to get your work done quicker and more easily. That's accomplished two ways:

- Applications can share data so that you have to create the data only once, or change it once, and that change is reflected everywhere that the data is used, regardless of the application. Such integration saves you the trouble of creating or changing the same information separately in each application that uses it.

- Data can call up the application used to maintain it so that every time you work with that data, no matter where you are, the proper application leaps into action. Such integration saves you the time and trouble of locating and opening the required application when your documents contain a variety of types of data, such as text, numerical data, and sound and video clips.

The principle vehicle for this kind of integration in Windows 95 is Object Linking and Embedding (OLE, pronounced *olay!*) Version 2.0. In the next several pages, you'll discover the basics of using OLE to share data among applications. You may find that the basics are all you ever need. OLE can be programmed to do some pretty amazing stuff, however, especially across a network. For advanced OLE programming information, see Chapter 12.

Summary

Windows 95 isn't a program, it's an environment—a big one, which you can customize in a hundred different ways. Fortunately, you're not forced to do much customizing at all. You can use the Windows default color scheme, keep track of your Start Menu, and you're all set.

Of course, if you're so inclined, you also can tweak all of your colors and screen fonts, slap up some wallpaper, size and move your taskbar, scale your icons, tune your Start Menu, integrate your applications, and even create a completely different configuration for every mood. You're the boss.

In the final chapter of Part II, you'll learn how to tune your Windows setup for maximum performance and reliability.

Tuning Windows 95 for Optimal Performance and Reliability

6

by Ned Snell

IN THIS CHAPTER

Speed is no trivial factor. The cost of your PC has a direct relationship to its speed. If you paid top-dollar, you would want to make the most of that investment. If you went cheap, you would want to make your PC perform *as if* you paid top-dollar. Either way, you recognize that the more responsive your PC is, the more productive you are.

Like that of all large, complex programs, Windows 95's performance can vary greatly, depending on your hardware configuration and other factors. This chapter shows which factors affect Windows' performance, and also which factors may lead to problems with speed and reliability. The information here equips you to make informed choices when selecting hardware and configuring your system, so you can strike your own balance between performance and economy—or maybe even achieve both.

Why Tune a *Self-Tuning* System?

Microsoft calls Windows 95 a *self-tuning* system and, compared with Windows 3.1, it is.

Left to its own, Windows 3.1 was configured for conservative performance; you had to manually tune the disk cache (SmartDrive) and swapfile (virtual memory) and a few other settings to allow Windows 3.1 to take full advantage of your hardware's performance capabilities. Using conservative defaults was Microsoft's answer to some reliability problems that became less common when the system never shifted past second gear. Microsoft figured that, given a choice between reliable, mediocre computing and crash-prone, snappy computing, most users would choose the former.

Windows 95, however, dynamically tunes the swapfile as you work and sets other configuration options (such as 32-bit disk access) during setup to the best-performing choice available for your hardware. More importantly, Windows 95 features a new approach to memory allocation for the graphical interface. The new design makes Windows 95 far less prone to run low on system resources, a problem that persistently drained Windows 3.1's performance and was the culprit in most lockups, crashes, Not Enough Memory failures, and the ever popular Unrecoverable Application Errors (UAEs, in Windows 3.0) and General Protection Faults (GPFs, in 3.1). Of course, as you know, Windows 95 is (mostly) a multitasking, multithreaded, 32-bit operating system, so it tends to perform better than 3.1 even when it's *not* perfectly tuned.

So, if you've followed the setup steps carefully (so that the Setup Wizard accurately identified your hardware and configured your system properly), you probably don't *need* to tune your system. Still, there is some tuning that can be done to squeeze that last drop of performance from your system. Wouldn't you like to have it? Look at it another way: As far as I know, a Ferrari runs pretty fast on regular gas. But if you had a Ferrari, why wouldn't you fill up with premium and get all the performance you paid for?

There are other, less gaudy reasons to look into the tuning options available in Windows 95. You may want to tune up if:

- You want to make sure that the Setup Wizard properly identified and configured your hardware for top speed.

- Your system is equipped with minimal memory or disk storage and you want to make the most of it.

- Since you set up Windows, you've upgraded your hardware with non-Plug and Play devices (Windows auto-tunes Plug and Play items).

- You begin experiencing locked applications or Not Enough Memory error messages.

- Network access begins to crawl.

- You notice a slow-down in performance over time, particularly during file and disk activities such as loading applications.

The last reason may be the most important. When properly tuned, most parts of your system stay tuned. Your hard drive, however, requires regular tune-ups and maintenance to remain speedy. Because of its dynamic swapfile and huge memory demands, Windows 95 is actually more dependent upon hard-drive speed for overall performance than was Windows 3.1.

This chapter shows how to tune up and maintain your Windows system for maximum performance and reliability.

Hardware Selection and Configuration

I'll assume that, as you read this, you have already purchased your PC and installed Windows 95 on it. So, now may not be the best time to talk about what hardware you need. Still, knowing how your hardware choices affects Windows performance is important for three reasons:

- No matter how carefully you may tune your software, your hardware is the ultimate limiter of your system's performance.

- If you are *seriously* dissatisfied with your performance, it's unlikely that tuning Windows 95 will rev things up enough to make you happy. You need to upgrade your hardware, or perhaps invest in faster applications (if application performance is the main problem).

- When you *do* upgrade your hardware, it's important to know what Windows wants.

Processors

Windows 95 runs on every x86-class processor from the anemic 386SX to the feisty Pentium. (Sorry you 286 users—your upgrade is *long* overdue.) Following are notes on how Windows 95 performs on the two principal PC processors available today.

386-Class Processors

Microsoft says Windows 95 runs on a 386-based PC, even a 16MHz 386sx. That's true, technically; but in reality, running Windows 95 on a 386 should be considered a very temporary stop gap until your credit is approved for a faster PC. Windows 95 is incredibly slow on 386 machines, and is likely to lock up or crash there, as well. This is exacerbated by the fact that few 386s are equipped with more than 4 MB of memory—while the reasonable minimum for Windows 95 is 8 MB.

Also, Windows 95 won't run at all on older 386s. If during setup you see the message

```
Setup fails with error B1
```

your 386 is incompatible with Windows 95. A version of the Intel 386 chip manufactured before April 1987 had a bug; it made math errors during 32-bit operations. If you open your PC's chassis and look at the chip, you might see the message, "For 16-bit Operations Only." Most of the time, that presented no problem for Windows 3.1 applications, which were mostly 16-bit programs anyway. Windows 95, however, does too much 32-bit processing to survive the flaw. You must purchase a new PC or, at the very least, upgrade your processor. Note, however, that upgrading your processor to a newer 386 or even a 486 may make your PC *compatible* with Windows 95, but will do nothing to significantly improve the poor performance you can expect from an older PC built in the 386 era.

486-Class Processors

Although Windows 95 incorporates both 32-bit and 16-bit code, it uses substantially more 32-bit code than Windows 3.1 did. Intel 386 processors are technically 32-bit processors, but they were developed in the age of 16-bit code and they're optimized for 16-bit operations. Because 486 processors are optimized for 32-bit, protected-mode operations, under Windows 95 they show a significant performance advantage over 386 processors—even more than under Windows 3.1. Although Windows 95 runs reliably on 386 processors, for practical purposes, a 486SX processor should be considered the minimum requirement for acceptable Windows 95 performance. A 486 DX2 66MHz is recommended.

Pentium-Class Processors

At this writing, the Intel Pentium processor is the most powerful PC chip on the market. To the extent that the Pentium is a faster processor than a 486, it will indeed run Windows 95 with performance superior to that of most similarly equipped 486-based PCs. Nevertheless, having no 64-bit code, the current implementation of Windows 95 takes no advantage of Pentium's 64-bit processing capability. By all user-perceptible measures, PCs equipped with fast 486 chips, such as the 486 DX4, will run Windows 95 as quickly as mid-level (90MHz) Pentium machines and faster than entry-level Pentiums (60–66MHz).

In fact, other parts of the system—in particular, memory and disk speed—have more impact on overall Windows 95 performance than the difference between 486 and Pentium processors. When there is a price difference between a 486 and similarly configured Pentium, the difference is probably better spent on faster peripherals or extra memory; these will likely boost performance more than the Pentium alone. For example, a 16MB 486 DX2 PC with a PCI bus will likely outperform an 8MB Pentium in most scenarios.

Microsoft has confirmed rumors that a Pentium-optimized version of Windows 95, featuring some 64-bit code, is in the works. At this writing, no word has been made public about *how much* 64-bit code will be used, or when (or even *if*) the Pentium version of Windows 95 will debut. In any case, it's likely to be a 32-bit system with a few 64-bit components, which means that it's unlikely to blow the doors off the standard issue of Windows 95.

> **NOTE**
>
> In 1994, a design flaw in some Pentium processors was discovered. This glitch caused errors in the results of some high-level mathematical calculations and affected only a small proportion of Pentium buyers, but it nonetheless set off a firestorm in the trade press so hot that the news broke in the mainstream media as well and inspired Pentium paranoia.
>
> If you've heard about this, you should know that the problem's been fixed and won't appear in any recently manufactured Pentium PC. And for most older Pentiums, a replacement chip can be ordered from the manufacturer. So, just as there's no compelling reason to invest in Pentium for Windows 95 computing, there's no reason *not* to, either.

Other Performance Choices

Following are tips for selecting or upgrading hardware for top Windows 95 performance.

Memory

As with processors, the official "minimum" RAM requirement for Windows 95 would be better described as the "technically workable but actually insufficient" RAM requirement. Although Microsoft lists 4 MB as the minimum requirement, the practical minimum for Windows 95 is 8 MB. Installing as much as 16 MB in a client PC or 32 MB in a server will reward you with superior performance because the extra memory reduces performance-robbing paging to and from the disk-based Windows swapfile.

A measly 4 MB will indeed *run* Windows 95, but the operating system itself consumes almost that much simply to function. Running even a single application in a 4MB PC may require heavy paging, degrading performance significantly. Depending on the requirements of the applications that you use and the amount of free disk space available for the swapfile, a 4MB PC might multitask so slowly that, for all practical purposes, it must be used as a single-tasking machine—and with applications that use very little memory, at that.

Hard Disk

Traditionally, the hard disk is the bottleneck in most systems; it's the slowest system component and therefore the part whose tuning benefits the overall system the most. In a system running Windows 95, the importance of a fast hard disk is even greater than in Windows 3.1. A demand paging feature used by Windows 95 during multitasking swaps entire applications to the swapfile on disk when other applications demand more memory than is available. A slow hard disk could seriously drag system performance during such operations and others as well, such as Windows start-up, application start-up, and various file operations.

The ideal Windows hard drive features a fast access time (<12ms) and a fast interface (PCI or SCSI 2 bus will both perform well, though PCI has the extra advantage of being easily configurable from within Windows). It's also compatible with Windows's 32-bit disk drivers. (See Chapter 4, "Installing Windows 95.") Most newer drives are, but some older drives rely on partitioning software that Windows must run in real mode (dubbed "compatibility mode" in Windows 95), instead of Windows's own 32-bit device drivers, which run in protected mode. Also, drives compressed with utilities that aren't compatible with Windows 95's compression routines cause the same problem. Any drive that requires a real-mode driver, no matter what its other specifications, will seriously degrade the performance of Windows 95 and should be replaced at the first opportunity.

The ideal drive is also large (>500 MB), not simply because Windows 95 and its applications tend to require a lot of space, but also because of the following:

- A larger disk can accumulate more applications and files before beginning to show performance degradation from overcrowding.
- A larger disk is less likely to require compression (see the "DriveSpace" section later in this chapter), which can slow down some types of operations.
- Windows 95's dynamic swapfile (see "Virtual Memory (Swapfile) Management") can, if necessary, allocate all of the free space on a disk to the swapfile; more free space may mean the ability to multitask more applications.

No matter what its specifications, *any* hard disk used by Windows 95 requires proper configuration and regular maintenance to perform quickly, consistently, and reliably.

Parallel Port

Windows 95's accelerated 32-bit print routines enable it to prepare and send documents to the printer more rapidly than Windows 3.1 could. For fastest printing, an Enhanced Communication Port (ECP) is recommended to support rapid sending to the printer.

Display Adapter

Increasingly, PC users are turning to coprocessor-based "accelerator" display adapters for Windows computing. These remain a good choice for Windows 95. What's crucial, however, for display performance under Windows 95 is compatibility with Windows 95's miniport display drivers. For top performance, use a display driver included with Windows 95, or get a new Windows 95 driver from the manufacturer of your display adapter. Windows 3.1 drivers are supported by Windows 95, but using them will result in slower display response.

NOTE

You can control the extent to which Windows takes advantage of accelerated display adapters. (See the section later in this chapter, "Graphics Optimization.")

Tuning for Performance

This section leads you through the steps required to monitor your system performance and tune your configuration.

Using System Monitor

System Monitor is a new Windows utility that records and charts the extent to which various hardware and software components are using system resources. It's not a beginner's tool; you have to have some technical expertise to make use of the information that System Monitor reveals, especially because it can report on minute, highly specific system activities. Its greatest value is as a diagnostic and performance tool on a network; network administrators can use System Monitor to check the performance of remote computers and the performance of the network. Some users also may find it useful for tracking the effects of changes in their configuration. For example, after using System Monitor to evaluate performance under one configuration, you can change your configuration, restart the system (if necessary), and then reopen System Monitor to observe the changes.

To use System Monitor, choose Run from the Start Menu and enter sysmon. (You also may find System Monitor in the System Tools group in your Accessories folder). A screen like the one shown in Figure 6.1 appears.

Choose Edit and then Add Item to select any of the several dozen system resources tracked by System Monitor. The categories and items vary somewhat, depending upon the computer's configuration (also, System Monitor has an extensible interface, so third-party manufacturers can add new items), but standard items for the file system, memory, system kernel, and network are included. (See Table 6.1 for explanations of some of the items available.) To monitor a remote computer, choose File and then Connect, then choose items for that computer.

FIGURE 6.1.

Using System Monitor.

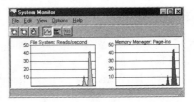

For each item selected, a separate chart is created. You can chart as many different items as you like, although the more items you track at once, the smaller and less useful each chart becomes.

You also have your choice of chart types on the View menu and on the toolbar. You can display bar charts, line graphs, or numeric reports that merely show the number values for each activity. All charts displayed at once must all be the same chart type; you can't mix bar charts and line graphs on the same screen. You can, however, edit the color used for an item, and choose whether the scale on each chart should be automatic—changing as necessary, based on the data charted—or fixed, with a user-defined maximum value and a minimum of 0. To edit the color and scale, double-click the chart, or choose Edit and then Edit Item, and click the item to change. A dialog box appears for you to select a color, choose between an automatic and fixed scale, and enter a value for the top of a fixed scale.

System Monitor remembers your choices. When you open System Monitor again, it will automatically display the charts that you configured the last time you used it.

Table 6.1. Important resources tracked by System Monitor.

Category	Item	Description
Kernel	Processor Usage	Percentage of time the CPU is busy.
	Threads	Number of threads active.
	Virtual machines	Number of virtual machines active.
File System	Dirty Data	Total number of bytes in cache blocks containing changed data waiting to be written to disk (true bytes of "dirty data" will actually be less because they may not be full.)
	Reads per second	Number of read operations delivered to the file system per second.
	Writes per second	Number of write operations delivered to the file system per second.
Memory Manager	Disk cache size	Current size of the cache in bytes.
	Free memory	Total amount of free memory in bytes.
	Page-ins	Number of pages of swapped into memory per second.

Category	Item	Description
	Page-outs	Number of pages of swapped out of memory per second.
	Swapfile in use	Number of bytes in the current swapfile.

NOTE

For explanations of other categories/items tracked by System Monitor, choose Edit, select the category and item, and then click the Explain button.

Using the Performance Page

Many of the tuning procedures that follow begin on the Performance property page. To reach it, open Control Panel, open System, and then click the Performance tab. You'll see a screen like the one shown in Figure 6.2.

FIGURE 6.2.

The Performance page.

RESOURCES

Under Windows 3.1, in a PC with at least 4 MB of memory, a reasonably fast hard disk, and a permanent swapfile, most performance problems and system failures resulted from the fact that Windows allocated small, 64KB memory blocks, called *heaps*, for storing and managing standard graphical interface information required by applications when using Windows application program interfaces (APIs). Complex screens loaded with Windows and icons, or poorly designed applications that failed to release heap space when they were finished with it, tended to exhaust these heaps, resulting in "not enough memory" and "insufficient resources" errors. These errors seemed mysterious because, usually, there was plenty of system memory available when these problems occurred.

Windows 95 has all but eliminated these problems by switching most of the heaps from 16-bit memory to 32-bit memory, and by raising—or in some cases, eliminating—the limits on the size of the heaps that the graphical interface and other APIs are permitted to use.

Memory Management

Your PC's memory is Windows' workspace. Give it a large, uncluttered area to work in, and Windows can fly. Give it a small, messy room and Windows sits there feeling sorry for itself. The next few pages show you how to provide Windows 95 with a memory space that lets it soar.

Freeing RAM

As mentioned earlier, there is no substitute for equipping your PC with sufficient memory to run Windows well—8 MB or more. If you must run Windows with only the minimum 4 MB, however, the tips that follow may help you live more comfortably in that space by reducing the size of the Windows 95 working set, the program code that Windows keeps active in memory at all times. If you have 8 MB but run into heavy paging (see "Virtual Memory (Swapfile) Management") when multitasking certain applications, you might also try the following suggestions to free RAM and reduce the need for swapfile paging.

Make sure that Windows's background print rendering feature is turned off . (See "Printing Performance" later in this chapter.)

- Run only one network client and no more network protocols and services than you absolutely require. Each client and each protocol takes up some memory, even when you're not logged onto the network.

- Don't put any programs in your Startup folder. Run programs when you need them and close them when you're done.

- When running lengthy operations that can run unattended, such as disk defragmentation, disk compression, or file downloading, minimize the program window until the operation is complete. Minimized programs use less memory than windowed or maximized ones because they save the memory required to report their progress to you.

■ Seek out and use low-demand applications. When writing a document, must you use Word or WordPerfect? WordPad, or even Notepad, will make fewer demands on your overtaxed system.

Virtual Memory (Swapfile) Management

By default, Windows 95 manages the virtual memory swapfile dynamically, expanding it and contracting it as the demand for memory rises and falls. This sounds suspiciously like Windows 3.1's default "temporary" swapfile, which was a major performance inhibitor. Performance-minded 3.1 users always switched over to a permanent swapfile as Step 1 in boosting performance.

So, it's natural if your first temptation is to distrust Windows's defaults and start monkeying with the swapfile—but restrain yourself. New high-performance algorithms make the dynamic swapfile the best performing choice for almost all users. There are only a few instances when an adjustment to the swapfile may result in improved performance, and these really only come into play in machines with more than one hard disk drive.

By default, Windows 95 sets up the swapfile on the same disk where Windows is stored. If another drive in your system is

■ Faster

■ Less full

■ Uncompressed (and the drive containing Windows is compressed)

then you can speed up your system by relocating the swapfile to the other drive. You can use the same procedure to move the swapfile to or from a compressed disk on the same physical drive.

To change your virtual memory settings, open the Performance property sheet and click the Virtual memory button. You'll see a screen like the one shown in Figure 6.3.

FIGURE 6.3.

Changing virtual memory settings.

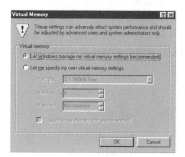

To change the location of the swapfile, click the radio button next to Let me specify my own virtual memory settings, then select the Hard disk from the drop-down list. Note that the list also indicates the amount of free space on each disk.

After you select a disk, you'll notice that the Minimum allowable cache size remains at 0, whereas the value for Maximum will be the entire amount of free space on the disk. There's no real reason to change either of these. The Minimum of 0 allows your system to run free of any swapfile when none is required, which will often be the case if your system has a healthy amount of RAM and you tend to use only one application at a time. The default Maximum expressed here isn't really valid; what it should say is "all the free space on the drive," because this value will dynamically grow and shrink as the actual amount of free space on the drive changes. If you change the Maximum value manually, the size of the swapfile will never exceed the value you entered *or* the amount of free space, whichever is smaller.

> **CAUTION**
>
> Never check the box at the bottom of the Virtual Memory page that reads "Disable virtual memory" and then adds, correctly, "not recommended." This box is provided so that you can shut off virtual memory at the request of a Microsoft tech support person when trying to isolate a problem. If you check it on your own, your performance will certainly suffer and your system may not even restart. There is no circumstance under which disabling virtual memory can improve performance. What was a useful option in Windows 3.1 is an integral, essential part of the operating system in Windows 95.
>
> When finished, click OK.

Disk Tuning

As noted earlier, the hard disk is almost always the principle bottleneck in a Windows system. As the only mechanical device in an otherwise solid-state machine (OK, your floppy drive doesn't count), it requires the most careful tuning, and the most maintenance. An undermaintained, undertuned hard disk does more to drag your system down than any other single element.

Beyond choosing a fast disk in the first place, you can do the following to ensure that your disk performs as quickly and reliably as possible under Windows 95.

- Make sure that 32-bit disk access is enabled.
- Make sure that the disk cache is configured properly.
- Remove unnecessary files.
- Check and correct disk flaws and fragmentation.

> **CAUTION**
>
> When Setup installs Windows 95, a number of your old DOS external command executables are deleted from disk. You need to do the same with old versions of Norton Utilities, PC Tools, and the like. Windows 95's new Installable File System is backwardly compatible with previous versions of DOS, but utilities that delete, sort, defragment, or in some way alter the structure of your hard disk were created *before* Windows 95 and know nothing of the new VFAT file system and its support for long filenames.
>
> Using old DOS utilities can be hazardous to the health of your data because they can corrupt your disk's structures.

32-Bit Disk Access

True to its conservative leanings, Windows 3.1 employed 16-bit disk operations by default, even in PCs equipped with a fast 32-bit data path to the disk. Users had the option of switching to a 32-bit disk driver called Fastdisk, but few knew about it, and the experts never agreed about whether Windows 3.1's 32-bit disk access really helped or hindered. Windows 95, however, enables its robust 32-bit disk access by default, unless it can't access the disk in 32-bit protected mode.

When Windows can't use its 32-bit drivers to access a disk, performance suffers tremendously. Windows accesses the disk in 16-bit real mode, called *compatibility mode* in the Windows 95 lexicon. Not only is the 16-bit access inherently slower, but Windows must switch into compatibility mode every time it accesses the device, and back to protected mode afterwards—an operation that wastes resources and further degrades performance.

Windows enables compatibility mode when the Setup Wizard determines that the disk requires a real-mode disk driver for which Windows has no compatible 32-bit replacement. Disks compressed with older versions of Stacker or another disk compression utility may use such drivers, as may disks protected by some security or encryption software and older FAT disks partitioned with unusual third-party utilities.

To find out whether your hard disk is afflicted, open the Performance page, which is shown in Figure 6.4.

Note that, on my system, drive D is listed in the box titled Select an item. Anything listed in this box is an instance where Windows had to forego its default performance settings to accommodate hardware with compatibility problems. Any reference here to *compatibility mode* means that Windows could not replace an existing real-mode driver with a compatible protected-mode driver, and therefore must access the hardware in compatibility mode. Note also that, above the box, File System indicates that a drive is running in compatibility mode.

FIGURE 6.4.

Checking 32-bit disk access.

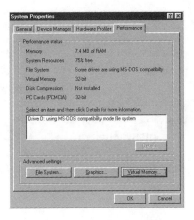

In my case, it's my CD-ROM drive (drive D) that uses a DOS-based real-mode driver for which Windows 95 had no replacement. (I need to acquire a Windows 95 driver from the manufacturer.) Fortunately, my hard disk (C) isn't listed here, which means that Windows is using 32-bit access for it. Further proof of that appears above the box; because my computer is using 32-bit virtual memory, I must have 32-bit disk access.

If your hard disk turns out to be using a real-mode driver, you must locate and install a new driver that is compatible with Windows 95.

■ If the driver was bundled with your hard disk or PC, contact your hard disk or PC manufacturer and request an updated driver. You also might try Microsoft Tech Support. After you've acquired a new driver, install it by opening Control Panel and then opening Add New Hardware.

■ If the driver is part of a compression or security software package, you have several options: You can contact the software manufacturer to find out whether you can upgrade to a newer, Windows 95-compatible version, or you may be able to remove the compression or encryption (follow the software manufacturer's instructions), and then use Add New Hardware to re-install the disk using Windows 95 drivers.

Cache Tuning (or Not!)

Another tuning favorite in Windows 3.1 was SmartDrive, the disk cache that boosted system performance by caching disk data in RAM to allow Windows to access the hard disk less frequently. Users with plenty of RAM and modest application requirements found that they could increase the size of the cache from the defaults and boost performance.

Windows 95 has a new disk caching system, VCACHE (*virtual cache*), which dynamically configures itself according to system demand just as the swapfile does. In fact, the swapfile and the cache work together to balance memory demand with system performance.

VCACHE is not user-configurable except in one sense. You can choose from among three basic profiles that select the algorithms Windows applies in managing the cache. Each tunes the cache to the most effective settings for the usage patterns of the PC:

- Desktop
- Mobile or Docking System
- Network Server

TUNING PORTABLES

The Mobile or Docking profile compromises some performance aspects of the cache to accommodate the power-saving requirements of portable PCs and their tendency to be equipped with less memory than their desktop counterparts.

If your portable PC has at least 8 MB of memory and you typically use it plugged in (not on batteries), you'll improve your cache performance by switching to the Desktop profile.

However, if you use a docking station that's equipped with another hard drive and has Plug and Play BIOS (see Chapter 11), you may find this cache selection valuable. The Mobile or Docking selection automatically retunes your cache settings for the docking station's hard drive whenever you dock, then retunes for your portable's internal drive when you undock.

During setup, Windows selects the proper setting. If you change the way that the PC is used, you'll want to change the Hard Disk optimization setting as well so that Windows will manage the cache in the best way for the role your PC plays.

To change the setting, click the File System button on the Performance tab. You'll see a screen like the one shown in Figure 6.5.

In the Hard Disk optimization box, choose one of the Typical role profiles in the drop-down list, and then click OK.

NOTE

For CD-ROM drives, Windows has a separate cache. (See the section titled "CD-ROM Performance," later in this chapter.)

FIGURE 6.5.

Changing the hard disk optimization settings.

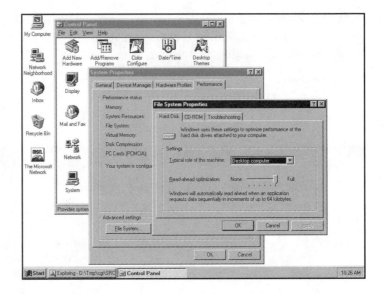

Freeing Storage Space

Tuning and maintenance of your hard disk go hand in hand. Fast 32-bit access and the correct cache settings are of little value if your disk is overcrowded, badly fragmented, or infected with accumulated errors and defective sectors.

Regular disk maintenance is a three-step process described as follows. Note that the order of the steps is important:

1. As you know, you should make regular backups of your hard disk. Avoid performing the other steps listed here until you have a recent and complete backup set so that any mistake made during disk maintenance can be corrected. The most common error is accidentally deleting an important file, and the Recycle Bin provides some safety from that. Still, the Bin is not permanent and not foolproof; regular backups are your only guarantee.

2. Having a complete backup set available, you should regularly "clean out" your hard disk, deleting (or archiving to floppy disk or tape and then deleting) old, unwanted data files and applications. Opening Explorer from the Programs menu is an excellent way to do this; you can hunt through your entire folder/directory structure to delete files and even entire directories. This maximizes free space on your disk, which can improve your disk's performance and also offers the swapfile more room to provide more multitasking capability.

3. Check your disk regularly for fragmentation, and defragment the disk anytime Windows recommends that you do so. Over time, the files on a disk are broken up and spread in pieces around the disk, and the free space on the disk is broken up, as

well. This fragmentation isn't technically a flaw; your computer can still use the files and free space. As a disk becomes more fragmented, however, disk operations start to slow down because of the extra seek-and-retrieval time caused by the fragmentation. This also makes the disk work harder, which may eventually cause data errors and premature disk failure. Because Windows 95 can use fragmented free space for the swapfile, paging is slowed by fragmentation as well. Always defragment *after* disk clean-out, not before, because deleting files after defragmenting gives your disk a head start on becoming fragmented again.

4. If and when you find that you're running low on space, Windows 95 has a built-in disk compression utility for expanding the amount of space available on a disk.

Backup

Windows 95's Microsoft Backup applet is a full-featured backup utility. To begin, choose Microsoft Backup from the System Group in the Accessories folder. The first time you use backup, it automatically creates a *file set*, or listing of files to be backed up, that includes your entire hard disk. It does this to encourage you to perform a complete backup first so that you'll have a starting point from which to perform quicker *incremental* backups later. An incremental backup backs up only files that have changed since your last backup so that your backup set is made current without the time and trouble of a complete backup.

> **TIP**
>
> Because you can create and name different file sets, you can make backups for special purposes. For example, if you want to back up the files used in a particular project more often than you back up your whole system, you can create a special backup set including just those files.

Backup also can compress data as it backs up, which is an especially valuable feature if you're backing up to floppy disks, or even if you have a tape drive, if your hard drive is well-loaded. Be aware, though, that the amount of compression will vary with the file type, and that, overall, you're unlikely to cut the space required for files by more than half. If you have more than 100 MB of files (and few Windows users have less than this) you may want to consider investing in a tape drive to avoid backing up to 30 or more floppy disks.

> **SCSI TAPE DRIVE SUPPORT**
>
> At this writing, Microsoft Backup doesn't support SCSI tape drives, though it's reasonable to expect support to be made available through a patch or upgrade. If you have a SCSI tape drive, contact Microsoft to find out whether an upgrade is available.

After the first-time note about the full backup set, you'll see a screen like the one shown in Figure 6.6.

FIGURE 6.6.

Microsoft Backup.

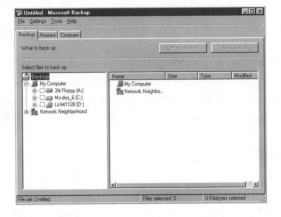

The three tabs allow you to create a file set and backup, restore from a backup set, or compare files on your hard disk to files in a backup set. The Compare option can be useful for deciding whether to restore from a backup set or use an existing file in the case of a corrupted, lost, or accidentally altered file.

To create a new file set and backup files:

1. Click the Backup tab. An Explorer-style listing of your computer's contents appears, with checkmark boxes next to elements that you can back up. (Note that you can create a file set containing everything on your hard disk by clicking the checkbox next to it.)

2. Select the files to be included in the file set by double-clicking the icon for your hard disk, then navigate among the folders and files, placing checkmarks next to items that you want included in the file set.

   - To include all files and folders within a folder, check the folder.
   - To select only some of the files or folders within a folder, double-click the folder icon, then place checkmarks next to the items that you want to include.
   - To remove a checkmark, click the box again.

   When you check any box, Windows immediately adds the names of the file and folders to the set, displaying a File Selection in Progress box whenever you make a large selection that requires a little time to collect. As you work, the status bar at the bottom of the Backup window tracks the number of files that you have selected and their uncompressed size. (The files may require less disk space to back up than the size suggests if you use the Compress data option; see the "Backup Options" section that follows.)

3. After creating the file set, click Next Step. Windows shows you the available devices to which you can back up. Typically, you can back up to a tape drive (usually the best choice), to floppy disks (best for small file sets), to another hard disk in your system, or even to free space on the same hard disk. (This last option provides protection in the case of accidental deletions or corrupted files, but not in the case of a dead hard disk, of course. And it cuts into disk space that your swapfile may need.) After choosing a device, click Start Backup.

4. Windows prompts you to supply a name for the file set and provides an option to password protect the backup so that no unauthorized user can restore from it later. After you enter the name, Windows begins the backup.

REUSING A FILE SET

In the future, if you want to back up the same group of files that you've backed up before, choose File | Open File Set, and then choose the file set from the list provided.

Using Explorer or My Computer, you also can back up a previously created file set by dragging it and dropping it on the Backup icon. Unless you've stored them elsewhere, you'll find your file sets in the Accessories folder, using the extension .SET. If you open My Computer and navigate through Program Files to the Accessories folder, you'll find Backup.exe and all of your file sets together in the same Window, making it easy to drag a file set and drop it on backup.

■ To restore from a backup, load the tape or first floppy disk of the backup set (unless you back up to hard disk), choose the Restore tab, select the device on which the backup is stored, select the name of the backup set from the list provided, and click Next Step. Windows shows the files included in the file set and allows you to check or uncheck files to restore. Select the whole set or specific files and folders and then click Start Restore.

■ To compare a backup set to files on your hard disk, load the tape or first floppy disk of the backup set (if necessary) and choose the Compare tab. In the left side of the window, click the drive on which the original files are stored. On the right, select the name of the backup set. Click Next Step, check the files that you want compared in the list provided, and click Start Compare.

Backup Options

Microsoft Backup offers a number of optional controls and settings that affect how backup activities are handled. You'll find these in the Settings menu and in the Options box that you can open from the Settings menu. These include:

- **File Filtering:** You can easily modify the list of files to be included in a new backup set or restored from an existing set by the date that files were last modified or by file type.

- **Drag and Drop:** You can control how drag-and-drop backup operations are handled. In particular, you can choose to run backup minimized so that you can conveniently back up by dropping a file set on the Backup icon and never see the Backup window at all.

- **Options:** This choice brings up a four-page Settings-Options sheet that enables you to choose between full and differential backups, whether to use data compression, whether to automatically format tapes or erase old files on floppy disks, and other options for Restore and Compare operations. You make your selections simply by selecting radio buttons and checking checkboxes.

Disk Defragmenter

To defragment your hard disk, choose Disk Defragmenter from the System Tools group in the Accessories folder. (You also can choose Run and enter defrag.) A box appears from which you can select the disk to defragment.

> **NOTE**
>
> Disk Defragmenter works with drives compressed by Windows' DriveSpace or DOS' DoubleSpace. It can't, however, defragment disks compressed by third-party disk compressors, such as Stacker. It also doesn't work with network drives, read-only drives, locked drives, FFS drives, and those created with DOS' ASSIGN, JOIN, and SUBST commands.

When you choose a drive, Windows analyzes that drive to determine the extent of fragmentation. If your drive is not badly fragmented, Windows displays its recommendation that defragmentation isn't necessary. (If you disagree, you can click Start to proceed to the next step.) If Windows determines that the disk is fragmented badly enough to benefit from defragmentation, it recommends defragmenting. To start defragmenting with the default defragmentation options, click Start.

To change the options, click Advanced. A box like the one shown in Figure 6.7 appears.

FIGURE 6.7.

Defragmentation options.

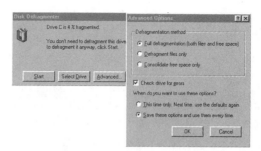

■ Full defragmentation performs both of the choices listed below it. Full is always the best choice but, of course, it takes the longest. If you've got a big hard disk and not enough time for a full defragmentation but you want at least half a tune-up, choose one of the other options that appears below Full defragmentation (described in the following bullets).

■ Defragment files locates any file that is broken up into pieces and moves the pieces together so that the whole file occupies a single, contiguous area on disk, which can speed disk reads and writes to and from existing files. This option defragments files without regard to where the free space is so that, after this option is used, the files are defragmented but the free space may be broken up and spread around the disk.

■ Consolidate free space moves all the data on the disk into one contiguous block so that all the free space occupies one contiguous block as well. This speeds paging operations, improving performance overall when the swapfile comes into play. This option consolidates free space without regard to file fragmentation so that, after this option is used, the free space is consolidated but the files may still be fragmented.

TIP

When you perform a full defragmentation on a badly fragmented disk, the process can take minutes or more than an hour, depending upon the speed and size of your drive and the extent of fragmentation. The process runs quickest when you minimize Disk Defragmenter while defragmenting because, when it's minimized, the utility doesn't use extra resources to show you its progress.

DriveSpace

Like its late, lamented DOS parent DoubleSpace, DriveSpace creates a *compressed drive* on an existing hard disk in your system to increase the amount of data that you can store there. The actual amount of the increase varies but you may be able to nearly double the workable size of a hard disk; for example, you may be able to use a 200MB disk as a 400MB disk.

PERFORMANCE AND COMPRESSION

Because this chapter is about performance and reliability, I have to point out that there is no performance advantage to using DriveSpace, except in one case. To the extent that a disk has little free space, compressing files can make room for a larger Windows swapfile, which will improve your multitasking capabilities and may improve system performance under certain circumstances.

The jury is still out on whether DriveSpace, like its compression predecessors, has a measurable negative impact on performance. Because compression forces your PC to add the extra work of decompressing data before using it and recompressing before writing it to disk, there is always some performance degradation—very slight, in the case of DriveSpace—when compression is used.

Perhaps more important, though, using DriveSpace is really an admission that you've run out of disk space and probably need another hard drive. Before using DriveSpace, make sure that you've already cleaned out old, unnecessary files and applications. If you have files that you never use but still want to keep, back them up to tape or floppy disk and then delete them from your hard disk. You may find that you don't need DriveSpace after all.

If you still need DriveSpace, go to it, but don't use it as an excuse to forget that you have a storage shortage. Compress and then start saving for a bigger hard drive.

DriveSpace creates a new logical disk in a compressed volume file (CVF), which is stored on an uncompressed disk, the *host* drive. The compressed disk has its own drive letter and is seen by Windows and by applications as a separate hard disk. (Typically, DriveSpace renames the uncompressed host drive to drive H and uses the original physical drive letter for the compressed drive.) Because the data stored within the CVF is compressed, the CVF can hold more data than the space it occupies on the host drive. A CVF holding 100 MB of data may take up only 50 MB on the host drive. Note that a compressed drive can't hold more than 512 MB, so to compress more than a few hundred MB, you'll have to create multiple compressed drives on the physical drive.

To use DriveSpace:

1. Choose DriveSpace from the System Tools group in the Accessories folder. From the list that appears, select the drive that you want to compress. Note that you also can create compressed drives on floppy disks to increase the amount of data they can hold. You also can create a "new" compressed drive out of free space on an existing drive.

2. Open the Drive menu and choose Compress. A box appears like the one shown in Figure 6.8.

This box illustrates the effects of the compression using the current default options. To accept the defaults and create the compressed drive, click Start. Windows prompts you to back up your files. If you have not already done so, click Back Up Files to start Microsoft Backup, which is described earlier in this chapter. To create the compressed drive, click Compress Now.

FIGURE 6.8.

Compressing a drive with DriveSpace.

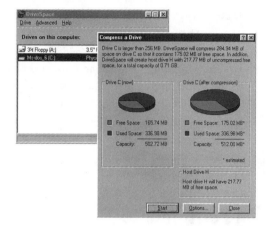

DriveSpace automatically runs ScanDisk (see the "ScanDisk" section that follows) to check the disk for errors. Then it begins compressing, which may take a few minutes or several hours, depending upon the size of your disk and the speed of your system. You can start DriveSpace when you have files open, but as DriveSpace encounters open files, it will pause compression and prompt you to close the files. It's simplest to run DriveSpace by itself when you've no other work to do, while occasionally checking the screen for any prompts or problems.

ScanDisk

ScanDisk checks disk drives for problems and fixes them when it can. It thoroughly tests the integrity of the file allocation table (FAT), filenames (including long filenames), directory trees and file system structure, the physical surface of the disk, and DriveSpace or DoubleSpace files and structure. Use ScanDisk routinely to make sure that errors aren't piling up on a disk, or whenever you suspect a problem. Note that ScanDisk can analyze and repair not only hard disks but also floppies, RAM drives, and memory cards. ScanDisk can't check or fix CD-ROMs, network drives, or drives created with DOS' ASSIGN, JOIN, SUBST, or INTERLNK commands.

To use ScanDisk:

1. Choose ScanDisk from the System Tools group in the Accessories folder. (You also can choose Run and enter scandisk.) From the list that appears, select the drive that you want to scan.

2. Choose a Type of Scan. Standard, the quicker method, checks files and file structures for errors, whereas Thorough checks the file system and the entire physical disk surface (including free space) for flaws. If you run ScanDisk routinely and you know that your disk is in good working order, you can use Standard scanning most of the time and use Thorough once or twice a year to give your disk a good going over.

Under the Advanced button, you can choose from among advanced options related to how ScanDisk reports its findings and how it goes about fixing errors. For example, you can instruct ScanDisk to convert lost file fragments to files (the default), or to Free (delete) them.

If you choose Thorough scan, you can choose from among a few options available when you click the Options button. In general, the defaults are the best choice here. But if you're trying to track down an error and you think you know where it might be encountered (for example, in the data area, or only during reads), you can use these options to save time by restricting the scan to the suspected disk areas or activities.

3. To instruct ScanDisk to automatically repair any disk or file errors it encounters, check the box next to Automatically fix errors. If you don't check this box, ScanDisk reports any errors that it finds and gives you the option to repair or ignore them.

4. Click Start.

CD-ROM Performance

Windows has a separate cache from the disk cache for speeding up CD-ROM access. You can tune the access pattern that Windows uses for the CD-ROM, and the size of the cache, from the File System property sheet shown in Figure 6.9. Open this sheet by choosing File System from the Performance page.

FIGURE 6.9.

*Optimizing your
CD-ROM drive.*

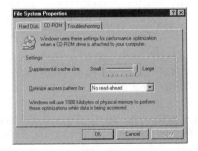

The Supplemental cache size is the amount of system RAM used for the cache. The cache is used only when you're using your CD-ROM drive, so it doesn't affect the RAM available to applications when your CD-ROM drive is idle. The top and bottom values of the slider control change according to the selection that you make in Optimize access pattern…, getting higher as disk speed increases.

In general, the larger the cache, the better your performance. Depending upon the choice you make in Optimize access pattern…, you may allocate up to 1,238 KB for the cache. If you multitask while running CD-ROM applications, or discover problems with your CD-ROM applications related to low memory, reduce the cache size. Also, if your CD-ROM drive produces unusual errors, such as seeming unable to locate files on a CD-ROM, try choosing the next lower speed.

For example, if you experience problems with a triple-speed drive, try choosing Double-speed. The errors that you have encountered may result from the cache anticipating quicker work from the drive than the drive supplies. Note that choosing the slower setting has no effect on your CD-ROM drive's speed; it simply retunes the cache access pattern for a slower drive, which may slightly decrease performance but may also increase reliability.

Graphics Optimization

If you have an accelerated display adapter, Windows 95 typically can exploit all of its acceleration features to squeeze out top performance. If you experience certain types of display-related problems, however, you can selectively "turn off" some acceleration functions, trading some performance for better reliability.

If you encounter display problems or want to check whether Windows is exploiting your graphics hardware, click the Graphics button on the Performance page. A box appears like the one shown in Figure 6.10.

FIGURE 6.10.

Advanced graphics settings.

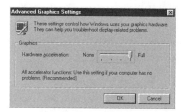

On the slide control, the recommended setting is Full; Windows uses all the graphics acceleration features of your hardware. If necessary, change the setting:

- **Back 1/4:** Most accelerator functions are enabled, but those that may cause mouse pointer problems are disabled.
- **Back 1/2:** Some basic accelerator functions are enabled, but those that may cause other errors, including program errors, are disabled.
- **None:** All accelerator functions are disabled. Graphics hardware will function properly but at greatly decreased performance.

Printing Performance

Printing performance presents a classic example of the maxim, "performance is in the eye of the beholder." As you know, Windows 95 processes and prints documents in the background. When you print any document of reasonable size and complexity, however, you'll still have to wait a few moments while Windows prepares the document for print spooling. When you spool documents to a printer, *performance* can mean either of two things when you choose to print:

1. You return quickly to your application while print processes happen slowly in the background (and overall system performance slows during printing).

2. Your document transfers quickly to the printer while you wait for Windows to return you to your application.

Sorry, you can't have both. When spooling from an application to a printer, Windows prepares the source document in two stages. First, the document is rendered in Enhanced Metafile Format (EMF), a device-independent rendering that can be produced fairly quickly. Next, Windows renders the EMF into the printer-specific language as it "despools" to the printer. You can choose to have the initial EMF rendering and despooling performed together so that, as each page is being despooled to the printer, the next is being rendered into EMF. Or you can choose to have the whole file rendered to EMF and temporarily stored on disk, then slowly despooled to the printer, in the background, after Windows returns you to your application.

Performing the rendering and despooling together cuts overall printing time and uses little disk space but may leave you waiting longer before Windows returns you to your application. Performing the whole EMF rendering first and then despooling returns you to your application quicker but temporarily eats up some disk space (for storage of the prepared print file before spooling), and usually causes printing to take longer overall. Moreover, depending upon the overall performance of your system, you may notice a degradation in overall system performance during background printing.

Of course, you also have the option to avoid spooling altogether and send documents to the printer without spooling. That choice prints the fastest but locks you out of your application until the entire job has been transferred to the printer.

> **TIP**
>
> If you print through a file or print server, you'll usually get better performance if the server is running Windows 95 than if it's a NetWare or Windows NT server. A Windows 95 server can take over the second rendering so that the client PC can simply render to EMF, send the job to the server, and get back to business. Other servers require the client PC to do the whole job of rendering the file in the printer language before sending it to the server.

To choose your own version of performance printing, open the Printers folder in My Computer, right-click the printer, choose Properties, and then click the Spool Settings button. A screen like the one in Figure 6.11 appears.

FIGURE 6.11.

Choosing spool settings for print performance.

To use Windows's background printing, click the radio button next to Spool print job. Then choose one of the following:

- Start printing after last page is spooled (to return to your application more quickly but print more slowly).

- Start printing after first page is spooled (to speed up overall printing but return to your application more slowly).

In general, if your documents are fairly small and don't contain many different fonts or graphics, and if your printer has a large buffer (as many laser printers do), you'll find that you can choose the second option and not be left waiting for your applications to recover.

Of course, some people don't keep working when they print. They send a job to the printer and don't continue working until they've seen the results. These folks may want to try selecting "Print directly to the printer" for fastest printing. This option switches off background printing and won't return you to your application until the whole document has been sent to the printer. Again, if your documents are small and your printer has sufficient memory, this may happen quickly enough to suit you.

SPOOLING DOS PRINT JOBS

If you use DOS apps that print documents, you may want to choose to have Windows 95 spool the jobs along with any Windows 95 application's print jobs to avoid conflict and keep each print job's integrity. The drawback to spooling DOS print jobs, however, is that most DOS apps don't send an end-of-job signal, so Windows 95 ends up waiting for the end signal until the time-out is reached. The result is that Windows 95 waits 45 seconds or so before even processing a DOS print job.

If you print from a DOS app only when no Windows 95 application is using the printer, turning off the spooling of DOS print jobs lets you see the document sooner.

You can edit the length of the time-out in the Details dialog of your printer's properties dialog. Clicking the Port Settings button enables you to select and deselect DOS print spooling.

Tips for Network Performance

Network performance is that unfathomable equation in which the relative speeds of too many parts—network adapters, buses, servers, clients, applications—together define the performance of the whole. True network performance management is beyond the scope of this chapter. Then again, it's also beyond the scope of most books and many network administrators.

Fortunately, Windows 95 self-tunes its network processing in most respects, including network caching, which is automatic and dynamic, just as local disk-caching is. There's little that a user—or a network administrator—needs to do in the way of tuning to ensure good performance. There are some basic hardware/software choices, though, which have a major impact on network performance:

- **32-bit, protected-mode drivers:** Just as these provide the best local-machine performance when used for display and disk access, they also provide the best performance on the network. Windows own protected-mode Microsoft Client for NetWare outperforms other NetWare clients that are supported under Windows 95 but require real-mode operations. The same goes for network adapter drivers and for drivers for server disk drives.

- **Network adapters:** Obviously, faster network adapters improve performance. Consider using multiple adapters in machines that access multiple networks; some integration may be sacrificed, but performance on each of the networks will benefit. Also, use the Network program in Control Panel to disable network adapters that aren't currently in use to improve performance by cutting the number of packets that must be broadcast.

- **Clients and servers:** Make sure that they're tuned and equipped according to the instructions in this chapter. Configure the network so that most of the file and print serving comes from the machines with the most memory and the quickest hard disks.

Maintaining Top Performance

After you've tuned up, stay on top of it. Your PC's snappy performance will deteriorate over time without regular tune-ups. Here are a few final tips.

- Back up, clean out, and defragment your hard disk regularly. This is your best hedge against sluggish disk access and the poor overall performance that results from it.

- Recheck your Performance settings any time you install new hardware or software. Carefully selected settings can be reset to defaults or otherwise altered by some setup routines.

■ When you buy new applications, buy those designed for Windows 95. These will perform and multitask better than Windows 3.1 applications. They also will save Windows the extra effort of consulting .INI files for information that should be in the Registry.

■ When you upgrade hardware, choose what's best for Windows (see "Hardware Selection and Configuration" earlier in this chapter). Consider devices compatible with Windows's Plug and Play features, not simply because they're easier to install but also because Windows automatically tunes them, when possible, for best performance in your system.

Summary

Windows 95 is a much more performance-smart system than Windows 3.1. Many users will never even bother to tune up and, in most cases, they'll experience reasonably good performance and reliable Windows computing.

Those who want to make the most of an investment in hardware and software will find that a little tuning and a few smart habits reward them with responsive, reliable computing. Those who've experienced that rarely go back to their old ways.

Exploiting
Windows 95

Windows 95 has a breadth and depth much larger than any previous version. This section of the book shows you how to exploit the power of Windows 95 on your system.

One of Microsoft's goals in developing Windows 95 was to provide performance equal to or better than Windows 3.x, even on low-end systems, and at the same time expand the capabilities of Windows. Microsoft has largely succeeded in meeting this goal.

The biggest change in Windows 95 is the move to 32-bit code that takes full advantage of the 386/486 processor. A good example of the kinds of improvements in Windows 95 is the file system, which has been totally overhauled in Windows 95.

Gone is the reliance on DOS to provide so basic a service as disk access, which proved over the years to be a major performance bottleneck. Instead, Windows 95 now uses a 32-bit subsystem known as the Installable File System (IFS). Through the IFS architecture, Windows 95 can gain access to files written in almost any structure.

The default file structure for Windows 95 is an updated version of the old DOS File Allocation Table (FAT) that provides support for long filenames, yet still retains a measure of backward compatibility with DOS, enabling you to continue reading all your old floppy disks and to transfer files to folks who haven't yet installed Windows 95.

As you will see in the chapter detailing Windows 95's architecture, other file systems can be installed on your computer for the purpose of reading CD-ROM disks, file formats on network servers, and the like.

There are new and improved subsystems for communications, printing, legacy applications written for DOS and earlier versions of Windows, as well as a host of completely new features.

Improved Device Support

Along with the new 32-bit subsystems, Windows 95 also sports a supporting cast of 32-bit device drivers that run in protected mode, have no conventional memory footprint, and provide improved performance even on older, slower machines with limited memory resources. One of the ways Microsoft has achieved these improvements is by modeling other subsystems after their successful Unidriver architecture first introduced in Windows 3.1.

The basic concept of the Unidriver architecture is to have a single device driver that provides nearly all the code needed for the devices' functionality. Drivers for specific hardware play off the Unidriver, translating instructions to meet the needs of specific hardware. Thus the drivers that must be produced by hardware vendors are usually smaller, don't duplicate functionality with other drivers, and are easier to develop. The benefit to you, the user, is simple: Device drivers are more standardized, less likely to contain bugs, and can be brought to the market more quickly.

Chapter 7, "Windows 95 Device Support—Printer, Comm, Fonts, and Video," will give you the information you need to make the most of your system and its resources.

Registry-Based Configuration

In previous versions of Windows, a great reliance was placed on WIN.INI and SYSTEM.INI to store configuration information. In Windows 95, these files remain strictly for compatibility with applications that are unaware of the new Registry. The Registry is a hierarchical database of configuration information that can be accessed by Windows 95 and applications alike; it replaces the old Windows 3.x registration database. Unlike the Windows 3.x registration database, which was used primarily for registering OLE and DDE functionality of applications, the Registry maintains almost every setting that affects your system's configuration.

In the Windows 95 Registry, which is very similar to the Registry found in Windows NT, not only are OLE functions registered, but so is just about everything else about an application including its default icon. By concentrating all of the configuration information in a single repository, INI files are made all but obsolete, even for applications, and the information once stored in Program Manager group (.GRP) files is consolidated. Under the new system, applications can place entries in the registry specific to the application.

Application Support

Windows 95 supports three distinct classes of software applications: 32-bit applications, 16-bit applications designed for previous versions of Windows, and applications written for DOS. Despite the fact that DOS development is all but dead, support for DOS applications is better than ever in Windows 95.

Applications created with 32-bit development tools run faster, use preemptive multitasking, are better isolated from one another, and can multithread. 32-bit applications run faster because they can perform more work per clock tick than Win16 (programs written for Windows 3.x) applications. Also, 32-bit apps are each given their own address space and message queue, so they are better isolated from ill-behaved applications that might otherwise crash other running programs. When running 32-bit applications, the new multitasking code in Windows 95 is able to preempt applications, meaning that Windows 95 assigns just so much processor time and then switches to something else. This model is in stark contrast to Win16 applications that rely on an application notifying Windows 3.x that they are willing to yield to another program. As icing on the cake, 32-bit applications are able to spawn multiple threads, meaning that an application can have more than one process running at the same time.

Your old 16-bit (Win16) applications run similarly to the way they always have. All running Win16 applications share a single address space and a common message queue, and cooperatively multitask, just as they did in Windows 3.x. A special layer of code, called the *thunk layer*, enables Win16 applications to make use of the 32-bit subsystems in Windows 95, so they gain a performance edge from the environment they are running under—Windows 95. The thunk layer thunks (translates) 16-bit parameters into 32-bit parameters, Windows 95 acts on the request for service, and then thunks the resulting codes back into 16-bit format. As you will see in Chapter 9, "The Architecture of Windows 95," the Windows 95 Architecture chapter, there are some 16-bit services that remain in Windows 95, but for the most part your old Windows applications will run even better in the new version.

In the years since the introduction of DOS, way back in 1981, hundreds of thousands (if not millions) of DOS applications have been written. With very few exceptions, all of them will run under Windows 95. There is a common misconception that Windows 95 no longer does DOS, but the truth is that Windows 95 does DOS better than DOS ever did. While it is true that Windows 95 doesn't rely on DOS for operating system services, as it did in previous versions, there is still a copy of DOS floating around inside Windows 95 to provide support for real-mode device drivers, and to support the running of DOS applications. Among the improvements to DOS support are better windowing (including a toolbar in DOS) apps, better graphics support, and better memory management. For those applications that just flat refuse to cooperate with Windows 95, there is a special MS-DOS mode where Windows almost completely vacates memory, leaving just enough of itself in memory to restart—so an unruly DOS application can hog the whole machine.

Find out how Windows 95 supports software applications in Chapter 10, "Application Support in Windows 95."

The Windows 95 Architecture

Windows 95 retains the best features of Windows 3.1 and borrows the best of Windows NT to bring you a full 32-bit operating system that provides long filename support, preemptive multitasking, multithreading, and full protected-mode operation. The new user interface aside, the feel of Windows 95 is very different from earlier versions. Windows 95 is snappier and much more agile. You can finally format a floppy, download a large file, print a hundred pages, and play Solitaire all at the same time—and still feel like your system is peppy and responsive. The difference is that the core of Windows 95 is a full, 32-bit, protected-mode operating system that doesn't have to switch back and forth between real mode and protected mode.

Changes to the architecture of subsystems such as the multitasker, the printing and communications subsystems, and refinements to the video subsystem all play a role. Of course, Windows 95 won't scream along on a 386SX with 4 MB of RAM (what will?), but if you have a reasonably fast 486 with 8–16 MB of RAM and a decent video card, you should see a noticeable improvement in performance. Chapter 9 will tell you why.

The Rest of the Story

Other chapters in this section deal with specific aspects of exploiting the power of Windows 95. Chapter 14, "Microsoft Plus! for Windows 95" tells you about Microsoft's add-on product for Windows 95 that includes among its features font smoothing for better type, improved disk compression in the form of DriveSpace 3, system agents that schedule regular housekeeping chores to keep your system fine-tuned, and a host of other features that expand the capabilities of Windows 95.

Chapter 13, "Family Computing," gives you the information you need to involve your whole family in using your home computer. This chapter covers both productivity software such as Works and Bob, as well as educational and entertainment titles such as Encarta 95 and Gus Goes to Cybertown.

You will see how to take Windows 95 on the road in Chapter 11, "Mobile Computing." In this chapter, you will learn how to keep your notebook files current with your desk-based hard disk, keep e-mail and communications manageable with Exchange, and take advantage of Windows 95's battery power management and hot docking capabilities.

In Chapter 12, "OLE," you will see how to use Windows applications to create compound documents that bring tools and data from one application to another, even though they may be thousands of miles distant from one another.

In short, this section of the book is a fount of information that will enable you to get the most from Windows 95. So curl up, enjoy, and have a good read.

Windows 95 Device Support—Printer, Comm, Fonts, and Video

7

by Ed Tiley

IN THIS CHAPTER

The job of an operating system like Windows 95 is to bring together all the disparate devices attached to your computer and make them function together as a system. Despite the fact that no two devices in your computer come from the same factory, Windows 95 provides the glue that binds them together to create a working computer system.

In this chapter you will learn how Windows 95's device support integrates and attaches disk drives, communications ports, modems, printers, and other devices into a working system, and how the architecture of Windows 95 supports various classes of devices. You will also see in this chapter how Windows 95 provides various fonts to support printers and display devices.

Windows 95 Devices

When speaking of the devices managed by Windows 95, most people automatically think of hardware such as modems, video cards, and so on. Not all Windows 95 devices involve user-installed hardware, however. There are a number of system devices used by Windows 95 that are set up during startup. Examples include the CMOS/Real Time Clock, times, interrupts, the system board, and the direct memory access controller. Although these devices seldom give users any trouble, once in a great while you may be called upon to make some small adjustment or check on one of the system devices to see if there is a conflict with other hardware.

Well over 95 percent of the time, the term *device* indeed refers to hardware. There are three main categories of device that Windows 95 manages. Take a moment to consider each type:

    Legacy devices

    Plug and Play devices

    PCMCIA devices

The term *legacy device* is a catch-all that refers to printers, modems, video cards, hard disk controllers, keyboards, network interface cards, and so on, designed or manufactured before Plug and Play standards were adopted. In all likelihood, your computer itself is a legacy device unless it is very new, because it probably doesn't contain a Plug and Play BIOS.

Legacy devices often utilize DIP switches and jumper blocks to change settings, so you can have a difficult time getting them to work correctly. You usually adjust the settings for port addresses, IRQ, and DMA by configuring switches and jumpers to conform with default settings, and then installing drivers that are aware of those settings. Problems can occur when two cards want to use conflicting settings.

Plug and Play devices have no true default values. The Plug and Play standard says that devices must be self-aware and configurable through software. You simply plug the card into the system and let Windows 95 survey the installed hardware. Based on what Windows 95 finds, it will arbitrate between the devices and assign non-conflicting values to each.

PCMCIA devices present their own set of problems. The PCMCIA standard, used mostly in notebooks and other mobile computers, enables hot docking of cards without rebooting the system. Not only does Windows 95 have to configure the hardware on the fly, it also has to load and unload device drivers in memory.

Device Drivers

To some, the term *device driver* is very foreign and somehow scary. Device drivers, especially poorly written ones, can be a real pain to deal with, but their concept is simple.

Figure 7.1 shows a simplified view of how devices, device drivers, and Windows 95 all fit together. Every hardware device that is manufactured performs a specific type of operation in your system: printers print, video cards render the screens, and comm ports communicate with other devices.

FIGURE 7.1.

A simplified view of device support in Windows 95.

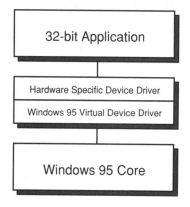

Life would be simple if every modem worked exactly the same as every other modem ever manufactured. Microsoft could include a single device driver to interface all modems, and this chapter would be unnecessary. Life, however, isn't simple. In the race to win the hearts and minds of the computer-buying public, manufacturers are constantly adding new features to their hardware.

What is needed then, is a program to control the hardware and make it conform to the standards required by the operating system. That is the purpose of a device driver. As you can see in Figure 7.1, the interface between Windows 95 and the hardware is a device driver layer that includes both a driver that is specific to the hardware and a virtual device driver that provides the layer with which the Windows 95 operating system interacts. This arrangement is typical, even though it is simplified.

Windows 3.1 used what are sometimes called monolithic device drivers, which handled everything having to do with a specific device. In Windows 95 the architecture is built around the idea of having a universal driver for a device type and a minidriver to provide device-specific code for hardware.

Under this scheme, the universal driver (unidriver) contains most of the programming needed to use a particular type of device, such as printers, modems, video cards, and so on. It is the universal driver that the operating system interfaces with. Minidrivers are usually provided by hardware manufacturers, and contain any additional programming necessary to operate the device. As you might imagine, the minidriver usually remains quite small because all it has to do is fill in the blanks, so to speak, leaving it up to the unidriver to contain the code to operate the most common standards for the device type. Thus, the communications unidriver contains all the code needed to operate modems that use the standard Hayes AT commands.

The Device Manager

If you double-click System in Control Panel or right-click My Computer and select Properties from the context menu, you will see a dialog similar to the one shown in Figure 7.2.

FIGURE 7.2.

The Device Manager is the place to go to view and edit device settings.

Each device listed has its own property sheet. As you can see in Figure 7.2, you can expand major categories of devices by clicking the plus sign icon. Each of the entries in a category, not the category itself, has a property sheet that contains information specific to the device.

For example, Figure 7.3 shows the Properties dialog generated when display adapter property settings are selected. The General tab of the dialog tells you what driver is installed, what the working status of the device is, and what hardware profiles use the device. Hardware profiles enable the same system to have multiple hardware configurations. For example, a docking station computer system usually leaves behind network cards, scanners, tape backup units, and the like when it is undocked for travel. Using multiple profiles enables Windows 95 to properly configure the system, and avoid loading unnecessary drivers into memory, when the system is undocked.

FIGURE 7.3.

The General tab provides overall information about the device and its working status.

When you click the Driver tab a dialog similar to the one shown in Figure 7.4 appears. In this dialog, the names of the driver files that are loaded for the device are listed. A single device may make use of several driver files, which divide the code for handling the device between drivers supplied by the manufacturer of the device and Microsoft supplied drivers. The information displayed in this dialog helps you to figure out what drivers are used for your hardware, and whether they are the latest versions. As you highlight each driver filename, information about the origin of the driver is listed. If you click the Change Driver button, the Select Device dialog shown is revealed.

FIGURE 7.4.

The Select Device dialog enables you to change the drivers used for hardware in your system.

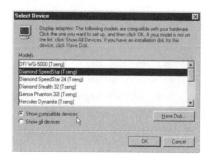

At the bottom of the Select Driver dialog are two radio buttons that change the view from all devices in the class, or just compatible devices. You shouldn't try to change drivers, even in the compatible category unless you know exactly what you are doing, have loads of life insurance, or a darned good backup with spare time on your hands. If you install incompatible drivers, or even semi-compatible drivers, you may render a device unworkable. Before changing drivers, make sure that the new drivers are compatible with the hardware.

Of course, different devices have different functions, so the properties of each device type will vary accordingly, and those differences are reflected in the varied property dialogs you will find when you go exploring. Almost all devices, however, have a Resources tab in their Properties dialog. Figure 7.5 shows you a typical Resources dialog.

FIGURE 7.5.

The Resources dialog enables you to inspect and adjust settings for memory addresses, IRQ, and the like.

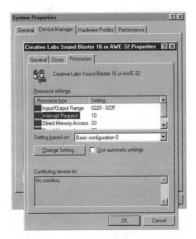

CAUTION

Do not change resource settings in the Device Manager unless you are an advanced user or have been instructed to do so by a support technician. Changing settings can create conflicts with other devices, which may prevent your system from operating properly.

In addition, if you have Plug and Play devices, changing settings for P&P devices limits the options that Windows 95 has in arbitrating settings among devices. By manually entering a value for a device, you lock that device into those settings. Later, if you add another device, Windows 95 may have problems setting up the new device because it is blocked from changing manually entered settings even though they conflict with settings needed by another device.

Hardware Profiles

In addition to the General and Device Manager tabs, the System Properties dialog has two other tabs. The Hardware Profiles tab is intended primarily for those users who have docking station-type systems where there is a disparity between what devices the system has access to when docked versus what devices are available when the system is undocked and on the road. Quite often, the cards for network interface, scanners, video capture boards, and so on are left behind when the system is undocked.

To avoid errors that might occur when Windows 95 tries to load drivers for hardware that isn't present, and to avoid using memory on absent devices, you can create a second device profile to be used when you are on the road.

> **NOTE**
>
> Multiple profiles are unnecessary when your system is Plug and Play-compatible. The P&P BIOS is able to detect when the system is docked and when it is not.

Like everything else in Windows 95, information about device management and multiple configurations resides in the Registry. The Registry divides information into units called keys. These keys are names that can be searched by Windows 95 at runtime for information about the system, user configuration, and so on. For those readers keeping a box score, multiple configurations are found associated with the Hkey_Local_Machine group of Registry entries. The Hkey_Local_MachineConfig key contains information about multiple users of the system, as well as multiple device configurations.

Windows 95 tries to automatically detect when hardware is added or removed from the system. The time spent scanning the system is part of those few moments during boot-up when nothing seems to be happening. Auto-detection is performed on both P&P devices, but also on legacy devices. When booting a docking system, if Windows 95 finds a new hardware configuration at startup, you will be prompted to enter a new name for that configuration. If you give a name, that configuration will be added to the Registry's configuration mapping table. Each configuration has a unique ID.

One of three results can be obtained when Windows 95 performs the hardware auto-detection routine:

- The proper unique configuration ID is found and automatically selected.
- If the system is being started for the first time in a new hardware configuration, a new configuration is created and added to the Registry. This occurs, for example, the first time you boot an undocked system.
- If Windows 95 cannot properly detect which configuration is correct, you are asked to choose the appropriate one.

Performance

The Performance tab of the System Properties dialog enables you to change settings for the file system, graphics, and virtual memory.

Device Support in Windows 95

Windows 95 sports improved device support architecture over previous versions of Windows. The three most notable examples are the subsystems and device drivers that control communications, printing, and video display. In the next few sections, each of these subsystems is covered in detail.

Communications

The refinements and improvements to the communications subsystem of Windows 95 would probably win the "Most Improved" award, if such awards were given. Among the improvements are

32-bit Communications Subsystem: The Windows 95 communications subsystem is full 32-bit code. When compared to Windows 3.x, Windows 95 communicates faster, supports multiple threads, and takes advantage of preemptive multitasking.

UniModem Driver: By changing the communications subsystem architecture to use a single universal driver (Unidriver) called UniModem, which is similar to the Windows 3.x printer unidriver, you need to set up the modem only one time. Any Windows 95-compliant program can then use the modem without requiring modem-specific setup.

TAPI Support: TAPI (Telephony Application Programming Interface) provides a standardized way of controlling any kind of telephone interaction. TAPI also arbitrates conflicts between applications requesting use of communications ports, modems, and so on.

MAPI Support: MAPI (Messaging Application Programming Interface) provides a standardized way of controlling the flow of messages such as LAN-based e-mail (Microsoft Mail, Internet, and so on), online e-mail services (Compuserve, MSN, and so on), faxes, and other remote messaging.

Better UART Support: Windows 95 supports the 16550A UART (Universal Asynchronous Receiver/Transmitter) chip, as well as the older 8250s. UART chips are the part of your computer's COM port that actually does the communicating between the CPU and whatever is attached to your COM port.

> **TIP**
>
> Upgrading your comm ports to the 16550 chip will dramatically improve Windows 95's capability to multitask while heavy communications are in progress.
>
> The advantage to using the 16550 chip is that it employs a larger buffer and is faster than the older 8250s. The result is that the system is better able to multitask other applications because it can reduce the amount of CPU time dedicated to communications.
>
> Depending on the hardware configuration of your machine, UART chips may be found on the motherboard, if your system supplied the comm ports, or on the card that adds the comm port to your system. Many systems use multiple I/O cards that combine comm ports, printer ports, hard disk controller, and floppy disk controller circuits on a single card. Internal modems supply UART chips on their card.

Enhanced Communications Capabilities: Windows 95 contains the support necessary for communications devices that transmit at speeds far greater than conventional RS-232 COM ports. For example, ISDN vendors can supply you with drivers that enable communication speeds ranging from 64 to 128 kilobits per second. TCP/IP and improved networking protocol support expand the available options for, and the speed of, LAN-based communication.

Support for the Future: Windows 95 already has support in the communications subsystem for Voice View modems (you'll see one soon) that enable people to talk to one another on the same line they are using to exchange files. Windows 95 also supports Enhanced Capabilities Ports (ECP) that will one day support parallel modems to achieve much higher baud rates than can be achieved using a serial port.

The Architecture of Windows 95 Communications

Figure 7.6 shows a view of the basic Windows 95 Communications Subsystem. As you can see, the architecture is constructed as software layers between the application that wants to use the device and the hardware that performs communications tasks.

As you can see Figure 7.6, there is a difference between the way 32-bit applications and 16-bit applications behave. 32-bit applications address the TAPI and COMM API layers. These drivers provide functions that applications can call to have communications services provided for them.

One of the duties of the TAPI layer is to arbitrate among running threads that want to use COM ports and modems. For example, while Dial Up Networking is waiting for a call, you can send an outgoing fax without first unloading the Dial Up software. If two applications want to use the modem at the same time, the second one in line is told to wait, which causes the application to present you with a message box informing you that the device is busy.

FIGURE 7.6.

The architecture of Windows 95 communications.

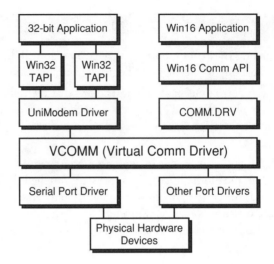

The TAPI and COMM layers, in turn, make calls to the UniModem driver, which is responsible for generating commands to modems. UniModem is a universal driver, meaning that it includes most of the programming code necessary for controlling standard modems. UniModem works with all modems that use the Hayes-compatible AT command set.

As you can see, 16-bit applications take a different execution path because they are unable to utilize the new architecture. How could they? The architecture didn't exist when the applications were written. Communications software written for Windows 3.x relies on being able to find the Win16 API to request services, and also expects to find COMM.DRV. COMM.DRV provides the same functionality as the Windows 3.x driver of the same name.

Both 32-bit and 16-bit applications eventually end up having their service requests processed by VCOMM, the virtual communications driver. VCOMM provides protected-mode support for high-speed data ports, as well as conventional RS-232 serial ports (COM ports). VCOMM can support up to 128 serial ports.

The last layer of software between the application and the hardware are device-specific drivers for modems and COM ports. It is the job of these minidrivers to accommodate any quirks or incompatibilities between standard Windows 95 communications support and a specific piece of hardware.

Installing a Modem Minidriver

Usually, Windows 95 Setup will detect a modem attached to your system and run the Install New Modem Wizard as part of setting up Windows 95 to run on your system. If you need to change modems or you acquire a modem after Setup is finished, you can easily run the Modem Installation Wizard by double-clicking Modems in the Control Panel. You can also get to the modem wizard using Add/Remove Hardware, but doing so takes longer. You will also activate the wizard if you try to run a program that attempts to initialize a modem that doesn't exist. Inserting a PCMCIA modem card into a portable system will also invoke the wizard.

Figure 7.7 shows the Install New Modem wizard in action. A checkbox in the opening screen of the wizard enables you to bypass automatic detection if you know exactly what kind of modem is installed on your system. Especially when you are dealing with internal modems, which are installed in a slot and usually hidden from view, allowing Windows 95 to auto-detect the type of modem is advisable, unless you actually like taking the cover off of computers.

FIGURE 7.7.

The Install New Modem wizard scans your system for a modem automatically, or lets you manually specify the modem type.

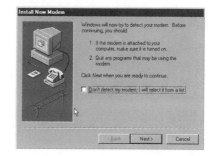

Figure 7.8 shows the wizard's appearance while it is auto-detecting the modem. The wizard first scans COM ports to look for a modem. After it finds a modem, it tries to figure out what kind of modem is installed. The wizard is usually able to read the signature burned onto the chips in the modem in order to find out what modem is installed.

FIGURE 7.8.

The wizard's auto-detect mode scans ports for modems, and then scans the modem it finds to figure out what type it is.

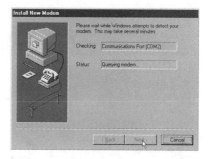

Occasionally, the wizard is unsuccessful in detecting the type of modem, or wrongly detects the modem as a different unit. If the modem has been detected properly, click the Next button to finish installation. If, for some reason, the modem you have isn't properly detected, you can click the change button to specify a different modem. You will then be asked to select a manufacturer and then select a model from the manufacturer's list. If you have a disk with a Windows 95 driver on it, you will be able to click the Have Disk button and install the modem from that disk.

Modem Properties

After the wizard has identified the proper modem, all that remains is to check out, and alter if necessary, is the Modem Properties. This dialog, shown in Figure 7.9, appears just after the Install New Modem wizard closes.

FIGURE 7.9.

Most of the time the modem's properties are automatically set for optimum performance without user intervention.

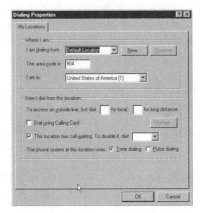

Most of the time the modem's properties are set for optimum performance, but you will need to make sure the Dialing Properties conform to your locale. The second window in Figure 7.9 shows the settings you can make in this dialog. These settings can be customized for several different dialing locations. You can set the modem driver to properly dial out using a PBX exchange that requires you to dial 9 for an outside line, and also lets you disable call-waiting services when your local phone company provides an access code to dial.

> **TIP**
>
> The settings for Modem Properties can also be reached using the Device Manager, so there is no need to reinstall the modem to change these settings.

Windows 95 Printer Support

The Windows 3.1 Printer Subsystem was the first major Windows subsystem to utilize the Unidriver architecture that has been adopted for other subsystems in Windows 95. The Unidriver concept has the advantage of providing system-wide setup, meaning that individual applications can just send print jobs to Windows 95 without knowing what kind of printer the job is being sent to.

There are a number of improvements to the Windows 95 Printer subsystem. Here's a quick rundown:

32-bit Code: Because the Windows 95 Printing subsystem has been rewritten in 32-bit, it is faster, runs better in the background, and is compatible with the Windows NT Printing subsystem. Support is included for printers capable of bi-directional communications, so you get more information about what is going on with the job than just an offline message when there is a problem. The printer can inform you of when it jams, runs out of toner, or has some other problem finishing the job.

Enhanced Metafile Support: The way Windows printing works is relatively simple. The printing application makes calls to the Graphic Device Interface (GDI), one of the core components of Windows 95, to prepare the print job as an Enhanced Metafile, which is then spooled out to disk. During this process, printing is done in the foreground. After the job is spooled, control is returned to the user and the rest of the printing process occurs in the background. The EMF is translated into the commands necessary for the printer to render the pages, and the job is printed. Using this method enables Windows 95 applications to regain control much quicker than under previous versions.

Better DOS Support: Under Windows 95, DOS print jobs can be placed into the spool alongside Windows application print jobs. The result is better conflict resolution when multiple programs are trying to print.

Point and Print Support: Point and Print means that you can install remote printers on your system as easily as you might connect to them. This hands-free installation can be done with printers on other Windows 95 machines using peer-to-peer networking, and also with printers on Windows NT and Novell NetWare networks.

NetWare PSERVER Support: Systems running Windows 95 can load PSERVER, a utility that enables the Windows 95 system to receive spooled print jobs from other workstations.

Image Color Matching (ICM): ICM is a new standard that better matches colors seen on-screen with colors generated by color printers, thus expanding the scope of WYSIWYG (What-You-See-Is-What-You-Get).

Deferred Printing: What do you do when you're away from your desk and printer? With Windows 95 Deferred Printing, you can spool print jobs to the hard drive to be printed when you get near a printer again.

Extended Capabilities Port Support: The Parallel Extended Capabilities Port standard, discussed briefly in the section on communications earlier in this chapter, also has printing ramifications because ECP provides higher performance for all kinds of I/O, including very fast printers capable of communicating with the operating system.

No Penalty for Having Lots of TrueType Fonts: In Windows 3.1, each registered TrueType font loaded a small program into memory in order to make the font available to the system. Windows 95 changes that by storing font installations in the Registry. Memory resources are conserved, and you pay no penalty for installing a large number of fonts, other than the hard disk space used to store them.

234

You will find that printing is easier and quicker than ever before. The Windows 3.*x* Print Manager is gone. In its place is a more tightly integrated 32-bit spooler that handles multiple print destinations as easily as it does the local printer.

> **NOTE**
>
> There is a difference in fonts distributed on the disk builds of Windows 95 versus the CD-ROM version, which contains fonts that provide about 650 characters to provide European language support.

The Architecture of Windows 95 Printing

Figure 7.10 show a diagram of the architecture of the Windows 95 Printing Subsystem. As you can see, applications that want to get to the printer go through the Graphic Device Interface (GDI) to get to the printer. GDI is part of the Windows 95 API that provides services to applications. The job of the GDI layer is to render graphics for the screen, the printer, and any other device that needs graphical manipulation.

FIGURE 7.10.

The Printing Subsystem is a software layer that lets applications hand a print job to Windows 95 and forget it.

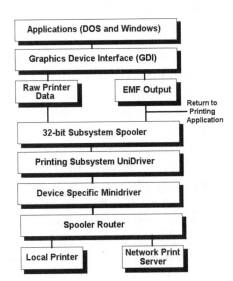

Perhaps the biggest change in the Windows 95 Printing subsystem is the use of EMF spooling for all print jobs, except those destined for PostScript printers. The Enhanced Metafile format stores the commands necessary to draw the page, using the GDI. In effect, the EMF is a device-independent page description language. In PostScript, there is no need for the EMF because the output is sent to the printer uncooked.

The two best-known and widely used page description languages are PostScript and Hewlett Packard Page Control Language (HPPCL). A page description language is really a very specialized programming language designed to turn graphic images into printed images. Page description languages consist of commands and functions that tell the printer's engine where to put ink (toner). The differences between PostScript and HPPCL are great.

PostScript printers receive print jobs as a text file of instructions on how to print the page. The printer's engine executes the commands to form the printed page. The HP method of doing things is to have the printer driver convert the print job into the printer engine's native commands, thus offloading most of the intensive computing work to the system instead of the printer. Both methods are valid and successful.

If a print job is destined for a PostScript printer, the print job is created as raw printer data (PS commands) and forwarded to the spooler to be sent to the printer as a text file for the printer to interpret. All other print jobs are created as an EMF file. After the EMF file is created, the file is sent to the spooler and control is returned to the application, which means the user can go back to work.

After the EMF version of the print job is in the spooler, it can be extracted by the Unidriver and converted to the page description language used by the printer. The print job is then routed to the target printer.

Universal Printer Driver

The printing Unidriver shipped with Windows 95 includes support for a number of page description languages including HPPCL, Epson ESC P/2, Canon CaPSL, Lexmark PPDS, monochrome HP GL/2, as well as support for interfacing with older dot matrix printers. PostScript is handled with a Microsoft-supplied minidriver.

The Unidriver supports use of printer resident Intellifont fonts, as well as resident TrueType fonts, including downloading TrueType outline fonts to PCL printers that have TrueType rasterizers. Support for 600 dots-per-inch and expandability to higher resolutions is built into the Unidriver.

Bidirectional Communications with Printers

A new generation of printers is much more able to communicate with the operating system and individual applications. In much the same way that multimedia applications can query devices to determine their capabilities, printers that conform to the IEEE 1284 standard can be queried about available memory, installed fonts, duplexing, and other capabilities. This enables applications to more easily identify printer models and to take advantage of all of the printer's functionality.

Additionally, printers can send detailed messages back to the operating system in real time to let users know that the paper is out, toner is low, or some other condition.

Installing and Uninstalling Printers

Windows 95 Setup creates a system folder named Printers on the same drive on which Windows 95 itself is installed. You can easily open this folder from the Settings item in the Start Menu, from the Printers object in Control Panel, or by using Explorer. Figure 7.11 shows this folder after the Add Printer Wizard has been launched. As you can see, more than one printer can be installed. Several applications, such as WinFax Pro (seen in the Printers folder) install themselves as alternate printers.

FIGURE 7.11.

The Printers folder after the Add Printer Wizard has been launched.

TIP

Many applications support drag-and-drop printing, which enables you to drag a file to be printed onto the printer object's icon and drop it. This will launch the application that created the file, and the file is sent to the printer automatically.

To make drag-and-drop printing easier, you might consider placing a shortcut to your printer(s) onto the desktop where you can easily drop a file to be printed.

The Install wizard, in its second screen (shown in Figure 7.12), lets you choose the printer you want to install. Select the manufacturer in the left pane, and the specific model in the right pane. If you have a manufacturer supplied driver disk, you can click the Have Disk button to install from the disk.

When you click the Next button, the wizard asks you to select a port where the printer is attached. (See Figure 7.13.) Note that one of the choices is FILE. This selection enables you to send printer output to a file instead of to a physical printer. The file can then be printed later simply by copying the file to PRN, the generic device name for a local printer. You can also use the drag and drop method to print files generated by the driver.

FIGURE 7.12.

The Add Printer Wizard makes installing printers simple and easy.

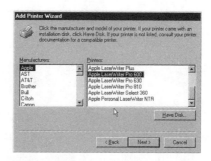

FIGURE 7.13.

You can add multiple installations of your printer, customizing each installation for specific purposes.

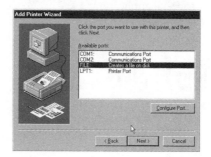

You have the ability to create multiple installations of the same printer driver in order to customize them for particular purposes, such as printing to file. You can also install printers you do not have physically attached to your system.

One interesting use for this would be installing a PostScript printer like the Apple LaserWriter, which is a generic PS implementation. Because PostScript printers work from a file of commands rather than device-specific commands, you can create output that can be printed on any PostScript printer, regardless of resolution. This means, for example, that you could create a poster or flyer in CorelDRAW! and print the image to file using a PostScript printer driver.

You can then take the resulting file to your local print shop or service bureau where they can feed the job to a high-resolution output device such as a Linotronic. Some of these professional devices have the capability to produce output at resolutions greater than 2,000 dots per inch. In this way you can use PostScript to create high-quality output suitable for even the most demanding print standards without the expense of buying a second printer.

Figure 7.14 shows two interesting things. First, note that the icon for the newly installed printer shows that its output will be directed to disk. Second, by right-clicking the printer object and selecting Properties from the context menu, you can easily customize the settings for any installed printer.

FIGURE 7.14.

You can easily customize your printer settings by right-clicking objects in your Printers system folder.

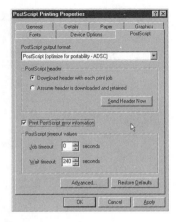

Uninstalling Printers

Right-clicking the objects in your Printers system folder is also the way to uninstall printer drivers. Just select the Delete item from the context menu and answer Yes to the confirmation message, and the printer is removed from your installation.

If any files were copied to your system during installation that are not used by any other installed printers, you will see a message box asking if these files should be deleted. If you plan to reinstall the printer at a future date, you may want to leave the files intact to make reinstallation a bit faster. However, if you do not intend to reinstall the printer, answering Yes reclaims disk space.

> **TIP**
>
> If you have a printer set to create files instead of directly printing documents, you may want to create an entry in your SendTo folder to accommodate copying files directly to the printer. Here's the way to do it:
>
> In a folder that is on your PATH, create a DOS batch file called COPYFILETOPRN.BAT, and add the single line COPY %1 PRN.
>
> Open your SendTo folder (if it is hidden, just type SendTo in the RUN box) and Copy a shortcut to the batch file into the SendTo folder.
>
> Rename the shortcut "PRN (Printer)" to be consistent with the SendTo floppy disk entries.
>
> Right-click and choose Properties. Edit the shortcut's properties by selecting Close on Exit, and choose to Run Minimized.
>
> Now all you have to do to send a file directly to a printer is right-click the file and select PRN from the SendTo option.

Windows 95 and Fonts

When TrueType fonts were introduced to Windows in Version 3.1, the type world literally changed overnight. Previously, fonts were rendered as files full of bitmaps called soft fonts that had to be downloaded to the printer. Each variation on the font needed to be in its own file. If you wanted Times Roman in 8, 10, 12, and 18 points, you had to install four files. To have bold, italic, regular, and bold italic in each point size you were up to 16 files, and that didn't cover the screen font files needed to render Times Roman on-screen. Windows 95 still contains support for soft fonts (and others, as you will see), but TrueType reigns as the most versatile type format in Windows because TrueType fonts are device independent, meaning that the same font file serves both screen display and printing.

> **WIZARD NOTE**
>
> The art of typography divides fonts into three styles: serif, sanserif, and decorative. Serif typefaces are formed so that the letters rest on little flourishes that appear to be pedestals. Serif typefaces are derived from Greek and Roman carvings of letters. Sanserif typefaces have straight lines at the bottom and do not flair out into pedestals. Arial is a the classic example of sanserif. Decorative typefaces include script letterforms and special purpose type meant for headings that exaggerate the forms of letters to evoke an emotion or a mood.

How TrueType Works

TrueType fonts are scaleable and resolution independent because they are not bitmaps of letter shapes. The problem with using bitmap-based fonts is that most devices have their own resolution. For example, letters on a VGA screen are 96 pixels by 96 pixels, but most laser printers use 300 by 300, not even a multiple of 96.

Instead of bitmaps stored in files, TrueType fonts are mathematical formulas for a collection of points and hints. *Points* form a basic outline for the letter. *Hints* are equations that alter the outline to give its best look at a specified resolution.

When an application uses a TrueType font for the first time in a session, Windows 95 opens the font. As the user types, letters are rendered as bitmaps and placed into memory in a font cache. If the letter has been rendered previously, it can simply be read from memory; it doesn't have to be rendered again.

Because TrueType fonts are scaleable outlines, they appear the same on both screens and the printed page. This capability to look the same in different resolutions is sometimes referred to as WYSIWYG (pronounced WhizzyWig) and stands for What-You-See-Is-What-You-Get.

240

A starter set of TrueType fonts is included with Windows 95. Table 7.1 shows the fonts that are installed by Windows 95.

Table 7.1. Supplied TrueType font files in Windows 95.

Font name	Normal	Bold	Bold/Italic	Italic
Arial	ARIAL.TTF	ARIALBD.TTF	ARIALBI.TTF	ARIALI.TTF
Courier New	COUR.TTF	COURBD.TTF	COURBI.TTF	COURI.TTF
Times New Roman	TIMES.TTF	TIMESBD.TTF	TIMESBI.TTF	TIMESI.TTF
Symbol	SYMBOL.TTF			
Wingding	WINGDING.TTF			

Viewing and Installing TrueType Fonts

In Windows 95, TrueType fonts are installed in a special folder, WINDOWS\FONTS. You can use Explorer to gain access to this folder, or double-click the shortcut to this folder in Control Panel.

The Control Panel launches a single pane view of the folder, shown in Figure 7.15. Each of the font files is listed. To view a font, all you need to do is double-click a font object in the window. As you can see in the figure, the font is opened, and type samples are displayed.

FIGURE 7.15.

Double-clicking a TrueType font will cause font samples to be displayed in a window.

Choosing Install New fonts from the File menu of the Fonts folder will bring up the Add Fonts dialog shown in Figure 7.16. Here you can specify the location and names of TrueType fonts you want to install.

Note the checkbox labeled Copy fonts to Windows folder at the bottom of the Add Fonts window. When this checkbox is selected, the font files are copied to the WINDOWS\FONTS folder. When the checkbox is unselected, a shortcut to the original copy is placed in the Fonts folder. Using the shortcut method enables you to place your font files in a folder on another drive with more room when your Windows drive is cramped for free space.

FIGURE 7.16.

The Add Fonts dialog box lets you select the TrueType fonts you want to install.

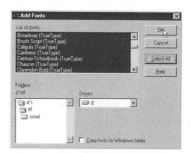

TIP

In earlier versions of Windows, FOT files were constructed in the WINDOWS\SYSTEM folder to correspond with each installed TrueType font. At startup, these FOT files, containing information about the font, were loaded in order to make the actual TrueType fonts, stored in TTF files, available.

Under Windows 95, however, all that changes because the installation of TrueType fonts is done in the Registry. Thus, there is no memory use or performance penalty to be paid for having lots of TrueType fonts installed. TrueType fonts are loaded into memory only when they are used in an application.

To remove fonts from your Windows 95 installation, simply delete them from the system folder as you would any other file.

Other Fonts in Windows 95

Not every situation can be handled with TrueType fonts. Two other font types are supported in Windows 95 to handle these special cases.

Raster Fonts

Raster fonts are files containing bitmaps of letters. Examples of raster fonts include HP Downloadable Soft Fonts and Adobe Type Manager Type 1 fonts. Soft fonts were used in versions of Windows previous to Windows 3.1 to provide typeset quality fonts with HP LaserJets and compatibles. Adobe Type Manager can be used to produce typeset quality output, and is especially suited to working with PostScript printers that are standardized on Adobe Type 1 fonts.

In addition, Windows 95 ships with some raster fonts that are used mainly to provide compatibility with devices that require fonts in a specific resolution. Four raster fonts are used to create screen displays. They are MS Serif (similar to Times Roman), MS Sans Serif (similar to Helvetica), Courier (similar to the default DOS font), and System, which is a lower resolution font similar to MS Sans Serif. System is used by default to display menus and labels for controls.

Raster fonts are device-dependent in terms of resolution, so several resolutions of raster fonts are provided in some cases. For example, MS Serif and MS Sans Serif are both provided in six point sizes and resolutions compatible with CGA, EGA, VGA, and 8514 display devices, as well as some dot matrix printers. Several variations on raster fonts can be installed by Windows 95 depending on the type of display and printer you have. Table 7.2 shows these varied raster font resolutions.

Table 7.2. Raster font resolutions.

Letter	Output device	Resolution	x size*	y size*
B**	EGA display	1.33:1	96	72
C**	Printer	1:1.2	60	72
D**	Printer	1.66:1	120	72
E	VGA display	1:1	96	96
F	8514 display	1:1	120	120

* Pixels per inch.

** These fonts are not included on the Windows 95 installation disks. They can be downloaded from the Microsoft Download Service BBS (see Appendix A, "Microsoft Technical Support Services"), or picked up from previous versions of Windows.

When installed, these raster fonts can be identified by the way the letter that signifies the resolution is attached to the filename. For example, COURE.FON signals that it is a VGA resolution version of Courier.

Another group of raster fonts are supplied for compatibility with devices and applications (mostly older applications that expect raster fonts from previous versions of Windows) that may require fonts in specific resolutions. Table 7.3 lists these fonts.

Table 7.3. Compatibility fonts used by Windows 95.

Font name	8514 Res.	VGA Res.
System	8514SYS.FON	VGASYS.FON
Fixed	8514FIX.FON	VGAFIX.FON
OEM	8514OEM.FON	VGAOEM.FON

In addition, a number of fonts are provided for displaying DOS applications in a window and for simulating fonts used in previous versions of Windows. They are CGA40WOA.FON, CGA80WOA.FON, DOSAPP.FON, EGA40WOA.FON, and EGA80WOA.FON. Note that WOA in the names of these fonts stands for Windows Old App, and are used for applications that expect the fonts used in versions of Windows previous to 3.1.

Vector Fonts

Vector fonts are provided with Windows 95 for backward compatibility with some applications and to support output devices, such as plotters, that are not capable of using bitmapped raster fonts. Vector fonts are created using formulas and algorithms that plot points and connect them with lines to form letters.

Vector fonts can be scaled to a wide range of sizes, but are crude when compared to TrueType and raster fonts. Vector fonts can also drag down printing performance because they require a lot of computation to render. Before the introduction of TrueType fonts in Windows 3.1, vector fonts were often used to create large letters for printing and display.

There are only three vector fonts supplied with Windows 95. They are

ROMAN.FON	A Serif font similar to Times Roman
SCRIPT.FON	A cursive, decorative script
MODERN.FON	A Sans Serif font similar to Helvetica

Video Display Devices

Video display support in Windows 95 has also been improved over previous versions of Windows. The display driver architecture has been reworked to include support from the new 32-bit Device Independent Bitmap (DIB) engine, which provides speedier graphics drawing than ever before.

By using the Unidriver/Minidriver architecture, Windows 95 is able to provide more stable and reliable drivers that run in protected mode. The Microsoft development team wrote many of the new protected mode minidrivers in cooperation with video card manufacturers, and assisted other OEMs to produce drivers to optimize capabilities and performance. Support for the new "green" Energy Star standard for reduction of power consumption is also included for monitors that are Energy Star compatible.

Standard mode grabbers used in previous versions of Windows are a thing of the past, because Windows 95 doesn't support standard mode any longer. Configuring your display is as easy as editing properties, and some video drivers are capable of changing resolutions on-the-fly without restarting Windows 95.

> **NOTE**
>
> Unfortunately, one feature missing from Windows 95 video support is the capability to hot dock video drivers. There are just too many potential memory and I/O port address conflicts among the various display adapter standards in common usage to create dynamically loadable VXDs.

Supported Video Modes

Depending on the capabilities of your display adapter, Windows 95 can display bitmap using as many as 4.2 billion colors. Of course, displaying large numbers of colors requires much more memory to be allocated for rendering bitmaps. Table 7.4 shows the number of bits per pixel required for each of the supported color depths. The more bits per pixel, of course, the more memory is required to place the image in memory.

Table 7.4. Color depths.

Bits per pixel	Color Depth
1 bpp	Monochrome
4 bpp	16 colors
8 bpp	256 colors
15 bpp	32,768 colors (High Color)
16 bpp	65,536 colors (True Color)
24 bpp	16.7 million colors
32 bpp	4.2 billion colors (more than you can see)

When selecting video display adapters for Windows 95, you will want to compare the number of resolutions the adapter can produce versus the number of colors that can be displayed in each resolution. Generally speaking, the more memory the video display adapter contains, the more colors it can produce. You have to be careful, though, because some resolutions might not produce as many colors as you might want to use.

Most video adapters are built around proven chip sets. That is, the manufacturer of the card buys the core components of the card from a company such as Tseng Labs or Chips and Technologies, and then builds their card, with its unique features, around the capabilities of the standard chip set. Table 7.5 lists several of the most popular video cards, and the resolutions and color depths they can render.

Table 7.5. Video cards and their capabilities.

Chip Set	*Resolutions and Color Depths*
Standard VGA	
640×480	monochrome and 16 colors
SuperVGA	
640×480	16, 256, 64K, and 16.7 MB
800×600	16, 256, and 64K
1024×768	256
ATI VGA Wonder	
640×480	16, 256, 64K, and 16.7 MB
800×600	16, 256, and 64K
1024×768	256
ATI Mach 64	
640×480	16, 256, 64K, 16.7 MB, and 4 GB
800×600	16, 256, 64K, 16.7 MB, and 4 GB
1024×768	16, 256, 64K, 16.7 MB, and 4 GB
1280×1024	16, 256, and 64K
Chips & Technologies Super VGA	
640×480	16 and 256
800×600	16 and 256
1024×768	256

continues

Table 7.5. continued

Chip Set	Resolutions and Color Depths
Chips & Technologies Accelerator	
640×480	16, 256, 64K, and 16.7 MB
800×600	16, 256, 64K, and 16.7 MB
1024×768	16, 256, and 64K
1280×1024	256
Cirrus Logic	
640×480	16, 256, 64K, and 16.7 MB
800×600	16, 256, 64K, and 16.7 MB
1024×768	16, 256, and 64K
1280×1024	256
Cirrus Logic 5429/5434	
640×480	16, 256, 64K, and 16.7 MB
800×600	16, 256, 64K, and 16.7 MB
1024×768	256, 64K, 16.7 MB
1280×1024	256
Oak Technology	
640×480	16 and 256
800×600	16 and 256
1024×768	256
S3 Inc. 911/924	
640×480	16, 256, and 64K
800×600	16, 256, and 64K
1024×768	256
S3 Inc. 801/928/964	
640×480	16, 256, 64K, and 16.7 MB
800×600	16, 256, 64K, and 16.7 MB
1024×768	16, 256, 64K, and 16.7 MB
1280×1024	16, 256, 64K, and 16.7 MB
1600×1200	256

Chip Set	Resolutions and Color Depths
Trident Microsystems	
640×480	16 and 256
800×600	16 and 256
1024×768	256
Tseng Labs ET4000	
640×480	16, 256, 64K, and 16.7 MB
800×600	16, 256, and 64K
1024×768	256
Video Seven VRAM / VRAM II / 1024i	
640×480	16 and 256
800×600	16 and 256
1024×768	256
Western Digital	
640×480	16, 256, 64K, and 16.7 MB
800×600	16, 256, 64K, and 16.7 MB
1024×768	16 and 256
1280×1024	256

Video Installation

During Setup, Windows 95 will identify your video card and install the proper drivers. After the base driver set for your display is installed, you can use the Display Properties dialog to customize and configure your display characteristics.

> **CAUTION**
>
> Some video cards and monitors are subject to damage if you feed them the wrong settings. If you are unsure of what video equipment is installed, get help before installing different video drivers.

If, after initial Setup, you change video display adapters, Windows 95 will detect the new card and take you through the Install Wizard 99 percent of the time. If the new card is similar to the old one, or if you get a new set of drivers from the manufacturer, use the Add New Hardware dialog in Control Panel to install the new drivers.

Figure 7.17 shows the Add New Hardware Wizard in action. The Add New Hardware dialog can autodetect devices for you, or you can choose the hardware you want to change manually. If have a specific task in mind, such as changing video drivers within the same family of adapters, or you are changing the monitor, see the section later in this chapter, "Changing Drivers Using Display Properties."

FIGURE 7.17.

If you have new Windows 95 drivers from the manufacturer, click the Have Disk button.

Video Configuration

In Chapter 5, "Customizing the Desktop and Integrating Windows 95 Applications," you saw how you can right-click the desktop and choose Properties from the context menu, or double-click the Display object in Control Panel, to bring up the Properties dialog for your display. Using this dialog, you can set wallpaper, screen savers, color schemes, and so on.

The Settings tab of the Display Properties dialog, shown in Figure 7.18, is used to adjust settings for color depth, resolution, font sizing, and to configure Windows 95 for your monitor. The bitmap of the monitor at the top of the dialog changes to reflect the settings you have established.

FIGURE 7.18.

The Settings dialog enables you to configure both the display adapter and the monitor.

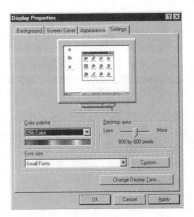

To change the color depth and resolution, all you have to do is select them using the list box and the slider bar. If your new selections require the same or fewer resources as your old setting you will see the message box shown in Figure 7.19. This message appears when restarting your system isn't necessary to put the new settings into effect.

FIGURE 7.19.

If Windows 95 can change the settings without restarting, you will see this message.

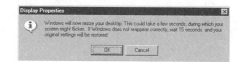

Once the changes you have made are put into effect, the message shown in Figure 7.20 will appear. You have 15 seconds to answer Yes; otherwise, Windows 95 will put your old settings back into effect automatically.

FIGURE 7.20.

Once the changes have been made, you have 15 seconds to decide if you want to keep them. If you do nothing, Windows 95 will revert to the old settings.

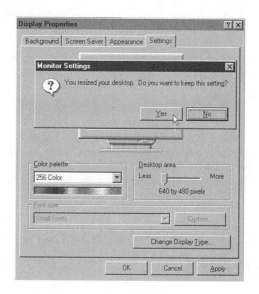

Changing Font Sizes

Font sizes have always been an elastic sort of arrangement. If you look in typography textbooks for the definition of a point, they always say approximately 1/72 of an inch equals a point. The measurements for type fonts that are used today are descended from cold type technology invented in the last century. In those days, point sizes were measured as the height of the small metal block (called a slug) that the letters were cast onto. Thus, two different type fonts, at the same point size, may actually be different heights.

Using today's font technology, you can adjust the sizing of the fonts used for displaying title bars, menus, and other Windows 95 generated output when using some video cards and monitors at resolutions above 640×480. Adjusting the size of fonts can produce a more readable image.

Generally, one of the choices from the list box, small fonts or large fonts, will give you screen proportions that are easy on the eyes. If you have poor eyesight, you will definitely want to try using large fonts to see if they help.

If, however, you want to customize the sizing of fonts, you can click the Custom button, which will bring up the dialog shown in Figure 7.21.

FIGURE 7.21.

You can easily scale the size of fonts used in menus, title bars, and so on.

Changing Device Drivers Using Display Properties

The Settings dialog in Display Properties gives you an additional method of adjusting drivers and settings for monitors via the Change Display Type button. As you can see in Figure 7.22, clicking this button brings up the Change Display Type dialog shown in the upper-left of the figure. This dialog enables you to select either a new video card or a new monitor. The Set Device dialog in the lower-right shows the monitor settings being changed. Two radio buttons appear under the list box. If Show compatible devices is selected, the Set Device dialog will show only a single list box of available choices. If Show all devices is selected, the dual pane view shown in 7.22 is used.

FIGURE 7.22.

The Change Display Type dialogs let you adjust settings for the video card and the monitor.

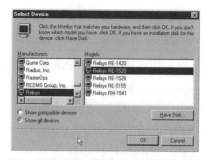

> **NOTE**
>
> Energy Star is a computer industry standard designed to reduce power consumption on newer systems. When the system is unused, Energy Star-compliant monitors can switch to a standby mode, or even turn themselves completely off in order to save money on the electric bill.

Monitors and Refresh Rates

The monitor attached to your system displays images using very nearly the same technology as your TV set. An electron gun sends a stream of energy particles to strike phosphors that glow. The electron gun is controlled by an electromagnetic yoke that sends the beam across lines on the screen. When the end of the scan line is encountered, the beam is shut off and re-aimed at the beginning of the next scan line. The capability to synchronize the movement of the electron beam with the phosphor dots that make up the image at different frequencies is crucial to displaying the various standard screen resolutions.

Most modern monitors have the capability to use several different synchronizations to produce images on the screen. Matching the display adapter's frequencies with the refresh rate of the monitor is required to generate the highest possible video output. If they are mismatched, the screen image may be distorted, and/or a visible flickering of the image may occur.

Flicker is extremely hard on the eyes. Adjusting refresh rates on your monitor to synch up with the video adapter is the only way to reduce eyestrain. Most video adapters come with a utility that adjusts the output of the adapter to match the optimum settings for the monitor. Usually, you need to run this utility only one time to set the frequencies. The data is then stored in the BIOS of the display adapter, or the settings are placed into effect by calling a utility from AUTOEXEC.BAT during startup.

Check with your display adapter's documentation to see if such a utility is supplied. Table 7.6 shows some of the most common of these utilities.

Table 7.6. Display adapter utilities.

Video Card	Utility Filename
ATI	INSTALL.EXE
Cirrus Logic	MONTYPE.EXE or CLMODE.EXE
Diamond Stealth	STLMODE.EXE
Tseng Labs	VMODE.EXE
Western Digital	VGAMODE.EXE

For example, the VMODE utility used with adapters based on the TSENG ET4000 chip set is a DOS app that lets the user visually pick the frequency settings for each resolution the card is capable of producing. After the settings have been established, adding the line VMODE CUSTOM in AUTOEXEC.BAT will cause the settings to be established each time the computer is booted. This loads VMODE as a TSR that requires 1 KB of memory. When the display adapter is required to change video modes, it can check on the information stored in memory by VMODE so the proper refresh rate frequencies are selected.

Summary

In this chapter you have seen how Windows 95 supports all of the different hardware devices attached to your system. Right-clicking the My Computer icon on your desktop will bring up the System Properties dialog, which includes the Device Manager.

You have also seen how Windows 95 provides particular support to communications, printing, and video displays, as well as font support for both printing and screen display.

Customizing Your System Using the Registry

8

by John Mueller

IN THIS CHAPTER

Very few people get an optimized installation using the default settings provided by Windows 95. The very proliferation of books and articles that help the user optimize his or her system speaks to this fact. There are all kinds of tricks you can use to get Windows 95 to help you get the most from your system, but in the final analysis, you will have to rely on a detailed knowledge of the registry if you want "race car" performance from your system. For example, the registry will allow you to probe the depths of OLE support provided by many Windows applications. Optimizing this support translates into improved efficiency.

Even if you decide that you don't need the very best performance from your system, you may need to fix problems that crop up from time to time. Windows 95 does provide a wealth of utilities to help you do this. However, there are some occasions when you will not find the utility you need to fix some problem. For example, what if you wanted to change the individual colors of the 3-D controls used by Windows 95. There isn't any way to do it. The same holds true for renaming some system objects like the Recycle Bin. Editing the Registry is the only way to fix these kinds of problems.

How Does the Registry Help You?

The Registry has appeared in many forms over the years. It's in Windows 3.1 in a very simple form: It provides the means for storing file associations. In Windows NT, the registry is an extremely complex method for completely configuring your system. This Registry contains everything from every desktop configuration to all the administrator settings for the network. Windows 95 provides much of the same functionality of the Windows NT registry, but it's a little simpler to use because it needs to store less information. Anyone familiar with the Windows NT Registry will see a lot of same types of entries here. The big difference is that Windows 95 is a single-user operating system. This chapter will tell you what the Registry is and how to use it to your benefit.

Many people take one look at the Registry and think that it's too complex for the average human to figure out. One look at Figure 8.1 and you may tend to agree. This is about how the Registry Editor will look when you first start using it. (Of course, the screen will differ a little between machines because the equipment they contain is different.)

Although it's true that only a programmer could love many aspects of the Registry, there is plenty there for the average user to look at, too. The first thing you need to figure out when looking at the Windows 95 Registry is what it can do for you.

Windows 3.1 uses two configuration files to store application and hardware configuration information: WIN.INI and SYSTEM.INI. These rather cryptic files contain a wealth of information about your machine and the applications you use. Unfortunately, every application adjusts these files to meet its own needs and doesn't tend to remove the adjustments when you remove the application or update it. As a result, the information contained in these Windows

3.1 configuration files doesn't always reflect reality. After a while, you can end up with two immense files that the average user can't decipher. The end result of all this manipulation is decreased Windows performance at best, instability or even total failure at worst.

FIGURE 8.1.

This screen shows a typical Regedit opening screen. Note the six main categories (or HKEY) entries in this display.

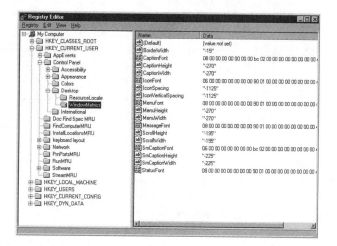

Added to the problem of cryptic entries is a lack of organization. There are major headings, but every application seems to add yet another heading of dubious value. Overall, WIN.INI and SYSTEM.INI are files constructed by a committee of applications that couldn't decide what they should look like. Trying to figure out this undocumented mess can give the best system administrator nightmares.

The final insult comes in how you have to clean up these files. After Windows gets to the point where it won't work properly, you have to edit these files with a text editor to remove the accumulated junk that applications leave in them. What a counterintuitive way to manage a GUI environment!

Windows 95 does away with these two files (except for legacy applications) by using the Registry. It uses two hidden files, USER.DAT and SYSTEM.DAT, to accomplish approximately the same functions as these previous files did. The Registry is a lot easier to use because it organizes the entries that applications need to make in a hierarchical format. You can keep your eye on the overall system picture and still edit the details needed to make your system perform better. The best part about this format is that it's self documenting. Even if an application vendor does need to add a new entry, the purpose of that entry is clear when taken in context of the entries surrounding it. For that matter, the Registry makes it easier for applications to do the job of removing old entries for you automatically. A vendor can remove its entries without affecting entries made by other vendors. One problem with the old WIN.INI and SYSTEM.INI files was the interactions that could take place because of the lack of organization.

> **TIP**
>
> Windows 95 stores the previous copy of your Registry in the USER.DA0 and
> SYSTEM.DA0 files. If you find that you make a mistake in editing the Registry, exit
> immediately, shut Windows 95 down, and then boot into DOS mode. Change
> directories to your Windows 95 main directory. Use the ATTRIB utility to make the
> SYSTEM.DA0, SYSTEM.DAT, USER.DA0, and USER.DAT files visible by using
> the -R, -H, and -S switches. Now, copy the backup of your registry to the two original
> files (that is, SYSTEM.DA0 to SYSTEM.DAT and USER.DA0 to USER.DAT). This
> will restore your Registry to its pre-edit state. Make sure that you restore the previous
> file attribute state by using the +R, +H, and +S switches of the ATTRIB utility.

Not only does the Registry contain hardware and application settings, but it also contains
every other piece of information you can imagine about your machine. You can learn a lot about
Windows simply by looking at the information presented by this application. For example,
did you know that you can use multiple desktops in Windows 95? Of course, that leads into
another problem: maintaining those separate desktops. The hierarchical format presented
by the Registry editor helps the administrator compare the differences among the various desktops. It also allows the administrator to configure them with ease. Best of all, editing the
Registry doesn't involve a session with a text editor. Windows provides a GUI editor that the
administrator can use to change the settings in the Registry.

Knowing that the Registry contains a lot of information and is easy to edit still doesn't tell you
what it can do for you. When was the last time you used the Explorer to check out your hard
drive? I use it a lot because it provides an easy way to find what I need. The Registry can help
you make the Explorer easier to use. For one thing, you can edit the registry to associate files
with a specific application. Even though the Explorer can help you associate files with an application, the Registry is a lot more powerful. Say that you want to associate a graphics editor
with PCX and BMP files. That isn't too difficult to do. What if each file type requires a different set of command line switches, however? Now you get into an area where using the registry
can really help. Using the Registry to edit these entries can help you customize file access.

Adding REGEDIT to Your Start Menu

Now that you have some idea of what you can use the Registry for, it's time to do something
with it. The first step, of course, is to make the editor easy to access. You may wonder why this
application doesn't appear in one of the folders on the Task Bar. Microsoft doesn't add
REGEDIT to your Start Menu for a reason. In the wrong hands, the registry editor can do a
lot more harm than good. A novice user could accidentally destroy his or her entire Windows
setup by modifying the wrong entries.

Use the Start | Settings | Task Bar command to display the dialog box shown in Figure 8.2.

FIGURE 8.2.

The Properties for Taskbar dialog box.

Select the Start Menu Programs page and click the Add button. Figure 8.3 shows the program selection dialog that you'll see next. Notice that the example already has the path and filename of the Registry Editor in place. Fill in this blank with the path to your Windows 95 installation. The main Windows 95 directory contains REGEDIT.EXE. As an alternative, you can click the Browse button and search for the file using Explorer.

FIGURE 8.3.

The Create Shortcut dialog box.

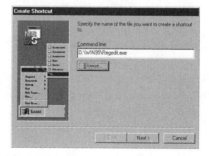

Click the Next button to select a folder. I placed the Registry Editor in the Accessories folder, but you can put it anywhere you like. Figure 8.4 shows a typical folder selection dialog box.

FIGURE 8.4.

The Select Program Group dialog box.

Click the Next button. The final dialog asks you for an application name. All you need to do is click the Finish button here. Calling the Registry Editor REGEDIT is good enough. That's all there is to it. You now have quick access to the Registry Editor from the Start Menu.

A Centralized Database of Setup Information

It's time to take a look at how the Registry is organized. To start the Registry Editor, simply open REGEDIT as you would any another application on the Start Menu. Start Regedit now to better understand the discussion in the following sections.

Before you go much farther, it's time to back the Registry up. You can use this backup file to restore the Registry later if you run into difficulty. Unfortunately, this method won't help much if you permanently destroy the Registry and reboot the machine. Windows 95 needs a clean registry to boot.

> **WARNING**
>
> REGEDIT is an application designed to assist experienced users in changing Windows 95 and associated application behavior. Although it will allow you to enhance system performance and make applications easier to use, it can cause unexpected results when misused. Never edit an entry unless you know what that entry is for. Failure to observe this precaution can result in data loss and even prevent your system from booting the next time you start Windows 95.

Highlight the My Computer entry of the Registry. Select the Registry | Export Registry File... menu entry, as shown in Figure 8.5.

FIGURE 8.5.

The Registry Editor menu allows you to import and export registry settings.

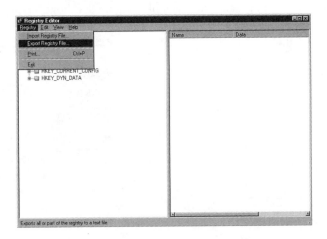

You should see an Export Registry dialog box similar to the one in Figure 8.6. Note that the filename field already contains a save name. You can use any name you wish; I selected OLDENTRY to designate a pre-edited Registry. Notice that the All radio button is selected in the Export Range group.

FIGURE 8.6.

The Export Registry dialog box allows you to save your current registry settings.

Click the Save button to place a copy of the Registry on disk. The OLDENTRY.REG file in your main Windows 95 directory now contains a complete copy of your original Registry.

There are a few terms that I need to get out of the way before proceeding. Table 8.1 provides you with a list of REGEDIT-specific terms and tells you what they mean.

Table 8.1. REGEDIT terms and definitions.

Term	Definition
Category	One of the six main keys under the My Computer key.
Key	A REGEDIT topic. Think of a key as the heading that tells you what a particular section will contain. Looking at all the keys shows an outline of a particular topic. Each key provides a little more detail about that particular topic. The keys always appear on the left side of the REGEDIT window.
Value	The definition of a REGEDIT topic. Think of a value as the text that fills out the heading provided by a key. There are three types of values: binary, string, and DWORD. Only applications use the binary and DWORD value types. They usually store configuration data in a format not in human-readable form. The string values provide a lot of information about the application and how it's configured. Values always appear on the right side of the REGEDIT window.

Each Main Heading Has a Specific Purpose

The first thing you'll note when looking at the Registry display is that there are at least six main headings in the Registry. Clicking the plus box connected to the folder associated with the heading opens that category. The following paragraphs describe these categories in more detail.

HKEY_CLASSES_ROOT

The HKEY_CLASSES_ROOT category is the one that presents some of the best opportunities to enhance application ease of use. Figure 8.7 shows a typical HKEY_CLASSES_ROOT structure. Note the distinct difference between file extension and file association keys. Also note the ShellX subkey below the TXT key.

FIGURE 8.7.

A typical HKEY_CLASSES_ROOT display.

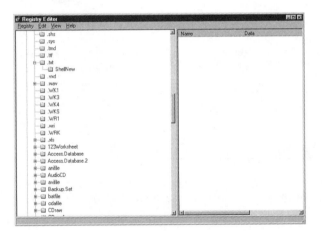

There are two types of entry in this category. The first key type (remember that a key is a REGEDIT topic) is a file extension. Think of all the three-character extensions that you used in the past, such as .DOC and .TXT. The file extension entries normally associate a data file with an application or an executable file with a specific Windows 95 function. You should change your application file entries to make your working environment as efficient as possible. Never change an executable file association. Changing an executable file extension such as DLL could make it difficult for Windows 95 to start your applications or could even crash the system. I look at the procedure for changing an application file association in the "Modifying File Associations" section later in this chapter.

SPECIAL EXTENSION SUBKEYS

Some file extensions such as .TXT provide a ShellX subkey. (See Figure 8.7.) In the case of .TXT and .DOC, the standard subkey is ShellNew (the most common key). This ShellX key is a shell extension. There is a variety of other shell extensions available; the actual number is limited only by your application vendor.

A shell extension is an OLE hook into Windows 95. Only an application that supports OLE extensions can place a ShellX key into the registry; don't add one of these keys on your own. When you see this key, you know that the application provides some type of extended, OLE-related functionality. For example, if you double-click a shortcut to a data file that no longer exists, an application with the ShellNew shell extension will ask whether you want to create a new file of the same type. (If you look at the values associated with ShellNew, there is always a NullFile entry that tells the shell extension what type of file to create.)

You can use this shell extension behavior to create new files just by double-clicking an icon on your desktop. All you need to do is create a temporary file and a shortcut to it on your desktop, and then erase the temporary file. (Make certain that the application provides a ShellNew shell extension before you do this.) Your application will always create a new file for you. This behavior also works if you place the file shortcut in the Start Menu folder.

There are other, more generic shell extensions as well. For example, the * extension has a generic Shellex subkey. Below this you'll see a PropertySheetHandlers key, and finally a 128-digit key that looks like some kind of secret code. Actually, the 128-digit value *is* a secret code. It's a reference identifier for the DLL (a type of application) that takes care of the * extension. You'll find this key under the CLSID key. (CLSID stands for class identifier.) The secret code is for the "OLE Docfile Property Page." Looking at the value of the next key will tell you that it exists in DOCPROP.DLL. This DLL provides the dialog that asks which application you want to use to open a file when there is no registry entry associated with that extension.

As you can see, shell extensions are a powerful addition to the Windows 95 Registry. Suffice it to say that you should not change or delete these shell extensions; let the application take care of them for you.

The second type of entry is the file association. After you tell Windows 95 about a file extension, you have to tell it what to do with that extension. For example, adding a file extension key tells Windows 95 that that file extension exists. Now you have to tell it what application to use with that extension. These entries modify things such as the menu you see when you right-click a filename in Explorer. They also provide the means for modifying how an application interacts with the file when performing a particular task. For example, to print a file, you normally need to open the application with the /P parameter. The "Modifying File Associations" section of this chapter explores this topic in detail.

HKEY_CURRENT_USER

The HKEY_CURRENT_USER category contains a lot of "soft" settings for your machine. It is slaved to the settings for the current user, the one who is logged into the machine at the time. The registry copies the contents of the HKEY_USERS category into this category, then updates HKEY_USERS when you shut down. This is the area where Windows 95 obtains new setting information and places any changes that you make. That makes this category particularly useful if you make a mistake when changing a configuration setting. With enough patience, you can return the current settings to match those of the previous session, erasing the error before it's recorded permanently. Of course, that's just one use for this particular Registry category.

> **NOTE**
>
> Using a common setup for all users means that HKEY_CURRENT_USER settings automatically reflect the default setting in HKEY_USERS. (Click the first radio button in the User Profiles tab of the Passwords selection in the Control Panel.) See the HKEY_USERS discussion for more details on these settings.

As you can see from Figure 8.8, the keys within the HKEY_CURRENT_USER category are pretty self-explanatory in most cases. All the entries adjust some type of user-specific setting, but nothing that affects a global element such as a device driver. The following paragraphs describe each key in detail.

FIGURE 8.8.

The HKEY_CURRENT_USER category contains all the user-specific settings.

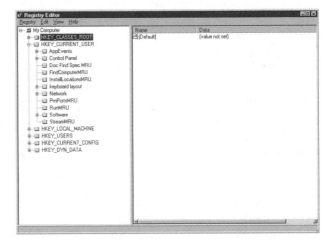

AppEvents

This is a listing of the application events defined for the current user. There are two subkeys under this one: EventLabels and Schemes. The EventLabels key holds the general definitions for these events. The Schemes key is the one that you'll probably want to explore. This is where the settings for your sound files appear.

Control Panel

This is probably the most familiar Registry key. It won't contain entries for all the icons in the Control Panel, but it will contain keys for all the icons that control user-specific settings. For example, the Registry contains a subkey called Colors. This entry controls all the colors displayed on-screen. In fact, you may find a few surprise entries here. The Registry allows you to control a wider variety of color settings than the Control Panel does. How would you like to individually change the component colors of the 3-D buttons? The Registry allows you to do that. Unfortunately, you'll have to insert color numbers instead of using the Control Panel's convenient interface.

InstallLocationsMRU

This Registry key contains the most recently used locations of installation files. This doesn't pertain to the location of software installation files, but to device- or service-related installation files. For example, installing a new set of network drivers would place an entry here but installing a new word processor would not. This key also contains a MRUList value that maintains a list of which order Windows 95 should use to search for install file locations.

Keyboard Layout

This Registry key provides information about the keyboard currently attached to the machine. It doesn't really change from user to user unless one user needs to use a different language or keyboard layout than another. The preload key under the keyboard section reflects the different languages in use. The substitutes key reflects the keyboard layout. For example, you could use English (United States) as a language and English (Dvorak) as a layout. The toggle key tells you which control key combination you can use to switch between languages.

Network

Unfortunately, most of the contents of this key are network specific. Essentially, it tells your machine how to configure itself for the network you have in place. The one key that remains the same across networks is the recent key. This key contains values for each of the network drives that you recently accessed.

Software

This Registry key should contain plenty of configuration information for your software. Until you upgrade to 32-bit versions of your applications, however, it will probably contain a few default entries for Windows 95-specific applications. This section replaces all those entries that you used to have in WIN.INI and SYSTEM.INI. The hierarchical structure of this key makes it very easy to remove application-specific information from your Windows 95 installation. There is one subkey of particular interest. The MS Setup (ACME) | User Info key (Figure 8.9) contains the user's name and company information. Many 32-bit programs use this information as a default during installation for burning the user information into the application. Other applications will look at this entry during installation in the future. This is the only place that you can change this information in Windows 95. If you need to change the user name for software installation purposes, this is the place to do it.

FIGURE 8.9.

The User Info key normally contains two entries: one for the user name and another for the company name.

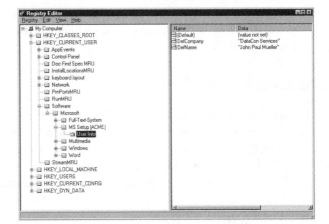

HKEY_LOCAL_MACHINE

The HKEY_LOCAL_MACHINE category centers its attention on the machine hardware. This includes the drivers and configuration information required to run the hardware. There is a lot of subtle information about your hardware stored under this category. For example, this category contains all the Plug and Play information about your machine. It also provides a complete listing of the device drivers and their revision level.

This category does contain some software specific information. For example, a 32-bit application will store the location of its setup table here. The application uses this table during installation. Some applications also use it during a setup modification. Applications such as Word for Windows NT store all their setup information in SFT tables. Figure 8.10 shows a typical HKEY_LOCAL_MACHINE category setup. The following paragraphs describe each key in detail.

FIGURE 8.10.

*The HKEY_LOCAL_
MACHINE category contains
everything you need to
know about your hardware.*

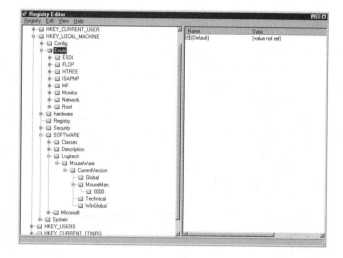

Config

The Config key provides specific information needed to set up the machine during boot. The two main references configure the display and the printer. The printer settings appear under the System key. In most cases, the only printer configuration information that you'll see is the specific name of the printer attached to the current machine. This key doesn't provide any network-specific information.

> **NOTE**
>
> Windows 95 copies the contents of the Config key to the HKEY_CURRENT_CONFIG category. It will overwrite any changes you make to the values in this key during logout or shut down. Make any required changes to the HKEY_CURRENT_CONFIG values. Fortunately, having a backup copy of the configuration under the HKEY_LOCAL_MACHINE | Config key means that you can easily correct editing mistakes in the HKEY_CURRENT_CONFIG key values.

The display settings include the resolution and fonts. The settings under Display key are a lot more detailed than the printer settings. There are two subkeys under the main Display key. The Fonts key provides a list of default font requirements and the name of the font file that satisfies that need. In most cases, you can change these settings using the Display utility in the control panel. The Settings key provides information on the current number of colors (as bits per pixel) and the display resolution. It also provides the names of the default display fonts.

Enum

This Registry key enumerates the hardware connected to your machine. Figure 8.10 provides a picture of a typical installation. Some hardware receives special attention through the use of separate keys. For example, an IDE hard drive and the floppy drives fall into this category. Other hardware falls into the Plug and Play category. The actual Plug and Play hardware listing appears under the root key. The subkeys under the root key also appear in the Device Manager listing. Figure 8.11 shows a typical set of values for the COM ports. A typical Plug and Play Registry entry doesn't provide much information. It does, however, provide important clues for the network troubleshooter. One of the most important pieces of information is the location of the INF file associated with the device.

FIGURE 8.11.

A typical Plug and Play Registry entry showing the COM port settings.

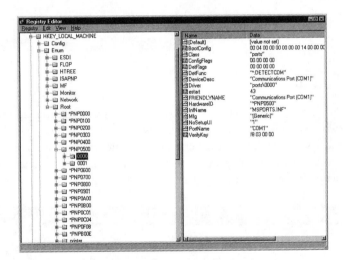

As you can see, the Device Manager display is much easier to read. The Registry display does provide one important piece of troubleshooting information, however. It provides the name of the INF file that holds the COM port configuration information (MSPORTS.INF). These INF files provide a wealth of information about the default port interrupts. They also provide information about the DLLs and VXDs used to support them. You also can modify the INF files for any device to provide support for nonstandard devices or additional port/interrupt configurations. Think of an INF file as an INI file for devices.

Hardware

In most cases, you can ignore the Hardware Registry key. Its only function is to list the communication ports attached to the machine. This key doesn't contain any actual configuration information.

Security

This Registry key is network specific. Refer to your network manuals for additional information. As a general rule, it contains pointers to files holding account and other network security-specific information.

SOFTWARE

NOTE

You have seen another section in this chapter for another Software key. The Registry contains numerous examples wherein the same key name appears more than once. Each instance of a key performs a different task that might or might not appear similar to other keys of the same name.

The SOFTWARE Registry key contains device driver and global application information. Figure 8.10 shows a typical setup. Note that the subkeys include a variety of vendor-specific information.

The Logitech key provides mouse setup information as well as the driver version. For example, under the MouseMan | 0000 key are values that determine which buttons become assigned to various mouse functions. The default setup program enables you to assign a left- or a right-handed setup for the mouse. What if you wanted to exchange the right and middle button functions (essentially creating a two-button mouse)? You could do so by transposing the MappingButton2 and MappingButton3 Registry values, even though the configuration utility doesn't provide the means to do so.

The Microsoft section of the SOFTWARE key provides some useful information as well. One of these keys is the New Users Settings key. Most 32-bit applications and some 16-bit applications can provide an entry in this area. A new user inherits these settings when you set up a new login on the machine. In essence, this key contains the global settings that everyone uses with this application (at least until users customize their setup). This key also provides the location of shared tools and any global network settings required to make the application work.

One of the interesting subkeys is Classes. Opening this key reveals a list of file extensions and associations just like the one in HKEY_CLASSES_ROOT. The purpose behind this listing is totally different. Windows 95 uses this list to locate application- or device driver-specific files instead of creating links for Explorer. If you change this listing, it won't affect your Explorer display.

The Description key also provides some interesting information. A default setup always contains the Microsoft remote procedure call (RPC) listing. A network could use this section, however, to describe other links between machines as well.

System

The last Registry key in this category is also the most destructive when edited incorrectly. Figure 8.12 provides an overview of the subkeys associated with the System key. The System key provides a lot of information and opportunities for system optimization. However, along with the opportunities comes a price. A bad entry in any value under this key can kill your installation.

FIGURE 8.12.

An overview of the System key and its subkeys.

Microsoft split these keys into two categories: control and services. The control key contains all the subkeys that change how the user reacts to the system. For example, the national language support (NLS) keys appear here. Remember the keyboard setting discussed previously? This is where all the language settings came from. If you had the correct driver, you could add support for Martian by changing the value of one of these keys. The network administration-specific keys appear here as well. One of the first keys that you'll see is the computer name used to log onto the network.

There are several subkeys that provide the advanced user with an opportunity to tune system performance. One of the most interesting keys to look at is the Known16DLLs key under the SessionManager key. The values in this key tell you where you can optimize the system. A 16-bit DLL doesn't perform as well as its 32-bit counterpart. Finding 32-bit DLLs to replace the 16-bit DLLs in this section will improve system performance without buying any new hardware.

One of the more dangerous keys in this section is the PwdProvider key. It tells Windows 95 the location of any password or user account files. This key also contains the name of any DLLs or VXDs required to implement system security. Just try to log into the network if this key becomes deleted.

The System Monitor utility (installed during network installation) gets some of its input here as well. Look under the PerfStats | Enum key. Here are all the statistics from which you can choose in the System Monitor utility. Each subkey in this section contains a description, differentiate flag, and name. You could theoretically add a performance-monitor statistic here, and it would show up in the System Monitor utility. Of course, you wouldn't get any useful information out of it. There are other Registry entries required, and you would need to write the supporting software. You could, however, remove statistics from here to prevent network users from monitoring areas that you don't want them to touch. You also could change the name or description of a statistic to meet your needs.

On to the second part of the System key, Services. This group of keys does just the opposite of the Control key section; it allows the user to change the way the system reacts. There are a few keys in this group that you should never touch. They include Arbitrators, Unknown, and nodriver.

The majority of the Class key subkeys provide useful information. For example, the CDROM key can tell you about the drivers associated with the CD-ROM drive. In some cases, it may provide clues about why the CD-ROM drive fails to play music or interface with the system in some other way.

The Display key contains several subkeys related to the display adapter. This includes specifics about resolution and color combinations that the driver supports. (In one case, I was actually able to change this entry and provide 256-color support at 1024 × 768 resolution on one machine even though the driver originally showed that it didn't support this combination.) Of course, editing the values for these keys, like any other keys in this group, can result in a boot failure or other unforeseen occurrences.

HKEY_USERS

The HKEY_USERS category is the one category that you should never edit unless you need to maintain a network environment. None of the entries here will take effect until the next time the user logs in to Windows 95. Changing the settings for the current user is a waste of time because Windows 95 will overwrite the new data with the data contained in HKEY_CURRENT_USER during logout or shut down. All the entries in this section match the HKEY_CURRENT_USER category, so I won't go over the individual keys again. There are a few network specific issues to attend to, however.

This category contains one major key for each user that you create on the local machine (not including remote access users). Each of these major keys contains an exact duplicate of the contents of the HKEY_CURRENT_USER category. Figure 8.13 shows a setup that includes the default key and one user key. When a user logs into the network, Windows 95 copies all the information in that user's profile to the HKEY_CURRENT_USER area of the Registry. When the user logs out or shuts down, Windows 95 updates the information in the user's specific section from the HKEY_CURRENT_USER category.

FIGURE 8.13.

Windows 95 creates one entry in the HKEY_USERS category for each user who logs into the machine.

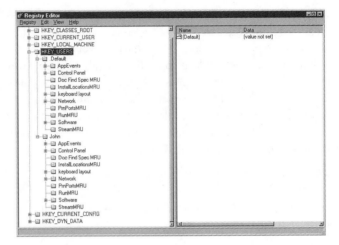

So, where does the original information for each user come from? The registry contains one entry called .Default. (Note the period in front of the key name; Default without a period is an actual user name.) Windows 95 takes the information in this key and copies it to a user-specific key when the user logs in for the first time. (The initial login does more work than create a simple registry entry, but I won't cover that in this chapter.) There are a few Registry-related tips that you should follow when setting up your network.

- Always configure the workstation for the minimum possible access rights for the .Default user. This allows you to create new users without the risk of circumventing network security.

- Consider renaming the .Default user entry so that other people can't log in without a password. (Windows 95 will come to a screeching halt if it can't find the default user.)

- Use the System Policy Editor in place of the Registry Editor whenever possible to make changes to the network setup.

- Make a backup of both the USER.DAT and SYSTEM.DAT files before you set the network up. Failure to take this step means that you will have to reinstall Windows 95 from scratch if the network setup fails.

HKEY_CURRENT_CONFIG

The HKEY_CURRENT_CONFIG category is the simplest part of the registry. It contains two major keys, the same keys that you saw under the Config key of the HKEY_LOCAL_MACHINE category. Figure 8.14 shows the major keys in this category.

FIGURE 8.14.

The HKEY_CURRENT_ CONFIG category echoes the settings under the Config key of the HKEY_LOCAL_MACHINE category.

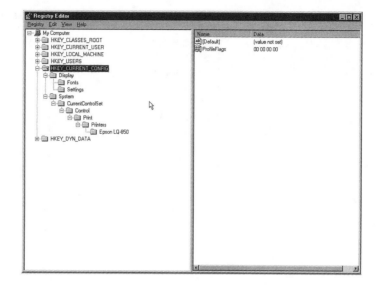

The Display key provides two subkeys: Fonts and Settings. The Fonts subkey determines which fonts that Windows 95 uses for general display purposes. These are the raster (non-TrueType) fonts that it displays when you get a choice of which font to use for icons or other purposes.

The Settings subkey contains the current display resolution and number of bits per pixel. The bits per pixel value determines the number of colors available. For example, 4 bits per pixel provides 16 colors, and 8 bits per pixel provides 256 colors. The three fonts listed as values under this key are the default fonts used for icons and application menus. You can change all the settings under this key using the Settings tab of the Properties for Display dialog found in the Control Panel.

The System key looks like a convoluted mess. Only one of the subkeys under this key has any meaning, however. The Printers subkey contains a list of the printers attached to the machine. It doesn't include printers accessed through a network connection.

HKEY_DYN_DATA

The final category, HKEY_DYN_DATA, contains two subkeys: Config Manager and PerfStats. You can monitor the status of the Config Manager key using the Device Manager. The PerfStats key values appear as statistics in the System Monitor utility display. Figure 8.15 shows these two main keys and their subkeys. The values in these keys reflect the current, or dynamic, state of the computer.

FIGURE 8.15.

HKEY_DYN_DATA contains registry entries for current events.

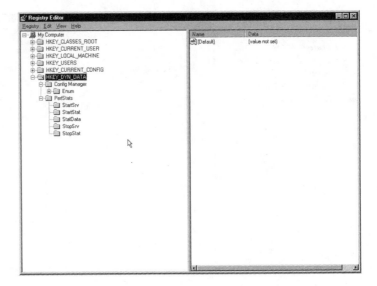

The Enum key contains subkeys for every device attached to the computer. Each one of the subkeys contains the same four values. The Allocation value shows which process has control of the device. The HardwareKey value contains an entry that matches the Plug and Play values that we talked about for the HKEY_LOCAL_MACHINE | Enum | Root key. Essentially, this value identifies the device. For example, a PNP value of 0500 matches the first serial port. The Problem value should equal 0 in most cases (unless the hardware experiences a fault). This value always contains an error number during a hardware failure. The final key, Status, contains a value of 4F 4A 00 00 when the hardware is error free.

The PerfStats key contains five subkeys. The first two subkeys control the starting time for gathering server and statistical data. The last two control the stopping time. The only interesting key in this group is the StatData key. It contains the current usage level data for each of the categories that the System Monitor utility tracks. In fact, if you press F5 to refresh the registry data, you can watch the data values change. Keeping the System Monitor utility open at the same time will show how these numbers track the information that you see in the utility.

Modifying File Associations

Explorer is the Windows 95 alternative to the Windows 3.1 File Manager. It goes a long way toward making Windows 95 truly usable. Just like any other tool, however, you'll probably want to customize this one to meet your needs. One of the first things that you'll want to do is change the file associations.

Open a copy of Explorer and the Registry Editor. If you don't have the Registry Editor on your Start Menu, look at the procedure at the beginning of this chapter for help.

Select the View | Options… command from the Explorer menu. Click the File Types tab. You should see a dialog box similar to the one in Figure 8.16.

FIGURE 8.16.

The Options dialog box of the Explorer utility.

In this case, the Word for Windows 6.0 Document is highlighted, but you could just as easily apply this to any other application. Note that there are three file types associated with a Word for Windows 6.0 Document. What happens if you want to associate a fourth file type with Word? Clicking the Edit button shows that you can add additional commands but not additional associations to this existing file type.

The only choice is to click New Type to create a new file type. Use the New pushbutton to create the actions listed in the Actions section of the dialog box. Figure 8.17 shows the dialog box that appears. Note how the blanks in the screen shot are filled out.

FIGURE 8.17.

Adding a new file type to the Explorer menu.

Note that you duplicated the Microsoft Word 6.0 Document entry exactly. Because this is an exact duplication, you should simply see a new file extension associated with the one Microsoft Word 6.0 Document entry, right? Wrong! Click the Close button, and you'll see the results.

There are two identical Microsoft Word 6.0 Document entries in the Explorer Options dialog now. To understand the reason for this, you need to look in the Registry Editor.

Open the Registry Editor and then click the HKEY_CLASSES_ROOT key. Highlight the .ASC file extension key. You should see a display similar to the one in Figure 8.18.

FIGURE 8.18.

The .ASC file extension entry.

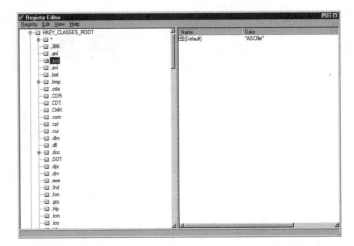

Note that the .ASC file extension that you created in Explorer is associated with the ASCfile type, not the Microsoft Word 6.0 Document type. If you look at the value for the DOC file extension key, you'll see "Word.Document.6." Looking at the .ASC and the .DOC file extension entries in the registry shows the reason for two Microsoft Word 6.0 Document entries in Explorer.

Go back up to the ASC file extension entry. Right-click the Default value entry and select Modify. Type Word.Document.6 in place of ASCfile. Make certain to use the same capitalization and add the periods as needed to the new value. You should see a display similar to the one in Figure 8.19.

FIGURE 8.19.

Changing a key value in the registry.

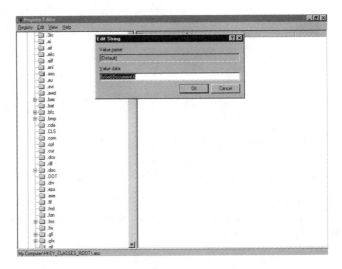

Click OK and minimize the Registry. Close the old copy of Explorer and open a new one. This will force a read from the edited Registry entry. Open the View | Options... | File Types dialog box again. Highlight the Microsoft Word 6.0 Document entry and you'll see the new Word file association shown in Figure 8.20.

FIGURE 8.20.

The new Microsoft Word 6.0 Document association contains all four file types.

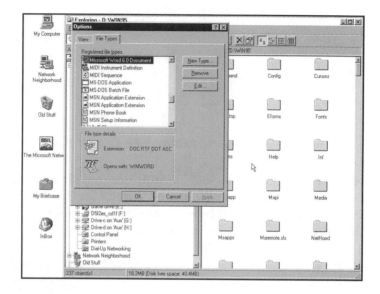

Note that you can see all four file types now. In addition, the new file type automatically inherits the right-click menu settings of the original file types. There is one last step needed to complete this task. You need to clean up the extra registry entry (ASCfile).

Maximize the REGEDIT utility again. Find the ASCfile key in the HKEY_CLASSES_ROOT category. Highlight it and press Delete. Make sure that you don't accidentally delete the wrong key. Exit the Registry Editor.

Importing and Exporting Registry Data

One of the problems with using a Registry for everything is that you have to get the configuration data into a form that the Registry can accept. Quite a few mainstream applications create a REG file that you can import into the registry. Even the REG files created with 16-bit legacy applications are compatible with the Windows 95 Registry.

Importing Data

There are several techniques that you can use to import your current Registry information into the Registry. First, you can open a copy of Explorer and find the Registry file that you want to import. Figure 8.21 shows a typical example.

FIGURE 8.21.

A typical Registry file entry. This one is for Word for Windows 6.0.

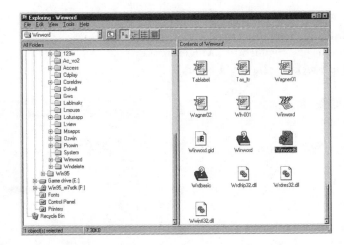

All you need to do is double-click the REG icon, and REGEDIT automatically enters it into the Registry. Note that the REG file icon looks like the Registry Editor icon with a document behind it. After the Registry enters the new configuration information for your application, it displays the dialog box shown in Figure 8.22.

FIGURE 8.22.

The Registry signals a successful configuration data entry for Word for Windows 6.0.

A second technique comes in handy when you have the Registry Editor open. Simply click the Registry | Import Registry File... command. The Registry Editor will display a dialog box similar to the one shown in Figure 8.23.

FIGURE 8.23.

You can use menu commands to import configuration into the Registry when Regedit is open.

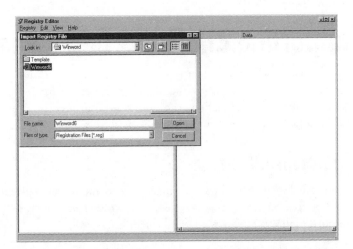

Click the Open pushbutton to complete the task. You should see the same dialog box shown in Figure 8.22 when REGEDIT completes the task.

Exporting Data

What happens when you want to save some of those configuration changes that you made in the past? You can export either all or part of the registry by using the Registry | Export Registry File... command in the Registry Editor. Figure 8.24 shows the Export Registry File dialog box. You can edit the exported data using any standard text editor such as Notepad.

FIGURE 8.24.

The Registry provides the means to export configuration data into a pure ASCII text file.

Note that this dialog box shows the Branch radio button selected and a branch name filled in. You can either highlight the branch that you want to save before you open the Export Registry File dialog box, or you can type the path later. The other radio button selection, All, saves the entire Registry to a text file. This option comes in handy if you want to save the Registry before you start editing it.

All you need to do to complete the process is to click the Save pushbutton. REGEDIT doesn't provide any kind of feedback after it exports the registry to disk. You'll probably want to view the saved file before you make any changes to the registry.

Viewing the Saved File's Contents

Exported Registry data files contain pure ASCII text. They don't contain any control characters that you need to worry about. You normally need to use Wordpad to view a save of the entire Registry. (A full Registry export file normally takes between 400 and 500 KB of storage.) Notepad will probably do the job if you want to look at a saved branch.

Figure 8.25 shows a typical saved Registry branch. Note that there are three lines in this file. Each line serves a specific purpose during the import process. The first line contains REGEDIT4. This identifies the version of the Registry Editor that created the file. It also prevents you from importing the file into an older version of the registry. Application REG files normally don't contain any version numbers as part of the REGEDIT entry. This allows you to import them using any version of REGEDIT.

FIGURE 8.25.

This saved Registry branch contains a mere four lines of data.

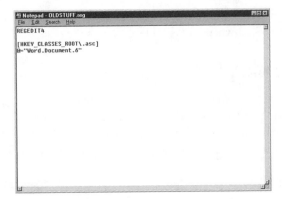

The real second line of the file contains a blank. REGEDIT uses this blank line as a delimiter between Registry key entries. The second line of text (third line of the file) contains the registry key. Note that it looks like a hard disk directory listing. Each backslash tells REGEDIT to create a new key level.

The final line of text contains the actual key value. The @ symbol at the beginning of the line tells REGEDIT that this is the default entry. Any other value begins with a value name. The double quotation marks around the value itself tells REGEDIT that this is a string value. Binary values begin with the word *hex* followed by a colon, whereas DWORD values begin with the word *dword* followed by a colon.

EDITING A BRANCH

You might find that you need to add the keys from one branch to another branch in the Registry. It seems as though REGEDIT should provide some type of cut-and-paste capability to take care of this task, but it doesn't. The fastest, most efficient way to add the contents of one branch to another is to export the Registry, use a text editor to cut and paste the values you need, and then import the modified registry file. Of course, you could find yourself with a machine that won't boot using this method. Make sure to keep an unmodified copy of the Registry handy just in case.

Summary

In this chapter you learned what function each part of the registry performs and how to use the Registry Editor to maintain your machine's setup. The Registry can look complex until you take it apart one piece at a time. The big thing to remember is that you always have to edit the part that holds the current copy of the data, not the static portion. Make a note of which sections of the description contained static data and which sections are dynamic.

The second rule of thumb is to make a backup of the Registry before you edit it. You either can export a copy of the entire Registry or make a copy of the USER.DAT and SYSTEM.DAT files. Remember that Windows 95 always makes a copy of the Registry during startup.

Finally, you saw how you can use the Registry Editor to make some significant changes in your computing environment. The key here is to use every other tool first, and then fall back on the Registry Editor. This is a powerful tool that can wipe out your entire installation in a single keystroke; make sure that you give it the respect it's due.

The Architecture of Windows 95

9

by Ed Tiley

IN THIS CHAPTER

To fully appreciate Windows 95, you need an understanding of how it's constructed. If you're one of those people who isn't interested in how it works, preferring instead just to turn on the machine and work with a single program all day long, then you probably want to skip this chapter and the few that follow.

If, on the other hand, you're interested in getting maximum performance and in understanding what makes Windows 95 tick, settle back and dig in for a good read. In this chapter and the few that follow, you'll learn what's "under the hood" of Windows 95, from a user's perspective, without getting into the minutiae of the bits and bytes (except where absolutely necessary). The material that follows is more concerned with teaching you the concepts than in teaching you stuff that programmers need to know.

What Is Windows 95?

Windows 95 is Microsoft's newest version of the popular Windows operating environment. This time around, Windows has grown up to become not just an operating environment but a complete operating *system*.

NOTE

The term *operating system* refers to software that serves as the foundation for all of the operational things that a computer needs to do, such as reading and writing disks, sending data to the printer, managing the screen, and taking input from the keyboard. An operating system's primary job is to boot up the computer and to create a platform that provides system services to the applications (such as word processors, paint programs, and spreadsheets). Without an operating system, you couldn't launch the programs you use daily.

In its earlier versions, Windows provided many of the same services as an operating system; but technically it remained an operating environment, because the DOS operating system was required in order to boot the computer, manage disk drives, and provide other services. With the release of Windows 95, however, you no longer need a separate copy of DOS to boot first before you go into Windows. That doesn't mean that DOS isn't there. Instead, it means that Windows 95 boots up the computer and lets you run a copy of DOS (if you want to) as just another program.

The Windows 95 operating system is designed to run only on Intel-based computer systems having a 386, 486, or Pentium processor. Unlike its big brothers Windows NT and Windows NT Server, Windows 95 is intended as Microsoft's mainstream operating system for the vast majority of desktop and notebook computers in use today. Much of the core of the Windows 95 operating system is taken from NT, and any application written to the Windows 32-bit specification will run on both operating systems.

Nearly every program ever written for the DOS-compatible computer is supposed to be able to execute in Windows 95. That's a tall order. If Microsoft could get away with dropping DOS and Windows 3.1 support, Windows 95 would be a whole lot less complex. But there would be a whole lot fewer copies sold too. Fortunately, the history of the Intel processor and its backwards-compatibility problems has less impact on Windows 95 than on any previous version. Nonetheless, you need to know a few things about the architecture of your basic "Intel Inside" computer.

A Very Short History of the PC

Before the IBM PC was introduced in 1981, most serious business-oriented computing was done with the Zilog Z80 8-bit processor, using an operating system called CP/M (Control Program for Microprocessors). Most machines had 32 or 64 KB of RAM. Monster machines had 128 KB.

As legend tells it, IBM originally approached Digital Research, the company that created CP/M, to provide the operating system for its new 16-bit computers; but eventually IBM settled on a then-fledgling company called Microsoft. Microsoft's operating-system interface was in many ways a knock-off of CP/M, and thus we inherited the command-line interface of CP/M and commands such as DIR, FORMAT, and so on.

The brains of the new IBM PC were supposed to be the Intel 8086 processor, a slightly faster version of the 8088 that was used in place of the 8086 for some reason. One legend has it that the 8088 won out because of a shortage of 8086 chips. Another version of the story (though less kind to IBM) is that IBM didn't really think of the PC as much more than a toy, so they opted for a less capable chip set that was cheaper to produce. Whichever legend eventually ends up in the history books, the 8086 and 8088 were capable of addressing up to 1 MB of RAM, which at the time seemed to be more memory than any software program could ever ask for. It was so much more extra memory, in fact, that 384 KB of the possible 1 MB was reserved for system usage, thus the infamous 640KB barrier was born.

For several years, the system area of the memory structure housed video memory, ROM instructions, and little else. The 640 KB of program-usable memory in the original PC became known as conventional memory, and most early PCs were sold with only 256 KB of memory installed.

Expanded Memory

What the engineers who designed the original IBM PC hadn't counted on were the thousands of loyal Lotus 1-2-3 users who, freed from the restraints of 64 KB, began to build monster spreadsheets and databases that ran right into the 640KB limit. A way was needed to exceed the 640KB barrier without breaking anything else.

What eventually happened was that a method of expanding usable memory was devised by Lotus, Intel, and Microsoft. The Lotus/Intel/Microsoft Expanded Memory Specification was adopted as a near universal standard. This is the standard referred to when you hear about LIM memory or the EMS (Expanded) specification.

The mechanics of the LIM specification were relatively simple. A card containing memory was inserted into an expansion slot in the computer, and a page frame of 64 KB was placed into the mostly unused area between 640 KB and 1 MB. The page frame was used as a window into the additional memory. Data stored in the RAM chips on the board got copied into the page frame, where the processor could access it. If the data was changed, it was rewritten back to the memory card before it was written over. This early swapping technique is a very distant cousin to Windows 95's Virtual Memory Manager.

The Intel 80286

Around 1985, Intel replaced the 8086/8088 with a new processor called the 80286. (Intel *did* release an 80186 chip but it was never widely adopted.) The 80286 chip retained the 16-bit design but it was much faster than the 8088/8086 chips. Plus, the 80286 sported a radical new feature: the capability to run in *protected mode*, a memory-management scheme designed to enable more than one program to share the resources of the machine. As the name implies, programs are supposed to be protected from each other when the computer is operating in this mode. In theory, an ill-behaved program can't crash the entire system, disrupting programs that are following the rules. IBM adopted the 80286 chip as the processor for the IBM PC-AT, and a whole new generation of clones was born.

When you turn on a computer equipped with an 80286 chip, it by default emulates an 8086. This emulation of the 8086 chip was named *real mode* to differentiate it from protected-mode operation. The truth is, the name wasn't needed because most AT-class machines lived and died without ever having their protected-mode operation switched on.

Despite the fact that protected-mode operation enabled the 286 chip to address up to 16 MB of RAM using the Extended Memory Specification (XMS), no mainstream operating system used the protected-mode operation, and Expanded memory remained the solution of choice for addressing more memory. One of the main reasons was that the 286 lacked a way of easily returning to real mode. After the processor was switched to protected mode, programmers had to literally hack a way to reboot the processor to get back to real mode.

The Intel 80386 and Beyond

The 80386 chip was introduced, with much fanfare, in 1987. The 80386 incorporated a 32-bit architecture that promised to greatly enhance the potential for computing. This new chip could address up to 4 GB of memory in protected mode and it introduced a new feature: the virtual machine.

The 80386 chip has the capability to create an emulation of an Intel-based computer entirely out of memory. Each virtual machine is totally separate from any other virtual machine that is running, it can run programs in protected mode, and it further isolates other parts of the system from renegade programs that would otherwise cause all of the running programs to crash. There are even features built into the chip set to make it easier for an operating system to arbitrate requests for hardware services from multiple running programs.

Windows 3.*x* uses the virtual-machine capability of the 80386 to run all of Windows in one virtual machine and to run each DOS program by launching it into its own separate virtual machine. The virtual-machine capability of the 80386 was so well designed that it has been inherited by both the 80486 and the Pentium chips.

Windows 95 is a close cousin to, and shares a fair amount of core code with, Windows NT 3.5. Unlike NT, however, Windows 95 is designed to run only on the Intel family of processors (386 and higher). One of the major goals of Windows 95 is to provide a 32-bit, preemptive multitasking operating system for mainstream computers and users that retains backward compatibility with all of the software that has come before. Windows 95 will run DOS, Windows 16-bit, and Windows 32-bit programs, and it will run them all at the same time.

> **NOTE**
>
> During the remainder of this discussion, the term *386* is used to refer not only to the Intel 80386 processor but also the 80486 and the Pentium.
>
> It's a simplification, to be sure, but for the purposes of this discussion, the 80486 is simply a faster version of the 386, with the capabilities of the 80387 math coprocessor built in. Also, for all practical purposes, the Pentium as it's used by Windows 95 is simply a faster version of the 80486, because the Pentium's capability to support multiple processors is not used.

Another of the capabilities of the 386 chip is to define privilege levels for running software. Each different privilege level is called a *ring*. Ring 0 is the highest level and has the highest level of privilege. Code running in Ring 0 can perform any task the processor is capable of doing, and it can manipulate any memory address in the machine. Ring 1 has more privilege than Ring 2, which has even more than Ring 3.

Where We Are Now

Instead of being a graphical extension of DOS, Windows 95 is an integrated, 32-bit graphical operating system that boots up your computer and provides all of the services necessary for running your computer system. The need to first boot to DOS is gone, sort of. As you will see later in this chapter, DOS is actually alive and kicking.

Here is a short list of the major features of Windows 95:

- **32-bit, protected-mode graphical operating system:** All of the memory management, process management, and hardware management is performed by Windows 95.

- **Preemptive multitasking and multithreading:** 32-bit applications are scheduled differently than Win16 (16-bit Windows 3.*x*) applications. Win32 applications do not depend on other programs yielding time to them. The capability to separate tasks into multiple threads means that background operations are much less noticeable.

- **System-wide Registry database:** Replaces initialization files such as AUTOEXEC.BAT, CONFIG.SYS, WIN.INI, and SYSTEM.INI. AUTOEXEC and CONFIG are needed only to load real-mode drivers for hardware components that don't have protected-mode drivers. Environmental settings in these files are passed along to any DOS sessions you might launch. The .INI files are needed only for compatibility with those Win16 applications that expect to be able to use them.

- **32-bit installable file system (IFS):** The IFS provides support for multiple simultaneous file-storage formats, including VFAT (Virtual File Allocation Table) with long filename support, CDFS (Compact Disk File System), and network redirectors that enable users to connect to multiple network protocols simultaneously.

- **Unidriver support:** For printing, communications, and video services.

- **Dynamic loading and unloading of protected mode 32-bit device drivers:** This allows for hot docking of PCMCIA devices, as well as unloading device drivers to gain more memory for working applications.

- **Support for Plug and Play devices and legacy devices:** The Plug and Play specifications provide a standard for add-in cards that do not require the user to perform the configuration steps that can be so maddening. Under Plug and Play, the system automatically recognizes new cards added to the system and automatically assigns IRQ settings, DMA settings, address settings, and the like, which do not conflict with other devices already in the system. Windows 95 also has better support for older cards that were built before Plug and Play. When these cards are detected, Windows 95 will do as much automatic configuration as possible.

- **A completely reworked user interface:** Windows 95 has a completely new user interface that combines the best features of Windows with the best ideas from other GUI interfaces to create a new way of working that is easily learned by new users, yet delivers the power that old timers demand.

Booting Windows 95

When you flip on the big red button to power up your computer, a number of steps must be taken before you can begin working with Windows 95. As always, the Power On Self Test (POST) routine built into your hardware scans the system and makes sure that memory appears to be working correctly and all the settings in CMOS are correct. Then the system goes looking for an operating system. This section provides a simplified, nontechnical description of the Windows 95 boot process.

When your system finds Windows 95, it begins to load program code from the hard disk to memory in order to run Windows 95. Keep in mind that Windows 95 must support not only 32-bit applications and Win3.*x* 16-bit applications, but it must also support running DOS applications.

Because Intel processors initialize in real mode (the mode of operation compatible with the original IBM PC), and because most DOS programs run in real mode, Windows 95 first loads an updated real mode version of DOS. This copy of DOS is used to support device drivers that run in real mode, and also supports any DOS applications that might be run by the user.

Next, Windows 95 loads what are known as static VxDs. VxD, according to Windows folklore, stands for Virtual Anything Driver. A static VxD, then, is a device driver that remains in memory the whole time Windows 95 is running. One good example of this is the video driver that Windows 95 uses. You cannot unload the video driver and replace it with another one while the system is running.

Windows 95 switches into protected mode next, which effectively puts the real mode DOS that has been loaded to sleep, and begins loading the core components of Windows 95 into a virtual machine. A virtual machine is an area in memory that looks like a real computer to software. As you will see later in this chapter, there are a lot of components that work together to create Windows 95. These components include the very heart of the Windows 95 operating system such as the Virtual Machine Manager, installable file systems, dynamic VxDs, and other operating system services.

Finally, the Windows 95 shell is loaded, and you are presented with a working desktop from which you can launch applications. In the sections of this chapter that follow, you will see how Windows 95 is constructed so that you have a better idea of what is under the hood of Windows 95.

The Windows 95 Architecture

One of the hallmarks of Microsoft operating systems over the years has been the way they are put together out of modular components that work together. Windows 95 continues in that tradition. The benefit of this modular approach is that many of the operating system's components can be easily replaced by the user in order to provide non-standard or enhanced capabilities. Take a look at Figure 9.1 and you'll see how the components of Windows 95 are fitted together to create the overall architecture of Windows 95. As you can see, the basic configuration of Windows 95 is layered so that a single subsystem manages a single group of related activities.

FIGURE 9.1.

The Windows 95 system components and their relationship to each other.

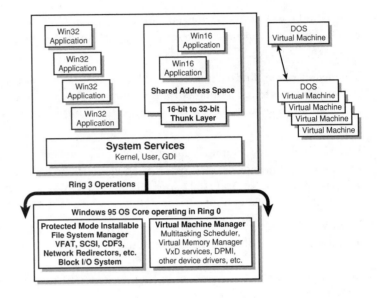

Perhaps the first thing you noticed in Figure 9.1 is the line of demarcation between the parts of Windows 95 that run in Ring 0 and those that run in Ring 3. This division of the operating system and its running application programs into separate rings takes advantage of the protection-ring architecture built into 386 processors and is a new feature in Windows.

As you move from Ring 0 down to Ring 3, running programs are progressively restricted in the processor instructions they can use and the memory locations they can address. The portions of Windows 95 that run in Ring 0 provide the base services that are normally thought of as the core of any operating system. Figure 9.2 shows you a simplified view of the way these rings are laid out within the architecture of the 386 processor.

Windows 95 only uses Ring 0 and Ring 3. Unlike Windows NT, which uses all four ring levels to adapt itself to different processors, the mid-level rings are not used at all in Windows 95. The reason for this is that there is quite a bit of processor overhead involved in shifting between rings. The processor in a computer can only cycle (perform one instruction) each time the computer's clock ticks.

Calling a routine that is running in another ring takes about 3.5 times as many clock ticks as calling a routine that is running in the same ring. The number of processor cycles it takes to return a result takes a similar amount of time. For this reason, the number of ring transitions in Windows 95 is kept to a minimum wherever possible. Properly managed, however, the division of Windows 95 into Ring 0 and Ring 3 components more than makes up for the overhead of ring transition by providing a robust environment that makes it difficult for an errant program to bring down the whole system. The trade off is stability.

Windows 95 is designed to be a mainstream operating system suitable for the vast majority of users. By limiting its operation to Ring 0 and Ring 3 and allowing non-Microsoft code to run in Ring 0, it is possible for a third-party programmer to create a flawed device driver that can crash the system.

Microsoft is working with device driver programmers to educate them in an effort to reduce the possibility that an ill-behaved device driver will crash the system, so there should be few problems of this sort. However, you should be aware that if you need absolute iron-fence protection for mission-critical or high-security applications, you need to pick up a copy of Windows NT.

FIGURE 9.2.

Software executing in Ring 0 has the highest privilege level, Ring 3 the least.

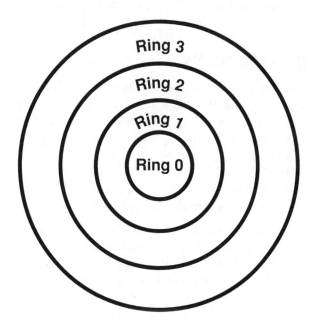

The Ring 0 Components

The Ring 0 components of Windows 95 are the heart and soul of the operating system. They include the file-management subsystem and the Virtual Machine Manager.

The file-management subsystem is divided into three basic layers. The Installable File System (IFS) manager, which is responsible for managing any installable file systems in memory. When a call is made to read or write a file, the IFS manager determines which IFS should be used and routes the request to the appropriate installed file system. The IFS then handles the request by turning it into the proper format for the Block I/O subsystem, which is responsible for directly addressing the hardware.

The Virtual Machine Manager (VMM) provides a number of basic services including memory management, task scheduling, and device-driver management. Details of the VMM are provided later in this chapter.

Perhaps the Achilles' heel of Windows 95 is the fact that VxDs (virtual device drivers) can also run in Ring 0. Because Microsoft has documented how to build VxDs, third-party (non-Microsoft) software vendors can place code into your system that, if ill-behaved, can crash your entire system. This situation is one of the few major compromises in the design of Windows 95.

Any code running in Ring 0 has permission to do anything it wants. A relatively simple bug in a VxD could bring down the whole system. Windows 95 could have been designed so that VxDs run in Ring 1 to offer better protection, but the designers opted for better performance by avoiding ring transitions.

Ring 3 Components

The portions of Windows 95 that reside in Ring 3 are the System Virtual Machine and any DOS virtual machines that may be launched to run non-Windows programs. The System Virtual Machine is a standard 386 virtual machine that supports both 32-bit Windows 95 programs as well as Windows 3.x 16-bit programs. Additionally, the System Virtual Machine contains the three traditional segments of the Windows API (Application Programming Interface): KERNEL, USER, and GDI. All of the Windows applications you have running are contained in the System Virtual Machine. 32-bit applications each get a separate address space, whereas 16-bit Windows 3.x programs share a single address space.

When you boot Windows 95, a single DOS virtual machine is created, but it's never used by any program. Instead, this "phantom" virtual machine is used as a template to create the environment for any DOS applications that are run. When you launch a DOS program, a new virtual machine is created, and the content and configuration of the phantom VM is copied into the newly created VM. The DOS program is then loaded and run. More details on this process can be found in Chapter 10, "Application Support in Windows 95."

The third component that resides in Ring 3 is the Windows API. The API is itself divided into three parts: GDI, USER, and KERNEL. The Windows API is a group of functions that can be called by any Windows program to request services. GDI handles calls for graphical services such as drawing on the screen and printing. USER is responsible for managing windows and controls within windows. KERNEL basically takes care of everything else.

> **NOTE**
>
> Keep in mind that Windows 95, because it retains compatibility with 16-bit versions of Windows, actually divides the API into six parts. GDI, USER, and KERNEL all have both 16- and 32-bit versions. More details on the division between 16- and 32-bit components are found later in this chapter.

The Windows 95 Virtual Machine Manager

If you refer back to Figure 9.1, you'll see that the Virtual Machine Manager is constructed of several parts. Here is a quick rundown of each:

Scheduler: The scheduler is the part of the Windows 95 core that provides multitasking.

Memory Manager: Each task that is running under Windows 95 is allocated memory to use. Windows 95 virtualizes memory by using page tables that convert the memory addresses referenced by programs into the physical memory locations where program code and data are actually stored. The Windows 95 memory manager also controls swapping of code and data in and out of the Virtual Memory swap file.

VxD Manager: VxDs are virtual device drivers, which in Windows 95 can be dynamically loaded and unloaded as needed. In Windows 95, hardware devices such as the keyboard, video card, mouse, CD ROM drives, sound cards, scanners, and so on, are virtualized. That is, software interfaces with the driver as if it were the hardware itself, and the driver in turn arbitrates conflicting requests for device services and deals with the hardware directly.

DOS Virtual Machine Manager: Each DOS program launched is contained within its own 386 virtual machine. Since DOS programs usually assume that they are the only program running, they have no inboard mechanism for multitasking or sharing system resources. The DOS VMM provides these services.

Each of these aspects of the Virtual Machine Manager deserves to be looked at in greater detail. The sections that follow do just that.

CAUTION

Perhaps the most overused and potentially confusing term applied to Windows 95 is *virtual.* Virtual memory, virtual device drivers, virtual machines, and other such terms can be ambiguous, leading users to think that nominally unrelated parts of the Windows 95 core have more in common than they really do.

In fact, the term *virtual* refers to the technique of using memory and layers of software to create entities that appear to the running programs to be hardware devices or memory. Instead, virtualization creates a level of indirection that insulates hardware from being directly manipulated by running programs.

For example, a virtual device driver that controls a Sound Blaster card appears to programs to be a real Sound Blaster. Any attempts by programs to access the available services of the Sound Blaster are directed to the virtual device driver (VxD). The VxD intercepts these requests for services, arbitrates conflicting requests, and translates the requests into calls to the Sound Blaster card itself. This way, if two programs simultaneously request a sound to be played, the VxD captures the requests and only one of the requests is honored. The other process must wait until the hardware becomes available again. Each program thinks it is independently controlling the Sound Blaster without interference from any other program.

Multitasking, Multithreading, and the Scheduler

Multitasking is the apparent capability of a single processor to run more than one program at a time. Of course, a processor cannot actually do more than one thing at a time, but by slicing up the processor's resources and letting each running program have a share, the illusion of simultaneous execution can be created. It's the scheduler's job to create that illusion.

Those readers familiar with Windows NT or OS/2 are probably already familiar with the concept of multithreading, but most Windows 3.x users are not. Simply stated, a *thread* is the smallest unit of program execution in Windows 95. New functions in the Windows 95 API enable 32-bit programs (applications and VxDs) to seat themselves in memory and then spawn small subroutines that share the parent program's code and data.

Using multiple threads, programs can divide up the tasks they must perform. For example a word processor might use one thread to print in the background and another thread to accept keystrokes from the keyboard. Or perhaps, a program might spawn a thread to perform a lengthy task, such as opening a large file, and use another thread to put up a message box with a Cancel button that the user can click if he or she decides not to open the file. That way, the file-open routine doesn't have to waste clock cycles to check to see whether the user has tried to cancel the opening of the file.

Under Windows 95, the scheduler is primarily concerned with threads instead of the parent process. A running program of any type is simply a thread to the scheduler. Old-style Win16 programs and DOS programs cannot multithread. 32-bit programs, on the other hand, can spawn multiple threads. The ability of 32-bit software to split itself into multiple threads could potentially enable 32-bit programs to monopolize the scheduler and put the squeeze on Win16 and DOS programs, but the scheduler is too smart to let that happen.

The Windows 95 Multitasking Model

There are basically two flavors of multitasking: cooperative and preemptive. Cooperative multitasking is the model used in Windows 3.x, and it relies on programmers to construct software that gracefully yields processor time to other running programs. Preemptive multitasking is under the control of the operating system's scheduler, which assigns each running process a slice of the processor's time. The process gets that amount of time only, before the scheduler preempts it in favor of another process. Windows 95 uses both models.

Under Windows 95, 32-bit programs are preemptively scheduled. Preemptive scheduling creates a smoother, more reliable transition from process to process, which ensures no single process can hog the computer's resources to the detriment of other running programs.

Cooperative scheduling is reserved for 16-bit Windows 3.*x* programs. Without going into the bits and bytes, you should know that Windows programs traditionally contain a window procedure (`MainWndProc`) that processes the event messages addressed to that program. When this procedure is executed, and it is executed often, Windows 3.*x* takes it as a signal that the program can be suspended to allow another program to gain access to processor time without interrupting a critical section of code.

The Windows 95 Scheduler

When you speak of processor resources, you are really speaking of time. The speed at which the processor can carry out instructions depends on the speed of the clock that drives it. All other things being equal, the faster the clock, the faster the computing that can take place. Processor performance is measured in MIPS (Millions of Instructions Per Second). The processing power of the CPU is divided into segments called *timeslices*. The job of the Windows 95 scheduler is to assign timeslices to waiting threads.

The scheduler in Windows 95 is a very complex bit of software engineering that is divided into two parts: the primary scheduler and the timeslice scheduler. The job of the primary scheduler is to assign priorities to each of the threads awaiting execution time. The timeslice scheduler calculates the percentage of each timeslice to be given to threads. These two parts of the scheduler work together in four steps:

- The primary scheduler assigns priorities to each waiting thread. Priority values are integers between 0 and 31. Priorities are reevaluated approximately every 20 milliseconds.

- The primary scheduler suspends any thread that doesn't have the highest priority value. For example, if two threads have a priority value of 17, they are handed off to the timeslice scheduler, and all other threads are suspended. If only one thread has the highest value, it's sent to the timeslice scheduler by itself.

- The timeslice scheduler assigns a percentage of the current timeslice to each of the threads it's handling. Calculations are based on values (`VMStat_Exclusive`, `VMStat_Background`, and `VMStat_High_Pri_Bacground`) that are contained in the virtual machine that houses the thread.

- The threads are run, and the process begins all over again.

Each timeslice is a fixed number of clock ticks, and the scheduler can gain control of the processor whenever a clock interrupt occurs. The next timeslice is given to the thread that has the highest priority value.

Priorities are assigned at the process level (the program itself) and at the thread level. Processes have one of three priority classifications: high, normal, and idle. In addition, individual threads can have their priority values dynamically adjusted. When a program receives input from the mouse, keyboard, or the message queue, all of its threads are boosted to a higher priority. Also, the program running in the foreground is automatically boosted to a higher level in anticipation of increased activity. Thus the program that the user is actually working with at the moment is given extra processor time so that the user won't perceive it as being slow.

A thread that has been given a boost is subject to a timed decay. Each time the thread receives a timeslice, its priority value is reduced until it eventually returns to its base priority. Threads that have been passed over for processor time have their priority level boosted. This way, each thread that is running tends to be prioritized so that it gets all the timeslices it needs in order to do work, but not so many timeslices that processor time is wasted.

Memory Management in Windows 95

It's all too easy in discussing memory issues to fall into the trap of framing the discussion in terms of bits and bytes, segments and offsets, and all the other minutiae that only a programmer could love. That level of discussion, however, quickly leaves all but the most advanced computer users in the dust. This section of the chapter attempts to give you a broad overview of memory management issues as they relate to the everyday use of Windows 95. If you are interested in the bits and bytes, you'll need to refer to a book that deals with memory management on a programmer's level.

From a user's point of view, the way Windows 95 handles memory is completely different from the way it's done previous versions of Windows or in DOS. Gone is HIMEM.SYS and EMM386.EXE. Gone, too, is SmartDrive and the necessity of setting up Windows' virtual memory settings. But, as the spaghetti-sauce commercial says, "It's in there." The functionality of the "missing" components is built right into the core of Windows 95.

32-Bit Addressing of Memory

Unlike previous versions of DOS and Windows, memory under Windows 95 is not divided into Conventional, Expanded, and Extended memory specifications. Instead, Windows 95 uses a built-in capability of the 386 (and higher) chip to address memory using a linear addressing model, also known as a flat memory model, that provides access to up to 4 GB of RAM. That's four *billion* bytes of memory. Simply stated, the first byte of RAM is byte 0, and the last byte of RAM is byte 4,000,000,000, (well 4,096,000,000 to be technically exact) and it's counted straight through. And yes, because everything else in Windows 95 seems to be virtualized, why not memory management, too?

Virtual Memory Management

Of course, few if any computers outside research facilities have ever been blessed with 4 GB of memory. Most machines these days have between 8 and 32 MB of RAM. Windows 95 takes advantage of a feature of the 386 chip design called *paging*. When the paging feature of the 386 is turned on, the 4 GB of potential addresses is divided into 4KB chunks, each of which is called a page. A page table is used to map virtual addresses to physical memory locations. The page table is used to keep track of the condition of the information stored in physical memory.

When Windows 95 is launched, it requires somewhere in the neighborhood of 1 MB of RAM for the basic Virtual Machine Manager, the Windows 95 shell, and the normal complement of device drivers for the keyboard, video card, and the built-in cache VxD that replaced SmartDrive. In addition, Windows 95 is capable of dynamically loading and unloading device drivers in the form of VxDs. Most of this memory is locked down for the entire session.

As you launch programs and open data files, physical memory is allocated for the purpose. At some point, especially if you only have 4 or 8 MB of RAM, a program will request more memory than is physically present in your computer. That is when Windows 95 will call up a least-recently used (LRU) algorithm that determines what portion of memory it can free up by writing the contents to a disk-based swap file if necessary. Once the swap file is updated, the physical memory addresses can be overwritten with the data requested by the program.

The "if necessary" part is determined by looking at the page table to see whether the data has been changed since it was placed into memory. Each memory page has a flag that indicates the condition of the data contained in physical memory. This flag indicates whether the contents of the physical memory has accessed or changed. For example, if you launch a word-processing program and open a large file, one part of physical memory is filled with the code for the program and another portion of the memory holds the document (or a portion of the document).

As you work with the program, the memory containing the program's code is accessed, but it isn't usually changed. On the other hand, as you make changes to the document, those changes are reflected by altering the contents of the memory that is used to store the document. The virtual memory manager keeps track of when memory locations are read and whether the contents of a memory location have been changed.

As you continue to work, launching other programs and opening other documents, you'll probably reach a point where the virtual memory manager is asked to allocate more memory than physically exists in the system. That's when it uses the LRU algorithm to determine what can be swapped out.

If the code for a loaded program hasn't been used in a while, the physical memory it occupies can be given over to another use without saving it to a swap file. Because it already resides on disk, all Windows 95 has to do is make a note of what the memory contains before it's overwritten. The same also is true of a document that hasn't been modified. It already resides on disk, so there is no reason to duplicate the document in a swap file.

Of course, if the contents of the document have changed, the story is different. Windows 95 can't just write the alterations to the document to the disk file, because you may decide not to keep the changes. Instead, the memory image of the file is stored in the swap file (sometimes also called a page file).

Later, when you go back to working with a program whose code or data have been swapped out of memory, the virtual memory manager then determines what is currently in memory that can be swapped out, so the information you need can be placed back into physical memory.

Disk Caching and the Virtual Memory Manager

Previous versions of DOS and Windows used a disk-caching program called SmartDrive that uses a portion of your system's memory to provide read and write caching. In Windows 95, the cache software is provided by a VxD (named Vcache) that is part of the virtual memory manager.

Cache software dedicates a piece of memory to storing everything that is read from disk or written to disk. Because even today's fast hard disks are excruciatingly slow when compared to the speed of accessing memory, a cache can dramatically increase system performance. When a program requests data to be read from disk, the cache is first checked to see whether the data has recently been read. If it's found in the cache, the data is placed into working memory for the program to use. In Windows 95, the cache and the virtual memory manager work together. Just because you have closed a program doesn't mean that the memory it occupied is immediately overwritten. If there is enough memory, and the demands on memory are small enough, chances are that the information is still in memory.

Try this: Launch Windows 95 and immediately double-click My Computer. When it comes up, close it immediately, and then double-click My Computer again. You should notice two things. First, Explorer launches again, even faster than the first time. Second, you should notice that the hard disk light doesn't come on while the program is launching the second time. The reason is that the memory it occupied previously is still intact. All the virtual memory manager has to do is reassign the same physical memory addresses and reinitialize them before running the code.

How Windows 95 Uses Memory

Figure 9.3 illustrates how Windows 95 uses a map of all 4 GB—the maximum amount of addressable memory—to place code and data into memory. This map is used regardless of the actual amount of memory installed in your system.

As you can see in Figure 9.3, the first megabyte of memory is used for MS-DOS virtual-machine operations. This is a throwback to the old conventional-memory days. The area between 1 and 4 MB is unused except in very special cases, and you would need programming knowledge to understand those cases, so just consider those addresses a wasteland.

FIGURE 9.3.

The Windows 95 memory map.

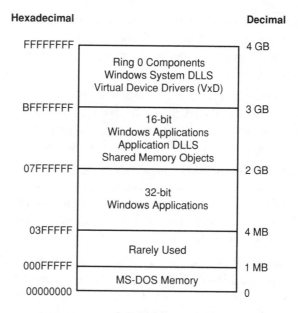

Hexadecimal		Decimal
FFFFFFFF	Ring 0 Components / Windows System DLLS / Virtual Device Drivers (VxD)	4 GB
BFFFFFFF	16-bit / Windows Applications / Application DLLS / Shared Memory Objects	3 GB
07FFFFFF	32-bit / Windows Applications	2 GB
03FFFFF	Rarely Used	4 MB
000FFFFF	MS-DOS Memory	1 MB
00000000		0

The address area is the portion of the map that gets a real workout. The addresses between 4 MB and 2 GB are used by 32-bit programs as their base of operations. Each running 32-bit app gets its own local map of these two gigabytes of addresses. Each 32-bit program that is running believes that it has 2 GB of memory to work with. In effect it does, because when memory starts to get full, the virtual memory manager is able to swap the current contents of memory out to the swap file.

The area between 2 and 3 GB is used by 16-bit Windows 3.*x* programs and by shared-memory configurations such as dynamic link libraries (DLL) and OLE objects. Windows 3.*x* programs were written to share the same address space and Message queues with other programs. Theoretically, each 16-bit program could be given an individual address space, but it would only complicate matters and slow things down.

The area between 3 and 4 GB is used to house the core of the Windows 95 operating system, VxDs, and any system DLLs that might need to be loaded. All of the Ring 0 components have their addresses in this area.

Seldom, if ever, do the memory addresses used by program threads correspond to the physical memory installed in the system. Instead, when a thread calls an address, it's translated internally by the Windows 95 virtual memory manager into the physical memory address that contains the information the thread wants to access.

Virtual Memory

The term *virtual memory* refers to the way Windows 95 uses the physical memory of the computer and hard-disk resources to create a memory allocation system that allows for multiple running applications to request and receive allocations of memory, even when memory is at or near capacity. Windows 95 itself requires at least 1 MB of memory in order to launch, and it may require more depending on the types of devices and network protocols you have installed.

Each program that is running addresses memory using local references to memory addresses. The addresses that the program believes it's using are actually mapped to the program's Local Descriptor Table. The descriptor table translates the addresses used by the program into the physical memory addresses the program is actually using.

In addition, the Local Descriptor Table keeps track of some information about the usage of memory. When data or program code is first read into memory, it's considered clean, meaning that there have been no changes made to it. The descriptor table indicates whether the memory has been accessed, when it was last accessed, and whether the data has been changed since it was last written to disk.

If a program needs memory and no physical memory is available, the Windows 95 pager is called upon to do its stuff. The act of temporarily storing memory contents on disk is called paging, or swapping. The pager will first look for empty memory locations. Failing that, it will look to see what memory locations have gone the longest without being used. The formula for determining what memory to swap to disk is known as the LRU (Least Recently Used) algorithm.

Simply because a portion of a program's memory allotment is swapped to disk doesn't mean that the program or its threads are suspended. If the program should happen to try accessing a chunk of its memory that is swapped out, a condition known as a page fault occurs. A page fault simply means that the program can't find something it owns in memory. It's the job of the pager to find out what is needed and to find a spot for it in memory.

Because modern software applications use tremendous amounts of memory compared to their ancestors (believe it or not, WordPerfect used to come on two disks), it's easy to see that having two or three programs running can require more than 4 MB of memory, and even 8 MB might not be enough when large applications with large data files open are being run.

Because more swapping is required when memory is low, it's easy to see why throwing more SIMM chips into a system quickly improves performance. Despite the fact that they are getting faster all the time, hard disks are relatively slow, and network transmission can be even slower. That's why reading and writing to disk is perhaps the most time-consuming task your computer performs.

The Windows 95 Swap File

Under previous versions of Windows, virtual memory was often a hassle. You couldn't put your swap file on a drive that was using disk compression such as Stacker or DriveSpace, temporary swap files were very sensitive to disk fragmentation, and permanent swap files were large and hidden.

All of that changes under Windows 95. In fact, the virtual-memory swap file should be all but invisible to users. Under the default scheme, Windows 95 selects the location of the swap file and manages its size, which can range from 0 bytes to all available disk space. Indeed, if you look at the System Properties' Virtual Memory dialog box shown in Figure 9.4, you'll see that you are strongly warned against customizing virtual-memory settings.

FIGURE 9.4.

If you don't know what you're doing, you can actually impair system performance by customizing the swap file settings.

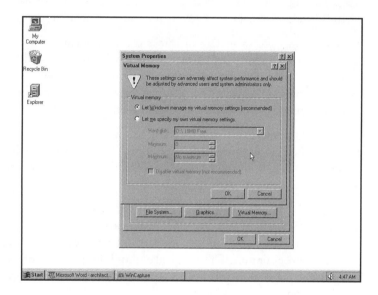

Under Windows 3.x you have two choices: a permanent swap file or a temporary one. The permanent swap file is a hidden file (SPARTPAR.386) of several megabytes that cannot be fragmented or written to a compressed drive. The temporary swap file is limited in performance and slow. Windows 95 changes all that by providing an entirely rewritten Virtual Memory Manager that dynamically allocates space for the swap file depending on the needs of the system at runtime. The size of the swap file can be increased and decreased as needed. The Windows 95 swap file can be written to a fragmented hard disk without taking a huge performance hit, and can even be written to a compressed disk.

TIP

Just because the swap file doesn't slow down too much on a fragmented disk drive, don't use this as an excuse not to regularly defragment your disks using the Microsoft supplied Defrag utility.

Most of the time you do not need to worry about the swap file. There are times, however, when you might want to override the default swap file settings. One example would be when the disk drive where Windows 95 is installed has relatively little free space, while another drive in the system has plenty.

16-Bit Versus 32-Bit Memory and the Thunk

Although Windows 95 is very much a 32-bit operating system, there are still some 16-bit components that remain. As has been mentioned before, the Windows API is divided into GDI, USER, and KERNEL. Where changing to 32-bit code would have resulted in greater memory usage without significant performance benefit, the 16-bit code has remained. Other portions of 16-bit code are retained to provide backward compatibility.

Without going into the details of Intel's processor architecture, you need to know that the methods used for addressing 16-bit memory locations are very different from the way 32-bit addresses are treated. Obviously, programs written for previous versions of Windows lack the capability to run in 32-bit mode. Yet they must be able to address memory in a machine that is running mostly 32-bit code and to call functions in the Win32 API.

What all of this means is that there must be a way of translating requests from 16-bit applications into their 32-bit equivalent. In Windows 95, this translation is called a *thunk*, a term that started out as a joke among Microsoft programmers. Somehow the name stuck, and now we are stuck with using it.

From a user standpoint, you don't need to worry about thunks in any way. All of the thunking is done automatically by Windows 95. The reason it's important for you to know about thunking is that the translation from 16-bit addresses and data types to 32-bit equivalents and back again consumes processor time. The overhead of thunking is just one of the reasons you'll usually see a noticeable boost in performance when you upgrade from a 16-bit software package to its 32-bit version.

Installable File System Architecture

The Installable File System (IFS) is a complex bit of programming that makes Windows 95 simpler to use, especially for users who don't understand all the details of data storage. When a program requests a disk read or write, the IFS Manager determines what type of device the data is stored on and calls the appropriate installable file system driver.

Floppy disks and hard disks use a clever variation on the old DOS File Allocation Table (FAT) scheme to store data using long filenames. This 32-bit driver is known as the VFAT, or Virtual File Allocation Table driver. CD-ROM disks, on the other hand use, the ISO 960 format to store information. NetWare has a proprietary file structure, as do other network protocols, and SCSI devices have their own quirks.

By enabling multiple file systems to be managed simultaneously, Windows 95 can deal with turning almost any data format into the specific Block I/O requests that are needed to interface to hardware such as disks, network cards, and so on. Figure 9.5 shows the architecture of the IFS.

FIGURE 9.5.

The IFS concept enables a wide variety of different file systems.

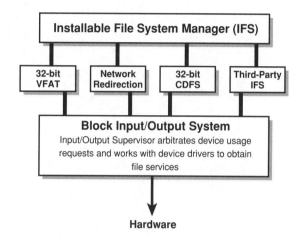

There are a number of uses for an installable file system. An IFS will let you more easily connect to other systems that don't support the VFAT file system. Disk compression schemes, mainframe databases, online services, and so forth can use the IFS to create data structures that look just like standard files to a user. In short, the IFS is a complex subsystem that makes it possible for users to forget the details and simply work with their data, wherever and however it may be stored.

Summary

In this chapter you have seen how Windows 95's new 32-bit architecture creates a very different environment for users. Windows 95 has graduated into a 32-bit operating system that provides superior multitasking. The capability of 32-bit programs to break tasks up into multiple threads also ensures better performance and smoother operation of background processes.

You also have gained an insight into the way Windows 95 is constructed. This knowledge will help you grasp the finer points of how Windows 95 supports DOS, 16-bit, and 32-bit software, which is the topic of the next chapter.

Application Support in Windows 95

One of the problems with establishing a worldwide standard such as MS-DOS is that you build up an incredible legacy that you must maintain support for. Microsoft is doubly blessed—or cursed, depending on how you view the situation. The incredible success over the years of DOS and Windows creates two legacies that must be maintained. Microsoft's claim for Windows 95 is that it will run virtually every program ever written for Intel-equipped computers, which is quite a feat.

Because there were relatively few Windows 2.x users, Microsoft was able to make some changes for Windows 3.0 that rendered many 2.x applications obsolete. They simply wouldn't run properly in the new environment. Microsoft does not have the luxury of making anything obsolete in Windows 95 because of the number of DOS and Windows 3.x programs in regular use.

There are three distinct classes of software that must be supported in Windows 95: 32-bit applications, 16-bit applications, and DOS applications. Each class presents a unique set of circumstances because of the era it represents.

The differences between text-based DOS applications and their graphical Windows cousins are manifest, but still that's only part of the story. Intel processors have three separate and distinct ways of addressing memory: real mode, 16-bit protected mode, and 32-bit protected mode. It is no coincidence that the three types of software that Windows 95 must support correspond exactly with the evolution of the 80x86 processor line.

Thanks for the Memories

The real mode operation of every Intel processor is based on a *segment:offset* method of addressing memory, which uses two hexadecimal numbers to represent a memory address. Remember, hexadecimal numbers use letters to represent the numbers 10 through 15 (A is 10; F is 15). Memory is divided into chunks of 64 KB, and the first number identifies the segment of memory to be addressed. The second number specifies how many bytes offset from the beginning of the segment to address. When you see something such as 1ACD:113F, you know it is a memory address. The 1ACD is a segment, and the 113F is the number of bytes away from the beginning of the segment that the actual memory is located.

DOS applications that use the *segment:offset* method of addressing might require Expanded memory support (EMS) and might even have the capability to run in protected mode.

All 16-Bit Windows 3.x applications use a modification of the *segment:offset* addressing scheme, use only Extended memory, and always run in protected mode.

All 32-Bit applications use a linear addressing scheme that is free of the 64KB segment limit and free of both Expanded and Extended memory architectures. It's no wonder that each of the three classes of software is treated very differently in Windows 95.

Windows 95 and 32-bit Applications

There are a number of qualifications that applications must possess in order to be certified as "designed for Windows 95." They must adhere to the Win32 Application Programming Interface (API), have Registry awareness, and support OLE where practical, among other specifications.

Because applications designed with the Win32 API take full advantage of the Windows 95 architecture, they generally provide the best performance. Whenever possible, you should update your applications with the Windows 95 specific version. Here is a quick list of the benefits of using 32-bit versions of your favorite programs.

- **Performance:** 32-bit applications require less overhead and fit right into the 32-bit architecture of Windows 95 so that you get the fastest possible execution speed.

- **Preemptive multitasking:** Because the Windows 95 scheduler assigns specific timeslices to 32-bit applications, greedy applications cannot hog processor resources and drag down overall system performance.

- **Multithreading:** Because 32-bit applications can spawn threads that are separately scheduled by the Windows 95 scheduler, multitasking (especially of background operations) is a lot smoother.

- **Long filenames:** 32-bit applications can take full advantage of long filename support in Windows 95.

- **Extra protection:** Each 32-bit application runs in its own protected, private address space. Each application also has a private message queue. Other applications' errors cannot intrude on memory locations or block messages from reaching the application.

- **Registry aware:** Applications designed for Windows 95 are aware of the registry and do not require WIN.INI, SYSTEM.INI, or any startup files such as CONFIG.SYS. Also Windows 95 compatible apps can uninstall themselves without leaving files orphaned in the Windows or System folders.

Windows 95 and 16-bit Applications

The success of Windows 3.x is illustrated by a single statistic. In 1993, sales of Windows applications outstripped sales of DOS applications for the first time. Although the major software companies will have 32-bit versions of their products available at about the same time Windows 95 ships, there are still many thousands of 16-bit programs in circulation.

Microsoft promises that Win16 applications will run under Windows 95 without modification, and they will run as well or better than under Windows 3.x. You will find that many 16-bit applications actually run better because Windows 95's new 32-bit subsystems provide a better, faster level of operating system support that Win16 apps translate into better performance.

Although Win16 applications run in the same System Virtual Machine as 32-bit applications, they do not receive the same treatment. Just as they did under Windows 3.x, 16-bit applications share the same address space and message queues. Each running 16-bit application is a single thread of execution that cooperatively multitasks just like Windows 3.1.

Some portions of the Windows operating system still contain hand-tuned 16-bit assembly code to provide essential services to Win16 applications. These portions of 16-bit support code remain because converting them to 32-bit code would have increased the size of Windows 95 without offering any substantial increase in performance. Win16 applications can access the new 32-bit subsystems through the Thunk layer, which converts 16-bit addressing and data information into 32-bit equivalents.

Windows 95 continues to place files named WIN.INI and SYSTEM.INI into the Windows folder to maintain compatibility with Win16 applications that expect to find and use these files. Whenever possible, Windows 95 detects changes to these files and incorporates the changes into the Registry.

TIP

Some Win16 applications do not install correctly because they used the services of Program Manager to update the Windows 3.x registration database and initialization files. If you encounter such an application, open Program Manager and install the application from there. When the application is installed, the proper settings will be made in the Registry and you can run the application normally without using Program Manager to launch it.

Windows 95 and DOS Applications

Supporting DOS software under Windows has always been a thorn in the side for Microsoft. The DOS environment is so different from Windows that special exceptions have to be made for DOS applications at every turn.

The problem is simply that as DOS grew up over the years, programmers were always pushing the edge of DOS's capabilities to get things done. Also DOS was never intended as a multitasking environment, so DOS programmers always made the assumption that hardware was theirs to do with as they pleased. By the time Windows came along, the DOS world had evolved numerous conventions and programming practices that are in direct conflict with the Windows way of writing software. Compared to Windows applications, most DOS software is greedy, inconsiderate, and memory-hogging—the proverbial 600-pound gorilla. Incredibly, the support for DOS applications gets stronger with each new version of Windows.

Windows 95 continues that tradition by providing better windowing capabilities for DOS applications. New features include a toolbar in DOS sessions, the capability to spool print jobs, and better support for DOS-based graphics.

Because each running DOS application resides within its own DOS virtual machine, the Windows 95 scheduler treats each one as a single thread and schedules each VM preemptively. The new 32-bit VDD (Virtual Device Driver) architecture arbitrates access to hardware resources. Thus, each running DOS application is fooled into believing that it is running its own individual computer, and applications that were never written to multitask with other applications perform flawlessly.

Another boost to DOS support in Windows 95 is the replacement of real mode device drivers with 32-bit versions that have no need to load in conventional memory, or in an Upper Memory Block (UMB). Old favorites such as HIMEM.SYS, EMM386.EXE, and SmartDrive are all history. In their place are 32-bit versions that are loaded automatically by Windows 95 at startup when it loads the file IO.SYS, which helps to make CONFIG.SYS all but obsolete unless you have hardware that requires real mode drivers. DoubleSpace and DriveSpace compressed disk drives have new protected mode drivers, and protected mode drivers are supplied for all but the most marginal of hardware.

There is almost no need for hand-tuning upper memory to make room in conventional memory for DOS applications to run, even for applications that require an Expanded memory page frame. On a system that uses Windows 95's 32-bit protected-mode drivers, there can be a savings of as much as 225 KB in conventional memory, compared to a similar system using real mode drivers for the network, mouse, CD-ROM disk, and so on.

The benefit to having more room in conventional memory is that it isn't unusual to find that DOS applications that wouldn't run in Windows now run flawlessly. Many DOS applications run faster in Windows 95 than they do under any previous version of DOS. Also, Windows 95's support of DPMI (DOS Protected Mode Interface) in the operating system core also accommodates protected mode DOS applications that have become popular in the last couple of years.

Dealing with Problem Applications

Windows 95 is a very different animal from the previous versions of windows that were designed to sit on top of DOS. It shouldn't come as a surprise that some applications written for Windows 3.x and for DOS can be a problem to run. The reason is that they try to take advantage of some part of the environment that doesn't exist anymore.

For example, some Win16 applications use the title bar to put buttons on the window. Under Windows 95, such doodads belong on the toolbar, and Windows 95 might not correctly handle the application. Another example is Terminate and Stay Ready (TSR) software, designed for

DOS, that monitors a particular DOS interrupt and reacts when the interrupt is called. Because Windows 95 doesn't rely on DOS interrupts like previous versions did, TSR programs might fail to operate correctly.

CAUTION

When Windows 95 installs, potentially harmful DOS utilities are removed from your DOS directory. If you have third party utility programs similar to the Norton Utilities or PC Tools, be very careful about how you use them. Most of these tools are incompatible with the new VFAT Long Filename file system. Writing to disk with these utilities can damage your hard disk's data structure, making the disk and its data unreadable.

Fortunately, Windows 95 contains programming that attempts to give problem applications what they are looking for. Here are some examples of the legacy support offered by Windows 95.

Real Mode Device Drivers, TSRs, and Windows 95

In DOS, system services are provided by interrupts. An interrupt is a program function designed so that the processor can stop application processing, provide an operating system service, and then pick up again with the application. In some ways, the interrupt system is a little like crude multitasking. One of the tricks of the trade in DOS programming was to create a program that responded to specific interrupt events by waking up. For example, pressing Ctrl+Alt made the infamous Sidekick program stop everything in the computer and pop up a menu. When you were finished with Sidekick, it went to sleep and whatever was going on before continued.

Unlike Sidekick, most TSR programs are invisible to the user because most TSR programs are real mode drivers of one sort or another. Of course, you should use 32-bit protected mode drivers whenever possible so that you get top performance and configuration information can be stored in the registry. After you eliminate real mode drivers, you can get rid of AUTOEXEC.BAT and CONFIG.SYS completely.

During Setup, Windows 95 will replace any real-mode drivers that it can with 32-bit, protected-mode versions. For example, DBLSPACE.BIN is removed from CONFIG.SYS, and DBLSPACE.VXD is loaded as a replacement. Other examples include DOS drivers such as MSCDEX.EXE, EMM386.EXE, and HIMEM.SYS. Windows 95 maintains a safe list of drivers that can safely be replaced with Windows 95's protected mode replacements. This file, IOS.SYS, can be found in the Windows folder and examined with Notepad, WordPad, or some other similar applet.

> **CAUTION**
>
> Windows 95 does not maintain version numbers of replaceable drivers. If, for some reason, you must use a real-mode driver, you should closely inspect any new versions before installing them. To be compliant, the vendor must change the name of the driver whenever a version is created that changes the safe/unsafe status of the driver.
>
> To some extent, however, you can probably ignore this warning because real mode drivers are soon to be a thing of the past. Any hardware for which a protected mode driver isn't soon available is probably so near the end of its product life that no new real mode drivers are forthcoming anyway.

By default, a real-mode driver is considered to be safe if it is a DOS 5.0 compatible block device driver, if it monitors or replaces interrupt 13 (INT 13 -- Disk Services) without directly accessing hardware, and if it is compatible with ASPI (Advanced SCSI Programming Interface) or CAM (Common Access Method). Unsafe drivers are those that perform tasks not supported by protected mode drivers. Examples include drivers that do data compression that isn't compatible with DriveSpace, data encryption, disk mirroring, mapping of bad sectors, and so on.

If you know you have a real mode driver that offers some feature not available from a protected-mode 32-bit driver, remove the driver's entry in IOS.SYS. On the other hand, if you know that a 32-bit driver is available that has the same functionality, add an entry in IOS.SYS

Using DOS TSR Utilities

If, for some reason, you have a TSR that you must continue to use, create a shortcut to the EXE that launches the TSR. Double-clicking the shortcut will open the program in a window. Use the program in the normal way. When you are done, press Ctrl+C when the window is active to close the TSR program and remove it from memory.

Version Checking Errors

One of the most common incompatibilities with Windows 95 is the failure of Win16 applications to correctly check the version of Windows that is running. The Windows version is stored in memory and can be checked by any program that is version-sensitive. One byte contains the major version, and another byte records the revision level.

Perhaps the most common mistake is for an application to invert the bytes that provide the version information so that version 3.10 appears to be version 10.3 to the application. Because most applications check to see that the version is higher than *x*, Windows pulls a sneaky trick by reporting itself as version 3.95. If a program tries to check for a version greater than 3.10 or the reversed, 10.3, the Windows 95 version will always return a greater number so that the program can run.

The second most common error is for an application to look for a specific version. If the version number returned by Windows isn't exact, the program won't run. You can solve this problem by finding out the compiled module name for the application and placing an entry into the [Compatibility] section of WIN.INI.

To determine the module name of an application that reports it can't run in Windows 95, find the EXE file using Explorer and right-click the file object to display the context menu. Select the Quick View option from the context menu. You will get a display similar to the one shown in Figure 10.1.

FIGURE 10.1.

Choosing Quick View from the context menu of an executable file provides the compiled module name.

For the record, CorelPHOTO-PAINT! is not an application that requires a specific version of Windows or any compatibility entries at all. This program was selected because the entry for Expected Windows Version indicates the expected Version is 3.0. Usually this entry means that the program will run properly on Version 3.0 and higher, as is the case with CorelPHOTO-PAINT!.

However, if this program did check specifically for Version 3.0 and refused to run, you would simply find the module name in the Quick View (in this case, CORELPNT) and add a line like the following to the [Compatibility] section of WIN.INI:

```
CORELPNT=0x00200000
```

When the entry has been placed in WIN.INI and the file is saved, you should be able to run the program without further problems. The problem is that figuring out what the proper entry should be is nearly impossible. Unless you are given a value from a reliable source, such as Microsoft Tech Support, you are going to have to do some research. One place to start your research is the undocumented utility called MKCOMPAT.EXE, found in the Windows\System folder. With this utility, you can try changing major settings, and most of the time this will get an application working.

Application Protection

No software program of any size is perfect. Some are much less than perfect. Despite the best efforts of programmers, occasionally software programs experience problems running and they hang up. A hung program stops responding to the operating system and becomes unusable.

Because 32-bit applications have a private memory space and DOS applications run in a virtual machine, there is usually plenty of insulation to keep program A from interfering with program B. Therefore, the problem is seldom incompatibility with other 32-bit or DOS applications.

Win16 applications, on the other hand, do present some possibilities for interfering with each other because they share the same address space. More commonly, however, an application hangs because it tries to use some resource that it doesn't own. Sometimes an application is incompatible with a particular device driver, and sometimes the device driver is the one causing the problem, because device drivers run in Ring 0 and can access anything in the system.

Whatever the reason, you can easily remove hung applications from memory, most of the time without the hassle of restarting Windows as was so frequently the case under Windows 3.x. Windows 95 is much more efficient at cleaning up after errant programs.

Resources are allotted to 32-bit applications on a per-thread basis. When a thread passes out of existence, the System Virtual Machine Manager automatically cleans up any system resources the thread was using. If an application hangs up and stops responding to the system, a local reboot can usually be performed instead of having to reboot the entire system.

To unload from memory an application that has stopped responding to the system, you can perform a local reboot by pressing Ctrl+Alt+Del. Instead of rebooting the entire system, as it would in DOS, this keystroke brings up the Close Programs dialog.

NOTE

While the Close Programs dialog is onscreen, all activity in the system is halted. There is no illustration of this dialog simply because a screen capture program freezes along with everything else.

To see the Close Programs dialog, make sure no programs are running that are sensitive to interruptions, and then press Ctrl+Alt+Del. The dialog has a list of the currently running applications and three buttons. The End Task button closes the currently selected application. The Shut Down button performs an orderly shut down of the computer so that unsaved data can be preserved, and Cancel closes the dialog without taking any action.

Select the application to close and click the End Task button. The System Virtual Machine Manager will automatically reclaim any memory resources allocated to the application.

There are times, however, when a restart is indicated. Restart the system if any of the following circumstances occur:

- You get a message box telling you the shell might have been affected.
- Performance of the system seems slow after a local reboot.
- The percentage of available resources, shown in Explorer's Help About box after a local reboot, is low relative to the number of applications you have running.

Installing and Removing Applications

A common complaint among Windows 3.1 users concerns how installing applications bloats the WINDOWS and WINDOWS\SYSTEM folders with files. Many applications write DLL files into the SYSTEM folder, initialization files into the WINDOWS folder, and who knows what else. That is the problem.

What files get written where is controlled by the software's creators. Some applications have documentation that states what files the setup program writes to disk, but all too often they don't. The result is that you can never completely uninstall an application that you decide you don't want any more. The SYSTEM folder becomes bloated with DLL files having cryptic names, and you don't dare delete them because you aren't sure what applications they belong to.

Happily, Windows 95 comes very close to solving the problem for applications designed for Windows 95 by including the Add/Remove Programs dialog in the Control Panel. Add/Remove is a three-tabbed dialog that lets you install applications, refresh Windows 95 installations, and create a bootable floppy diskette.

The Install/Uninstall tab presents a two-part dialog. A button marked Install is at the top of the window. Clicking this button causes Windows 95 to seek out the floppy and CD drives of your system for SETUP.EXE, the most common name for installation programs.

Applications designed for Windows 95 that get installed by the Add/Remove Control Panel Applet leave a record of the files they write to your system. These applications will be listed in the window at the bottom of the pane.

> **NOTE**
>
> Although only applications specifically written to take advantage of the new installation features will list themselves in the box at the bottom of the window, it is a good

idea to get in the habit of using the Add/Remove Programs applet to install new applications. Doing so ensures that any application that can uninstall is set up to do so, and prevents out-of-date files from infecting your system.

Installing an Application

Often, especially on CD-ROM disks, the installation program is in a folder below the root. If Windows 95 fails to see SETUP.EXE in the root folder of any of the drives it checks, it offers a dialog similar to the File Open dialog so that you can browse through your disks. This dialog is shown in Figure 10.2.

FIGURE 10.2.

The Browse dialog lets you point to the installation program for an application you want to install.

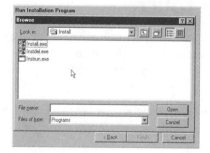

Whether Windows 95 finds the setup program on its own or you use the Browse dialog to point to it, the Install wizard automatically runs the application's normal installation program. All you have to do is follow the prompting of the installation program. If the application installs successfully and it is designed for Windows 95, the application's name is added to the list of software that can be automatically uninstalled.

TIP

Using Add/Remove to install DOS applications enables you to specify a custom icon for the application, and creates a PIF (Program Information File) for the application. Information about the special requirements of many applications is stored in APPS.INF. If an application has an entry in this file, it is used as the basis for the PIF; otherwise, the default PIF is used.

Removing an Application

Keep in mind that only applications designed for Windows 95 will present themselves in the list of software that can be removed automatically. If you want to delete an application that appears in the list, all you have to do is highlight the name of the application and click the Remove button. Of course, you can also double-click the application's filename.

Allowing Windows 95 to automatically delete the application removes any files the application keeps in the WINDOWS or WINDOWS\SYSTEM folders, removes the application's folder or shortcut from the Start Menu, and deletes the folder that contains the application. Of course, Windows 95 checks the Registry to see whether one or more files is shared by another application. Shared files are not deleted.

A Nice Touch

One other common complaint addressed in Windows 95 occurs when you install software that places out-of-date files on your system, sometimes with disastrous results. The beauty of the DLL (dynamic link library) is that multiple applications can share the same programming code without duplicating the code on disk multiple times.

Some DLLs are designated as distributable, meaning that they can be freely distributed by an ISV (independent software vendor) as a part of its application. Most DLLs in this category originate from Microsoft, and occasionally, new versions are issued to update and upgrade the capabilities of a DLL.

If you install an older application, it might write a version of a distributable DLL to your disk that is older, and assumedly less capable. In previous versions of Windows, this condition went unnoticed until you ran an application that was dependent on the newer version's capabilities. Your first notification of a problem was delivered when the application crashed, taking your data with it.

To remedy this situation, Windows 95 monitors the overwriting of system files such as DLLs. The nice touch about this feature is that it doesn't interrupt the application's setup. Instead, after everything is complete, the dialog shown in Figure 10.3 appears to ask you how to handle the situation.

The System File dialog presents three options you can take. The first option is to simply restore the latest version of the file. Just click the Restore button to retain the newer version. This is usually the best choice because the newer file probably has all the capabilities of the older version and also usually contains bug fixes, optimized code, and improved capabilities.

Some applications, however, could be incompatible with the newer version by relying on some behavior of the older DLL that is no longer supported. If you are unsure which version to retain, click the button marked Test. The dialog goes away until the next time you restart Windows. If you experience no problems with any of the applications that rely on the listed files (DLL or other system files), you can safely use the older version.

FIGURE 10.3.
The System File Error dialog provides three options for handling out-of-date system files.

If you know the older version is acceptable to use, either through testing or information from the vendor, you can click Ignore to keep the older version in your system. Usually, however, you want to retain the newest version of any system files or DLLs that are used by your system.

File Associations

One of the most convenient features of Windows has always been the capability to double-click on a document file and have the parent application automatically launched. Using the Windows 3.x File Manager, files were associated with a parent application by selecting Associate from the File menu.

In Windows 95, you can create associations with Explorer, but now the term is registering a file type. If you right-click a document file, the first item in the context menu will be Open if the file type is registered. If the file type is unregistered, the first item will read Open With. Unregistered file types are represented by an icon that looks like a sheet of paper with a Windows logo in the middle.

Unregistered File Types

If you double-click a file that is unregistered or select Open With from its context menu, a dialog similar to the one shown in Figure 10.4 appears. This dialog enables you to specify an application capable of editing the data contained in the document.

Three major elements make up this dialog. A list box in the middle of the window pane lets you select an application to open the document. Above the list is a text box in which you can type information about the file, but you only want to take the time to fill in this box if you select the checkbox below the list of applications. This checkbox, when checked, specifies that the chosen application should always be used to open documents of this type.

FIGURE 10.4.

*The Open With dialog
specifies an application to
use in opening the
document.*

The Open With dialog is probably the simplest way of changing the contents of the registry. By default, the checkbox is always selected. If it remains checked when you click OK, the Registry will be updated to reflect that the chosen application is always to be launched to open any document of this type. All of the document objects of this type in Explorer will have their icon changed to reflect the application you have associated with the document.

File Registration Using Explorer

During an Explorer or My Computer session, if you choose View | Options from the menu, the Options dialog appears. Click the File Types tab, and you will see a dialog similar to the one shown in Figure 10.5. This dialog provides a way to make registry entries that do more than just associate a document type with an application.

FIGURE 10.5.

*The File Types dialog
enables you to associate
applications with document
file types, change icons, and
more.*

As you can see, the dialog shown in Figure 10.5 is very similar to the Open With dialog. In the File Types dialog, however, the list box contains the file types that have been registered instead of their parent applications. Also, a trio of buttons have been added to enable you to create new file registrations, remove a file type from the Registry, and edit the current settings of a particular file type.

> **CAUTION**
>
> Using the File Types dialog improperly can really screw up the Registry. One of the Registry entries for documents contains information on how the parent application supports OLE (Object Linking and Embedding). Editing this information without fully understanding what you are doing can render the OLE registration for a file type unusable.
>
> If you are a novice user (or a cautious old hand), make sure you have backup copies of USER.DAT, SYSTEM.DAT, and (if you are networked) POLICIES.DAT. POLICIES.DAT might not reside on your system. USER.DAT is your personal settings in the registry. There are also Windows 95 generated backups of these files that have the extension DA0.

Adding New File Types

If you click the New Type button of the dialog shown in Figure 10.5, the Add New Type dialog shown in Figure 10.6 will appear. This dialog enables you to specify information about the document file type you want to register.

> **TIP**
>
> The only action you can safely specify for a document without knowing a little bit about OLE is the open action. (See Chapter 12, "OLE.") Applications that are capable of registering OLE activity can add support for drag-and-drop printing, and more. See the section "Using a Registration File to Associate an Application," later in this chapter, for more information on using registration data files.

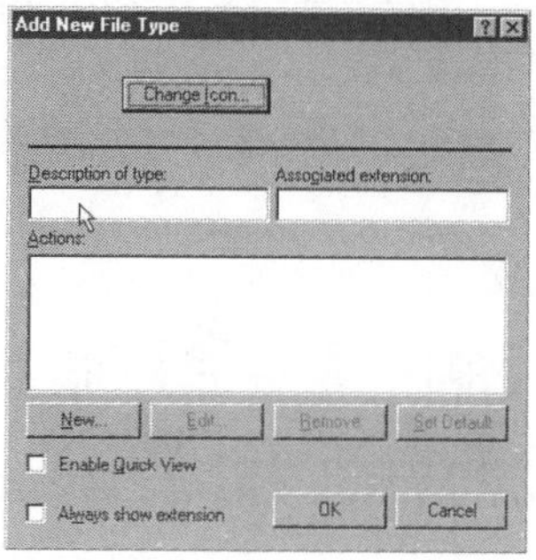

FIGURE 10.6.

The Add New File Type dialog registers documents, associating them with a compatible application.

In general, unless you know command-line syntax for applications that support drag-and-drop printing, OLE, and so on, the only registration you should make is to tell Windows 95 how to open a document with the parent application. Take a look at the controls found in the Add New File Type dialog pictured in Figure 10.6.

At the top of the dialog is the Change Icon button. Save this one for last. You might like the default icon. Two text boxes enable you to enter information about the file type. The description text box lets you type a description of the file type you are registering. The description is displayed when you display file objects in Explorer as a list. The extension text box lets you enter the filename extension that uniquely identifies the document type. Filename extensions, although they are often hidden from view by the file system, are used just as they are in DOS to identify file formats. Examples include DOC for Word for Windows files, DBF for dBASE 5.0 data files, and TXT for text files.

For example, if you want to associate PCX bitmap files with Paint Shop Pro, you might enter PCX -- Paint Shop Pro as the description and type PCX as the extension to identify the file type.

> **TIP**
>
> Occasionally, you will have an application that can open and edit more than one document type. To specify more than one extension, put a space between each extension you register.

When you have the description and extension information entered, click the New button under the Action list box. This brings up the New Action dialog shown in Figure 10.7. Type open in the Action text box. If you know the full path and name of the application, you can type it into the Application text box, or you can click the Browse button to point and click a file using an Open With dialog.

FIGURE 10.7.

The New Action dialog enables you to specify the application to associate with the file type you are registering.

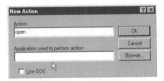

When you have specified the new action, click OK. The Add New File Type dialog now shows the default icon for the application you have selected. If you want to use a different icon, click the Change Icon button to reveal the dialog shown in Figure 10.8. In this dialog, the source of the icon is listed in the text box, and the icons available from the source are shown below them.

By default, Windows 95 shows you the icons available in SHELL32.DLL. You can also find interesting icons in PROGMAN.EXE, which is found in the Windows folder. After you select an icon, click Close in the Add File Type dialog, and then click OK to close the Options dialog and return to Explorer. Until you change its registration, the file type you have registered will automatically launch the specified application whenever a file object of that type is double-clicked or Open is selected from the file's context menu.

FIGURE 10.8.

You can browse through the icons displayed to select the one you want to associate with the file type.

TIP

One of the tabs of the Options dialog is marked View. Using this dialog, you can specify whether DLL files and other system files are visible to the Windows 95 browsers such as Explorer and the File Open dialog. If you have this dialog set so that DLL files are visible, you can also use the file MOREICONS.DLL, which is found in the Windows\System folder. After you have associated an icon from a DLL with an application, you can then reset the View dialog to hide DLLs and other system files.

Editing and Removing File Type Registrations

If you click the Remove button of the Options dialog, the registration information of the currently selected file type will be erased. Before Windows 95 deletes the registry entries, however, you must confirm that you really want the file type removed. This prevents you from erasing a file type's registration information by accident.

If you click the Edit button of the Options dialog, you will see the same dialogs that the Add option presents, except that the current information will already be filled in.

Using a Registration File to Associate an Application

Many Windows applications, both 16-bit and 32-bit, supply a file with the extension .REG that gets written into the application's folder or one of the folders in the application's branch of the tree. Figure 10.9 shows an enlarged version of the icon that represents these file objects.

FIGURE 10.9.

Double-click files with this icon to register the file types that an application can manipulate.

REG files contain registration entries for the file types that the application can edit. If you right-click a REG file object, you see that Merge is the first entry in the context menu. Selecting Merge from the context menu, or double-clicking the file, automatically places the entries for the application into the registry. Using the registration file to register the application's file types is usually preferable to manually entering a new type, because often the registration file contains the information necessary to let Windows 95 know how the application can support OLE, drag-and-drop printing, and so on.

DOS Applications and Windows 95

Despite the fact that the market for DOS software is quickly sinking into oblivion, there are still millions of computer users who hang on to their favorite DOS applications even when Windows versions are available. Support for DOS apps has always been problematic in Windows, because of the way most DOS apps are written. There are basically two issues: resource allocation and hardware usage.

DOS was never intended to be a multitasking environment when it was first released in 1981. Only TSR software was designed to expect other programs to be running. TSRs were usually loaded at bootup via AUTOEXEC.BAT. They allocated just enough memory to do their job, and then returned control back to the operating system.

Applications, on the other hand, were designed quite differently. DOS programmers, over the years, came to expect that any unallocated system resources in the computer were exclusively theirs to control. DOS applications routinely ask for, and expect to get, all remaining memory when they are launched. Because no other programs are supposed to be running, DOS programs almost never check to see whether printer ports, comm ports, disk drives, or any other hardware are in use. If the application isn't using the printer, the printer is idle. At least that's the assumption.

The assumption that there are no other running programs leads to one other practice that was common in the heyday of DOS: Bypassing the DOS interrupts in favor of directly accessing hardware. Sometimes there is a performance penalty to following the rules and calling the proper DOS interrupt functions to perform actions such as writing data onscreen. So, quite often, DOS applications directly access the video card. It makes the application run faster but plays havoc with trying to build an operating system that will multitask DOS applications.

How Windows 95 Supports DOS Applications

Emulating DOS text-based screens has never been a problem for Windows. The problem has always been that DOS applications want to take over the machine so completely and are sensitive to low conventional memory situations. By running each DOS application in its own DOS Virtual Machine, each application has a "machine" of its own to hog up. Because VMs are insulated from each other, several DOS apps can happily run, letting Windows 95 intercept and arbitrate any screen writes, disk activity, printing, communications, and so on.

Lack of conventional memory has been, by far, the biggest impediment to running DOS applications under Windows. By the time the machine gets booted up, DOS, network redirectors, and other TSR software can eat up so much precious memory below 640 KB that many DOS applications simply don't have enough free memory to run reliably. Because Windows 95 replaces all kinds of drivers with 32-bit replacements that occupy zero bytes of conventional memory, many programs that wouldn't run before behave perfectly under Windows 95.

> **TIP**
>
> When you boot up Windows 95, the core components of the operating system are loaded, and a DOS virtual machine is created. This VM is used by Windows 95 as a template for any virtual machines spawned when you run DOS applications. Thus, each new DOS virtual machine inherits whatever settings are established by AUTOEXEC.BAT and CONFIG.SYS at startup.
>
> For more information about configuration files such as AUTOEXEC and CONFIG, see Chapter 4, "Installing Windows 95."

In addition to providing more available memory, Windows 95 has a number of improvements in the way DOS applications are supported. Here's a quick rundown:

- **Flexible booting:** Chapter 4 contains information on how you can set Windows 95 to boot to a previous version of DOS, the Windows 95 DOS prompt, or directly into Windows 95. You can even dual boot with Windows NT.

- **MS-DOS mode:** For those DOS programs that will not run any other way, Windows 95 will swap out to disk and remove itself from memory almost totally. Only a small stub remains in memory to reload Windows 95 when you are finished.

- **DOS toolbar:** Windowed DOS applications have a toolbar that makes support features easy to use.

- **Print spooling:** To avoid conflict with other running applications, DOS print jobs can now be sent to the Windows 95 spooler.

■ **Dynamically adjustable properties:** The Windows 3.x PIF (Program Information File) Editor is gone. In its place is a property sheet that can be used to adjust the environment for DOS applications. Many settings can be adjusted while the application is running.

■ **New commands:** The capabilities of the DOS command line have been expanded in Windows 95. New commands have been added, and old commands are able to use the new long filename support of the 32-bit VFAT.

MS-DOS Mode

Some DOS programs (notably games) just can't be made to run under Windows 95. For these programs, Windows 95 employs the MS-DOS mode. When you run an application or a DOS session in MS-DOS mode, Windows 95 all but removes itself from memory. Of course, this means that any applications running in the background are suspended until you return to Windows 95, but even the most troublesome applications can be made to run. See the section titled "Dynamically Adjustable Properties," later in this chapter, for more information.

Usually, however, Windows 95 is able to integrate DOS applications into the environment, enabling them to be multitasked alongside Windows applications. There is even support for the DOS Protected Mode Interface (DPMI), which allows DOS applications to run in protected mode. Windows 95 also adds enhanced support for applications that run in the various DOS graphic mode standards.

You should only run applications in the MS-DOS mode when you experience problems with them. More than 99 percent of all the DOS applications ever written will perform perfectly in a Windows 95 virtual machine.

DOS Toolbar

When you run DOS applications in a window instead of in a full screen, you have the option of displaying a toolbar at the top of the window. Figure 10.10 shows the toolbar.

Here's a rundown of the toolbar from left to right.

■ The pulldown list box enables you to specify the font (raster or TrueType) to be used when displaying the window. Selecting Auto resizes the font automatically as you adjust the window size.

■ The three buttons to the right of the list box are the Mark, Copy, and Paste buttons, which enable you to work with the Windows 95 Clipboard. Click the Mark button and drag text to mark it for transfer. The Copy button, places marked text onto the Clipboard, and the Paste button reads in text from the Clipboard as if it were being typed from the keyboard.

■ The Full Screen button has four arrows to show you that it will run the application in a full DOS screen instead of a window.

■ The Properties button pictures a hand pointing to the property sheet. This button brings up the same dialog as the Properties item in the context menu for the DOS app.

■ The Background button determines whether the application is suspended when it is not the active window. If the button is depressed, the application continues to run in the background.

■ The rightmost button is a second method of determining what font should be used. It differs from the list box method by calling up the font dialog of the property sheet, which enables you to preview any changes you make.

FIGURE 10.10.

Windowed DOS applications now have a toolbar.

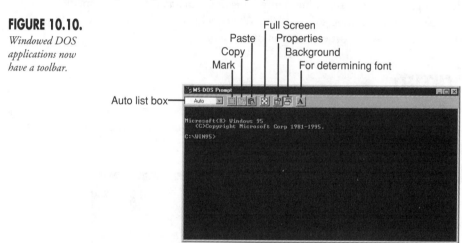

Print Spooling

In the past, users had to be on guard not to have two DOS applications try to print at the same time. Windows 95 eliminates this problem by providing better device contention handling, and by enabling DOS print jobs to be spooled to the Windows 95 print queue. Although DOS applications cannot take advantage of Windows 95's Enhanced Meta File printing capabilities, you'll find that background printing of spooled print jobs is much smoother than in past versions of Windows.

Dynamically Adjustable Properties

Previous versions of Windows used the PIF Editor to create and maintain Program Information Files. Although Windows 95 still uses PIF files, the way they are created and maintained is different. Settings, once handled with the editor, are now maintained in the property sheet for an application.

When you double-click a DOS application to run it the first time, Windows 95 checks a file called APPS.INF to see whether there are any known compatibility issues with the application. If entries are found, the settings in APPS.INF are used; otherwise, Windows 95's default property settings are used. The next time you go to run that program, you will find that a PIF file of the same name has been created automatically and placed into the folder as a shortcut. This shortcut PIF file reflects any changes you made to properties the first time the app was run. The next time you want to run the app, use the shortcut.

Right-clicking the PIF shortcut and choosing Properties from the context menu, or clicking the Properties button while the application is running, presents you with the dialog shown in Figure 10.11. As you can see, there are five tabs. Each tab presents a specialized dialog for one aspect of the PIF settings for the application. The sections that follow do not fully cover each possible setting. Instead, the most important settings are explained. To get information on other settings, right-click the setting to reveal the What's This box. Clicking What's This causes Windows 95 to display a short explanation of the item.

Program

The Program settings, shown in Figure 10.11, provide a description to be used in displaying Explorer lists, the command line used to launch the application, its initial working directory, and so on. The Batch File list box presents a particularly useful feature.

FIGURE 10.11.

Six tabs control the properties for DOS applications.

If you are running only protected mode drivers, you no longer need AUTOEXEC.BAT and CONFIG.SYS, except in rare circumstances. If you want to initialize DOS environment variables, load TSR programs, or perform similar tasks, you can create a standard DOS batch file. Entering the name of the batch file in this dialog causes the batch file to be run before the application is launched.

The Advanced button reveals a subdialog, as shown in Figure 10.12. In this dialog, you can keep DOS apps from sensing that Windows is running, have Windows 95 notify you whenever it thinks the application should be run in MS-DOS mode, and also control how the configuration of the virtual machine should be arranged. The replacement settings for AUTOEXEC and CONFIG apply only to applications running in MS-DOS mode. The Configure button activates a wizard that lets you set configurations for Expanded memory, mouse settings, load DOSKEY, and so on.

FIGURE 10.12.

Clicking MS-DOS mode causes the application to be run in MS-DOS mode and replaces current settings for AUTOEXEC.BAT and CONFIG.SYS.

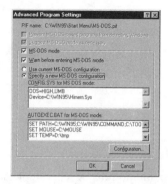

NOTE

When DOS applications check to see what version of the operating system is in use, the version reported is MS-DOS 7.0. Applications that require a specific version might display an error message. Applications that are absolutely version specific and can't be satisfied by SETVER must be run by using a boot floppy to start the machine with the required version of DOS, and cannot be run under Windows 95.

Font

The Font dialog, shown in Figure 10.13, enables you to specify the types and sizes of fonts you want to use in rendering DOS applications run in a window. Selecting a type style from the list box previews the size of the window relative to the full screen and shows a sample of the font in the panes at the bottom of the dialog.

TIP

Windows 95 does not load EMM386.EXE at boot-up by default. EMM386 is only required when you run DOS applications that require Expanded (EMS) memory. If you need Expanded memory, you need to load EMM386 via CONFIG.SYS.

FIGURE 10.13.

FIGURE 10.13.

The Font dialog lets you adjust the size and type style of windowed DOS apps.

Memory

The Memory configuration dialog lets you put specific limits on the use of memory by DOS applications. You should seldom edit these values. Leaving the settings in the pulldown list boxes set to Auto lets Windows 95 dynamically allocate and adjust memory usage. However, if you find yourself running several DOS applications on a system with low memory, you can sometimes optimize overall system performance, at the expense of app performance, by restricting the amount of memory available to DOS apps.

Screen

The Screen dialog lets you specify whether the app should open in a window, whether a toolbar should be visible, and so on. The Restore checkbox specifies whether the registry should be updated with changed settings so that the application is launched next time in the same condition it was in when last closed.

Misc

The Misc (miscellaneous) dialog contains a group of very important settings. This dialog is shown in Figure 10.14 and shows the default settings.

The mouse settings are a bit unusual. Checking QuickEdit causes the mouse to be active only for marking text in a window and is unavailable to the application. If it is unchecked, you have to click the Mark button in the toolbar. The Exclusive setting means that the app has total and exclusive use of the mouse and that the mouse can no longer serve as the Windows 95 pointing device. Leave that one alone!

The Idle sensitivity determines how the Windows 95 scheduler reacts to long periods of idleness by the application. If the slider is set lower, the scheduler waits longer to reduce the priority level of the application. If a DOS app running in the background needs more CPU time, move the slider lower. To lower the app's priority and reduce CPU usage by the app, move the slider higher.

FIGURE 10.14.

This dialog controls a number of options concerning shortcut keys, screen savers, and other behaviors of the application.

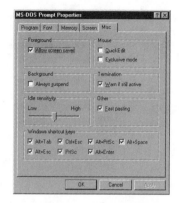

Getting Rid of Configuration Files

You need to keep only the AUTOEXEC and CONFIG files under limited circumstances, such as the following:

- For loading real mode drivers at start-up
- For loading EMM386 to provide Expanded memory
- For overriding settings contained in IO.SYS
- For customizing the DOS environment for all DOS applications

If you run only a couple of DOS applications on your system, it is probably better to use the application's property sheet to specify a batch file to run before launching the application. For more information on configuration files, see Chapter 4.

Summary

In this chapter, you have seen how Windows 95 supports each of three classes of applications. The 32-bit applications designed for Windows 95 make the fullest use of the operating system by running in a private address space, preemptively multitasking, and using multiple threads to provide smoother program operation.

The 16-bit applications, which were written for previous versions of Windows, work much as they have in the past for cooperatively multitasking and sharing a common address space.

DOS applications are run in individual virtual machines and enjoy support for high-level graphics operation and protected mode operation. They might even run faster under Windows 95 because they have more available memory.

In the next chapter, you will learn how Windows 95 helps you move off the desktop and into the real world with mobile computing.

Mobile Computing

11

by Ned Snell

Windows 95 acknowledges that a portable PC—usually a notebook PC, but sometimes a subnotebook or other battery-operated variant—is both an acceptable Windows platform and a platform that demands its own set of tools and other special configuration considerations. Compared to a typical desktop PC, a portable PC might need the following:

- Access to a corporate network not only from a local node but also from anywhere on the road or across the world
- Access to e-mail messaging and fax services, from anywhere to anywhere
- A way to maintain the same files that are on a separate desktop PC and keep both sets of files up-to-date and synchronized
- To synchronize files and change configuration every time it docks or undocks with a docking station
- Use of PCMCIA cards
- To run on a more power-stingy set of configuration settings when running on batteries

Windows 95 is the first PC operating system with built-in tools for addressing all of the issues faced by mobile computers and their users. This chapter describes how to set up and use Windows 95's mobile computing features.

NOTEBOOK CONFIGURATION

Notebook PCs increasingly rival desktop machines in basic hardware specs. Still, a notebook always costs more than a desktop PC with the same processor, RAM, hard disk size, and other similar specifications. As a result, most notebook users compromise when choosing a machine, saving money by accepting a smaller hard disk, less memory, a slower hard drive, or a monochrome display.

Regardless of the platform, setup does its best to tune and configure the PC for the best performance and reliability. Still, if your notebook is underpowered for Windows 95 (having less than a 486 DX, 8MB RAM, and 200MB hard disk), you'll want to check out Chapter 6, "Tuning Windows 95 for Optimal Performance and Reliability," to learn about which upgrades are the most important and how to tune your notebook for best performance within its limitations. You'll also want to check out Chapter 5, "Customizing the Desktop and Integrating Windows 95 Applications," to learn how to customize a small, fuzzy, or colorless display for the best clarity and usability. For example, Chapter 5 shows how to do the following:

- Enlarge icons
- Enlarge the text on title bars and other standard screen elements
- Make the pointer and cursors easier to see and work with
- Select a high-contrast color scheme to brighten up an LCD display

Setting Up

During Windows setup, you choose a Setup Type so that Windows can best configure your PC for the type of work it does—Typical, Portable, Compact, or Custom. When you choose Portable, the setup Wizard installs tools it thinks portable users need, leaves out tools it thinks they don't need, and sets a few configuration options in ways it assumes are advantageous to users of portable computers.

Specifically, Portable setup installs support for power management, Briefcase, Dial-up Networking, PCMCIA card support (if your notebook does not have Plug and Play BIOS, you must manually enable PCMCIA), and Quick Viewer. It also leaves out support for multimedia (unless it detects multimedia devices such as built-in or PCMCIA sound cards), WordPad, Microsoft Exchange, and Image Color Matching support. Finally, the setup Wizard configures the dynamic disk cache performance settings for portable computing. (See Chapter 6 to learn about configuring the disk cache.)

The setup Wizard bases all of these choices on the typical uses and limitations of notebook PCs; it assumes the PC sometimes runs on batteries, accesses a network from a remote site while on the road, and is used in concert with a docking station or desktop PC whose files must be kept in sync with the notebook's files. Obviously, any or all of Windows's assumptions might be wrong for you and your portable PC. Increasingly, notebooks are being used as desktop PCs, rarely (or never) being used on batteries, taken on the road, or used in support of a desktop PC. That scenario makes Windows' power management, Direct Cable Connection, and Briefcase tools unnecessary, and might make the Desktop disk cache setting more appropriate for the way you use your PC. Your notebook might not use PCMCIA cards, or you might want WordPad and Exchange on your system—especially if you want to use Microsoft Fax, which requires Exchange.

If the choices made by Portable setup aren't relevant to the way you use your portable PC, you can always choose Desktop for the setup type and then make whatever specific changes you want later. (See the following Tip to learn how to add or remove Windows programs.) Or, you can choose Portable setup and then add or subtract tools later. If you're short on disk space and RAM and don't need mobile computing tools, you can choose Compact setup for the minimum, space-saving Windows 95 installation.

The point is that Portable setup is not required for a portable PC. A portable will work just fine if you choose Desktop setup, although if you want to use any mobile computing tools, you'll have to set them up manually one by one. Either way, it's your PC. You're in charge.

> **TIP**
>
> Windows 95's Mobile Computing tools—power management, Briefcase, Dial-up
> Networking, PCMCIA card support, and Quick Viewer—are installed automatically
> by Portable setup. If you do not use Portable setup, you can choose any of these
> programs individually, using Custom setup. (See Chapter 4, "Installing Windows 95.")
>
> To add or remove mobile computing tools after setup, open Control Panel, choose
> Add/Remove Programs, and click the Windows Setup tab. Then select the programs
> you want to install, and click the Install button.

Synchronizing Files with Briefcase

The Windows Briefcase applet provides a convenient way to keep the files on two computers
in sync. It's intended use is to update files on a desktop PC, docking station, or network from
those on a portable PC when the portable returns from the road, or to update the portable's
files before it leaves. That's the scenario used in this chapter to illustrate how to operate
Briefcase.

However, Briefcase can be used in any scenario in which keeping multiple copies of the same
file in sync is valuable. For example, in an office without a network, Briefcase can be used to
keep files in sync when two different users are collaborating on the same document and use
floppy disks to trade the document files back and forth. Of course, Briefcase also comes in handy
for keeping office files in sync with *home* office files.

Briefcase supports any method of file transfer: network, direct cable connection, or floppy disk.
Any time it's possible to move a file from one Windows 95 PC to another, Briefcase can be
used to keep files in sync.

The Briefcase is really just a special folder that functions as the intermediary between computers. To understand Briefcase, it helps to think of it as a true briefcase—a temporary, portable
container. Before going on the road, you remove from your desk the papers you'll need on the
road, and put them in your briefcase. During your trip, you change those papers. When you
return, you put the changed papers back in your desk and, if necessary, replace any original
copies of those papers with the updated ones. Windows Briefcase works the same way.

Files that are needed on the road are copied into the Briefcase folder on the desktop PC from
its hard disk or from the network. The Briefcase folder is then moved to the notebook. When
the notebook comes home with the files changed, the Briefcase folder is moved back to the
desktop PC, where you can instruct it to update the original desktop files with a few quick
menu choices.

Filling Your Briefcase

To put files in a briefcase and take them on the road, follow these steps:

1. On the desktop PC, copy the files to Briefcase. You can use Edit menus to copy files from one location (Explorer or My Computer) to the Clipboard. Then open the Briefcase folder and paste the files into the Briefcase folder. Or, you can drag files and drop them on the Briefcase folder icon, but be sure to *copy* the files to Briefcase rather than *move* them there.

   If you're using Briefcase between computers that will remain connected, you're done; edit the files within the Briefcase, and when you want to synchronize the files on the other PC, move on to Updating Files. If you're using a portable PC that is (or will be) disconnected from the desktop PC or docking station, perform Step 2.

2. Move the Briefcase folder (don't copy it) to the portable PC through any available method:

   - Move the folder to a floppy disk and then transfer the floppy to the notebook PC.

   - Move the folder through a Direct Cable Connection (see the "Direct Cable Connection" section later in this chapter).

   - Move the folder through a network connection.

TIP

So, you've already landed in Des Moines, checked into the hotel, and suddenly you realize you forgot to pack your Windows Briefcase before you left. No problem.

Use Dial-Up Networking (see Chapter 26, "Remote Access") to connect to your office PC or network, fill the Briefcase, and move it through the modem connection into your notebook PC. If your dial-up access privileges prevent deleting files, you might have to copy the Briefcase rather than moving it. If so, when you return to the office, be sure to delete the briefcase from your office PC or network before starting the file synchronization procedure.

While on the road, edit the files in the Briefcase folder using any application compatible with those files. It need not be the same application used on the desktop or network; for example, files created in Word for Windows 6.0 on the desktop can be edited on the road in WordPad, because WordPad can edit and save Word files.

Updating Files

When your trip is over, synchronize the files:

■ If the two computers are connected, right-click the Briefcase folder or open Briefcase and pull down the Briefcase menu. Choose Update All to synchronize all files to the latest versions. You can also select individual files and choose Update Selection.

■ If using a floppy disk, transfer the floppy back to the desktop PC. On the desktop, open Briefcase and pull down the Briefcase menu. Choose Update All to synchronize all files to the latest versions. You can also select individual files and choose Update Selection.

TIP

If you use a floppy disk for file transfer, you can edit the files on the floppy or drag them from the Briefcase folder on the floppy to your notebook's hard disk. If you choose to edit on the hard disk, you must perform the file synchronization procedure (see the "Updating Files" section, later in this chapter) twice: First, on the notebook, open Briefcase on the floppy, and then choose Update All to bring the files on the floppy into sync. Then transfer the floppy to the desktop, and use Update again to update the files there.

TIP

If you use a portable with a docking station that has Plug and Play BIOS, Briefcase automatically synchronizes files on the portable with the files on the docking station's hard disk each time you dock. If your docking station is not Plug and Play compatible, follow the steps for using Briefcase with two connected computers.

Direct Cable Connection

Direct Cable Connection enables you to set up an instant network by plugging two Windows 95 computers together through a serial or parallel cable. When they are connected, the two computers can share resources, such as sharing data files and transferring files between the computers. Also, if one of the two computers is on a network, the other can access the resources of the network as well.

This feature is particularly useful to mobile computer users, because it provides an easy way to tap into a corporate network or the resources of any Windows 95 PC. Direct Cable Connection is also a handy way to connect computers in order to use Briefcase for synchronizing files. (See the "Synchronizing Files with Briefcase" section, earlier in this chapter.)

To use Direct Cable Connection, you first must make sure it has been installed on both of the computers that you plan to connect to one another. It is not installed automatically through any setup option; you must choose Custom setup and select it from the list of Windows components. After installation, you can install Direct Cable Connection by choosing Add/Remove programs in Control Panel, and then choosing Windows setup.

When you use Direct Cable Connection, one computer is designated as the *guest* and the other as the *host*. In a typical scenario, your portable would be the guest, while the other computer (especially if it is connected to the network) would be the host.

NOTE

When the files on the host computer are protected by user-level security, the user of the host must change sharing options to give you access to them. To do that, the user must do the following:

1. Select the folder that contains the file to share.
2. Right-click to bring up the Explorer menu.
3. Click Sharing and then click the Sharing tab.
4. Click Add Users and add you to the list.

Also, before you can transfer files from a host, the sharing options must be set as described earlier, and File and Print Sharing for Microsoft Networks or NetWare Networks must be enabled on the host PC. The user of the host enables File and Print sharing through the Network option in Control Panel.

To set up the connection, you must first physically connect the two computers through their parallel or serial ports. You can use any standard RS-232 serial null modem cable for the serial ports. To connect the computers through their parallel ports, you can use any of the following:

- A Standard or Basic 4-bit parallel cable.
- An Enhanced Communications Port (ECP) cable. This type of cable requires ECP ports on both PCs and requires that these ports be configured as ECP ports in Windows.
- A Universal Cable Module (UCM), which enables you to connect two different types of parallel port; for example, one PC might have a regular parallel port, and the other might have an ECP port.

Note that parallel connections support faster data transfer, but they are limited to shorter cable lengths (typically 15 feet or less) and usually require bulkier, heavier cables. Serial connections can be made through longer, lighter cables, but they're slower.

When the connection has been established, you must enable Direct Cable Connection on each computer, beginning with the host:

1. Open the Accessories menu and choose Direct Cable Connection to start the Direct Cable Connection Wizard.

2. When prompted, choose Host.

3. Respond to the prompts asking which port you're using for the connection and whether you want the connection to be password-protected. (If you say Yes, you'll need to supply a password.)

When the Wizard displays a message that says it is waiting for the guest computer, repeat the procedure on the guest by choosing Guest in Step 1.

PCMCIA Support

Most modern notebooks and subnotebooks feature one or more sockets for swappable PCMCIA (Personal Computer Memory Card International Association) cards. During setup, Windows 95 detects PCMCIA sockets, but it does not automatically enable them. If you have a PCMCIA socket, you must run the PCMCIA Wizard after setup to enable the socket and configure your PCMCIA devices.

The PCMCIA Wizard enables the PCMCIA socket, and when a device is compatible with Windows 95 32-bit drivers, the Wizard removes real-mode PCMCIA drivers from AUTOEXEC.BAT and CONFIG.SYS. The Windows drivers—which support all Intel- and Databook-compatible sockets and most types of PCMCIA cards—will deliver the best performance not only for the PCMCIA devices themselves, but for the whole notebook because using any real mode driver slows down Windows. (See Chapter 6, "Tuning Windows 95 for Optimal Performance and Reliability.") If your PCMCIA sockets and cards are all supported by Windows drivers, the PCMCIA Wizard automatically configures them, and Windows runs them in enhanced Plug and Play mode, allowing *hot swapping* and fast 32-bit access. Hot swapping means Windows dynamically loads and unloads the proper drivers from memory when you switch PCMCIA cards or dock with a docking station.

You can check whether the Setup Wizard detected your PCMCIA socket by opening Control Panel, System, and the Device Manager tab.

- If no PCMCIA socket appears in the list of devices, Windows did not detect your socket; you must run Add New Hardware from Control Panel and choose the Install specific hardware button to manually direct Windows to the location of your PCMCIA socket drivers.

- If a PCMCIA socket appears on the list, you can run the PCMCIA Wizard to configure and enable your socket.

NOTE

If you use a PCMCIA network adapter, your PCMCIA socket driver and the driver for your network card must both be Plug and Play compatible or both be Plug and Play incompatible. If one is compatible and the other is not, your portable could crash or bring down the network. If only one of these is Plug and Play compatible, use Add New Hardware to reinstall its real-mode drivers. Note that using real-mode drivers will cause your portable's performance to suffer, and can cause reliability problems as well. However, in this case, the real-mode drivers are a safer bet than mixing real-mode and 32-bit drivers.

Note, also, that a few portables have shipped with Plug and Play-compatible devices but without the necessary Plug and Play BIOS. These must use the real-mode drivers until the BIOS can be updated by the manufacturer. See Chapter 3, "Plug and Play."

When Windows can't replace your PCMCIA drivers, it still allows your PCMCIA cards to run using their own real mode or protected mode drivers, but Windows might not enable some enhanced PCMCIA features. It also can't configure the devices automatically, which means you must manually resolve any configuration problems such as conflicting IRQs (see Chapter 7, "Windows 95 Device Support—Printer, Comm, Fonts, and Video"). Of course, you can avoid all of this by acquiring Windows 95 drivers from your hardware manufacturer. If you plan to upgrade unsupported real-mode drivers to manufacturer-supplied Windows 95 drivers, upgrade the drivers first and then run the PCMCIA wizard.

To run the PCMCIA Wizard, open Control Panel and open the PCMCIA icon. You can also start the Wizard by opening System, clicking the Device Manager tab, and double-clicking the PCMCIA device.

TIP

If you've run the PCMCIA Wizard to enable PCMCIA but one or more of your PCMCIA cards doesn't work, the card is probably using a manufacturer's driver and doesn't match Windows' default memory region and IRQ settings for non-Plug and Play PCMCIA cards. (Windows can't automatically configure such devices, so it supplies defaults that work for most cards.) To enable support for the card, you must install a new Windows 95 compatible driver, or alter the configuration settings manually.

To begin, consult your hardware manual, README files, or hardware manufacturer to determine the supported memory address and IRQ settings for the card.

338

To manually configure the address for a PCMCIA device, follow these steps:

1. Open Control Panel, open System, click the Device Manager tab, and double-click the device listing for the PCMCIA device.

2. Click the Global Settings tab. You'll see a screen like the one in Figure 11.1.

FIGURE 11.1.

Manually configuring a PCMCIA card.

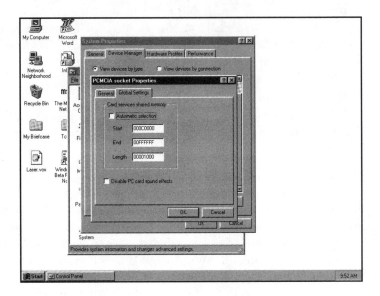

The Automatic Selection checkbox should not be checked, because this device is not Plug and Play; if the box is checked, uncheck it.

3. Enter the correct Start address for your PCMCIA card, and click OK. If you don't know the address, try a start address above 100000.

4. Restart Windows.

To change the IRQ setting for a PCMCIA device, follow these steps:

1. Open Control Panel, open System, double-click the Device Manager tab, select the PCMCIA device, and click Properties.

2. Choose a new IRQ that is supported by your card and does not conflict with other devices on your system. Then click OK.

3. Restart Windows.

Remote Network Access

If you use a network in the office, you should be able to access it from the road, too. Windows 95 provides support for such remote network access through its Dial-Up Networking feature.

In effect, Dial-Up Networking turns your modem into a network adapter, enabling you to dial into a remote access server on your office network and use your office network exactly as you would if you were there. You use the same logon procedures (username and password), have access to the same applications and files, and so on.

For more about remote networking, see Chapter 26.

TIP

Another useful feature for portable users is Deferred Printing. Deferred printing accepts print jobs from Windows applications but stores them on disk until you choose to print them. You can prepare printed documents on the road, and then quickly print them out when you return home and reconnect to a printer.

To use Deferred Printing, open Control Panel and then Printers. Double-click the icon for the printer on which you eventually want documents printed. Then choose Work Offline from the File menu on the Printer window. The icon for that printer dims in the Printers folder, and all documents printed to that printer will be written to disk.

When you return to the office, reconnect the printer, double-click the dimmed printer icon in the Printers folder, uncheck Work Offline, and click Resume to print the documents you have deferred.

Using Microsoft Exchange

Exchange is a *universal messaging client*, a centralized messaging engine that brings all your e-mail (whether to and from the network or an online service), faxing, and file transfer activities under one umbrella. Exchange retrieves all types of electronic messages, regardless of their source, and allows you to manage them from within a single universal Inbox. You can also compose a message within Exchange and send it out as a fax, e-mail, or both. Exchange is required for using Microsoft Fax, Microsoft Mail and Windows CompuServe Mail client.

From within Exchange, you maintain a one-stop Personal Address Book containing the e-mail addresses and fax numbers of your important contacts, and a unified Personal Information Store containing all your e-mail messages and fax files. The store operates exactly like an Explorer view, providing options for sorting, filtering, and viewing your stored message files.

To link information sources, Exchange uses Messaging API (MAPI) drivers. Any service for which a MAPI driver is available can be hooked into Exchange. Windows 95 ships with MAPI drivers for Microsoft Fax, CompuServe Mail, Microsoft Mail, the Microsoft Network, and the Internet. However, additional MAPI drivers will be made available through Microsoft and other parties to allow Exchange to manage messaging to and from other online services and other e-mail systems.

Each user has an Exchange Profile that includes the installed messaging services and information Exchange requires to use the service. For example, a user's profile might include the Microsoft Mail client configured with the user's ID, the network address of the Mail Post Office, and any other information Exchange requires for routing messages to and from Microsoft Mail.

Setting Up Exchange

Microsoft Exchange is automatically installed at Windows setup if you choose Typical setup and can be optionally installed if you select Custom setup. It is not installed if you choose Portable setup.

TIP

To install Exchange after setup:

1. Open Control Panel, choose Add/Remove Programs, and click the Windows Setup tab.
2. Check the checkbox next to Microsoft Exchange. Click details, and make sure that you check any clients (CompuServe, Internet) you want. Click OK.
3. Check the checkboxes next to Microsoft Fax and Microsoft Network if you want those services, and click Install.

Follow the prompts. When the Exchange Setup Wizard begins, follow the instructions in the next paragraphs.

To use the Exchange Wizard, begin by gathering the basic access information for the services you will use: for example, your user IDs, the location of your Microsoft Mail Post Office, the number to dial for CompuServe (or the disk/directory location of your CompuServe settings file, if you use CompuServe Information Manager), and so on. Exchange will request this information to build your profile.

The Exchange Setup Wizard opens, prompting you for the necessary information for building your profile. After you complete Exchange Setup, restart Windows so your changes can take effect.

Using Exchange To Create and Manage Messages

After you set it up, Exchange adds an Exchange selection to your Programs menu. Through that menu item, you can do the following:

- Check and read all of your waiting e-mail and faxes, regardless of their source
- Respond to new messages or old ones in your Personal Store

■ Create and send e-mail messages and faxes

To begin, select the Exchange item from your Programs menu. You'll see an Explorer-style view like the one shown in Figure 11.2.

FIGURE 11.2.

Microsoft Exchange.

In your Personal Information Store, you'll find these items:

- **Deleted Items:** Messages you've deleted from the other folders in your Personal Store. This folder works something like the Recycle Bin; delete a message elsewhere in the store, and it moves here. Delete it here, and it's gone. The nice thing about having the messages here is that you can recall them and then reply to or forward them.

- **Inbox:** Messages you've received but not deleted yet.

- **Outbox:** Messages you've prepared but not sent yet.

- **Sent Items:** Copies of messages you've sent.

In any of these folders, you can double-click any message to view it. You can also select any message and have immediate access to the message management features on the toolbar and in the menus. These include

- **Reply:** A window opens into which you can type a message to be automatically e-mailed or faxed back to the sender of the message you selected.

- **Forward:** Send a copy of the message to another recipient, with a note attached that you forwarded it.

- **Print:** Print the current message on your local printer.

These functions are also available on context menus that appear when you right-click a message, and they're available from toolbars and menus when you're viewing a message.

Choices on the Compose menu enable you to write a new message and send it by e-mail or fax (although you can use any MAPI-compatible Windows word processor or text editor to create and send e-mail or faxes, as described later in this chapter in the section, "Using Exchange from Within Applications").

Using Exchange To Receive Mail

From Exchange's Tools menu, choose Deliver Mail Using to collect your waiting e-mail. This option allows you to select the messaging service from which you want to collect new mail, or to choose All services. When you choose All services, Exchange establishes the appropriate connection for each e-mail source in your profile; for example, it might poll the Microsoft Mail post office for any new messages, dial CompuServe, log in, collect your e-mail, and log off. When Exchange finishes delivering mail, your new messages are listed in the Inbox folder.

Using Exchange with Dial-Up Networking

Mobile users can use Dial-Up Networking with Exchange to send and receive messages from the road. To do this, you must create two different Exchange profiles: one containing the information necessary to access messaging services locally, and another with the changes necessary to access the same services through phone lines and Dial-Up Networking.

To set up Exchange for Dial-Up Networking, follow these steps:

1. Open Control Panel, Mail, and Fax.
2. Click Copy to copy your existing profile and give it a new name. This way, you only need to make the changes necessary for Dial-Up Networking; you won't need to re-enter information that doesn't change.
3. Select the new profile, and click Properties. A screen appears like the one in Figure 11.3.

FIGURE 11.3.

Changing connection information on services.

From the screen shown in Figure 11.3, select your messaging services one at a time, click Properties, and make any profile changes required for Dial-Up Networking. For example, I would click CompuServe and then Properties to edit my CompuServe connection information. I would then enter the CompuServe access number used in the city I planned to visit. (Because this is a bit of a chore, if I tend to travel to several cities from which I need CompuServe, I could create a separate profile for each.) Note that you can remove services that aren't required for this Dial-Up profile.

TIP

If you use Microsoft Mail, Exchange offers you some helpful options for using Mail remotely. To configure these options, open the profile as described earlier, select Microsoft Mail, and click Properties. A screen appears that is like the one shown in Figure 11.4.

The tabs on the sheet shown in Figure 11.4 allow you to enable and configure special Mail remote access options. Begin by clicking Connection and clicking the radio button next to Remote. Edit the path to the post office, if necessary, to allow Exchange to find it from a remote site. After you've completed the Connection tab, you're configured for Dial-Up Mail. Other tabs on this page enable useful options:

- Remote Configuration enables a Remote Preview feature that downloads only the headers for new messages, and then allows you to selectively download only the messages you want to see. This saves you the online time for downloading messages that can wait until you return to the office. This tab also lets you use a copy of the Mail Post Office Address Book on your notebook so that your notebook won't attempt to access the post office every time you need an address.

- Remote Session enables automatic dial-up/logoff procedures to make messaging quicker and more convenient. For example, you can force Exchange to automatically disconnect the Dial-Up session as soon as all messages have been sent and/or received.

- Dial-Up Networking configures dialing and connection options, such as the number of times to retry a connection.

FIGURE 11.4.

Remote options for Microsoft Mail.

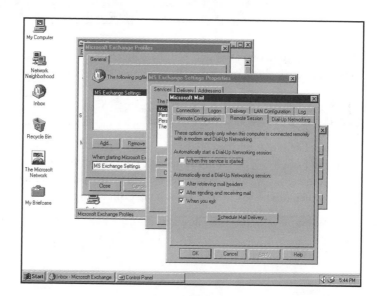

Using Exchange from Within Applications

You can use any MAPI-enabled Windows application to send messages and faxes through Exchange from within the application itself:

- To send the current document as a fax, select Microsoft Fax as the printer, and then print as described later in the section "Using Microsoft Fax."
- To send the current document as e-mail, choose Send from the File menu. If you have more than one profile, Exchange prompts you for the profile to use. Otherwise, Exchange opens a dialog like the one shown in Figure 11.5.

FIGURE 11.5.

Sending e-mail through Exchange from within an application.

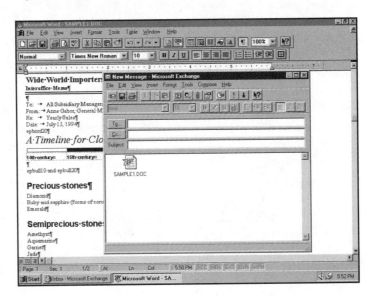

Double-click To in order to open your Personal Address Book and select an addressee for your message, or enter the name and Address manually.

Using Microsoft Fax

Fax works like most commercial fax packages: it installs as a Windows printer. To fax a document, you print it to Fax, fill in the necessary address information, and you're all set. Receiving faxes is a matter of opening Exchange to enable Fax receiving, allowing it to idle on your desktop, and then double-clicking it when a fax is incoming (you can also set it to auto-answer).

In the Windows 95 landscape, however, Fax does a few very special things:

- Fax can send document files that the recipient can open and edit like any data file, as opposed to ordinary fax graphic files, which are not editable (see the "Fax Sending Options" section, later in this chapter).

- Fax enables you to compose and send a new fax from within most OLE-compliant Windows word processors or text editors, from within Exchange, or through a Compose New Fax item on the Accessories menu.

- Fax enables you to key encrypt or password-protect, for privacy, the faxes you send (see the "Fax Sending Options" section).

- Fax sends and receives faxes through a shared fax modem on a network.

Fax requires Microsoft Exchange; whether you install Fax during Windows setup or later, you must also install Exchange.

Setting Up Fax

Setting up Fax is simple. Here's how to do it:

During Windows setup, choose Custom setup, and check the boxes next to Microsoft Exchange and Microsoft Fax.

Or, after Windows setup, open Control Panel, open Add/remove programs, and choose Windows setup. Select Microsoft Fax (and Exchange, if you have not already installed it), and click Install. Run the Exchange setup Wizard (described earlier in this chapter), being sure to include Microsoft Fax among the services in your Exchange profile.

> **NOTE**
>
> In addition to installing and configuring Fax, you must also properly install and set up a compatible fax modem. Windows 95 supports most Class 1 and Class 2 fax modems. For more information about configuring your fax modem, see Chapter 7.

When Fax is included in your Exchange profile, you can complete configuration by supplying information about your modem, dialing instructions, and more. You can also supply information about yourself and your return fax number; this information is used by Fax in creating cover pages and header information on faxes you send.

Open Control Panel, open Mail and Fax, select Microsoft fax from the list of services, and click Properties. Click each tab and supply any information required. Click OK when you're done.

Sending a Fax

Exchange enables you to prepare and send a fax in four ways. Although the method of composing the document and initiating Fax differs among them, after that the steps are the same and are controlled by the New Fax Wizard. The Wizard leads you through the steps to prepare the fax:

- It prompts for address information, which you can enter or copy from your Personal Address Book.

- It lets you select one of Windows's predefined cover pages, or no cover page.

- It lets you choose among special options (described later in this section).

- It lets you initiate dialing and send the fax.

FIGURE 11.6.

The Fax Cover Page Editor.

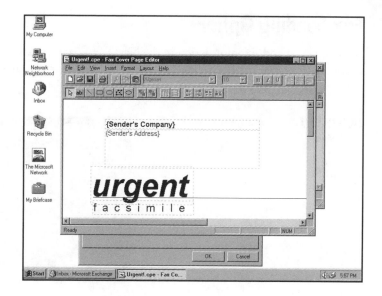

You can send a fax in one of four ways:

- **By printing:** Create a document in a MAPI-compatible application (such as Microsoft Word, Excel, or most other OLE-compliant applications), and choose Print from the File menu. If the Print dialog doesn't show Microsoft Fax as the printer, click Printer, select it, and click Close. Then click Print. Windows starts the New Fax Wizard. (In this case, the Wizard does not provide a window for composing the fax, as it does when you start it in some other ways.)

- **Through Exchange:** Open Exchange, choose Compose, and choose Fax. Windows starts the New Fax Wizard with a Compose window into which you can type the fax copy.

- **Through Compose New Fax:** Open Compose New Fax from the Fax folder in Accessories. Windows starts the New Fax Wizard with a Compose window into which you can type the fax copy.

- **By drag and drop:** In Explorer or My Computer, select a document file created in a MAPI-compatible application. Drag it and drop it on the Microsoft Fax icon in the Printers folder (or on the desktop, if you've moved it there). Windows starts the New Fax Wizard. (In this case, the Wizard does not provide a window for composing a fax, as it does in some other cases.)

Fax Sending Options

After you enter address information in the New Fax Wizard, a screen appears prompting you to select a cover page or No cover page for this fax. On that screen, an Options button appears. Clicking Options displays a screen like the one shown in Figure 11.7.

FIGURE 11.7.

Fax options.

In Message format, you tell Fax to query the recipient's fax hardware to determine whether your fax can be received there as an editable file, and to send it as an editable file if possible. Editable files can be sent from MAPI-compliant Windows applications to recipients using Windows 95, Windows for Workgroups, or Microsoft at Work Fax. Fax transmission is used as the vehicle for these files, but the message sent and received is not a fax; it's simply a data file that can be opened and edited on the recipient's computer in the appropriate application. If you choose Not editable, the fax is sent as a noneditable graphic regardless of the recipient's capabilities. If you send Editable only, the fax will not be sent if the recipient can't receive it as an editable file.

In the Time to Send box, you can choose to send the fax as soon as you complete the New Fax wizard, or you can schedule a time to send the fax automatically (provided your PC is switched on, Exchange is open, and your modem is connected to a phone line). This feature is useful for sending files at night, when long-distance rates are lower and most office fax machines are less likely to be tied up.

- In the Cover Page box, you can browse for a cover page (.CPE) file other than those found in the Windows directory.
- In the Billing code box, you can enter an office billing code if your company uses these to track fax and phone usage.

Clicking the Security button brings up a screen like the one in Figure 11.8. These security options work only when the fax is being exchanged between two fax modems in PCs using Windows 95, Windows for Workgroups, or Microsoft at Work Fax.

FIGURE 11.8.

Protecting a fax trans mission.

- The Key-encrypted selection encrypts your fax using RSA public key encryption. Before you can use key encryption, you must create your own public key, and your recipient must also have your key to decrypt the fax.

- The Password-protected selection enables you to enter a password for the fax. The recipient must know your password to open the fax.

Receiving a Fax

To set your fax modem to receive faxes, open Exchange. The phone icon appears in your Taskbar, indicating that it is prepared to receive files. When setting up Fax, you choose between auto-answer and manual answer. If you chose auto-answer, Exchange answers the phone after the selected number of rings and attempts to receive the fax. (Obviously, this option works best on a dedicated phone line.) If you chose manual answer, when you answer the phone and hear a fax tone, double-click the telephone icon to start receiving.

After the fax has been received, it appears in your Inbox, where you can view it, reply to it, forward it, and so on.

Summary

When Windows 3.1 debuted, notebook computers were a novelty and Windows was built with little recognition that it might end up in a mobile computer. Windows 95 was built under the assumption that it would certainly end up in portable computers; the proof of that is the rich array of mobile computing tools, plus setup options that make living within a notebook simpler.

OLE

12

by Wilfred Smith

IN THIS CHAPTER

During the past few years, Microsoft has invested heavily in usability studies. Essentially, companies do usability studies to observe people at work in order to find insight on how to improve productivity. Sometimes, they find simple improvements such as floating toolbars. Occasionally, they develop an entirely new technology that threatens to revolutionize the industry, like OLE. In this chapter, you'll learn how OLE can make you more productive with Windows 95.

Pretend that you've been put in charge of your company's Independence Day party. One of your duties is to make an informal invitation and mail it to everyone. The invitation should include the date (in case anyone forgets), time, and directions to your house (because you were nice enough to volunteer your back yard).

Last year, you were forced to make an emergency trip to the grocery store because nobody brought hot dogs. This year, you want to be sure that everyone knows what to bring. You intend to keep a list of all the volunteers and their respective culinary masterpieces. As a reminder, this list will be sent out along with the invitation to the party.

That seems simple enough. Off to the computer you go. First, you start your favorite word processor and begin typing in the details. While entering the directions to your house, you remember that the main road will be closed during the week of the party. Concerned that someone may get lost, you decide to make a map of your neighborhood. After all, a picture is supposed to be worth a thousand words. So, you fire up your favorite drawing program and draw your heart out. Next, you make up the volunteer list. After a few clicks, your spreadsheet program appears and you enter everyone's name. Just in case you need to make any changes later, you decide to save the three files (invitation and directions, map, and volunteer list) to your hard disk drive. Call the files July 4th Invitation.doc, July 4th Map.bmp, and July 4th volunteers.xls. Thanks to the long filenames in Windows 95, you may be able to find them later.

Unfortunately, you don't have a printer at home, so you copy the three files on a diskette. Tomorrow, you can use the laser printer at work.

Review the steps involved in completing the invitation:

1. Start the word processor.
2. Enter the party details.
3. Save the party details to a file (July 4th invitation.doc).
4. Start the drawing program.
5. Sketch the map.
6. Save the map to a file (July 4th map.bmp).
7. Start the spreadsheet program.
8. Enter the list of attendees and what they're bringing.
9. Save the spreadsheet to a file (July 4th volunteer list.xls).

The next day, when you are ready to print the invitation, you will need to go through almost as many steps:

1. Start the word processor.
2. Find and load the party details file (July 4th invitation.doc).
3. Print as many copies of the party details as you need.
4. Start your drawing program.
5. Find and load the map file (July 4th map.bmp).
6. Print the number of copies of the map you need.
7. Start your spreadsheet program.
8. Find and load the volunteer list (July 4th volunteer list.xls).
9. Print the number of copies of the volunteer list you need.

If you were watching someone do this, you would notice that he or she was spending a great deal of time starting programs, swapping between programs, and finding files. Imagine writing a book with many illustrations and graphs. At some point, you would run out of filenames and start calling the pictures Picture 22 or Graph on page 40. Yes, those are legal filenames, but they aren't very descriptive. The larger the project you're working on, the more likely you are to have several files. At some point, there would be too many files to keep track of. Fortunately, there is a better way to do this and it involves using OLE.

What is OLE and How Can It Help Me?

OLE stands for Object Linking and Embedding. It is a tool that enables you to use information without having to worry about filenames and loading applications. Many of the advances in Windows 95 improve its file-handling capabilities. OLE may be the most important feature of Windows 95, because it almost lets you forget files exist.

Before you continue, read a brief history lesson on the evolution of OLE. Then, you'll explore how OLE can make creating your invitation easier.

Most operating systems (the software that manages your computer) are *file-oriented*. If you want to load a spreadsheet, you must find and start the spreadsheet program. Then, you must tell the spreadsheet program to load the file in which you're interested. Every time you save a spreadsheet, you must give it a filename, even if the best name you can come up with is "More data." If you forget the name of your spreadsheet, you may have a hard time finding it again, so it's best to be descriptive. Worse still, if you try to load a file into the wrong application, the application won't be able to read it; in fact, it may damage the file by trying.

Files worked well before Windows, when most people used only one program. If all your files were made by Lotus 1-2-3, you probably would never want to exit the program unless you were about to turn the computer off. Finding files was simpler because all you needed to know was the filename. Now, everyone has a word processor, spreadsheet, CAD program, accounting package, and more. All the files are incompatible, and they're scattered across the disk drive so that you must spend a great deal of time finding the information you need.

O Is for Objects

Windows 95 is touted as an object-oriented operating system. That means that you won't need to know any filenames unless you specifically want to; instead, you can concentrate on the task at hand. Windows 95 also enables you to work the old-fashioned file-oriented way, if you prefer. But that's not where the power lies.

In Windows 95, an OLE *object* is anything on the screen that responds to a right-click. If you want to see typical OLE objects at work, try right-clicking different places on the screen. You may be surprised. For example, the desktop (the area behind the windows and menus) is an object. If you right-click it, a list of *verbs* will appear. (See Figure 12.1.) They are called verbs because they describe actions that an OLE object can take. If you want the desktop to do something, such as arrange the icons on the screen, just select what you want it to do.

FIGURE 12.1.

The verb list (context menu) for the Windows 95 desktop.

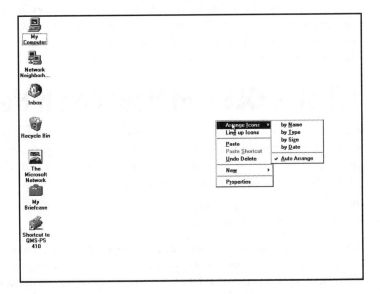

Windows 95 provides both objects and documents. Objects can be printers, sounds, pictures, maps, spreadsheets, and much more. Documents are objects that can contain other objects. In the example in this chapter, you'll play with both types. If you aren't sure whether something is an OLE object or document, right-click it. If it displays what it knows how to do, you've found an object.

Creating a New Document

Take a look at how your invitation would be created if you didn't want to play with filenames. First, you need to create an empty document. To do this, you must tell the desktop object that you want to create a new object. Just right-click anywhere on the exposed desktop (that is, where there are no windows or icons displayed). The desktop will display a list of things you can tell it to do.

Click New and you will see a list of the types of things the desktop can make; this list will vary from machine to machine, depending on which OLE programs you have installed. When the screen shot in Figure 12.2 was taken, only Microsoft Excel was installed. You can also make a new Paint, Notepad, or Wordpad object if you installed those applications during Windows 95 Setup.

FIGURE 12.2.

New object types available from the desktop.

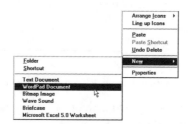

Notice that some of the new objects that can be created are called documents or workspaces. Most of the information for your invitation will be in text form, so you could select Text document or WordPad document. WordPad is completely OLE-capable, so select WordPad document.

Windows 95 will wait for you to describe what the document will contain (Figure 12.3). Enter `Independence Day '95 Party Information`.

FIGURE 12.3.

Describing a new document.

Having the file in the middle of the screen isn't very convenient, so drag it off to the side. If you tell the desktop to auto-arrange, new objects will automatically line up against the left side of the desktop. You can do this by telling the desktop to Arrange | Auto-arrange (Figure 12.4).

FIGURE 12.4.

Turning on auto-arrange.

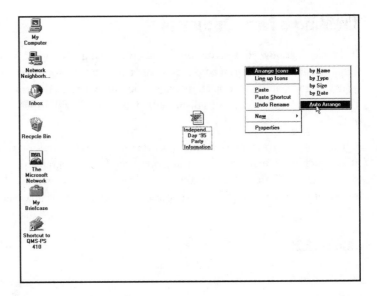

Review the steps involved in creating a new object:

1. Right-click the exposed desktop. This will display a list of verbs, which are things you can tell the desktop object to do.

2. Select New to display the different types of objects you can make. Some of the object types will be called documents or workspaces. This means that they can hold other objects.

3. Select the type of object you want to create. Remember that only document or folder objects can hold other objects. Normally, you will want to choose a document object at this point.

4 Give the new object a name. The name can be as long as 250 characters, so it's OK to be descriptive. For example, "Party Flyer for Sue's Birthday 1995" is fine.

5. Press Enter. Your new object will be left on the screen. Feel free to drag it wherever you'd like.

Using Your New Object

Remember when you read that all OLE objects respond when you right-click them? Try out your new WordPad object. It can do many things, even before you put any text into it. With one click you can open it, rename it, even destroy it (Figure 12.5). You can do almost anything with only two clicks.

FIGURE 12.5.

*New WordPad object
displaying its verbs.*

Notice that the top verb, Open, is displayed in boldface. This is your document's default action. If you double left-click an OLE object, it performs its default action. If the object were some type of sound or video object, it might play itself as a default action.

Now get back to your comparison and open your new WordPad object. It's time to enter some text into it. Double-click your WordPad document and it will display itself in a window (Figure 12.6). From here, just enter the text. Notice that your new-fangled object behaves just like an old-fashioned word processor.

FIGURE 12.6.

*The WordPad document
displaying itself.*

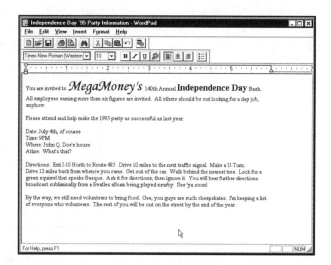

If you've used Windows 3.1 before, the Windows 95 title bar should look strange. If you were using a Windows 3.1 application, the title bar would say WordPad - Independence Day '95 Party Information instead of Independence Day '95 Party Information - WordPad. This reversal is another effect of using OLE.

In Windows 3.1, the title bar displayed which file was loaded into your application. After an application, such as Excel, had been loaded, it was easy to tell Excel to open another file. Also, only Excel could open most Excel files. If you want to, you can use Windows 95 to open applications just like Windows 3.1.

However, in this example you've opened an object in Windows 95. Your object could be anything from a sound to a picture of Eleanor Roosevelt. With so many possibilities, it's nice that you don't have to figure out which application to open. In fact, your object could be displayed by more than one application. For example, if you have Word for Windows on your computer, Windows 95 can display your document in Word.

If an object is a document, the objects inside can each be shown by a different program. You'll see how this works shortly. For now, finish entering your text, and then close the document.

So far, you haven't seen a single .doc anywhere. But, before you believe that the filenames aren't somewhere behind the scenes, take a look at your document's properties. Right-click your document again, and select Properties. A set of tabbed folders appears, describing your document (Figure 12.7). Next to the entry "MS-DOS name," you can see a filename and extension. All along, Windows 95 has been keeping track of your document's filename for you. In fact, its real filename is something like C:\win95\desktop\Independence Day '95 Party Information.doc. INDEPE~2.DOC is a synonym that Windows 95 maintains for programs that can't handle objects or filenames more than eight letters long.

FIGURE 12.7.

WordPad document properties.

While you're in this menu, click the Summary and Statistics tabs. The type of property information available will be different for each object. For example, Word and WordPad objects will display their word count and author on the Statistics tab. Occasionally, the Properties information can save you from having to open the document.

Folders are Objects, Too

Once you've played around with Windows 95 for a while, you'll realize that nearly everything is an OLE object. Try making a new folder object. Just like before, right-click the desktop; then, select New and Folder. You can even name the folder the same way you named your document. Call this one 1995 Parties. Just type the name of the folder and press Enter. Then, you're free to drag it anywhere you'd like.

Folders are also documents. They aren't listed as folder documents, but they function the same way.

Try this. Grab your party information document and drag it on top of the folder you just made. You'll notice that the document disappears, leaving only the folder on the desktop. The party information document is now inside the 1995 Parties folder. Double-click the folder and you'll see your document sitting there, waiting for you to look at it (Figure 12.8).

FIGURE 12.8.

Viewing the contents of a folder.

Here's something else to try. Right-click the empty space inside the 1995 Parties folder. Notice that the list of verbs is almost the same as the desktop's. Click New. You can stick a new document or object right here in the folder, without having to move it in from the desktop. Just point to where you want the new object. It doesn't get any simpler.

E is for Embedding

If you're thinking "It would be nice to do that to your invitation," guess what? It works there, too. You can stick an object directly in the document. Unfortunately, the steps are a little bit different.

This entire operation, by the way, is called embedding. As long as your object is a document, you can embed other objects into it.

Now you can embed your map. First, you need to open your document again by double-clicking it. Move the cursor between the directions and the request for volunteers and click Insert Object from the menu.

A list of object types is displayed (Figure 12.9). Notice that there are more items on this list than the desktop or folder could create. Some older OLE objects aren't fully implemented and cannot be presented properly by Windows 95. Usually, these older OLE objects must be inserted into certain types of documents. As Windows 95 becomes more popular, you will see far fewer of these malformed objects. There are a few other things you can do here, which you'll learn about shortly.

FIGURE 12.9.

Inserting an object into WordPad.

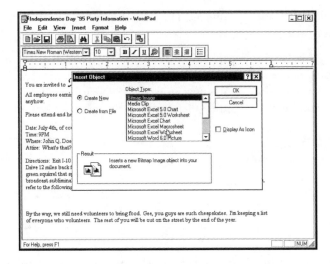

Select Bitmap Image, and a square frame should appear inside the document. Suddenly, the WordPad toolbars are replaced with a color palette and painting tools. It's time to draw a map! A little bit of scribbling and there's your map (Figure 12.10). If Bitmap Image is not in the object type list, go back to Setup and install Paint.

FIGURE 12.10.

Drawing a map in the document.

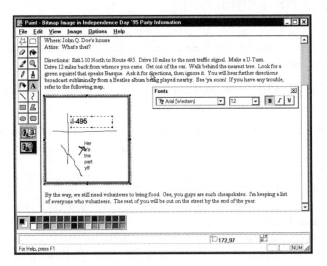

Be sure to notice what has happened to the title bar this time. Now, you're looking at Paint, but it says that it is displaying a bitmap in Independence Day '95 Party Information (Figure 12.11). It won't be necessary to name the map you drew, it's just part of the party information.

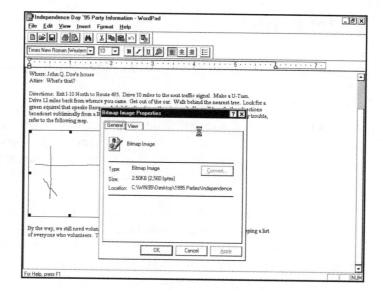

Click the text you typed earlier. Notice that you can move through the text, even though the picture is between two paragraphs. Even better, the document will print exactly as displayed. Instead of three pages to send out, you can fit the map and the directions on the same page.

If you choose to, you can insert your volunteer list in the invitation the same way, except this time you'd choose to insert a Microsoft Excel Worksheet. But that would be too easy. You need to learn the other options on the dialog in Figure 12.10.

Recap

OLE embedding enables you to place objects inside certain other objects (container objects). These container objects are called documents. Objects placed inside a document do not need to have a separate filename or title. Subject to the constraints of the document type, objects may be positioned anywhere inside a document.

If an object supports visual editing, you can modify it without opening a separate window. Otherwise, you must double-click the object to edit it. When you save a document, the objects it contains are saved inside it.

Objects can also be embedded as icons. Some objects do not know how to display themselves and must be embedded as icons. To use these objects, double-click them. You'll see an example of this in the next section.

L Is for Linking

OLE embedding is pretty nifty, but there are several occasions when embedding is not the right thing to do. At other times, it just isn't possible. Here are three situations in which embedding is not appropriate.

- You use a program that doesn't know how to handle objects. This may be an MS-DOS program or a Microsoft Windows program that was written before Microsoft began pushing OLE at software developers. These programs only know how to handle files. Objects are not in their vocabulary. In most cases there will be a newer, Windows 95 version available, but it isn't fun to be forced into buying software you already own.

- You want an object to be part of more than one document. Each time you embed an object, it consumes disk space. If you have five copies of an object in different objects, it will consume five times as much disk space. This could be a problem if, for example, you wanted to place your map in all your documents.

- Those who view your file will frequently need to run a certain program. You want them to be able to start that program from within your document.

Linking a File to Your Document

In the example, you want to use the volunteer's list in two separate documents. The first document is the invitation and the second is a letter to the president of the company. If you embed the list of volunteers in both documents, twice as much disk space will be used. True, your list of volunteers isn't that large, but it could be.

It would be cumbersome to ensure that both documents always have the same information. You don't want to get into a cycle of updating one document, only to take the same steps to update the other.

That's where linking comes in. OLE linking enables you to refer to an object (or file) without placing it inside another object. Instead, you place a *link* to the other object that says where the information is. For this example, you'll create the list of volunteers as a separate object. Then, you'll place links to it in both the invitation and letter documents.

There's a significant side effect to doing this. Because there is only one copy of the list of volunteers, changing the list affects both documents. If you were to create five hundred documents, all containing a link to the list of volunteers, they would all be up-to-date all the time.

Make your spreadsheet and link, so that you can play with linking.

1. Make a new spreadsheet object. Any OLE spreadsheet should be fine. Label it List of Volunteers for July 4, 1995, and leave it out on the desktop for now.

2. Enter the volunteers' names and what they are bringing.

3. Close the spreadsheet. You can leave the spreadsheet open, but closing it reduces screen clutter.

4. Open the invitation document.

5. Drag the list of volunteers to the invitation document. Release it when you have it positioned at the end. Notice that the caret (where the next letter appears when you type) moves to indicate where the spreadsheet will be inserted (Figure 12.12).

6. Follow the same procedure for the letter.

FIGURE 12.12.

Creating a link to the volunteers' list.

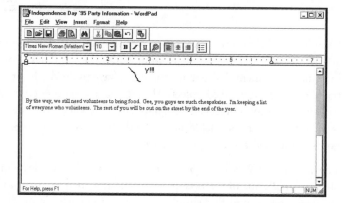

As soon as the link is established, the spreadsheet object appears, just as if you had embedded it. In fact, you can edit linked objects exactly as you would edit an embedded object.

The easiest way to determine whether an object has been linked is to view its properties. Go back to the invitation and right-click the spreadsheet you just linked in. When the verb list appears, select Object Properties. A dialog titled Linked Spreadsheet Properties appears.

Click the link tab and you'll learn about link updates (Figure 12.13). Windows 95 supports two types of links: automatic and manual. If you create a manual link to information in another object, the information in your document will change only when you press the Update Now button in this dialog box. If you decide that you will never want to update your link, press the Break Link button to embed the object in its current state.

Try automatic updating. Open the volunteers list and change something. Say that Chelsea has decided to bring unsalted pretzels instead of German beer. Then, save the spreadsheet. If you go back to the invitation or the letter, you'll see that the information has auto-magically been updated in both documents. If you double-click the volunteers list in the document, make changes, and save, the other document will be updated. Why? There's only one file.

FIGURE 12.13.

Link update options for the volunteers list.

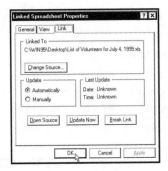

If you're on a Microsoft-compatible network, you can create links to objects on other computers. This means that you can collaborate with others and have your combined work contained in a single document. Note that you would have to divide the document into parts, each composed of a separate, linked object. Also, if one of the other computers leaves the network, you will lose access to its objects. If this happens, you will need to show Windows 95 where the file is when the object is available again. To do this, display the link properties, click Browse, and point to the object. (See Figure 12.14.)

The designers of Windows 95 realized that it will take a while before all programs support OLE objects. That's one of the reasons why they included linking in OLE. There will always be a few programs around that simply must have filenames. Wouldn't it be nice if you could tell your document to pretend your file is an object, even though it isn't?

Windows 95 enables you to make a link to a file just as easily as you can insert an object. There is one major restriction, however. Since the file is not an OLE object, it won't know how to display itself. Instead, the file will be displayed (and will print) as an icon. You can still double-click the file object icon to view your information, however. In fact, you can view your file object with any program you wish.

Say that you have an ancient program called XYZ Text in which your boss has written some personal comments about the Independence Day party and his great granddaddy being a founding father. He's a bit long-winded, but he wants his comments sent out to everyone. Being environmentally conscious, you decide that sending everyone electronic mail would be better than laying waste to a forest the size of Texas. What a great opportunity to try out Windows 95's file linking!

The procedure for linking to a file is similar to linking to an object. The difference is that when the dialog appears, you select Create from file. Notice that Display as icon is an option. When you link to a file, Windows 95 doesn't know whether the file can be displayed as an OLE object; that requires an OLE-capable program that can display the file. If it finds out that the object isn't OLE-capable at display time, Windows 95 will display an icon anyway. In your case, you know that XYZ Text uses a completely arcane file format developed by the Egyptians. There is no OLE-capable program that can display its files, so check Display as icon.

FIGURE 12.14.

About to link to a file.

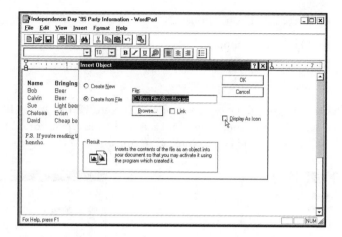

When you close the dialog, the icon appears (Figure 12.15). When you try to double-click it, you get a message stating, "No application is associated with this file" from the object packager.

FIGURE 12.15.

Linked icon.

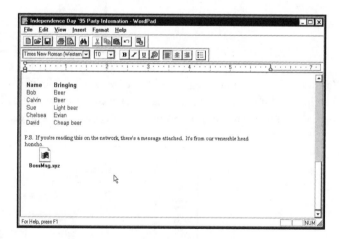

An *object packager* is a program that helps files pretend they're objects. Essentially, it stands in for them and lets you change things like the icon displayed for the file and the title underneath it. It is also responsible for starting the correct program (application) in cases such as this.

What does "No application associated with this file" mean? With file-oriented programs, the three-letter extension following a filename normally indicates the program that created it. For example, letter.doc is a document file such as those created by Microsoft Word. finance.xls is a spreadsheet file created by Microsoft Excel. Windows 95 uses the file extensions to determine which program to start when you want to look at a file. Unfortunately, it has never seen an XYZ Text file, or any file with an .XYZ extension. You need to tell it which program to use.

Look at the list of associations:

- Open My Computer.
- Select View from the menu, and then select Options.
- Select the File Types tab.

A list of registered file types will appear (Figure 12.16). In the file type details box, you'll see the extension and application for each of the file types. For example, text documents have a .TXT extension and cause Notepad to run when they are opened.

FIGURE 12.16.

Associating a file with an extension.

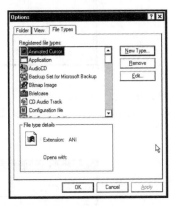

You want to create a new registered file type, so click New Type. Enter XYZ Text as the type description. Enter xyz as the associated extension (Figure 12.17). Notice that you can enter more than one extension. For example, you could enter xyz qqq 123.

FIGURE 12.17.

Adding a new registered file type.

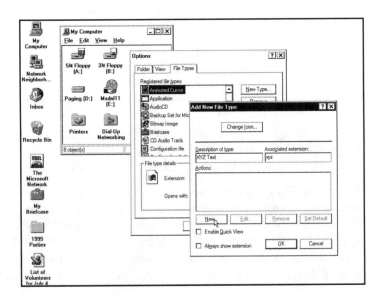

Under Actions, click New. The actions are the verbs to which an object can respond. Enter Edit as the action and xyztext.exe as the application used to perform the action (Figure 12.18). Then click OK. Notice that Edit has appeared here on the list of actions. As you can tell by the buttons, you can change and delete actions from here. At this point, you have told Windows 95 that when Edit is selected on an XYZ Text file (object), fire up xyztext.exe.

FIGURE 12.18.

Creating a new action for XYZ Text.

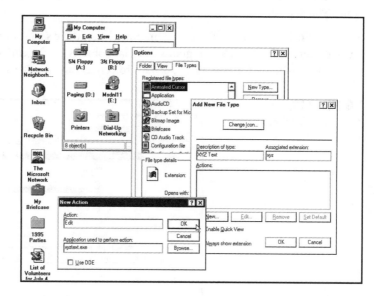

Highlight Edit and then click Set Default. When a file or object is double-clicked, Windows 95 performs its default action (verb). You set your default action to Edit.

Now, go back to the linked file object and try to start it.

Linking to Part of a File

Occasionally, you will want to include part of an object in a document. If you'll never need to update the object, you can use the clipboard. However, sometimes cut and paste isn't enough. What if you need to have the document update automatically?

Windows 95 supports linking (and embedding) via the clipboard as well. Say that you want to create a new WordPad document with only the names of the volunteers. The spreadsheet containing the names will change, so you want the new document to automatically keep itself current.

Open the spreadsheet and select just the volunteer names. Use the Edit | Copy menu item to put the names on the clipboard. Now right-click the desktop and make a new WordPad document. Just below the Edit | Paste menu item is the Edit | Paste Link or Edit | Paste Special menu item. In some programs, like WordPad, both are available. Select Edit | Paste Special and a dialog will appear.

From here, you can select Paste Link and a link to the contents of the clipboard will be pasted into your document. By default, the link will automatically update itself. Take a look at the text titled Source near the top of the dialog. That text identifies the area of the document from which you copied.

While you're here, click the Paste button. Notice that there's a list of things you can paste, or embed (Figure 12.19). Most programs can place objects on the clipboard in several formats. This can be useful if, for example, you want to convert an area of a spreadsheet to a picture.

FIGURE 12.19.

Using the clipboard to paste a link.

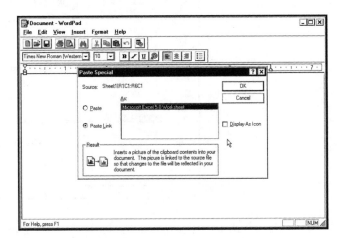

Dragging and Dropping and Scraps

As you have noticed, Windows 95 treats objects as if they were, well, objects. You can examine them, put them in other objects, tell them to do things, and more. You can even have different types of objects, capable of doing different things. Yet, one of the niftiest things about objects is that you can move them around and combine them with each other. This is affectionately called "drag and drop." You've already played with this by dragging your document around and dropping it on a folder or the desktop. However, you can also drop your objects on other things.

For example, you can place a shortcut (similar to a link) to your printer on the desktop and drag objects to it. Everything you drop on the printer will then print. That makes sense doesn't it? This works because, just as you learned earlier, almost everything in Windows 95 is an OLE object.

Here's how to put a printer on your desktop.

1. Open My Computer by double-clicking it. A list of your computer's disk drives will appear along with folders for its other resources.

2. Open Printers the same way. A list of all the printers you have available will appear. In Figure 12.20 there is only one printer; that's the QMS PS-410 you see in the screen shot. If you have a different type of printer, you'll see its name there instead. You'll also see a Fax object that may seem out of place; it's there because Windows 95 treats fax modems as if they were printers. That way, you can "print to fax" from any program you wish.

3. Drag onto the desktop the printer you use most often. You'll get a message about not being able to move or copy the printer. If you click OK, Windows 95 will make a *shortcut*. (See Figure 12.20.) Shortcuts are just like links. You can tell a shortcut by the little arrow below the icon. Just like a linked object, you can treat a shortcut just like the actual object.

FIGURE 12.20.

Creating a printer shortcut.

To print an object, all you need to do is drag it to the printer shortcut you just made. This is great if you have several objects or documents in a folder and you need to print (or fax) them all. It's far better than opening each file and manually printing them. As an added bonus, you can build up your wrist muscles by printing files during your coffee breaks.

So, if you want to print the invitation document when you get to work tomorrow and you have created a shortcut to your printer there, it only takes four steps:

1. Insert the floppy.

2. Open My Computer by double-clicking it.

3. Open your floppy drive's folder, either A: or B:, depending on the computer.

4. Drag the invitation document to the printer (Figure 12.21).

FIGURE 12.21.

Printing the invitation.

There is another way to quickly print a document. You may have guessed that most objects should know how to print themselves. If so, you have earned some brownie points. After you have opened the floppy drive's folder, right-clicking the invitation document will display its verb list. One of the things the invitation document can do is print.

This is much faster than having to find, open, and print three separate files.

Scraps

One nice thing about Windows 95 is that it occasionally surprises you. While showing OLE to a friend, I selected text from a document and, accidentally, dropped it on the desktop. To my surprise, a "scrap" document appeared where I released the mouse button. When I opened the document, it contained what I had selected. Windows 95 had automatically turned it into an object!

It isn't every day that you stumble on a useful feature, but it happens frequently with Windows 95 and its OLE objects. I have quickly learned that if it would make sense for an object to behave a certain way, it probably will. Don't be afraid to experiment. You might discover something useful.

Think about how useful scraps can be. Say that you want to create an object containing the directions you wrote and put it into your 1995 Parties folder. There are many ways to accomplish this task. Yet, the most intuitive is to select the text of the directions and drag it to the folder. Guess what, it works! Windows 95 even creates a title for it using the first few words. (See Figure 12.22.) You could just as easily have dragged the directions to a printer, a fax, or another document.

FIGURE 12.22.

Your scrap of directions.

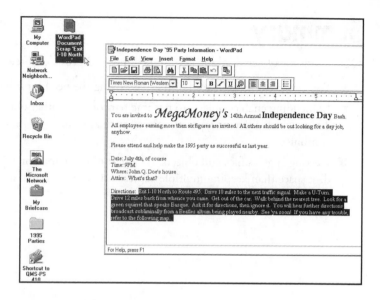

Old OLE

If you install an application that uses old-style (Windows 3.1) OLE under Windows 95, it might not act the way you expect. For one thing, it won't show up on the desktop's verb list. The application must be opened before a new file can be created.

Once created, the old-style OLE object cannot be dragged and dropped onto a document. It can only be copied and pasted from the clipboard.

Inside a document, you cannot move the cursor over an old-style OLE object and edit it. You must double-click the object, which opens the object's application in a separate window.

Converting Objects

When you must move a document to another computer, it's often useful to move an object to some other kind of object. You might want to do this because the other machine doesn't have the same applications loaded; or it might not use Windows 95. If an object knows how to convert itself, it will have *convert* in its list of verbs. Click *convert*, and you will be able to choose from a dialog. Suppose you have a Microsoft Excel object with a Microsoft Word object embedded inside and you need to give the file to a friend who only has Excel. You could convert the Word object to a Notepad object, so that your friend will be able to look at your text.

Summary

OLE stands for Object Linking and Embedding and provides three major benefits:

- You can use objects instead of files, removing the need for keeping track of filenames.
- Embedding enables objects to become part of some other objects, called documents. This enables different types of objects, such as sound, text, and graphics, to be combined.
- Linking enables files and objects to be part of more than one document. This uses less disk space than keeping multiple copies and permits several documents to be updated from a single source.

Family Computing

13

by Ed Tiley

As long as there have been computers, there have been ways of playing with the computer. From the earliest mainframe versions of Tic-Tac-Toe to classic games like Wumpus Hunt, to reproductions of Playboy Playmates printed on old daisywheel and dot matrix printers, computer users have always augmented the business productivity capabilities of the machine with entertainment and diversion.

In these, the last days of the twentieth century, people's desire to use the personal computer for education and entertainment has blossomed into a billion-dollar business. Nearly one-fourth of all homes in the United States have a home computer, and thousands more are sold every week.

Perhaps the single most important reason to have a computer at home, however, is for family computing. Family computing can be defined as running software on the computer that provides fun and learning, and has the tendency to bring people together.

More and more people are choosing to forego the passivity of watching TV and movies, choosing instead to join the digital Renaissance. An explosion of new multimedia titles is fueling the Renaissance, making learning for the sake of learning entertaining and fun.

In this chapter you will get to see the tip of the iceberg. There is no way to definitively cover the subject of family computing in a single chapter. Instead, this chapter focuses on representative samples of the kinds of software you can find on the shelves at your local computer store. The first order of business is the hardware you need to make family computing all it's cracked up to be, but that is a short subject. The remainder of the chapter is devoted to play, not work.

The Family Computer

There are a wide range of choices available when it comes to selecting hardware for the family computer. There is a tendency to get hung up on bits and bytes when selecting hardware, but there are really only two major considerations. Will the computer run Windows 95 fast enough to make you happy, and does it have multimedia capability? If you answer both questions with a yes, you have a suitable home computer.

If you are in the market to buy a complete system, here are a few specifications that you can use as a checklist to make sure you're getting a system that will handle almost anything you throw at it for the next five or six years:

- The CPU should be an Intel 80486/66 or a Pentium.
- The system should have at least 8 MB of RAM.
- If you plan to communicate with online services or surf the Internet, you will need a modem capable of performing at 14400 baud or better.
- You will want a sound card and a CD-ROM drive.

Add a mouse, trackball, maybe a joystick for games, and a printer of your choice, and you have a system that will deliver years of fun and education, as well as being capable of taking the load when you bring "just a few things home from the office."

> **TIP**
>
> Don't give the kids the fuzzy end of the lollipop. All too often when an adult buys a computer for a combination of home productivity work and family computing the kids get short shrift. The tendency is to make sure the system has the horsepower to do the office work, but things like a sound card or a CD-ROM get put off until later, or worse, are dismissed as frills.
>
> Just keep in mind that providing tools such as a multimedia encyclopedia, or edutainment titles like Multimedia Beethoven or Dinosaurs provides educational benefits equal to any private school, and the cost is much less.

If you have an older machine that meets the basic requirements but is not multimedia-capable, you should investigate the growing number of multimedia upgrade kits. One example that is covered a little later in this chapter is Creative Labs' Digital Schoolhouse. In one box you get a sound card, a double-speed CD-ROM drive, speakers, and a microphone. Along with the hardware, you also get a big bundle of software goodies that make your system come alive as soon as you install the hardware.

> **TIP**
>
> Don't worry so much about the hardware. Get your hands on the fastest, best-equipped system you can afford, and then concentrate on what you can do with the computer.
>
> Folks who get hung up on hardware get a special kind of kick out of tinkering, comparing, and playing with gadgets. For the rest of us, playing with the software and connecting to the outside world is the main focus, and, incidentally, the most fun.

Of course, the choice of hardware isn't trivial. To make intelligent choices you need some idea of what you intend to use the machine for. If you work at home, and the machine will be a combination work and play system, you will want to skew your choices toward the top end of the spectrum. If all you want is a play machine, you can safely stay a bit closer to the middle of the road, although the faster the machine, the faster your programs will run. That's an important consideration if you play complex, highly graphic games like Doom or Wolfenstein.

In any case, you will want to check out what hardware choices are available, and make sure that what you purchase is suitable. There are a few tips and things to watch out for that you may want to take into account before signing on the dotted line.

Whenever possible, avoid computers that are not component-based, meaning that the basic functionality is built into the motherboard, but items like disk controllers, serial ports, and the like are provided as cards in the bus slots. A number of computer manufacturers are able to offer low-cost machines "designed for family computing" by building everything in the system onto the motherboard. There are two problems with computers of this type.

First, you may have difficulty upgrading components later. If the video card is built into the motherboard of the system, replacing it with the next great innovation in video may be impossible.

Second, if a component fails, your repair costs may be higher. A single card that controls the hard drive, floppy drives, printer and communications ports usually costs less than fifty dollars. If your COM port goes bad, you get another card and plug it in, and away you go. If, however, the COM port hardware is embedded in the motherboard, you may end up spending hundreds of dollars to repair the computer because the entire motherboard has to be replaced.

Pay special attention to the video and monitor specifications. Many an otherwise acceptable system fails to please because the video display is weak. Windows 95 puts a heavy burden on the video card. A slow or outdated video display card will slow the system down. You can have all the RAM in the world and the fastest CPU in town, but a slow video card will make the system run like a dog because the rest of the system will have to wait for the video display to catch up before it can continue. Also make sure the card can display multiple resolutions (640×480, 800×600, 768×1024), and that it can display more than 256 simultaneous colors.

When choosing the monitor itself, the dot pitch of the monitor—the actual size of the dots on the screen that form images—should be .28 or less for the most pleasing video imagery. Multisynch monitors enable the video card to use scanning and refresh rates that eliminate flicker and provide the best video display possible with as little eyestrain as possible. Remember, you are likely to spend many hours staring at that screen. Low radiation and energy efficiency are good things to look at, too. Saving a few dollars by compromising on video quality is usually no bargain in the end.

Free and Nearly Free

OK, so you just popped for a couple of grand and bought a shiny new computer for the family room. You've got it installed, Windows 95 is up and running, but the hard disk is empty. You've seen lots of software at the computer store you want to get, but your wallet is empty. What you need is good low-cost freeware and shareware.

Games

The first place to look is in Windows 95. Several high-quality games are distributed as applets along with WordPad, the Calculator, and so on. Assuming you don't have a network at home, Minesweeper, Freecell, and Hearts are going to get the most vigorous workout. Just click the Start button and find the Games group contained in Accessories. If you didn't install the games during setup, no problem. Install them using the Add/Remove Programs dialog in Control Panel. Don't forget that the CD version of Windows 95 contains a cool game called Hover, and Microsoft Plus! For Windows 95 contains 3D Pinball.

Minesweeper

The Minesweeper game was first introduced with Windows 3.1. It is a real challenge for even the most logical minds. The game loads into a window filled with small square buttons. Each button potentially hides a mine. Click the wrong button and kaboom. Figure 13.1 shows a game in progress.

FIGURE 13.1.

Try to uncover the safe squares without exploding a mine.

There are four levels of difficulty: beginner, intermediate, advanced, and custom. The game plays exactly the same way in all levels, but the more advanced levels have more mines to find.

When you click a square, one of two things will happen: a mine will explode or you will reveal a number that indicates how many mines the uncovered square touches. A blank square means you aren't touching a square with a mine. The counter in the upper-left corner counts down how many mines you have left to find. Right-click a square to mark it as a bomb. Right-click again to put a question mark there so you can decide later. If you uncover all the squares that are mine-free, you win!

Freecell

Freecell has to be the most addictive game of solitaire ever devised because it is more a game of skill than a game of luck. Theoretically, every game can be won. Theoretically!

Figure 13.2 shows a game in progress. At the top left of the screen are four free cells where you can place cards temporarily. The cells on the right side are where you build your four suits, aces up, to get cards off the table. When you make a card on the table unneeded (meaning that there are no cards left in the stacks that can be played on it), it will automatically fly into the proper cell at the top right if the next lower card is already there.

All of the cards are dealt face up into the eight piles on the table. Red sixes go on black sevens, black queens go on red kings, and so on, just like regular solitaire. Unlike regular solitaire, however, any card can be placed into an empty pile. You can click a pile of cards to mark them, and then click the pile where you want them to go. If there are enough free cells, the cards will be moved.

FIGURE 13.2.

The object of the game is to move all the cards to the four cells in the top-right corner. Your reward is the dancing card show.

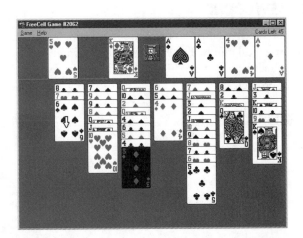

TIP

Pressing the numbers 1–8 will let you see the cards in each pile.

If you see the title bar begin to flash, beware! It means you are just a move or two away from doing something entirely stupid that will lose the game for you. You can move bigger piles of cards when you have an empty pile. Have fun.

Hearts

Hearts can be played by four people on a network, but is just as much fun when played against three computer personalities. All 52 cards are dealt out. Each player passes three cards to another player and play begins. Whoever holds the two of clubs plays that card first to begin the hand. You must follow suit if you are able.

The object of the game is to score the fewest number of points. Each heart card is worth a single point, and the queen of spades is worth 13. Figure 13.3 shows play in progress. Figure 13.4 shows the automatic score card.

FIGURE 13.3.

Play of the cards is like bridge or spades, but the object of Hearts is very different!

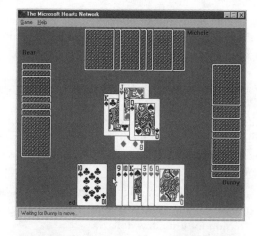

FIGURE 13.4.

Take the fewest tricks, and you will usually take the fewest point cards. The player with the fewest points when another player tops 100 points is the winner.

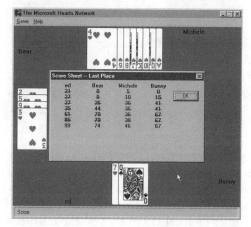

You pass three cards to an opponent three out of four hands. The first hand you pass left, right, and then across. On the fourth hand you play the cards you were dealt. You want to take the fewest number of heart cards you can. You also want to avoid taking the queen of spades, usually. Usually because if you can take all thirteen hearts and the queen of spades, you earn 0 points while giving 26 points to each of your opponents. Taking everything, however, is difficult to do, and the risk is high that you will get stuck.

Other Sources for Low-Cost Games and Programs

There are literally thousands of places you can go to look for free and low-cost software that rivals anything being produced by the top software companies. Freeware and shareware programs for fun, productivity, and entertainment abound.

> **NOTE**
>
> The difference between freeware and shareware is simple. *Freeware* has been released by its author to the public. Sometimes freeware authors retain the copyright instead of placing it in the public domain, but the distinction is that the author isn't looking for payment.
>
> *Shareware* is released by small entrepreneurs on a try-before-you-buy concept. You can check out the program, and if you like it you can register it and usually get an enhanced version for just a few dollars.
>
> Like any human endeavor, writing software produces mixed results; some shareware is lousy, some is pretty good, but there are also some that qualify as world-class, quality software. PKZIP, which has become a worldwide standard for archiving and compressing files, McAfee's virus protection programs, which are available as shareware, and several commercial programs like ProComm Plus for Windows started life as shareware. When you find good shareware and register it, you help to support the system, and ensure that good, low-cost software will be available in the future.

Where to go for freeware and shareware is a difficult subject to cover because it is everywhere. Just about any town of any size in the United States has one or more local bulletin board services in operation. Online services such as CompuServe, America Online, Prodigy, and the Microsoft Network are all sources for the latest releases. Around the world, there are thousands of File Transfer Protocol (FTP) sites on the Internet were you can download freeware and shareware programs. Some FTP sites can be visited using the World Wide Web, too.

One Word of Caution

A word of caution is in order before you fire up the modem and start surfing cyberspace looking for goodies. Most sysops (system operators) of online sources are dedicated and responsible folks who do their level best to screen out bad software.

Unfortunately, there are immature jerks who own computers, too. These are the same folks who kick over gravestones, spray-paint cars, and vandalize schools. Their computerized brethren love nothing more than to catch folks unawares by putting virus-infected files into the public's reach.

The first two bits of shareware you want to acquire are WinZip, which can be found on the CD-ROM that comes with this book, and a virus protection program like McAfee. Most freeware and shareware programs are distributed by wrapping up all their files into a single compressed archive file with the extension .ZIP. By combining WinZip with a virus scanner and using them to screen every file you download, you will save yourself a lot of grief. Oh, and don't forget to do your backups.

WinZip has way too many features than can be discussed here, but Figure 13.5 shows its most useful features. When you open a ZIP file with WinZip, you open a list of all the files in the archive to see what they contain, or to edit them. All you need to do is double-click the file you want to open. If you make changes to the file, WinZip will offer to update the ZIP file with the new version.

Reference and Learning

One of the basic truths of the Digital Renaissance is that computerized reference works are a lot easier to use than printed reference works. Through the miracle of hypertext, you can jump to related information with a single click of the mouse instead of having to find another book in the stacks at the library. Not that having a digital encyclopedia will make the library obsolete, mind you. Like any encyclopedia, the information is summarized and condensed. You will find the bibliography quite useful, however, when you need to head to the library; you can go armed with a list of reference works on the subject you are researching.

Probably the two best known encyclopedisks are Grolier's and Encarta. Because this book isn't about comparing and reviewing products, no comparisons are drawn between the products. It's up to you to do that for yourself.

The New Grolier Multimedia Encyclopedia Release 6

When you open Grolier's, the initial screen appears as it does in Figure 13.5. As you can see, there are twelve buttons that lead you into twelve different views of the contents of the encyclopedia. Included in the information are sound clips, videos, maps, and of course, the standard textual entries you might find in a printed encyclopedia.

FIGURE 13.5.

The starting screen for Grolier's. Each button represents a specific view of the information in the encyclopedia.

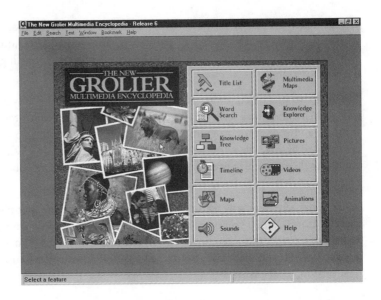

Each of the buttons has an icon associated with the category. As you can see in Figure 13.6, you can find these same icons in the toolbar when you drill down into a category. This way, you can easily jump between views.

In Figure 13.6, a video on the exploration of space is playing. The beauty, and most of the fun, of a digital encyclopedia is the ability to jump around from subject to subject. As you can see in Figure 13.7, even the text part of the encyclopedia gets into the action.

FIGURE 13.6.

Clicking the Knowledge Explorer enables you to find a video on the exploration of space.

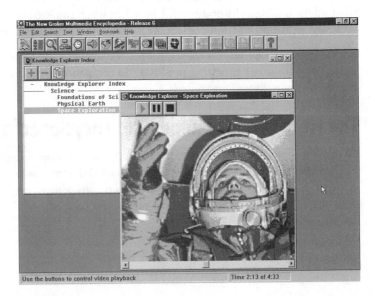

FIGURE 13.7.

Picking subjects from the Title List brings up a written report on the subject. Clicking the map icon in the title bar opens a window to display the associated map.

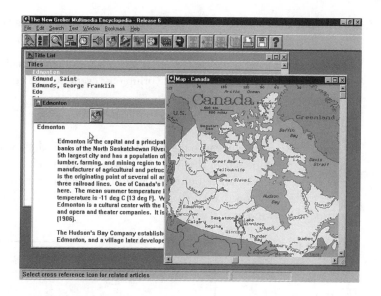

When you make a selection from the Title List, a window opens with an article about the subject displayed. You can click the map icon in the title bar to see an entry from the atlas, or you can highlight a date, click the time line button (obscured by the map), and see where events lie along the time line of history.

Most encyclopedia disks highlight words in the text that can be searched to find other entries. Grolier's is different. All you have to do is double-click any word to pop open a window similar to the one shown in Figure 13.8. This window presents all the topics that you can jump to that contain the word *Hudson*.

FIGURE 13.8.

Potentially any word in an article can be used as a search key for finding related topics.

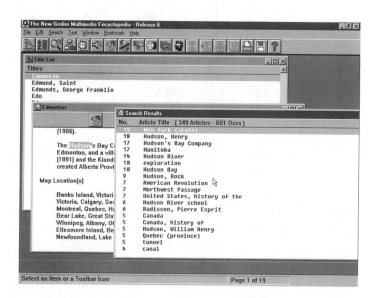

By double-clicking words in each successive article presented, you can easily find yourself drawn into reading about all sorts of things related and unrelated to your original topic.

When you find the information you are seeking, you can copy small chunks of the text to the clipboard, send the entire article to the printer, or even save the article to disk in a file.

Encarta '95

Encarta is Microsoft's entry into the digital encyclopedia field. As you can see in Figure 13.9, there is a startup title screen that you can bypass by unchecking the box in the bottom-left corner of the window. Three buttons below the name Encarta give you a quick tour of the features of this encyclopedia. You begin to explore Encarta by clicking the Enter button on the right side of the window.

FIGURE 13.9.

The title screen lets you explore Encarta's features. Once you are familiar with them, uncheck the box in the lower left to bypass this screen.

One of the options you can set in Encarta is whether you return to the same point you left off in your last session. This feature makes it handy to switch to another disk, or even leave off for the day and come right back to the same point when you return to Encarta.

As you can see in Figure 13.10, the information in Encarta is divided into ten main areas of interest, and that each area of interest is again subdivided into categories.

Words and phrases in the text that have a link to a related topic are highlighted. Clicking a highlighted word takes you to that subject. Double-clicking other words will let you read the dictionary and thesaurus entries for the word.

FIGURE 13.10.

Each area of interest is divided into categories.

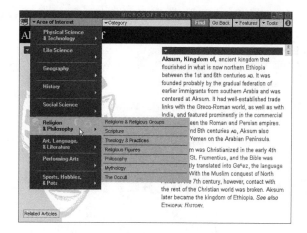

Many entries have sound or video presentations that accompany them, and multimedia entries have controls on them so you can view or listen to them.

When you pull down the Areas of Interest menu and select a category, the Pinpointer window is opened. This window gives you a list of the keywords you can search to find topics you want to read. Figure 13.11 shows the Pinpointer in action. All you have to do is type the word or phrase on which you want to search. When you press Enter or click an entry, the main window's view changes to that topic.

FIGURE 13.11.

The buttons on the right side of the Pinpointer window let you filter out unwanted information.

There are several buttons on the right side of the Pinpointer window. These buttons let you restrict your view of the data. Clicking the Time button, for example, lets you narrow the view of titles so that only those articles that deal with a specific historical period appear. In Figure 13.11, the Category button has been clicked, giving you a quick way of changing areas of interest and categories. The Word button helps you assemble very specific word searches.

Once you get the hang of Encarta, you will find that you can quickly find almost any topic. You will also find that you are soon just jumping from one topic to another, engrossed in all the facts and figures at your disposal.

Family Computing Tools

If you use a computer at work, you likely use top-of-the-line business applications. If you work with words, you probably use WordPerfect, Word for Windows, Ami Pro, or some other high-end word-processing program. Number crunchers tend to settle on Lotus 1-2-3, Excel, or Quattro Pro. Programs such as dBASE 5.0 for Windows or Access are used to create data management forms and applications. Programs like these are used in business because they offer maximum flexibility and support for the broadest range of features.

In addition, there is a tendency these days for software packages that compete with one another to enter into feature wars. WordPerfect adds a feature, so all the other word processors add the same feature plus their own special variation or enhancement. The result is that the software used day-to-day in business gets ever more complicated with each new version. Family computing, however, usually dictates a simpler software model that lets beginning computer users and kids share the same tools.

Microsoft Works for Windows

Over the years, a second tier of software products has emerged, often using the name Works. This class of software combines the capability to create several document types into the same program. These kinds of programs are ideal for high-level family computing because they have enough features to enable Mom and Dad to do business-type work, yet are simple enough for the kids to use in doing their homework.

A good example of this type of package is Microsoft Works. Works combines the basic features of a word processor, a spreadsheet, a data manager, and a communications program into a single integrated program. Each of the document types that Works can produce is designed to share data with each of the other document types.

Figure 13.12 shows a Works document, a spreadsheet, and a data entry form, all within the same window. Each application is limited in what it can do when compared to top-of-the-line products like Word 6 for Windows, Lotus 1-2-3 or Excel, or dBASE 5.0 for Windows. Still, each application has more than enough features and horsepower to do real work, both office work and homework. The word processor is perfectly suited to writing letters and doing essay reports for school.

FIGURE 13.12.

Works gives you the big three in software: word processing, spreadsheeting, and data management.

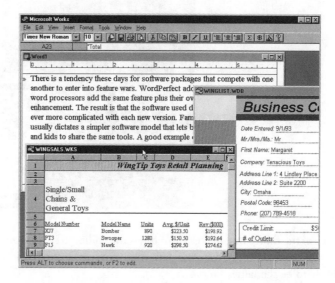

In fact, most folks who use programs like Works do so because they are easier to learn and use than full-blown software packages. Automated wizards can give you step-by-step tutorials in how to enter and use information, and you can cut and paste figures from one type of document into another.

Microsoft BOB

It is worth bearing in mind that folks who have mastered high-end software find programs like Works easy as pie. For raw beginning computer users, however, even stripped-down versions of the classic software types seem intimidating. It is for users like these that Microsoft BOB was designed.

When you start BOB, your computer is transformed into an everyday scene like a den office, or even the garage. Some rooms can be used by every member of the family, but each user in the house can set up private rooms where they can enter their own private data. Yes, girls, you can hide *his* special phone number from your little brother's prying eyes!

BOB is a collection of programs. Figure 13.13 shows how each of its available programs is disguised as an object in the public study room. To use a program, just click the object associated with it. Each person who uses BOB gets to choose their own personal guide. A personal guide is an animated character that tells you just about everything you need to know to use BOB. Some guides offer more help than others, and each has a distinctive personality.

FIGURE 13.13.

To use the programs in BOB, all you do is click one of the items in the room.

One of the things that makes BOB fun is the ability to customize. You not only get your choice of guides, but you can decorate your rooms to suit your taste. No two installations of BOB are likely to be the same.

BOB comes with a group of programs for doing specific tasks. You can also use BOB to start other programs on the computer. The following is a rundown on the programs that come with BOB:

Letter Writer: This program lets you personalize your correspondence. Letters can be sent via e-mail or printed. (See Figure 13.14.)

Calendar: This helpful companion remembers all your important appointments and things to do. You can set it to notify you of an event up to a week in advance.

Checkbook: The checkbook is more than just a digital representation of your real checkbook. The BOB checkbook can keep track of bills that need paying, send payments online, and track multiple accounts.

Household Manager: Track entries in more than a dozen categories from gifts to personal growth. Household manager even suggests activities you can do with the kids.

Address Book: The BOB address book lets you keep track of your friends and family. It tracks phone numbers, mail addresses, e-mail addresses, birthdays, and more.

E-mail: BOB can act as your interface to a number of e-mail sources. As you might expect, it's just about the easiest way of exchanging e-mail there is.

Financial Guide: This is the serious part of BOB, where you can track your investments and plan for retirement.

GeoSafari: GeoSafari is a fun game for the entire family. Test your knowledge!

BOB can be customized to start other programs as well as the ones that come with BOB. For the true cyberphobics in your life, you can create a login that contains BOB in the Start folder, so that every time they start the computer, BOB is launched and the standard Windows 95 shell is bypassed.

FIGURE 13.14.

The letter writing module of BOB.

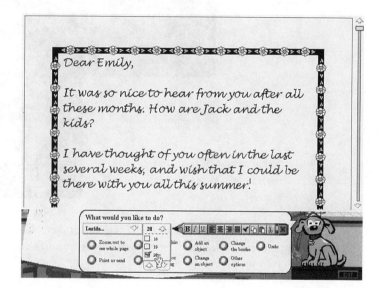

Serious Play

Games make up the lion's share of software titles on most family computers. Here are a couple of titles that will appeal to older family members.

The Magic Death

If you are one of those types who spends countless hours, usually alone and in the darkness, devouring murder mysteries by the score, The Magic Death is for you. Here's your chance to compete on an even footing with Sherlock Holmes, Nero Wolfe, Hercule Poirot, and their ilk.

Most murders in the United States are solved within the first six hours. Those hours are critical to collecting and interpreting evidence. You are in a race with the clock to single out the murderer from a dozen dirty suspects.

So, here's what you've got. You have a dead academic who specialized in studying Voodoo and magic. She's laying on a carpet in her apartment (see Figure 13.15), apparently poisoned. Next to her is a weird symbol drawn on the carpet with white powder, an altar containing a bottle of poison, a dead chicken, and the body is smeared in mud and chicken blood.

FIGURE 13.15.

One body, twelve suspects. Can you figure out the mystery of The Magic Death?

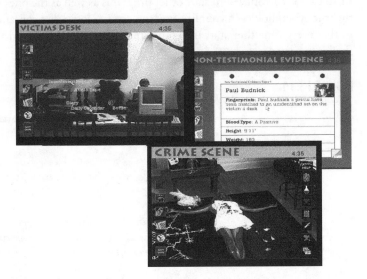

It won't be easy because there is something fishy going on here. Can you tell the real stink from the red herrings? The Magic Death is available from Creative Multimedia of Portland, Oregon, (503) 241-1530.

Chessmaster 3000

There is great debate over where the game of chess originated. India, China, and Persia all claim the distinction for themselves. What is not in dispute is that chess is the greatest game of all time. A true war of wits, with the health and life of the ego at stake, that can take a lifetime to master.

Like anything in life, constant practice is required to build skills in chess. The single biggest obstacle to learning to play the game well is the perennial lack of partners to victimize. Chessmaster 3000, from Software Toolworks in Novato, California, (415) 883-3000, never gets tired of taking on all comers.

Along the way, players can customize the board and pieces, although the standard Staunton set shown in Figure 13.16 is the easiest on the eyes. Players can also set parameters for how the computer plays, ask advice, switch sides, and listen to the analysis of the Chessmaster.

FIGURE 13.16.

*Chessmaster 3000 is a
multimedia chess partner
that never tires of playing.*

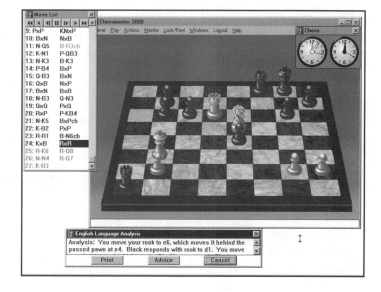

Don't get the idea that the Chessmaster is a pushover, either. Although the default settings
give you a chance, the day you whip the Chessmaster when he is on his most difficult settings
is the day you should register for some major chess tournaments.

Microsoft Complete Basketball

If there is a basketball fan in your house, this disk has your name written on it. Complete player
profiles, biographies, videos of the game's greatest plays, and more come packed onto this CD.
Figure 13.17 shows the awards page for the 1980-1981 season.

FIGURE 13.17.

*Player profiles, statistics,
awards, and live action
videos make Complete
Basketball come alive.*

Microsoft Complete Basketball, from the Microsoft Home division, is like owning thousands of basketball cards and shelves of reference works and video tapes. For fans of the giants of the greensward, try Microsoft Complete Baseball.

Just For Kids

The remainder of the titles covered in this chapter are just for kids. Uh-huh! You can bet there are lots of parents who will send the kiddies off to bed, just to get their hands on a few of these.

Scholastic's The Magic School Bus Explores the Human Body

This program almost didn't make it into this chapter because my daughter Laurel wouldn't let me have it. Based on the Magic School Bus book series, written by Joanna Cole and Bruce Degen, this disk combines classic interactive techniques and a school bus ride through the body of classmate Arnold.

When the program begins, you are looking at a classroom. Kids love exploring the classroom by clicking randomly on the various objects depicted (see Figure 13.18). There's even a model volcano on one of the desks that will erupt on command. Click the hot air balloon and it takes off on a merry ride around the classroom until you click it enough times to make it drop all its ballast and float off the top of the screen.

FIGURE 13.18.

The classroom is full of interactive objects that come to life when you click them.

Click on the goldfish bowl, off the left edge of Figure 13.18, and the fish leaps into the air. Beware, however, because sometimes he misses and lands on the floor. Drop him back in the bowl to make him happy. Of course, if your kid is normal, the thought will come to them to drop the poor fish into the volcano! No worries, though, because the volcano will harmlessly spit the fish back into his bowl.

Clean off the desk and put the proper items in the trash can and the recycle bin, and you can open the desk to play the games. The games are introduced in The Magic School Bus' tour of Arnold's body.

Figure 13.19 shows the inside of Arnold. You are the bus driver, and you have to navigate around through all of the major organs. Your kids will take to this disk like mine did.

FIGURE 13.19.

Can a school bus really fly into a kid's mouth and take a trip? This one can. In a companion disk, the bus explores the Solar System.

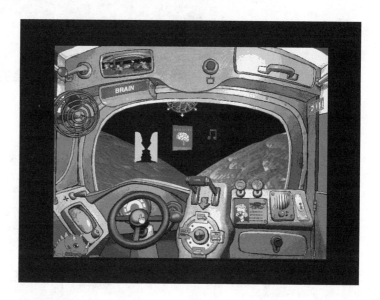

Just Grandma and Me

Written by Mercer Mayer, Just Grandma and Me is one of the titles in Broderbund's Living Books Series. Critter and his Grandma, seen in Figure 13.20, take a trip to the beach.

Unlike most CD products, Just Grandma and Me requires no installation, just click the Grandma icon and you're off. The title screen lets you choose one of three languages and lets you choose to simply read the book, or to play inside the story. As each page is read, in play mode, the child can stop and click on objects that react in sometimes strange and humorous ways. Broderbund, of Novato, California, (415) 382-4600, is the same company that does the highly popular, Where in the World is Carmen Sandiego?

FIGURE 13.20.

The story can be viewed in English, Japanese, and Spanish.

Gus Goes to Cybertown

Gus Goes to Cybertown is bundled in the Creative Labs Digital Schoolhouse Multimedia Kit mentioned earlier in this chapter and is produced by Modern Media Ventures of San Francisco, California, (800) 530-5080. This program is suitable for young school-aged children. As you wander through Cybertown (see Figure 13.21), you can enter shops or stroll in the park with Gus. In the park, you can explore the timeline of history, comparing things as they were to things as they are. In the shops, you can click objects to see what they do. Find the hidden object in each shop and play a game like the counting game shown in the figure.

FIGURE 13.21.

Gus Goes to Cybertown is a multimedia romp through learning.

Although there are lots of facts and learning games in Gus Goes to Cybertown, it is so entertaining that kids won't even realize they are doing something good for them.

Do Your Homework!

The last two programs covered in this chapter are both created by Davidson and Associates of Torrance, California, (800) 556-6141, and are part of the bundle with the Digital Schoolhouse Multimedia Upgrade Kit. There are many others in this bundle that are not covered in this chapter.

Kid Works 2

Just as Microsoft Works, covered earlier in this chapter, is a softer, less-complicated version of traditional business software, Kid Works 2 is a simplified starting place for elementary school-aged children to learn to use software (see Figure 13.22).

FIGURE 13.22.

Kids Works 2 lets you write stories, illustrate them, create icons, and more.

Anyone who remembers the old Macintosh Talking Moose program will recognize an old friend in a new package in the story writing part of Kid Works 2. As your child enters words and picks up pictures out of the boxes, you can click to have the words spoken. Pictures can be translated into words, and vice versa. The Story Illustrator lets your child experiment with a kid-sized drawing program, and the Icon Maker lets them draw Windows 95 icons.

The Cruncher

The Cruncher is a kid's first spreadsheet program designed to make working with numbers fun. There are spreadsheet games that act as tutorials (see Figure 13.23), and projects for kids to do like tracking baseball statistics.

FIGURE 13.23.

The tutorial games found in The Cruncher make working with numbers and formulas fun and accessible.

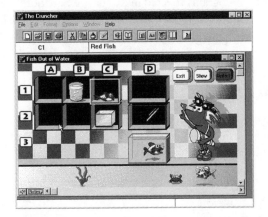

Don't be mislead by the simplicity of The Cruncher. This is a kid-sized spreadsheet that anyone, even you, can use.

Summary

In this chapter, you have had a chance to explore Family Computing. Along the way, you have seen only the tip of the iceberg when it comes to the amazing variety and sheer number of titles that are available. Keep in mind, too, that you can download many useful and entertaining programs from online services and bulletin boards.

Microsoft Plus! for
Windows 95

Microsoft Plus! for Windows 95 is an add-on package for those users of Windows 95 who have high-end systems, meaning that they have a 486 or Pentium processor, at least 8 MB of RAM, and a video setup capable of displaying at least 256 colors (although a video/monitor combination capable of 16-bit High Color rendering is recommended). A sound card and modem are also needed to utilize everything that Plus! has to offer.

What does Microsoft Plus! have to offer? Here's a quick rundown:

- **System Agent**: An agent, in computer terms, is a bit of software that you can preset to perform a needed service. In the case of System Agent, you can schedule events to occur at times when you are not likely to be at your system, so that ScanDisk or Disk Defragmenter can be run automatically.

- **DriveSpace 3**: This is the latest revision of Microsoft's disk compression utility. DriveSpace 3 can be used to compress drives up to two gigabytes in size, as well as drives previously compressed with DoubleSpace or earlier DOS or Windows 95 versions of DriveSpace. Compression can be tuned to balance disk space and performance. In addition, a DriveSpace agent can be scheduled to apply extra compression during idle times.

- **Internet Jumpstart Kit**: With Plus!, you can be surfing the Net within minutes of installation. Whether you want to use MSN as your gateway to the InfoBahn or have a provider-supplied account elsewhere, the Internet Explorer extends the Windows 95 user interface to include the World Wide Web.

- **Dial-Up Network Server**: You can extend the dial-up capabilities of Windows 95 to include incoming dial-up connections that let you, or other users you authorize, dial into your system.

- **Desktop Themes**: Plus! moves Microsoft into the interior decorating business in a big way. With Desktop Themes, you can accessorize your system with matched sets of wallpaper, color schemes, sounds, pointers, and screen savers. If you have a fast machine and High Color video installed, you can choose from a list of themes that range from Dangerous Creatures and Travel, to the hippie Sixties or the more refined Golden Era.

- **Visual Enhancements**: A lot of folks will acquire Plus! for the simple reason that it lets you easily change the icons associated with My Computer, Network Neighborhood, and Recycle Bin without hacking the Registry. In addition, Plus! gives your system the capability to do full window dragging (instead of dragging just a frame), screen font smoothing, display icons using more than 16 colors, and stretch wallpaper bitmaps to cover the entire Desktop.

- **3-D Pinball**: What would a product like Plus! be without some diversion? Not nearly as much fun. To that end, the kids at Microsoft have included 3-D Pinball, a video homage to the old-style quarter suckers of a bygone era. For all of you who have always wanted to own a pinball machine but have never seemed to find the way, 3-D Pinball is the next best thing. You can even tilt and nudge to gain the most ball control.

Installing Microsoft Plus!

Installation of Microsoft Plus! is so easy that, as the famous billiards author Robert Byrne put it, "even a drunken child can do it." All you have to do is insert Plus! into your floppy or CD drive, find Setup, and double-click on it. The Setup Wizard takes you through the usual filling in of information and selecting of a folder that accompanies most installations; then you are asked to perform a Typical or Custom install. Typical gives you everything, and Custom lets you choose those parts of Plus! that you want to be installed.

Of course, if you leave something off during your initial install, you can always go back and use Custom to add the features you didn't install before. Figure 14.1 shows the Custom dialog of the Setup Wizard. To leave a feature uninstalled, remove the check from the box to the left of the feature's name.

FIGURE 14.1.

Some of the Plus! features have a submenu of options. If the Change Options button is active, you can click it to access the submenu.

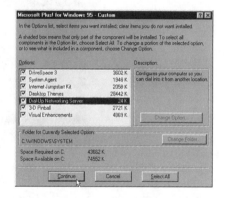

When you have selected the portions of Plus! you want to install, the Setup Wizard copies the files from your disk to your hard drive. If you have chosen Internet Jumpstart Kit or Desktop Themes, wizards will be run to let you install these items in more detail.

As you can see in Figure 14.2, there are two paths you can take, depending on how you plan to get into the Internet. If you do not already have an account established with an Internet provider, you can elect to use the Microsoft Network (MSN) as your onramp.

FIGURE 14.2.

You can access the Internet through either the Microsoft Network or a service provider.

If you elect to use MSN access, all you need to do is set up the dial-up parameters just as you would do in Windows 95. If you elect to gain access to the Net using an independent service provider, you need to follow the Wizard through the same steps as for setting up a Dial-Up networking client. See Chapter 21, "The Internet," for details.

Figure 14.3 shows the setup dialog for Desktop Themes. After setup, an object appears in Control Panel that lets you access the same choices. In this dialog, you are able to choose whatever desktop themes you want to preview. If your video setup only supports 256-color mode, you should avoid selecting High Color themes because they will render poorly onscreen.

FIGURE 14.3.

Setup for Desktop Themes is simple. Choose a theme then uncheck any features in the list on the right that you don't want applied.

After Setup completes, you are prompted to restart Windows 95. When the restart is completed, you are ready to enjoy the benefits of Microsoft Plus! for Windows 95.

System Agent

If there is any identifiable trend in personal computer use, it is that computers are turned on more often and stay on longer than ever before. This is a trend that is destined to continue as more and more computers are connected to the phone network. Many folks just leave the computer running 24 hours a day to receive voice mail, e-mail, and incoming faxes. A byproduct of this trend is the fact that computers often spend long hours waiting for the human touch.

The concept behind System Agent is to provide stimulation for the millions of lonely computers by scheduling those system housekeeping tasks that users just never seem to get around to, such as running ScanDisk and defragmenting their drives. System Agent is also used to schedule those everyday forgettable chores such as picking up e-mail, picking up the kids, and just about anything else that you might want to have done. In short, with System Agent, you can turn your computer into a self-maintaining extension of yourself by offloading tasks that you don't have time to do.

How System Agent Works

From the time you install System Agent, a small object appears in the taskbar (near the clock) to show that System Agent is running and to provide you access to the schedule. Figure 14.4 shows the window that pops up when you double-click the taskbar object.

FIGURE 14.4.

The System Agent enables you to add, edit, delete, or suspend scheduled activities.

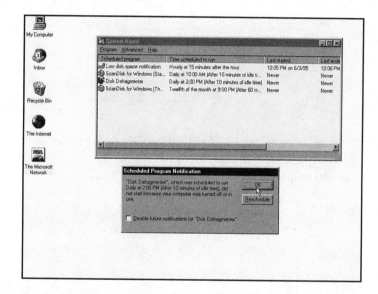

Online documentation for Plus! is added to the online documentation for Windows 95. To see the online documentation, select Help from the Start Menu and click the book marked Microsoft Plus! for Windows 95.

Also visible in Figure 14.4 is a notification dialog, which informs you that a scheduled activity has not taken place. Clicking OK keeps the activity in the queue; clicking the checkbox labeled Disable Future Notifications eliminates notifications from the scheduled event. Notifications normally occur when you boot up a system that was turned off at the time the activity was scheduled.

To edit scheduled events, simply right-click on the event's object to bring up the context menu, and select Properties. This presents a dialog similar to the one shown in Figure 14.4. Four bits of information are in this dialog. The first is a command line for the program to be run. There is also a checkbox that determines whether the results of running the program are logged to the file SAGELOG.TXT, found in the Programs\Plus! folder. The Description text box lets you enter the description displayed in the System Agent window to identify a scheduled activity.

The Run list box lets you specify whether the program is run minimized, maximized, or in a normal window.

FIGURE 14.5.

Each scheduled activity creates an event object that can be edited using a Properties sheet.

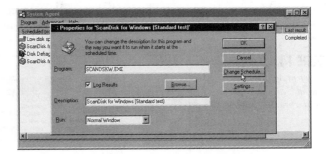

As you can see in Figure 14.6, clicking the Change Schedule button enables you to specify how often you want the scheduled event to happen, and at what time. The Advanced button enables you to specify what to do when the event hasn't occurred by a certain time.

FIGURE 14.6.

Scheduling the event to occur is just a few mouse clicks away.

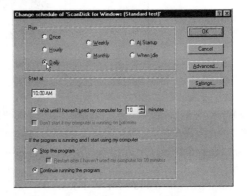

Creating Your Own Events

To schedule an event of your own choosing, select Schedule a New Program from the Program menu. The dialog in Figure 14.7 shows how you fill in the same information that you saw in editing a scheduled event. Clicking the Browse button lets you scan your system to find the program you want to run.

The most difficult part of creating a scheduled event is deciding what you want to have done. In the example shown in Figure 14.7, Sound Recorder is tapped to play a WAV file.

FIGURE 14.7.

Creating new events is a simple task that takes only a minute or two.

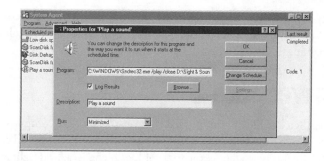

System Agent is aware of some programs such as ScanDisk, and it lets you set parameters using the Settings button. However, if the Settings button is dimmed, you need to enter all the details on the command line. For example, the command line needed to play a sound might read something like this:

```
C:\WINDOWS\Sndrec32.exe /play /close D:\Sight & Sound\WAV\affair.wav
```

This sample command line specifies the name of the program to run and several command line parameters. The Play and Close parameters tell Sound Recorder that you want the sound played when the applet is launched and closed when the sound has finished playing. The final parameter specifies the WAV file to be played.

WIZARD

If you are not experienced in creating command lines for Windows applications, the previous example might look a bit intimidating, but it is really simple to put together once you know the trick.

What happens when you double-click a sound file? By default, the Sound Recorder is opened, the sound file is played, and the Sound Recorder is closed. To see what the command line for that cycle looks like, all you have to do is access the Explorer menu and select View | Options | File Types. In the list of file types, double-click WAV, and then double-click the Play entry in the Action list. Viola! That's where the command and first two parameters come from. With a right-click on the Play command line (note that it is selected and highlighted), you can copy the command to the Clipboard and paste it into the System Agent's command line text box.

The filename specification can be easily obtained by right-dragging the wave you want played to the desktop as a shortcut, and then repeating the Copy and Paste routine to add the second half of the System Agent command line.

Any application or applet for which you can assemble a valid command line can be scheduled by System Agent. What do you want to bet that one of the next big shareware categories will be programs designed to be run by System Agent?

DriveSpace 3

After Stacker Electronics proved that on-the-fly disk compression was a viable and popular addition to the computing environment, Microsoft introduced compression as part of the MS-DOS operating system in the form of DoubleSpace. A cat fight and litigation ensued, with the result that Microsoft reworked its compression software and introduced DriveSpace. Windows 95 contains support for all three via conversion and updating.

Microsoft Plus! for Windows 95 gives you DriveSpace 3, the most sophisticated disk compression utility yet released by Microsoft. DriveSpace 3 can upgrade compressed volumes created with DoubleSpace and DriveSpace from previous versions of DOS and from Windows 95. During Setup, Windows 95 should have already upgraded compressed drives created with DOS versions of Stacker. There is support for hard disks up to two gigabytes in size, and you can control the way DriveSpace 3 is tuned. The full benefit of DriveSpace 3, UltraPack compression, is a feature pretty much limited to Pentium-equipped systems for performance reasons. However, DriveSpace 3 should provide 486-equipped systems a better compression ratio than previous versions.

> **NOTE**
>
> How does disk compression work? Almost everyone is familiar with compressed files. Common examples include ZIP files, the CAB files Windows 95 uses in Setup, self-extracting archive files, and so on.
>
> Each of these archive types can store multiple files within the archive. So imagine that you have a big ZIP file sitting on your hard disk, except its name is G or any other available drive letter.
>
> That's basically how compressed drives work. When you tell DriveSpace 3 to compress a disk drive, it creates a huge file and archives all the files on the hard disk in this single file. As you work, files are read by pulling them out of the archive and uncompressing them. When an application writes to the disk, the data is compressed and written into the archive.
>
> When you compress a whole drive, a small uncompressed area is reserved and renamed by the system as another drive letter. The original drive letter is assigned to the compressed archive. For example, if you compress C, DriveSpace assigns another letter such as E to it and calls it the host. On that host drive, a big archive file is created and the contents of the drive are compressed and written into the archive. DriveSpace, by default, assigns the next available drive letter that is two letters higher than your last

real drive. The archive file is then presented by Windows 95 as C. It looks and acts just the same as it always did, but now it is a virtual drive with much more space for storing files.

You can also compress only a portion of a drive to create a virtual drive with another letter. For example, if you create a new compressed drive using 100 MB on drive C, an archive file is created and assigned a letter that is two letters higher than your last real drive. An archive file (hidden) is created on drive C, and this virtual drive is presented by Windows 95 as a virtual disk drive having much more than 100 MB available.

It only makes sense that the extra computing required to compress and decompress files on the fly, as they are written to and read from the hard disk, will have an impact on overall system performance. There is no free lunch, but because DriveSpace 3 supports three different compression levels, you can adjust the performance costs to a level that you can be comfortable with. DriveSpace 3 supports Standard, HiPack, and UltraPack (three different compression densities), and also supplies Compression Agent.

Compression Agent is a program that can be scheduled by System Agent. As you work, you can use Standard compression, which is the least dense and fastest compression level. Still, Standard is more efficient than any previous version of DriveSpace. HiPack provides even denser compression than Standard, and UltraPack provides the densest level of compression available. While your system is idle, Compression Agent will activate and go through your hard disk, crushing files compressed using Standard into HiPack or UltraPack format.

NOTE

When you use DriveSpace 3 to compress a disk, a driver is loaded that requires approximately 115 KB of conventional memory. Although this use of memory will not affect the amount of RAM available to DOS applications run under Windows 95, you might find that some memory-intensive programs (such as highly graphical games that must be run in MS-DOS mode) will have problems.

There are several ways that you might increase available memory for these programs. Here is a list of things to try:

Add EMM386 to your CONFIG.SYS file using the NOEMS parameter to eliminate the 64KB Expanded Memory page frame, which resides in upper memory.

Include a line similar to

```
DEVICEHIGH=C:\WINDOWS\COMMAND\DRVSPACE.SYS /MOVE
```

that allows the driver more flexibility in the way memory is used. If you are sure that your upper memory blocks are configured properly, and you already have a DRVSPACE.SYS line in your CONFIG.SYS file that uses the /L:0 parameter, try removing the /L:0 parameter.

If all else fails, you can press F8 at boot up and choose to confirm each driver as it loads. When you are asked to load DriveSpace, answer no. Until you reboot, however, you will not have access to the compressed portions of your disks. You need to install the DOS program into an uncompressed volume.

Compressing Drives

As you can see in Figure 14.8, there are two choices available to you when creating a compressed drive on a currently uncompressed hard disk. Each method has advantages and disadvantages.

The first method is to simply compress the whole drive. The advantage is that you get the maximum available compression, while retaining the same drive letter. The disadvantage is that you have no area of the disk that remains uncompressed for writing finicky DOS applications that cannot coexist with compression, or for other uses such as temporary storage of files.

FIGURE 14.8.

The two methods for compressing disk space.

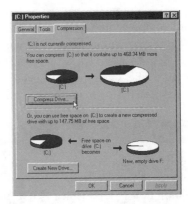

The second method is to create a new virtual drive, using only part of the free disk space on the drive. The advantage is that you get a "new" drive that is compressed. The disadvantage is that because a portion of the drive remains uncompressed, you don't get the maximum compression available.

CAUTION

After installing DriveSpace 3 on your system, be sure to go to Control Panel and double-click the Add/Remove Programs icon. Click the Startup Disk tab and create a new emergency Startup Disk. Otherwise, you will lose access to your compressed drives when you boot from the Startup Disk you made during the initial setup.

Figure 14.9 shows the dialog that is displayed when you click the Create New Drive button in order to use only a portion of the hard disk to create a new virtual drive (method two discussed earlier). As you can see, the dialog is very straightforward and even does all the math for you.

FIGURE 14.9.

The Create New Drive dialog lets you choose how much disk space to give over to a new virtual compressed drive.

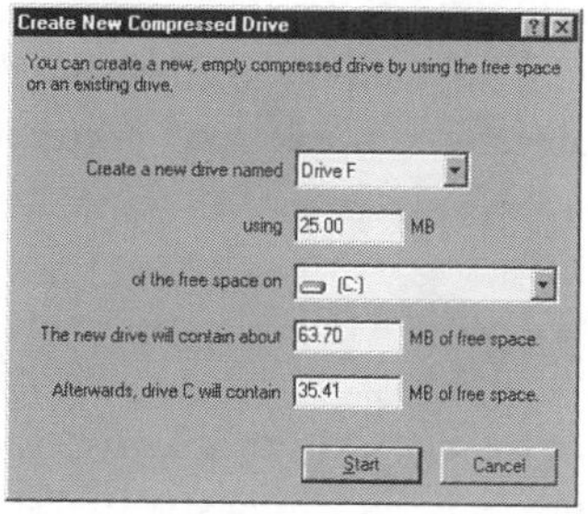

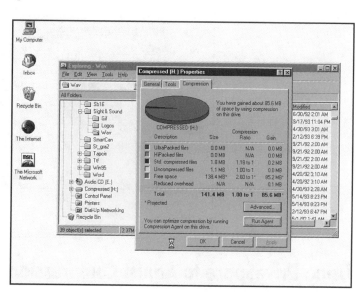

When you click the Start button, the drive is first searched for errors. If errors are detected, the Help Wizard for running ScanDisk is automatically launched, which makes it easy for you to fix what is wrong and then restart the process.

After the compressed drive is created, right-clicking on the drive's object in Explorer and then selecting the Compression tab displays a dialog similar to the one shown in Figure 14.10. As you can see, there are only a few files written to the compressed drive, and they are all compressed using Standard compression.

FIGURE 14.10.

You can visually inspect the compression ratios using the Compression tab of the drive's Properties sheet.

Clicking the Advanced button opens a dialog that has a checkbox that allows you to hide the host drive and a button for starting DriveSpace, in order to fine-tune your compression ratios.

Hide Host Drive

Disk compression creates a single large file on the hard disk and presents that file to the user as a virtual drive, which looks and acts just like a real hard disk. DriveSpace requires a small amount of uncompressed space as a workspace on the host drive. If you have compressed the vast majority of a drive, you might want to click this checkbox to hide the host drive so that it won't show up in Explorer, for example, and clutter up your display with what are essentially unusable hard disk objects.

The New Drive

As you can see in Figure 14.11, after DriveSpace 3 has finished creating the new compressed drive, a message box appears telling you to restart Windows to finish installing the new drive. At the same time, Windows 95 Help is opened to present you with the wizard for adjusting the drive's compression settings.

If Windows 95 Help is set to always be on top (as in Figure 14.11), you might be confused about the next step. The help file is open at this time so that it will be reopened automatically when the system is restarted. Do the restart before adjusting the settings.

FIGURE 14.11.

You need to restart the computer for the changes to the drives to take full effect.

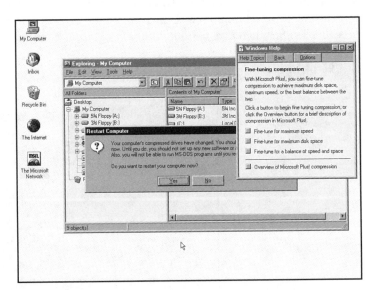

Using DriveSpace to Adjust Compression

When the system has restarted, the Help window should be redisplayed in essentially the same way it was in Figure 14.11. There are four buttons in the window. They let you tune the compressed drive for maximum speed, maximum space, or a balance between the two. The fourth button explains compression and your options. All of these choices lead to launching DriveSpace 3 to make settings.

If Windows 95 fails to reopen Help for some reason, you can get to the Settings dialog (shown in Figure 14.12) by launching DriveSpace 3 from the Start Menu. You'll find it in Accessories | System Tools. Highlight the new drive and choose Settings from the Advanced menu. As Figure 14.12 shows, there are four basic settings. Here is a quick explanation of each:

- **HiPack**: This setting is recommended only for users with Pentium processors. Using HiPack compression on the fly requires extra processing that might degrade the performance of 486 systems to an unacceptable level.

- **Standard**: This setting tells DriveSpace to use Standard compression when working on the fly.

- **No Compression Unless**: If your drives are not already cramped, you can plan for the future without sacrificing performance. With this setting, you tell DriveSpace not to do any compression unless the drive is a certain percentage full. This way, compression only kicks in when absolutely needed. Until compression is applied, you get the fastest possible performance.

- **No Compression**: This setting turns off disk compression but doesn't uninstall the compressed volume.

FIGURE 14.12.

You can balance your setting to arbitrate between fastest performance and maximum space.

The checkbox seen in Figure 14.12 is mainly intended for troubleshooting purposes. Unless a compressed drive is mounted, it cannot be accessed or even seen. Only rarely will you ever need to touch this checkbox.

Compression Agent

When you create a compressed drive, Compression Agent is automatically placed into System Agent so that you can benefit from the second level of compression features. Using Compression Agent, your system waits until the scheduled time to go through the files on the compressed drive and recompress files into one of the denser formats.

If you double-click System Agent on the Taskbar and then double-click the Compression Agent, you get a dialog that has a Settings button. Figure 14.13 shows the Settings dialog. This is where you control how compression is done on your system.

FIGURE 14.13.

This dialog controls how Compression Agent acts.

There are three levels of compression available from DriveSpace 3: Standard, HiPack, and UltraPack. Although users with slower systems should not attempt to use UltraPack on the fly, the Compression Agent can HiPack and UltraPack files while the system is idle. This way you get maximum disk space and don't take such a performance hit while working. The dialog shown in Figure 14.13 lets you control how files are handled by Compression agent.

The first set of choices determines when files are UltraPacked. If you have an older, slower system, clicking the top radio button turns off UltraPack completely. On faster systems, you probably should choose the second radio button to use UltraPack all the time. This setting is not recommended unless you have a Pentium-equipped system. The third radio button in the group lets you tell DriveSpace 3 to UltraPack only files that aren't often used. You can set the number of days as a threshold so that only files not used in a certain number of days will be UltraPacked. This third setting is probably the one you want if you have a 486 processor.

The second set of choices determines how other files are packed. The first radio button specifies that HiPack should be used on all other files, while the second button tells DriveSpace to leave them alone.

While you are working, if you access a file that has been HiPacked or UltraPacked by the Compression Agent, the file is uncompressed on the fly, so it might take a second or two longer to read. Later, if the file is then written back to disk, the settings you have in DriveSpace 3 for on-the-fly work are used (usually Standard density). The file is then HiPacked or UltraPacked again later when Compression Agent runs again.

Creating Exceptions to the Settings

If you click on the Exceptions button in the Settings dialog, you will see a dialog similar to the one shown in Figure 14.14. This dialog lets you point and click individual files or folders to be singled out for special treatment, and it also lets you specify the way specific file types (such as bitmaps and databases) are handled.

Controlling how compression is done can enable you to fine-tune compression even further. Files and folders that present performance problems when UltraPacked can be limited to the faster HiPack, or even no compression at all, which yields the fastest performance.

FIGURE 14.14.

Any settings you apply to folders are extended to all the files in the folder, as well as all the files in subfolders.

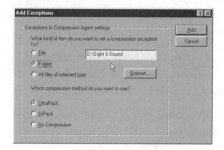

Use the Browse button to locate files and folders that you want to have special handling. For each entry, you can specify that Compression Agent use UltraPack, HiPack, or no compression at all.

The Internet JumpStart Kit

Figure 14.15 shows the Internet Explorer in action. Internet Explorer is an application in the category Web Browser, which means that it can be used to navigate the graphical parts of the World Wide Web, currently the hottest ticket in all of cyberspace.

FIGURE 14.15.

Internet Explorer is Microsoft's version of a web browser.

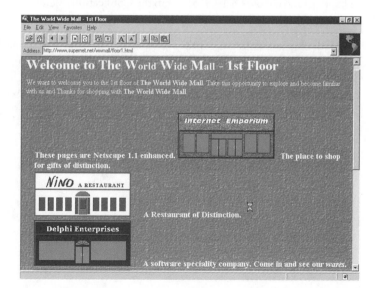

The World Wide Web is available for academic research, shopping, and game playing, as well as downloading software, sounds, images, and animations. If humans did it, do it, or only think about doing it, *it* can be found on the Web.

The World Wide Web is a loose configuration of servers, all of which can talk to each other. Each server handles the folks who have accounts there. People publish themselves on the Web using a home page. A home page is an address that contains a script of what should be displayed. The script is written using a simple editor such as NotePad (although more elaborate tools are available).

The contents of the home page are written using HyperText Markup Language (HTML), which uses symbols to indicate how text should be displayed. It doesn't take long to catch on to creating pages using HTML; almost anyone can figure it out in a few hours.

For more information about installing and using Internet Explorer, see Chapter 21. There, you can learn how to establish dial-up connections to The Microsoft Network and to other TCP/IP service providers.

Dial-Up Network Server

The capability to create dial-up connections that enable you to connect your system to Internet providers, company network servers, and other remote resources is built right into Windows 95. Information on dial-up clients can be found in Chapter 11, "Mobile Computing." What Plus! provides is a way of setting up your system so that you can log on when you are away or let others log on to share data and resources with you.

To create a dial-up server after Plus! is installed, double-click the Dial-Up Networking folder in Explorer and choose Dial-Up Server in the Connections menu. You should see a dialog similar to the one shown in Figure 14.16.

Two radio buttons at the top of the dialog let you determine whether Dial-Up Server is active. If Allow Caller Access is selected, the modem will answer and prompt the caller to log in using the password you specify by clicking the Change Password button. To disable Dial-Up Server, come back to the Dial-Up Server dialog and click the No Caller Access button.

Clicking the Server Type button brings up the small dialog shown in Figure 14.16, which lets you specify the type of protocol to use. Available protocols are determined by the settings for your Dial-Up Adapter, found under Network in Control Panel.

FIGURE 14.16.

*Configuring Dial-Up
Server takes less than two
minutes.*

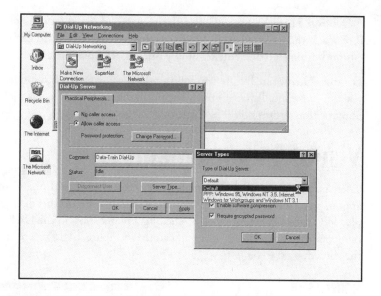

Desktop Themes

After Plus! is installed, you will have an icon in Control Panel labeled Desktop Themes. Double-clicking this icon displays the dialog shown in Figure 14.17. At first, this might seem to be a complex dialog, but it isn't.

FIGURE 14.17.

*Select a theme to display its
preview, and then uncheck
the elements of the theme
you don't want.*

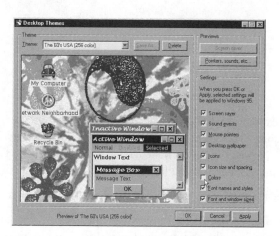

The large picture is just a preview of a Desktop Theme. You can select other themes using the Theme listbox. Each theme is labeled to tell you whether it is 256 color or High Color. If your system is set up as 256-color display, the High Color graphics will not render correctly.

A Desktop Theme is a made up of all the elements listed on the right side of the preview picture. Each theme supplied in Plus! contains customizations in each element. To remove the customization to that element, simply uncheck the box next to the element's name.

Desktop Themes are like instant interior decorating for your system. After a theme is installed, you can make small changes using the normal Windows 95 tools such as the Display Property Sheet or the Sounds object in Control Panel.

Visual Enhancements

There is only one really simple dialog to control the Visual Enhancements features of Plus!. It appears as a tab on the Display Properties sheet. Bring up this dialog by double-clicking Display in Control Panel, or by right-clicking a blank spot on the Desktop and selecting Properties from the context menu. As you can see in Figure 14.18, there are only a few choices, but the choices tend to be tasty.

FIGURE 14.18.

The Display Properties sheet is the home of Visual Enhancements.

At the top of the dialog is a feature bound to be popular with all users who fall into the anti-My Computer camp. There are four desktop icons that can be changed in this dialog: My Computer, Network Neighborhood, and Recycle Bin's full and empty icons. Click an icon and then click the Change Icon button.

At the bottom of the dialog are four checkboxes. Here is a rundown of what they do:

■ **Show window contents while dragging**: By default, when you move or resize a window, the original window is displayed onscreen and Windows 95 shows you a representation of the final position or size by showing you an empty frame. If this checkbox is marked, Windows 95 will drag or size the window in real time instead without using the frame representation.

■ **Smooth edges of screen fonts**: Font smoothing is a technique by which the jagged edges on letters can be reduced or eliminated. For example, open WordPad and place a very large (72-point) capital letter A into the document. Note how jagged the diagonal lines are. Then turn on font smoothing, click Apply, and check out the difference by deleting and retyping the capital A. Font smoothing is most apparent on large type.

■ **Show icons using all possible colors**: Icons do not have to be restricted to the 16 primary Windows colors. Rendering icons with more colors, however, can be a big drain on video resources if your system isn't up to the job. If you have a high horse-power system and want to use icons with lots of colors, check this box.

■ **Stretch desktop wallpaper to fit the screen**: Windows 95's capability to resize graphic images is exploited by this feature, which enables you to display wallpaper that is smaller than your screen by stretching it to reach the edges.

3-D Pinball

Check out the Games section of the Start Menu to find 3-D Pinball. If you miss the old silver ball, this excellent rendition of the classic pinball machine will keep you entertained for hours. The keys used to hit the flippers and tilt are fully configureable. It's a good thing this game is free, otherwise you'd never have any quarters in your pocket.

Summary

Microsoft Plus! for Windows 95 is an add-on product that enhances Windows 95 in some significant ways by adding better disk compression, dial-up server capability, Internet Explorer, System Agent, and more. Using the Desktop Themes feature enables you to select from a variety of atmospheres for your system.

Windows 95 and Multimedia

The home computer market has grown tremendously the last few years—in part because of the growth in availability of multimedia hardware and software. Whether folks want to create their own home movies using a Windows-based editor or examine "Ancient Lands," the addition of video, music, and hypertext links to informational and educational programs has made them easier and more entertaining to use.

Windows 95 is capitalizing on this trend by adding several features to make creating and playing multimedia software easier. The next several chapters explain these changes, and their impact, in detail.

A quick summary of the changes to be found in Windows 95 follows.

Plug and Play Support for Multimedia Devices

Examples of Plug and Play support are audio adapter cards, CD-ROM drives, and video overlay devices. The big plus here is that you can have a higher comfort level that the multimedia hardware add-ins your title depends upon have been installed correctly.

New File System for CD-ROMs

Windows 95's new 32-bit CD file system (CDFS), which is modeled on the 32-bit, fixed-disk file system, adds reliability and enhanced performance.

AutoPlay of CD-ROMs

When you close the door on the CD-ROM drive, it automatically launches the CD-ROM's player application. Windows 95 looks for a file called AUTORUN.INF in the CD-ROM's root directory. If the file is present, the script is run to start a game or another CD-ROM-based application.

More Effective Compression of Digital Audio Files

This comes from two new software audio *codecs* (coders and decoders) for Windows 95 that use ADPCM techniques. A special codec for music that provides about 2:1 to 4:1 compression without noticeable loss of fidelity also is included with Windows 95.

Improved MIDI Performance

Windows 95's new Polymessage MIDI feature enables fast transmission of complex MIDI messages, with very little processor overhead. This is especially important for users who use message-intensive MIDI exotica, such as polyphonic aftertouch.

Built-In Support for Digital Video

This includes a variety of software video compression codecs that support the most important video file formats. Microsoft's Video for Windows 1.1 is now a standard feature in a 32-bit version. The upgraded Media Control Interface (MCI) now provides remote control for VCRs and other video devices that comply with Sony's VISCA standard. (A video overlay card is needed to watch analog video from VCRs and laser disc players on your PC.)

A New Display Control Interface (DCI)

This interface, developed jointly by Microsoft and Intel, takes advantage of the capabilities introduced by using VLB and PCI display adapter cards. The new DCI is aimed at further improving digital video performance and offers built-in chroma-keying and other special effects.

The WinG APL

Windows 3.1's graphic device interface (GDI) was designed to make it easier to control graphic displays in a standardized manner. This abstraction from the hardware level also resulted in slower screen updates, which has allowed the DOS game industry to remain much larger than the Windows game industry. The new WinG (Windows Game) application programming interface is designed to change that by letting game publishers create 32-bit titles for Windows 95 that rival the performance of DOS-based products. In addition to WinG, there is a new Game SDK that Microsoft has begun distributing to developers who are writing games for the 32-bit Windows world. This includes additional tools for working with animations and games, and is available to MSDN (Microsoft Solutions Developer Network) Level II subscribers.

In addition to these changes, Microsoft has also introduced new tools for creating multimedia titles (MediaView 1.3) and made changes to its existing tools (such as the new WinHelp 4.0) to allow for more flexibility in creating titles, and to make it even easier for casual users to create and enjoy their own multimedia creations.

Read through the next few chapters and start thinking about what you can do with the new multimedia features of Windows 95.

Installing Multimedia Devices with Windows 95

15

by
Bill Montemer

IN THIS CHAPTER

In the Beginning, There Was the Mac

Multimedia has been considered an emerging technology since early 1991. Pundits called it the doorway to a new world of experience and information, while critics moaned that it would never live up to its promise and potential. A scant five years later, it seemed likely that the naysayers had been right all along. But Windows 95 is looking to change all that.

Before Windows 95, multimedia on the PC seemed to be an afterthought, at best. At worst, it was simply a new source of agitation between the more visually literate Mac users and the "Mac-Wannabe" Windows camp. To the PC users, the arguments were more about capability and resourcefulness. But to the Mac devotees, the discussion centered on using the right tool for the job. Between the two camps reality beckoned: The PC was a poor step-child in the world of multimedia, digital video, and all the rest.

The PC's problem was speed, or the lack of it. The PC could crunch numbers and process words with any machine, but moving large amounts of data—like multimegabyte-sized digital audio or video files—brought even the fastest processor to its knees.

The reliable but dated 16-bit PC architecture was built for a kinder, gentler time. There were problems with the slow ISA bus, which was originally designed to handle 8 MHz worth of data throughput. On top of that, one of the very mechanisms that gave Windows such universal appeal among both program users and program developers—graphics device independence—also made it virtually impossible for Windows to display or draw graphics quickly. For good measure, Windows 3.1 was more of a shell operating over MS-DOS than a true operating system, and had to work around the 640KB DOS real-mode memory limit. In many ways, multimedia was out of the PC's league.

The Macintosh, on the other hand—with its 32-bit architecture, directly accessible video memory, and efficient, well-supported graphics and QuickTime digital video formats—seemed to be built for speed, high-fidelity, and motion. The Mac's dominance was further enhanced when Apple introduced a QuickTime for Windows digital video format that significantly outperformed Microsoft's first attempt at digital video—Video for Windows (VFW) and the AVI format (audio video interleave).

The PC with Windows 3.1 AVI format struggled to display 1/8th screen, postage stamp-sized (160×140 pixels) digital video—jokingly referred to as "dancing postage stamps." For sound, the Multimedia PC specification had standardized on 8-bit digital audio, which was fine for Space Invader games but truly forgettable otherwise. It was easy to see why both developers and serious multimedia users flocked to the Macintosh as the platform of choice. In fact, most of the current PC multimedia titles originate on the Macintosh, a fact Mac users take great pride in.

But just when it seemed that multimedia PC users were in their worst nightmare, some positive signs started to appear. First and foremost, in spite of the Macintosh's lead in multimedia technology, the PC was the clear leader in the marketplace. And as the market for PC multimedia expanded, the PC's technology improved by leaps and bounds, reaching "critical mass" with the wide acceptance of 16-bit audio cards, double-speed CD-ROM drives, affordable accelerated video cards, and local-bus motherboards. The better technology, in turn, triggered an exponential growth in multimedia titles developed for the PC, which guaranteed the obvious: Windows would be the delivery platform for multimedia, at least for the rest of this century. For Windows enthusiasts, the change seemed to happen overnight.

In early 1994, Microsoft began unveiling significant pieces of its multimedia master plan. First came Video for Windows 1.1, which worked with an accelerated graphics library called WinG. This understated minor release displayed quarter-screen, postcard-sized video (240×340 pixels), called, appropriately enough, "dancing postcards." This VFW release outperformed Apple's QuickTime for Windows 1.1.1 and several multimedia content developers considered VFW to be an acceptable alternative to QuickTime.

Christmas that same year found Disney Interactive, in a bold and surprisingly ambitious step, shipping 300,000 copies of The Lion King Animated StoryBook using a brand new Video for Windows and WinG technology called WinToon. This digital "blue screen" technology proved that at last PC multimedia could offer something the Mac could not. Soon, other WinG-enabled titles—including DOOM, the infamous 3-D "shoot-em-up" phenomenon—began appearing on Windows, months ahead of their Mac counterparts. In some cases titles were Windows only and cross-platform (Mac and Windows) development was never an economic consideration, another acknowledgment of the dominant size of the Windows market.

With each technological success and every marketplace victory, it became clear that Microsoft's multimedia strategy was formidable and well-constructed. When Windows 95 was finally released, PC users would no longer be in the Macintosh shadow. It was time for a role reversal.

A First Taste of Windows 95 Multimedia

If your PC matches the Multimedia Personal Computer Level II specification (MPC2)—if it contains a 16-bit sound card, a high-color (thousands of colors) video display adapter, and a double-speed or better CD-ROM drive—your first experience with multimedia in Windows 95 should be uneventful. Windows 95 will install and configure itself and your multimedia hardware with little or no user intervention.

Wizards

As you have probably seen by now, Windows 95 provides a very powerful set of installation and configuration utilities called *Wizards*. Wizards are designed to give both novice and experienced users quick access to Windows 95's more powerful and complex features.

The first Wizard you are likely to encounter when you enter the world of Windows 95 is the Setup Wizard shown in Figure 15.1. The Setup Wizard's clean and simple graphic interface is deftly designed to hide the details of Windows 95's powerful setup routines. In fact, in a fashion very similar to the Macintosh's "ease-of-use" approach, Windows 95 has taken great strides to make even the most complex and confusing computing tasks appear simple.

FIGURE 15.1.

The much improved Windows 95 Setup utility uses Microsoft's Wizard approach to handling installation. Notice that you can always cancel an operation before the system carries it out.

For the multimedia user, this new Setup approach means that rather than struggle with which IRQ to use, what DMA channel is available, or what the I/O address should be, Setup Wizard will determine what resources are needed, what are available, and who gets what—almost automatically.

The Setup Wizard breaks the installation routines into four logical phases. The first two—detecting hardware and asking configuration questions—can be used to optimize and customize the Windows 95 multimedia environment. The last two—copying Windows 95 files and setting the final configuration—do most of the real work.

The hardware detection phase uses a number of Windows 95's potent autodetection mechanisms. One method involves querying a Windows 95 database of known devices and then using that data to automatically test the PC ports and addresses. Another method uses the Plug and Play specification discussed later to accomplish basically the same thing. Whatever method or combination of methods Windows 95 uses, the end result is easier, more efficient installation.

In the configuration questions phase, Windows 95 presents a list of the detected (or selected) devices and components. As Figure 15.2 shows, the user is asked to confirm which components should be installed or removed. If you select the Multimedia component from this list, the system configuration information is displayed by component type.

Clicking the Details button opens a new configuration window and takes the user down into an even deeper configuration level. At this level, shown in Figure 15.3, the user adds or removes components by simply clicking the check boxes—definitely an easy and intuitive way to customize an environment.

FIGURE 15.2.

This hierarchical configuration questions dialog box shows Windows 95's improved user interface. Notice that you can move back to the previous screen if you change your mind.

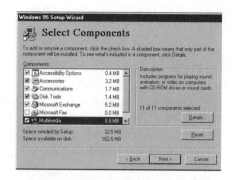

FIGURE 15.3.

The configuration questions dialog. This view shows the specific components that make up the selected multimedia component. Using check boxes and image lists make selecting options much more intuitive.

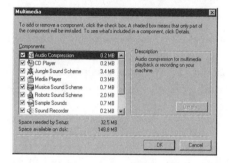

The remaining phases of the Setup Wizard—copying the selected Windows 95 files and setting the final configuration—are vitally important to the operating system, but effectively transparent to the user. Once again, the expressed goal of the Windows 95 user interface is to make the complex appear simple. Whether it's a simple audio game card or a complex MPEG video capture system, installing multimedia with the Setup Wizard could hardly be easier.

But of all the Windows 95 innovations—graphically interfaced wizards, true 32-bit operating systems, preemptive multitasking, multithreaded processing, and installable component architecture—perhaps nothing is as important to multimedia users and developers as Plug and Play.

Plug and Play

Just as the Setup Wizard makes configuring and allocating resources easy at installation time, Plug and Play promises to make reconfiguring systems and resources just as simple, all the time. This miraculous Plug and Play functionality is made possible by combining the robust Windows 95 operating system with smart, affordable hardware. But to appreciate why Plug and Play is so important to PC multimedia, you have to look back at Windows 3.1.

Order Out of Hardware Chaos

As the number of multimedia applications and titles under Window 3.1 began to skyrocket, a sizable flood of multimedia upgrade kits also hit the market. Most were Multimedia Personal Computer Level II (MPC2) compatibles with 16-bit sound cards and double-speed CD drives. And almost all the kits came bundled with "value-added" diskettes or CDs full of drivers, applications, and utilities. In the open-standard PC world, many devices are poorly documented clones of *de facto* market leaders. Because they are usually the result of clean room reverse engineering, they may emulate the operation of a more popular device, but their internal functions may be totally different. To work in a market-leading environment such as Windows, the manufacturers write (or buy) proprietary or third-party drivers, specifically designed for their hardware.

Installing proprietary drivers in Window 3.1 usually is not difficult if you have the right installation data and a good install program. Unfortunately, receiving a bundle of disks and software does not guarantee that you have everything you will need. For various reasons then, setting up and configuring PC multimedia became somewhat of a black art, best left to the professional practitioner.

Fortunately, Microsoft saw the chaotic state of the hardware marketplace and decided to do something about it. Windows 95 tackles the system configuration problem by implementing Plug and Play support. Simply put, Plug and Play makes the Windows 95 operating system and hardware manufacturers responsible for setting things up correctly.

Fully Plug and Play Enabled

Full Plug and Play support means that if you buy a Plug and Play sound board and plug it in, it will play in Windows 95 automatically, just as it's supposed to do. What's even more impressive is that if you swap peripherals—for instance, suppose you plug in an external PCMCIA CD-ROM card—Windows 95 will automatically sense the new device, reconfigure the system on-the-fly, and enable you to use it as if it was always connected.

This kind of power and flexibility is not without cost, however. Fully enabled Plug and Play devices require special firmware or flash ROM code to identify a device and enumerate the resources the device requires. Windows 95 operating system code then stores the necessary configuration data in the Registry, where it is used by the device and configuration managers to dynamically load and unload virtual device drivers.

The key element in Plug and Play is dynamic allocation. Because the user doesn't always know just what part of a multimedia system they want or need to use at a given time, the system itself must be able to make the necessary adjustments. Giving the Windows 95 operating system the responsibility and the power to make these kinds of arrangements brings the multimedia PC up to the level of a trusted household appliance. With Windows 95 Plug and Play, switching on a multimedia title could soon be as easy as turning on a TV set.

Windows 95 and Legacy Systems

Although Plug and Play–enabled peripherals are neat, and definitely the way to go, you may not want to scrap your existing multimedia system to enjoy the benefits of Windows 95. Fortunately, Microsoft considered that possibility, too.

Older, pre-Windows 95 devices—at the time of this printing most PC devices fit into this category—may still be able to benefit from some parts of the Plug and Play specification. Microsoft calls pre-Windows 95 peripherals *legacy* hardware, probably because they are inherited from the previous PC generation. To account for this large base of existing hardware, Windows 95 follows a find, assign, and fix course of action.

At system bootup, Windows 95's autodetection first looks for legacy peripherals, giving them first choice over available system resources and device allocations. The remaining resources are then assigned to the more flexible, dynamically loaded devices. Finally, if there are any device conflicts remaining, Windows 95 will inform the user and offer to fix the conflict if possible. Also, even if a device is non-Plug and Play, Windows 95's built-in configuration and management tools make it a lot easier to add new hardware and software—a far cry from the chaotic Windows 3.1 days.

Adding New Legacy Hardware

To add a new piece of legacy multimedia hardware to Windows 95, the first step (after buying the hardware, of course) is to plug the board in, just as in Windows 3.1. This is where the similarity ends.

If Windows 95 correctly recognizes the new hardware, it will probably be able to configure it automatically. Otherwise, the user can step through another of Windows 95 wizards called, appropriately enough, the Add New Hardware Wizard.

You use the Control Panel window to access the Add New Hardware Wizard. Several Control Panel objects (shown in Figure 15.4) deal with multimedia properties; these will be discussed later. For now, click the Start button on the taskbar and then point to the Settings pop-up menu. Click the Control Panel entry of this menu.

From the Control Panel, click the Add New Hardware icon. This opens the Add New Hardware Wizard shown in Figure 15.5, which works just like the previously described Setup Wizard. If you follow the simple prompts, this Wizard will guide you through the entire hardware installation process and enable you to customize the Windows 95 multimedia subsystem.

FIGURE 15.4.

The Control Panel contains a number of objects used to configure Windows 95.

FIGURE 15.5.

The Add New Hardware Wizard leads users through hardware installation with easy-to-understand screens that greatly simplify the process.

NOTE

With Windows 95, some of your present PC hardware may need to be replaced. Fortunately, much of your so-called legacy hardware will work just fine. If the board is well-known and well-established, plugging it in may be all that's necessary, because Windows 95 will be able to recognize and configure the board. For instance, even the early beta versions of Windows 95 could recognize a Sound Blaster 16 legacy sound board. Setting this board up was a pure no-brainer.

If the board is new, it should be at least partially Plug-and-Play–enabled. If the board is not new, consider exchanging it for one that meets the new specification. The time and trouble you save will be worth the extra effort.

If the board if older, it may still be easy to configure. It shouldn't hurt to plug it in and let Windows 95 try to find it. For example, Windows 95 recognized an early MediaVision PAS-16 (Windows NT would not) and set it up as easily as a new board.

Other more obscure and exotic boards might take more research. First, find the manual and look for the manufacturer's technical support phone number. Also, check the online services (AOL, CompuServe, or Microsoft Support Group) for information about your particular board.

If the board was expensive and high-quality, the manufacturer will probably have some Windows 95 information available. One word to the wise: creating, testing, and supporting a new 32-bit driver is not trivial or inexpensive. It may not make sense economically for a manufacturer to create Windows 95 drivers for an old board, especially if they plan to market a new 32-bit Plug and Play peripheral. This reality exists in the video capture board market, where newly designed 32-bit hardware significantly outperforms their older 16-bit predecessors.

If the board was a bargain-basement, end-of-the-production-line special, you might be able to find a better board that is supported for a bargain price. But remember that video capture boards are an altogether different story; many will probably never see 32-bit drivers. As a last-ditch effort, you could set Windows 95 to dual boot and install a minimal version of Windows 3.1, but that defeats the purpose of this book, so we won't get into that.

Once again, all the older legacy boards are virtually obsolete and most suppliers will be restocking with the newer models. There will be a lot of good hardware available for good prices. It goes without saying that there will be a lot of junk too. As always, to find a bargain, you have to do more research.

The next installation page, shown in Figure 15.6, lets you select how Windows 95 identifies the new hardware. The first option uses one of Windows 95's automatic detection mechanisms. This is probably the easiest method, but not necessarily the safest.

FIGURE 15.6.

This Wizard dialog page enables the user to autodetect or manually install the new piece of hardware. Select the second option to manually specify the device.

NOTE

Autodetection relies on being able to distinguish one kind of peripheral from another. If the jumpers on two boards are physically set to the same IRQ or I/O address, there is no way Windows 95 can tell one from the other. Also, if a clone board emulates another electronically different type of board, the clone may confuse the autodetection scheme.

If autodetection fails, your system will sit and wait for an OK signal that will never come. Under Windows 95, this is not as bad as it seems; it's not that uncommon, either. Simply turn off your machine and begin again. This next time, however, do not try autodetect; install the new device manually.

If you have the board and manual available, it is probably more straightforward to choose the second method and select the type of device from the supplied list. To manually install the hardware, select No and then click the Next button. A list of possible hardware additions appear. Because you are interested in multimedia hardware, scroll down and select the sound, video, and games controller item.

After you select the type of device, a new dialog box appears (see Figure 15.7), which lists the device manufacturers and their supported devices. As Windows 95 matures, this list will surely grow.

FIGURE 15.7.

This next dialog box presents two list boxes to users: the left box lists manufacturers and the right box lists their model numbers.

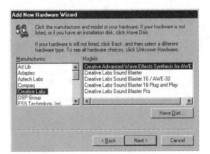

After you select the manufacturer and model of the new device, click the Next button to bring up the final dialog shown in Figure 15.8. As in most of the new Windows 95 dialogs, the user is given a final chance to either commit to making the changes or to cancel.

FIGURE 15.8.

The last step in the Add New Hardware Wizard gives the user one final chance to cancel the installation.

Adding Software Components

By now you've seen how easy it is to add new multimedia devices using the Add New Hardware Wizard. The Add New Hardware Wizard is also used to install certain types of software components called codecs.

You usually add new software to a Windows 95 system through the Add/Remove Programs Properties object located on the Windows 95 Control Panel. As Figure 15.9 shows, this ubiquitous sheet provides a standardized program Install/Uninstall launching point, a place to add or remove components of Windows 95, and a place to create Startup boot disks. However, it is not used for adding or removing one of the most vital multimedia components: the codec.

FIGURE 15.9.

The Add/Remove Programs Properties sheet seems to be an uncharacteristically multiheaded utility that is used for installing programs, customizing Windows 95 configurations, and creating System boot disks.

Codec is short for compressor/decompressor. A codec, which is explained more fully in the section "Codecs," acts as an intermediary between the Windows 95 multimedia subsystem and the PC display or audio driver. Codecs are software components used to compress motion video (or audio) data during the recording and file creation process or decompress it for playback. Because software-only codecs replace hardware compression/decompression devices, you install a new codec just like you would install new hardware—using the Add New Hardware Wizard. Although codecs are software binary objects, they are used like hardware devices, so installing them with this wizard is not entirely out of place.

The line between hardware and software gets more and more blurred, especially in the multimedia realm. For instance, in digital audio, it is possible to process audio signals in the traditional analog form, or in a straight digital format. In much the same way, digital video processing has advanced far enough that highly specialized and expensive hardware devices can be simulated with relatively inexpensive software.

Using the Windows 95 System Tools for Multimedia

Although automatic configuration is nice, there may be times when you need to get "under the hood" and tweak a configuration. For instance, suppose you are adding an older overlay card to a Windows 95 system that already contains legacy sound and video controller cards. The two previously installed boards may have required juggling hardware jumpers and DIP switches to find a combination that worked.

Under Windows 3.1, to add the third card you might need to physically remove the other cards, note the current jumper settings, and juggle some more to find compatible settings for all three cards. The task would take at least a couple hours, and you might find that in the end you can't get even the first two cards to work together. (This is just another situation in which Plug and Play peripherals can save both time and frustration.)

Even without Plug and Play cards, Windows 95 provides several tools that can significantly speed up the adding, swapping, and upgrading of peripherals. Most of these tools are accessed through the now-familiar Control Panel.

If you double-click the System icon, Windows 95 displays the System Properties property sheet shown in Figure 15.10. This property sheet provides access to devices, configuration profiles, and performance optimizing characteristics of the Windows 95 system. For multimedia configuration you are interested in the Device Manager.

FIGURE 15.10.

The System Properties page gives the user access to all the configuration data required for Windows 95 multimedia.

Clicking the Device Manager tab displays an image list, which can be ordered by device type or by type of physical connection. To look at the multimedia devices, scroll to the sound, video, and game controllers item and click. The hierarchical list expands to display the current sound, video, and game devices, as shown in Figure 15.11.

FIGURE 15.11.

The sound, video, and game controller entry expands to show the current multimedia devices.

When you select one of the available devices and then click the Properties button, a property sheet for the device appears. The property sheet gives the user an unprecedented amount of detail about the selected device, including the various parameters, driver names, file dates, and assigned system resources.

Now, to install your third board into Windows 95 you would open the property sheets for the first two devices and find a set of compatible jumper assignments for the new board. Although this approach would still not provide an automatic solution, it is still a vast improvement over the Windows 3.1 scheme.

> **NOTE**
>
> The Device Manager Property Sheet provides a lot of useful configuration data. The following screens illustrate the type of detail found in the property sheet of a typical multimedia device, the Sound Blaster 16. The arrangement and type of data available through the object property sheets varies by manufacturer and type of device. Still, having convenient access to this data is a definite win for multimedia troubleshooting.
>
> The most useful information on the General properties page (shown in Figure 15.12) is the Device status box. Hopefully, a good device will show up as properly working.
>
> As shown in Figure 15.13, the Driver properties page contains valuable configuration information: driver names, version numbers, and dates. This information is used to keep the drivers consistent with the hardware. Usually, newer drivers are better, but once in a while new drivers are not completely backward-compatible.
>
> The Resources properties page gives the user access to the infamous Input/Output addresses, Interrupt Request settings, and Direct Memory Access channels, just as in the old Windows 3.1 drivers control panel. For complex multiboard setups, the conflicting device status listing—as shown in Figure 15.14, there are no conflicts—is a definite timesaver.

FIGURE 15.12.

The General properties page displays device type, manufacturer, version number, and the all important Device status field.

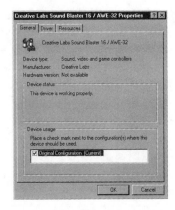

FIGURE 15.13.

The Driver properties page displays important name and version information for the current device drivers.

FIGURE 15.14.

The Resources properties page accesses all device-specific information for the Sound Blaster 16: I/O addresses, IRQ settings, and DMA channel.

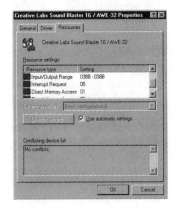

Inside the Windows 95 Multimedia Subsystem

While using the various Windows 95 Wizards and Help systems, you may have noticed that there are many ways to get to a specific configuration or setup module. This is because Windows in general, and Windows 95 in particular, is a collection of software subsystems that plug into one another like a child's Lego blocks. This approach provides lots of interconnectivity, so that the same configuration module can be called seamlessly from a wizard or a device manager.

Figure 15.15 shows a simplified view of the Windows 95 Multimedia system and its various component pieces. This open, modular architecture enables the easy integration of new leading-edge hardware and software technology. In quickly advancing technologies like multimedia, this type of flexibility is necessary to keep Windows 95 vital and up-to-date.

FIGURE 15.15.

The Windows 95 multimedia system consists of these basic software components.

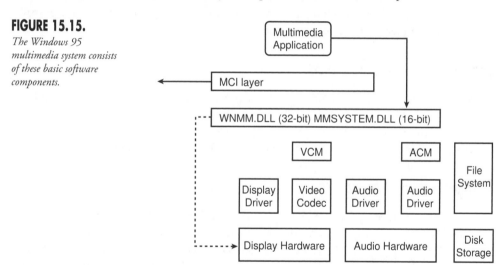

The Components of Windows 95 Multimedia

From its inception, Microsoft has intended to make Windows 95 the leading force in multimedia technology. To that end, the Windows 95 multimedia subsystem uses an open, expandable architecture that provides state-of-the-art multimedia services today and the promise of even greater support to come.

The Multimedia Application

A running multimedia application sits on top of the PC and Windows 95 operating system, interacting with the PC user, any external hardware devices, and the PC hardware itself. For instance, a reference title may play a digital video in response to a user's mouse click. Or a video editing application may sequence the playback of two VCRs into a third "master recorder." All applications use the same general interface to the multimedia system, making application development easier and more consistent.

The Media Control Interface

The Media Control Interface (MCI) provides applications with a standard way of controlling media devices. It provides both a high-level (human-language intelligible) and a low-level (parameterized code) method of talking to media recorders, players, and other similar devices. The high-level set of commands provides easy-to-use general commands such as "play sound from 30 seconds to end." The low-level interface provides efficient commands and parameter structures to enable robust device communication.

Core Multimedia Systems

The central code engine for Windows 95 multimedia is contained in two Dynamic Link Libraries: WINMM.DLL and MMSYSTEM.DLL. WINMM is a new 32-bit collection of multimedia functions, and MMSYSTEM is its 16-bit counterpart from Windows 3.1. Both libraries provide services to capture, edit, and play back video, audio, and image data.

Compression Managers

Multimedia image files are large. A single, full-screen color image frame, such as a 640×480, 256-color Windows bitmap, is over 300 KB in size. If you do the math on a 30-second sequence at 15 frames per second, the sequence comes out to be a hefty 135 MB. These file sizes cannot be handled very well on any system, let alone a PC. Therefore, compressing multimedia data files is mandatory, and developing the best, most efficient compression method is big business.

Windows 95 contains two compression managers: The Audio Compression Manager (ACM) handles audio, and the Video Compression Manager (VCM) handles video and image data compression. Both compression managers work with software compressors/decompressors called codecs.

Codecs

Codecs are compressors/decompressors. Codecs are used in both the creation of AVI or WAV files and in their playback. In file creation, codecs take large uncompressed files and produce smaller compressed versions. In playback, codecs take compressed files and expand them. How close these expanded file copies come to the original files depends on the compression method and its compression parameters. Several compression methods for audio and video are provided by Windows 95. Because of Windows' installable compression architecture, other codecs can be added.

Display Control Interface

The Display Control Interface (DCI) is a new device driver interface created jointly by Microsoft and Intel. DCI-compliant drivers provide fast access to the video frame buffer enabling multimedia and game applications to draw faster, with less demands on the CPU. In addition, it enables digital video playback to take advantage of the hardware assistance built into certain display adapters. This assistance may include hardware stretching and color space conversion, which can reduce the amount of work a codec must perform by up to 30 percent.

Back to the Fun Stuff

By adding all this power and complexity to the operating system, Windows 95 tries to shield the user from the detail and minutiae of multimedia technology, while at the same time using the technology to create engaging, interactive, multisensory experiences. In theory, after being freed from the drudgery of hardware and software specifics, the Windows 95 user will finally be able to concentrate on the more interesting, aesthetic, and just plain "fun" aspects of multimedia.

In the next chapters, you will examine the various elements of multimedia and see how Windows 95 is poised to turn the PC into a world-class multimedia machine.

Using Windows 95's Multimedia Applets

16

by Ewan Grantham

IN THIS CHAPTER

Introduction

Along with the overall changes to the operating system in Windows 95, Microsoft has also strengthened Windows' Multimedia capabilities by improving the Media Player and Sound Recorder applets, and adding Volume Control and CD Player applets. In this chapter, you will learn about all four of these applets, how to use them, and how to make the most of them.

CD Player

One of the first changes you may notice in Windows 95 occurs the first time you put an audio CD into your CD-ROM drive. While you're going through the start menu trying to find the CD player applet, all of a sudden it shows up on the toolbar and starts playing your CD automatically. This feature (Auto Play) is just one of the niceties of the built-in CD Player applet.

The CD Player is designed in many ways to act like a stereo CD player. If you look at Figure 16.1, you'll see what the applet looks like with a CD in the drive that has not been set up in the CD Player database before. The first item to look at is the display, which in this figure is shown with the Small Font. The track that is currently ready to be played is displayed (the [01]), followed by the amount of time the track has been playing (00:00 in this case). As each track is played, the number in brackets changes accordingly.

FIGURE 16.1.

CD Player applet with a "new" audio CD loaded.

To the right of this display are the controls for manipulating the playing of the CD. The top-left control in the control panel is the Play button. Clicking this starts the CD. As the dotted box around the button indicates, this is the default action when CD Player is started.

To the right of the Play button is the Pause button. This is the button you click when the phone rings at an inconvenient time. It is grayed out in this figure because the CD isn't playing at the moment, so there is nothing to pause.

The last button in this row is the Stop button. This stops the CD and returns it to the beginning of the CD, not to the beginning of the current track. If you don't want to lose your place, you should hit the Pause button. Again, like the Pause button, the Stop button is grayed out because the CD is not playing.

On the next row of controls, starting at the left again, is a button with a line and two arrows pointing to the left. This is the Previous Track button. Pressing this will take you to the beginning of the track if the CD is currently playing. If you hold it down or press it when the CD is stopped, it will take you backward track-by-track. Pressing it when the CD is already at the first track has no effect.

The next button to the right has two arrows pointing to the left without a line. This is the Rewind (or as Microsoft calls it, the Skip Backwards) button. Clicking this will rewind the track one second. Holding it down will keep you going backward through the track (as opposed to skipping tracks). If you get to the beginning of a track, it goes to the previous track and continues rewinding from the end of that track.

Continuing to the right, the next button is the Fast Forward (or Skip Forwards) button. A click on the button advances you one second on the present track. Holding it down will keep you going forward through the track, and at the end of the present track, take you to the next.

The last button on this row is the Eject button. Assuming your CD-ROM drive is properly equipped, pushing this button will cause the tray to extend out with your CD in it.

Below the controls and the Track/Time display are three informational fields. This is where you are shown the Artist, the Title of the CD, and the names for each Track. You actually enter this information from the Disc | Edit Play List menu option, which you'll learn about in a bit. Again, in the preceding example, you can tell that this CD has not been entered into the CD Player's library.

At the bottom of the applet are two fields. On the left is the total play time for the CD in minutes and seconds. On the right is the play time for this particular track, also in minutes and seconds.

All of this is based on the default setup for the applet and a new CD. You can leave everything alone and simply play your CDs without any additional effort, and you'll have the same basic functionality of a simple stereo CD player. However, you'll notice there are some menu options; these enable you to control the appearance and the function of the CD Player applet. In the next section, you will learn how to do this.

Customizing the CD Player Applet

As mentioned previously, there are four menu options for the CD Player applet. The first three, Disc, View, and Options, enable you to customize how the tool works or appears. The fourth option, Help, enables you to look at the online help for the applet.

The first menu option, Disc, enables you to select from two menu items: Edit Play List and Exit. Selecting Edit Play List takes you to the screen shown in Figure 16.2.

FIGURE 16.2.

CD Player Edit Play List requestor.

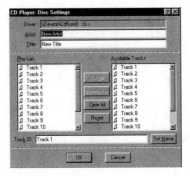

The first three fields on this window are the Drive (which shows both the Windows 95 device name and the DOS drive mapping), Artist, and Title fields. Only Artist and Title are editable. Below these are two listings of the tracks available on the CD. The listing on the left side is the play list, and the listing on the right is a list of the tracks on the CD. By default, these two lists are the same. They don't have to be, though, and that is something you will learn later.

Artist is the first highlighted field, so you can type in the musician or group here; pressing Enter will take you automatically to Title. Enter the CD's title, and then click the bottom field so you can enter the song title for Track 01. If you press Enter after the title instead of clicking in the bottom field, you are taken back to the main CD player screen. Pressing Enter in the bottom field automatically puts into both windows the title you typed to replace track 1, and changes the prompt for the bottom field to Track 02, as seen in Figure 16.3.

FIGURE 16.3.

Edit Play List after the first track has been entered.

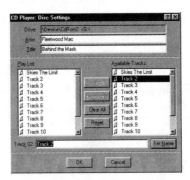

At this point, you can keep entering titles, one after another, until you hit the last track of the CD. Pressing Enter after typing in the title for the last track will bring Track 01 back up. You can then click OK to save the information about the CD into the CDPLAYER.INI file in your Windows 95 home directory, which looks like Figure 16.4 for the CD in this example. Notice that the header for the entry (the number in the brackets) is the CD's ID entry, which is unique for each title. Below that is the information that you entered, though you'll notice that the entries start at 0 instead of 1. Because of this, you can expect to see catalogs coming out with all this information already typed in.

FIGURE 16.4.

CD Player .INI file.

One other item to note is the line that says `order=` and then has the track numbers in the order they are to be played. You might decide that you would rather hear tracks 2 and 3 after track 12 (or 3 and 4 after 13 if you count starting at 1). You can either edit this file directly or go back to the Edit Play List screen and change the order graphically.

The way you do this graphically is to first remove the track, or tracks, from the Play List side of the screen. You do that by double-clicking the track you want to remove. Then, you mark the track on the Play List side after which you want the song to be inserted. Now, on the Available Tracks side, double-click the track you want to add back to the Play List. You'll now see the track listed on the Play List after the track you had highlighted with your mouse click.

If you want to make more than one or two changes, it is probably faster to click the Clear All button, which removes all the entries from the Play List side. Then start double-clicking the Available Tracks side in the order you want them to play.

Of course, if you end up deciding that the original order was best, click the Reset button to place the Play List in the same order as the Available Tracks list.

As if that weren't enough flexibility, while the CD is playing, you can go to the Track field of CD Player, choose the track you want from the drop-down list, and CD Player will jump to that track and start playing from there.

In addition to editing the Play List, you can also edit the way the applet looks by using the options on the View menu. Looking at Figure 16.5, you can see three options: Toolbar, Disc/ Track Info, and Status Bar. You can have these enabled or disabled in any combination to get the look you want.

Figure 16.6 shows the CD Player applet when all three of these options have been selected. The toolbar buttons from left to right are Edit Play List, Track Time Elapsed, Track Time Remaining, Disc Time Remaining, Random Track Order, Continuous Play, and Intro Play.

FIGURE 16.5.

CD Player View menu.

FIGURE 16.6.

CD Player with toolbar.

In fact, the next three View options are on the toolbar, and are designed to enable only one to be selected at a time. In other words, you can view Track Time Remaining, but not Disc Time Remaining, unless you use View to change the option.

The last View option is a jump to the Volume Control applet, which is discussed later in the chapter.

Next on the menu bar is Options. Here you can directly affect how the applet works. Figure 16.7 shows the Options menu.

FIGURE 16.7.

CD Player Options menu.

The first three options are different ways of playing the CD. The first option, Random Order, is exactly that: the tracks on the CD are played in a random order. This option can be very useful if you have a multi-CD changer, or just want to hear an old CD in a new way. The next option is Continuous Play. This plays all the tracks on the CD, in Play List order, and then starts all over again. This continues until you change the option or close the applet. Finally, Intro Play goes to each track and plays the first 10 seconds of the track. You can change the length of time that each track will play from Preferences, which is detailed shortly. Intro Play is good for quickly previewing a CD. In all three cases, you click the choice or toolbar button, and then click the Play button.

Preferences, the last option on the Options Menu, has a number of choices that affect how the CD Player handles certain things. Figure 16.8 shows these choices.

FIGURE 16.8.

CD Player Preferences.

The first three checkboxes enable you to have the applet automatically stop the CD if you exit the program, save any changes you have made when you exit the program, and choose whether or not to show tool tips, which are the little help boxes that appear when you leave your mouse pointing at a button on the screen for more than a second or two.

Next is a box to define how long you want Intro Play to play each track when that mode is selected. The default is 10 seconds, but you can select any value between 5 and 15 seconds.

Finally, there is a pair of options for selecting either the small or large font for the panel display. The box to the side shows what your choice will make it look like.

In addition to all the changes you can make from within the applet itself, you can also affect the way things happen using the system settings for the CD device. The only time you will usually do this on purpose, though, is to disable or re-enable the AutoPlay function.

To disable AutoPlay, follow these steps:

1. Double-click the My Computer icon.
2. Select the View menu, and then select Options.
3. Click the File Types tab.
4. Click the AudioCD type, and then click Edit.
5. From the Action List, click Play, and then click Set Default.

To re-enable AutoPlay, simply run through the same steps.

NOTE

To disable AutoPlay for a single CD, press the Shift key when you insert the audio CD.

Now that you know about all these options, you should be able to set up Windows 95 to play your favorite CDs just the way you want them. Just remember that the options to change the way the interface looks are under the View menu, and the options that change the way the interface works are under the Options menu.

Media Player

Media Player has been around for a while, but in Windows 95 the applet's interface has been cleaned up and given quite a bit more power through the addition of more tools for editing and altering the playback of multimedia objects.

Using the Media Player Applet

Figure 16.9 shows Media Player after it has first been brought up. Notice the addition of an Edit menu, as well as several additional controls along the bottom.

FIGURE 16.9.

Media Player.

At this point, all the controls are grayed out. To change that, load an example .AVI file (.AVI is Microsoft's Video for Windows format), and let it play a bit. The end result can be seen in Figure 16.10, which shows the Media Player box, and behind it the stopped .AVI file.

FIGURE 16.10.

Media Player with an open Video for Windows (.AVI) file.

Something else to notice is the way that "Welcome.avi" shows up twice on the taskbar. The button that has "Welcome.avi - Media Play..." is for the Media Player applet, while the other button is to the window where the .AVI is being displayed. Even though there are two buttons showing on the taskbar, closing Media Play will also close the .AVI being displayed.

The main idea behind Media Player is to give various multimedia files a similar interface for the end user. So, you can pull up a MIDI file, as in Figure 16.11, and notice that for the most part, the player looks the same as it does when playing an .AVI file. The only real differences are that there is a different name for the file, and there isn't a separate window open.

FIGURE 16.11.

Media Player with an open MIDI (.MID) file.

Regardless of the underlying file, the basic interface remains the same. Going through the menu, File is similar to the File option on most Windows applications; it has Open, Close, and Exit options. Print is not available because some objects would be difficult to print; though it would be interesting to see this added in the future and have, for example, MIDI files get a printout of the score while a Video file could print out the current frame.

At the bottom of the applet are the buttons for controlling the playback of the files. Going from left to right these are

Play	Starts the playback of the current clip.
Stop	Stops the playback of the current clip.
Eject	Ejects a CD or tape if the Device driver supports it.
Previous Mark	If you have made a selection in the current clip (for editing, copying, and so on), this will take you to the beginning of that selection. Otherwise, you are returned to the beginning of the clip.
Rewind	Move backward through the clip. This will continue as long as you keep the button clicked, or until you hit the beginning of the piece.
Fast Forward	Moves forward through the clip without playing (as opposed to Play). This continues as long as you keep the button clicked, or until you hit the end of the piece (notice how rewind and fast forward differ in Media Player from CD Player).
Next Mark	If you've made a selection in the current clip, this takes you to the end of the selection. Otherwise, this moves you to the end of the clip.
Start Selection	This defines the point in the clip from which you are starting your selection (for copying, editing, and so on). Also creates the beginning mark.
End Selection	The point in the clip where the selection you are making from the clip ends.

You now know how to play back your files, but to really make "music" with them, check out the next section on customizing Media Player.

Customizing

When you customize Media Player, most of what you can change affects the playback or the copying and embedding of files in other applications. You do this customization through the menu choices that come after File.

The Edit menu, which is new in Windows 95, comes after the File menu. The options here are Copy Object, Options, and Selection. Copy Object enables you to grab the entire file and insert it into another application—like a help file or a memo. Figure 16.12 shows an example of this using Microsoft Word. Here the Video file has been pasted into a document, and by right-clicking the mouse over the inserted object you get a menu for handling the video clip. Double-clicking this same pane starts the playback of the clip.

FIGURE 16.12.

A file copied into a document using the Media Player Edit menu.

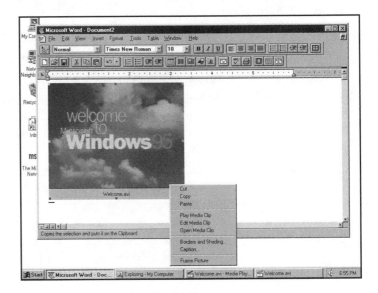

Choosing the next Edit option of Options presents a requestor like the one shown in Figure 16.13. This requestor has options that affect how the file appears and is played back.

FIGURE 16.13.

The Media Player Edit menu: Options requestor.

The first two options on this requestor enable you to have the file perform a certain function at the end of the clip playback. Auto Rewind will position the clip at the beginning, ready to be played again after the selection has played. Auto Repeat will make the clip play over and over again until the Stop button is clicked. This option is great for building one of those continuous demos you are always seeing at the store. The default behavior is for the file to remain stopped at the end of the selection after it has been played.

The other options affect how the file will appear if it is embedded in another document (as was described earlier). By turning all of these off you can make the selection appear to be an almost seamless part of your document. The flip side is that if you turn off the control bar option, the user will have to wait for the selection to stop; there will be no way to manually intervene with the playback.

Finally, the Edit menu also has a Selection option. Clicking this option brings up the requestor shown in Figure 16.14, which gives you the ability to control which parts of the clip will be copied.

FIGURE 16.14.

The Media Player Edit menu: Selection requestor.

As you might guess, the All option simply means that the default behavior of the copy command—to copy all of the file—will occur. The None option means that nothing will be copied. More useful are the remaining options, which enable you to specify a starting point and then either an ending point or a duration. Changing either the start or end will affect the Size option, whereas changing Size will affect the end point.

Device is the next Media Player menu item. The first group of options will be somewhat different depending on which devices you have installed. By default, you should see at least the group of devices shown in Figure 16.15, as well as others you may have on your system.

FIGURE 16.15.

Media Player Device menu.

Currently, Video for Windows is checked because you have that file open already. If you didn't have a file open, clicking one of these items would cause the Open requestor to appear with a filter for that type of file.

The Configure option takes you to a screen with configuration options that are appropriate for each particular device.

The last option jumps you to the Volume Control applet, which you will learn about later in the chapter.

Next on the menubar, and the last option that enables you to configure Media Player, is the Scale menu. As you can see in Figure 16.16, this option enables you to control the scale used for the playback options.

FIGURE 16.16.

The Media Player Scale menu.

Again, depending on the device, each of these three options (Time, Frames, and Tracks) may be enabled. Clicking one of these changes the scale used to determine where you are in the clip being played. So, again in Figure 16.16, notice that the scale shows playback Time. Clicking Frames would change the numbers and marks below the bar to frame numbers for the clip rather than time segments.

Now that you have mastered these Media Player basics, you have the basic tools you'll need to begin creating multimedia documents and files, not to mention some fairly cool ways of making your computer more fun.

Sound Recorder

The Sound Recorder applet has changed little from its Windows 3.1 version. This is partly because so few people currently record their own sounds, and those who do tend to use multi-track editing software. However, if you are just trying to pick up some additional .WAVs for your system, or doing an annotation for a document, Sound Recorder is definitely enough to do the job. Sound Recorder is also a way to do some simple editing on your sound files, although you will probably prefer to use Media Player for this.

Using the Sound Recorder Applet

Figure 16.17 shows what Sound Recorder looks like. It looks basically like it did in the Windows 3.1 version.

FIGURE 16.17.

Sound Recorder.

To actually use Sound Recorder, you will need to have an audio card with a microphone or a system that has a built-in microphone. To begin using the applet to record, first go to the File menu and select New. Then answer the requestor questions for the Name, Format, and Attributes of this recording. Finally, click the Record button (the one on the far right with the red circle) to begin recording. When you are done, click the Stop button (the one just to the left with the square).

After you have a sound recorded or have loaded a sound using the File menu's Open option, you can play it back using the other buttons on the bottom of the applet. These are (from left to right)

Rewind (Seek to Start)   Move to the beginning of the clip

Fast Forward (Seek to End)   Move to the end of the clip

Play   Play the clip

You can also customize how Sound Recorder plays back sounds, which is covered in the next section.

Customizing

For this section, look at how Sound Recorder would look just after you have recorded or loaded a sound file. The example is shown in Figure 16.18, which shows Sound Recorder with the Chord.wav file that is in the Media folder.

FIGURE 16.18.

Sound Recorder with Chord.wav loaded.

Now look at what you can do using the Edit menu. This example will look like what is shown in Figure 16.19. Notice that there are eight options that enable you to modify the current sound clip or use it in other documents.

FIGURE 16.19.

Sound Recorder and the Edit menu.

Copy enables you to grab the clip and insert it into another document. This is similar to the example in the Media Player description earlier in the chapter.

Paste Insert and Paste Mix enable you to take sound clips you may have copied from another application or another instance of Sound Recorder, and add them to the current clip. Insert places the new clip at whatever point you are at in the current sound file. Mix will lay the new clip over the present clip.

After these choices are Insert File and Mix with File. These do the same thing as the previous two options using an existing file. For a fun experiment, load Chord.wav as in the example, and then use the Mix with File option and select Chimes.wav. The end result is amusing.

Note that you can't mix into or with the other two .WAV files in the Media folder because they are compressed .WAV files. Insert and Mix only work with noncompressed files.

The next two options cut the clip. Delete Before Current Position removes anything that occurred before the current point in the clip. Delete After Current Position removes anything that is in the clip after the current point.

Finally, Audio Properties produces a screen similar to the one in Figure 16.20. Your screen might be different depending on what sound card and/or microphone you use.

FIGURE 16.20.

Sound Recorder and the Edit menu's Audio Properties.

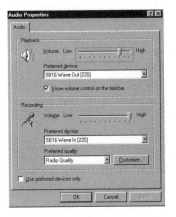

You should leave most of these options the way they are, although you can have quite an impact on the size and quality of the file by changing the Preferred quality option. Radio is usually a good compromise, and Telephone is good enough for annotations or other voice recordings. CD Quality is generally only something to use if the recording is really important or very intricate. Also be aware that you can lower the quality from what was originally recorded, but upping the quality above the original recording will have no effect.

Sound Recorder's next menu option, Effects, enables you to play with the clip to get the sound you want. These options are shown in Figure 16.21, in which the menu has been pulled down for the example clip.

FIGURE 16.21.

Sound Recorder's Effects menu.

The first two options, Increase Volume and Decrease Volume, let you work with the volume of the clip. This is the baseline volume, which is then affected by your settings for the Volume Control for your system.

The next two options, Increase Speed and Decrease Speed, affect the speed of the playback. In other words, you can use this to turn your favorite song into a chattering "animal" rendition or into a slow, plodding version.

The last two options should be something you try with the Chord.wav sound as in the example. Add Echo gives you a delayed additional track that gives an echo effect. Reverse enables you to click the Play button and hear the clip in reverse. A great way to check out what folks really did say in their musical selections.

Rounding out the menu, as usual, is the Help option for getting additional information about using and customizing the applet.

Volume Control

Volume Control is a little applet with a *big* effect on your machine. If nothing else, you want to be familiar with it to keep from waking the house at 2 a.m. The following section explains more about how to use this applet.

Using Volume Control

There are two interfaces to the Volume Control applet. The first one is the one you get if you click the little speaker in the right corner of the toolbar. It only enables you to set the Master volume, and appears as shown in Figure 16.22.

FIGURE 16.22.

Volume Control toolbar interface.

The other interface is what you see if you call Volume Control from the Start menu (Start | Programs | Accessories | Multimedia | Volume Control), or from one of the other multimedia applets. This interface looks like Figure 16.23, although, as you'll see later, you can make it appear differently.

As Figure 16.23 shows, you can adjust the master volume (the Volume Control slider), as well as the volumes of various output devices relative to the Master volume. Volume Control can also affect the volume of input devices through the use of the Options menu and the Properties command. Figure 16.24 illustrates the various choices you can make on the interface.

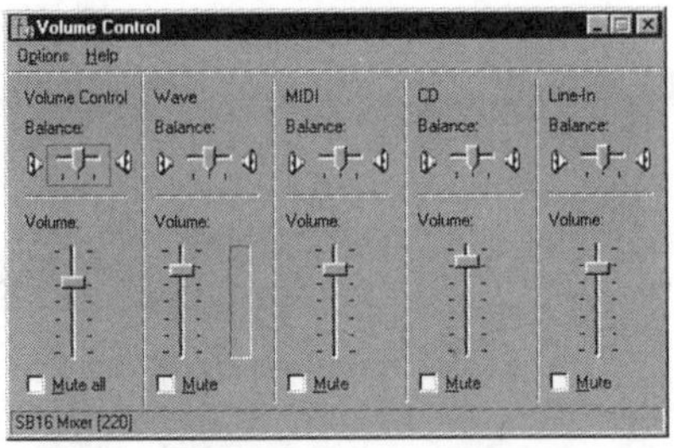

FIGURE 16.23.

Volume Control full interface.

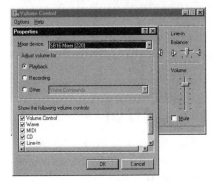

FIGURE 16.24.

Volume Control Properties requestor.

Each of the Adjust volume choices gives you a different set of control panels with which you can work.

A little experimentation should help you decide which settings are right for your machine's capabilities and personal tastes.

Summary

This chapter has covered the various multimedia applets that are available to you in Windows 95. They enable you to control and customize the multimedia portions of your environment, as well as let you edit and integrate multimedia into your documents. If you are familiar with these applets, you should be more productive, and be able to make your computer a little more fun as well.

Using Sound in Windows 95

by

Multimedia and Sound

Windows has supported sound since Version 3.0's Multimedia extensions, but Windows 95 takes this support to a new level. In Windows 95, sound is controlled at the system level, which means that rather than struggling with a number of sound cards and proprietary sound mixer applications, you need to learn only one applet—the Volume Control—to make sound work. But to use sound effectively, it helps to know something about digital audio and how Windows 95 supports it.

Imagine watching your favorite television show with the sound turned down. Or try watching MTV without the music. (Of course, you might prefer it that way.) Obviously, we expect sound to accompany these experiences. Without the sound, we find something lacking. Similarly, when we look at multimedia on a PC—especially for the first time—we quite naturally expect the experience to be lifelike. If the sound is shrill, scratchy, or out of sync with the visuals—or if there simply is no sound—we come away with a less than positive impression of multimedia.

One of the difficulties of using or producing multimedia on the PC is that television has produced a generation with quite a sophisticated audio-visual appetite. Our expectation levels are high and we are seldom impressed with silent slide shows. We want sound and we want effects, and we expect our PCs to deliver them.

Sound adds a dimension to multimedia that viewers expect. Before Windows 95, working with sound and images was difficult. The PC's constant juggling of resources and memory was like trying to squeeze an elephant through a mail slot: only part of it will fit, and then things get really ugly. Often, as you added more sound, more imagery, and more effects to your crisp new multimedia project, things only seemed to get worse. Full-screen graphics and animation would crawl, motion video looked like bad slide shows, and the audio would stop and stutter at all the wrong times.

Great Audio on a PC

Windows 95 promises to make these performance deficiencies, a thing of the past. When you install Windows 95, your PC's multimedia performance is instantly upgraded. The powerful 32-bit multitasking operating system easily handles graphics and audio, and makes synchronizing a variety of multimedia elements a snap. With Windows 95's improved 32-bit file input/output component, accessing and moving large amounts of multimedia data is no longer a limiting factor. You can get as much data as you need; now you have to decide what to do with it.

By now, you're probably convinced that Windows 95 can deliver great audio where and when you want it. Before you see how to get and use great audio on Windows 95, let's examine what makes audio great.

Supporting the Main Action

When the audio is right, it adds to a scene without becoming overly noticeable. Like a great supporting cast member, the audio seldom takes the spotlight. It acts more to support the main action or event.

For instance, in Steven Spielberg's classic thriller *Jaws*, the rising and pulsing string section makes the moviegoer anticipate another shark attack. Yet it works unconsciously, in the background, supporting and building the story—and the unseen horror.

Sound Behind the Scenes

Sound fills in behind-the-scenes and communicates impressions and moods—things that make for a more complete and satisfying experience. For instance, in the romantic comedy *Sleepless in Seattle*, several classic love songs set the mood for the final intimate encounter, which most of the time doesn't happen. The sound gets us leaning one way, allowing the story to move in the other direction, which is exactly the comedic effect the director was after.

In multimedia, sound is even more important because it is one of the easiest elements to edit and control. When it's done right, sound creates a context for the images you use.

Controlling the Viewer's Focus

Sound can also control the viewer's focus. Reading text along with a spoken narration has been shown to help reading comprehension. Accenting key moments in a presentation with music "stings" effectively adds a nonverbal exclamation point. Even a change in dynamics—a sudden unexpected silence, for example—draws and focuses a viewer's attention.

Intelligent use of sound can communicate information that the viewer might not otherwise notice. And because the audio track is so subtle and nonintrusive, viewers very often get the message before they're even aware that there is a message.

But don't think that slick audio can make up for poor design or sloppy graphics. Unfortunately, good audio goes unnoticed by most people. And, in most cases, that's what you want. It almost goes without saying that although good audio will go overlooked, almost everyone notices bad sound. That leaves you with only two choices: use great audio that possibly no one will notice, or use bad audio that no one will forget.

Digital Audio Primer

Before you can work intelligently with digital audio, you need a basic understanding of traditional audio and how it works. Once it is gained, this insight will help you understand the choices (especially the subtle ones) that you must make in the digital audio realm.

What we call *sound* is the rapid movement of air molecules caused by a physical air disturbance. What we call *hearing* is the perception of this air movement by our eardrums. But how are the two related?

Just as the age-old question "Does a tree falling in the forest, with no one to hear, make any sound?" points out, hearing and sound might be separate events but they are intrinsically related. For our purposes, one is of little use without the other. But as it turns out, the choices you make based on a sound's physical characteristics directly affect the way we perceive it.

Waveforms

As shown in Figure 17.1, a sound vibration causes a microphone to emit an electrical signal. If you graph the signal, you might get a waveform like the one shown. This analog waveform can be represented by a series of smooth curves. If it is amplified and sent to a speaker system, this waveform reproduces the original sound.

FIGURE 17.1.

A sound vibration causes a microphone to emit an electrical signal.

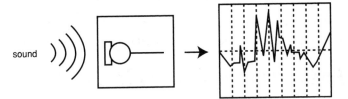

The waveform has an amplitude, which is measured from the zero midpoint to a plus or minus peak, and a period, which is the smallest nonrepeating unit in the wave. (See Figure 17.2.) The number of these periods per second determines the number of times it repeats or the frequency of the wave. This frequency is measured in cycles per second or hertz (Hz).

FIGURE 17.2.

A sound waveform has an amplitude, which is measured from a zero midpoint to a plus or minus peak, and a period, which is the smallest nonrepeating unit in a waveform.

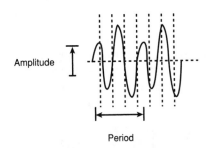

Figure 17.3 shows a digital representation of the same wave. Notice that the digital version resembles the original, but it is made up of a series of sample rectangles. Each rectangle represents the value of the wave at a particular moment in time. The width of the rectangle sample is the sample period, and the frequency is the number of sample periods in one second.

FIGURE 17.3.

The digital waveform is a series of rectangles. Each represents the value of the waveform a particular time.

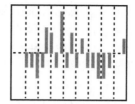

Once again, although this might seem boring and unnecessary, this basic understanding will help you to create and manipulate a digital audio waveform intelligently.

Sample Frequency

You might notice that the series of rectangles resembles the original analog wave (except for the squared-off corners). How closely the digital wave resembles the analog one depends on how many rectangular samples you use. The higher the sample rate, the better the digital copy.

As shown in Figure 17.4, each *sample* is actually a piece of the original wave that is passed through a switch. The sample frequency represents the rate at which the switch is opened and closed. When you convert an analog wave to a digital one, you are basically taking a series of small pieces and stringing all the pieces together over time to represent the original. For this reason, digitizing analog waves is called *sampling*.

FIGURE 17.4.

Passing the analog wave through a switch that is opening and closing at a frequency rate of Z kHz produces this digital waveform.

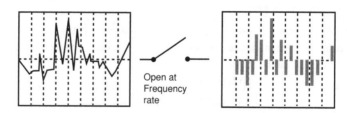

Open at
Frequency
rate

A digitized wave then has a sample frequency (the number of sample periods in one second). Each sample also has an amplitude, the height of the sample from the midpoint in either plus or minus Y direction.

In addition to creating a better quality copy, the more samples you take, the larger the digital wave becomes. Ideally, you want to limit the number of samples and use just enough to make a good copy.

Fortunately, instead of choosing a sample rate and resorting to trial and error, you can use a mathematical theorem from statistical analysis to help you choose. Simply put, the theorem states that you can faithfully reconstruct a waveform if the sample rate is at least twice the highest expected frequency.

The result might not seem very useful, but consider this: The range of human hearing is roughly 20 Hz to 20 kHz. The sample rate of CD quality audio—which we can assume is enough quality for most anything—is 44.1 kHz. As you see, the digital audio on a CD is sampled at roughly twice the range of human hearing, which is more than good enough to guarantee high fidelity.

In practice, you might not know the highest frequency to expect. However, you can make an educated guess. For instance, in a human voice-over, the highest frequency is typically in the 5 kHz range. If you sample the voice at 12 kHz, you should capture a reasonable facsimile.

As you will see, this little bit of knowledge about digitizing audio can make a big difference between noisy, forgettable audio tracks and powerful, full-bodied sound.

Bits, Size, Samples, and Throughput

Another factor that is affected by the choice of sampling frequency is the size of the sampled wave. The higher the sampling frequency, the larger the resulting waveform. But sampling frequency isn't the only factor affecting a sampled waveform's size.

Bits per sample, or the number of bits used to represent the zero to peak amplitude, also affects the sample size. The number of bits per sample also determines how much information is contained in a sample. For instance, in an 8-bit sample, the range can run from 0 to 256, which means that the digital amplitude value can represent 256 discrete levels. In a 16-bit sample, the range runs from 0 to 65,536. A 16-bit sample value can represent over 65,000 levels—a considerably larger range.

In PC's, there are two choices for bits per sample: 8 bits or 16 bits. Choosing 16 bits per sample creates a more high-fidelity wave. An 8-bit sampled waveform is smaller and easier to access and manipulate.

Obviously, the choice of sampling frequencies and bits per sample affects the final size and quality of the resulting sampled waveform. As Table 17.1 shows, raising the bits per sample (or the sampling rate) changes the resulting waveform size by a factor of two. The final size affects some areas of multimedia production significantly. In particular, since large unedited original files must be kept for any required rework, archiving the originals becomes more difficult. Also editing large audio files takes longer and eats up more disk space. Finally, to distribute large files, you must use multiple diskettes and sometimes even multiple CD's—a more expensive and unattractive proposition.

Table 17.1. Raising the sampling rate.

	Sample Frequency		
Bits per sample	*11.025*	*22.05*	*44.1*
8 bits	3.30 MB	6.615 MB	13.2 MB
16 bits	6.615 MB	13.2 MB	26.46 MB

The following formula can be used to estimate the approximate file size when sampling audio.

```
File size/minute = (Sampling rate x bits per sample)/8 x 0.060
```

As shown in Table 17.2, Windows 95 also defines three standard digital audio quality levels. The lowest one, telephone quality, is meant for simple voice annotated memos and voice mail. The next level, radio quality, is better and is usually used for presentations in which both quality and system performance are important. The last level, CD or Authoring quality, is the highest level and is used for creating audio tracks for desktop video or high-quality CD titles. On Windows 95, the standard multimedia output device is CD-ROM, with a throughput of roughly 300 kilobytes per second. CD-ROM can easily support any of the audio formats we have discussed. As the WAV quality level increases, the required throughput in kilobytes per second increases. This means it becomes more difficult to push the audio data through the PC.

Table 17.2. Standard digital audio quality levels.

Quality	Bits/Sample	Sampling Frequency	Throughput Requirements
Telephone	8	11 kHz	10 KB/Sec
Radio	8	22 kHz	21 KB/Sec
CD	16	44.1 kHz	172 KB/Sec

To create high-quality audio on the PC, balancing file size and quality is essential. It's a choice you must make with understanding and experience.

Windows 95 Audio

The robust 32-bit Windows 95 operating system enables your PC to play back audio in multimedia applications and CD titles much more efficiently than in previous versions of Windows. With Windows 95's broad support of Object Linking and Embedding, however, the line between multimedia apps and more traditional productivity applications is quickly disappearing. As it matures, Windows 95 promises to make using and manipulating audio data as easy as cutting and pasting text.

Built-In Sound Support

Like its Windows 3.1 predecessor, Windows 95 offers built-in support for sound. Windows 95 provides system-level tools and applets that make the basic creating, editing, and playing of digital audio straightforward and easy. The well-designed audio tools rival third-party commercial applications in feature set and power.

Assigning Sounds to System Events

As in Windows 3.1, audio sounds can be assigned to specific Windows events such as Windows Startup, Exit, or Exclamation. Double-clicking on the Sounds icon in the Control Panel brings up the Sounds Properties sheet shown in Figure 17.5. To assign a sound to an event, click on the event in the Events image list and select a sound in the Sound edit list. Repeat the process for other events and sounds. For user customization, a set of sound event assignments can be saved using the Scheme/Save As button.

FIGURE 17.5.

The Sounds Properties sheet is used to assign sounds to system events.

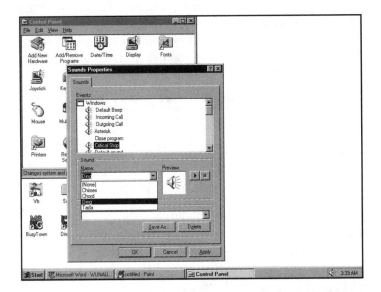

Audio is truly integral to Windows 95. For example, notice the Sound icon in the Taskbar hardware window. As shown in Figure 17.6, left-clicking this icon brings up a small Volume slider, which enables the user to immediately control the audio playback level.

Right-clicking the icon brings up a submenu to access the Windows 95 Volume controls (detailed in the next section), or the system audio properties sheet as shown in Figure 17.7.

FIGURE 17.6.

Left-clicking the Sound icon in the Taskbar hardware window brings up a system master volume control slider.

FIGURE 17.7.

The Audio Properties sheet can be accessed by right-clicking the Sound icon in the Taskbar hardware window and selecting the Adjust Audio Properties item.

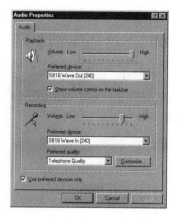

The Volume Control

Unlike Windows 3.1, Windows 95 provides a system-level Volume Control (as shown in Figure 17.8). This centralized control greatly improves on the chaotic approach of 3.1 and manages the different audio lines installed on a computer. The number of audio lines you can mix depends on whether you are using the control for input or output.

FIGURE 17.8.

The Windows 95 Volume Control simulates a professional audio mixer in both look and function.

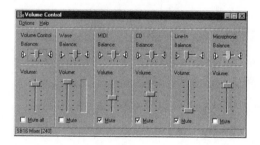

The Windows 95 Volume Control module simulates a professional multichannel audio mixer in both look and function. It contains a Master Volume control, which affects the level of all audio signals, and separate channel controls for WAV digital audio, the internal MIDI synth, CD audio playback, audio Line-In, and the internal PC speaker. In addition to a volume slider, the control includes a Balance slider for panning from left to right and a mute control for cutting. Of course, these software controls function only if the physical audio lines are connected properly. Refer to the documentation of your sound card for appropriate connection instructions.

As in other Windows 95 system applets, the display view of the various volume channels can be customized by the user. Clicking on the Options item of the main menu brings up a submenu that accesses the Volume Control property sheet. As shown in Figure 17.9, this property sheet is used to adjust volumes for playback and recording, as well as providing another control option for future expansion. Individual audio inputs are displayed by checking (or unchecking) the option box in the scrolling device list.

FIGURE 17.9.

Checking items from the scrolling device list on the Volume Control Properties sheet configures the display of the audio volume controls.

The Volume Control applet is an example of the flexibility gained by using Windows 95's extensive OLE (Object Linking and Embedding) capabilities. It can be accessed as a separate application from the Windows Start Programs | Accessories | Multimedia programs group, or called from the various Windows 95 audio playback applications—Sound Recorder, CD player, or the Media Player. These applications also act as OLE servers, making it possible to add multimedia support to any OLE-enabled application.

Audio support is integral to Windows 95. It provides a set of full-featured applets that can be used to record, edit, and play audio—either as stand-alone applications, or as embedded OLE servers.

The Sound Recorder

The Sound Recorder is a 32-bit version of the Windows 3.1 applet. It provides a convenient way for users to record, play, and even edit audio. As shown in Figure 17.10, the VCR-style controls are easy to use and understand. To record, simply click the Record button (the red dot). To stop, click the Stop button (the black square). The recorded wave will appear in the waveform window, where it can be edited.

Although a more powerful audio editor is necessary for professional application, the Sound Recorder provides a fair amount of editing capabilities for the occasional audio user. And, as a bundled utility, it can't be beat.

FIGURE 17.10.

The Sound Recorder provides digital audio capabilities for the occasional audio user.

The CD Player

The Windows 95 CD Player (shown in Figure 17.11) looks and works like a standard consumer audio CD player. It includes advanced features that are modeled on higher-end

CD players, such as random play, repeat, and programmed playback. The programmed play list enables the user to easily define and edit a play sequence that includes Artist and Title information.

FIGURE 17.11.

The CD Player is modeled on a higher-end consumer audio CD machine and features random play, repeat, and a programmable play list.

The Media Player

The Media Player (shown in Figure 17.12) is the Windows 95 general multimedia play application. It also uses a VCR-like interface to control the installed multimedia devices. Despite its rudimentary appearance, the Media Player accesses most devices controlled through the Windows 95 Media Control Interface.

FIGURE 17.12.

The Media Player uses a VCR-like interface to access media devices, which are controlled through the Windows 95 Media Control Interface.

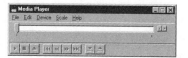

Hardware Issues and Conversion

A sound card must be installed to use the Windows 95 sound capabilities. As detailed in the chapter on Multimedia Installation, the sound card can be configured at Installation time, or through the Control Panel's Add New Hardware Wizard.

After a sound card is installed and configured, you can start sampling—converting audio into digital audio. As Figure 17.13 shows, digital audio on the PC requires two conversions: an ADC, or analog to digital conversion, on the input side; and an opposite DAC, or digital to analog conversion, on the output side.

Most cards include both a microphone input for low-strength signals and a line level input for stronger line-level signals. Plugging a microphone into the microphone input is the simplest method of recording digital audio. Taking the output of an audio tape recorder and feeding it into the line input is another method. As we shall soon see, the choice of sampling method and input level also affects the quality of the digital audio wave.

FIGURE 17.13.

PC digital audio requires two audio signal conversions: An analog-to-digital conversion (ADC) occurs at the sound card's input, and a digital-to-analog (DAC) conversion occurs at the sound card's output.

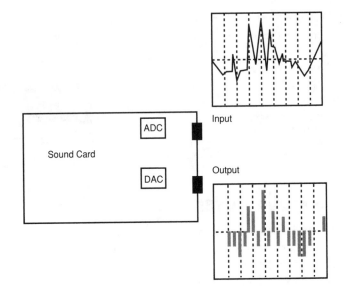

You might be wondering why you would use a tape recorder at all, instead of recording sound *direct to disk*. That's a simple question, but the answer is not so simple. The method you use to record depends on several factors, but the most important has to do with keeping copies of your work. As we've already seen, even good radio-quality digital audio files can get very large. In contrast, you can record radio-quality or better on a fairly inexpensive stereo cassette recorder for pennies. You are more likely to need the hard disk space before you need to record over the audio cassette, so archiving your work on tape is obviously preferable.

If you use recorded music in your multimedia project, it probably comes on CD. In that case, you have two ways to digitize it: Use your sound card's internal CD connection (assuming you have the hardware and have set it up correctly), or use a PCM to WAV conversion program. Because the audio on a CD is already in digital form, it is possible for a program to access and convert the CD audio track into a WAV file. There are several shareware utilities that do exactly that.

CD Audio, Red Book, Yellow Book, and CD+

When you discuss CD audio and multimedia, there are three formats that come into play. Redbook, which is presumably named for the color of the definition standards book, is the standard specification for consumer audio. Digitized music and sound is burned on the CD, which can hold up to 74 minutes of 44.1 kHz sampled 16-bit audio. Nearly all popular music is released on this format, and Windows 95 supports it directly. In fact, the Windows 95 CD Player applet uses the PC's installed CD and emulates the look and function of a standard consumer CD machine.

The Yellow Book standard defines how discs store data. The format allows the same CD peripherals to be used in Windows 95/NT, UNIX, MS-DOS, and Macintosh computers. Although the success of audio CDs is responsible for the wide acceptance and affordability of the CD format, the computer data CD has opened up new fields of information and software distribution, and it promises to open even more as multimedia and interactive CD-ROMs gain momentum. As far as audio and the PC go, Yellow Book CDs are simply data containers for standard WAV files.

A newcomer to the music and CD markets is CD+ (plus). CD+ is a combination of the Red Book audio format and the Yellow Book data format. It is designed to alleviate the problem caused by having a data track on CD audio track 1. In the track 1 data situation, placing a music and data combination CD in an audio player caused the audio circuitry to play the data! The sound of data playing is extremely unpleasant and, when played on a powerful home music system, it is very dangerous to expensive speakers.

The CD+ format places the data on track 0, where audio CDs cannot find it. Windows 95 supports CD+ and similar formats. If the music and entertainment industry solidly back CD+, it could be the format for another new type of musical expression.

The Audio in Digital Video

Another audio source in Windows 95 is the audio track in digital video. The idea of a *track* in any computer data file is more conceptual than physical. Both Quicktime and AVI digital video are, in fact, data holders or containers for *streams* of information (which is yet another conceptual description). On the PC, these containers can also hold an audio WAV file.

To get down to the details, a WAV file is really a RIFF (Resource Interchange Format File). It contains chunks of encoded information with embedded Header Tags. The tags define the type of resource and where things are in the file. An AVI file is also a RIFF file, so adding a WAV to an AVI is fairly straightforward. Because the audio is really an embedded WAV file, digital video does not have its own volume on the mixer or a separate routing control; you control the video volume through the WAV volume control. Quicktime operates on a similar principle, although it is technically very different.

What About MIDI Music?

Our final audio source—and the one that most PC users overlook—is MIDI. MIDI stands for Musical Instrument Device Interface and is universally implemented in the musical instrument manufacturing business.

A MIDI music file is not actually a sound file at all. MIDI is more like sheet music than anything else. A MIDI musical instrument sends out a stream of control codes, which are MIDI messages. If you send these messages back to a MIDI musical instrument or synthesizer card, the original notes and timing are played back. The actual sound, or voice, might differ widely depending on the technology used in the instrument. Many sound cards use FM synthesis to simulate other sounds. The more expensive cards use digitized samples to reproduce the original sounds.

Professional MIDI on the PC is gaining momentum all the time. Windows 95 includes support for a new MIDI implementation called *polymessage MIDI*. This technology solves the problem of MIDI message bottlenecks, in which so many controls messages are sent in the MIDI stream that notes and command events are dropped.

Using Audio I: A Multimedia Memo

In the previous sections, you analyzed digital audio waveforms and examined the effect of various sampling frequencies. You found that there is a relationship between quality and file size for both 8- and 16-bit digitized waves. Now it's time to put your newfound knowledge to work.

The first practical example is to create a multimedia memo. You will build the memo with the Windows 95 "freebie" applets because they are full-featured, OLE-enabled, 32-bit programs. You will also need a sound card with a microphone attached to input.

Begin by opening a new file in WordPad and typing out demo text as shown in Figure 17.14. Save the file as MyMemo.Doc

FIGURE 17.14.

WordPad—Windows 95's OLE-enabled, 32-bit replacement for Notepad and Write—can be used to generate compound multimedia documents.

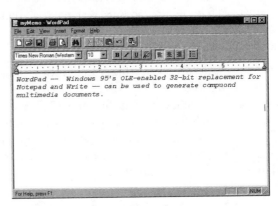

Next, choose Insert New Object from WordPad's Insert menu. Accept the Create New option on the Insert Object dialog box, and scroll down the Object Type list to Wave Sound. (See Figure 17.15.) To close the dialog box, click the OK button. Figure 17.16 shows the open Sound Recorder and the new Sound icon in the WordPad document.

FIGURE 17.15.

In the Insert Object dialog box, select Wave Sound to create and insert a new audio file.

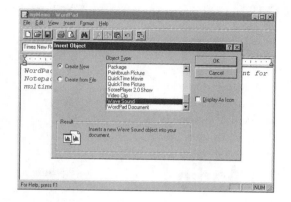

When the Sound Recorder opens, you will record and save a voice annotation. But first you must set the quality level for your resulting audio file. To set recording quality, select Audio Properties from the Sound Recorder's Edit menu. (See Figure 17.16.) Because your memo is an informal note to a friend, choose telephone quality (8 bit, 11 kHz). This is a good choice for informal e-mail applications, because they are reasonably sized and play well even on lower power PCs.

FIGURE 17.16.

Closing the Insert Object dialog box opens the Sound Recorder within the WordPad document.

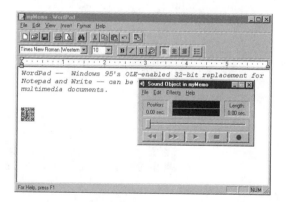

From the Audio Properties sheet, select Telephone Quality from the Preferred Quality list box. (See Figure 17.17.) Also be sure that the Recording level slider is up reasonably high.

Just like on a consumer tape recorder, clicking on the red Record button initiates the recording process. If the microphone is correctly connected, talking into the microphone should create a new audio WAV file. (See Figure 17.18.) To close the Sound Recorder, choose Exit & Return to myMemo from the Sound Recorder File menu.

FIGURE 17.17.

To set recording quality, select Telephone Quality from the Preferred quality list box on the Audio Properties sheet.

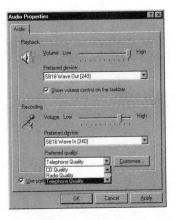

FIGURE 17.18.

Recording a sound wave in Windows 95 is as easy as using a portable cassette recorder.

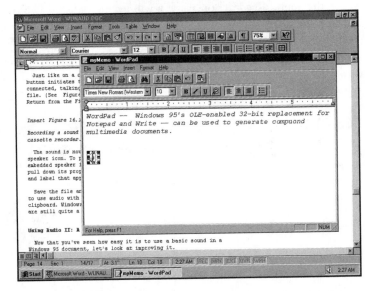

The sound is now embedded in the memo and is represented by the speaker icon. To play the sound, the user double-clicks the embedded speaker icon. As a final touch, select the sound object and pull down its property sheet. From here, the user can change the icon and label that appears on the sound object.

Save the file and send it to a friend. As you can see, it's as easy to use audio with Windows 95 as it is to cut and paste from the clipboard. Windows 95's OLE implementation does the work. But there are still quite a few things you can do to improve your project.

Using Audio II: A Business Presentation

Now that you've seen how easy it is to use a basic sound in a Windows 95 document, let's look at improving it.

Obviously, one way to improve the sound is to use a higher sampling rate. If you redigitize your vocal message using the next Windows 95 supplied level (radio quality), the resulting file would already be a major improvement. Figure 17.19 shows the Audio Properties sheet with radio quality selected.

FIGURE 17.19.

Using Radio Quality audio (8 bit 22 kHz mono) is an improvement over the Multimedia Mail project.

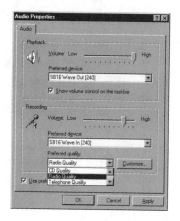

Another improvement would be to use a more formal presentation program, something more impressive than WordPad. Use PowerPoint because it is already OLE-enabled, integrates nicely into Windows 95, and is very easy due to the application Wizards. The PowerPoint Wizard template system works just like the Windows 95 versions. (For the most part, what worked well in Microsoft's Office applications found its way into the operating system enhancements.) Besides, adding audio to PowerPoint is very similar to adding sound to WordPad. For your purposes, let the PowerPoint Wizards build a multiple slide show for you. (See Figure 17.20.) Then you can get back to using audio.

For higher quality audio, it is best to prepare your media elements separately. Even if you are limited to a small production operation (even a one-person crew), breaking a larger multimedia project into stages helps you focus on each stage. For good audio, set your levels and run some tests to determine whether you are getting a good strong signal. If you are using a microphone that came with your sound card, it might be adequate if you record under perfect conditions. Otherwise, consider picking up a better quality microphone or using an external mixer to raise the signal level.

FIGURE 17.20.

PowerPoint is a formal OLE-Enabled Presentation application. Still, inserting audio is remarkably similar to WordPad's method.

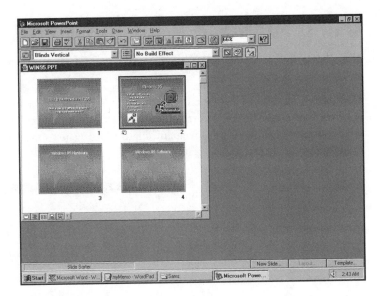

Once again, if you use the resources you already have, you should at least try to set up a good recording environment. Try a few different record settings to check the results. After you get a strong, clean voice recording, you might mix some music under it to mask any rough edges and provide a little ambiance. Sound Recorder lets you mix music with the voice (mix the music wave with the voice wave) using the Mix with File option on the Edit menu. If you are attempting this, you must prepare the music and the voice before the mix. The music level should be about half as loud as the voice, but it all depends on what you are trying to do.

You might also consider adding a short musical opening and closing section, which is commonly known as a *sting*. Short musical stings add a touch of polish to your presentation. Again, these do not have to be long—maybe three or four seconds. They should be just long enough to let the viewer recognize that something is happening. When all the pieces are ready, you begin assembling them.

In PowerPoint, you add sound by adding a Sound Object in the Slide view. As shown in Figure 17.21, the Insert Object dialog box appears when you select Insert | Object from the main menu. Click the Create from File radio button and browse to your first multimedia wave. At this point, you have an option to link the wave file to the PowerPoint file or embed it. If you embed the file, it becomes part of the PowerPoint .ppt file; the PowerPoint file increases in size, sometimes dramatically, but it always goes with your presentation file.

If you link the file, you must distribute the wave file as a separate file with your PowerPoint file. Linking enables you to use the same file—for instance, a musical sting—several times, without increasing the file size. Also the WAV file can be updated and changed separately from the presentation file.

FIGURE 17.21.

Inserting a sound object into PowerPoint is as simple as browsing for the WAV file and clicking OK.

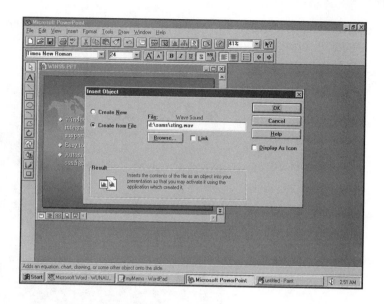

After selecting the wave file in the Insert Object dialog and choosing OK, an icon representing the new object appears on the current slide. (See Figure 17.22.) With this object selected, click the Tools/Play Settings item to bring up the Play Settings dialog.

FIGURE 17.22.

An icon representing the new sound object appears on the current slide. This icon can be hidden while the slide plays.

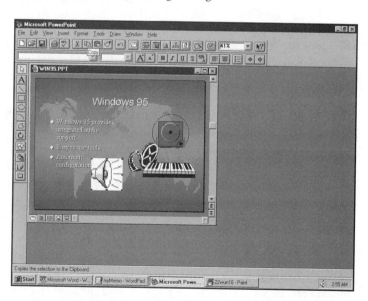

The Play Settings dialog, as shown in Figure 17.23, provides some control over when the sound plays. The Start Play options in particular enable the user to define when a sound (or other multimedia element) plays. A musical sting might be played when a transition starts, whereas a voice annotation might be played after. The Ends Plus text edit box provides a place to add timing (in seconds) before a sound plays. The Hide While not Playing option does not apply to a sound object.

FIGURE 17.23.

The Play Settings dialog box controls when Windows 95 plays a sound file. The amount of timing control is limited however.

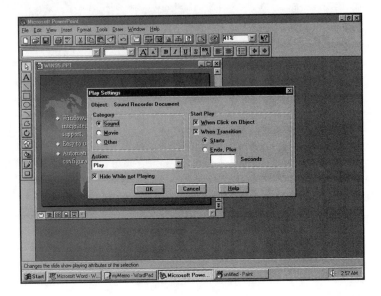

To add more sound to the other slides, simply insert sound objects on each following slide and adjust the Play Settings. As you can see, what separates business presentation audio from voice annotated e-mail is sound quality, preparation of the sound media elements, and playback control.

Using Audio III: Authoring Quality

To move up to the next quality level, Authoring quality, simply apply the same principles that were discussed earlier in the "Using Audio II: Business Presentation" section, but even more rigorously. Figure 17.24 shows some steps you might use in producing a professional multimedia production. Notice that the basic steps can be broken into more and more steps. The figure simplifies much of the process to concentrate on the audio tasks.

Although it is possible to create a business presentation on the fly with maybe only an outline and using unscripted dialog and narration, a quality multimedia production will always have a script. The script enables you to plan changes, develop a storyboard, and create artwork and animation. The script also enables you to record the audio separately and edit it offline.

FIGURE 17.24.

Creating a professional multimedia production involves several steps. Audio production, however, uses the same principles discussed earlier.

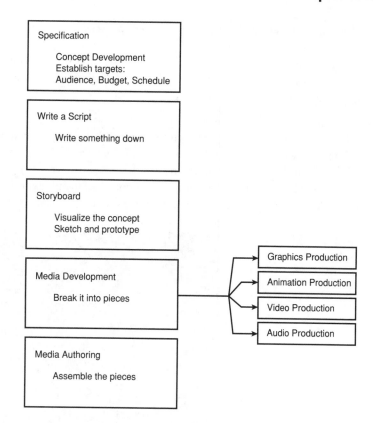

The audio can be recorded directly to disk, or it can be laid down on audiotape and digitized later. As far as sampling rates go, what Windows 95 calls CD quality (44.1 kHz at 16 bits) is not necessarily *authoring quality*. CD-quality audio requires a throughput of approximately 172 kilobytes per second, which is over half the throughput allotted by a double-speed (300 kB/sec) drive. CD audio doesn't leave a lot of headroom for animation or video files.

In practice, 22 kHz 8 bits can provide good quality audio, if you work at it. First, the signal must be strong and clean as possible. Next, digitizing must be correctly setup. Depending on your source material, you might want to add graphic equalization before digitizing. (There are no hard and fast rules, but test runs are mandatory.) A good step is to digitize at 16 bits and let the software convert the signal to 8 bits. This always works better because electrical noise and hum at 8 bits is "louder" than the same noise at 16 bits; the smallest increment (hum) at 8 bits is twice the smallest increment at 16 bits. Of course, adding the extra digitizing step takes extra time and a lot more hard disk space.

However you digitize, the next step is to set up a separate editing session. The editing session is crucial to a finished and polished production, because it gives you time to edit out mistakes or timing differences. (In multimedia, a professional is not someone who doesn't make mistakes, but someone who doesn't show them.) The editing session gives you a chance to prepare the wave files and make them perfect.

A professional production will also use an application program that gives you the ability to synchronize audio. Programs that give you control over audiosyncing usually have some kind of Timeline view to control what happens at any moment. Others such as MacroMind Director (shown in Figure 17.25) are frame-based and control what happens at every frame. Again, creating quality sound for these programs is not basically different than creating sound for our PowerPoint project. In both, preparation is everything.

FIGURE 17.25.

With MacroMind Director's frame-based timing system, the times at which images and sounds play can be controlled very precisely.

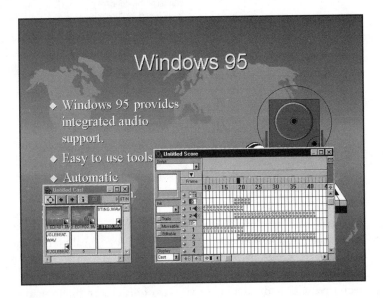

After preparing the audio, you're ready to place it into the production. In Director, the audio is imported as a cast member and becomes embedded into the Director projector file. Other programs might embed waves, link them, or both. The key element in this part of audio production is controlling when the wave plays. Rather than letting the elements play out any way they fall, planning is the key. Figure 17.26 shows one audio track beginning, followed by a new image. Then they both end together—in sync!

FIGURE 17.26.

MacroMind Director allows the multimedia producer to control synchronization of events, which is a must for professional multimedia production.

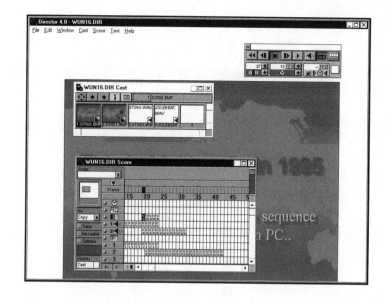

Summary

Sound in Windows 95 has surely improved. With sound support integrated at the system level, sound control is finally consistent and available anywhere it is needed—not just in audio applications. As OLE-enabled applications continue to make the distinctions disappear between *multimedia* and *normal* apps, productivity and communications capabilities promise to rise. With the improved multimedia performance of Windows 95, multimedia titles and games look to be more involving, exciting, and fun.

Today, in Windows 95, multimedia technology might finally live up to its promise. Soon, playing high-performance multimedia might become so easy and commonplace that users will at last be able to concentrate on the content and not the technology.

For multimedia users and developers, that prospect is truly worth waiting for.

Using Video and Animation with Windows 95

18

by Ewan Grantham

Introduction

Whether it's part of one of your favorite games, part of a business presentation you are preparing, or just a particularly interesting rendered cartoon, computer animation has become a part of most systems. The same technology that allows for animation playbacks can also be used to edit and playback video. This chapter covers using these technologies within Windows 95 and guidelines for using them, as well as some of the tools that are available.

Understanding the Different Available Formats

AVI (Video for Windows)

Video for Windows is a joint Intel/Microsoft product that is built into Windows 95. It is a 32-bit version of the product, which means that it runs more efficiently than its 16-bit cousins. This also will result, in most cases, in speedier playback as well. In general, Video for Windows movies run in a 320×240 resolution box; however, the first time you run Video for Windows, it will profile your display to try and determine the best internal setup for maximum speed and performance.

One concern that might affect your decision to use this format if you are developing video or animations is the lack of players for Video for Windows AVI files on non-Windows platforms. The other two standards have players on multiple platforms. However, being tied to Windows also gives Microsoft an edge in tuning the application.

Two examples of Video for Windows screens can be found in Figures 18.1 and 18.2. In Figure 18.1, you see an animated clock (clock.avi), which is used in this case to track the capability of your machine to keep sound in sync with the display.

FIGURE 18.1.

An example of using Video for Windows for animation.

Figure 18.2 shows how the same player and the same technology can also be used for digital video. In this case, you see the sample skiing.avi, which is found in the Media folder under your Windows folder.

FIGURE 18.2.

An example of using Video for Windows for digital video.

Figure 18.2 unfortunately shows one of the downsides of current digital video technology: the fact that the world has a lot more color and resolution than our computers currently can provide. Nonetheless, it still serves as an effective way to make a quick presentation or deliver other video content. Keep these pictures in mind for comparison with the next format.

MOV (QuickTime for Windows)

QuickTime is a standard for creating video and animations that was first developed for the Macintosh computer by Apple. However, a Windows version was produced not long after the product began shipping, and it is now at Version 2. Unlike AVI files, which can be played by the Video for Windows built into Windows 95, MOV files require that you get a copy of the necessary player software to view them. This can be a concern if you are developing animations or videos in this format. These files are relatively easy to find (the MACMULTI forum on CompuServe is one place to find them), and Apple can also license you to redistribute them.

QuickTime has a big plus in its support for multiple platforms, which has made it the most popular standard for movie studios that are distributing clips, as well as for game designers. As with the Video for Windows examples earlier in this chapter, there are two examples of the QuickTime for Windows (QTW) format showing both animations and video.

Figure 18.3 shows an animation in QTW format. Notice that the default behavior is for the file to play from within QTW's Movie Player.

You can see how video is handled by QTW in Figure 18.4, in which a train is roaring down the tracks. Compare these two clips to the AVI clips, and the main difference you'll notice is that the current version of QTW supports somewhat clearer video, although animation seems virtually identical.

Also for comparison purposes, check out the train video as played using Windows' own Media Player as shown in Figure 18.5.

FIGURE 18.3.

An example of using QuickTime for Windows for animation.

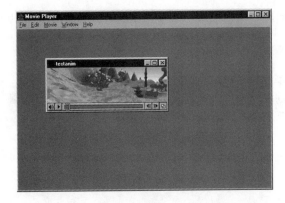

FIGURE 18.4.

An example of using QuickTime for Windows for digital video.

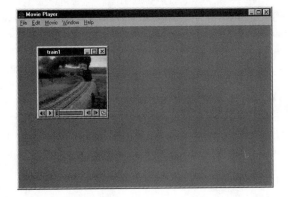

FIGURE 18.5.

An example of using Media Player to play a QuickTime digital video.

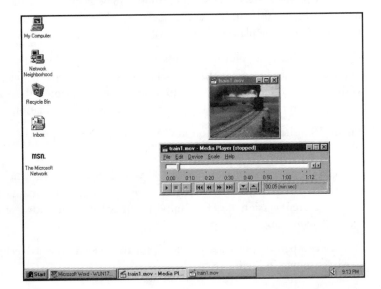

If you are downloading QTW's MOV files from a BBS or online service, you should make sure that they have already been *flattened*. This means that the Resource fork (which the Mac adds to its files by default) has been placed into the main file before distribution. This is something that can only be done on the Mac side, although there are some utilities (which work most of the time) that will place a default resource fork into the file that can be run from DOS/Windows.

The reason that this has to be done is because of a major difference in how the Macintosh and Windows handle files. A Windows binary file has all of its pieces in one contiguous file (ignoring fragmentation). On the Macintosh, binary files have a Data fork where program code and data reside, and a Resource fork where information about dialogs and other *metadata* (data about data) resides. So, for a Mac file to be completely brought over to a PC, you would have to discard the resource fork (which works for Word Processing and Text files) or flatten the file by putting the resource file into the main file.

FLC (Autodesk Animation)

The FLC standard (and its cousin FLI) were designed by Autodesk to support the animation side of its CAD (and other) products. Because the specifications for the standard have been published, there are players for almost every operating system out there. If cross-platform is your main concern, this standard has a lot going for it.

FLC also allows 640×480 screens with reasonable playback, although the 320×240 size used by the other standards is most prevalent. Because of its history, almost all FLC or FLI files that you are likely to download or receive will be animations, but there is the occasional video as well.

Figure 18.6 shows a still frame from a 640×480 animation in FLC format.

FIGURE 18.6.

An example of using FLC to play a 640×480 animation.

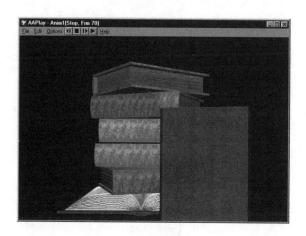

Figure 18.7 shows a video example, also in FLC format.

FIGURE 18.7.

An example of using FLC to play a digital video.

As with QTW files, you need to pick up a separate player to be able to view FLC files. There are literally hundreds of shareware and commercial products available that can playback FLC files. Autodesk has a freeware player—AAPLAY—that can be downloaded from their forum on CIS, and can also be found around the Internet.

Optimizing Windows 95 For Video and Animations

As with any operating system, there are some things you can do that will make video and animation files run better on your system.

1. Have at least 16 MB of RAM on your system to ensure that a significant portion of a video or animation can be loaded at one time.

2. Make sure that you specify a minimum swap file size of at least 24 MB. Again, this makes enough room available in memory to allow a significant portion of the animation or video to be loaded at one time.

3. Make sure that you defragment your hard drive often, and that you run scandisk on it frequently as well.

4. Be sure that your autoexec.bat specifies both a SET TEMP = and a SET TMP = value, that the specified directory exists, and that these refer to a directory that's on a drive with plenty of free space.

5. If you have more than 16 MB of RAM, try setting up a 2 MB or larger RAMDISK into which you initially load your animation or video.

6. Try not to have much else running at the same time. Serial communications taking place during a playback can really make a mess.

7. Make sure your screen saver (if you have one) is turned off.

8. Keep an eye out for newer versions of the players.

9. Make sure to specify your Monitor as well as your Video driver in your Display settings. This allows for some rudimentary color correction.

Optimizing Your Video Card for Video and Animations

One of the best things you can do to help improve performance is to make sure that you have the most current Windows 95 drivers for your video card. If the card's manufacturer doesn't produce a Windows 95 specific driver, see whether one of the generic Windows 95 drivers will work for you. Here are some other things you can do with the video card to improve performance:

1. Disable VESA compatibility if it requires loading a DOS device driver. It doesn't help the animations or video, and it can cause up to a 10-percent slowdown in performance. (If you need this for something else you use, consider using Boot Manager to have alternate startup files.)

2. If your video card can hold more RAM, get it. This usually gives you more choices for resolution and colors, as well as somewhat faster playback.

3. Set your card to 640×480 and 24-bit if it is capable of this. QuickTime in particular will show an improvement by going above 256 colors. Note that if you have a monitor that is larger than 17 inches, you will probably want to go at 800×600. The reason for this is to speed up the redraws; fewer pixels means fewer things to redraw on each scan. Also, because most video and animation is done at 320×240, the apparent size of the window will be larger, which makes it easier to watch.

4. See whether the manufacturer of your video card makes a daughterboard for accelerating graphics and doing video capture. Third-party cards might also be available, but you usually see somewhat better performance by getting both cards from the same manufacturer.

Creating Videos and Animations

At some point, you will probably want to stop watching other folks videos and animations and start producing your own.

For animations, you will need an animation design product (either 2-D or 3-D oriented) that enables you to create frames and objects, set up keyframes (so that you don't have to draw each individual frame by yourself), and output the saved animation to one of the three formats discussed earlier.

For video, you will need to have a video capture board, a video source (camera, VCR, or TV), and software to manipulate the captured images.

Either way, you probably also want some production software to enable you to introduce various effects, synchronize sound to your actions, and mix multiple sources.

Before getting into the details of production, let's first review some basic concepts.

Basic Concepts

Tricking the Eye

Both video and animations use the same tricks on the eye to make motion appear from still images. The rate at which these still images flash before your eyes affects how realistic the motion appears.

Full-motion can be considered to be a playback of 30 frames per second, although even 15 frames per second (fps) can appear to be fluid if there isn't too much movement between frames. The number of frames per second directly impacts the size of the file. A one second playback at 15 fps will have fewer frames and, therefore, be smaller than a one second playback at 30 fps.

Keyframes

In the case of animation, you rarely want to draw each frame individually. Normally, the package you use will enable you to create what are called keyframes. These are reference points that the package then interpolates between to create the necessary frames to move the objects from keyframe A to keyframe B. In addition, you can get a *morphing* package, which enables you to set up keyframes that have an object taking on different appearances, and then fills in the intermediate frames to get there. In either case, you are basically having the package draw the intermediate frames between the frames you have created yourself. The better a package is at doing this, the better the end result.

The trade-off with keyframes is fluidity of motion versus time and effort to create frames. The more keyframes you have, the more fluid the motion will appear to be (in general). But that also means more time and effort that you have to put in as the author of the title. The trick is to find a happy medium between drawing every frame yourself and drawing the first and last frames and letting the computer do the rest.

Video Buffering

One of the big benefits of Windows 95 for animators is the addition of built-in support for off-screen video buffering. This allows an image to be assembled in a video buffer, and then displayed to the user after it has already been put together. This is one of the technologies that has gone into the WinG programming library that Microsoft has developed to help game programmers for Windows 95.

Video-Specific Basics

Because of the nature of video and the tools currently available for handling video on a computer, you will have to get a little more technical than is required with animation. As mentioned earlier, you first need to get some additional hardware to capture/input video into your system. Simple cards allow for the video capture. More expensive cards might also provide video *overlay* so that you can see what's going on as it happens: The video picture overlays (or is overlaid by) the computer-generated display.

Regardless of how the video gets into your system, you start out with a large file and have some pretty large temporary files as you go along, so having plenty of free disk space is a necessity. A good starting point would be to have 200 MB of free space available for a one-minute video capture at 30 fps and 320×240 resolution. You also need software that enables you to mix the video with any computer-generated titles or graphics you have, as well as to edit the stored clip. Sometimes the capture software allows for simple mixes and edits, but usually you want a full editing package.

Finally, you might also want to have a dedicated VCR to enable you to print back to film, as well as create digital videos. Almost all video capture boards also include a Video Out jack.

Compression (Codecs)

One major issue for both Animation and Video is storage, or how to fit enough information on the disk without requiring folks to buy jukebox CD-ROM drives. This is accomplished through various compression schemes known as codecs. Just as modem is short for modulate/demodulate, codec is short for compress/decompress.

The Windows 95 codecs are the same 32-bit codecs that were included with Microsoft Video for Windows 1.1; these codecs give about the same performance under Windows 3.1, Windows NT 3.5, and Windows 95. The following section describes these codecs, as well as other hardware and software codecs for computers running Windows 95.

To begin with, codecs come in two types: symmetrical and asymmetrical. Symmetrical codecs, also called interframe codecs, encode (compress) and decode (expand) video data at about the same speed. This allows symmetrical codecs to provide real-time capture and playback of small (320×240-pixel, 1/4-display) video images. The capture and playback rate, measured in frames per second, depends on the capability of your hardware.

Asymmetrical codecs, or intraframe codecs, use offline compression methods. Offline compression requires a professional-grade VCR or a laserdisc player that sends one video frame at a time to the compressing codec. Asymmetrical compression codecs spend most of their time comparing successive frames of the video sequence so that they can eliminate duplicate information. By doing this, only the changes from frame to frame are stored. Intraframe compression can reduce the video data rate by a factor of 100 or more, depending on the size and quality needed for the compressed digital video sequence. In addition to eliminating duplicate data, asymmetrical codecs also sacrifice some color fidelity for improved compression ratios. The human eye is much more sensitive to brightness than to color (in part because of how the rods and cones in your retina function), so some chrominance information can be discarded to allow more luminance data in the compressed stream.

The main symmetrical codecs are as follows:

- Indeo is a codec developed by Intel Corporation. Indeo has gone through several versions, three of which are found in Windows 95. The early versions provided about the same performance as Microsoft's original AVI codec; the latest version (3.2) gives about the same performance as Supermac's Cinepak, but compression is faster. Cinepak is one of the asymmetrical codecs described later in this section. Intel supplies a moderately priced video-capture adapter card that provides built-in hardware compression for real-time video image capture and compression using the Indeo codec.

- RLE (run-length encoding) is a simple codec primarily used for compressing still bit-mapped images, such as splash screens. RLE works well for simple animations of line art, such as dynamic bar charts, but it is inadequate for digital video.

- Video 1 is a codec developed by Microsoft that is reasonably efficient and provides full-motion video of moderate quality, together with adequate (not quite CD-quality) sound reproduction. This is the codec that is usually used for Video for Windows titles.

- QuickTime is the standard codec for Apple Macintosh computers. The recently released QuickTime Version 2.0 provides somewhat better performance than does Microsoft Video 1 and allows inclusion of MIDI messages, together with the audio and video data streams. As mentioned earlier, you need a separate application to play QuickTime movies on PCs, although after the full QuickTime for Windows software has been installed, you can play the titles with Media Player.

The main Asymmetrical codecs you are likely to see are as follows:

- Cinepak is an asymmetrical codec that was originally developed by Supermac Technologies and licensed by Microsoft from SuperMatch. Cinepak provides the highest quality images and frame rates of all the software-only codecs. To achieve this quality, however, takes very long compression times; 12 to 16 hours to compress 10 minutes of finished video is typical. You can see examples of the Cinepak codec in the *Cinemania '94* and *Dinosaurs* titles from Microsoft.

- DVI (Digital Video Interactive) is an Intel codec that can deliver full-screen, full-motion video. Encoding DVI requires a super-computer, and you need an adapter card to play back DVI-encoded video. DVI was adopted early on by IBM and other firms for use in multimedia kiosks and high-quality video presentations.

Available Tools

Here are some animation tools you might want to consider:

- trueSpace 2.0 (Caligari) is one of the premier animation packages for the PC that is still within the average person's budget. This package enables you to create 2-D and

3-D (emphasis on 3-D) animations and has a built-in modeler for simple object creation. This package allows for both camera-based (the animation path is the path the camera takes around or past the object) and object-based (the animation path is the path the object takes around or past the camera) animation.

■ Visual Reality 1.5 (Visual Software) is less expensive than trueSpace. This package also comes with a heavy-duty modeler, as well as a more focused rendering engine. It only supports camera-based animation.

■ Animation Studio and 3D Studio (Autodesk) are for the professional. These two packages enable you to create animations that rival what you see on those great TV ads. At approximately $4,000, this is not a recommended starting package. The big claim to fame of this package is the support for inverse kinematics, which enables you to define how a hand moves relative to an arm so that, when you move the arm, it handles moving the hand for you. It also has the capability to include add-on modules for doing special effects such as exploding particles.

For Video tools, you may want to look at the following products:

■ VideoBlaster RT300 (Creative Labs) is a video capture board that was created by the same folks who make the Sound Blaster. It has no overlay support and not the best-looking video, but it is one of the best sub-$500 cards around.

■ VideoStar Pro (Diamond Multimedia) is a great video capture/playback card made by your friendly video card makers. This card is somewhat more expensive, but it provides overlay capability as well as a significantly better image. It also includes a playback accelerator so that you get improved performance on what you watch as well as what you produce.

In both cases, you probably should pick up a production package such as Adobe Premiere, which enables you to mix and match material from various sources and edit them together into one clip.

Producing an Example of an Animation Title

To give you an idea of how this all flows together, here is a small animation project. Begin by laying out a short script or narrative of what you want to have happen. This usually helps you to identify what items, objects, or people you will have in your animation.

In this case, we'll do a 3-D animation, so the next step is to load a modeler to create the objects that are going to be used. Figure 18.8 shows the modeller from Visual Reality being used to create an airplane.

Next, the image is brought into a Renderer to give it a 3-D appearance and to add a suitable background, as shown in Figure 18.9.

FIGURE 18.8.

An example of creating a 3-D model.

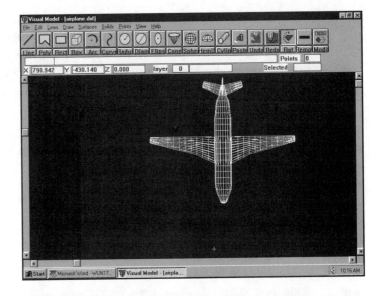

FIGURE 18.9.

An example of rendering a model for an animation.

Finally, you move the "camera" around to create an animation of a plane flying past by defining several keyframes. Figure 18.9 might be one of the keyframes around the middle of the animation. You could then have a beginning keyframe in which the plane appears to be further away from the viewer by making the plane smaller, and an ending keyframe in which all that can be seen is the tail so that the plane appears to grow and come toward the viewer. The sensation you are trying to create for the viewer is of a plane that is coming toward the camera. As the plane approaches, it passes beneath the viewer, and the final frame is the last bit of the plane that is seen before it disappears from view. This could also be a good place for a reverse shot where you pan the camera to see the plane flying away from you at this point.

At this point, you have your package Render To File, which directs the software to render each frame needed for the animation to disk. Even on a fast Pentium, this process takes several minutes for each second of animation.

When you have one scene completed, you should create the next scene, and then the next. This is where a package such as Adobe Premiere can help by allowing you to string the scenes together into a single animation file. So, using the previous example, you could then have a scene of the airplane coming in for a landing, and another scene of a modeled human or some luggage coming off the plane. Then, pull in all three of the scenes to create one scene where the plane flies by, lands at the airport, and something gets out.

Producing an Example of a Video Title

For this sample video, a video tape from a skiing trip is being used. The first step is to make sure that the video card has been properly installed, and then hook up either a VCR or the camera itself into the Video In port of the capture card you are using. Depending on the card, you might have a separate program for capturing, or you might use a program such as Adobe Premiere, which has capture built in. Figure 18.10 shows what the capture control looks like.

FIGURE 18.10.

A look at the Capture Control from Adobe Premiere.

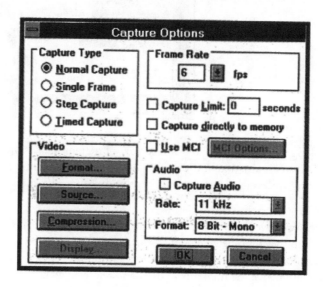

In this case, the output of a camcorder is connected using an RCA plug attached from its Video Out port to a Video Blaster's Video In port. Then, using the control shown in Figure 18.10, a segment is defined for capture.

Here is one example wherein having a Video Overlay board would have been helpful because it would have been possible to watch the Video being captured as it was played.

To capture the sound from the video, another RCA plug is needed to hook the Audio Out from the Camcorder into the Audio In of the board. Capturing the Audio at the same time makes it easier to keep things in sync, but also adds another 200–300 KB of disk space per second captured to your free space requirements.

After the raw video has been captured to disk, it's time to edit it to show what you want. Again, to do this, you should bring up a package that lets you integrate both video and computer graphics. Figure 18.11 shows an initial load of some of the parts into Premiere.

FIGURE 18.11.

A look at an example video project.

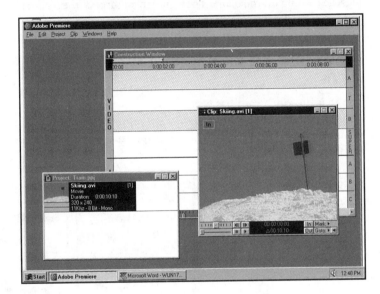

Looking at this example, you can see how a program such as this enables you to integrate various clips of animation and/or video, add graphics elements, and even work with tracks. By working with tracks, you can mix clips and use transition effects to go from one clip to the next.

When you have all the elements together, simply instruct the program to create an AVI or MOV file with the combined elements for playback or to distribute to others. The specifics of how this is done vary from program to program, but in general it is simply a matter of telling the program to save the final mix to disk, and selecting what format from an option requestor.

Summary

Whether you are creating animations, videos, or combinations of the two, you will use similar technologies to build and distribute your work. Depending on your audience and your requirements, you'll want to pick a format (AVI, MOV, or FLC), decide upon a codec for compression (if your tool gives you a choice), and then start putting together the various scenes into your final title.

Multimedia Authoring with Windows 95

19

by
Ewan Grantham

Multimedia publishing has been gaining ground since the Apple Macintosh was introduced in the early 1980s. Even then, it was possible (at a price) to put sound, video, and programs together. As machines have become cheaper in price, more powerful, and the operating systems that run them have incorporated better support for these elements, the multimedia market has exploded.

The definition of exactly what multimedia is depends on who is doing the defining. Certainly, a game such as DOOM or DESCENT has graphics and sound, but usually these aren't classified as multimedia titles. In general, this chapter considers multimedia to be computer programs that use hypertext, graphics, and other additions to help inform or entertain.

Windows 95 can run programs created by three of Microsoft's multimedia authoring systems: WinHelp, Viewer, and MediaView. This chapter will cover all three, with an emphasis on WinHelp because it has changed with Windows 95. Another networkable standard is HTML, which is the language used for the World Wide Web. There are also third-party tools for creating multimedia titles (such as IconAuthor and MacroMedia Director), but they are not covered in this chapter.

Finally, some general tips on design and distribution of your project should help you decide on which tool to use, as well as give you some ideas for creating a better title.

Publishing For Windows 95

WinHelp 4

Microsoft Windows Help (also known as WinHelp) is the standard program for the display of online Help files for programs that have been written for the Windows operating system. Because it is a standard piece of Windows, it has also emerged as a popular platform for delivering multimedia and hypertext titles. Along with the other improvements in Windows 95, Microsoft has reworked the Help engine to create WinHelp 4, which has been designed to be easier to use for the end-user and more flexible for the developer. Following is a list of the most significant changes between the Help engine in Windows 3.1 (also used in Windows for Workgroups and Windows NT versions prior to 3.51) and Windows 95. The same engine is also being used in the new Windows NT 3.51 release so that you can create one file for both platforms.

Product Changes

Full-text search with phrase searching (similar to that in Multimedia Viewer 2.0).

Graphics having up to 16 million colors without an additional DLL.

.AVI, .WAV, and .MIDI files without an additional DLL.

Separate window with an exploding table of contents (like the MSDN CDs).

Can display up to nine secondary windows at a time.

Configurable button bars in secondary windows.

Auto-sizable secondary windows to match the length of the topic text.

Authorable buttons (the kind that depress when you click them).

Can run macros when a user selects author-defined keywords from the index.

Integrates multiple .HLP files seamlessly.

New training card feature for running things step-by-step.

Programming Changes

The Help compiler (HCW) is now a Windows application—no more shelling to DOS to compile.

Provides 26 new macros.

Supports curly quotation marks, em and en dashes, and em and en spaces.

Number of permitted build tags is now 16,383.

Number of permitted entries in the [MAP] section of the .HPJ file is now 16,000.

The size limitation for a hot spot has been raised to 4,095 characters.

The [WINDOWS] section of the .HPJ file can have 255 window definitions.

All limits for macro length and nesting have been removed. Macro length is limited only by the amount of local memory available at the time the macro is invoked (typically 10 KB to 20 KB), and nesting is limited to the stack size.

A Help file can reference as many as 65,535 unique bitmaps.

Font names can be as long as 31 characters (were limited to 20), and you can now use the Wingdings font as well as other fonts.

Many of these changes are optional. In other words, you can take advantage of them or not take advantage of them, depending on the needs of your users and your own preferences. To support all these changes, Microsoft has changed the tools that are used to create Help files, as well as added some files to both the creation process (.CNT or CONTENTS file) and the runtime process (.GID files).

To give you an idea of what WinHelp 4 looks like, take a look at Figures 19.1, 19.2, and 19.3. Figure 19.1 is the opening screen of a WinHelp 4 file. At this point, there isn't much to indicate that this is not a WinHelp 3.1 file. Clicking on the Contents button shows the first major difference.

Figure 19.2 shows what the new Contents dialog looks like. The Help file's first or *parent* topic is shown as a book. Topics that are subordinate to it are shown as pages with question marks. Notice that subtopics can also have subtopics, which is why the topics are shown as books. You can expand or collapse headings by simply clicking on them. You can also use topics to provide jumps to multiple WinHelp files in a way that is transparent to the user. If a particular component of the program and its assigned Help file haven't been loaded, WinHelp automatically drops all references to the topics in that Help file from the Contents dialog.

Clicking the Find tab brings up the next major difference.

FIGURE 19.1.

The WinHelp Help file.

FIGURE 19.2.

*The WinHelp Help file's
Contents tab.*

Full-text search was one of the most requested features for this version of WinHelp. Figure 19.3 shows how the dialog appears that enables you or your user to find topics with specific words or phrases. This makes it much easier for the programmer, who doesn't have to remember to create an index or keyword for every possible combination of important terms. It is also easier for the user, who can find what he or she wants more directly.

FIGURE 19.3.

*The Sample Help file's full-
text search tab.*

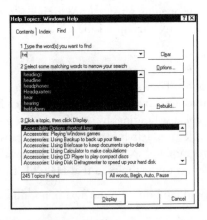

Although the sample file shows a hypertext help file, a WinHelp file can present online information using the following elements:

- Text with many fonts, type sizes, and colors
- Graphics, both for illustration and to serve as a hot spot jump
- Hypertext jumps for linking information
- Pop-up windows for presenting context-sensitive help or additional text and graphics
- Secondary windows for presenting information in a controlled format
- Keyword search capability for finding specific information
- Multimedia elements such as voice and video

To build WinHelp 4.0 files, you will need the following software on your computer:

- Microsoft Help Compiler version 4.0 (HCW.EXE and HCRTF.EXE)
- Microsoft Hotspot Editor version 2.0 (SHED.EXE)
- Microsoft Multi-Resolution Bitmap Compiler version 1.1 (MRBC.EXE)
- Microsoft Windows Help version 4.0 (WINHELP.EXE)
- A text file editor that handles rich-text format (RTF)

The Microsoft files are included with the Win32 SDK for Windows 95 or Windows NT. Most third-party WinHelp authoring packages that support Windows 95 also have the compiler and the other tools.

At this time (mid-1995), there are only two commercial third-party tools that support the creation of WinHelp 4 titles. These are Blue Sky's WinHelp Office (which includes RoboHelp and a video on creating WinHelp files), and Olson Software's Help Writer's Assistant. What is unique about both of these tools is that not only can you build both WinHelp 3.1 and WinHelp 4 files from them, but they both allow you to import your old Help files into the tool so that you can add, change, or delete material and build a new WinHelp file. Here is the contact and pricing information for these products:

Blue Sky Software
WinHelp Office
$599 (U.S.)
Toll Free: 800-677-4WIN
International: 619-459-6365
FAX: 619-459-6366

Olson Software
Help Writer's Assistant (Professional)
$199 (U.S.)
Phone: +64 6 359 1408
FAX: +64 6 355 2775
CIS: 100352,1315

Tools such as these really help in complex environments where keeping track of multiple jumps or building complex .HPJ or .CNT files would take a lot of time. Also, if you have to write Help files but don't really want to be forced to do all the RTF codes and building of HPJ and CNT files by hand, a third-party tool will come in handy.

Topic files for WinHelp files must be created in RTF (rich text format) to be properly compiled by the Help compiler (HCW). If you are familiar with RTF coding, you can prepare and save your topic file in any word processor or text editor that can create an RTF file. Coding RTF by hand, however, is time-consuming. Most WinHelp authors prefer to create the topic file within a word processor (either alone or as part of an integrated third-party tool), format the topic text the way they want it to look, and then save the topic file as an .RTF file. For this, you need a word processor that can do the following:

- Save files in rich text format (RTF)
- Insert custom footnotes
- Support single and double underlining
- Support hidden text

Microsoft Word for Windows (version 1.1 or later) and Microsoft Word (version 5.0 or later) can produce compatible .RTF files. The Microsoft WordPad program that comes with Windows 95 does not create compatible RTF files. Also note that although you can author WinHelp files on any version of the Microsoft Windows NT operating system, WinHelp version 4.0 does not run on versions 3.11 and 3.5, but only on Windows NT 3.51 or later.

After your RTF file has been generated, it is compiled with the HCW compiler—along with any graphics, sound, or other multimedia files you have specified—into the final HLP file. It is this final HLP file, along with its accompanying CNT file, that you distribute to your end users.

For more information about the specifics of creating WinHelp 4.0 files, be sure to pick up Sams Publishing's *Programming Windows 95 Unleashed*, which devotes an entire chapter to the subject.

Multimedia Viewer

Viewer is Microsoft's original multimedia authoring system. Unlike Windows Help, which was not designed to be a multimedia system originally, Viewer was designed from the start for electronic publishing and multimedia delivery.

Viewer was created after WinHelp 3.1 and before WinHelp 4, so it bridges the difference between the systems. It has some features that are not available in WinHelp (most notably the use of panes), but it is still very similar in terms of creating a title and some of its capabilities. WinHelp source files can be compiled by Viewer with very few changes.

As with WinHelp, most of the information for a Viewer title is entered by using Word for Windows in conjunction with Viewer programs that let you conduct technical operations, such as multimedia actions, through simple dialog boxes. Figure 19.4 shows the Project Editor for Viewer, which controls how Viewer applications are put together.

FIGURE 19.4.

The Multimedia Viewer Project Editor.

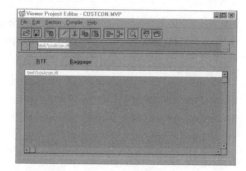

Viewer can be used to develop computer-based training and many other types of applications. It is especially suitable for references such as encyclopedias or more advanced multimedia applications. Microsoft used Viewer to produce its original versions of Bookshelf, Cinemania, and Encarta. Viewer has been optimized to create applications that will be distributed on a CD-ROM disc, while providing fast access to the material on the disk.

Viewer is a cross-platform system. The Viewer toolkit can create applications that run under Windows and Macintosh systems (although the Macintosh versions require the addition of a third-party toolkit). Viewer's Windows runtime programs can be distributed without paying any royalties.

Viewer applications can present the user with a combination of text, graphics, sounds, animations, and movies. Viewer applications offer the following:

■ A variety of display options, including master and secondary windows, panes (sections of windows), nonscrolling regions, and pop-up windows.

■ Many different ways to navigate through the application, including text and graphic hot spots, buttons that allow browsing through related application sections, a history list that permits returning to previous sections, and a keyword index.

■ The capability for users to print material from the application, or copy it directly to other programs.

■ The capability for users to annotate the application.

■ Full-text search capabilities that you can easily customize.

■ A configurable user interface incorporating standard or custom menus, buttons, and graphic elements that execute commands when clicked.

■ Functions that make multimedia events easy for you to create and the user to use.

A Viewer application is built as a group of related topics. A topic is the basic building block of a Viewer application. All of the material in a Viewer application, from the table of contents to menus and user instructions, is organized into topics. A topic can contain any combination of text, pictures, audio, animations, or movies. If a topic is too big to display all at once, scrollbars are automatically added to let the user see the rest of the material.

References to other topics are known as hot spots. A hot spot is a word, phrase, or picture that you design within the application to link to another topic or perform some action you define.

The general process of going from topic to topic is known as *navigation*. Because you can allow the user to follow an unstructured path through the application's material, you must help the user avoid getting lost. One way to do this is to provide consistent topic headings that help the user understand where the current topic fits into the overall application. Viewer also provides the user with a list that shows the titles of the last 40 topics displayed. The user can return to any of these topics by double-clicking on the desired entry. This is similar to the History button in WinHelp.

Viewer applications are displayed in a main window and can use one secondary window at a time. The programmer can set the size and position of both windows, and the user can adjust their sizes and positions. Each window can also be divided into multiple panes. There can only be one master pane, which is where topics are normally displayed. Topics can be displayed in any other pane, and the size and position of each pane can be controlled programatically. The user cannot adjust panes. Panes are useful for information that should remain visible along with the current topic, such as user interface controls, menus, or pictures. A nonscrolling region can also be created in topics that are displayed in the master pane. This stays displayed as the user scrolls through the remaining material in that topic. This is useful for headings or user interface controls.

A hot spot can also cause a pop-up window to be displayed on top of the normal window. A pop-up window can contain text or pictures, and it disappears when the user clicks anywhere outside the window. Pop-up windows are usually used to display definitions or explanations, but they can serve many purposes. Pop-up windows can even contain other hot spots.

The Viewer toolkit also makes it easy to include multimedia elements in your application. You can choose between two types of sound files: MIDI files or wave files. You can also play movie files that are created from video cameras or video tapes, or animations that are created on a computer. Viewer makes it easy to control playing a multimedia file. You can play the file automatically, or let the user start, pause, or stop the file. A simple dialog box in the Viewer toolkit lets you choose a multimedia file and set some basic options. Buttons bring up other dialog boxes that create a caption or define buttons that let the user control the playback.

Viewer also makes it easy to make your graphics look their best. You can use 8-bit (256-color) graphics, and you can decide whether you want them dithered or not on 16-color systems. Graphics can be used that are created in one video resolution such as VGA, and they will still display properly on other systems such as SVGA without doing anything special.

As mentioned earlier, Viewer is designed to create large applications. In fact, these applications are expected to be distributed on CD-ROM rather than disks. The following list of Viewer limits will help you appreciate how large and complex a Viewer application can be:

- A Viewer application file can be as large as 2 gigabytes.
- The number of topics in an application is limited only by disk space.
- Each RTF file can contain 32,767 topics.
- Up to 512,000 topics can be indexed if you use topic groups.
- Up to 10,000 files can be stored in Baggage.
- Up to 4 billion aliases can be used.
- Each topic can contain a total of 256 nonscrolling regions, scrolling regions, panes, and pop-up windows.
- Each application can contain 200 topic groups and word wheels.
- Each application can have 255 keywords, 255 windows, 255 panes, and 255 custom pop-up windows.
- There are two basic parts to Viewer: an authoring system that you use to create a Viewer application, and a runtime system that runs the application. You distribute the runtime programs with your application, usually using a setup tool to make sure the runtime program is installed properly on the user's system. The general steps to create a Viewer application are as follows:

    1. Design the application function and interface: Decide how you want to present information, select the material to be presented, decide how users will move through the application, and design the user interface.

    2. Design the details: Create the material to be presented and the topics it will belong to, designate groups of topics, and design menus.

    3. Create the document file: Create your text and the commands needed to display pictures, play sounds or movies, and perform other desired actions. This file is the heart of your application. It is created using Microsoft's Word for Windows. One of the programs in the Viewer authoring system, the Topic Editor, makes it easy to create nearly all of the special entries that control your application. It lets you enter most of the necessary information through easily understood dialog boxes.

    4. Compile the files: Execute the Viewer compiler to create a Viewer application file from your document and supporting files. This also creates a log file that lists any errors that were found.

    5. Test the application.

    6. Distribute: Prepare your files for distribution, including creating the setup program that will install the files on the user's system.

Viewer can also be extended through external programs in several ways:

- The embedded window interface is well-documented, which enables you to use this technique to develop additional capabilities.

- The standard search operation uses internal functions that are well-documented so that programmers can develop customized search dialog boxes and operations.

- An API function is provided that allows external programs to start a Viewer session and issue commands to control that session.

- A programming interface is provided that allows a program to be informed of actions taken by a Viewer application, such as changing the size of a window, displaying a new topic, or scrolling within a topic.

- Functions in external libraries (DLLs) can be defined and executed within Viewer just like internal commands. These can include Windows APIs, other commercial DLLs, and custom-written functions unique to your application.

With this introduction, you can see how Multimedia Viewer might fit into your plans for creating multimedia titles. To use it for this purpose, you need to get hold of the Viewer files, which can be done either through subscribing to the Microsoft Developers Network with a Level 2 subscription, or by sending an e-mail request to mmdinfo@microsoft.com. Include your shipping address (not a P.O. box) and phone number.

MediaView 1.3

MediaView 1.3 is Microsoft's latest offering for creating a multimedia title. Unlike the previous two toolkits, MediaView requires that you have either Visual C++ or Visual Basic in addition to the toolkit. This is because MediaView is a set of libraries and tools that help create the content and drive the design of the player application; but ultimately, the MediaView author is responsible for creating a player for the title. With WinHelp and Viewer, you primarily use the player that Microsoft has already created.

You use the MediaView libraries to develop a Windows-based application that can play your multimedia title through *media views*. A media view is essentially a window programmed to display multimedia using the MediaView libraries.

A MediaView title and title player built with MediaView can do the following:

- Print one or more topics.
- Display an index to the topics.
- Perform a search for any word in the application.
- Display topics containing text, graphics, video, audio, and other media.
- Quickly move from topic to topic at a stroke of the keyboard or a click of the mouse.
- Select text for copying or for looking up in an index.

■ Change the way text looks while playing the title.

■ Change the magnification ratio of the display.

■ Anything else the author desires, because the player is ultimately in the hands of the creating programmer.

MediaView integrates large quantities of text, images, and multimedia data into an easily accessible package. MediaView can create many types of information titles, and although the specific authoring tasks required for a project depend on the features that are implemented, most projects have many tasks in common. A MediaView project consists of a number of source files, including topic files, images, multimedia sequences, and other data. To keep track of the files, you create a project directory and project file. The project file lists options for the project, identifies the source files to include in the title, and defines such title resources as windows, search fields and data types, and external commands.

The project file is a text file divided into sections containing project options used by the MediaView compiler. Sections are identified by a bracketed title and contain lists of options (lines of data starting with a label and an equal sign) or lists of information (such as filenames).

Here are the tools you'll need to create a MediaView application:

■ A word processor capable of saving topic source files in rich text format (RTF) and an ASCII text editor for the title's project (.MVP) file. For topic files, you can use any editor that can save RTF files that are compatible with the MediaView title compiler.

■ Any tools you need to create media files for your title, such as a bitmap editor, a sound file editor, Video for Windows, and so on.

■ The hot spot editor for hot spots on graphics, MVSHED.EXE.

■ The MediaView title compiler, MVCC13x.EXE.

MediaView is similar in many ways to Viewer but was designed to split the data management layer away from the user interface and navigation portions of Viewer. This allows a MediaView programmer to do pretty much what he or she wants to with the MediaView runtime engine. A programmer must custom-code his own browser in C++ or Visual Basic and handle the user interface and navigation functions that were previously handled by Viewer. A programmer must also provide macro support and translation because MediaView does not provide these services.

Although MediaView is fairly new, it is the direction that Microsoft has chosen for developing its future multimedia titles, and it is also serving as the basis for the distributed multimedia titles being created for the Microsoft Network (MSN). As with Viewer, the MediaView 1.3 tools can be obtained from mmdinfo@microsoft.com or on the MSDN Level II CD-ROMs.

HTML

HTML (HyperText Markup Language) was designed to enable hypertext titles to be used remotely on the Internet. Changes to the definition of the language have allowed the inclusion of graphics and other multimedia elements into current documents, which makes HTML one of the most widely used multimedia formats currently available.

One of HTML's biggest advantages is that there are readers for virtually every computer platform available. This means that as long as you stick to "standard" HTML (in other words, you don't use the extensions that are specific to a particular browser), your application will run and look virtually the same on a Windows machine, an OS/2 machine, a Macintosh, a UNIX box, and so on.

Creating HTML is as easy or as complex as you care to make it. One of the cheapest, and fairly easy, ways to create an HTML document is using one of the many templates available for creating HTML in Microsoft Word for Windows. Figure 19.5 shows one document being created using the ANT_HTML template that can be found on CompuServe and on the Internet.

The HTML language is currently being revised to make it even easier to incorporate graphics, audio, and video files. Because the files can be read locally as well as remotely, the use of HTML for multimedia titles is sure to increase.

As mentioned earlier, you need to obtain a browser to read HTML documents. The two main players at this point are Mosaic (NCSA Labs) and Netscape (Netscape Communications). Single users can obtain these browsers for free from either the Internet or one of the online services. In addition, many of the online services (CompuServe, AOL, and so on) have their own browsers that work equally well.

FIGURE 19.5.

An HTML document (RADIUS magazine) being created in MS Word with a template.

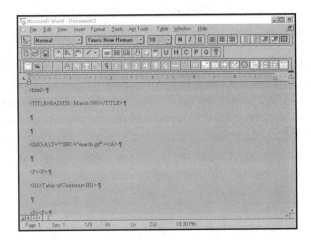

Design Considerations For a Successful Title

Because a multimedia title is composed of all sorts of diverse elements, you don't want to just jump into creating a file. You want to spend some time going through a design phase. This should include defining the contents and goals for the file. In the following subsections are some of the questions you need to consider.

Who Is Your Audience?

In other words, who are you planning to have view your completed application? A multimedia title that is intended to be used as an internal training system for a Fortune 500 company will have vastly different goals than a program designed to teach someone how to play the piano.

Knowing your audience helps you to make decisions on what is important to cover and what you can afford to leave out if space becomes a problem. It also helps you decide whether sound is more important than video, or maybe your application simply needs some hot-spot graphics.

You need to also decide how you know who your audience is. In other words, you don't want to invest a lot of time (and money) on a project based purely on who you think your audience is. So you will need to create a method for interviewing potential users or viewers on what they are looking for, and what they would want from something like you are planning to build.

For example, you might think that a multimedia magazine about famous artworks would be popular. But after talking with people you have identified as potential readers you might find that there is plenty of interest, but only if the price is so low you can't afford to produce the title.

You could then alter your focus to better fit what the folks you identified are willing to pay, or figure out a different profit scheme (perhaps selling advertising space to museums), or move on to a different topic.

The same holds true for games. You may have the latest, greatest version of some game ever designed, but if no one is interested in playing it because your ships look like bottle rockets...

What Platforms Will You Support?

When you know your audience, you will be in a good position to decide what operating systems and hardware should be able to run your multimedia title. In general, you want the audience to determine what tools you use. However, sometimes the tools you have available will constrain which platforms you will target.

When you are creating a multimedia title under Windows 95, it doesn't mean you can only support Windows 95 audiences. All of the tools discussed above have some way to be ported to at least the Mac; HTML can be run on any GUI platform.

One additional issue to consider if you do choose the HTML format is whether each platform you plan on reaching has the appropriate players for your multimedia elements. If you include sound files, but only Windows has a player for that sort of sound file, you're drastically limiting your audience.

How Will You Distribute Your End Product?

This usually comes down to one or more of three choices: electronic distribution, disk-based distribution, and CD-ROM distribution. Each of these methods has its advantages and disadvantages. Your decision will be heavily dependent on your answers to the two previous questions.

Again, the choice you make here will also have an impact on which tools you can use, and vice versa.

Summary

As this chapter has shown, there are a number of easy and fairly inexpensive ways to create your own multimedia title for Windows 95. Whether you choose WinHelp or HTML, the proper design of your title and the judicious use of graphics, video, animations, and hypertext will make your product a hit.

V

Connecting to the Outside World

If you thought the multimedia features of Windows 3.x were a hot topic, just wait until you get your modem fired up and start checking out the landscape beyond your desktop. This section of the book gets you started by giving you the information you need to get out and go online.

Ever since Ward Christensen wrote CBBS, the first bulletin board software for CP/M computers back in the late seventies, there has been a slow but steady growth in online services. Although only 4 percent of American computer users currently subscribes to a commercial online service, there is almost certainly such a subscription in your future.

CompuServe, America Online, Prodigy, and the new kid on the block—The Microsoft Network—are the major online services available in the United States. For a small monthly subscription fee and usually an hourly connect fee, you can find just about anything you might have an interest in. Whether you want to make a reservation on an airline, find recipes for eggplant, find out how to fix your car, download the latest device drivers, or just exchange information with other folks who have opinions too, the online services are simple to use and cost-effective.

Add the fact that each of the services is capable of acting as your onramp to the Internet, a worldwide computer network the size of which simply dwarfs the combined resources of all four major services, and you can see that there is indeed something for everyone at the other end of your modem line.

CompuServe, America Online, and Prodigy are covered in Chapter 20, "Windows 95 and Commercial Online Services."

There are other, some say preferable, ways of getting Internet access than using one of the commercial online services. Whether you access the Internet using an Internet service provider or you use one of the commercial services as an onramp, the information contained in Chapter 21, "The Internet," gives you the jump start you need to get cruising. Surf's up!

Windows 95 and Commerical Online Services

20

by David Geller

What Is an Online Service?

They arrive every month and are often attached to the popular computer magazines that you subscribe to or see blanketing bookstores and newsstands. They are the free trial packs for the popular online services: CompuServe, America Online, and Prodigy. Modem manufacturers also bundle similar offers with their products, providing buyers with a great way to take advantage of their new 14,400-baud or 28,800-baud fax/data modems.

Online services such as CompuServe, America Online (AOL), and Prodigy offer numerous reference materials, interactive chat areas, and of course, electronic mail. They also now provide access to the World Wide Web (WWW or Web for short), which is hosted on the Internet. Though Microsoft will undoubtedly impact this market with its entry into the online business, there will still be millions of customers for whom CompuServe, AOL, and Prodigy will play an important role.

All of the major online providers offer a range of useful, informative services including the following:

- **Electronic mail (e-mail):** E-mail enables you to communicate with both friends and business associates. It also helps bridge the gap between the home office and the traditional workplace, providing flexibility and, in many cases, increased productivity.

- **News:** The news carried by the online services is often from the very same sources that feed your local and national radio and television news programs. Reading news online is sometimes more dynamic and certainly more customized. And because of the computerized nature of the interface, online news enables you to search for topics that fit your criteria.

- **Databases:** Projects for school and work can benefit from additional information. Searching online using commercial databases can save you time and help you to discover new information. Databases are essentially online libraries that provide you with information at your fingertips 24 hours a day.

- **Online shopping:** Although it has been promoted for years, online shopping is on the verge of becoming more accepted. Shopping through CompuServe, AOL, and Prodigy offers you not only diversity and convenience but also security in terms of billing and credit card transactions.

- **Weather (and satellite images):** The traditional television weather report has a new competitor in the online services. Whether you're a fan of the outdoors, a private pilot, or simply planning a big outdoor event, you'll want to take advantage of accurate and detailed weather information provided online.

- **Interactive conversation and chat areas:** It isn't as lonely in cyberspace as you might have believed. Online chat areas make it easy to communicate with both individuals and entire groups of fellow online users. Subjects can range from the technical to the personal and there's almost always someone there that you can communicate with 24 hours a day, seven days a week.

■ **Product support areas:** If it's late in the evening or during a weekend and you're in need of technical support, you might find that a company's technical support department isn't available via the telephone. However, online support is almost always available, and the amount and variety of information might help you through a tough problem.

■ **And more:** The beauty of online services is that they're always changing—mostly to meet the needs and desires of their subscribers. The largest online providers have recently begun supporting the Internet, allowing customers to *surf* the Web. They've also engaged in a comprehensive effort to increase local access and support higher speed modems; in some cases, they now support ISDN.

Online services have been around for many years. Of the services covered in this chapter, CompuServe is the oldest. It was started in 1969 and began its online information services in 1979. America Online (AOL) was formed in 1985 but has quickly risen to the number two spot in terms of customer base. Prodigy, a joint venture between Sears and IBM, made its national debut in 1990. However, it has only been in the last few years that all three providers have seen a dramatic increase in the number of new subscribers. What do they offer the Windows 95 user? Should you be among their customers? What are the major differences between CompuServe, AOL, and Prodigy?

Electronic Mail (E-Mail)

Perhaps the most important feature that the online services offer, in terms of global reach and communications, is their electronic mail capabilities. All three providers offer extensive resources to enable their users to send electronic mail. Originally, the online services companies developed mail systems designed primarily to serve their own users. But the popularity of other mail environments, such as MCI Mail and the Internet, prompted support for external gateways. Today, users of CompuServe, AOL, and Prodigy enjoy the freedom to exchange electronic mail with almost anyone, anywhere in the world.

During the testing of Windows 95, electronic mail played an important role. It allowed Microsoft test engineers to communicate with beta testers. One of the best examples of this was an informational newsletter that Microsoft mailed electronically every few weeks. No matter what system users subscribed to—be it CompuServe, AOL or Prodigy—they were sure to get current information about Windows 95 through their e-mail. Microsoft employed a listserver program to automate the mailing. The Windows 95 newsletter became so popular that its readership reached into the tens of thousands. Of course, the beta test program for Windows had more than 50,000 participants. What if you had to send out that many newsletters? Would you rather be licking stamps for a couple of days or tapping away at your keyboard and sending them electronically?

> **NOTE**
>
> All three commercial services have seen enormous growth in the use of electronic mail by their users in the last few years. Their e-mail and chat areas are, by far, the most popular services they offer.

You might have a different use for e-mail. Perhaps you use it to communicate with family members living throughout the country or the world. E-mail has the advantage of being able to bridge far away places with ease and without regard to time zone differences or long distance telephone charges. Maybe you use e-mail to voice your opinion with your local, state, or federal political representatives. A growing number of elected officials and government agencies have realized the importance of being connected, electronically, to their constituents and have started publishing their e-mail addresses. Telephone your congressional representatives and ask whether they have an e-mail address that you can use to send comments and questions.

> **NOTE**
>
> Today, all the major broadcast television news networks provide e-mail addresses for feedback. Several also maintain pages on the World Wide Web. Another growing use for e-mail is spreading information through listserver programs.

> **TIP**
>
> Signing up on a particular list usually entails only sending a short message with the word subscribe in the body. For an exhaustive list of subjects covered by mailing lists, check out the Web page http://www.neosoft.com/internet/paml/.

Today, sending e-mail no longer means just being able to send text-based messages typed on your keyboard. E-mail enables you to send almost any form of digital information attached to your message. If you are sending e-mail to a friend or family member, you might attach a voice file recorded on your computer or an image that you scanned. For business users, attaching documents, spreadsheets, and other important items is now commonplace.

News and Information

When disasters occur, whether they're natural or man-made, the news services pulse with energy. Online services play an important role in disseminating this news to their subscribers. When the bombing of the Alfred P. Murrah Federal building in Oklahoma City occurred in April of 1995, all three online services began buzzing with the latest news almost immediately after the disaster occurred. Users of CompuServe, AOL, and Prodigy were able to learn, in detail, the tragedy that captured the attention of the nation. In addition to the raw facts surrounding the event, the online services provided more in-depth information that couldn't be obtained through other sources in such an easily accessible manner.

In the case of America Online, it had a special area dedicated to covering the Oklahoma City bombing in place by noon—just hours after the explosion. Besides being able to read news passed on by the wire services, AOL users were able to access photos of the devastation. There were also chat areas established so that users could communicate with one another about the event. Some online users were from Oklahoma City and contributed firsthand knowledge of the tragedy. AOL had also established an online folder where its subscribers could go to learn how they could donate to the rescue and support effort.

Of course, there's also a computer side to the news obtained through the online services. Users can access several of the popular computer-oriented magazines and obtain complete stories, additional information, and even utility software mentioned in those articles. Now that access to the Internet has been enabled, subscribers can also reach the thousands of Usenet newsgroups carried on the Internet. Never before has so much information been so easy to obtain.

There's an assortment of computer magazines and columns available online. You'll also notice that some publishers provide resources on more than one service. This makes sense when you consider the fact that all three of the services covered in this chapter continue to attract new users. There is also an increasing trend toward hosting information on the World Wide Web. Now that the "big three" all support Web browsing, information providers and publishers can prepare their information in a common format. In the past, they had to customize their information and interface for each service.

The following is a list of some of the magazines represented online.

CompuServe:

- *PC Computing* (GO ZNT:PCCONT)
- *PC World* (GO PCWORLD)
- *LAN Magazine* (GO LANMAG)
- *Internet World* (GO IWORLD)
- *Windows Magazine* (GO WINMAG)

America Online (AOL):

- *Family PC Online* (FamilyPC)
- *Home Office Computing*
- *HomePC* (HomePC)
- *Newsbytes* (Newsbytes)
- *PC World* (PC World)
- *Windows Magazine* (WinMag)

- *WIRED Magazine* (`Wired`)
- *WordPerfect Magazine* (`WPMag`)

Prodigy:

- Columns by Larry Magid and Steve Rosenthal
- *PC News* (accessed from the Computers menu)
- *PC Previews*
- *PC Trends*

> **NOTE**
>
> Windows 95 users can access the Microsoft WinNews electronic newsletter through all the popular online services. On CompuServe, type `GO WINNEWS`. For Prodigy, use the `Jump` command and the keyword `WINNEWS`. For America Online use the keyword `WINNEWS`. If you want to receive the newsletter via e-mail, compose a message with the body text `subscribe winnews` and send it to `news@microsoft.newnet.com`. WinNews is published twice a month, on the first and third Monday of each month.

Product Support

Although e-mail and news are important elements of the online experience, a great many computer users take advantage of the medium to obtain technical support for the products they buy and use. Seeking assistance online has become very popular due to the extraordinary growth of the software market. Probably everyone has, at some point, been through the maddening experience of trying to reach a company's technical support department by telephone. It's supposed to be easy but rarely is. Many companies have recognized this problem and have established support areas online to assist their users.

For example, Microsoft has a huge support area that it maintains on CompuServe. Virtually every product it offers is supported online. A Microsoft Excel user could, for example, reach the Excel support area by visiting the MSEXCE forum. Using WinCIM, the CompuServe graphical navigator, you simply press the traffic light GO button and enter MSEXCE. From there, you gain access to online documents, conversation threads started by users, updated files, and advice from the manufacturer.

Support areas exist on America Online and Prodigy as well. On AOL, users can reach the computer support areas from the main screen's Computing button. Like the rest of the AOL interface, you can reach your destination by navigating through a series of menus. Usually this can be accomplished with just a few mouse clicks. The AOL interface is highly polished and inviting for both expert and novice online users.

Answers to online questions don't always come strictly from the companies representing the forum or area you're visiting. Very often, the fastest responses will come from other users with similar experiences or expertise related to your problem. This online friendship and willingness to share information and help others is part of the reason that these services have become so popular. But, as in our own society, it's important to give back to the community that provides for you. If you know the answer to a question being posed online by another user, take a moment to respond. If your answer is general enough to be useful to others, consider posting your response. Otherwise, e-mail the person asking the question directly.

> **TIP**
>
> Learning to be a good *cyber-citizen* is an important part of being an online user. The difference between posting and responding is subtle enough to be overlooked but important enough to deserve an explanation. If you have a comment or answer that's suitable for general reading and would benefit others visiting the same forum or board, you should prepare a post that's available for everyone to read. On CompuServe, this is accomplished by replying to a forum message. However, if the content of your message is fairly specific and intended only to be read by one person, you should consider replying by e-mail. In addition to being more efficient, a direct response by e-mail helps reduce unnecessary traffic in busy online areas. Just as the carpenter's adage "measure twice and cut once" helps reduce costly mistakes, it is wise to review your message before sending it or posting online.

Software

For years bulletin board systems (BBSs) provided the best source for obtaining shareware and freeware software. Although thousands of independent BBS operators still exist, the base of software available on commercial online services has become far larger. Almost every conceivable utility or accessory can be obtained online. Some vendors even use online services to promote their products and use the medium as their primary distribution vehicle.

> **NOTE**
>
> One example of promoting products almost entirely through the online medium is McAfee Associates. For years they've been known as innovators in the software virus protection business. Acting like the software equivalent of the Centers for Disease Control, McAfee Associates has used online services, bulletin boards, and the Internet to spread its "try before you buy" message, popularized by the shareware industry. Their technique has been so successful that they're continually attracting new users and posting record sales.

For Windows 95 users, the online services offer a bounty of useful and sometimes critically important utility programs, shareware applications, and freeware products. As Windows 95 eclipses Windows 3.1 and NT in popularity, you'll begin to see a number of new forums dedicated to supporting its use on all the online services.

Here are some great places on CompuServe to check for Windows 95 software:

- The Windows Shareware Forum (GO WINSHA)
- The Windows NT Forum (GO WINNT)
- The Windows Fun+ Forum (GO WINFUN)
- WUGNET Forum (GO WINUSE)

On America Online:

- Windows 95 users can quickly jump to the Software Center where they will find categories for Windows Software and the Top Software Downloads. AOL also has a special area just for Windows NT and Windows 95 programs. You can reach it by accessing the Windows Software Libraries and then selecting the area Win95 and NT.

> **NOTE**
>
> There is an important flipside to downloading programs online, and that's uploading. If you're a creative programmer who has created a utility or application that you think would be useful to other Windows 95 users, you should consider uploading it to one or more of the commercial online services. In most cases, your connection-time charges will be suspended during your upload (as a form of encouraging file contributions). In addition to programs, you can also upload sound files, wallpaper, and animated cursors and mouse pointers.

Online Chat Areas

The most popular areas that the online services offer are their *chat rooms*. CompuServe calls its service the CB Simulator, a name taken from the days of Citizen Band radios, which were popular in the 1970s and early 1980s (long before any of us knew about cellular telephones). Both AOL and Prodigy refer to their online conversation areas as chat rooms.

Anyone who thinks that the online world (cyberspace) is a cold and lonely place hasn't visited a chat area at 2 a.m. At almost any hour of the day, you can find a variety of conversations being conducted by a few or even dozens of online users. Many different conversations can be going on at one time. Each service has a slightly different interface for joining and participating, but you'll find all of them to be intuitive and fairly efficient.

The cartoon character Dilbert's dog, Dogbert, once remarked something to the effect that "on the Internet, no one knows you're a dog." This applies similarly to the online chat arena, which allows participants to mask their identity through online names called *handles*. Spending time in these online chat areas can be both fun and amusing. It can also be terribly addictive. And the language and subject content can sometimes turn a bit racy.

> **CAUTION**
>
> Some online chat areas are for adults only and often cover mature themes. Even though the online services make a fairly good effort at warning and protecting unsuspecting users about these areas, it's ultimately the parents' responsibility to monitor their children's exposure to potentially strong language or subject matter that they might find objectionable.

Accessing the Internet

You can't escape the Internet. It's literally everywhere and has received the lion's share of attention in the press related to high technology. Although it has been around for almost two decades, recent advances in how information is stored and accessed through the Internet have created a sort of revolution in the online community. The part of the Internet that started this upsurge in popularity is the World Wide Web, also known simply as the Web or WWW.

What makes the Web so special is its simplicity. There are basically two components to the Web: clients and servers. As someone accessing (viewing) information online, you would be considered a client. You would use a program called a Web browser to view both graphics and text. Servers supply the information you read.

Until recently, almost all access to the Web was made through direct connections to the Internet using browsers such as NCSA Mosaic or Netscape. But the online service companies haven't stood by simply watching the tidal wave of Internet excitement escape them. Instead, CompuServe, AOL, and Prodigy have all taken aggressive steps to bridge access to the Internet for their customers. In fact, they collectively might have provided the easiest way that has ever been available for most people to access the Internet and Web.

> **NOTE**
>
> Access to the Internet for Windows users is traditionally made possible by using the TCP/IP protocol through PPP (point-to-point protocol) or SLIP (serial line IP) connections. Applications (such as browsers, Telnet, and FTP programs) access TCP/IP through the WINSOCK API. Before Windows 95, users were required to purchase their own TCP/IP stacks and tools from third-party vendors because the operating system didn't provide this support built in. However, even though Windows 95 now

comes with TCP/IP and PPP built in, the online services have chosen to control and route access to the Internet through their own networks—in essence, hiding much of the complexity from the user.

One immediate benefit of this arrangement is that with your single online account, you can reach the Internet from anywhere your provider offers access. Whether this solution allows you to use other Winsock-compliant applications and treat your connection as if it is a direct connection to the Net depends upon your provider. CompuServe's solution provides a WINSOCK.DLL that enables you to use any external program that's Winsock-compliant, such as shareware FTP programs and Internet Phone. AOL's and Prodigy's solutions are, for the time being, more restrictive, but both expect to provide a Winsock interface in the near future.

Online Manners: Netiquette

Have you ever typed out an e-mail message with the Caps Lock feature enabled. THE TEXT BECOMES KIND OF DIFFICULT TO READ. It's also considered rude in online circles and equivalent to shouting. There are numerous so-called "rules of the road" that one must learn when covering the online terrain. They're all bunched into a category popularly known as *Netiquette*, or *net etiquette*. Meet the Miss Manners of the 90's—your online partner.

E-Mail

As I said, typing an e-mail message with the Caps Lock feature enabled will cause more than a few heads to turn—especially if your message is a response. Other tips for e-mail include the following:

- Keep your message size to a minimum. Think about how much e-mail your recipient might receive and how long it will take him to read your message. The longer your message, the greater the chance that the reader's attention could stray.

- Get straight to the point. Although it surprisingly takes longer to write a short, concise, well-crafted message, your reader will appreciate your clarity and sense of proportion.

- Avoid using tabs or trying to include data in columns. Some readers will view your message with programs (such as Windows 95's Exchange) that display text using proportionally spaced fonts. Tables will come out all jumbled looking.

- Keep attachment sizes to a bare minimum. If you absolutely must send a huge chunk of data or a bunch of separate files, consider breaking them up and sending them in several different messages. Users retrieving mail "on the road" will appreciate not having to sit waiting while their PC downloads a single gigantic message through costly hotel phone systems.

■ Be mindful of your tone. Although it's usually very easy to discern someone's mood in person by observing body language and detecting speech inflections, no such subtle aids exist for e-mail. It's always a good idea to reread your message before pressing the Send or Transmit button. Catching a phrase or word whose tone might appear too angry could save you from explaining and perhaps even embarrassment later.

■ Avoid overusing silly character-based graphics. These arranged characters, called *smileys* (or *emoticons),* such as **:)** or ;>, can make your message difficult to read. Of course, every now and then, you're likely to encounter a clever gem that you'll want to save and pass on to friends. But you'll probably find a majority of users hoping for a fairly conservative and direct presentation of your message. Having just said that, however, there is a use for emoticons in messages. Sometimes they help the reader interpret the tone of your message. For example, a simple <g> (grin) following a strong statement lets the reader know that you're serious but not necessarily angry.

Online Chat Sessions

Similar to the etiquette rules you should follow for e-mail, online chat users frown when they see messages sent in all capital letters or filled with sometimes hard to follow graphics. Here are some other tips:

■ When you first enter a chat room, wait a little while and read a few of the responses from other online participants. Try to figure out what the subject is before blurting out an unrelated question.

■ Keep your responses short. There are usually several people wanting to communicate at once, and the more orderly the sessions, the easier and more enjoyable it is for everyone participating. Lengthy replies, naturally, take longer to read.

■ If you are responding to another person, start your message with that person's online name or handle. This will help keep the conversation thread organized and increase the chances of you receiving a reply.

Usenet News Groups

Now that access to Usenet news groups (which number close to 9,000) has become available through CompuServe and AOL, you'll learn that adhering to good netiquette is more than just a valuable suggestion; it's literally a requirement to peacefully coexisting online. Through the Usenet newsgroups, you'll be able to share ideas and information with millions of other users around the world. It is partly because of your audience's size that prescribing to a few online rules is wise. But don't worry about making a mistake such as writing an ANGRY/ SHOUTING message, or one that's too long or filled with goofy characters. Other users will surely let you know the evil of your ways. It's called being *flamed,* and it is part of earning your online wings.

Here are some tips you can follow to help you to gain some online respect. At worst, they'll decrease your chances of being flamed.

- Always ask yourself, "Is my response directed at the author of the message or everyone in the newsgroup?" If it's directed at the author, consider sending an e-mail message rather than a message to the group that everyone will have to see.

- Avoid offering advice that's virtually useless, such as "read the manual" or "ask your system administrator." If you're taking the time to prepare a response, make one that's worth reading.

- Avoid excessive signatures. These are the lines of text that usually follow your message and identify you by name, company, and e-mail address. You're going to see some very interesting and sometimes creative signatures online. But think about all the bandwidth being used. Some data communication experts say our networks are getting *maxxed out*. Could this be one of the reasons?

- Don't post private e-mail that was sent to you without first asking the author. The author might not want his or her comments put out for public viewing.

- Avoid inflammatory responses. They're just going to start online flame wars and add to the already bloated and, unfortunately, useless content plaguing some newsgroups.

- If you plan on shifting the topic of a thread, be sure you change the subject line for the message. This will help other readers weed out the topics that they're either tired of reading or want to outright avoid.

- Before asking a question online, check to see whether there's a FAQ (Frequently Asked Questions) document you can examine. Alternatively, try examining older message threads in the same newsgroup. The topic you're seeking answers to might recently have been covered.

Using CompuServe with Windows 95

CompuServe is currently the elder statesman of the online services. With more than 3 million members and hundreds of specialized forums, it offers an enormous wealth of information to its subscribers. Users of Microsoft's products can well attest to CompuServe's important role in providing a base for technical support. Microsoft manages numerous forums related to its products and has conducted almost all of its high-profile beta programs using the service as a depository for messages, files, and information.

The Windows 95 beta program, for example, relied heavily on CompuServe. A special forum devoted entirely to discussing features and reporting anomalies proved to be an exciting and energetic online spot. Discussion threads were created almost daily that involved both small and large groups of people. Ideas and comments flowed almost without abandon, and you could find other users online in that forum at almost any hour of the day.

WinCIM

CompuServe's most popular access tool is currently WinCIM. WinCIM was developed several years ago and has been revised a number of times to become an easy to use and powerful access tool. Its user interface popularized the *favorite places* paradigm that Microsoft adopted for its new online service.

> **TIP**
>
> If all of your access to CompuServe has been through a terminal program, you can download a copy of WinCIM by visiting the WinCIM support area. Type GO WINCIM and then select the item for downloading the most recent version of the program. At around 2 MB, though, it's best to have at least a 9,600- or 14,400-baud modem. You can also call CompuServe and request a copy of the program on diskette.

Navigator and Other Offline Tools

Whereas WinCIM is the consummate tool for interactive access, CompuServe Navigator is CompuServe's answer to the user's need for an offline tool. If you've used a commercial service, you'll know firsthand that charges are sometimes levied based upon how much time you spend connected. Although it might not be apparent, accessing an online service through a totally interactive user interface quickly eats up valuable time and begins to become expensive. Even if you think you know where to find what you want, it is unlikely that you can do it as quickly as an automated tool such as Navigator. And offline tools help you to avoid the all-too-easy mistake of getting sidetracked online.

If you find yourself checking your e-mail on a regular basis (which you should) or accessing specific forums for updated messages or files, you should consider using Navigator. It could save you a bundle. Although its user interface is somewhat strange and initially difficult to use, the nature of tools like Navigator is such that you really only have to learn them once. Luckily, after Navigator has been configured to access your selected forums and check for e-mail, it manages to go about its job quietly and efficiently time after time.

> **TIP**
>
> CompuServe Navigator can be obtained online by typing GO CSNAV at the CompuServe system prompt. Windows 95's Hyperterminal can get you connected to CompuServe, but after you obtain WinCIM or Navigator, you should use those tools because they offer a better, more reliable means of communication. CSNav carries a $20 purchase price, which is automatically added to your CompuServe bill when you download the program. However, when you buy it, you are given a $10 usage credit toward future online use.

Before Navigator was introduced, another offline navigation tool named OzCIS managed to become one of CompuServe's most popular tools with a large and loyal following. Last year the author, Steve Sneed, introduced a Windows version called OzWIN, and it too has become extremely popular.

> **· TIP**
>
> You can obtain a copy of OzWIN by visiting the OZWIN forum on CompuServe. The program is shareware and requires a $69 registration fee after a 30-day evaluation period.

E-Mail with WinCIM

With points of presence located throughout the globe and gateway support for all the popular e-mail formats, CompuServe users can exchange electronic mail with almost anyone, 24 hours a day, seven days a week, regardless of geographic distance. (See Figure 20.1.) Sending mail to other CompuServe users is as easy as typing in their comma-separated addresses. Sending to recipients on other services requires just a little additional knowledge. Table 20.1 will help you in preparing e-mail addresses for the various formats. You can reference this table when creating entries in your WinCIM address book or when creating one-time-only e-mail messages.

FIGURE 20.1.

The CompuServe e-mail interface is easy to learn and use. New versions of WinCIM allow binary files to be attached directly to outbound messages.

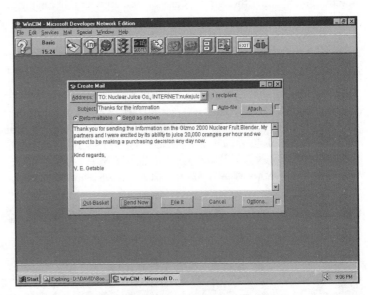

Table 20.1. E-mail address formats.

E-Mail System	Address Format
Advantis	X400:(C=country; A=IBMX400; P=private-domain; S=surname; G=given-name)
AT&T EasyLink	X400:(C=country, A=WESTERN UNION; P=private-domain; S=surname; G=given-name; D=ELN:easylink-number)
BT Messaging	X400:(C=country; A=BT; O=org; S=surname; G=given-name)
Cable and Wireless	X400:(C=country; A=CWMAIL; P=private-domain; O=org; S=surname; G=given-name)
Fax	FAX:fax-number
Internet	INTERNET:address@domain
MCI Mail	MCIMAIL:mci-id
NIFTY	X400:(C=country; A=NIFTY; P=private-domain; S=mail-id)
Telex	TLX:machine number

NOTE

You'll notice that the formats for X400 address types are all very similar. Additional formats and examples of their use can be found in WinCIM's online help under the topic Electronic Mail Address Formats. It shouldn't be surprising, though, to find that most people are beginning to use the Internet *address@domain* scheme for identifying their addresses. Even CompuServe users often identify themselves on their business cards and letterheads as *user-id@compuserve*.com, in which *user-id* represents their comma-separated CompuServe ID. However, it should be noted that when specifying your address in this manner, the comma should be replaced with a period. For example, 72667,1312 would be formatted as 72667.1312@compuserve.com and represent a valid Internet address for a CompuServe user.

Forums

CompuServe offers more than 850 forums. Almost every conceivable topic is represented, in one way or another, through an online forum area. The easiest way to locate a forum for a topic that you're interested in is to press the Find button on WinCIM's main toolbar. Enter one or more keywords and press the OK button. If you're not currently online when you do this, WinCIM automatically connects you and begins searching for your selected topic.

Searching for *Windows 95* turned up two forums. The first was the MS Windows News+ forum and the second was the Microsoft Windows Intl. D+ forum, which is an area dedicated to supporting Windows internationalization development efforts. Searching for forums related just to *Windows* turned up more than 150!

For programmers, there are a number of useful forums. Borland Delphi users can turn to their own forum by accessing the DELPHI forum. Visual Basic programmers can turn to the MS Languages forum (MSLANG). C and C++ users can turn to forums hosted by the vendors of those compilers such as Borland (BCPPWI), Symantec (SYMDEV), Microsoft (MSLANG), and Watcom (WATFOR). But don't think that the forums are only for work-related activities.

Internet Support

CompuServe chose a staged method of offering access to the Internet for its subscribers. (See Figure 20.2.) It started by allowing access to the Usenet newsgroups. Then, in the first half of 1995, CompuServe acquired Spry, Inc. of Seattle. Spry is a well-known vendor of Internet-related tools and the creator of the popular Internet-in-a-Box product. Through their joint efforts, CompuServe members were rewarded with the ability to access the World Wide Web using a special browser that communicated with the Internet through CompuServe's network.

FIGURE 20.2.

In addition to offering WWW access through a Web browser program, CompuServe also offers Telnet and FTP service. To reach the main Internet starting point type GO INTERNET.

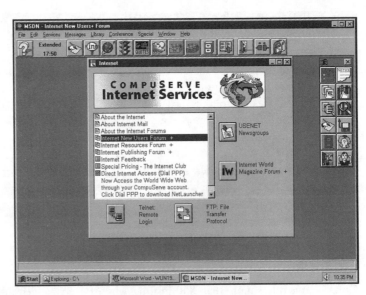

America Online and Windows 95

America Online currently has the most polished user interface of the services covered in this chapter. Whereas CompuServe started in the days of character-based or "dumb" terminals and Prodigy tried to preserve a graphics format originally designed for much slower networks, AOL largely grew up with Windows and the Macintosh. Although AOL technically started as a graphical DOS program, its interface migrated with ease to Windows and now relies heavily upon high-quality graphic images to enhance its presentation.

America Online's subscriber base, though not the largest, is probably the fastest growing. AOL engages in an aggressive marketing program that puts its starter kit in the hands of magazine purchasers, modem buyers, and new computer owners. AOL software comes bundled with many of the new PCs sold by IBM, Apple, Compaq, AST, Tandy, NEC, and Compudyne.

E-Mail

It would be hard to imagine a simpler interface for electronic mail than the one AOL provides. It is tightly integrated into the entire range of services that are provided—including AOL's new Web browser, which became available starting with Version 2.5 of the program. (See Figure 20.3.)

FIGURE 20.3.

The AOL e-mail dialog has iconic buttons that clearly point out how to attach a file, select names from an address book, and ultimately send the message.

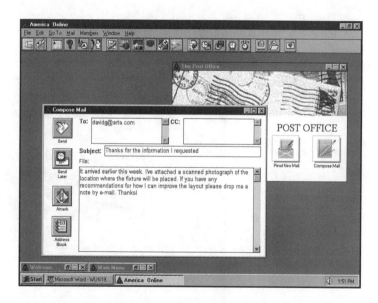

Just as you would expect, every time you connect to AOL, your mailbox is checked for new entries. If mail is available, you are alerted and given the opportunity to read it.

AOL offers *FlashSessions*, which are similar in purpose to the offline navigation tools described for CompuServe. These enable you to automate the collection (or delivery) of e-mail, as well as messages for newsgroups. FlashSessions have the added feature of being able to be scheduled, which is definitely a nice touch for the power online user.

Internet Support

Like their e-mail interface, AOL deserves credit for their superb Internet integration efforts. The AOL Web browser fits in so well with the regular interface that it is difficult to believe it hasn't been there all along. Unlike CompuServe and Prodigy, which launch external Web browser applications, the AOL browser is simply another window inside the main program. It can be resized like other windows and provide status feedback so that you know how long a page will take to download. On top of the browser, AOL has created what appears like an entire support area surrounding its Internet services. Instead of simply casting its users into the unfamiliar waters of the World Wide Web, AOL provides some very nice and helpful online guidance areas. For example, one such area helps users learn which Web sites are the most popular, and another area provides a list of sites representing computer magazines.

Starting the AOL Web Browser

As long as you have Version 2.5 or later of the AOL software, you can access the World Wide Web. From the main menu displayed when you first connect, press the button labeled Internet Connection.

FIGURE 20.4.

The AOL Web Browser, shown displaying the company's primary Web page, which is located at `http://www.blue.aol.com/`.

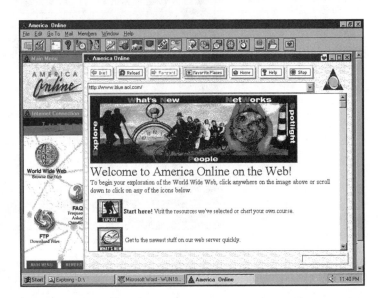

From the main AOL home page, you can access several different areas set up on the Web to assist in your online navigation.

■ Explore offers a sort of launching point for Web exploration. You'll find an up-to-date list of locations (represented by Uniform Resource Locators or URLs) broken down into categories such as Clubs and Interests, Computing, Education, Entertainment,

Games, Kids Only, Marketplace, Music, Sports, and Travel. Each click brings you deeper into the subtopic. For instance, the Travel link brings you to Sarah & Chris's Roadtrip, a story-like introduction to sites such as The Andy Warhol Museum in Pittsburgh, The White House, and *60 Minutes.*

- The What's New section, although it is still being enhanced, will highlight bright and interesting new spots on the Web. It currently provides links to an Internet Directory and AOL's Web Feedback area.

- If you've explored the Web before and have visited sites such as NCSA's What's New page or a collection and search resource called Yahoo, you'll recognize the format for Spotlight. It's basically a selection of Web sites that are new or interesting that is arranged chronologically. And, like other similar sites on the Web, AOL's Spotlight includes some small advertising.

- One day the People page will be a starting point for reaching AOL members' private home pages. Until that time, it offers a collection of home pages for AOL employees.

- The Networks page appears to represent AOL's mirrored FTP resources. FTP, or File Transfer Protocol, is the standard UNIX way of transferring files between computers. A mirror site is essentially a copy of a software library. By mirroring software locally, AOL is making it easier and faster for its members to obtain popular shareware and freeware software products, documents, and other Internet-based files.

- The Feedback page invites AOL Web browsers to provide feedback related to their Internet and Web services. Because the browser is so tightly integrated with the main AOL program, selecting the Feedback link launches the familiar AOL e-mail interface with the address of the AOL Webmaster (the person who maintains the Web-related resources) already filled in.

Transferring Files

Using FTP with AOL is almost as easy as accessing and downloading other files on the service. You reach the FTP services through the Internet Connection screen—the same way you access the Web browser. The screen that appears provides a list of common and popular FTP sites. These sites are known to have huge collections of software available for downloading. If there's a specific site you need to reach that's not on this list, you can reach it by pressing the button labeled Other Site and entering its name.

When you are connected to a remote FTP site, the AOL interface works like other FTP programs. It displays directories and their contents in a list fashion. Selecting and opening directories (which can also be done by double-clicking on them) navigates you deeper into the remote computer's directory hierarchy. When you reach a file that you want to retrieve, you simply press the Download button to begin the file transfer. A progress gauge provides status information during the transfer.

News and Information

News and information appear to be strong points with AOL. Its graphical interface lends an air of sophistication to the presentation. Accessing news can start from several points. The two easiest are the buttons labeled Today's News and Newsstand from the main menu. Today's News brings you right to a list of top stories being covered by the major news organizations, along with starting points for US & World news, Business news, Entertainment, Sports, and Weather. A Search News button offers a convenient way to search for specific stories.

Selecting the US & World news button displays another screen designed to provide you with more access to national and international news stories. You'll also see familiar icons for The New York Times, ABC News, and TIME Magazine—services all sponsored by those organizations.

The New York Times @times area provides an electronic equivalent to the world-renowned newspaper. Because it is broken down into familiar sections such as Arts & Leisure, Science Times, and NYT Classified, users will find it remarkably easy to locate current stories, research movies and restaurants (and see past reviews for both), and find apartments and automobiles. Of course, except for the news, most of the information is targeted at people living in or around the metropolitan New York City area. Still, the real-estate interface is slick and, because of its graphical imagemap-like format, easy to use. But with New York City real-estate prices the way they are, you might be better off living in the suburbs and telecommuting through AOL.

ABC's On Demand news area offers traditional access to online news and follows the format of ABC's television news program by offering a Person of the Week library, American Agenda, and Peter Jennings' Journal. A library of video clips is also included. Obviously, the faster your modem the better, because these files can be quite large. A video promo for ABC news that lasted just 6.5 seconds required the storage of a 552KB AVI file, which was itself compressed to only 464 KB. When you begin experimenting with online multimedia (both video and sound files), you learn to appreciate not only the benefits of having a fast modem (which, somehow, is never quite fast enough), but also the sheer size required to store things in a digital format.

NOTE

In an effort to increase its support for high-speed access, America Online has expanded its AOLNet service. Now becoming available in most major cities, AOLNet allows its subscribers access using 28,800-baud (V.34) modems. In the near future, it is expected that AOLNet will begin supporting ISDN for even faster access.

TIP

After downloading audio (.WAV) and video files (.AVI), you can use Windows 95's built-in *properties* feature, which is available through the floating menu displayed when the alternate (usually right) mouse button is pressed. The preview tab enables you to listen to wave audio (.WAV) files and preview video (.AVI) files.

The two largest business news partners on AOL are *Business Week* and *Investor's Business Daily*. Their services, collectively, offer AOL subscribers current business news, stock tips, and company profile information. You'll also find that they provide a good mix of stories relating to computers and high technology, both areas of interest to the business community.

Support Areas

AOL's support areas for computer users are vast. They have a comprehensive list of both software and hardware companies that maintain online support areas. It's quite likely that the technical question or problem you have can be tackled online through either the vendor's message board or by downloading one or more files from the vendor's software library.

Reaching online computer support begins through the Industry Connection. From there, you will find a category list containing items such as Applications, Desktop Publishing, Development, Graphics & Animation, Multimedia, and more. Suppose you're a Quicken user and you want to see whether there's an update to the program. Selecting the Application category presents another list containing software companies. Scrolling part of the way through the list, you find Intuit, the creator of Quicken. When you select the item, you are greeted with the Intuit welcome screen and can then access a message center, Intuit's software library (where updates are often placed), and a list of Frequently Asked Questions (FAQs). The same process can be applied to a number of other companies. Some companies have already shifted their support areas to the Internet and supply information through Web pages. Luckily, AOL's interface can take you there automatically.

TIP

If, after an exhaustive search, you still can't locate an online source of technical support, you can always turn to the original products vendor. But what if you don't know who that is or have lost their telephone number and address? You can turn to the PC Vendors Database on AOL. By entering a keyword such as the product's name, you can see of list of associated companies. Entering LapLink, for example, quickly brought up the name of the company that created it and sells it worldwide: Traveling Software, Inc. A more general search using the term video produced over a thousand matches, and a search using the keyword windows produced over two thousand! Clearly, it helps to be as detailed as possible when performing online searches. Still, it's nice to have an online reference for the thousands of computer hardware and software companies around the world.

Shopping

Now that you've purchased Windows 95, you might be thinking about upgrading your computer. Perhaps a little extra RAM or a larger hard disk would improve performance and add storage capacity. You could jump in your car and visit your local computer store or scour the local paper for specials. But wouldn't shopping online be more convenient? You'll be pleased to know that shopping online through AOL can be both convenient and easy. And you don't have to be shopping for just computer items.

AOL has shopping areas that offer grocery and pharmaceutical products, vitamins, flowers, miscellaneous gifts, a wide variety of books, specialty items from the Discovery Channel store and Hollywood Online, and more.

However, if you are planning to add a few gadgets to the family or office PC, you can check out Global Plaza or PC Catalog. Global Plaza has some excellent specials from time to time but PC Catalog focuses on offering only computer-related products and, thus, has a wider selection of high-technology items.

Prodigy

Like CompuServe and AOL, Prodigy offers a full range of online services including e-mail, online chat areas, entertainment, shopping, online banking and brokerage services, travel reservations, and Internet support. Prodigy claims to have more than 600,000 members enrolled to use its integrated Web browser.

Similar to the other networks, and in part because of the competitive nature of online services, Prodigy is racing forward to support high-speed, 28,800-baud access to as many of its users as possible, as well as testing delivery of its service over cable systems and through ISDN.

Prodigy's user interface and contents appear to be highly consumer- and family-oriented and they've attracted a huge and loyal following.

E-Mail

Sending e-mail with Prodigy is easy, in part because their interface is so simple. From any screen, press the button labeled Mail to enter into the mailbox resource. There you will see a list of messages waiting for you in your inbox, as well as another button labeled Write, which you can press if you want to begin composing a new message.

Prodigy's compose mail screen enables you to enter one or more Prodigy IDs or Internet addresses. In fact, a button marked Internet ID helps you format proper Internet e-mail addresses and also provides examples of how to send e-mail to users on other commercial services such as CompuServe, AOL, GEnie, and Delphi.

> **NOTE**
>
> The examples provided by Prodigy for sending mail to other online services are general enough to be useful no matter what e-mail software or service you plan to use. Sending mail to CompuServe users is performed by attaching `@compuserve.com` to their ID (provided you change the comma in their ID to a period), as in `77777.666@compuserve.com`. For AOL users, you attach `@aol.com` to their ID, as in `aoluser@aol.com`. Delphi users can be reached by `username@delphi.com` and GEnie users through `g.user1@genie.geis.com`.

The Prodigy e-mail interface enables you to attach up to three files, of any format, that get sent with your message. You can also import text files into the body of your message. One of the most interesting aspects of the Prodigy interface is an option that speaks your message. Using a very computer-like voice, Prodigy will actually say all of the words in your message. This might be a novelty for some, but it could be an important aid for users without sight.

> **NOTE**
>
> Prodigy offers two forms of offline e-mail support: one for DOS users, and one for Windows users. Both enable you to compose messages while disconnected from Prodigy. The windows software is a special version of ConnectSoft's E-Mail Connection.

Internet Support

Prodigy offers a complete selection of tools related to Internet access, including Usenet newsgroups and Internet mail; and FTP, gopher, and Web access through the integrated Web browser. Prodigy has also set up a special Internet Bulletin Board (BB), which is useful for beginners seeking advice and guidance from fellow Prodigy users.

The Prodigy Web Browser is a native Windows application that acts like other popular browsers, including NCSA Mosaic and Netscape. All communication with the Internet and Web is made through your Prodigy online connection, so you won't have to worry about establishing an account with an Internet provider. The Prodigy home page offers starting points for Internet exploration, searching, and technical support.

FIGURE 20.5.

Prodigy's integrated Web browser offers users access to the whole online world.

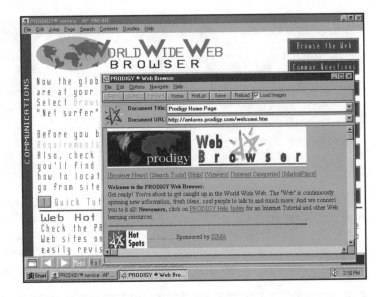

For example, selecting the Sports link from Prodigy's home page brings you to a list of sites covering professional sports such NFL football, soccer, tennis, and hockey, as well as recreational sports such as cycling, mountain climbing, and backpacking.

> **TIP**
>
> A great site to visit on the Web for outdoor activities is a Web-based magazine named *Outside Online*, which is offered by Starwave, a company started by Microsoft co-founder Paul Allen. You can reach it through the URL http://www.starwave.com/outside.

News and Information

Prodigy's online news and information resources are comprehensive. From the main menu, you can reach them by pressing the button labeled News/Weather. You then see a list of top stories that you can read in detail by pressing their jump buttons. The lead stories, like the news itself, are always changing. Other news and information features of Prodigy include the following:

- Online photos, many of which are in full color, download quickly with a 14,400-baud modem and offer you an immediacy unavailable through newspapers and regular television news.

- Newspapers and magazines offered online include *Access, Ad Age, American Heritage, Consumer Reports, Kiplinger's, Mac Home Journal, Newsday Direct,* and *Newsweek Interactive.*

- Polls taken by Prodigy put you in touch with the pulse (and opinion) of other online users and also let you cast an opinion on current topics. It's easy to participate and also easy to see detailed results of past polls.

- The Newstoons area has some of the best political cartooning available.

- Weather has online maps and city forecasts that provide quick and precise weather information.

Support Areas

Online computer support is available from several companies, including Acer, AST, Compaq, Dell, Gateway 2000, and IBM. The primary interface employed by these companies is a bulletin board where users can post questions and read comments made by other users and support personnel. Some also offer more complete interfaces and include file libraries. Access to support files usually incurs an additional hourly fee, but the files themselves are generally free.

> **TIP**
>
> To reach the computer support areas on Prodigy, press the button labeled Computers on the main menu. Next, press the Product Support button. From there, you can narrow your selection based upon company and type of support needed.

Shopping

With credit card in hand, you can shop until you drop online with Prodigy. Like AOL and CompuServe, Prodigy members can choose from a variety of vendors offering everything from automobiles (usually just information, unless your credit card limit is very good), to computers and entertainment products, to travel packages.

Reference Information

Looking for the perfect vacation spot or, perhaps, a good restaurant in your city? Prodigy's reference tools might be able to assist. By jumping to the Reference section online, you're introduced to a wide selection of possible reference materials including the following:

- The Academic American Encyclopedia.
- *Consumer Reports* magazine.

- A comprehensive political profile database, in which you can search for information about Congress.
- Software, travel, and movie guides.
- An online investment center.
- Homework Helper, which is a fee-based addition to Prodigy, offering student-oriented reference material. Prodigy bills it as its online library.

Remaining aware of current high technology issues and news (especially Windows 95) through active use of commercial online services is a wise and remarkably attainable endeavor. All three of the online services mentioned in this chapter are easy to join and use. If you're thinking more about accessing the Internet for e-mail and Web browsing through an independent Internet provider, rather than through one of these services, you might want reconsider. Now that CompuServe, AOL, and Prodigy all provide Web browsing, FTP (File Transfer Protocol), and Telnet, you'll find them to be, perhaps, the easiest way to become connected, electronically, to the world.

A great deal will be said about Microsoft's entry into the commercial online business during Windows 95's first year or two on the market. It's clearly a bold move and they've developed a remarkably well-integrated and potentially very powerful and attractive offering. But you'll find that the other, more established services, currently have a great deal more content to offer and a history of adapting to and servicing the needs of computer users.

Using online services is fun, sometimes challenging and almost always rewarding. If used properly, these resources can improve your communication capabilities and improve your chances of staying competitive.

The Internet

by

There's no hotter computer commodity right now than the Internet, that unmanaged, unfathomable "network of networks" that enables about 25 million people all over the world to exchange e-mail, post and read messages in topical newsgroups, perform research, and generally hack their way around the globe.

Knowing this (and being no slouch when it comes to trend-catching), Microsoft wanted to package a complete set of Internet tools in Windows 95. Unfortunately, as Windows 95's debut approached, Microsoft slowly backed off its commitments to supply the whole Internet kit and caboodle. Instead, Windows 95 comes equipped with the bare minimum software to get you online; the other Internet bells and whistles are offered separately in Microsoft Plus!

> **NOTE**
>
> The Microsoft Plus! add-on package for Windows 95 includes a number of enhancements—some related to the Internet, others not. The Internet enhancements in Plus! are described in this chapter, while the rest of Microsoft Plus! is described in Chapter 14.

About the Internet

To understand what's included in Windows 95 and what's not, you have to understand a little bit about how the Internet works. The Internet is made up of millions of computers and networks of every type and configuration in use today. This diverse community is able to intercommunicate thanks to a rather old, reliable internetworking protocol called TCP/IP. Every computer on the Internet must be running a TCP/IP protocol stack, or it must be connected to the Internet through a server that is running TCP/IP—though having a genuine TCP/IP Internet connection is not the only way to gain access to information on the Internet (more about that later).

Although TCP/IP binds the network together, it doesn't make all the resources available on the Internet behave in the same way. There are several distinct types of Internet resources, each requiring a completely different method of operation and each requiring some sort of software *client* or utility program. Among the types of Internet resources are

- **E-mail:** Exchanging electronic mail with any other Internet user anywhere in the world. In order to send and receive e-mail on the Internet, you need a program to compose, send, receive, and read the mail. That program can be Microsoft Exchange, the built-in Windows 95 messaging client, or it can be a third-party e-mail program.

- **Telnet:** Logging into a remote computer at a university, research firm, corporation, government, or other organization and using it as if you were a local user. Telnet requires the simplest software to get hooked up, but requires some experience to use, because every Telnet site has a different system of menus and/or commands.

- **Gopher:** Navigating among remote sites and visiting remote computers through a simple, standardized menuing system. In most cases, Telnet is happening behind the scenes, but Gopher menus mask the inconsistencies among many different sites and assist in locating and using the information stored there.

- **Newsgroups:** Reading and posting public messages in topic-centered forums, or newsgroups, most managed under the auspices of a loose affiliation of computers and networks called Usenet. There are thousands of Usenet newsgroups that enable interested users to exchange information about professions, hobbies, fetishes, and fandom. Using newsgroups requires a program called a newsreader that navigates among groups, sorts and searches through messages, and posts your messages so others can read them.

- **FTP:** Transferring files to and from remote computers set up as FTP servers. Using FTP, you can download (copy) files from remote FTP servers holding software programs, updated drivers, articles, books, photos, sound and video clips—you name it. Using FTP servers requires access to an FTP client program, either on your PC or on a server you share.

- **World Wide Web (WWW):** When you browse among sites on the World Wide Web, which is a subset of Internet sites that supports the use of "hypertext," you'll see highlighted words that, when selected, branch off to other sites and subjects. To use the WWW, you must have a program called a "WWW browser." WWW browsing also supports multimedia, so that full-color graphics, video, and sound can be incorporated into what you see and do there. Although the WWW does not encompass the entire Internet, it does make using the Internet more intuitive, flexible, and fun.

- **Talk, Chat, MUDs:** Various methods of online, interactive discussion. Talk supports one-to-one conversations, Chat enables group discussions, and MUDs and other interactive discussion games use the basic Chat facility to enable Internet users to join in elaborate online role-playing games. "MUD" stands for "multi-user dimension," "multi-user dungeon," or "multiuser dialog," depending on whom you ask.

You can find some or all of the client software required for these functions bundled in general-purpose Internet software packages like NetManage's Chameleon. You can also find separate programs for each function; many users prefer the "salad bar" approach, choosing the program they like best for each Internet resource type. Others take advantage of the fact that newsgroups and FTP file transfers can be performed from within a WWW browser. For that reason, a growing number of people access the Internet exclusively through their WWW browsers, which they regard as all-in-one Internet interfaces. That view is clearly in sync with Microsoft's, because between Windows 95 and Microsoft Plus!, Microsoft supplies a full-featured WWW browser and e-mail program but no separate tools for Gopher or newsgroup access.

About Connection Types

Some computers in large companies, universities, and research organizations have "dedicated" Internet access and are connected to the Net 24 hours a day. Users access Internet services from terminals or networked PCs and through a server that manages the dedicated connection. In this scenario, how the Internet is used and what users can do there is controlled through the server, and varies from site to site.

Increasingly, private users outside universities and large corporations have temporary, "on-demand" Internet accounts through which they connect to an Internet service (which itself has a dedicated connection) whenever they need Internet access. These temporary user accounts come in two types: basic "command-line" accounts and dial-up IP accounts.

In command-line accounts (also known as dial-up terminal accounts or shell accounts), users' computers are not officially connected to the Internet via TCP/IP. Instead, their computers are connected by an ordinary modem or network connection to a server that is connected to the Internet via TCP/IP, in much the same way as many users in universities are. Because they aren't using TCP/IP themselves, the users' computers aren't technically "on" the Internet, but they can access Internet resources supplied to them by the server. What the user can do is limited by the client software running on the server, which may provide a menu-based set of choices for accessing Internet resources or may offer only a command line from which users issue commands, one line at a time, to access Internet resources.

Command-line accounts have some great advantages. They're typically inexpensive (even free) and they can be used from even the most meagerly equipped PC, because the PC doesn't require an especially fast modem or the capability to run TCP/IP and client software. However, they're usually limited to basic Internet activities: Telnet, e-mail, and sometimes FTP or newsgroups. How you use these resources, and what you can and cannot do, is completely controlled by the server computer and the sysop who controls it—and there is a great deal of inconsistency in the way Internet tools must be used in these environments. Most importantly, these accounts do not support multiple simultaneous connections or Windows-based graphical browsing of the WWW. As the WWW becomes the hot spot on the Internet, command-line accounts are falling out of favor for the costlier, but more flexible, dial-up IP accounts.

> **TIP**
>
> In addition to command-line and dial-up IP accounts, there is one more way to access some Internet resources. By subscribing to some online services—in particular CompuServe, America Online, Delphi, and The Microsoft Network—you can gain access to some Internet resources through gateways provided by the service. At present, what's provided works like a dressed-up command-line account; the service provides menus for easily clicking your way through selected Internet resources (typically the newsgroups, sometimes FTP or Telnet), and the service controls the way you use them.

You don't need special software on your PC other than what the online service requires. All online services provide ways to send and receive e-mail to and from the Internet.

Internet access fees vary, and in most cases online services charge extra fees for Internet resources on top of their regular time-based or monthly access fees.

For Windows users, the preferred type of Internet account is a dial-up IP link, in which the PC is running the TCP/IP protocol stack and is actually connected to the Internet. Windows users still dial into a server to use these accounts (either through a modem or via a direct network connection to the server), but the server simply acts as a pathway, and typically imposes no limitations on the user, who can choose whatever client and utility software he likes for operating each Internet resource. These accounts come in two types, separated by the type of UNIX access/authentication protocol used: Serial Line Internet Protocol (SLIP, plus a compressed variant called CSLIP) and Point-to-Point Protocol (PPP). They require different configurations, but once set up, they appear the same to a user.

From a SLIP or PPP account, users have access to the full range of Internet services. They also have the capability to run their choice of Internet software on their own computers. Because you choose the tools, you can use the Internet through whichever windows you find easiest to use, or most powerful. A rich variety of tools is available, offering graphical browsing capabilities, online viewing of graphics and playing of multimedia, and near point-and-click Internet operation. These capabilities require a powerful PC (any PC that can handle Windows 95 acceptably is sufficient) and a fast modem (14,400 bps or faster).

Accessing a command-line Internet account involves only a simple modem connection to the server. You merely create a HyperTerminal session to dial the server. Dial-up IP accounts require a little more setup and configuration, but reward you with unlimited options.

The rest of this chapter pertains specifically to dial-up IP Internet accounts, because these are the preferred Internet accounts for Windows users.

TIP

In operation, there's little difference between SLIP and PPP connections. They both rely on TCP/IP, and both are supported by the same Windows sockets-based Internet applications.

However, Windows 95 offers several compelling reasons to favor a PPP account over a SLIP or CSLIP account:

- By default, PPP is available through Dial-Up Networking if you've also installed TCP/IP. SLIP/CSLIP is not automatically available; you must install it separately from the Windows 95 CD-ROM.

■ The files providing SLIP/CSLIP support are available only on the CD-ROM version of Windows 95. They are not included in the diskette version. (If you have the diskette version, you may be able to acquire the SLIP files separately from Microsoft support.)

■ Microsoft Plus! includes an Internet Wizard, described later in this chapter, that automates configuring Windows 95 for the Internet. The Wizard supports only PPP and Microsoft Network accounts. SLIP/CSLIP accounts must be configured manually.

Every time you log onto the Internet from Windows 95, a SLIP/CSLIP account requires at least one extra logging-on step, and sometimes two. That makes PPP accounts comparatively easy to log onto.

So while in the abstract, SLIP and PPP aren't that different, Microsoft has created a built-in bias for PPP as a Windows 95 Internet vehicle. Save yourself a headache, and do what Microsoft tells you to do—get a PPP account.

Resource List

This chapter pertains specifically to using Windows 95 to access the Internet, and can't comprehensively cover the range of resources and services available on the Net. Fortunately, there are several good books covering the Internet in greater detail, including the following, which are all published by Sams:

Navigating the Internet with Windows 95
Author: Ned Snell
Pages: 400

A comprehensive Internet guide featuring detailed explanations of Windows 95 Internet configuration, and directions for using many of the best and most popular Internet resources. Includes a list of access providers.

The Internet Unleashed, 2E
Authors: (40 Internet experts)
Pages: 1,390

A best-selling encyclopedia of the Internet and everything that's on it, geared not only to Windows users, but to Mac and UNIX users, as well. Includes a list of access providers and a disk of Windows-based Internet tools, plus a coupon for ordering Mac-based Internet tools.

The World Wide Web Unleashed, 2E
Authors: John December and Neil Randall
Pages: 1060

A comprehensive guide to using the WWW. Includes information about creating and publishing WWW pages online.

Your Internet Consultant
Author: Kevin M. Savetz
Pages: 550

A handy Internet reference guide organized in a useful "question-and-answer" format.

Teach Yourself the Internet
Author: Neil Randall
Pages: 675

A thorough, all-purpose Internet guide featuring scenarios for applying the Internet in business, education, and scientific tasks.

How is Windows 95 Built for the Internet?

Windows 95 includes the following Internet-related features:

- Dial-Up Networking, which supports network access through a modem connection. Dial-Up Networking can be used to access an Internet server and support TCP/IP and other required protocols.

- TCP/IP, for IP Internet access by dial-up or direct network connection. Windows 95's TCP/IP protocol stack runs in 32-bit protected mode, for top performance and minimal system overhead.

- SLIP (and CSLIP) and PPP protocols, so you can sign up for either type of IP account.

- Support for Internet e-mail in Microsoft Exchange, Windows 95's all-purpose messaging program.

- Very basic Internet access utilities, including
  FTP client
  Telnet
  Ping (a utility for checking your Internet connection)

- Software for accessing the Microsoft Network, which can be used as a gateway to some Internet resources (see "One-Stop Shopping—The Microsoft Network," later in this chapter). If you use The Microsoft Network to access Internet resources, you do not need any of Windows 95's other Internet-support features.

> **TIP**
>
> Most users will want to use third-party, Windows-based applications for these functions, instead of the more primitive command-line programs. Many third-party programs offer a more intuitive, Windows-style way to exploit Internet resources. More importantly, there are some Internet resources—such as the WWW, Gopher, and newsgroups—for which Windows 95 includes no client program or utility.
>
> Microsoft Plus! adds a number of Internet enhancements, including
>
> - Internet Explorer, a 32-bit graphical WWW browser capable of handling multimedia resources. Internet Explorer can be used with MSN Internet accounts or dial-up Internet accounts.
> - An Internet Wizard for conveniently configuring Windows 95 for the Internet.
>
> Both of these tools are described later in this chapter.

About Service Providers

You may know that no one owns the Internet and that using it is free, and that's essentially true. However, Internet access providers must lease high-speed telecommunications lines to the Internet, and they pass that cost on to their subscribers. In many cities, you can often find free Internet access through universities and through FreeNets, Internet gateways set up as a public service. As the Internet grows more popular, however, free access is becoming harder to find; and when you do find it, it's usually the less-capable command-line form and/or supplied by an underequipped, overtaxed, and therefore unreliable source.

Fortunately, options abound for reasonably priced ($15 to $25 per month) dial-up IP accounts. To find one in your area, check the Yellow Pages, or ask your local computer store or computer user's group. If you can't find a local provider, there are national providers that accept subscribers from anywhere. Be careful, though, to add the cost of long-distance phone charges when comparing prices, if the provider does not have a toll-free (1-800) number. Note too whether the voice number for technical support is toll-free. Also examine the pricing scheme; increasingly, providers charge a single monthly fee for unlimited access time, but some offer pay-by-the-hour, "time-based" plans. Some also offer budget plans with limited access, such as "E-mail only" accounts that let you send and receive e-mail and do nothing else.

You can find lists of local and national access providers in many Internet books, including *The Internet Unleashed* and *Navigating the Internet with Windows 95*, both published by Sams. These books include lists of access providers, plus suggestions for finding the names of more access providers.

One-Stop Shopping—The Microsoft Network

Microsoft's new online information service, The Microsoft Network (MSN), offers easy point-and-click access to some Internet resources.

There are two types of MSN accounts: Regular and Internet. At this writing, no pricing information is available for either type of account, but Internet accounts have a different pricing structure than regular accounts, and will, presumably, be more expensive than regular accounts. Fees for both types of accounts are billed to your credit card.

Regular MSN accounts offer access to a range of basic MSN services, including access to Internet e-mail and newsgroups. As part of its basic (non-Internet) accounts, MSN offers

- E-mail: Using Microsoft Exchange as a mail client, you can exchange e-mail with other MSN users and with Internet users as well. (You do not need an MSN Internet account to exchange Internet mail.)

- Bulletin boards: Users can post public messages or questions regarding a topic, and read other users' questions, comments, and answers in MSN bulletin boards. There are many different bulletin boards, each centering around a given topic. These are similar to Internet newsgroups, but they are *not* Internet newsgroups.

- Internet newsgroups: MSN packages the various categories of Internet newsgroups into folders. You can navigate to them, read messages, and post messages. (You do not need an MSN Internet account to use newsgroups through MSN.)

- Chat rooms: In chat rooms, MSN users communicate "live" with one another in groups by typing their comments in a window that all participants can read. This facility is similar to Internet Relay Chat, but it is *not* Internet Relay Chat.

- File libraries: MSN offers an extensive holding of files for downloading programs and files heavily slanted (for obvious reasons) toward Windows.

- Microsoft Customer Service: A hotline to Microsoft Customer Service so you can ask a representative why MSN's Internet access isn't complete.

- Information Services: The usual online information services folks have come to expect from online services: news, sports, weather, stock quotes, and special interest services.

NOTE

For more about Microsoft Network's regular accounts, see Appendix E.

MSN's Internet accounts offer all the same services included in regular accounts, plus access to the World Wide Web, Gopher menus and FTP file transfers, all through Internet Explorer, Microsoft's all-in-one WWW/Gopher/FTP tool. Note that having an MSN Internet account does not change the way you access Internet e-mail and newsgroups, which you still do in the same way as regular MSN users.

Note also that MSN's Internet accounts provide no way to access the Internet's live communications facilities: IRC, Talk, and MUDs. Finally, MSN Internet accounts, at this writing, do not allow you to select your own client software. You must use the MSN interface for newsgroup access, Exchange for e-mail, and Internet Explorer for all other Internet tasks.

Why Use MSN for Internet Access?

While MSN's Internet access is incomplete and restricted, there are reasons to go with MSN.

First of all, there are folks who only need, or only want, Internet e-mail access, and maybe newsgroups. If that's you, you don't even need an MSN Internet account—a regular MSN account supplies all the Internet functions you need, and at a cost that's probably favorable to most genuine Internet accounts. (Note that CompuServe and America Online also offer Internet e-mail and newsgroups, so shop around.)

For those who want more of the Internet, MSN's Internet account offers a very easy setup and configuration routine. You don't have to fiddle with TCP/IP, PPP, or SLIP on your PC. All you have to do is properly install your modem, and the Internet Wizard pretty much does the rest. Using MSN is also an advantage if you use the Internet while traveling. When away from home, you can switch to another MSN access number so the connection is still a local call. With most regular IP accounts, you'd have to dial the same number you dial at home, and pay the long distance charges.

MSN's Internet accounts do leave out live communications facilities, but comparatively few Internet users visit these anyway. The most important Internet services—e-mail, WWW access, FTP, and newsgroups—are all available. While you cannot select your own client software for accessing these resources, the tools MSN requires are fully capable, if not exceptional. Using MSN also saves you the hassle of finding, choosing, and configuring your own client software.

Setting Up an MSN Internet Account

You install a regular MSN account through the "Sign up for the Microsoft Network" icon that appears automatically on the Windows 95 desktop after setup. But to install an MSN Internet account, you need the Internet Wizard for setup, and Microsoft's WWW Browser, Internet Explorer. You can get these by purchasing Microsoft Plus!, or you can sign up temporarily for a regular MSN account, download the Wizard and Internet Explorer, and then run the Wizard to set up an MSN Internet account.

To install an MSN account, be sure you have already installed and configured a modem in Windows 95. Then open the Internet Wizard, and follow the prompts to select a dial-up number, username, and password, and to enter your billing information. When you finish, you're online.

Using Newsgroups Through MSN

Whether you have a regular MSN account or an MSN Internet account, you use Internet newsgroups through the standard MSN interface.

As a newsreader, MSN tries hard to mask some of the "techie" appearance of the newsgroup naming scheme. On the Internet, newsgroups are loosely categorized by general type through a series of abbreviations separated by periods: sci. (science), comp. (computers), soc. (social issues), alt. ("alternative" groups covering a wide range of interests), and so on. A real newsgroup name looks something like this:

```
alt.video.laserdiscs
```

or

```
sci.language.translation
```

Once you get used to them, these names are no big deal, and in fact, they're helpful. MSN hides them, though, in favor of gathering groups of a type together in a hierarchical folder structure. You'll find, for example, a .sci folder that holds other folders containing various subcategories under sci. Within a particular newsgroup, MSN also creates folders containing *threads*, messages that share the same subject line. Through this categorization, MSN lets you point-and-click your way through newsgroups until you find what you want.

To access newsgroups from the MSN Home Page, choose Categories and then Internet Newsgroups. A window opens offering a folder containing All Newsgroups, plus two other choices for basic newsgroup instructions and a course in *Netiquette*, the unofficial code of conduct for using the Internet without irritating others.

TIP

If you're a new user, be sure to acquaint yourself with Netiquette. Internet folks are basically hospitable, but they can be downright hostile to new users who break taboos.

A few years ago, when the America Online information service first offered access to Internet newsgroups, a flood of neophyte users (*newbies*) hit the newsgroups, ignored the rules, and were subsequently scorched by *flames* (online complaints, often hostile, and sometimes cruel) from ticked-off Internet types, who, to this day, grumble about AOL users. Some of the grumbling is pure snobbery—too many people are visiting the Internet users' playground. Still, like any community, the Internet has a code of

548

conduct (albeit unofficial and unenforced), and if you want to get along with your neighbors in cyberspace, you should observe it.

When you select All Newsgroups, you'll see more folders offering Regional and International newsgroups, Other newsgroups, and Usenet newsgroups. Most newsgroups fall under Usenet, but you may find interesting alternatives in the other folders.

When you choose Usenet, you'll see several icons grouping the available newsgroups by category. Each of these leads to several levels of other folders, until at last you arrive at a listing of messages for a particular newsgroup. Reading a newsgroup message is a matter of double-clicking on it. You'll see something like the screen shown in Figure 21.1.

FIGURE 21.1.

Reading a newsgroup message in the Microsoft Network.

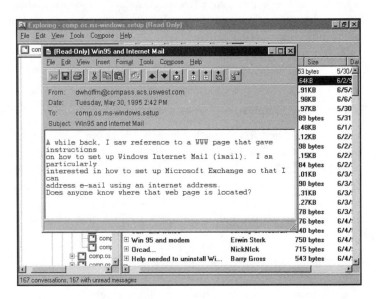

From the screen shown in Figure 21.1, you can reply to the message (which simply allows you to post a new message with the same subject line as the one you're reading), or compose a new message to be posted to this newsgroup.

MSN's method of hiding actual newsgroup names may frustrate experienced Internet users. Fortunately, few experienced users are likely to switch to MSN for Internet activities. For new users, MSN's approach makes newsgroup access a little more organized, but time-consuming. Also, because it masks newsgroup names, MSN prevents users from acquiring the skills necessary to use newsgroups in any other way but through MSN. Those wanting to make heavy use of newsgroups and not especially interested in MSN's other services should seriously consider a regular dial-up IP account and good newsreader software.

Using Internet E-mail Through MSN

MSN is integrated with Microsoft Exchange, so you manage your MSN e-mail through your Inbox—including any Internet mail routed through MSN. As with newsgroups, you perform Internet e-mail tasks through Exchange in exactly the same way whether you have a regular MSN account or an MSN Internet account.

Exchange requires that every *messaging service* you use be listed in your Exchange profile. When you sign up for the Microsoft Network, the messaging service "Internet through Microsoft Network" is added automatically to your Exchange profile.

To check and receive Internet Mail, open Exchange, choose Tools, then Deliver Mail, and then select Internet mail from the list of available services (see Figure 21.2). If you are not already connected to MSN, Exchange automatically dials MSN and connects to the service. It then downloads any waiting e-mail to your PC. Instead of first opening Exchange, you can simply sign on to MSN. When you do, it automatically checks for waiting e-mail, and asks whether you want to open your Inbox and read it. If you choose Yes, your Inbox opens, and the e-mail appears in the Inbox message list.

FIGURE 21.2.

Collecting Internet e-mail from MSN.

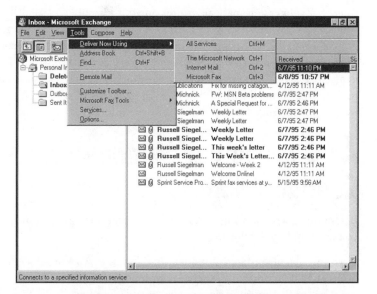

TWO WAYS TO GET E-MAIL

When you set up MSN, you can choose to have your e-mail delivered one of two ways:

■ Exchange can download just the message headers at first, and then download to your PC only the messages you choose to read

■ Exchange can automatically download the complete text of all messages when you choose to Deliver mail

Using the World Wide Web, Gopher, and FTP through MSN

OK, let's get this straight right here:

- "Windows Explorer" is the name of Windows 95's all-purpose file/folder access mechanism, the replacement for Windows 3.1's File Manager and Program Manager.

- "Internet Explorer" is the name of Microsoft's World Wide Web browser, which enables you to surf the WWW and Gopher menus, and download files through a dial-up Internet connection or an MSN Internet connection. It has no relationship whatsoever to "Windows Explorer," except for the fact that both were named without regard for the confusion they would create.

With that settled, the Internet Explorer described later in this chapter is a capable WWW browser. It does not have all of the high-end bells and whistles of popular shareware browsers like Mosaic or NetScape Navigator, but it has the most important features (except for a built-in newsreader).

Internet Explorer automatically stores on your PC copies of WWW pages you visit. That capability works with Windows 95's *auto-connect* feature to enable you to work offline. You can move through WWW pages that are stored on your PC without connecting to the Internet. When you get to an activity for which no page is stored on your PC, Internet Explorer automatically dials MSN to retrieve it. This feature is handy if you work at home, and don't want to tie up the phone line. It will be even more handy if, when Microsoft announces its pricing strategy for Internet access, it charges by the minute.

An Overview of Windows Internet Configuration

Before you can set up your Windows PC for dial-up access to a SLIP or PPP Internet account, you need to do the following.

1. Install and configure a modem in Windows. A 14,400 bps modem or faster is ideal; a 9600 may work in a pinch—temporarily. Modems running at 28,800 bps are great, but not all access providers support this speed yet. Still, 28,800 bps access is growing in popularity, so if you must buy a modem now, a 28,000 bps modem is a good investment, even if your provider supports only 14,400 bps. (Buy the faster modem, and then shop for a faster provider!) Anything slower than 9600 bps is unacceptable for this type of account, and 9600 bps modems will do only one thing quickly—exhaust your patience.

   If your modem was already installed in your PC before you installed Windows 95, it was configured during Windows setup. If you install a modem after setting up

Windows 95, you must use the Add New Hardware program in Control panel to configure the modem before it can be used by Windows 95.

2. Locate an Internet access provider and establish an account. Your proper Windows configuration is determined not so much by the Internet as by your service provider's Internet servers. The settings you need are entirely dependent on how that server is set up, and server configurations vary widely, even among those of type SLIP or PPP.

   Your access provider will tell you exactly which configuration settings you require. At the very least, the provider must tell you

   - The telephone number your modem must dial to access the server
   - Your user ID and password (you can probably choose one or both of these yourself) for logging onto the network
   - That the server assigns you an IP address and subnet mask automatically
   - Your unique IP address and subnet mask (and gateway, if necessary)
   - Your full Internet e-mail address
   - The DNS server address
   - The e-mail (SMTP) server address
   - The news server (NNTP) address

   You won't need the SMTP and NNTP server addresses for configuring Windows 95, but you will need them when configuring client software to use e-mail and newsgroups.

3. Install and configure TCP/IP.

4. Create a dial-up connection for dialing your access provider, and configure it to use the PPP or SLIP protocol.

> **NOTE**
>
> The following sections provide a simple overview of installing and configuring TCP/IP for Internet access, based on information supplied by your access provider. For advanced TCP/IP information, see Chapter 26, "Remote Access."

For users with local network connection to a server on the Internet, the procedures for configuration are essentially the same, except that TCP/IP should be bound to the network adapter instead of the Microsoft Dial-Up adapter, and no dial-up connection is necessary.

You can configure Windows 95 for the Internet in either of two ways:

   - The Microsoft Plus! add-on package includes an Internet Wizard for automating steps 3 and 4 of configuring Windows 95 for the Internet. It also creates some useful enhancements for Internet connections, and imposes some limitations. For information about using the Internet Wizard to set up your Windows 95 Internet accounts, see Configuring Windows 95 with the Internet Wizard.

■ If you don't have Microsoft Plus!, or don't want to use the Wizard, you can configure Windows 95's Internet access manually, according to the instructions that follow in "Configuring Windows 95 for Internet Access."

Configuring Windows 95 for Internet Access

You can install TCP/IP during Windows setup through Custom setup (see Chapter 1, "The Windows 95 User Interface"). TCP/IP is listed under the optional communications components among the Microsoft protocols.

After setup, you can install TCP/IP through Control Panel:

1. Open the Network icon and click the Add button.

2. In the list that appears, double-click Protocol. A dialog appears, listing manufacturers of protocols on the left and the protocols supplied on the right.

3. Select Microsoft from the Manufacturers list, and then Microsoft TCP/IP from the list of Protocols.

4. Click OK. Proceed to configuring TCP/IP, described in the next section.

Configuring TCP/IP

To configure TCP/IP for Internet access

1. Open Control Panel, and then the Network icon.

2. In the list of Network components, select TCP/IP and click Properties. A screen appears like the one shown in Figure 21.4.

In the tabs on the sheet in Figure 21.3, supply information required by your access provider. Note that you do not have to complete all the tabs; you need to enter only what your access provider requires.

> **IP Address tab:** Enter your IP address and subnet mask (provided by your access provider), or click Obtain an IP address from a DHCP server and leave the other fields blank.

FIGURE 21.3.

TCP/IP Properties.

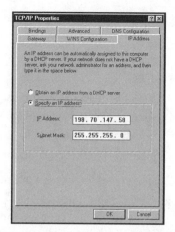

NOTE

Some access providers' servers are equipped with Dynamic Host Configuration Protocol (DHCP). DHCP automatically assigns an IP address and subnet mask to users each time they sign on to the network, so their TCP/IP configurations do not have to supply these values. If your access provider uses DHCP, you will not have to supply an IP address and subnet mask on the IP Address tab, as described previously. Instead, you simply click Obtain an IP address from a DHCP server, and leave the rest to your Internet access provider.

DNS Configuration tab: If your provider gives you a "DNS" value, you are required to enable and use DNS. The Domain Name System (DNS) is a database that translates a system of names, called "domains," into (and out of) numerical IP addresses.

Gateway tab: If your access provider gives you a gateway value, enter it here and click Add.

WINS (Windows Internet Name Service) Configuration tab: If your access provider gives you a WINS value, enable WINS and enter the value here.

After you finish supplying all required information in these tabs and click OK, you must restart Windows for your changes to take effect.

Making a Dial-Up Networking Connection for the Internet

After TCP/IP is configured, you need to create a Dial-Up Networking connection to initiate your modem, dial the access provider, and log into the server. If you've configured everything correctly, this final step puts you on the Internet.

How you configure dial-up networking depends on the type of server you're dialing into. If your access provider uses

- UNIX PPP servers, you must create a dial-up Networking connection and choose PPP as the Server type.
- UNIX SLIP (or CSLIP) servers, you must install support for UNIX SLIP from your Windows 95 CD-ROM, and then set up your dial-up Networking connection, choosing SLIP as the Server type.

To make a Dial-Up Networking connection for Internet access

1. Open Dial-Up Networking in My Computer or the Accessories menu.
2. Open Make New Connection. You'll be prompted to name the connection ("Internet," for example) and choose a modem (your default modem is pre-selected). Enter a name and, if necessary, change the modem selection, and then click Next.
3. Enter your Internet access provider's dial-up number, and click Next.
4. Click Finish to save your new connection. A new icon appears in the Dial-Up Networking folder.
5. Right-click the new icon to bring up its context menu, and select Properties. From the Properties menu, click Server Type. You'll see a screen like the one shown in Figure 21.4.

FIGURE 21.4.

Choosing a Server Type for an Internet connection.

Select the appropriate Server type for your Internet connection, and click OK.

- For UNIX PPP servers, choose PPP.
- For a SLIP or compressed SLIP (CSLIP) connection, choose SLIP or CSLIP.

NOTE

If SLIP and CSLIP do not appear on the list of Server Types, you have not yet installed the UNIX Connection for Dial-Up Networking option, described in the next section.

Installing and Configuring SLIP

You create a Dial-Up Networking connection for SLIP and CSLIP accounts exactly as you do for PPP accounts, as described earlier. The only difference is that SLIP support is not installed by default as a Server Type; you must install it before setting up your Dial-Up Networking connection.

NOTE

SLIP/CSLIP support is available only from the Windows 95 CD-ROM, not from the diskette version.

To install SLIP support, follow these steps:

1. Open Control Panel, and then open Add/Remove Programs.
2. Click the Windows Setup tab. A list of installed Windows components appears. Insert your Windows 95 CD-ROM and click Have Disk.
3. Enter the directory

   `d:\ADMIN\APPTOOLS\SLIP`

   and click OK. A dialog appears, listing Unix Connection for Dial-Up Networking as a Windows component. Make sure the component's checkbox is checked, and then click Install.
4. Perform the steps for setting up a Dial-Up Networking connection, described earlier in this chapter. When selecting a Server Type, choose SLIP for a SLIP server, or CSLIP for a CSLIP server.
5. On the Properties sheet for the Dial-Up connection, uncheck the checkbox for Logon to network. You must manually log into SLIP accounts, as described later in this chapter.

TIP

Your Internet access provider should supply you with complete and accurate configuration information. If you've followed the instructions in this chapter and entered exactly the information your provider has given you, you should connect to the Internet through the provider. If you still experience problems, your first step should be to double-check your configuration, making sure all your settings match the provider's instructions. Then you should describe your problem to your access provider's technical support department. Often, access providers make changes to their own server configurations that require matching changes in each user's configuration. Sometimes, they neglect to properly inform users of changes, and they sometimes distribute out-of-date instructions to new users. Also, because Windows 95 is a new operating system, many providers are themselves still learning exactly how their Windows 95 users should configure their communications.

If you can't get help from your provider, try the following:

1. Get a new provider with better technical support.

2. On some PPP accounts, you have to perform a manual terminal logon after connection, much as you do for SLIP accounts. To set this up, open the Properties sheet for the Internet Dial-Up Networking connection, click Configure, and then click Options. Check the checkbox next to Bring up terminal window after dialing. When you connect to your provider, the terminal window opens so the provider can prompt you for your logon ID and password.

3. On some SLIP accounts, compression settings may vary from Windows defaults. Consult your access provider about the proper settings. Open Control Panel, then Network, and then select Dial-Up adapter and click the Advanced tab. Change the selections for compression as necessary. Then click OK, and restart Windows.

Going Online

To connect to the Internet, double-click the icon for your Internet Dial-Up Networking connection, and click Connect. Windows displays a dialog showing your network user ID and prompting for a password. Enter your password and click OK. (If yours is a home computer and password security is not a concern, check the Save password checkbox so you won't have to enter it again.) Windows initializes your modem, dials your service provider, initiates TCP/IP communications, and connects to the server through your selected protocol.

If you're using SLIP or using PPP with the terminal logon option, a terminal window pops up after Dial-Up Networking has established a connection. You must complete the logon procedure as described next.

■ For PPP with terminal logon: Enter your user ID and password when prompted to do so. After entering your password, press F7 or click Continue to close the terminal window and enable Windows to complete the PPP connection.

■ For SLIP: Enter your user ID and password when prompted to do so. The server responds with your TCP/IP address, as shown in Figure 21.5. Make a note of the IP address, and then press F7 to enable Windows to complete the logon procedure. A dialog appears like the one shown in Figure 21.6.

FIGURE 21.5.

Logging on to a SLIP server.

FIGURE 21.6.

Verifying your IP address.

Make sure the address assigned to you in the terminal window (Figure 21.5) is the same as the one shown in the IP address dialog (Figure 21.6). If it is, click OK. If not, type the assigned IP address in the IP address dialog and click OK.

When Windows completes the logon procedure, it displays the message "Connected" and begins timing the connection. You are connected to the Internet. You can start any Windows sockets-based Internet applications to navigate to and use specific Internet resources.

Configuring Windows 95 with the Internet Wizard

Among other handy and cool add-ins, the Microsoft Plus! kit for Windows 95 features a setup wizard for Internet configuration of PPP accounts. The wizard leads you through the collection of all the information required for installing and configuring TCP/IP and PPP and creating a Dial-Up Networking connection. You can acquire the wizard by purchasing Microsoft Plus!. You can also download it from the Microsoft Network.

> **NOTE: THE "PLUS" MEANS "PLUS HARDWARE"**
>
> Microsoft Plus! requires a 486-based PC, 8 MB of memory, and a 256-color display adapter (a high-color adapter is strongly recommended). While these are reasonable requirements for any Windows 95-based PC, they exceed the official minimums required for Windows 95 (386, 4MB, 16 colors), so some Windows 95 users may not be able to run Microsoft Plus!. For more about Plus!, see Chapter 14.

Is Plus! a Plus?

Microsoft Plus! automates TCP/IP configuration and the creation of a Dial-Up Networking connection for PPP accounts in Windows 95. You still have to supply the same information to Windows that you would supply in a manual configuration, but the wizard leads you through the steps, making sure you've hit all the bases.

The wizard also deposits a nifty Internet icon on your desk, and links your Internet setup to a handy configuration management program, Internet Control Panel. Finally, the Internet Wizard configures your Internet connection to open the Microsoft WWW browser, Internet Explorer, when you connect to the Internet.

Of course, there's a downside. Using the wizard forces you to open Internet Explorer at the beginning of every Internet session. If you use a different WWW browser, or if you do something besides browsing the WWW when you start up, you'll still have to watch Explorer start up anyway. It's no big deal—you can open another program right on top of Explorer, or even close Explorer without closing the Internet connection—but it's not an elegant way to begin a session. This is yet another example of a Windows facility that ever so gently attempts to steer you Microsoft's way. Also, keep in mind that you cannot use the Wizard for SLIP accounts or Windows 3.1, or on computers with less than 8 MB of memory or a 386 processor.

Using the Internet Wizard

To use the Wizard, begin by installing Microsoft Plus!. When Plus! installation is complete, the Internet setup Wizard starts automatically. You can set up the Internet right away, or click Cancel and restart the Wizard at a later time. (To restart the Wizard later, open Accessories, then Internet Tools, and select Internet Setup Wizard.)

1. When the Wizard starts up, you'll see a Welcome screen. Click Next to continue.

2. A screen appears asking how you want to connect to the Internet—through the Microsoft Network or through your own account. Click the radio button next to "I already have an account..." and then click Next.

TIP

In Step 2, you can choose "Microsoft Network" instead, to set up a Microsoft Network Internet account. See "One-Stop Shopping—The Microsoft Network" earlier in this chapter.

3. A screen appears prompting you for the name of your provider. Enter any name here; this simply names the Dial-Up Networking connection used to access the Internet. I used the name of my access provider, but I could have simply used "Internet." Click Next, and a screen appears like the one shown in Figure 21.7.

FIGURE 21.7.

Entering the dial-up number of your Internet access provider.

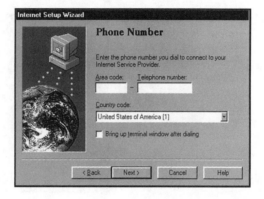

4. In the screen shown in Figure 21.7, enter the area code and number to dial to access your provider. (Windows needs the area code, but won't dial it if the number is local.) If your provider supports CHAP, do not check the checkbox next to Bring up terminal window after dialing. Otherwise, check the checkbox, and click Next.

5. In the next screen that appears fill in your username and password and click Next. Note that in many cases Internet servers are case-sensitive. You must use the exact combination of uppercase and lowercase characters your provider gives you. A screen like the one in Figure 21.8 appears.

6. If your Internet provider has assigned you a permanent IP address and subnet mask, click the radio button next to "Always use the following..." and fill in your IP address and mask. Otherwise, click the radio button next to "My Internet provider automatically assigns me one." Click Next. The screen shown in Figure 21.9 appears.

FIGURE 21.8.

Entering your IP address.

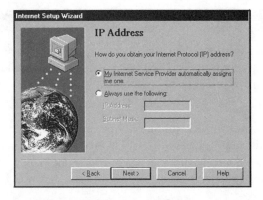

FIGURE 21.9.

Entering your DNS server address.

7. Enter the numerical IP address of your domain name system (DNS) server as shown in Figure 21.10. Note that you must type a numeric IP address, not a word-based Internet address. If your provider supplies the name of an alternate server (to use as a backup in case the primary DNS server has problems), enter it as the Alternate server. Click Next. The screen shown in Figure 21.10 appears.

FIGURE 21.10.

Setting up Internet e-mail.

8. If you plan to use Microsoft Exchange as your Internet e-mail program, leave the checkmark in the checkbox next to Use Internet Mail and fill in your full Internet e-mail address and e-mail server address. If you plan to use a third-party e-mail client, such as Eudora, un-check the checkbox and leave the address fields blank; you can set up your e-mail client later. Click Next.

9. If you un-checked the checkmark in Step 8, the next screen you see is a notice that your Internet setup is complete. If you checked the box, you see one more screen first, as shown in Figure 21.11.

FIGURE 21.11.

Choosing an Exchange Profile.

Microsoft Exchange supports the use of multiple user profiles, each containing its own list of supported messaging services and settings. The main purpose of this is to allow you to maintain a separate profile for accessing your messaging services from the road. Most users will maintain a single profile. In the screen shown in Figure 21.11, choose the profile from the drop-down list, and then click Next.

When the Wizard disappears, you'll find a few changes in Windows 95:

- A little globe labeled "Internet" appears on your desktop. This icon opens Internet Explorer, and then opens Dial-Up Networking and executes the connection created by the Internet wizard to connect you to the Internet.

- In Control Panel, a new item, Internet, appears. You use this item to change some of your configuration settings, as described in "Managing Your Configuration through Internet Control Panel," later in this chapter.

Connecting to the Internet

To connect to the Internet, double-click the Internet icon. The icon opens Internet Explorer, and then opens Dial-Up Networking and the connection for the Internet, as shown in Figure 21.12.

FIGURE 21.12.

Internet Explorer connecting to the Internet through Dial-Up Networking.

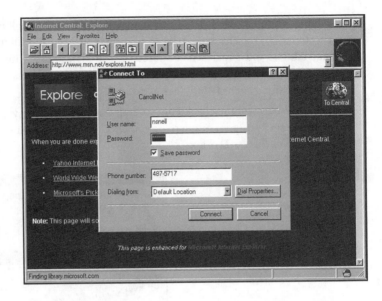

Click connect. Dial-Up Networking dials your access provider and attempts to connect to the TCP/IP network. If your provider supports CHAP or PAP, Windows completes the logon to the Internet.

If your provider does not support PAP or CHAP, a terminal window opens to display text received from the access provider's server. Fill in your username and password when prompted (be sure to follow the exact uppercase and lowercase characters your provider gave you). When the terminal window reports your IP address, press F7. The terminal window closes, and your Internet connection is complete.

Once connected to the Internet, you can immediately use Internet Explorer to access Internet resources (as described in later chapters). You can also minimize or close Explorer and open other Internet client software of your choosing.

Disconnecting from the Internet

While connected to the Internet, you see an "Internet" item minimized on the taskbar. You can open this at any time (as shown in Figure 21.13) to see how long you've been online.

FIGURE 21.13.

The Internet status box.

To disconnect from the Internet, click the Disconnect button.

Managing Your Configuration Through Internet Control Panel

The Internet Wizard creates a new Control Panel entry for the Internet. You can reach it through Control Panel, or by right-clicking the Internet icon on the desktop and choosing Properties (see Figure 21.14).

FIGURE 21.14.

The Internet Control Panel properties sheet.

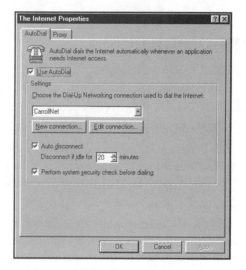

Check Use Autodial to allow Internet Explorer to automatically dial the Internet when necessary. As you discover in Chapter 11, Explorer stores WWW pages you've viewed, and can be used to examine stored pages offline. When Autodial is on, Explorer dials the Internet anytime you initiate an action that requires it.

You can also edit or create the Dial-Up Networking connection from the Control Panel. Selecting a connection and then clicking Edit or New opens the regular Windows Dial-Up Networking dialogs, from which you can control the number to dial, the opening of terminal windows and other Dial-Up Networking options.

Check Auto disconnect and specify a number of minutes if you want Windows to automatically sign you off the Internet if you are idle for a time. This feature is especially useful if you pay-per-minute charges for your Internet connection.

Finally, if you check "Perform system security check before dialog button", Windows prompts for your Windows username and password before allowing you to initiate an Internet connection.

> **NOTE: THE PROXY TAB**
>
> The other tab on the Internet Control Panel allows you to enter the address of a Proxy server. On a local area network (LAN), a proxy server is a computer connected to the Internet through which other computers on the LAN can access the Internet. Proxy servers are not involved in dial-up connections.

Internet E-mail

To send or receive e-mail across the Internet, you need a program for composing, addressing, sending, receiving, and reading e-mail. Most e-mail programs also offer such options as reply and forward, which save you the time of addressing messages when you forward a message or reply to a received message.

Your Microsoft Exchange Inbox is a fully capable e-mail program that can send, receive, and manage e-mail to and from any of the services it supports—which, at this writing, include Microsoft Mail, Microsoft Fax, the Microsoft Network, and the Internet.

The process for creating and sending an Internet message is the same as for any other service, except that you choose Internet in the New Entry dialog when creating a new address. When you select that address from your Personal Address Book in the future, any messages sent to that address are automatically routed through the Internet instead of the other supported services.

Windows 95 Internet Tools

As mentioned earlier, most Windows users will prefer to use one or more of the third-party Windows Internet access tools, or the tools bundled in the Windows 95 PlusPak, to the basic command-line tools included with Windows 95. If you need these functions rarely, however, or are accustomed to using the Internet from a command line, you may find them useful.

The commands described in the next few pages are basic Windows command-line TCP/IP programs. You execute these programs by entering them at the Windows command line. To access the command line, choose Run from the Start menu, or open an MS-DOS window.

Only the TCP/IP commands relevant to everyday Internet users are covered here. For more on TCP/IP, see Chapter 26, "Remote Access."

About Command Structure

Each command-line program has a "syntax," or basic rules for how you issue each command and its options, or "parameters."

In a syntax diagram, the command itself is shown first, exactly as you must type it. (Whether you use upper- or lowercase letters doesn't matter, however. Following the command are any optional parameters, shown in brackets. To use a parameter, you must type it exactly as shown, but do not type the brackets—they merely indicate that the parameter is optional. You may combine several parameters in one command line; just put one space between each. Although the syntax diagrams may be so long that they wrap to more than one line, note that you must enter in a single line the command and all parameters you use.

Words shown in *italics* represent items you must enter yourself. You don't type the word shown in italics; you type what it represents. For example, for a parameter like

`[name]`

I would type

`ned`

Note again that the brackets are not actually typed.

For each command described on the next several pages, the command's use is described, its syntax is shown, each of its parameters is defined and described, and then any commands are described.

> **TIP**
>
> If, after issuing the command-line command to start an Internet program, you can't remember the other commands for using the program, enter the word `help`, or just a question mark, to display descriptions of available commands.

FTP

FTP (file transfer protocol) is the basic file transfer mechanism on the Internet. Using the Windows FTP client, you can download program files, graphics, books, video and sound clips, or just about anything that can be stored in a computer file.

The files themselves must be stored on a computer configured as an "FTP server," of which there are many. FTP servers are prepared to display lists and directories of files available for downloading, and usually accept "anonymous" FTP login, so you don't need a password or user ID to download files.

FTP requires one command to establish the connection, and then enables you to issue other commands to navigate the site and download files while you are connected to the remote computer. To download a file through FTP, you connect to the Internet, and then issue the FTP command (including the FTP site address in the *host* parameter) to access the FTP site. After you are attached to the FTP site, you issue commands (see Table 21.1) to browse through the directories, download files, and quit the FTP session. A sample FTP session showing directories of files available from an FTP server is shown in Figure 21.15.

> **NOTE**
>
> Windows 95's FTP program enables you to group a list of FTP commands in a text file and then name that file in the command used to start up FTP. FTP automatically issues each command in the file after starting up.
>
> You can use this feature when you know the exact directory locations and names of files you want to download from a site. For example, you can enter the mget command (see Table 21.1), a list of filenames, and the quit command in a text file. Then issue the command to start FTP and include the name of the text file in the [-s: filename] parameter. FTP will log into the remote site, download the files, and then log off the FTP site and quit FTP, all while you get a cup of coffee.

FIGURE 21.15.

An FTP session.

The syntax is as follows:

```
ftp [-v] [-n] [-i] [-d] [-g] [host] [-s: filename]
```

-v	Turns off the display of remote server responses.
-n	Turns off automatic logon upon connection to the FTP site.
-i	Turns off prompting for each file during multiple file transfers (all files selected will be downloaded in succession without your involvement).
-d	Displays all FTP commands as they are exchanged between your PC and the FTP site.

-g	Prevents the use of wildcard characters in filenames. (You can also use the glob command, shown in Table 21.1, to control wildcard use.)
host	The name or IP address of the FTP site.
-s: *filename*	The name of a text file that contains a listing of FTP commands that will run automatically.

Table 21.1. FTP commands.

Command	Description
!	Runs a command on your computer instead of the remote computer.
?	Shows help for FTP commands.
append	Appends a file on your PC to one on the remote computer.
ascii	Enables ASCII as the transfer type (this is the default).
bell	Turns on a bell that rings after each file transfer.
binary	Enables binary as the transfer type.
bye	Quits the FTP session and FTP.
cd	Changes the directory on the remote computer.
close	Quits the FTP session with the remote computer, but keeps FTP active.
debug	Displays all commands sent to and received from the remote computer, to aid in troubleshooting.
delete	Deletes files on the remote computer.
dir	Displays a list of files and subdirectories on the remote computer.
disconnect	Disconnects from the remote computer; keeps FTP active.
get	Downloads one file.
glob	Turns "globbing" on or off. Globbing supports the use of wildcard characters in filenames and pathnames.
hash	Turns hash-mark printing for each 2048 bytes data block on or off.
help	Shows help for FTP commands.
lcd	Changes the working directory on your PC. (The current directory is the default.)
literal	Sends literal arguments to the FTP server.
ls	Shows an abbreviated list of files and subdirectories in the current directory on the FTP server.

continues

Table 21.1. continued

Command	Description
mdelete	Deletes multiple files on the FTP server.
mdir	Shows a detailed list of files and subdirectories on the FTP server, and lets you specify multiple directories.
mget	Downloads multiple files.
mkdir	Creates a new directory on the FTP server.
mls	Shows an abbreviated list of files and subdirectories on the FTP server, and lets you specify multiple directories.
mput	Uploads multiple files to the FTP server.
open	Connects to an FTP server.
prompt	Turns prompting on or off. Prompting pauses between multiple files being downloaded or uploaded (through mget and mput, respectively) so you can choose to transfer each or skip to the next.
put	Uploads a file to the FTP server.
pwd	Prints the current FTP server directory.
quit	Quits the FTP session and exits FTP.
quote	Sends literal arguments to the FTP server. (Identical to literal.)
recv	Downloads a file. Identical to get.
remotehelp	Shows help for commands on the FTP server.
rename	Renames files on the FTP server.
rmdir	Deletes a directory on the remote server.
send	Uploads a file to the FTP server. Identical to put.
status	Shows the status of all FTP connections.
trace	Turns packet tracing on or off. Packet tracing shows the route of each packet transferred by FTP.
type	Shows the file transfer type (binary or ASCII).
user	Names a user to the FTP server.
verbose	Turns verbose mode on or off. Verbose mode displays all FTP responses and a report of statistics following each file transfer.

PING

PING is used to verify Internet (TCP/IP) connections. It's a useful diagnostic tool when you're trying to determine proper Internet connections. When consulting your Internet service provider about a problem, the tech support person may ask you to use PING to check your connection.

Syntax:

```
ping [-t] [-a] [-n count] [-l length] [-f] [-i ttl] [-v tos] [-r count] [-s
➥count] [[-j host-list] ¦ [-k host-list]] [-w timeout] destination-list
```

-t	Queries the host repeatedly until interrupted.
-a	Switches off the resolving of addresses to host names.
-n *count*	Transmits four echo packets, or the number of packets specified in the optional *count*.
-l *length*	Transmits echo packets holding 64 bytes, or the amount of data specified in *length* (up to 8192 bytes).
-f	Prevents packets from being fragmented in gateways.
-i *ttl*	Sets Time To Live to the time (in milliseconds) specified in *ttl*.
-v *tos*	Sets Type Of Service to the type specified in *tos*.
-r *count*	Records the route of outgoing and returning packets. In *count*, you can choose from 1 to 9 hosts.
-s *count*	Turns on a time stamp for the number of hops specified in *count*.
-j *host-list*	Changes the routing of packets to the order of hosts (up to nine) listed in *host-list*. You can separate consecutive hosts by intermediate gateways.
-k *host-list*	Changes the routing of packets to the order of hosts (up to nine) listed in *host-list*. You cannot separate consecutive hosts by intermediate gateways.
-w *timeout*	Sets a time-out interval in milliseconds.
destination-list	Specifies the remote hosts.

Telnet

Telnet enables you to log onto remote computer systems as a guest, and work there as if you were a local user. The remote computer must be set up as a Telnet site, and it may place restrictions on what you're able to do there as a remote user. This is one of the more useful Windows command-line commands, because the command line is really used only to contact the Telnet server. Once logged in, you use the Telnet system as a local user would; in most cases, Telnet systems are simple menu-driven, terminal-style applications.

The steps required to connect to a remote Telnet server are fairly simple and consistent, but logging onto a Telnet computer and using it differs form site to site. Some require a username and password, some lead you through a first-time user routine to acquire a username and password, and still others require no username and password. The friendliest Telnet systems offer instructions, right from connection, to help you get logged on and working easily.

Many Telnet sites require your PC to be able to emulate one of the terminal types supported by the host computer. Windows' Telnet command emulates VT100, VT52, and TTY terminals.

To use Telnet:

1. Type `telnet` at the command line. (If you add the *host* name to the `telnet` command, you can skip Step 2.)

2. Choose Connect, and then Remote system.

3. Type the Host name, and then click Connect. Telnet establishes the connection (see Figure 21.16). From here, you must log onto and use the Telnet site according to instructions you've received elsewhere or according to any on-screen prompts the Telnet site supplies. While online, you can change your terminal emulation settings, screen font, and other options from the Preferences menu.

4. To end the session, log off the Telnet system, and then choose Disconnect from the Connect menu.

> **NOTE**
>
> Windows Telnet remembers every address you enter and stores the addresses in a drop-down list for easy retrieval. To use a Telnet site you've used before, enter `telnet` at the command line, then open the Connect menu, and then choose Remote System. A dialog appears, showing the drop-down list from which you can select a host address.

FIGURE 21.16.

A Telnet session.

The syntax is as follows:

```
telnet [host [port]]
```

> *host*   The Internet address of the Telnet system.
>
> *port*   The remote port. The default is the value listed in the registry under Services; if no entry exists, the default is 23.

Sample Third-Party Windows Internet Tools

A rich variety of software tools is available for Internet access through Windows, including tools for individually accessing specific types of resources (news readers for newsgroups, e-mail programs, Gopher clients, and so on) and WWW browsers, like those described next. Most of these are called "Windows sockets" applications because they conform to a standard for interfacing automatically to your Windows-based TCP/IP connection. As long as you have a properly configured IP connection, you can typically start up and use these applications without separately configuring any special communications parameters within them.

At this writing, there are no available Internet applications written specifically for Windows 95. Most Windows 3.1 and Windows NT applications will work fine, though. The WWW browsers described next are recent versions of the most popular WWW browsers. They're not Windows 95 applications by the book, but they work well under it.

Mosaic 2.0

Mosaic, shown in Figure 21.17, is an important application because, more than anything else, it is responsible for the Internet's recent popularity. Mosaic demonstrated to new users that the Internet could be friendly and fun. Microsoft's own WWW browser—featured in the Windows 95 PlusPak and as the browser on The Microsoft Network—is based on a commercial version of Mosaic called SpyGlass. But the original Mosaic has always been a freeware application, developed and distributed by the National Center for Supercomputing Applications (NCSA) at the University of Illinois at Urbana-Champaign.

A full-featured graphical WWW browser, Mosaic can display full-color graphics and play sound and video clips from the WWW. It's a 32-bit application, so it dovetails nicely with Windows 95 and performs acceptably on well-equipped machines. (Note: Mosaic can be sluggish on slower machines (486SX) and those with less than 8 MB of memory.)

Mosaic can be downloaded via FTP at

```
ftp.ncsa.uiuc.edu
```

FIGURE 21.17.

NCSA Mosaic.

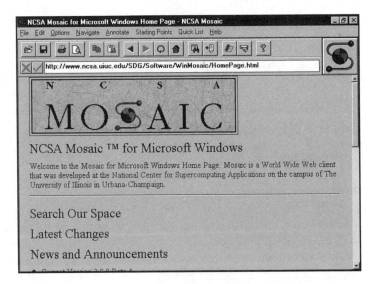

Netscape Navigator

A shareware WWW browser, Netscape Navigator (shown in Figure 21.18) is not quite as full-featured as Mosaic, but it tends to perform much better on less well-equipped PCs. It can be used free (without support) by individuals, or can be purchased for about $40 with technical support and documentation.

Netscape can be downloaded via FTP at

```
ftp.mcom.com
```

FIGURE 21.18.

Netscape.

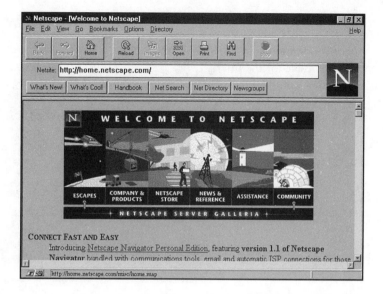

Internet Explorer

The Internet Explorer, shown in Figure 21.19, is the offspring of a rather strange lineage.

The early versions of the freeware browser Mosaic, the original graphical browser, were powerful and full-featured—so much so that the product's reliability and performance were questionable for its first few years, especially in its Windows 3.1 versions. A company called SpyGlass licensed the rights to modify Mosaic (as have many others) and to then license the result to others who wanted to market it as a commercial product. (SpyGlass also sells its own version, Enhanced Mosaic, which adds some features.) In an apparent effort to improve the product's ease-of-use, performance, and reliability, SpyGlass trimmed Mosaic of some of its features, and licensed out the pared-down, simplified program as SpyGlass Mosaic.

Finally, during Windows 95's development, Microsoft licensed rights to SpyGlass Mosaic, enhanced it for Windows 95, and released it as Internet Explorer, the official WWW browser for Windows 95 Internet connections and the Microsoft Network.

Is Internet Explorer the browser Microsoft really wanted, or is it the only one it could pick up and make ready in time? Microsoft cynic though I am, I'll choose the former; I think Internet Explorer's shallow feature pool is designed to appeal to Internet newbies who might be overwhelmed by the number of little tools and buttons in Mosaic or NetScape.

Despite its simplicity, Explorer is a full-featured browser that performs very well for two reasons: First, it's a 32-bit multithreaded Windows 95 application, a fact that not only boosts performance, but also supports simultaneous downloads. Second, it employs "progressive rendering" of graphics (which Navigator also does, but not Mosaic). That feature displays all text before the graphics, and then transfers the graphics in stages. It allows you to activate a link and jump to another page without first waiting for the graphics to appear.

FIGURE 21.19.

Internet Explorer, at Microsoft's Explorer home page.

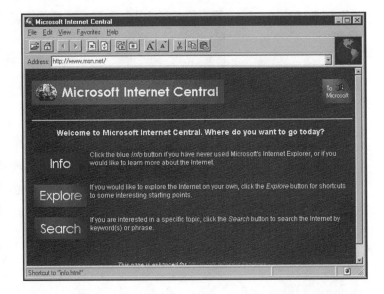

TIP

Internet Explorer includes a facility for creating shortcuts to WWW pages. When viewing a page, choose File, and then Create Shortcut. Explorer deposits a shortcut to that page on the Windows desktop. Double-clicking that icon opens Explorer and displays to page (if it is cached), or dials the Internet and retrieves the page (if the page is not cached).

Summary

The Internet is the place to be, and if you're not a user, it's likely you will be soon. Windows 95 doesn't offer a lot of built-in help with getting hooked on, but it does offer the most important underpinnings for successful Internet surfing—a 32-bit TCP/IP stack and support for PPP and SLIP protocols. Getting online is a matter of finding a service provider, configuring protocols in Windows, creating a Dial-Up Networking connection, and then running Internet software tools.

This chapter concludes Part V. In Part VI, you'll learn about Windows 95's networking support.

VI
PART

Networking with Windows 95

Windows 95 and Networking

If you've used Windows or Windows for Workgroups, you know that connecting to a local area network can be a bothersome task. Installing the hardware, configuring the kernel, loading the drivers, manually editing files, and incessant testing are all onerous tasks made more difficult by a lack of standardization across network protocols. Relax! Windows 95 makes these tasks much easier!

What's so hot about Windows 95 when it comes to networking? The primary feature is that Windows 95 supports more than one protocol at a time, so you can be connected and working on two or three different networks at the same time. This means you can use Novell NetWares IPX/SPX for your workgroup client/server system, and then switch to TCP/IP when you want to talk to the UNIX server with Internet access. You can transfer files between the TCP/IP network and the Novell NetWare network without having to reconfigure and reboot each time.

Windows 95 is more compatible with Novell's NetWare. Windows 95 has been designed to integrate as cleanly with NetWare as possible, making use of fast, efficient 32-bit drivers that take up no conventional memory. Instead of defaulting to the Windows for Workgroups NetBIOS network protocol, NetWare's IPX/SPX is the new default. Windows 95's NetWare drivers are even better than Novell's!

Peer-to-peer networking is simple with Windows 95. Slap in a hardware adapter card, select the software from a menu-driven list, and you're running as a full partner on most of the popular peer-to-peer local area network systems available today. Windows 95 supports several different peer-to-peer protocols directly, and older 16-bit drivers can be used for the rest.

For dial-up use, Windows 95 sets a new standard for ease. With the Remote Access Server, you can access your desktop machine or workgroup server from anywhere on the road, transfer files, and launch applications over a modem line. Automatic synchronization of your laptop and desktop machines means you don't have to worry about which files were modified while you were on the road.

Network device support has been improved, with network printing and network backup software all part of the Windows 95 package. With these features, you can effectively share network resources with everyone else on your LAN.

Best of all, the configuration and management processes have been streamlined to a few dialogs, common to all the network protocols. From one main network window you can add hardware and software, configure existing software, switch protocols, handle file and printer access, and control your network environment. Windows 95 has many new features that were missing in the older Windows 3.1 and Windows for Workgroups 3.11 releases.

New Default Protocol

Windows for Workgroups 3.11 used NetBEUI as the default network protocol. Windows 95 changes the default to IPX/SPX, which is Novell NetWare's protocol. You can, of course, still use NetBEUI as a protocol in a Windows for Workgroups network.

Microsoft made the change in network protocol for two primary reasons. First, Novell NetWare is the most widely used network, so the odds are good that a new Windows 95 system will be added to an IPX/SPX network instead of a NetBEUI. Secondly, IPX/SPX is a routable protocol, meaning it can work across multiple networks. NetBEUI isn't routable.

The new NetWare drivers included with Windows 95 are written in 32-bit protected mode, making them more robust. The network driver has been designed for faster performance for NetWare 3.x and 4.x systems.

Faster Network Interaction

Windows 95 uses a 32-bit architecture to provide for faster communications between your applications and the network. The network drivers in Windows 95 are implemented as Virtual Device Drivers (VxDs) that are 32-bit, protected-mode applications. Because they are 32-bit protected mode, they do not require any of your machine's conventional memory, leaving more of this vital resource for memory-hungry applications.

The 32-bit architecture is extended to all facets of networking support. Windows 95 includes 32-bit network client software, 32-bit network protocols, 32-bit network interface card drivers, 32-bit file and printer sharing software, and so on. This is combined with support for existing 16-bit software applications and DLLs currently in use with Windows for Workgroups.

More Robust Network Drivers

Because Windows 95 uses Virtual Device Drivers (VxDs) that reside in 32-bit memory for networking, there is much less chance of an application overwriting or affecting the network device driver (a process colloquially called *stepping on* the driver). This reduces the risk of network problems and machine lock-ups caused by driver corruption.

As Windows 95 is introduced, not all network operating systems support Virtual Device Drivers. However, most of those that do not have VxDs have announced they will be introducing such a driver shortly. The most popular networks, including Windows for Workgroups, Windows NT, Novell NetWare, and Artisoft LANtastic, have all released VxDs.

Multiple Networks and Multiple Protocols

Windows 95 lets you run several network protocols, network operating systems, and network cards simultaneously. For comparison, earlier versions of Windows provided support for only one network operating system and one network card at a time. Supporting multiple networks, multiple protocols, and multiple redirectors makes Windows 95 capable of fitting into many different heterogeneous network environments.

Windows 95 includes the network protocol drivers for the most popular networks, including IPX, NetBEUI, TCP/IP, SNMP, and DMI. With previous versions of Windows, you had to purchase separate products to provide some of these network drivers. Dial-up support for remote access is provided, as is support for PPP (Point to Point Protocol) and SLIP (Serial Line Interface Protocol), both widely used to connect to the Internet.

Windows 95 also provides excellent integration with Windows NT Server systems, offering fast client/server support in an NT environment.

Single Logons

Windows 95 enables you to set up networks so that you can access connected networks and any network peripherals using a single login account and password. Previously, if you wanted to move from one network to another, you usually had to log into a machine on each network, providing user names and passwords each time. If you used a number of different networks (such as a Novell NetWare and a UNIX network) regularly, this became a considerable annoyance.

Windows 95 makes it possible for the network administrators to establish your accounts on servers so that Windows 95 can do the logging in and password verification process automatically. This leaves you with a single login and password for all networks you have access to—a much simpler and user-friendly arrangement. (The same capabilities have existed on larger systems, such as UNIX networks, for many years, so Windows 95 is finally moving these features to the PC.)

As a side benefit, security has been enhanced with Windows 95, allowing for better network-wide security within Windows and LAN Manager networks. For other networks, Windows 95 relies on the native security methods.

Long Filenames and Server Names

The old eight-character, period, three-character filename that we know so well from DOS can now be replaced with longer, more descriptive names. (Again, this is a feature that has finally moved from larger systems—and the Macintosh—to Windows.) Your system must be set up to support long filenames; you can finally call your files by a useful name, instead of a cramped, compressed approximation of what the file is about.

The same is true for servers. Instead of short, simple names, a server can now have a more descriptive name. Names can be indicative of the owner, the department the server belongs to, or its physical location: It doesn't matter what the name really is, just that it is now more descriptive of the server.

Windows 95 also supports Universal Naming Convention (UNC), which means that the old technique of mapping server directories to a local directory (such as mapping the server's directory D:\user\tparker\book to the local drive E:) can be replaced.

Plug and Play Network Card Installation

You already know about Plug and Play capabilities within Windows 95. This makes it much easier to install network interface cards. With Plug and Play, you can just drop a network card in an available motherboard slot or to a PCMCIA slot and have Windows 95 detect the card type and the driver needed. Windows 95 will configure itself to the network card and load the driver without requiring intervention from you.

This is tremendously useful for portables, where you can run Windows 95 without network drivers until you plug in your PCMCIA network card. Windows 95 will sense the card and its network type, and load the proper drivers. When a network card is removed from a portable, it is not necessary to reboot the machine in order to keep working: Windows 95 adjusts itself automatically in most cases.

Simpler Access to Network Resources

Windows 95's My Computer window displays all the network resources you have access to, as well as your local machine's resources. This makes it as easy to print a file on a color laser printer attached to the network as it is to print the file on a bubble jet printer attached to your computer's parallel port.

Other network resources, such as tape drives, CD-ROM drives, scanners, high-speed printers, and plotters are all readily accessible through an icon in the My Computer window. As long as you have access to the resource, it will appear in the My Computer window.

Better Administration Tools

Most users don't notice the network until something goes wrong. That's when diagnostic and administration tools become important. Windows 95 enhances the tools that

Windows for Workgroups introduced, such as NetWatcher. The network tools let you watch the behavior of the network, see how efficiently it is performing, how heavily loaded it is, and perform simple troubleshooting tasks.

Most of the administration and configuration utilities can be run remotely, so a network administrator can manage a large network from one machine.

Windows 95 Networking Architecture

Windows 95 refines the network architecture used in Windows for Workgroups and Windows NT, resulting in better performance and reliability, as well as catering to the demands of different network requirements such as multiple protocol support. Because Windows 95 supports many different network protocols in 16- and 32-bit Virtual Mode Driver (VxD) versions, the architecture must provide the flexibility to accommodate a number of structures.

The Windows 95 architecture is layered. The network architecture is known as Microsoft's Windows Open Services Architecture (WOSA). WOSA was developed to enable applications to work with several different network types and includes a set of interfaces designed to allow coexistence of several network components.

The networking software components of Windows 95 are shown in their respective layers in Figure P6.1. Many of the network components will be familiar from earlier versions of Windows for Workgroups, Windows NT, or other operating systems and communications protocols. We can look at each layer in the Windows 95 architecture in a little more detail so that the function of each component is better understood.

FIGURE P6.1.

The Windows 95 networking software architecture showing the components.

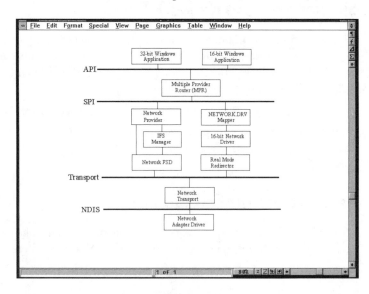

- **API:** The standard Win32 Application Programming Interface (API, the same system used with Windows NT). The API handles remote file operations and remote resources (printers and other devices). The Win32 APIs are used for programming applications.

- **Multiple Provider Router (MPR):** The MPR routes all network operations for Windows 95, as well as implementing network functions common to all network types. Win32 APIs communicate directly with the MPR, although some may be routed straight through. The MPR is a 32-bit, protected-mode DLL.

- **Network Provider:** The network provider implements the network service provider interface. Only the MPR can communicate with the network provider. The network provider is a 32-bit, protected-mode DLL.

- **IFS Manager:** The IFS Manager routes filesystem requests to the proper filesystem driver (FSD). The IFS Manager can be called directly by network providers.

- **Network Filesystem Driver (FSD):** The FSD implements the particular remote filesystem characteristics. The FSD may be used by the IFS Manager when the filesystem of the local and remote machines match. The FSD is a 32-bit, protected-mode VxD.

- **Network Transport:** The network transport is a VxD that implements the device-specific network transport protocol. Multiple network transports can be active at a time. The network FSD interfaces with the network transport, usually with a one-to-one mapping, although that is not necessarily the case.

- **Network Driver Interface Specification (NDIS):** A vendor-independent software specification that defines interactions between the network transport and device driver. Windows 95 supports both 32-bit and 16-bit NDIS versions.

- **Network Adapter Driver:** The network adapter driver VxD controls the actual network hardware device. NDIS communicates with the driver, which sends packets over the network. Windows 95 uses Media Access Control (MAC) drivers.

One of the key features of Windows 95 is the inclusion of support for multiple concurrent protocols. The new default protocol is NetWare's IPX/SPX. The NetWare IPX/SPX driver is faster than Novell's own driver and includes support for packet burst mode. Also included are NetBIOS and NetBEUI drivers, and a complete 32-bit VxD for TCP/IP. All these drivers are plug-and-play enabled, allowing dynamic loading and unloading.

Windows 95's support for multiple protocols is achieved through the Network Driver Interface Specification (NDIS), which is a superset of the NDIS used in Windows for Workgroups and Windows NT. The NDIS 3.1 driver has three parts: the protocol itself (which can be implemented by third-party vendors) and protocol manager, the MAC or mini-port, and the mini-port wrapper. The NDIS protocol manager loads and unloads protocols as needed.

The version of NDIS included with Windows 95 adds plug-and-play enhancements and new mini-drivers. The plug-and-play capability is added to the Protocol Manager and the Media Access Control (MAC) layer, letting network drivers dynamically load and unload. The mini-driver (which is compatible with the mini-driver models used in Windows NT 3.5) decreases the amount of code that must be written to support a network adapter.

Windows 95 enables support for many network servers concurrently. This is an improvement over Windows for Workgroups 3.11, which allowed only its own network and one additional network. The server support of Windows 95 is provided by the Network Provider Interface (NPI).

The Installable File System Manager (IFS) has a different role with Windows 95 than earlier versions such as Windows for Workgroups. Earlier versions of IFS managed only a single file system which was dependent on the operating system. Windows 95's IFS handles multiple file systems and supports loadable drivers for file systems Windows 95 knows nothing about.

What's in This Section

Networking is a relatively complex subject, but luckily you don't have to know much more than the basics to install and configure your Windows 95 machine on a local area network. This section shows you the essentials and provides step-by-step procedures for several LAN protocols to help you get going smoothly. This networking section of *Windows 95 Unleashed* is divided into seven chapters:

- Chapter 22 looks at the terminology and basics of networking, and then examines how to install network interface cards in your machine.

- Chapter 23 looks at peer-to-peer networking, the most common form of local area network for small groups of machine. With a peer-to-peer network, each machine can access others, and provide files directly to others without the need for a central server.

- Chapter 24 looks at the client aspect of local area networking, most common on larger networks where one or more servers is used.

- Chapter 25 examines Windows 95's sharing capabilities and shows you how to set your folders and printers for access from others. It also shows you how to protect your system from others gaining access.

■ Chapter 26 looks at Remote Access, and how you can call into your desktop machine from anywhere else with a modem. This chapter shows you how to set permissions and security properly, as well as how to set up your desktop machine.

■ Chapter 27 looks at network administration and how you can keep your local area network functioning smoothly.

■ Finally, for those experiencing problems, see Chapter 35, "Troubleshooting Communications and Networking."

Don't be scared of networking! Windows 95 makes it easy to install and configure. The thrill of transferring files from your machine to others, and vice versa, is one of the touch-stone events in everyone's computer career!

Installing Network Hardware with Windows 95

22

by Tim Parker

IN THIS CHAPTER

Windows 95 was designed right from the start with networking in mind. Microsoft knows that some users will use Windows 95 set up for stand-alone machines and not need networking services at all, but a sizable percentage of PCs are being connected to networks of all types, either directly or through a modem. By designing Windows 95 with the local area network (LAN) in mind, Microsoft makes it easy for users to connect their PC into a larger LAN or into a wide area network (WAN).

When Microsoft was incorporating networking into Windows 95, it was necessary to maintain backward compatibility with the 16-bit Windows and DOS applications that are in use today, as well as provide full support for existing DLLs. These compatibility issues had to be combined with the new 32-bit, protected-mode features of Windows 95 to provide a wide range of network product support.

Microsoft took into account the fact that there are many different types of networks in use: Novell's NetWare, Microsoft's own Windows for Workgroups, and Artisoft's LANtastic are all popular network systems for connecting PCs together. PC machines also connect to larger networks running software protocols such as TCP/IP, so Microsoft had to take all these network protocols into account and make Windows 95 support them all.

Getting the Terminology Right

Unfortunately, it's difficult to talk about networking unless the terms used are well understood. That's because there are a lot of terms in common usage that can mean different things, depending on the context. To avoid confusion, it's better to begin with the basic definitions that are used in this networking section.

Each of the following terms has a formal, rigorous definition, usually in some standard document. Standards are usually not written in easily understood language, so the terms have been simplified a little and generalizations are used where possible. This may mean that a term is not completely defined, but it does enable you to get on with the subject of networking a little faster.

Servers

A *server* is any machine that can provide files, resources, or services for you. That's a broad definition because any machine that you request a file from is a server. In fact, that's the essence of client-server systems, where one machine (the client) requests something from another (the server). One machine may be both the client and the server many times.

The more common definition for server is directly related to local area networks, where the server is a powerful machine that holds all the files and large applications. The other machines on the network connect to the server to access files. In this type of network, a single machine usually acts as the server and all the other machines are clients.

Large server-based networks might have special servers for specific purposes. For example, one server may handle files for the network (the file server), another handles all print requests (the print server), yet another connects to the outside world through modems (the communications server), and so on. One or more of these functions may be on any individual machine on the network, or you may have several machines on a large network acting as a specific kind of server. You may have two file servers, for example.

In this section, you will need to use both the central and client-server definitions of server, depending on the type of LAN and network services you are dealing with. Simply put, the server is the machine from which your machine requests something.

Clients

As you might have figured out from the definition of server, a *client* is any machine that requests something from a server. In the more common definition of a client, the server supplies files and sometimes processing power to the smaller machines connected to it. Each machine is a client. Thus, a typical ten PC local area network may have one large server with all the major files and databases on it, and all the other machines connect as clients.

In the term client/server, a client is the machine that initiates a request to the server. This type of terminology is common with TCP/IP networks, where no single machine is necessarily the central repository.

Nodes

Small networks that comprise a server and a number of PC or Macintosh machines connected to the server are common. Each PC or Macintosh on the network is called a *node*. A node essentially means any device that is attached to the network. Because each machine has a unique name or number (so the rest of the network can identify it), you will hear the term *node name* or *node number* quite often. It is more proper to describe each machine as a client, although the term node is in common use.

Local and Remote Resources

A *local resource* is any device (printer, modem, scanner, hard disk, and so on) that is attached to your machine. Because the machine doesn't have to go out to the network to get to the device, it is called a local device or local resource.

Following the same logic, any device that must be reached through the network is a *remote resource*. Any devices attached to a server, for example, are remote resources. A high-speed color laser printer that may be part of the network is also a remote resource.

Network Operating System

A network operating system (often called a NOS) controls the interactions between all the machines on the network. The network operating system is responsible for controlling the way information is sent over the network medium (a coaxial or twisted-pair cable, for example). It handles the way in which data from a machine is packaged and sent to others, as well as what happens when two or more machines try to send information at the same time. The NOS can also handle shared peripherals, such as a laser printer, scanner, or CD-ROM drive that is on one machine but is accessible by other machines on the network.

With local area networks that have a single server and many clients hanging off it, the NOS resides on the server. This is the way Novell's NetWare works. The main part of the NOS sits on the server, and smaller client software packages are loaded onto each client.

On larger networks that don't use a single server, such as a UNIX network running TCP/IP, the NOS may be part of each machine's software. UNIX, for example, has the networking code for TCP/IP built into the operating system kernel so the network code is always available. A PC that tries to connect to the TCP/IP network must have a software package that handles the TCP/IP protocol on it.

Networks like Microsoft's Windows for Workgroups and Artisoft's LANtastic do not use a single primary server (although they can). Instead, each machine acts as its own server, containing all the NOS that is needed to talk to any other machine on the network.

Network Protocols

The network protocol is the name of the communications system by which machines on the network interact. On a UNIX system, for example, TCP/IP (Transmission Control Protocol/ Internet Protocol) is the most common network protocol. (Actually, TCP/IP is a whole family of protocols, but you'll deal with that later.) Novell NetWare usually uses a network protocol called InterPacket Exchange (IPX).

The different protocols use about the same approach to communications: they assemble information into blocks of data called a packet, and send that across the network. However, the way the packet is made up and the type of information attached to control its routing differs with each NOS.

When you connect your Windows 95 machine to a network, you must have Windows 95 use the same network protocol that all the other machines on the network use. If you try to use a different protocol, your machine will not be able to talk with the other machines.

Some operating systems, including Windows 95, enable more than one network protocol to be used at one time. This enables the machine and the network to be more flexible.

Network Interface Card

The *network interface card* (NIC) is an adapter that usually sits in a slot inside your PC. Some NICs now plug into parallel or SCSI ports on the back of your system. These plug-in NICs are very useful for portable machines, although they are still rare for desktops.

The network interface card handles the connection to the network through one or more connectors on the backplane of the card. The most common network connectors are similar to telephone jacks, and coaxial cable connectors (like cable TV) are a close second. You must make sure that the network interface card you are using in your machine works with the network operating system.

Bridges, Routers, and Brouters

You may often hear the terms bridge and router. They are simply machines that connect two or more networks together. The difference between a bridge and a router is that a *bridge* simply connects two local area networks running the same network operating system (it acts as a bridge between two LANs). A *router* connects LANs that may be running different operating systems. The router can have special software that converts one NOS' packets to the other NOS' packets.

A router is more complicated than a bridge in that it can make decisions about where and how to send packets of information (routing them, and hence the name) to their destination. A *brouter* is a relatively new device that combines the capabilities of both bridges and routers (hence its name).

Gateways

A *gateway* is a machine that acts as an interface between a small network and a much larger one, such as a local area network connecting to the Internet. Gateways are also used in large corporations, for example, to connect small office-based LANs into the larger corporate mainframe network. Usually, the gateway connects to a high-speed network cable or medium called the backbone.

Network Basics

Once you understand the terminology, you can see how networks are designed both from a physical and a logical point of view. This includes the type of network topology (how the network looks), the type of cables used to connect machines, the type of interface drivers the machines will use, and the network protocol.

590

Network Topologies

A network topology is the way the cabling is laid out. This doesn't mean the physical layout (how it loops through walls and floors), but how the logical layout looks when viewed in a simplified diagram. You may hear many different names for the type of network you have: ring, bus, star, and so on. They all refer to the shape of the network schematic.

One of the most widely used network topologies (and the one most often used in medium to large LANs) is the bus network. A *bus* network uses a cable to which are attached all the network devices, either directly or through a junction box of some sort. The manner of attachment depends on the type of bus network, the protocol in use, and the speed of the network. The main cable that is used to connect all the devices is called the *backbone*. Novell NetWare, Windows for Workgroups, and most commercial small LAN packages use bus networks.

Figure 22.1 shows a typical schematic of a bus network. In this case, the backbone has a number of junction boxes or transceivers attached, with a computer or network device attached to the junction box. This allows for a high-speed backbone, which is usually also immune to problems with any network card within a device (because the junction box allows traffic through the backbone whether a device is attached to the junction box or not). Each end of the backbone (also called a bus) is terminated with a block of resistors or similar electrical device.

FIGURE 22.1.

A schematic of a bus network. The backbone has several junction boxes along its length, each of which can lead to one or more computers or other network devices.

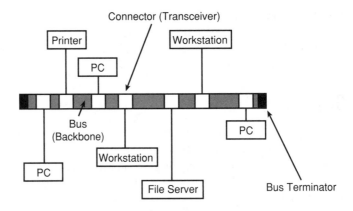

A popular variation of the bus network topology is found in many small LANs. This variation consists of a length of cable that snakes from machine to machine. Unlike the bus network in Figure 22.1, there are no transceivers along the network. Instead, each device is connected into the bus directly using a T-shaped connector on the network interface card, often using a connector called a BNC. The connector connects the machine to its two neighbors through two cables, one to each neighbor. At the ends of the network, a simple resistor is added to one side of the T-connector to terminate the network electrically.

This machine-to-machine (also called peer-to-peer) network is not capable of sustaining the higher speeds of the backbone-based bus network, primarily because of the medium of the network cable. A backbone network can use fiber optics, for example, with small coaxial or twisted-pair cables from a junction box to the device. A machine-to-machine network is usually built using twisted-pair or coaxial cable. Until recently, these networks were limited to a throughput of about 10 Mbps (megabits per second). However, a recent development, called 100VG or Fast Ethernet, allows 100Mbps on this type of network.

The problem with this type of bus network is that if one machine is taken off the network cable or the network interface card malfunctions, the backbone is broken and must be tied together again with a jumper of some sort. This can cause the network to behave erratically or all network traffic to fail completely.

A schematic of this type of network is shown in Figure 22.2. Each network device has a T-connector attached to the network interface card leading to the two neighbors. The two ends of the bus are terminated with resistors. Some devices on this type of network use a telephone jack (called an RJ-45) connection instead of a T-connector and BNC jacks. In this case, a special adapter must be coupled into the network backbone to accept the telephone jacks.

FIGURE 22.2.

A schematic of a machine-to-machine bus network. Each device is directly connected to its two neighbors by a cable attached to the network interface card.

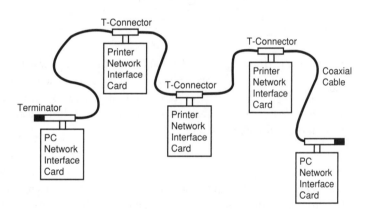

Another network topology is the ring network. Although most people think there is a physical loop made of the network cable joining into a large circle, that's not the case in the most common form of ring network called Token Ring. The ring name comes from the design of the central network device, which has a loop inside it to which are attached cables for all the devices on the network.

In a Token Ring network, the central control unit is called a Media Access Unit, or MAU. Inside the MAU is the cable ring to which all devices are attached, and which is similar to the backbone in a bus network. IBM's Token Ring is the most commonly encountered network system that uses a ring topology.

Figure 22.3 shows a schematic of a ring network; the MAU is at the center of the network containing the bus ring. Attached to the ring through junction boxes are all the network devices.

FIGURE 22.3.

A schematic of a ring network. Each device attaches through a junction box to the inner loop of the Media Access Unit.

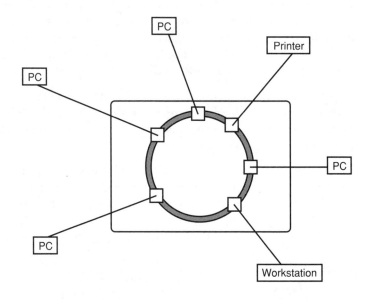

There are some true ring networks that have a physically closed loop of network cable. The ring network has some advantages from a design point of view in that network problems with traffic collisions are handled more easily than on a bus network. As with the bus-based machine-to-machine network, any problem with one machine's connection to the network cable can crash the entire network.

A star network is arranged in a structure that looks like a central star with branches radiating from it. As you will see shortly, this is a common layout with twisted-pair peer-to-peer networks. The central point of the star structure is called a concentrator, into which plug all the cables from individual machines. One machine on the network usually acts as the central controller or network server. A star network has one major advantage over the bus and ring networks: When a machine is disconnected from the concentrator, the rest of the network continues functioning unaffected.

Network traffic on a star network proceeds from your PC to the concentrator, then out to the target machine and vice versa. A star network needs a lot of cable because each machine must have a cable straight to the concentrator.

The last type of topology in this chapter is called the hub network. It is similar to the bus network, in that it uses a backbone cable that has a set of connectors on it. The cable in a hub network is called a backplane. Each connector leads to a hub device, which leads off to network devices. This enables a very high-speed backplane to be used, which can be as long and complex as needed. Hub networks are commonly found in large organizations that must support many network devices and need high speeds.

The hubs that lead off the backplane can support many devices, depending on the type of connector. For example, each hub can support hundreds of PC or Macintosh machines, so a hub network can be used for very large (tens of thousands of network devices) networks. The cost of a hub network is high, though. Figure 22.4 shows a schematic of a hub network.

FIGURE 22.4.

A schematic of a hub network. Each connection from the backplane leads to a hub or port connector, to which all the devices are attached.

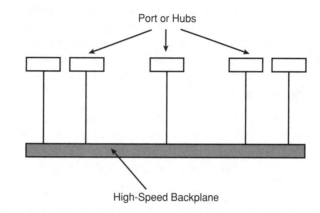

Port or Hubs

High-Speed Backplane

Network Media

The type of cabling used in a network is called the *network medium*. There are many types of cables used in networks today, although only a few are in common usage because of the cost of some of the more exotic types. The type of cabling can influence the speed of the network, although for most small- to medium-sized local area networks this is not a major issue.

Twisted-pair cabling is one of the most commonly used network mediums because it is cheap and easy to work with. Unshielded twisted-pair cables (often called UTP) look just like the cable that attaches your household telephone to the wall jack. As the name suggests, twisted-pair cables have a pair of wires twisted around each other to reduce interference. There can be two, four, or even more sets of twisted pairs in a network cable. Twisted-pair cables usually attach to network devices with a jack that looks like a telephone modular jack, but is a little wider (supporting up to eight wires). The most commonly used jacks are called RJ-11 and RJ-45, depending on the size of the connector (and hence the number of wires inside). The RJ-11 connector is the same as the modular jack on household telephones, and holds four wires. The RJ-45 jack is wider than an RJ-11 and holds eight wires.

A variation on unshielded twisted-pair cables is shielded twisted-pair, often called STP. The shielded twisted-pair cable has the same basic construction as its unshielded cousin, but the entire cable is wrapped with a layer of insulation for protection from interference, much like a cable for connecting speakers to your stereo system. The same types of connectors are used with both forms of twisted-pair cables.

Twisted-pair cables have one major limitation: They support only one channel of data. This is called *baseband* or *single-channel* cabling. Other types of cables can support many channels of data, although sometimes only one channel is used. This is called *broadband* or *multiple-channel* cabling.

The other popular network medium is coaxial cable. Coax cable is designed with two conductors, one (usually a number of strands intertwined) in the center surrounded by a layer of inner insulation, and the second a mesh or foil conductor surrounding the insulation. Outside the mesh is a layer of outer insulation. Because of its reduced electrical impedance, coaxial is capable of faster transmissions than twisted-pair cables. Coax is also broadband, supporting several network channels on the same cable.

There are two types of coaxial cable in use: thick and thin coax. *Thick coax* is a heavy cable (usually yellow colored) that is used as a network backbone for bus networks. This cable is formally known as Ethernet PVC coax, but usually called 10Base5. Because thick coax is so heavy and stiff, it is difficult to work with and is quite expensive.

Thin coax is the most common type of cable used in Ethernet networks. It goes by several names, including thin Ethernet, thinnet, 10Base2, and somewhat derogatorily as cheapernet. Formally, thin coax is called RG-58. Thin coax is the same as your television cable. The inner connector can be made of a single solid copper wire or fashioned out of thin strands of wire braided together. Thin coax is also used in other networks such as ARCnet, although the specification for the coaxial cable's construction is known as RG-62.

Thin coax is quite flexible and has a low impedance, so it is capable of fast throughput rates. Because of its flexibility, it is not difficult to lay out, and it is easy to construct cables with the proper connectors at each end. Thin coax is broadband, although most networks use only a single channel.

Fiber-optic cables are becoming popular for very high-speed networks (which is why telephone companies use it). It is very expensive, but capable of supporting many channels at tremendous speeds. Fiber-optic cable is almost never used in local area networks, although some large corporations do use it to connect many LANs together into a wide area network. The supporting hardware to handle fiber optic backbones is quite expensive and specialized.

Finally, wireless networks are becoming more popular as technology has increased their bandwidth and reduced noise levels. A wireless network has no cable; instead, it uses a small transceiver that uses radio frequencies or infrared light to talk to a hub. Wireless is still expensive, but it does provide a solution where network cabling is difficult to lay.

Network Interface Drivers

The network interface driver (also called a LAN adapter driver or network driver) is the software that lets the network interface card talk to the network protocol. The network interface card is the physical card to which the network cable is attached. Most network card manufacturers provide a driver with their product, although many operating systems include drivers for most network cards as well. The drivers are usually designed specifically for a single network card, and cannot be interchanged. There are many network interface drivers in existence, although there are only a few in common use.

NDIS (Network Driver Interface Specification) was originally developed by Microsoft and 3Com, but is now in common use with many vendors. NDIS requires a program called a protocol manager (PROTMAN.SYS on DOS systems) to connect the network drivers to the network protocol. The protocol manager handles packets of information coming in and being sent through the network card. NDIS enables multiple protocols to be supported; the protocol manager decides which protocol gets the traffic.

ODI (Open Data-Link Interface) was developed by Novell as a competitor to NDIS, and is used primarily on NetWare networks. Like NDIS, ODI supports multiple protocols. ODI is composed of two parts: the Multiple Link Interface Driver (MLID) and the Link Support Layer (LSL). The MLID is the driver supplied by the network card manufacturer, and the LSL is provided by Novell.

Packet drivers were developed for TCP/IP and other networks. They are sometimes called Clarkson drivers. The packet driver is a single piece of software that supports multiple protocols, checking incoming and outgoing packets for the protocol it needs and routing it as required. Packet drivers are specific to each network card.

Adapter Support Interface (ASI) was developed by IBM for the Token Ring network. Token Ring cards need a driver supplied by the vendor, and the driver is not compatible with other network schemes.

Network Protocols

There are many network protocols in common use, each with its own proponents. The type of network protocol that can be used depends on the manufacturer of the network operating system, although some cross support is available. The most commonly used network protocols (and the ones most likely to be encountered in a Windows 95 network) are TCP/IP, IPX/SPX, NetBIOS and NetBEUI, and SNA.

IPX/SPX (Internetwork Packet Exchange/Sequenced Packet Exchange) is the protocol used by Novell's NetWare (and now the default with Windows 95). It is actually a subset of a protocol called XNS (Xerox Network Services) developed several years ago by Xerox. IPX works with several different network drivers, although it does seem to prefer ODI.

NetBIOS (Network Basic Input Output System) and NetBEUI (NetBIOS Extended User Interface) were developed by IBM. NetBIOS and NetBEUI have become common for simple PC-based networks like Windows for Workgroups, LANtastic, and LAN Manager. NetBIOS is not really a communications protocol in the formal sense, because it establishes sessions and provides transfer capabilities. NetBEUI acts more like a formal communications protocol.

SNA (System Network Architecture) was developed by IBM as an overall networking model for all sizes of machines. It became a standard with IBM minicomputer and mainframe systems because of IBM's dominance in that market.

TCP/IP (Transmission Control Protocol/Internet Protocol) is a standard in the UNIX and minicomputer world, as well as on the Internet. TCP/IP is actually a family of protocols, working together to package and route data to its destination safely. TCP/IP is popular because of its wide support, well-documented specifications, reliability, and speed.

What You Need to Install Networking

What do you need to have ready to install networking with Windows 95? You need to have a network interface card that is compatible with the network operating system you are using, and you need to know the type of network protocol that the network uses. These were all discussed earlier in this chapter.

If you are connecting to an existing network, you should consult other users or the network administrator to ensure you install the correct system on your Windows 95 machine. If you are just starting to install a network, decide what type of network and the protocol to be used ahead of time to eliminate a lot of redundant work and simplify the configuration process.

Once you have this ready, you can install the hardware and software. Most networks need you to have a unique name or number for your machine, so you may want to consider this in advance. If you are connecting to a TCP/IP network, you also need additional information, which is discussed in more detail in Chapter 25, "Sharing Files and Resources."

The way you install and configure Windows 95 for your network will depend on whether you are installing a brand new system, already have Windows 95 installed without networking, or are upgrading an existing Windows for Workgroups system.

Installing a New Network

If you have installed Windows 95 and decide to install a network, or if you want to install the network while loading Windows 95 for the first time, the process is much the same. After you plug in your network card, Windows 95 may recognize it automatically if it is a plug-and-play type. If Windows 95 doesn't recognize the network interface card, you'll have to install it manually.

To install the network card into Windows 95, open the Control Panel and double-click the Add New Hardware icon. This starts the New Hardware Installation Wizard. A dialog will appear that gives you the option of letting Windows 95 try to detect the network interface card or enable you to select it manually. You can always let Windows 95 try and find the card itself, and then use the manual approach if that fails.

To install the new network interface card manually, click Next, and then select Network Adapters from the list. This dialog is shown in Figure 22.5. Double-click the Network Adapters item, or highlight it with a single click, and then click the Next button.

FIGURE 22.5.

The Add New Hardware Wizard lets you add new devices to your Windows 95 system. In this case, add a new network adapter manually.

The window that appears next shows a list of network card manufacturers on the left, and a more detailed list of network interface cards the selected manufacturer offers on the right. Find the manufacturer of your network interface card, single-click it, and then select the name that matches your specific card. You must be careful to match the names exactly, because some drivers will not work on other cards from the same manufacturer. This dialog is shown in Figure 22.6. If you can't find the model name you are using but have a driver supplied on diskette, use the Have Disk button to read the driver.

FIGURE 22.6.

The Select Device window lets you choose the manufacturer of your network interface card, then the specific model. If you have a diskette with a Windows driver from the manufacturer, use the Have Disk button to read the driver.

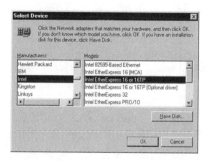

Windows 95 will display a window with configuration information in it. This may be a list with the currently detected settings or recommended settings. You need both an interrupt number (IRQ) and a memory address for the network interface card. This dialog is shown in Figure 22.7.

You will next see another window that lets you enter the settings you want. Use the scroll buttons to move the IRQ and address to the correct values, and then click the OK button. The scroll lists for the IRQ and address will show you which settings are recommended and which will cause conflicts with currently installed hardware.

FIGURE 22.7.

The network configuration screen for an Intel EtherExpress 16 card shows the recommended settings.

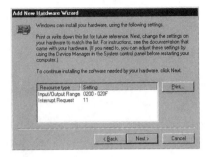

After setting the parameters, Windows 95 will make the necessary modifications to the configuration files and prompt you for a system restart. You must restart Windows 95 to make the new adapter card available.

If you made a mistake in the configuration or want to change settings, you can simply repeat the process and alter the parameters you chose. You can abort the installation of new hardware at any time with the Cancel button.

Plug and Play Network Cards

Many of the popular network cards are designed to be supported as plug-and-play devices. These network cards use 32-bit VxD drivers, although older 16-bit drivers can also be employed. Most 32-bit drivers supplied with Windows 95 or by a well-known network card vendor will be fully enabled for Windows 95 Plug and Play. Updates should be available for existing network cards that Windows 95 does not support directly.

If you are using a Plug and Play network card and a 32-bit driver, most of the network configuration steps will be performed automatically for you. The only steps you will usually have to perform is checking the settings of the network card to avoid conflicts (Windows 95 can't always set the IRQ, DMA, and I/O address to avoid all existing cards, especially when the card is not used in Windows 95) and adding the services and protocols.

If you plan on using 16-bit drivers supplied with Plug and Play network cards, there are a few things you should bear in mind to prevent problems. Windows 95 doesn't turn on a Plug and Play network card until it needs it, and 16-bit drivers tend not to support Plug and Play capabilities. For this reason, a 16-bit driver that was installed after Windows 95 recognized and configured a Plug and Play network card may not function properly. The network connection may appear dead. This is especially prevalent with NE2000-compatible cards, may of which cannot properly emulate Plug and Play capabilities.

To solve this problem, you must either replace the 16-bit driver with a 32-bit driver that supports Plug and Play properly, or turn off the Plug and Play capabilities of the network card. Usually, you can turn Plug and Play off with a utility supplied as part of the network card diagnostics. After the card's Plug and Play capabilities have been disabled, remove the network card and any associated protocols or services, and reinstall the card manually from scratch, supplying configuration information. This should clear up the hung network problem.

Parallel-Port Network Adapters

Windows 95 will function properly with network adapters that plug into parallel ports. This type of adapter is frequently used with laptop and portable computers, which can't house a full-size network card. Windows 95 will recognize many parallel-port adapters automatically, especially if they are configured for Plug and Play capabilities. Some 32-bit VxD drivers are supplied for parallel-port adapters.

However, many parallel-port adapters do not have plug-and-play, and most lack 32-bit drivers. You may have to manually install the parallel-port adapter card using utilities supplied either with the adapter or through the Windows 95 network window. Bear in mind that parallel-port adapters tend to be much slower than normal network cards, and some protocols will refuse to work properly because the slow nature of the parallel port prevents proper acknowledgments of transmitted packets before a timeout.

PCMCIA Cards

Windows 95 supports PCMCIA network cards. Most of the PCMCIA cards will function as a normal network card, and many are recognized automatically by Windows 95 during the installation process. Because Windows 95 allows dynamic loading and unloading of the VxD 32-bit drivers, PCMCIA network cards can be added or removed while Windows 95 is functioning as long as they are Plug and Play compatible and run a 32-bit driver.

Some 16-bit drivers will function properly with Windows 95, although most do not support Plug and Play properly. In these cases, you should not remove or insert the PCMCIA network card while Windows 95 is operational; otherwise Windows may experience lockups from drivers communicating with non-existent cards.

Upgrading from Windows for Workgroups

When you installed Windows 95 over your existing Windows for Workgroups system, Windows 95 will have detected the network parameters in use before completing the installation. There is usually very little you have to do to complete the Windows 95 installation, because Setup will complete the changes to the configuration files for you.

Setup will make changes to the WIN.INI and SYSTEM.INI files based on the previous settings, upgrading to new Windows 95 features where possible. For example, if your system used Windows for Workgroups or Novell NetWare, Windows 95 will use new 32-bit protected-mode drivers when it can. If there are no new 32-bit drivers currently available with

Windows 95, your older 16-bit drivers will be retained and used. If Windows 95 can't find some information or needs a clarification, it will ask for it. Any drive mapping you had established with Windows for Workgroups will be retained, although you may want to check that directories are still valid.

Once installed, Windows 95 should behave just like the previous Windows for Workgroups system did, at least as far as networking is concerned. The dialog and windows are different, of course, but the overall process remains the same.

If you have to make changes to the configuration, or if Windows 95 doesn't connect to the network properly, read the steps in the previous section for installing a new network card, and follow the entire procedure again.

If Windows 95 Fails to Boot

If you made a mistake in the configuration of a network interface card and Windows 95 doesn't boot up properly, it's probably because it is trying to communicate with a network interface card that doesn't respond. You can restart the machine and bring up the Fail Safe Boot messages. This lets you bring the Windows 95 system back up without attempting to establish communications with the network interface card.

Once Windows 95 is running in Fail Safe mode, you can go through the configuration process again to change the parameters. When the configuration information matches the card's settings, Windows 95 should boot completely. You can also make changes to the network interface card's parameters from the Network icon in the Control Panel.

To remove a driver for a network interface card, enter the Control Panel and double-click the System icon. This will display a window that shows you what Windows 95 knows about your system. Select the Device Manager sheet. This will show a window with all the known devices installed. Figure 22.8 shows a Device Manager window with three Intel EtherExpress boards installed by accident. Two of them are marked with a yellow icon to show that Windows 95 does not recognize them.

FIGURE 22.8.

The Device Manager window shows all devices Windows 95 has in its configuration files. In this example, three Intel EtherExpress cards have been installed by accident, when only one should exist.

You can see each network card's settings by clicking the Properties button. To remove a network adapter card from the list, highlight it and click the Remove button at the bottom of the window. A warning dialog, shown in Figure 22.9, asks you whether you are sure you want to remove the adapter card from the system. Clicking the OK button removes all the drivers from Windows 95.

FIGURE 22.9.

Before you remove a network adapter card from the Windows 95 configuration files, the system double-checks that this is what you want to do.

Windows 95 will then ask you whether you want to reboot the system at that point. In the case of the three Intel EtherExpress cards, you can remove the other unused card first, and then allow the system to restart.

Summary

This chapter has explained some of the terminology that you will encounter when you set up your networks, as well as general terms about local and wide area networks. This should help you understand *netspeak*, the acronym-laden language of networking.

In this chapter you also learned how to set up the network interface card. After you do that, Windows 95 recognizes the network interface card, and you must select the protocol. The process for this step differs depending on the type of network protocol your local area network will use. In the next two chapters, you will learn the steps involved in setting the network protocols for peer-to-peer and client networking.

Peer-to-Peer Networking with Windows 95

23

by Tim Parker

IN THIS CHAPTER

If you are thinking of setting up your own network, peer-to-peer is probably the best choice you can make. Peer-to-peer networks are relatively simple to install, set up, configure, and work with. If you have a small number of machines and the need to share files among them, peer-to-peer networks are also inexpensive and fast.

This chapter looks at peer-to-peer networking with Windows 95. You will learn how to configure Windows 95 specifically for peer-to-peer use. You will also learn several important things to keep in mind when you are installing a network for the first time.

If you have to connect to an existing network, you should check the network's type. If it is peer-to-peer, this chapter will help you connect to the existing system. If the network uses TCP/IP, NetWare, or other network operating systems, you should read the next chapter for more information on connecting your Windows 95 machine to the network.

What is a Peer-to-Peer Network?

Peer-to-peer networks are the most widely used network system for small numbers of machines that need to share files and, sometimes, resources such as a printer, CD-ROM drive, or backup tape unit. Peer-to-peer networks are usually set up as a simple bus topology with machine-to-machine connections. The peer-to-peer network is ideal for small companies or workgroups that have powerful PC machines, don't need a server to provide files or applications, but that do want to be able to easily and quickly transfer files between machines.

The name *peer-to-peer* originally derived from the fact that there was no single server on the system (with the other machines acting as clients). Instead, each machine on a peer-to-peer network acted as its own server, in a sense, in that it could connect to any other machine (and other machines could connect to it) in an *ad hoc* manner. Usually, machines connected to each other for simple tasks like file sharing, although peer-to-peer networks have since become much more powerful.

Peer-to-peer networks can use a central server, but each machine on the system still has the capability to connect to other machines directly. This capability is the indicator of a true peer-to-peer network.

The first peer-to-peer network product was IBM's PC LAN, developed with Microsoft. Other companies could easily see the utility of a peer-to-peer network (no more copying files to diskette and then physically moving to another machine, for example) and began introducing software with more features than PC LAN. Novell's NetWare is a peer-to-peer network, although it has the capability to add servers to provide better support. Novell's NetWare Lite product is a more classic peer-to-peer network. Other vendors introduced competitive products, like Artisoft's LANtastic and Performance Technology's Powerfusion.

Microsoft eventually introduced its own peer-to-peer network software incorporated into Windows for Workgroups. Windows for Workgroups (Windows 3.11) was notable for being very simple to install, completely integrated with Windows, user friendly, and easy to work with. The successor to this product is Windows 95.

Peer-to-Peer Network Limitations

Peer-to-peer networks are much simpler to install, configure, and maintain than other network types, but they do have some limitations because of their very simplicity. Before looking at the advantages of peer-to-peer networks, examine the problems associated with them.

Peer-to-peer networks are not for all network systems. Because of the high traffic involved when machines talk to each other, peer-to-peer networks work best for only a small number of machines. Many people recommend 10 to 25 machines maximum on a peer-to-peer network, depending on the amount of traffic between connections. If the network traffic is light, such as occasional connections to transfer files, then the network can grow quite large. However, if the network users are going to stay connected to each other and do a lot of work on remote machines, the network traffic will quickly lead to bottlenecks, slow performance, and occasional network crashes.

Shared resources help reduce overall costs, but they incur their own performance costs. For example, if you have a color laser printer attached to your PC and it is available for anyone on the peer-to-peer network to address through your machine, your system's CPU is involved in the processing of the information incoming from others (as is your RAM, hard drive, and expansion bus). This all slows down your machine as far as your applications are concerned because of the increased amount of background processing that must occur.

Finally, peer-to-peer networks are not very useful as application server-based networks. An *application server* is a machine that holds the applications users frequently access, instead of having them reside on their local hard drives. Because applications frequently must load modules or overlays, application servers involve a huge amount of network traffic—more than most peer-to-peer networks can support.

Peer-to-Peer Network Advantages

Peer-to-peer networks have a few limitations, but do their advantages overcome the problems? For most small networks, the answer is a resounding yes. That's why peer-to-peer networks are the favorite small network for most installations.

The primary advantage of a peer-to-peer network is its convenience. It greatly simplifies file transfers. Instead of copying a file to floppy, and then carrying it over and loading it from the floppy onto another machine's hard drive (a process affectionately known as "sneaker net"), you only have to open the File Manager, click a couple of menu items and dialog buttons, and you can drag-and-drop the file on the remote machine. The time is much shorter, as is the hassle. This is especially true of large files that don't conveniently fit on a floppy.

The capability to share a machine's resources is important, too. If one of the machines on your network has an optical drive used for high-speed backups, you can access it over the network quite easily to back up your user directories. It is much more effective than either buying several optical drives or physically moving the device to your PC and attaching it to an adapter. Heavily used resources can bog a peer-to-peer network down in traffic, but a seldom-used resource is ideally shared in this manner. Other typical examples of peer-to-peer resources are backup tape drives, CD-ROM jukeboxes, high-speed printers or plotters, and scanners.

Peer-to-peer networks are very easy to install and configure. Usually, you only have to insert a network adapter card in each machine on the network, string a cable between each machine, figure out a unique name for the machine, and select the type of network protocol in a configuration window. Windows for Workgroups and LANtastic have made the entire software installation process so easy that a Windows novice can do it. When you add a new machine to an existing peer-to-peer network, you only need to run more cable to that machine.

A useful feature of peer-to-peer networks is that they can be upgraded to more complex networks with little effort. For example, moving from a Windows for Workgroups NetBEUI-based peer-to-peer network to a full Novell NetWare network is usually a matter of installing the NetWare software on each machine and changing the configuration to use IPX as a protocol. The same applies for more complex protocols like TCP/IP. To add a UNIX-based server to an existing peer-to-peer network, you must change each PC network protocol to TCP/IP and make minor configuration changes. The investment in network interface cards and cabling is preserved, and the time required to upgrade a network is minimal.

For many managers and businessmen, a very attractive aspect of peer-to-peer networks is their low cost. Network interface cards are available for less than $50, and cable costs less than $5 for 10 feet, so a small peer-to-peer network can be established with a very small investment. Larger network systems require much more investment, and sometimes require specialized equipment. As already mentioned, because the peer-to-peer network can be easily upgraded, the small investment in cards and cables is preserved. A peer-to-peer network also saves time (always a precious commodity): a complete ten-machine peer-to-peer network can be installed and working in about four hours of one person's time.

Peer-to-Peer Networking Hardware

There are two components of hardware required for establishing a peer-to-peer network: the network interface card (NIC) and the network medium. As with most things in life, you can buy an inexpensive card and medium, or spend a lot more money for full-featured items. As the amount you spend increases, you get more functionality and benefits, although usually with diminishing returns for your dollar. Luckily, choosing the right balance of costs and features is not difficult with peer-to-peer networks, because the prices for even the more expensive products are still reasonable.

Before you decide on the type of network interface cards to use (unless you already have some), you should decide on the type of cabling the peer-to-peer network will use so the connectors on the network interface card can match. There are really only two cables that you'll want to consider, because the alternatives are much more expensive or require special hardware. The two are called 10Base2 and 10Base-T.

10Base-T is a twisted-pair cable, just like telephone cable. It is unshielded, and tends to have a wide telephone jack called an RJ-45 connector on each end. One end of the cable plugs into a jack on the network interface card, while the other end must plug into a special box called a distribution box, concentrator, or hub. These hubs generally have a number of connectors for incoming cables (the most popular units have 8, 12, or 16 connectors). The hub contains the circuitry needed to amplify signals, as well as to convert the connectors to other cable types if necessary. Several hubs can be joined together, commonly with two twisted-pair cables.

The alternative is 10Base2, which is also called Thin Ethernet. Thin Ethernet uses coaxial cable, just like your cable television feed or the cables from a VCR to a television. Each end of the coax cable has a twist-on connector called a BNC. (BNC connectors are easier to work with than the screw type of connector television coax uses.) A 10Base2 network interface card has a male plug jutting out from the back to which is attached a T-shaped connector. Both ends of the T are attached to cables running to the two neighboring machines. If the machine happens to be at the end of the chain, a terminating resistor plug is attached instead to electrically terminate the cable.

Which cable type is best? Different people will give you different answers. Because 10Base-T is usually unshielded, it can be more susceptible to interference. However, 10Base-T is much easier to work with and feed through walls, along the floor, and under carpets because it is much thinner and more flexible than Thin Ethernet coaxial cable. 10Base2 (Thin Ethernet), on the other hand, is well shielded from radiation, difficult to accidentally disconnect, and doesn't require a hub concentrator (which can cost several hundreds of dollars).

Speed is no longer a factor in choosing the cable type. In early local area networks, coaxial cables would outperform 10Base-T cables because of their inherent higher bandwidth, but both 10Base-T and 10Base2 cables can easily support the speeds used with modern peer-to-peer networks. Indeed, both can use the new Fast Ethernet 100Mbps system, so speed isn't a deciding factor.

Cost may help you decide which cable to use. Neither cable is expensive, but twisted-pair is less expensive than coaxial cable. However, unless you are buying a thousand feet or so of cable, chances are the difference in price won't be much. If you use twisted pair, though, you must purchase a concentrator, which can add a few hundred dollars to the network price for each hub.

Connectors are a little more difficult to hand-attach to twisted pair, whereas a pair of pliers is all you need to attach BNC connectors to coaxial cable. Many network installers buy a large reel of coaxial cable and a bulk supply of connectors, and then cut the cable to length as needed.

A simple guideline is that for only a few PC and other network machines (such as five or so), Thin Ethernet is less expensive because 10Base-T requires a concentrator. Above that number, the costs become more competitive and the choice really becomes one of convenience for layout of the network. Personally, the author prefers coaxial because of its shielding and better connections to the network interface card.

Once you've decided on the type of cabling, you can choose network interface cards with the proper connectors. (You can use RJ-45 connectors with a 10Base2 network, and vice versa, although you have to purchase special adapters, which cost more than a new network interface card.) Network cards are usually sold individually and in bulk packs of three, five, or ten cards (with some minor savings for the bulk packs because of reduced packaging and supporting documentation). Don't forget to check the bus architecture (local machine, not network architecture) for which the card is designed, because the same manufacturer may have ISA, EISA, and MCA versions in the same packaging.

There are many manufacturers of network interface cards on the market; some are provided by name-brand vendors (such as Novell, Artisoft, Intel, SMC, and Hewlett-Packard), and some by OEM (original equipment manufacturers) and lesser-known brands. The latter are usually cheaper because you don't pay a premium for a brand name. Most network interface cards are clearly labeled as to the type of connector (RJ-45 or BNC) and the network systems they support. Novell NetWare-compatible network interface cards are usually clearly labeled as such, for example. (Any network interface card that is compatible with NetWare will work with practically all peer-to-peer network operating systems.)

Many network interface cards provide more than one connector on the back plane of the card. It is not unusual to have both a 10Base2 BNC and 10Base5 AUI (thick Ethernet, used for much larger networks) connector on a single card, with either available for use. The same applies to RJ-45 and 10Base5 AUI connectors. A few cards provide 10Base2 BNC and 10BaseT RJ-45 connectors in addition to the 10Base5 AUI connector. These provide the ultimate in flexibility for the user and enable you to change your network from one format to the other as your network grows or shrinks.

Some network interface cards require you to manually select the card's parameters, such as the interrupt (IRQ) and interface address, by changing jumpers on the card. This can be daunting for novices, as well as difficult if you are not sure whether a setting will conflict with another card in your system. Recently, auto-configuring cards have been appearing (such as the Intel EtherExpress series), which use software to set the parameters. This enables you to change the settings at any time, experimenting to avoid conflicts with existing or newly added cards. Of course, you can expect to pay a little more for auto-configuring cards.

The latest feature of the more expensive network interface cards is flash memory, which enables you to load new drivers into the card from a diskette or downloaded software program. This can update the card's capabilities as new features are added to the network. Although flash memory is not important for many users, it does ensure the network interface card will not become obsolete quickly and can take advantage of new advances. For example, Intel's

EtherExpress LAN Adapter with flash memory now incorporates virus protection. Free updates to the virus software are available at regular intervals from bulletin boards.

You don't have to obtain all your network interface cards from the same manufacturer, as long as the cards support the same protocols. Shopping around for the best price and feature support whenever you need new cards will probably result in a variety of manufacturer's cards in your network, although there are some network administrators who prefer to stay with one vendor for convenience.

Installing a Peer-to-Peer Network

In the last chapter you saw how to install the network interface card and network card drivers into Windows 95. When Windows 95 starts up, it should recognize the card, although you won't be able to do anything with it because you don't have a network driver.

> **NOTE**
>
> If Windows 95 won't start up properly or it wants to enter Fail Safe mode after you've installed a network card, either Windows 95 can't communicate with the network card properly (check the settings) or it can't get signals from the network (no cable attached). You may have to start Windows 95 in Fail Safe mode until the network is properly attached and terminated.

The next step in the installation of a peer-to-peer network (or addition of your machine to an existing peer-to-peer network) is to configure the network software.

Identifying Your Machine

You can begin the peer-to-peer software installation by identifying your machine. Each machine on a network must have a unique name or number so that other machines will know how to send messages to you, and know that the messages you send are from you.

Most networks will let you use a common English (or any other language) name, although some protocols insist on numbers for each device on the network. The length of the name depends on the protocol, but as a general rule you have eight characters. Machine names are usually case-independent, but a few systems do allow a mix of upper- and lowercase characters in the system name.

To name your machine, double-click the Network icon in the Control Panel. You will see the Network window, with three pages available: Configuration, Identification, and Access Control. When the window first opens, it will show the Configuration screen. Figure 23.1 shows this screen, configured to use an Intel EtherExpress 16 card.

FIGURE 23.1.

The Network Configuration screen showing an Intel EtherExpress 16 configured, but no network drivers.

At the top of the window are three tabs for the different pages available. Click the Identification window and you will see a screen that lets you add a Computer name, a Workgroup name, and a Computer Description. This screen is shown in Figure 23.2 with blank entry fields. Your system may have one or more of the fields with default information already entered.

FIGURE 23.2.

The Network Identification screen lets you uniquely identify your machine. There may be some names already inserted into the three fields, depending on how Windows 95 was installed and configured.

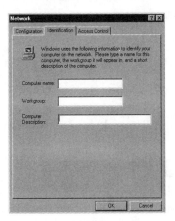

The Computer name is the unique name your machine will have on the local area network. Windows 95 enables you to enter up to 15 characters, none of which can be a blank character. Choose any name that is unique and enter it in the Computer name field.

You can use a computer name that is based on your own name (such as TimParker_PC or Tim's_Super_PC), or something you want to be identified with (such as DeathStar or Frobozz). You may want to identify your machine to indicate your location (such as Rm_134) or your position in the company (Windows_guru, network_admin, or Bottle_Washer). Remember that other users should be able to identify your machine from the name when they want to connect, so try not to make the computer name too obscure.

TIP

A handy trick is to use underline characters instead of spaces to make the computer name a little more readable.

The Workgroup name is the name of the local area network to which your machine will belong. Usually, this is a name that all the machines in your LAN will agree on, or it may already have been assigned. Workgroups enable local area networks that are connected to other LANs to identify where network traffic comes from and should be routed to. The Workgroup name also helps organize companies into departments or areas.

You can use up to 15 characters in a workgroup name, none of which can be spaces. If you are connecting to an existing network, make sure you use the name that is currently assigned (assuming the protocol you will use supports workgroup names), otherwise you may not be able to access other devices on the LAN.

If there are several workgroups in use, you should enter the name of the one to which you will connect the most. This may be the workgroup where the network resources (printers, modems, scanners, and so on) are located, or the workgroup where you will connect most often to transfer files. Once you are on one workgroup, you can switch to others without too much trouble, so don't feel as though you are restricting your options by joining a single workgroup. The Workgroup name represents your default workgroup.

Like computer names, workgroup names vary considerably, although they are seldom as creative as computer names. A workgroup name that represents everyone on the local area network ("programming" or "accounting") or a company name (XYZ_Widgets) is preferable to an obscure name that won't mean anything to others.

Finally, you can specify a description that other users will see when they look at your computer on the network. You don't have to enter anything here, but it is usually a courtesy to others to have your name, department, or location entered for quick lookup.

The Computer Description can be up to 48 characters long, but cannot contain commas (it can contain spaces). It makes the most sense to put your name, department (if there is one), and telephone number or extension in this space. This is especially useful if you chose an obscure machine name, because people may not immediately recognize your machine from the name Frobozz.

After completing all three pieces of information, you should verify that they are correct. Figure 23.3 shows a sample entry. Clicking the OK button at the bottom of the window enters into Windows 95's configuration files the information you provided.

FIGURE 23.3.

*The Network Identifi-
cation screen with all areas
filled. You can't use spaces
in the Computer or
Workgroup name fields,
or commas in the Computer
Description field.*

After that is done, your machine's identification is complete. The next step is to identify the
network protocols and services to be used.

Configuring the Network Software

Return to the Network Configuration screen (if it's not already displayed) either by selecting
the Configuration page from the Network window or double-clicking the Network icon in the
Control Panel. Doing this opens the Network window, which shows the hardware and any
software settings that the machine currently knows about. You saw this window earlier in Figure 23.1.

From the Network Configuration window, add the network services and protocols. Click the
Add button at the bottom of the window to display another window that asks for the type of
network component you want to install. This screen is shown in Figure 23.4.

FIGURE 23.4.

*This window lets you
select the type of network
component to add. Because
you have only installed the
network interface card
so far, you have to add
Client, Protocol, and
Service software.*

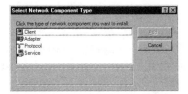

There are four options listed in the window: Client, Adapter, Protocol, and Service. Each is a
necessary part of the network configuration. Here's what each option means:

■ Adapter—The network card used to connect to the network cable (you've already
installed this option)

■ Protocol—The manner in which information is packaged for transfer across the network

■ Client—Lets you access other machines and devices on the network

■ Service—Special software-based capabilities, such as backing up your machine across the network, password verification, and many more

For this example, start by defining the protocol to be used. Double-click the Protocol line in the window, or highlight it with a single click and click the Add button. This will display a window with a list of all network protocols that are available with the Windows 95 software.

If your network protocol is not listed but you have the software available on diskette, click the Have Disk button and follow the instructions. You will rarely need to use this option, though, because practically every LAN protocol in use is supplied with Windows 95.

Your sample peer-to-peer network will involve other machines that are running Windows for Workgroups, so choose the Microsoft option. The right side of the window lists the network protocols Microsoft uses. If you are adding your machine to a Novell NetWare network, you would choose Novell. (You will look at Novell NetWare in more detail in Chapter 26, "Remote Access.") Figure 23.5 shows the Select Network Protocol window with Microsoft's networks displayed.

FIGURE 23.5.

Adding the software drivers for a Windows for Workgroups network involves choosing Microsoft from the list of LAN vendors, and then selecting the proper network protocol.

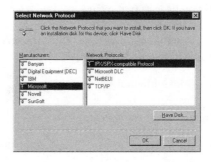

As you can see in Figure 23.5, Microsoft supports the most popular network protocols including NetWare's IPX, UNIX's TCP/IP, and Windows for Workgroups NetBEUI. To complete the selection of the protocol, double-click the protocol name or highlight the name with a single click, and then choose the OK button.

The last step in completing the initial network software configuration is to choose the Client option from the Select Network Component screen (you may have to choose Add again from the Network window to get there). This will display the Select Network Client window, shown in Figure 23.6. It is very similar to the Select Network Protocol window, except it lists the different types of clients.

FIGURE 23.6.

*Adding the client type for
the local area network
completes the basic network
configuration.*

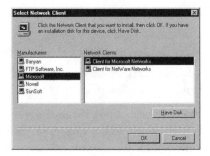

For the sample network using Windows for Workgroups NetBEUI, select Microsoft from the
list of vendors, and then choose Client for Microsoft Networks. After clicking OK, Windows
95 will make all the changes necessary to the configuration, and then ask if you want to reboot
the system to implement all the changes you've made.

When the system reboots, check the settings by double-clicking the Network icon in the Control Panel, and then everything should be ready for you to use your network.

Adding Services

The last option in the Select Network Component Type window is the Services window, which
lets you configure new services for the network. The list of currently available service manufacturers will be shown in the left window, while the services they offer are listed in the right. This
window is shown in Figure 23.7.

FIGURE 23.7.

*The Services window lists
all available special
network services. The lists
may change as new services
are added to Windows 95.*

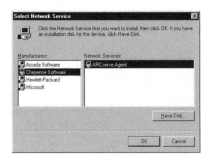

If you want to add a service that is not listed, you can click the Have Disk button (assuming
you have an installation disk for the service).

The services available can be added to your network configuration, although you do not need
to have any of them installed. It is recommended that you know what each service does before
you install it, or you may be adding configuration information that your system doesn't need
and which may affect performance. Check the documentation for each service.

Controlling Access to Your Machine

There are two windows that you want to make changes to in order to enable others to use your machine. The first is from the Network window, which has a button labeled File and Print Sharing. Click this button to display the File and Print Sharing window shown in Figure 23.8.

FIGURE 23.8.

The File and Print Sharing window lets you activate sharing of your files and printer.

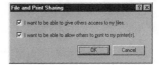

A checkbox next to the first item enables others to access your files. You must select the files or directories they will have access to from the File Manager. The second option enables others on the network to use your printer. Sharing your printer can slow down your system, so you may want to carefully consider using this option.

You can further control what other people on your local area network can do on your system by changing the type of access they have. There are two broad types of access: share-level and user-level. You can select either of these types through the Access Control page of the Network window. This is shown in Figure 23.9.

FIGURE 23.9.

Access Control lets you control the way in which other users on the network can use your machine's files and resources.

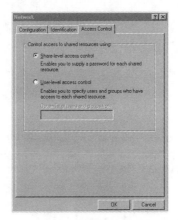

Share-level access control sets a password to each file or peripheral you have set to be shared. (You set the files or peripherals to be shared through the File Manager.) With share-level access control in place, users who try to access your machine must provide a password to perform the file transfers or use a local peripheral. The password can be set to null (nothing) to enable wide-open access.

User-level access control lets you set the users who have access to your files and resources. They don't need a password to get through to the files. However, there must be a master list of these users located somewhere, indicated by the Obtain List field entry.

Starting Windows 95 when the Network Isn't Running

When your machine isn't attached to the network or the network is not operating, Windows 95 may not start up properly. Windows 95 may want to enter Fail Safe mode. You can avoid this problem by entering the Network Configuration screen and changing the setting for the Primary Network Logon.

The Primary Network Logon controls how Windows 95 will behave when it starts up and checks the network for connections. The normal setting will be the Client (such as Client for Microsoft Networks) for the network software you have selected. In this setting, Windows 95 will prompt you for a logon when your system boots. It may also ask you for the name of the domain you want to use. This window is shown in Figure 23.10, with the two options available for the Microsoft network shown. There may be more options available depending on the type of network you have installed.

FIGURE 23.10.

Changing the Primary Network Logon can prevent Windows 95 from displaying error messages when it attempts to connect to the network.

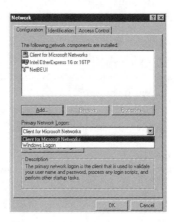

The Windows Logon option is useful for disabling the problems when the system starts up and the network is not complete. Selecting Windows Logon will start up Windows 95 but not display error messages if the system can't connect to the network.

The Windows Logon option is useful not only when you know the network is not operating, but also when you have a portable computer. When you are on the road or moving the machine about, switch to Windows Logon to disable the error messages.

Changing Network Settings: Using Properties

You have seen the basics of using the Network window, but there are more levels of detail available to fine-tune your peer-to-peer network and the software the network uses. These are accessed through the Properties button on the Network window. There is a property for each item in the current configuration list on the main window.

Network Card Properties

If you select the network interface card in the Network window list, and then click Properties, you will see a window that lets you fine-tune the behavior of the network card. Figure 23.11 shows the main Properties window for the Intel EtherExpress 16 card installed earlier.

FIGURE 23.11.

The Properties window lets you fine-tune the network interface card—in this case, an Intel EtherExpress 16. There are four pages available from this window. This figure shows the first page, which specifies the driver type.

There are four pages for the network interface card, which you select using the tabs at the top of the window. The first page is for the driver type. In Figure 23.10, you can see that the Intel EtherExpress card supports three different drivers: an Enhanced mode NDIS (32-bit and 16-bit), a real mode NDIS driver (16-bit only), and a real mode ODI driver (16-bit only). Windows 95 will set the default value for the card, which is usually the enhanced mode driver if the card can support it. If you are not sure which driver to use, leave the selection that Windows chooses for you as the default.

The Bindings page, shown in Figure 23.12, lists the protocols the network interface card will use. Because Windows 95 can support several protocols at once, there may be more than one protocol listed (you must have added the protocols using the procedure shown earlier). This window lets you deselect a protocol from use without removing it from the configuration files. This can be useful when you move across networks, such as with a portable computer.

The Advanced page lets you control a few of the special parameters involved in communicating with the network. This window is shown in Figure 23.13. It is highly recommended that you leave the default values unless you know what you are doing. Changing these settings can affect network performance. If you are going to change a parameter, note the default value so you can restore it later.

FIGURE 23.12.

The Bindings page lets you select which protocols are to be used with the network card. Multiple protocols can be active at once.

FIGURE 23.13.

The Advanced page controls the behavior of the network card. You should not experiment with settings in this window.

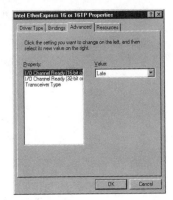

The last page available through the Properties window sets the IRQ and address for the network interface card. This window is the same as the one you saw when you installed your network card. If your network card is working, don't change these values.

Client Properties

To display the Client properties window, click a client in the Network window, and then select the Properties button. The Client properties window is a single screen, but its appearance and title will depend on the type of client you have installed. A Client Properties window for Microsoft Network Client is shown in Figure 23.14.

The top section of this window (labeled Logon validation) is off by default. Clicking the checkbox turns logon validation on. This displays a message if you make an error when typing a domain name or password during the logon process.

The lower section of the window controls how Windows 95 restores network connections from one session to the next. The default setting tries to reestablish all the connections that existed the last time you were logged on. Changing this to the top option, called Quick logon, doesn't reestablish your old connections; you must make them all over again.

FIGURE 23.14.

The Client Properties window lets you make adjustments to the behavior of the client software.

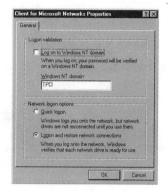

The Quick logon, as its name suggests, starts up Windows 95 faster because it doesn't have to use the network to communicate with other machines. However, if you regularly connect to other machines or resources, you may wish to have Windows 95 do the connections for you to ease the amount of work required to get to the other network machines.

Protocol Properties

The Protocol properties window is displayed whenever you select a protocol from the Network window and click the Properties button. This window lets you see more information about the protocols being used by the network. There are two pages available from the Protocol Properties window: Bindings and Advanced. The Bindings page, shown in Figure 23.15 for a NetBEUI protocol, is displayed first.

FIGURE 23.15.

The Protocol Properties window has two pages; this one shows the bindings that are currently in use by the network.

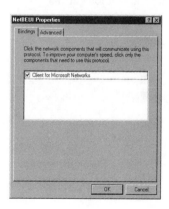

If you have configured your Windows 95 system to use only one protocol, it will be the only one displayed. If you have more than one protocol configured, though, they will all be displayed. You can disable (but not remove) a protocol by deselecting the checkbox. At least one protocol should be active at all times for the network connections to work properly.

The Advanced page of the Protocol Properties window includes more specific information about the behavior of the protocol. This window is shown in Figure 23.16 for the NetBEUI protocol. The parameters listed in the left window have a matching value slider control in the right. For the most part, unless you know exactly what you are doing, you should leave the default values.

FIGURE 23.16.

The Advanced page controls the behavior of the network protocol. You should leave the default settings unless you know what you are doing, or the network's performance may be adversely affected.

Summary

With the information in this chapter, you should have managed to install the hardware and software to set up a peer-to-peer network. The last step in setting up your peer-to-peer network machine is to select the files, directories, and local resources that will be available to others on the network. You will look at that in detail in Chapter 27, "Administration."

Windows 95 as a Client

24

by Tim Parker

You will often connect your Windows 95 machine to an existing network that doesn't run one of the protocols for peer-to-peer networking that we looked at in the last chapter (most commonly NetBEUI or NetBIOS). Instead, your network might require a widely used protocol such as TCP/IP, which enables you to connect to a high-performance server.

In most of these cases, your Windows 95 machine will not act as a peer, which is both a server and a client to other machines on the network; it will act only as a client to a larger server or other machines. In many cases, other users can connect to your machine, but in a more limited role.

There are several of these client-server networking systems in common use. The most common PC-based network is Novell's NetWare, which ties PC machines together, usually using a protocol called IPX/SPX. A widely used protocol is TCP/IP, which is popular because it is the default networking protocol of the Internet as well as all UNIX systems.

This chapter will show you how easy it is to tie your Windows 95 machine into a client-server network such as NetWare or TCP/IP. The steps are much the same as with peer-to-peer networking, so there's nothing really new about the process. The process for installing adapter cards, protocols, services, and clients was explained in the last chapter, but it is presented again here for convenience. This should make it easier for you to set up your system without flipping back and forth between chapters. However, a lot more detail about the installation process is explained in Chapter 23, "Peer-to-Peer Networking with Windows 95." If you have problems or are not sure of the steps, refer back to that chapter.

Using Windows 95 as a TCP/IP Client

TCP/IP (Transmission Control Protocol/Internet Protocol) is the most widely used networking protocol in the world. After originally being developed for tying UNIX machines together to form the Internet, it became the dominant UNIX network protocol because of its simplicity, standardization, and speed. TCP/IP is not a single protocol but a whole family of several protocols with different purposes.

You will often find these protocols referred to in books and networking systems because of their widespread use. Some of the information about the protocols is also required for Windows 95 configuration. You don't have to know all the details about each protocol, but knowing what each does and what the acronyms stands for will help you sort out the barrage of terms used in networking. (It will also make you look very learned at your next cocktail party!) The TCP/IP protocol family is listed here:

Transport: These protocols control the movement of data between two machines

TCP (Transmission Control Protocol): A connection-based service, which means that the sending and receiving machines are communicating with each other at all times.

UDP (User Datagram Protocol): A connectionless service (the two machines are not communicating with each other).

Routing: These protocols handle the addressing of the data and determine the best routing to the destination. They also handle the way large messages are broken up and reassembled at the destination.

IP (Internet Protocol): Handles the actual transmission of data.

ICMP (Internet Control Message Protocol): Handles status messages for IP, such as errors and network changes that can affect routing.

RIP (Routing Information Protocol): One of several protocols that determine the best routing method.

OSPF (Open Shortest Path First): An alternate protocol for determining routing.

Network Addresses: These services handle the way machines are addressed, both by a unique number and a more common symbolic name.

ARP (Address Resolution Protocol): Determines the unique numeric addresses of machines on the network.

DNS (Domain Name System): Determines numeric addresses from machine names.

RARP (Reverse Address Resolution Protocol): Determines addresses of machines on the network, but in a manner backward from ARP.

User Services: These are applications to which users have access.

BOOTP (Boot Protocol): Starts up a network machine by reading the boot information from a server. BOOTP is commonly used for diskless workstations.

FTP (File Transfer Protocol): Transfers files from one machine to another without excessive overhead. FTP uses TCP as the transport.

TFTP (Trivial File Transfer Protocol): A simple file transfer method that uses UDP as the transport.

Telnet: Allows remote logins so that a user on one machine can connect to another machine and use the remote machine's resources.

Gateway Protocols: These services help the network communicate routing and status information, as well as handle data for local networks.

EGP (Exterior Gateway Protocol): Transfers routing information for external networks.

GGP (Gateway-to-Gateway Protocol): Transfers routing information between Internet gateways.

IGP (Interior Gateway Protocol): Transfers routing information for internal networks.

Other Categories: These are services that don't fall into the categories mentioned earlier, but they provide important services over a network.

NFS (Network File System): Enables directories on one machine to be mounted on another machine and then accessed by users as though the directory was on the local machine.

NIS (Network Information Service): Maintains user accounts across networks, simplifying logins and password maintenance.

RPC (Remote Procedure Call): Enables remote applications to communicate with each other using function calls.

SMTP (Simple Mail Transfer Protocol): A protocol for transferring electronic mail between machines.

SNMP (Simple Network Management Protocol): An administrator's service that sends status messages about the network and devices attached to it.

Windows 95 and TCP/IP

Windows 95 includes as part of the basic distribution package a 32-bit VxD driver developed by Microsoft. The use of a 32-bit driver means that no conventional memory is used. The TCP/IP implementation included with Windows 95 is complete, offering all the services associated with the protocol, including the commonly used utilities FTP and Telnet. Basic TCP/IP diagnostic tools are also included. The Microsoft TCP/IP drivers are compatible with the 16-bit and 32-bit WinSock TCP drivers.

There are several commercially available TCP/IP packages available as well. The most widely used TCP/IP systems are ftp Software's PC/TCP and NetManage's Chameleon. Most third-party TCP/IP will work with Windows 95, but if it is not designed with 32-bit VxD drivers, it will chew up some conventional memory. Windows 95-specific versions of third-party tools are available, although the default TCP/IP drivers supplied by Microsoft should be sufficient for most client machines.

Before you begin installing TCP/IP for Windows 95, you must obtain a few pieces of information first. The most important information is your machine's IP address. Every device on a TCP/IP network has a unique number called an IP address. The IP address is written in *dotted-quad* notation—four numbers (between 0 and 255) separated by a period. For example, 127.0.0.1, 243.123.3.72, and 82.28.3.7 are all IP addresses.

If you are connecting to an existing network, you must ask your system administrator for your IP address; don't make one up! If your IP address conflicts with another device on the network, your machine will not function properly. Also, IP addresses are assigned using a special convention so that all network devices have similar numbers in the first one, two, or three parts of the dotted-quad notation.

The second piece of information that is necessary is the subnet mask. The subnet mask essentially indicates to TCP/IP which part of the IP address is used to identify your network, and which part is used to identify each device on that network. A subnet mask is composed of the numbers 255 or 0; you should obtain the subnet mask from your system administrator. If you are very familiar with IP addresses, you can determine your subnet mask based on the class of your network.

Installing TCP/IP for Windows 95

To install the TCP/IP drivers included with Windows, use the Network icon in the Control Panel to display the Network dialog (shown in Figure 24.1). The window shown has no network configuration at all. Your window might list existing network drivers, protocols, services, and adapters.

FIGURE 24.1.

The Network window enables you to configure your system for a network.

The steps to configure your system as a TCP/IP client first require you to specify your network adapter, load the protocol, and configure the system; then you test your settings after rebooting Windows 95. To install your network adapter, select the Add button on the Network window to display the Select Network Component Type window (shown in Figure 24.2).

FIGURE 24.2.

The Select Network Component Type window lets you add adapters, services, protocols, and clients to your Windows 95 installation.

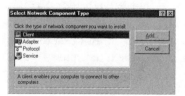

Select Adapter from the Select Network Component Type window. You will see the Select Network Adapters window shown in Figure 24.3. This window lets you select the manufacturer of the adapter card with which your system is equipped. After you select the manufacturer, a list of all adapter cards (more commonly called network interface cards, or NICs) is displayed. If your network card is not on the list, you need a driver disk from the manufacturer.

FIGURE 24.3.

The Select Network Adapters window shows you a list of all manufacturers and cards that have drivers supplied with Windows 95. Other cards require a driver from the manufacturer.

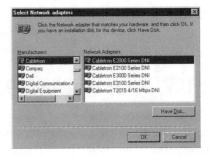

After you select the adapter card from the list and click the OK button, you are returned to the Select Network Component Type window. (Or if you double-clicked the adapter card name, you are back at the Network window.) The Network window now has the adapter name, as well as several services and protocols loaded by default (because you didn't give any specific protocols). This populated window is shown in Figure 24.4.

FIGURE 24.4.

After selecting a network adapter card, if you return to the Networks window without selecting a service or protocol, Windows 95 fills in the default values for you.

When you exit this window by clicking the OK button, you are asked for configuration information about your network adapter. This window is shown in Figure 24.5. Many adapter cards have DIPs or switches that must be set to specify the IRQ (interrupt) and memory address, whereas others (such as the IntelExpress 16 card used in the example) are configured by software. You can also change these settings by selecting the Properties button on the Network window after highlighting the adapter name. Choose the Settings page from the four Properties pages.

While the network drivers are loaded into the Windows 95 configuration, you might be asked to insert your distribution media so that Windows 95 can copy the files it needs. Finally, Windows 95 asks you to reboot your system. Rebooting is necessary to make sure that the new drivers are loaded. Because you still have to install the TCP/IP protocol, you don't necessarily have to reboot; however, doing so immediately shows you whether the network adapter was found by Windows 95.

FIGURE 24.5.

This window requests information about your network adapter's IRQ and memory address settings. These must match your hardware card for the network connection to succeed.

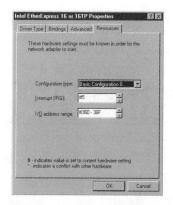

NOTE

When Windows 95 reboots, it tries to access the network adapter card. If it can't, an error window is displayed. If this happens, go into the Network window from the Control Panel, highlight the adapter name, select the Properties button, and then choose the Settings page. These values are incorrect and must be changed to match the network adapter card's settings. Make the necessary changes, click OK, and reboot Windows 95 to make sure the card is accessible now.

After you have configured your adapter, you can move on to the network protocols. (These can be loaded at the same time as the adapter, but a step-by-step process ensures that each component is properly loaded and configured.) From the Network window, select the Add button to display the Select Network Component Type, and then choose Protocol. The Select Network Protocol window (shown in Figure 24.6) will appear.

FIGURE 24.6.

The Select Network Protocol window lets you choose the proper protocol, such as TCP/IP, for Windows 95. If you are using a third-party TCP/IP product and the drivers are not part of Windows 95's distribution set, you need a vendor-supplied driver disk.

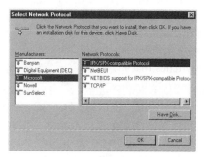

From the Select Network Protocol window, select the manufacturer of the protocol you want to use. If you are using a third-party product that is not listed, use the Have Disk button to read the drivers from a vendor-supplied disk. In this case, let's assume you are using the Microsoft-supplied TCP/IP protocol drivers. Click Microsoft and move to the right window, which lists all the protocols supplied. Choose TCP/IP. Either double-click the TCP/IP entry or highlight it and choose OK. You are returned to the Network window, and TCP/IP is now listed as a protocol.

Configuring Microsoft TCP/IP

Now that the protocol has been selected, the configuration must be completed before TCP/IP can be used. To start the configuration process, select the TCP/IP protocol entry in the Network window and click the Properties window. The TCP/IP Properties window appears, as shown in Figure 24.7.

FIGURE 24.7.

The TCP/IP Properties window has six pages of configuration information. At minimum, you must supply an IP address, shown on the first page when the TCP/IP Properties window appears.

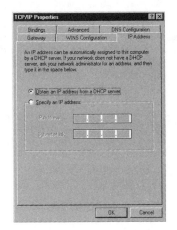

There are six pages of information that can be completed from the TCP/IP Properties window. Luckily, for most installations, you need to be concerned only with a minimum amount of information. Start with the IP Address page, which appears whenever the TCP/IP Properties window is displayed. For most installations, you should know the IP address and subnet mask. If this is the case, select the Specify and IP address button and enter the IP address and subnet mask in the spaces provided, making sure you keep the parts of the dotted-quad notation separate.

Some larger networks assign IP addresses automatically using a special protocol. This is usually used for machines that connect to the TCP/IP network occasionally. If your network uses one of these assignment systems, called Dynamic Host Configuration Protocol (DHCP) servers, you can select the first button on the IP Address page and let Windows 95 obtain your IP address and subnet mask for you. Most networks do not use DHCP.

Figure 24.8 shows the TCP/IP Properties page with a fictitious IP address and subnet mask entered. You should, of course, use a real IP address for your configuration.

FIGURE 24.8.

The IP Address page of the TCP/IP Properties window has been filled in with the machine's IP address and subnet mask. You must use real values for these numbers instead of randomly choosing numbers; otherwise, the network will not function properly!

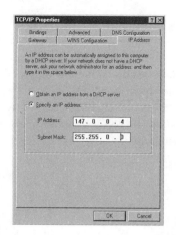

The WINS Configuration page of the TCP/IP Properties window is required if your network uses the Windows Internet Naming Service (WINS). WINS lets you use the NetBIOS protocol on a TCP/IP network. Most networks don't use WINS, so you can ignore this page unless your system administrator instructs you otherwise or you know you will use WINS. If WINS is required, enter the IP address of the primary (and secondary, if used) WINS servers, as well as the Scope ID.

The Gateway page (shown in Figure 24.9) lets you tell your Windows 95 system where the TCP/IP network's gateways are. Gateways are used to connect to other networks, including the Internet. If you are using a gateway, enter the IP address of the primary network gateway machine and click the Add button. You can enter many gateways, but you should provide the primary gateway IP address first. When searching for a gateway, Windows 95 goes down the list of gateways in order. If you are not sure about gateways on your network or don't know the IP address, you can leave this page until later. It is necessary only when you want to connect to another network through a gateway.

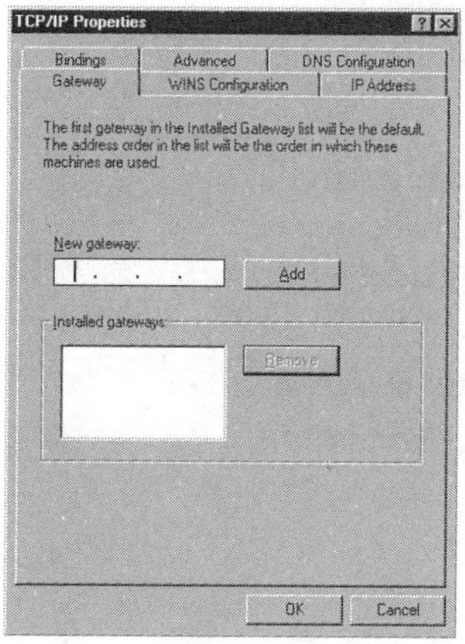

FIGURE 24.9.

The Gateway page of the TCP/IP Properties window lets you enter the IP address of all gateways on your TCP/IP network. Gateways are used to connect to other networks, as well as to the Internet.

The DNS Configuration page (shown in Figure 24.10) must be filled in if the Domain Name Service (DNS) is used on your TCP/IP network. DNS is a special TCP/IP protocol that converts the dotted-quad IP addresses to more common names. With DNS, you can call your machine Bob's_PC instead of a more complex IP address. It is also easier to connect to other machines, because you only need to know the name of the machine and not the IP address. DNS does the conversion between IP address and symbolic name. However, DNS requires a special configuration and server setup, so small networks are unlikely to use DNS. However, large networks often use it.

FIGURE 24.10.

If your network uses the Domain Name Service (DNS), you want to fill out the DNS Configuration page of the TCP/IP Properties window. You can specify your machine's symbolic name in this page.

If you are running DNS on your network, you can enter your machine's symbolic name, the domain name (the name of your workgroup or entire company), and the IP address of your DNS server. After Windows 95 has connected to the DNS server and told it of your IP address and symbolic name, other users of the network will be able to connect to your machine using your symbolic name. Similarly, if you know the symbolic name of a remote machine, you can use that to connect.

The Advanced page of the TCP/IP Properties window lets you select the TCP/IP protocol as the default protocol for your machine, as shown in Figure 24.11. Because you are using TCP/IP to connect to a TCP/IP network, you should select this option to prevent Windows 95 from using NetBIOS or IPX/SPX on the network.

The last page of the TCP/IP Properties window is the Bindings page, shown in Figure 24.12. This page lists all the network components that will use the TCP/IP protocol to communicate over the network. In this case, there is only the Microsoft client component in the list, and it should be selected.

FIGURE 24.11.

To use TCP/IP as the default network protocol, select this option from the Advanced page of the TCP/IP Properties window.

FIGURE 24.12.

The Bindings page of the TCP/IP Properties window specifies which components of Windows 95 are to use the protocol. In this case, only the default Microsoft client is listed and should be selected to use TCP/IP.

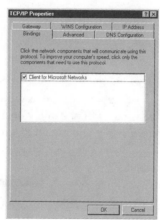

If you have installed other networking components and protocols, there might be more entries in the Bindings list. Select only those that are to use the TCP/IP protocol. Minimizing the number of bindings to the protocol helps improve efficiency of the Windows 95 networking software.

When all of the configuration information has been supplied in the different pages of the TCP/IP Properties window, select the OK button and you will be returned to the Network window. To finish the installation of the protocol and write the configuration information to the Windows 95 network files, click the OK button. Windows 95 now tries to load the drivers for the protocol, and probably asks you for the distribution disks.

After the drivers have been copied and the configuration information has been written, Windows 95 suggests that you reboot the machine to let the drivers take effect. You should reboot to make sure everything works properly. When Windows 95 starts up again, any problems with the adapter or protocol will be displayed as messages during startup. Read any warnings or error dialogs carefully, and then go back into the TCP/IP Properties window to correct problems with the protocol.

Testing Your TCP/IP Connection

To test your new TCP/IP protocol, one of the best utilities is a diagnostic tool called ping (which actually stands for Packet Internet Groper). The ping system works by sending little packets of information to another machine and waiting for a reply. The amount of time the reply takes is displayed, or error messages are shown. The system keeps sending packets until you tell it to stop.

To start ping, you must first find the utility. An easy way to locate it is to use Windows 95's Find command. From the Find window (shown in Figure 24.13), enter the word ping and click Find Now. Matches are shown in the window below. From there, double-click the ping icon to launch it.

The ping utility is a DOS application, not a Windows application, so you might have to launch it by opening a DOS window first. If you launch through the Find window or by clicking the icon within a Windows folder and the DOS window immediately closes, some configuration information is lacking. Don't panic. Open a DOS window and run ping from there.

FIGURE 24.13.

The Find utility is a good way to locate some of the TCP/IP network utilities such as ping and FTP.

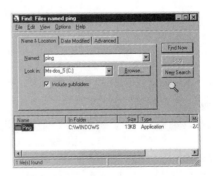

To use ping, you need to know the IP address or symbolic name of another machine on the network. Simply enter the name or address after the command, and watch as ping sends and receives packets of information. If you receive messages such as Bad IP Address, ping can't connect or resolve the name or IP address you supplied.

Figure 24.14 shows a ping session connecting to another machine on the network. You can see that it keeps pinging the remote machine four or five times. In the example shown in Figure 24.14, four pings were performed and took two milliseconds to return over the network. There are a number of options in ping that enable you to keep pinging, use different sizes of packets, and control the behavior. To see the available options, type the ping command name by itself in a DOS window, and a help screen will be displayed.

FIGURE 24.14.

The ping utility is sending packets to the machine with the IP address 147.0.0.2 and receiving them back in 2 milliseconds. It sends four packets total, in this example.

If you provided the IP address or symbolic name of a gateway (only valid if your network uses DNS), you can use ping to test any other machine on the networks connected to yours (including the Internet). Simply provide its IP address or domain name, and ping will attempt to connect through the gateway to the remote machine.

If you receive errors from the ping utility, you should verify that your IP address is valid. If it is, try using another machine on the network to ping your Windows 95 machine. If you can't, the network adapter or protocol is not loaded properly and you should return to the configuration screens.

As a final test of the network, you can use File Transfer Protocol (FTP) to connect to a remote machine, log in, and copy files back and forth. Use the Find utility to locate the file called ftp, or type its name from the DOS prompt. When launched, a window that looks like a DOS session appears, as shown in Figure 24.15. To exit FTP, type the command bye.

FIGURE 24.15.

The FTP utility lets you transfer files to other machines. The window looks like a DOS session.

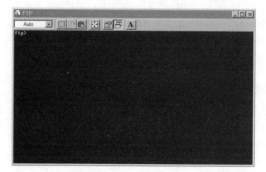

To obtain a list of valid FTP commands, just type the word help. FTP is not difficult to use, but it does require some familiarity with the utility. We can't go into enough detail here, so check a good TCP/IP book for more information. To connect to a remote machine, enter its

IP address (or symbolic name if your network uses DNS). If the connection to the remote machine is successful, you are prompted for a login name and a password. If they match the remote machine's information, you are connected and can move around the file system and transfer files (assuming you have permission). Figure 24.16 shows an FTP session established to a remote machine.

FIGURE 24.16.

FTP has been used to connect to a remote machine, and a login has been performed successfully. From here, you can transfer files or move around the remote system (assuming you have permission to do so).

If FTP can't connect to a remote machine at all, it could be because the remote machine hasn't been set up to allow FTP access. Many machines will not allow remote access for security reasons. If you can connect to the machine but can't log in, it's because you don't have a valid account on the remote machine. You should get the owner of the remote machine to create privileges for you.

You can also use the Telnet command, which lets you log in to other machines as though you are a user sitting in front of that machine. Telnet is widely used in UNIX but not as common in the DOS environment.

Sharing Your Files with Others

If you want to allow other users to connect to your machine and access files, you must turn File Sharing on. This is done through the File and Print Sharing button on the Network window. When you click the button, you will see a dialog that lets you select whether to share files and local printers. This dialog is shown in Figure 24.17.

FIGURE 24.17.

If you want to share your files or local printers with other network users, you must turn File and Print Sharing on by using this dialog.

Select the options you want from the File and Print Sharing dialog (notable files in this case, because we want to allow remote users to access our local files). Click OK and then click OK in the Network window, and Windows 95 prompts you for distribution disks so that it can load the sharing files. Finally, Windows 95 asks you to reboot so that the sharing of drivers can take effect.

After the drivers have been loaded, Windows 95 should allow others to connect to your system. You must set the file and printer permissions properly to allow access. For more information, see the Sharing chapter later in this section.

Windows 95 and Windows NT

Windows 95 has been closely integrated with Windows NT, and both share many of the same 32-bit components. Windows 95 can act as a client to Windows NT and Windows NT Server systems, and can also act as a peer if necessary.

The configuration of Windows 95 as a client to a Windows NT network is similar to that for TCP/IP, which was discussed earlier. The network adapter card is installed in exactly the same manner. The protocol installed with Windows 95 to access a Windows NT network depends on the protocol the NT network uses: Usually it is NetBIOS, but it could be running TCP/IP or IPX/SPX. After you have determined which protocol is used (probably NetBIOS), you can configure the protocol in the same manner as for a TCP/IP network (discussed earlier) or a peer-to-peer network (see Chapter 23).

If you want to log into a Windows NT network, you have to enable the Windows NT login process. This is done from the Network window. Double-click the Client for Microsoft Networks name in the list of installed components to display the Client for Microsoft Networks Properties window (shown in Figure 24.18).

FIGURE 24.18.

To set up Windows 95 to access Windows NT networks, use the Client for Microsoft Networks Properties windows to enable Windows NT logins.

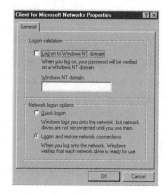

The Windows NT Domain on the Client for Microsoft Networks Properties window lets you enter the name of the Windows NT domain or workgroup that you will be logging into, and where your login information is stored. Whenever you log in, the login information is verified with the server for this domain or workgroup. The entry above the name, titled Logon Validation, indicates that you want to receive error messages if your login was not successful. If you want to validate your logins, complete this section of the window.

The lower part of the Client for Microsoft Networks Properties window, titled Network Logon Options, indicates how you want Windows 95 to connect you to the Windows NT network. If the default action, labeled Logon and restore network connections is selected, Windows 95 logs you into the Windows NT network when your machine first starts. This adds some time to the startup but ensures that the network is available without delay whenever you are using Windows 95. The alternative, labeled Quick logon, doesn't complete the connection process when Windows 95 starts. Instead, it ensures that a connection is possible, but it doesn't actually initiate the connection until you use it. If you use the network occasionally, this is the best choice.

When you log into the Windows NT network, you receive the same type of network login dialog as with any other network. Only the name changes to indicate a Microsoft Network. The window asks for your user name, password, and the domain you are connecting to. When the information has been verified with the server, you are connected.

Windows 95 and Windows NT servers work very well together because of the similarities of their architecture and the common NetBIOS interface. As noted earlier in this section, you can have more than one network configured at a time. Therefore, you could be connected to both a Windows NT NetBIOS network and a TCP/IP network at the same time.

Windows 95 and Novell NetWare

Windows 95 was designed with NetWare in mind, because NetWare is the most used local area networking system in the world. By changing the default configuration from NetBIOS to IPX/SPX, Windows 95 has acknowledged Novell's network dominance. For this reason, setting up Windows 95 as a client to a NetWare network is relatively easy. Windows 95 provides client support for both Novell NetWare 3.*x* and 4.*x* products. The NetWare protocols can also coexist with other protocols, so you can be simultaneously on a NetWare and TCP/IP network, for example.

Microsoft has supplied 32-bit drivers for NetWare integration, although existing 16-bit drivers such as VML shells and NETX can also be used. The 32-bit drivers are preferable, because they do not require any conventional memory. They are also faster than the older 16-bit drivers.

Installation of the network adapter card for Novell's LAN is the same as with other networks, although the same network card can't always be used with Novell NetWare as can be used with

Ethernet, for example. Check with the adapter card manufacturer to ensure that the card is Novell NetWare compatible. The installation process begins from the Network window, which is accessible through the Control Panel. Choose the Add button to display the Select Network Component Type window. This window is shown in Figure 24.19.

FIGURE 24.19.

The Select Network Component Type window lets you add NetWare adapters, services, protocols, and clients to your Windows 95 installation.

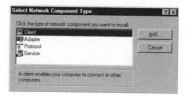

Select the Adapter option from the Select Network Component Type window. The Select Network Adapter window (shown in Figure 24.20) appears. You can use the scroll list in the left half of the window to select the manufacturer of the adapter card you will use. After you select the manufacturer, all adapter cards for which Windows 95 has drivers are displayed. If your network card is not on the list, you need a driver disk from the manufacturer, or you can select a driver that is compatible with your card. Most NetWare-capable cards can be configured as a Novell/Anthem NE2000 network card.

NOTE

Most network cards manufactured and sold by Novell are listed under Novell/Anthem in the scroll list. This includes the popular NE2000 card.

FIGURE 24.20.

The Select Network Adapters window lets you choose the manufacturer of your network card from the left scroll list and the actual card (or a compatible model) from the right scroll list.

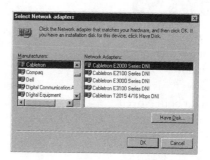

Figure 24.21 shows a network installation with the Novell/Anthem NE2000 card added. Many network cards are compatible with the NE2000, so this is a good default selection if your NetWare card is not listed. As you can see, Windows 95 automatically installed the default clients and protocols for use with the Novell NetWare IPX/SPX operating system.

> **TIP**
>
> If you are trying to install a NetWare/Anthem NE2000 card that has added functionality (such as the NE2000 Plus card) and are experiencing difficulties in getting the card to function properly, use the generic NE2000 card driver.

FIGURE 24.21.

Adding a Novell/Anthem NE2000 network adapter to the list of installed network components results in this window.

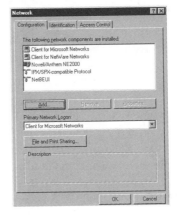

When you exit the Network window by clicking the OK button, you are asked for configuration information about your network adapter. This window is shown in Figure 24.22. You can also access this window by selecting the Properties button on the Network window after highlighting the adapter name.

FIGURE 24.22.

This window asks for information about the network card's IRQ, DMA, and I/O address settings. Some cards will be properly configured automatically, while others will need you to set DIP switches or jumpers.

If you exit the Networks window after configuring the network card, Windows 95 asks whether it can reboot to enable the new network settings. While Windows 95 reboots, it tries to access the network adapter card. If it can't, an error window is displayed. If you see an error, go into the Network window from the Control Panel, highlight the adapter name, select the Properties button, and choose the Settings page. The values you entered are incorrect and must be changed to match the network adapter card's settings.

After the adapter card has been installed and recognized by the system, you can install the Microsoft Client for NetWare drivers. These usually load automatically when the adapter card is installed, although they might not be set as the default protocol.

To configure the Microsoft Client for NetWare, double-click its name in the Network window. The Client for NetWare Networks Properties window (shown in Figure 24.23) appears. This window asks for information about the NetWare server to be used, the drive letter of the first network drive to be mounted on your Windows 95 machine, and whether a logon script should be processed when you log into the NetWare network.

FIGURE 24.23.

The Client for NetWare Networks Properties window lets you set the configuration information for connections to a NetWare network.

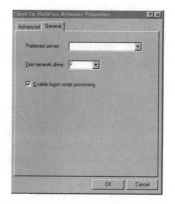

To complete the Client for NetWare Networks Properties window, enter the name of the NetWare server and the first drive letter to be used (usually the next available drive letter on your system, although some users like to set the letters higher to make it clear that they are network drives). Logon scripts, which are executed when you first connect to the network, let you tailor your system according to NetWare parameters. If you want a logon script to execute automatically, check the box next to this option. Figure 24.24 shows a completed Client for NetWare Networks Properties window.

When you log into a NetWare network, you are prompted for the same login information as any other network accessible through Windows 95: your user name, your password, and the name of the server to which you want to connect. After you supply the information, Windows 95 verifies the user information with the NetWare server and (assuming you are a valid user) gives you access. If you elected to run a logon script, it is executed immediately.

File and Printer Sharing is turned on by selecting the File and Printer Sharing button in the Network window. This shows the window seen earlier. (See Figure 24.17.) If you want to let others on your NetWare network gain access to your files, you must turn file sharing on.

FIGURE 24.24.

A completed Client for NetWare Networks Properties window that tells Windows 95 to connect to a remote server called Wizard and enable a logon script. Any mounted drives from the server are assigned as drive M or above.

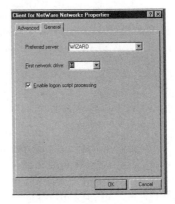

When file sharing is active, you still have to set your files or folders to be shared. This is done through the Properties sheet under each drive or folder. Select the Sharing page from the Properties sheet and you can specify the name of the drive or folder that remote users will see, and the types of access they will have. Figure 24.25 shows the Properties sheet for the C drive on a system.

FIGURE 24.25.

To let other NetWare users access your files, you must turn file sharing on and then set the folders or drives to be shared. The Properties window lets you give the drives or folder a name, as well as specify the type of access users will have.

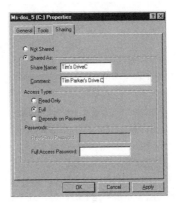

Printer sharing under NetWare is also set up through the File and Printer Sharing button on the Network window. You can specify a network printer through the Printer Add routine. Installing a network printer displays a window that asks for the network path name of the printer, as shown in Figure 24.26.

FIGURE 24.26.

To use a network printer, you must add it using the Printer Add routine. Specify a network printer when the Printer wizard asks whether the printer is local or remote, and then fill in this window with the name of the path to the network printer.

Network Print Servers

Windows 95 includes a 32-bit driver for PSERVER, the Novell NetWare print server. PSERVER lets Windows 95 machines handle print requests on any printer, in addition to the usual access from the NetWare server. PSERVER print queues can be shared between the NetWare server and Windows 95 machines.

When Windows 95 connects to a remote printer on a NetWare, Windows NT, or Windows 95 peer-to-peer network, the PSERVER drivers are automatically installed and loaded. The installation can occur transparently across the network from a server, if necessary. By installing in this manner, the most recent version of the PSERVER drivers can be made available every time a print request on a remote printer is issued. Printer installation for networks is also made much easier by PSERVER.

With PSERVER, when a network printer is disabled or goes off line for any reason, all print requests for that device are held in a queue. If the printer later becomes active again, the print requests are then printed. While in the queue, the print requests can be redirected to other printers, if desired. Windows 95 lets you manage remote printers as if they are local, which is much easier.

To manage a remote printer, double-click its icon. If you have the correct access permissions, you can affect any of your requests in the queue, either canceling or holding them.

Summary

As you have seen, Windows 95 can act as a client on any type of network as long as a driver is available for the network protocol. In this chapter, you've seen how to connect to a TCP/IP network. The same principles apply to Windows NT and Novell NetWare networks. As a client, Windows 95 can access files, printers, and machines on entirely different networks.

Although it isn't as powerful as a peer-to-peer network in terms of accessing other machines, a client-server network is the most commonly occurring local area network type. Windows 95 is ideally suited to act as a client, especially when you are accessing more than one type of network at a time.

Sharing Files and Resources

25

by Tim Parker

IN THIS CHAPTER

You've gone to a lot of trouble to install a network interface card, configure Windows 95 for a network protocol and service, and uniquely identify your machine. Now it's time to actually use the network to access other machines, as well as let other network users access some of your files and resources. This chapter shows you how to set your own system to allow others to gain access, and how you can access other systems.

Universal Naming Convention (UNC)

Windows 95 uses the Universal Naming Convention (UNC) to help make network access to files, machines, printers, and other devices a little easier. Without UNC, you would have to map a drive letter to a particular machine and drive (and sometimes directory), loading up your own machine's drive mappings.

UNC enables you to refer to remote machines and files using the format

```
command \\server\share_name\path_name
```

in which `server` is the name of the remote machine, `share_name` is the name of the device, and `path_name` is the path and filename, if applicable. Any DOS command (`COPY`, `DIR`, `DEL`, and so on) can use UNC when dealing with remote machines.

For example, to get the directory of the C drive (called `Bob_C` by the owner) on the remote machine Foofie, you could issue the command

```
dir \\Foofie\Bob_C
```

Of course, the owner of the remote machine must have set shared access to the drive on; otherwise, you would not be allowed to obtain a directory listing. You can only access shared resources on other machines.

> **NOTE**
>
> If the server you are connecting to supports long filenames (those with more than eight characters, a period, and three more characters, as in DOS's naming convention), you can use the long filenames with UNC as well. Windows NT, UNIX, and Novell NetWare all support long filenames.

You can use UNC to display shared remote folders and drives easily. From the Command Line text box in the Run dialog, fill in the command to be executed. If you are obtaining the remote directory in the previous example, a new window will open with the contents displayed. This is a little easier than going through the Network Neighborhood window, clicking the remote machine, and then clicking on the remote drive.

Resources, Workgroups, and Machine Names

We should begin with a quick check of terminology so that the chapter's contents are not ambiguous. Your machine is only one of several on the local area network. Each machine on the network is called a *node*. Depending on the way your network is set up, some nodes might be servers, some might be clients, and some might be both or neither.

Any machine that shares its resources, including files and printers, is a *server*. It is serving its resources to others. Any machine that uses another machine's resources is a *client*. Windows 95 lets a machine be both a client and a server. For example, another user could be logged into your system to copy a number of files, while you use a third user's machine to print your own files. In the former instance, you are the server; in the latter, you are the client.

Any resource that is directly attached to your machine is a *local resource*. This can be a file, directory, entire hard disk, or any peripheral such as a scanner, printer, CD-ROM drive, or tape drive. If the resource is set with permissions that allow other machines on the local area network to access it, it is a shared resource. You might have no shared resources on your machine. You can use any other machine's shared resources as long as your permissions allow you access. Windows 95 does not let you share all types of peripherals. (It really only allows sharing of hard disks and printers.) However, other operating systems that reside on your LAN might not have any restrictions.

Resources are usually assigned names to make it easier for identification. Just like each machine on the network has a name (always a unique one), each resource can be assigned a name, although it doesn't have to be unique. For example, you might call your hard drive `Tim_Drive_C` to make it obvious to others whose hard drive they are accessing. If you were to connect to drive C of four different machines and they all were called C, you would have a hard time knowing which one belonged to which machine. Identifying the resources with a name helps solve this problem.

A *workgroup* is a number of nodes that are grouped together into a single organizational entity and assigned a unique name for the group. Usually, the workgroup is based on your department, location, or company. For example, all the programmers in your company might belong to one workgroup, or separate workgroups might exist for each project that the programmers are working on. The division of a local area network into workgroups is for convenience when it comes to sharing resources. You can be a member of many workgroups.

Why use workgroups? Imagine you have a local area network with 80 users, each with a printer attached to his or her PC. Several of the printers are high-speed laser printers that you occasionally require to print out a large document. When you view the list of printers on the network, you would have to go through a list of 80 of them to find the one you want. It's much easier to break the 80 machines into smaller organizational groups so that you only have to search through your own workgroup for the printer.

Windows 95 uses workgroups as its network organizational element. All displays of resources are by workgroup name. Usually, workgroups are assigned so that you will spend most of your time inside your own workgroup, which minimizes the network traffic over the whole network and also saves you time.

Sharing Disks, Directories, and Files

Local area networks were originally designed to ease the problem of file sharing, and this is still their primary purpose. Windows 95 lets you share individual directories or an entire disk drive with others on the network. To share any of these items, you must use the Properties system to indicate that they can be shared.

Enable File and Printer Sharing

In order to share files and resources, you must have the file sharing options enabled. To enable them, open the Network window from the Control Panel (double-click on the Network icon). In the lower portion of the window is a large button labeled File and Print Sharing. Click the button to open the File and Print Sharing window shown in Figure 25.1.

FIGURE 25.1.

The File and Print Sharing window lets you enable the sharing of your resources with others on the network.

There are two entries in this window, one to allow sharing of your files and the other to allow sharing of printers attached to your machine. To activate the options, click the box next to the entry you want active. A checkmark will appear in the box. You must click the OK button to activate file and printer sharing (or either one if you select to share only one of your resources). Windows 95 will then install the file and printer sharing software on your system. During this process you might be asked to load software from your Windows 95 distribution media. When all the software is loaded and the configuration files are updated, Windows 95 prompts you to reboot your machine to make the changes effective.

After you have enabled file and printer sharing, the Network window will have a new entry for File and Printer Sharing, as shown in Figure 25.2. If you click the File and Print Sharing item in this list, and then click the Properties button, you will see a Properties sheet for the sharing service. This window is shown in Figure 25.3.

FIGURE 25.2.

File and Print Sharing now appears as a service on the Network summary window.

FIGURE 25.3.

The File and Print Sharing Properties window enables you to adjust parameters, although you should leave the default values as they are unless you are sure of your changes.

The File and Print Sharing Properties window lets you adjust some parameters of the sharing service. To adjust a parameter, highlight the name in the list to the left of the window, and then use the scroll buttons to the right to set the new values. Unless you know what you are adjusting, don't make any changes! You could adversely affect the behavior of your system's sharing service.

Now that you have activated the file and print sharing service, others can access your machine and make use of its resources. Usually, you won't want to let other users access everything on your machine, though, so you should decide which folders, files, or drives will be shared.

Sharing an Entire Disk Drive

If you want to share an entire disk such as your C drive, you have to highlight the disk drive name in the My Computer window as shown in Figure 25.4. Don't open the drive to display the contents; just highlight the name with a single-click.

FIGURE 25.4.

To share an entire drive, first select the drive in the My Computer window. You don't have to display the contents of the drive.

When the drive name to be shared is highlighted, select Properties from the File pull-down menu. This will display the Properties window, shown in Figure 25.5. There are three pages to the Properties window: the General page, the Tools page, and the Sharing page. The General page is always shown first.

> **NOTE**
>
> If you do not see a Sharing Page when you open the Properties window, File and Print Sharing is not active.

FIGURE 25.5.

The General page of the Properties window enables you to give a unique name to the drive you want to share.

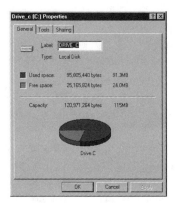

From the General page, you can assign a unique name to the drive. This name isn't visible to others on the network; it applies only to your own machine's name displayed in the Windows 95 My Computer window. However, many users find it convenient to have the same name for the local machine as for others on the network. You might want to change the name to match the shared drive name (which we change on the Sharing page).

It is often useful to include your name or your machine's name, as well as the drive letter in the name (such as `Tims_Drive_C` or `FroBozz_C`). The General page also shows you some information about the drive, such as the amount of free space available and the total size of the drive.

WARNING

It is usually a bad idea to share an entire drive. Instead, create a shared folder underneath the root directory into which you can transfer files. This is much safer and prevents accidental (and intentional) damage.

To change the name of the drive, highlight the current name (if it isn't already highlighted when you enter the Properties windows) and enter your new name directly. Name changes take effect immediately. You should enter a name for each drive you will share, and preferably be consistent in the naming convention.

The second page available through the Properties window is the Tools page. This page has nothing to do with sharing the drive, but it includes some basic disk utilities for checking the media and defragmenting the drive.

The Sharing page of the Properties window is where you can set the type of sharing you want for the drive. This window is shown in Figure 25.6. The default value selected when you open the window for the first time is No Sharing, which means that no one else on the network can access this drive. To allow others to access the drive, you must select the Share As button.

FIGURE 25.6.

The Sharing page of the Properties window lets you set the sharing characteristics of the entire drive.

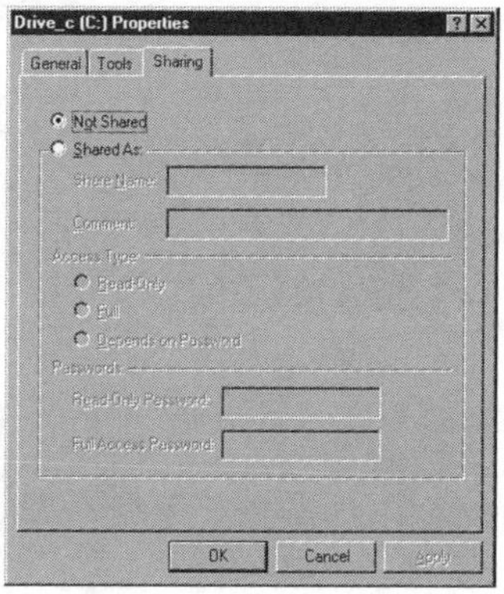

When you select the Share As button, the rest of the window becomes active. There are several parameters you can supply to control the way your drive is shared. The first thing to supply is a Shared Name. This is the name that other users will see when they connect to your machine. As mentioned earlier when we were naming the drive for your own desktop, there are many users who like to keep the names consistent. Whether you have separate names for your desktop and remote users is up to you; there is certainly nothing wrong with different names.

To supply a name, you should position the cursor inside the Shared As field and type a name. It is advantageous to use a name that indicates your machine's name or your name so that users over the network will know which drive they are using. You can use names like `Tims_C_Drive` or `Frobozz_C`, for example. Naming drives with strange names that have no relationship to you or your machine might seem amusing to some people, but it leads to confusion for others accessing your drive.

The Comment area lets you supply a general comment, perhaps about the drive or its contents. The Comment is seen by users of the network only when they use the Details view of the network. If your Shared As name is descriptive, you can probably skip the Comment.

The Access Type controls what other users on the network can do with your drive. If you set it to Full, users can make changes to your drive's contents, such as deleting files and adding them. If the access is set to Read-Only (the default), users can only read the drive contents and copy files from it. They cannot copy to your drive.

The Depends on Password option lets you assign access permissions through a password. You could allow everyone to read your drive, for example, and a few people who know a special password to write to your drive. The password they will use is specified on this screen, too. Figure 25.7 shows the Sharing screen filled in to allow password-based access to the local machine's C drive. You can have separate passwords for read-only and full access as well, to really control access to your drive.

FIGURE 25.7.

The Sharing page of the Properties window is set to require a different password for Read-Only and Full access to the local machine's C drive.

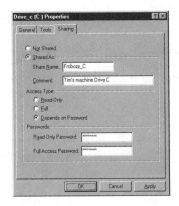

If you are using the Depends on Password option and you enter a password for either access level, when you click the OK or Apply button you will be prompted to verify the passwords in another window (shown in Figure 25.8). If you enter the same passwords, the password-dependent security is in place, and you must give your password to all users whom you want to be able to write to your drive.

Unless you expect people to copy files onto your drive, it is wise to set access permissions to Read-Only at first. You can always change settings temporarily if you must have another user copy files to your drive. There are few things more annoying than having another user delete important files on your drive by accident (or intent).

Chapter 25

FIGURE 25.8.

Windows 95 prompts for verification of the access passwords with this window. When the passwords have been verified, access protection is in place.

Sharing a Folder

You can select specific folders (directories) on a disk drive to share instead of sharing an entire disk. To share a folder, the process is similar to sharing a disk drive. Expand the disk drive that contains the folder to show the contents, and then highlight the folder to be shared (as shown in Figure 25.9). You don't have to open the folder to share it. You can work with more than one folder at a time when you select them in the drive window. Hold down the Shift key each time you click a folder, and they will all be highlighted.

FIGURE 25.9.

To share a folder, highlight its name and choose Properties from the File pull-down menu.

When the folder name is highlighted, choose Properties from the pull-down menu (or use the Alt+F, R keystrokes). This will display the Properties window for the folder, as shown in Figure 25.10. The folder Properties window has two pages: General and Sharing. (If only one page appears, File sharing is not active.)

The top portion of the folder Properties window shows you the name of the folder, as well as some basic statistics about the number of files and the total size used in the folder. The bottom portion of the screen has four check boxes labeled Read-only, Hidden, Archive, and System. For folders, the System box is grayed out and is unavailable (it is used for files). These boxes are not directly related to file sharing but control the attributes of the file. If you are working with multiple folders, when you enter the Properties window all the selected folders will be listed. The attributes at the bottom of the Properties window will have a checkmark if all folders have that attribute. If the box is gray, it means that only some of the folders have that attribute.

FIGURE 25.10.

The Properties window lets you see the folder's attributes.

The Sharing page is where you can control access to the folder. This window is shown in Figure 25.11. It looks and works exactly as the drive Sharing page does (which is mentioned in the previous section). You can set passwords for the folders, if you want, at both read-only and full-access levels.

FIGURE 25.11.

The Sharing page of the Properties window lets you control access to the folder in much the same way as with entire drives.

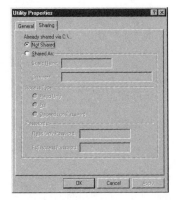

When a folder is set to full access, other users can place new items in it and delete existing items. They cannot enter folders that are not marked for sharing.

Sharing Files

Windows 95 doesn't allow you to tag individual files for sharing. It only allows folder and drive sharing. However, if you want to share only one or a few files, the easy means to achieve this goal is to create a new folder on your drive that is dedicated specifically to shared files. For example, you could have a public folder that is available to everyone on the network. You can refine this a little by creating both in and out folders, the former with full permission so that others can load files on your machine, and the latter with read-only permission so that no one can delete the contents.

It is quite common in peer-to-peer networking for each node on the machine to have public or in/out folders. This approach was actually developed from the Macintosh world but has been found useful and very workable for all types of peer-to-peer networks.

One important aspect to consider when tagging folders and drives for sharing is that others on the network can then access whatever is marked as shared, which potentially includes your e-mail, private files, and so on. Make sure you consider the fact that you will have no privacy for your files that are shared.

Sharing a CD-ROM Drive

You can share your CD-ROM drive and any other read-only devices the same way as any other drive. You don't have to differentiate between read-only and full access, however, because the device is read-only by its nature.

Some devices can be toggled between read-only and full access modes, such as some magneto-optical and CD-R (CD-Recordable) drives. They normally are read-only, but they can be set into write mode either through software or a panel switch. If you are using one of these devices, make sure users who connect to it know the limitations and dangers of running the device in write mode; otherwise, they might overwrite important data.

Removing File Sharing

To remove access to folders or drives that are currently marked as shared, open the Properties sheet for the item in question and click the Not Shared button. This takes effect as soon as you leave the Properties screen.

Marking folders on and off for sharing whenever you need them might seem cumbersome and time-consuming, but usually you will not have to change permissions that often.

When Others Access Your Shared Files

You can tell when someone is accessing a folder or drive that you have marked as shared because the icon of the item will have an outstretched hand underneath it. Figure 25.12 shows the C drive on a machine that has no sharing. Figure 25.13 shows the same drive with full sharing turned on.

FIGURE 25.12.

The My Computer window of a machine with no sharing of the drives.

FIGURE 25.13.

This window shows that Drive C of the machine has been set for sharing. The hand cradling the drive is an indication that sharing is set to be on.

The same change in icons applies when only folders are shared. Figure 25.14 shows that a single folder called Utility is shared on this drive.

FIGURE 25.14.

The folder called Utility is shared with others on the network, as indicated by the hand cradling the icon.

You can't tell from any of the My Computer menu items how many people are sharing a drive or folder. When you try to shut down your machine, though, you will see a window that warns you of other users connected to your system and gives you the option to continue the shutdown or cancel and leave your machine on.

Accessing Another Machine's Shared Files

To access a drive or folder on someone else's machine, you should know that machine name (or be able to figure it out from a list of all machines in the workgroup).

To connect to a remote machine, first open the Network Neighborhood window by clicking on its icon. You see a window that looks like the one shown in Figure 25.15. This particular network is very small, containing only two machines (one of which is yours).

You can see the Comment fields that were entered as part of the network configuration by selecting the Details menu option from the View pull-down menu. This can help you identify the machines on the network if the machine names don't help. You can also see some information about the remote machine by selecting the Properties screen from the File pull-down menu. This usually shows you the type of network software the remote machine is running. The properties window (shown in Figure 25.16) shows that the remote machine is running Windows for Workgroups.

FIGURE 25.15.

The Network Neighborhood window shows all the machines that are attached to yours through a network. This window has only two machines displayed.

FIGURE 25.16.

The Properties window shows you some details of the remote machine. In many cases, this includes the type of operating system it is running.

To connect to a resource such as a disk drive on another machine attached to the network, double-click the machine's icon. This opens a window that shows all the shared folders and drives on the remote machine. (See Figure 25.17.) The window doesn't differentiate between drives (megan_c) and folders (megan_opus). This particular window also shows that the CD-ROM drive attached to the remote is shared.

FIGURE 25.17.

Double-clicking a remote machine's icon displays a window with all the available shared resources, including folders and drives.

To use the remote drive or folder, double-click it and continue using the folder and files as though they are on your system. If the shared item is password-protected, you are prompted for the password. An option in the password window is to save the password for automatic use when you reconnect to the remote. This can save you a little time and prevents you from having to remember a lot of passwords.

After you have double-clicked the resource icon you want to use, the remote machine is now connected to yours through the network, and the remote folders or drives act as though they are on your system. If you try to do something that is forbidden by access permissions, you receive an error message.

To finish using the remote resource, close it as you would any other folder. Your connection to the remote is removed when you close all active connections.

Mapping a Network Drive

If you are going to use a remote machine's drive or folder often, you can make it behave as though it is permanently attached to your system by mapping it. Mapping a remote drive means assigning it a letter on your system. You could connect to a remote folder and have it logically attached to your system as drive E. Remember that because Windows 95 uses UNC, you don't have to map drives. However, if you will be using the remote resource a lot, mapping can help keep your desktop better organized.

To map a drive, use the Map Network Drive option under the File pull-down menu. This displays the Map Network Drive window, shown in Figure 25.18, which lets you choose the drive letter that the remote machine will take when mapped to your machine. Windows 95 automatically assigns the next logical drive letter, but you can override it if you want.

FIGURE 25.18.

The Map Network Drive window lets you treat a remote drive or folder as though it was one of your local drives by assigning a letter to the remote resource. This makes it easier to transfer files.

The Reconnect at Logon box, when checked, instructs Windows 95 to reattach the remote resource as the same drive letter when the operating system starts up each time. If you use the remote resource often, this can save you time. However, it does take Windows 95 longer to start up when it has to attach to remote drives. If you don't plan on using the remote resource during most sessions on your computer, don't use this option.

Creating Shortcuts

A shortcut is a fast way of accessing a remote resource. There are two ways to create the shortcut. You can use either of the methods because they all result in the same shortcut.

The first method of creating a shortcut involves dragging a folder or drive from the remote machine's window to your desktop background (anywhere that doesn't have an icon on it). This generates the error dialog shown in Figure 25.19, which warns you that you can't move or copy the item, but you can create a shortcut by clicking on the Yes button.

FIGURE 25.19.

This dialog is displayed when you drag a remote resource to your desktop. You can use this to create a shortcut.

The second method involves highlighting the resource name in the remote machine's window, and then choosing the Shortcut item from the File pull-down menu. This displays the dialog shown in Figure 25.20, which warns you that you can't create the shortcut there but you can place one on the desktop instead. Click on the Yes button and you proceed to the shortcut window.

FIGURE 25.20.

Another method of creating a shortcut is to use the Shortcut item in the File pull-down menu on the remote machine's window. This dialog is displayed.

Using either of these two methods creates an icon on your desktop called Shortcut To, followed by the name of the remote resource (as in Shortcut to Skywalker on Star_Wars). When you click the desktop top, its window opens. You can rename the shortcut as you rename any item on the desktop: click on the name and wait for the edit box to appear around it.

Sharing Printers

Windows 95 lets you share printers across networks. This means that you can print to a printer attached to any other machine on the network (assuming the attached PC's user allows access), and you can let others use any printers attached to your machine. Setting up and using shared printers is similar to sharing files.

Sharing Your Local Printer

To share a printer, you must first have File and Print Sharing turned on. You must have selected the option to share a printer, although you don't have to have file sharing active.

To set your local printer for sharing by others, you need to set the Properties of the printer.
Open the Printers window from your desktop, and select the printer (or printers) you want to
share. When a printer has been highlighted in the Printers window, choose the Properties option from the File pull-down menu. This opens the Properties window shown in Figure 25.21.
There are seven pages available from this window if Print Sharing is enabled. The first page is
the General page.

FIGURE 25.21.

*The Properties window for
a printer lets you alter its
sharing characteristics. The
General page lets you add
comments about your local
printer for other users to
read.*

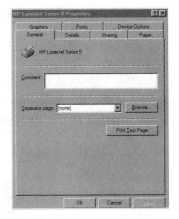

The Comments field on the General page lets you add a comment about the printer. This
comment will be viewable by other network users when they want to use your printer. Comments might be about the type of paper in each tray, special drivers needed, or the type of printer
emulation it uses. Figure 25.22 shows a comment added for a Hewlett-Packard Color LaserJet
printer that will help other users on the network use it properly. You don't have to add a comment to the printer, so usually they are used only when special information is necessary to use
the device.

The Sharing page of the Properties window is where you can set the printer to be shared. This
window is shown in Figure 25.23. The default setting is to not share the printer. If you decide
to share your printer, click on the Share As button, and then fill in the fields below so that the
printer has a name others can recognize. You can assign a password to the printer, which forces
network users to know the password before they can print on your local printer.

FIGURE 25.22.

The Comments field of the General page lets you add important information for other network users.

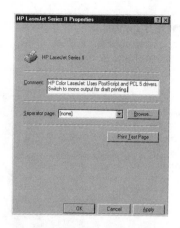

FIGURE 25.23.

To share a printer, click the Share As button and add a name and description. This helps identify the printer to other network users.

When a printer has been set for sharing, it appears in the Printer window with a hand cradling it. This is shown in Figure 25.24.

FIGURE 25.24.

A hand cradling a printer indicates that it has been set for shared access by others.

Using a Network Printer

To see which printers are available to you through the network, open the Networks window. You have to add the network printers to your Printer window by selecting Add Printer. Double-click the Add Printer icon to display the wizard that helps you configure the printer.

The process of configuring the printer is the same as for a local printer, except on the second screen you specify Network Printer instead of Local Printer. This screen is shown in Figure 25.25.

FIGURE 25.25.

To use a network printer you must first add it to your list of available printers. Select Network Printer from this printer wizard window.

When you select the Next button after clicking Network Printer, the printer wizard displays a window asking for the network path or queue name. This window is shown in Figure 25.26. If you know the network name of the printer, enter it in the field. The format of the printer name is \\machine_name\printer_name.

FIGURE 25.26.

To add a network printer, you must know its network path.

If you don't know the exact pathname of the printer you want to use, select the Browse button. This displays a window that shows all machines on the network and whether they have attached printers. This window is shown in Figure 25.27. When you select a printer, the window automatically puts the name of the printer in the Path field for you.

In the Browse window, a plus sign in a small box next to the machine name indicates that there are peripherals attached. Click the box to show the details. This lets you collapse and expand the view on large networks. From the browse window, select the printer you want to set as the network printer.

One screen in the printer wizard prompts you for a printer name. You can keep the default name supplied by Windows 95 or change it to any name you want. After you have finished with the printer wizard, the new printer appears in your Printers window. You can then use it as you would any other printer attached to your machine.

FIGURE 25.27.

The Browse button from the network printer window lets you see all machines on your network and whether they have printers attached.

Effects of Network Printing

Printing across a network to a remote printer means that you have to send the document to be printed through to the remote machine. This usually takes longer than printing on a local printer (unless you have a very slow local printer). Therefore, you should expect a slight delay before the printer will finish with your print request. Also, because your machine has to communicate with the network, you might notice a slight slowdown of your own Windows 95 session until the print request has been sent.

Letting others use your printer can have a more deleterious effect on your Windows 95 session. Your machine can slow down considerably when remote users queue requests to your local printer. This is because of the amount of background processing that your machine has to do to queue the printer properly.

If many people in your workgroup plan to use a remote printer often—especially if it is a special type of printer or plotter—you might want to consider putting it on the least used machine on the network, or even dedicating a special machine just to handle the printer. This can make the use of special print devices much easier and benefits the entire group by saving the cost of lots of local printers.

Summary

This chapter has shown you how to set up your own machine's resources for sharing with others, and how you can access other resources on the network. Sharing files and peripherals is one of the major advantages of networks and, when used properly, can make a working environment much more productive.

The next chapter discusses Remote Access, which lets you log into your desktop machine from a remote machine such as a laptop or another desktop.

Remote Access

26

by Tim Parker

What is remote access? It's a way to access your primary Windows 95 machines from another machine such as a desktop in another office or a laptop used in a hotel room. Remote access lets you connect to your primary machine and have the machine you are sitting in front of act as though its shared resources are on your primary machine.

Remote access is particularly popular with laptop owners who find themselves stranded in a hotel room with only a limited subset of their main machine on their laptop hard drive and the need to access files or services such as e-mail. Windows 95 lets you dial into your primary machine (whether at work or at home) from any other machine and, through a password-protected interface, access the machine easily and quickly.

With the increasing speed capabilities of modems, remote access to a Windows 95 system becomes realistic. Prior to high-speed synchronous modems, using Windows from a remote site could be torturously slow, forcing many users to abandon the whole idea.

Windows for Workgroups allowed a limited form of remote access to a Windows NT server, as well as remote access to a UNIX machine through a TCP/IP protocol that was an add-on software package. Windows 95 makes any machine a suitable client or server for remote access.

The remote access services are built into the Windows 95 operating system, as are the software protocols necessary to support remote access. This helps increase performance and reduce the need to depend on third-party software applications for remote access (some of which are remarkably good, but with Windows 95 they now become specialty items for specific requirements).

The simplest way to think of remote access is by analogy to a network system, except that with remote access, a couple of modems replace your network cable. When remote access has established a connection, it is as if you are using your networked machine. With remote access, you can also connect to a server (such as a Windows NT server) or a UNIX server, as well as to any machine on your local area network besides your own that allows access from RAS and has remote access enabled.

Setting Your System As a Remote Access Client

A remote access client calls in to a remote access server. The server can be a Windows 95 machine, Windows NT server, Novell NetWare server, a UNIX server, or another type of machine, as long as it is set up to receive calls from remote machines.

You can set your Windows 95 machine as a client quite easily by making a few simple changes to the configuration. The exact process depends on whether you are attached to a network that is already configured for remote access. The first step is to make sure that dial-up networking is enabled. When dial-up networking is active, install the Windows 95 PPP (Point-to-Point Protocol) driver.

Dial-Up Networking

Before you start setting up your system as a remote access client, you should have the dial-up network software installed on your system. Check your My Computer folder. If there is an icon labeled Dial-Up Networking, you can proceed to the installation of PPP.

If you don't see the Dial-Up Networking folder, you must install the dial-up networking software from your distribution media. To install a new component, use the Add/Remove Programs icon inside the Control Panel. This will display the Add/Remove Program Properties window, which has three pages. Select the Windows Setup page, as shown in Figure 26.1.

FIGURE 26.1.

The Windows Setup page lets you install components of Windows 95. In this case, the Dial-Up Networking option is underneath the Communications selection.

From the Windows Setup page, select the Communications option by double-clicking on it. This displays the different components of Windows 95 that are supplied with the distribution software. The Communications window, shown in Figure 26.2, has an option for Dial-Up Networking. Make sure there is a checkmark in the box next to the Dial-Up Networking title, and then click on OK. This returns you to the Windows Setup page. Clicking again on OK starts the installation process.

FIGURE 26.2.

The Communications options include Dial-Up Networking. This option should be checked. Windows 95 then prompts you for the distribution disks it needs.

Windows 95 prompts you for the disks or CD-ROM it needs to install dial-up networking. When the process is completed, Windows 95 reboots to enable the software drivers, and you can proceed to the PPP installation.

What is PPP?

PPP (or Point-to-Point Protocol) is one of the TCP/IP family of protocols. It is intended primarily for use over serial lines. PPP is related to another, somewhat simpler, protocol called SLIP (Serial Line Internet Protocol), which you might encounter with remote access. Both SLIP and PPP are available for most hardware platforms.

Both SLIP and PPP are intended to allow two computers to communicate over a serial line instead of a network cable. No network card is required for SLIP or PPP. PPP and SLIP support speeds up to 64.4 kbps (kilobits per second), although most serial ports won't work this fast. Because of the serial port limitations, most PPP and SLIP installations are limited to 19,200 baud, which can be boosted with modern modems to a much higher effective rate using software compression.

SLIP is used only for asynchronous communications and has none of the more sophisticated addressing and error detection features of PPP. For this reason, SLIP is usually used only when PPP can't be used. PPP can be both asynchronous and synchronous, although most users will never bother with synchronous communication over modems because of its high cost.

> **NOTE**
>
> If you plan to use RAS a lot, you might find asynchronous modems are too slow. Consider installing an ISDN line and purchasing an ISDN modem. They allow throughput of 64 kbps, which provides much better performance than asynchronous modems can provide. The cost is usually reasonable, although an ISDN line might be difficult to justify if you are not using RAS regularly. ISDN is also ideal for connecting to the Internet.

PPP handles multiple protocols, which allows it to be used with a variety of target hardware and operating system machines. It features built-in error detection and correction, as well as sophisticated handling of serial ports. Many connections to the Internet use PPP because of its speed and versatility. It makes an ideal protocol for remote access.

Installing PPP

Windows 95 treats the PPP driver and modem as though they are a network interface card. This makes it easier for the operating system to manage the configuration. To install the PPP driver, open the Network window from the Control Panel. Select the Add button to display the Select Network Component Type window. Either double-click on the Adapter entry, or highlight it and click the Add button. This screen is shown in Figure 26.3.

FIGURE 26.3.

To configure PPP, open the Select Network Component Type window and choose to add an adapter.

The Select Network Adapter window appears. Because Microsoft includes a PPP driver with the Windows 95 software, you should select Microsoft from the list of vendors. This will populate the list to the right of the window with Microsoft's list of products. (There might only be one because Microsoft doesn't make any hardware boards.) Select the Dial-up Adapter item and click on the OK button. This window is shown in Figure 26.4.

FIGURE 26.4.

Select the Dial-up Adapter from the list of Microsoft products in the Select Network Adapters window to begin installing PPP.

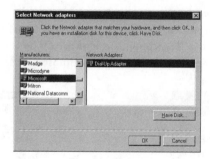

After you have clicked the OK button for Microsoft's Dial-Up Adapter, Windows 95 installs the PPP drivers and returns you to the Network window. You might notice that a number of new entries appear in the installed components list, as shown in Figure 26.5. These are the equivalent of a network interface board and protocol.

NOTE

If you use TCP/IP as the network protocol, you see two TCP/IP protocols listed in the network window—one for the network and one for dial-up. This is normal. NetBEUI uses the same driver for the network and dial-up.

FIGURE 26.5.

*After installing the
PPP driver, several new
components appear in the
Network Configuration
window.*

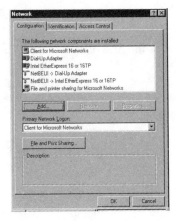

You can examine the properties of the new drivers by highlighting them in the Network window and clicking on the Properties button. The Properties window for the Dial-Up Adapter has three pages: Driver Type, Bindings, and Advanced. The Driver Type window, shown in Figure 26.6, lets you choose between 32-bit and 16-bit drivers. For the Microsoft PPP driver, only the·first option for 32-bit and 16-bit enhanced mode NDIS drivers is available. Commercial third-party PPP protocols might offer 16-bit real mode drivers (although the 32-bit enhanced mode driver is preferable in almost all cases).

FIGURE 26.6.

*The Properties window for
the Dial-Up Adapter lets
you select drivers. For the
Microsoft PPP driver, only
the first option is available.*

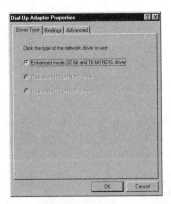

The Bindings page lists the Microsoft NetBEUI to Dial-Up Adapter binding, as shown in Figure 26.7. This should be left alone unless you are loading third-party PPP drivers.

FIGURE 26.7.

The Bindings page of the Properties window lets you use different protocols with the Dial-Up Adapter. For Microsoft's default PPP driver, only one protocol is usually used.

The Advanced page of the Dial-Up Adapter's Protocol window shows some of the parameters that can be adjusted with the PPP system. This window is shown in Figure 26.8. The parameters default to the best options for PPP performance. Therefore, you should avoid adjusting them unless you know what the parameters do and how they will affect your PPP sessions, and you can monitor the adjustments properly.

FIGURE 26.8.

The Advanced page of the Properties window contains parameter settings that should not be changed for most installations.

From the Network window, you can highlight the protocol line, which is usually labeled NetBEUI->Dial-up Adapter; then you can open the Properties window. This protocol Properties window has two pages: Bindings and Advanced.

The Bindings page of the NetBEUI Properties window shows that the dial-up protocol is bound to the adapter, which is the case for the file and printer sharing service in the window shown in Figure 26.9. Removing the checkmark from the box before each service deactivates the service component.

FIGURE 26.9.

The Bindings page of the NetBEUI Properties window shows all services that are bound to the protocol.

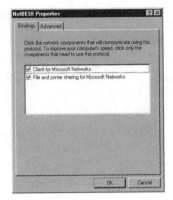

The Advanced page contains the adjustable parameters (shown in Figure 26.10). Like most of the Advanced pages, it should be left alone unless you know what you are doing.

FIGURE 26.10.

The Advanced page of the NetBEUI Properties window lets you adjust the behavior of the protocol. You should leave the default values as they are in most cases.

When you leave the Network Properties screen, make sure that you click the OK button to enable the remote access drivers. You might be prompted for the distribution software disk or CD-ROM if the drivers were not loaded during the original installation. After the drivers are loaded and the configuration files are updated, Windows 95 prompts you to reboot the machine so that the new drivers can take effect. You should reboot.

Telephone and Modem Settings

As a final step in setting up remote access, you must set the remote access parameters such as telephone number and modem characteristics. This is done with a wizard supplied with Windows 95. The easiest method of starting the process is to click on the Dial-Up Networking icon in the My Computer folder. This will display an information screen that looks like the one in Figure 26.11. Alternatively, you can install a modem using the wizard supplied in the Control Panel for Modems.

FIGURE 26.11.

This information screen is displayed when you first launch the remote access wizard by clicking on Dial-Up Networking in your My Computer window.

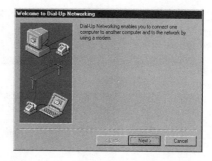

The next screen lets you set up your modem. You can either have Windows 95 try to detect the type of modem you have attached to your machine, or you can specify it directly. If you want Windows 95 to try to identify your modem, make sure it is plugged in and switched on (if it is an external unit). Also exit any application that might have the modem in use, such as communications and terminal programs. Windows 95 scans the serial ports testing for a modem, and then tests for supported speeds.

If you want to identify the modem yourself, choose the manufacturer and modem model from the list displayed when you select Don't Detect from the Install New Modem screen. This screen is shown in Figure 26.12.

FIGURE 26.12.

You can let Windows 95 identify your modem automatically, or you can specify it through this screen.

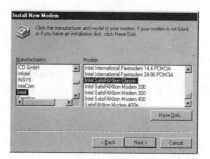

After the modem has been identified, Windows 95 installs the details of the speed, serial port number, and commands for driving the modem in its configuration files. If you want to fine-tune the behavior of your modem, you must use the Modems icon from the Control Panel. This will display the Modem Properties window shown in Figure 26.13.

Highlight the modem you want to configure and click on the Properties button. This will display the Properties window for your modem. Figure 26.14 shows the Properties window for the Hayes Optima 288 V.FC modem. The sliding scale enables you to alter the volume of the modem speaker when it is establishing or receiving a call. More importantly, the scroll list below the slider enables you to specify a maximum baud rate or lock the baud rate at a particular value.

FIGURE 26.13.

To alter the behavior of your modem (such as the baud rate or compression algorithms), use the Modems Properties window displayed by clicking on Modems in the Control Panel.

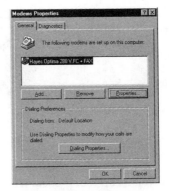

FIGURE 26.14.

The modem Properties window lets you alter baud rates, port values, and the speaker volume. You can specify a modem maximum speed or a single speed to use at all times.

It is a good idea to set your baud rate to the maximum allowed by your modem but not tick the connect speed lock box. Most modems try to connect at the maximum speed they are allowed, and then step down in increments until they find a speed that the modem at the other end and the telephone connection will allow. This ensures that you get the maximum speed possible each time. In some cases, such as with older modems or telephone lines, you might have to force the speed of the connection down using this scroll list.

Setting Up The Connection

Finally, you can specify details about your connection to the remote server. You can have many connections saved, but we will look at simply setting up one. The Make New Connection window, shown in Figure 26.15, is displayed after you have set up your modem. You can give the connection a name and select a modem connected to your machine. (If you only have one modem, you don't have to do anything about this field.)

You then see the screen shown in Figure 26.16, which asks for the telephone number and country dialing information (if applicable) for the connection you are creating.

FIGURE 26.15.

You can assign a name to each dial-up connection you use. It is useful to assign a name that tells you the system to which you are connecting.

FIGURE 26.16.

You specify the telephone number of your remote server as your first connection. Remember to set up area code or PBX prefixes if necessary.

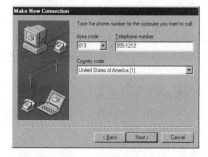

NOTE

If the telephone number you want to call is a toll-free 800 number, set the area code to 800 and the number to call as 1-800- followed by the usual seven digits.

After entering the telephone number, you see a screen that summarizes the addition of the new connection, after which the wizard terminates and you see your new connection in the Dial-Up Networking window (as shown in Figure 26.17). You can keep adding as many remote access connections as you want.

FIGURE 26.17.

Your new connection now shows up in the Dial-Up Networking window.

If you need to embed special codes or pauses in a telephone number, use commas to force a delay. A comma causes a half-second delay in the dialing process. This is often necessary when calling out from older PBX (Private Branch Exchange) switchboard systems.

You might need to alter the flow control used by some older modem systems. To do this, use the Connection page of your Modem Properties window and select the Advanced button. You can toggle between different flow controls in this window.

Connecting to a Remote Server

After you have set up a remote connection, all you have to do to connect is double-click on the connection name. You might see a window asking for your login name and password, depending on the type of connection. A series of dialogs keeps you informed of the status of the connection attempt.

When you are connected to the remote machine, the server's shared resources appear on your desktop. You can then use them as if they were directly connected to your current machine. Note, however, that operations such as browsing and opening large files can be much slower over a modem than on the actual server.

If you use a PCMCIA network interface card, Windows 95 detects whether the network is present and prompts you to use remote access to connect. For example, if you normally use a laptop at work with a PCMCIA network interface card adapter attached to a LAN, and then head home and try to start up a connection, Windows 95 will inform you that the network resources can't be accessed. Windows 95 will also ask whether you would like to use remote access to connect to the network. Of course, your laptop and the LAN server (or any machine on the LAN that has given you permission) must be set up for remote access.

Summary

Remote access is a really neat feature of Windows 95, because it lets you access your primary machine from another location and even from around the world. Setting up and using remote access is simple and fast. And, if you ever find yourself traveling, it is worth the effort.

Now we can look at some of the more advanced features of Windows 95, and how you can best administer your Windows 95 network.

Administration

27

by Tim Parker

Now that you have your Windows 95 networking component installed and working, it's time to take a look at some of the issues regarding maintenance and administration. The Windows 95 networking components require little operator intervention with Microsoft Windows-based networks (such as Windows NT, Windows 95 peer-to-peer, and Windows for Workgroups) because they are tightly integrated, but there are a few issues you should be aware of. With other network operating systems, the Microsoft tools are not quite as strong. Luckily, in those cases, the network operating system includes diagnostic and administration tools.

At the time of writing, all the utilities mentioned in this chapter were part of the Windows 95 distribution package. The final release version may be slightly different, and some of the tools may not be included with Windows 95 but will be available as add-ons. However, because these tools are all integral components of an administrator's arsenal, they are covered here.

Installation

For the most part, installing network interface cards, drivers, protocols, and services is a matter of letting Windows 95 copy the files it needs from the distribution media (either disks or CD-ROM). Windows 95 prompts you for the correct volumes when it needs them, assuming the drivers and software are part of the Windows 95 software set.

Even if you installed the entire software set when you first started Windows 95, you might still need the original disks or CD-ROM. By default, Windows 95 doesn't bother to load all the software during installation unless you select the options for networking during the load process. Even then, you will probably need to use the distribution media again. Multiple protocols, adapters, and services can be loaded at the same time.

Windows 95 no longer uses the same configuration .INI and .INF files it employed in previous versions of Windows. Instead, most configuration information is stored in the registry, which is dealt with elsewhere in this book. The hassles of editing PROTOCOL.INI and NET.CFG files, for example, are now history because the registry is much easier to work with. The registry replaces both PROTOCOL.INI and NET.CFG files. This change was necessary to allow better multiple protocol support, as well as to make user configuration easier.

You can also install Windows 95 from a remote machine or a server using the NetSetup utility. This is covered in more detail later in this chapter in the section titled, "Automating Installation from a Server."

PCMCIA cards

PCMCIA network cards can be removed from a Windows 95 machine without affecting the session. When you remove the PCMCIA card, Windows 95's Plug and Play drivers notice the change and automatically unload the driver. The opposite happens when you plug in a PCMCIA network card with a network connection.

The Plug and Play feature works for most PCMCIA network cards, although a few older cards might have some support problems. If you find the network does not adjust automatically to the presence or absence of the network adapter, check the Network window in the Control Panel to ensure that the drivers for the adapter are known. If you still experience trouble, contact the PCMCIA card manufacturer for a Windows 95 driver.

Third-Party Drivers

When you install standard networking software with Windows 95, Windows tries to use its own drivers for the network interface card, protocol, and service. The supplied Windows 95 drivers will work with the majority of installations, including Windows NetBEUI-based peer-to-peer, Novell NetWare, and many TCP/IP systems.

If you are using third-party drivers for a network interface card, a protocol, or a new service, you must use the disks supplied with the product. You might encounter some problems with Windows 95 recognizing older drivers, but most third-party software vendors are issuing updated disks with Windows 95 specific 32-bit protected mode drivers on them. You can still use older 16-bit drivers with Windows 95 instead of an updated version, but Windows 95 won't make optimal use of its memory.

Some network operating systems do not have a 32-bit protected mode driver as part of the Windows 95 installation. The two most commonly used network operating systems that fall in this category are Artisoft's LANtastic and Performance Technologies' PowerLAN. Microsoft does not have 32-bit protected mode drivers for these network operating systems, so you will have to rely on the 16-bit drivers used for Windows and Windows for Workgroups. Most of the vendors of network operating systems are working on new Windows 95 compatible drivers, so you should request them from the operating system vendor.

Other than a slightly less optimum use of Windows 95 memory and some issues regarding crash resistance, there is usually no problem using 16-bit drivers with Windows 95. If you have an existing network using 16-bit drivers, Windows 95 is not limiting you in any way. It wouldn't make sense to change the network operating system to one that has 32-bit protected mode drivers just for that issue.

A New Windows 95 Installation and Networking

When you install the Windows 95 networking components on a brand new system—installing Windows 95 from scratch, in other words—there is no backwards compatibility issue with previous versions of Windows. Windows 95 can obtain all the drivers and software to support the cards and services from its distribution disks. The configuration of the software was dealt with earlier in this section.

If you decide to use a third-party product that does not have software drivers built into the Windows 95 distribution software, you will need a driver disk from the product's vendor. To install the software, use the Have Disk option available through the Add button of the Network window, such as the Have Disk button in the Select Network Client window shown in Figure 27.1.

FIGURE 27.1.

To add third-party network software drivers to Windows 95, use the Have Disk button from the Network Add option.

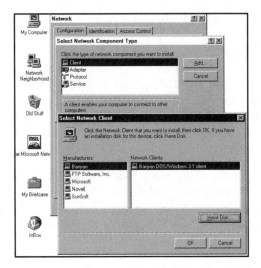

Clicking the Have Disk button starts an installation process that reads the disk your network product's manufacturer supplied. Windows 95 should read any driver for Windows, Windows for Workgroups, Windows NT, and Windows 95. You are prompted during the installation for necessary parameters, but otherwise the installation process is exactly the same as installing a Microsoft-supplied driver.

Dual-Boot Installations and Networking

If you decide to install Windows 95 in a dual-boot configuration so that you can still run older versions of Windows (and DOS), Windows 95 scans your existing Windows configuration files to look for network settings. These settings are carried over to the new Windows 95 configuration files.

In most cases, the configuration can be handled without problems. But if Windows 95 encounters difficulties reading your older Windows network or protocol information, a dialog will appear requesting the settings. You might have to supply new passwords and machine names when Windows 95 installs on a dual-boot system. You can set them to the same values as the other Windows installation on your machine.

When installed in a dual-boot configuration, Windows 95 tries to use 32-bit protected mode drivers even though your older Windows installation uses 16-bit drivers. If 32-bit drivers are not available or must be supplied from a vendor's disk, 16-bit drivers will be employed.

Upgrading Existing Windows and Networking

If you are upgrading from a previous version, Windows 95 attempts to retain all the configuration information that existed with your older Windows installation. After the installation of Windows 95, it is important to verify the settings of all the network components through the Properties windows to make sure that nothing was changed.

> **NOTE**
>
> Before upgrading your existing Windows networked system to Windows 95, note all the hardware and software settings. This will help you verify that the settings have remained unchanged after Windows 95 has been installed.

When Windows 95 installs over an existing Windows or Windows for Workgroups installation, Windows 95 checks the WIN.INI and SYSTEM.INI files for network configuration information. If the Windows 95 system has a 32-bit protected mode driver for the configuration item, it is used in place of the older one, and all references to the older driver are replaced.

Other network operating systems that do not have a 32-bit protected mode driver as part of the Windows 95 installation (such as Artisoft's LANtastic and Performance Technologies' PowerLAN) cannot be replaced by Windows 95 versions. In these cases, the 16-bit mode drivers currently in the WIN.INI or SYSTEM.INI files are retained and no changes are made to the drivers.

Passwords used on the older network operating system are retained by Windows 95 during an upgrade, as are machine names, domain names, and IP addresses. Drive mapping from the earlier versions is also retained from Windows for Workgroups. You should verify that all the configuration information is correct prior to connecting to the network, however, because a slight change in a name or IP address can cause problems with the network connection.

If Windows 95 encounters the line NET START in the AUTOEXEC.BAT file (which is used to start the network services in Windows for Workgroups and some other peer-to-peer LANs), it might change the line to explicitly point to the batch file that accomplishes the same purpose. The change lets Windows 95 run a 32-bit version of the NET.EXE binary instead of the 16-bit version supplied with older versions of Windows.

When upgrading some network operating systems, you might see additional dialog windows asking for locations of binaries or configuration files. These appear because Windows 95 can't find the files in question. They might be mounted on a network drive, for example, and not detected by Windows 95 during its boot. Supplying an explicit path to the files usually solves the problem.

To upgrade any older 16-bit network operating system drivers, a Windows 95-compatible driver should be requested from the operating system vendor. You can also download upgrades from most vendors through a bulletin board system or an online service such as CompuServe and America Online.

Upgrading Drivers

If you obtain new drivers from a network operating system, interface card, or software product vendor, you can replace your existing drivers with the new ones. The easiest methods to replace the drivers are to use the vendor's installation routine, or load the new drivers through the Add button of the Network window and then see whether the new version recognizes the older one and replaces it without any problems.

Some new drivers cannot recognize the older ones and can cause conflicts. In this case, you should remove the older drivers first, and then install the new ones. Make sure you note any existing settings so that you can duplicate them with the new drivers.

Removing Drivers

To remove drivers because you don't need them anymore, you have newer drivers, or you are changing network settings, use the Network window from the Control Panel. To remove a driver, highlight its name in the Network window list and click on the Remove button. This window is shown in Figure 27.2.

FIGURE 27.2.

To remove a driver, highlight the driver name by clicking in the list, and then click the Remove button.

Windows 95 displays no confirmation window. Instead, the driver is removed from the list. This can make it easy to accidentally delete drivers, so take extra care when working in this window. If you are not sure about the deletions or want to recover a driver you have deleted, exit the Network window without saving changes by clicking on the Cancel button. No changes are made to the network configuration when you use Cancel.

> **NOTE**
>
> As a safety precaution, make copies of the .INI files in a subdirectory before you start making changes to the network configuration. This will allow you to recover the old configuration in case of serious problems.

To make any changes permanent, click on the OK button. Depending on the drivers removed (or added), Windows 95 might take a few seconds to reconfigure the system. Windows 95 might prompt you to reboot your system to make any driver changes effective.

Windows 95 Network Protocols

Windows 95 is supplied with built-in support for Microsoft Networking and Novell NetWare, as well as support for several other real-mode networks such as 3Com's 3+Open, Artisoft's LANtastic, Banyan VINES, IBM LAN Server and PC LAN, SunSelect's PC-NFS, and TCS 10net. Other networks can be supported with third-party drivers. With Windows 95, you can run multiple protocols over a single network card, instead of the older approach of having a dedicated network card for each protocol.

The Windows for Workgroups NetBEUI protocol stack is available with Windows 95 as a 32-bit protected mode driver. It offers complete compatibility with Windows for Workgroups, Windows NT, LAN Manager, and other NetBIOS-based LANs. The NetBEUI driver has a NetBIOS programming interface built in.

Plug and Play Protocols

The primary protocols supported by Windows 95 are NetBEUI, NetWare's IPX/SPX, and TCP/IP. All three are implemented as Plug and Play protocols, meaning that they can be loaded and unloaded dynamically.

The IPX/SPX protocol used by Novell NetWare is the default protocol for Windows 95. The IPX/SPX protocol can be used to communicate with any NetWare server, as well as Microsoft Windows NT Server 3.5, which can use IPX/SPX. IPX/SPX is routable, so it can be run across bridges between networks. The driver for IPX/SPX that is included with Windows 95 has the capability to support packet burst transmissions, which improve network performance. Microsoft has also added Windows Sockets API support to the IPX/SPX driver, which allows any WinSock 32-bit application to run on top of IPX/SPX. The driver also has the more traditional Windows NetBIOS programming interface support as well.

The TCP/IP driver included with Windows 95 is a full 32-bit VxD, operating in protected mode. The protocol includes all the utilities needed by TCP/IP, such as ping, FTP, Telnet, and route; it also has troubleshooting utilities such as netstat, ipconfig, and traceroute. As with the IPX/SPX driver, Microsoft has added WinSock support to its TCP/IP driver as well as to the NetBIOS programming interface. The driver supports both 32-bit and 16-bit WinSock applications.

To enhance TCP/IP operation, Microsoft has added a BOOTP (boot protocol) backward-compatible protocol, which allows automatic allocation of IP addresses. Using the Dynamic Host Configuration Protocol (DHCP), a Windows 95 system can connect to a Windows NT DHCP server and obtain its IP address without involving the user. This makes configuration and setup much easier, although the DHCP server must be properly set up. Windows 95 cannot act as a DHCP server for other Windows 95 machines.

The TCP/IP system also includes support for the Windows NT Internet Naming Service (WINS) and the Distributed Computing Environment's Domain Name Service (DCE DNS), both of which provide mapping between an IP address and a common symbolic name. Windows 95 allows a single DCE DNS server or two Windows NT WINS servers to be accessed for name resolution.

UNIX Dial-Up Networking

You can install UNIX dial-up networking from the Networks window Add button. Dial-up networking lets you dial into a UNIX machine with a modem and connect as though you are a terminal. The installation procedure is the same as with any other protocol in the Network window. The dial-up networking protocol uses SLIP (Serial Line Interface Protocol), which is a reduced version of PPP (Point to Point Protocol) used for higher-speed communications. SLIP is usually used with asynchronous modems.

After dial-up networking has been added to the Windows 95 protocol list, you have to customize the installation to tell the dial-up driver which machine to connect to. Highlight the Dial-up Adapter entry in the Networks window list of installed components, and select the properties button. The Properties window you see is exactly the same as the one used to configure TCP/IP. This is explained in detail in Chapter 26, "Remote Access."

If you want to dial in to a remote UNIX machine, you must have the system administrator create an account for you. Otherwise, your logins will be rejected. An alternative is to use a guest account that has limited functionality, if the machine's administrator allows such accounts. Remember that guest accounts share their files with all users who log in as guest, so be careful what you leave on the UNIX system!

Windows 95's SNMP Agent

The Simple Network Management Protocol (or SNMP) is in wide use on UNIX networks, and Windows 95 includes an SNMP agent. SNMP is used to provide status information to a central server program about devices on a network, so that when a printer or network gateway crashes for some reason, the system administrator can know about it immediately. SNMP also allows some configuration actions to occur over the network. SNMP usually runs on TCP/IP.

SNMP uses a set of client software programs called agents on each device. Windows 95's SNMP agent relies on the WinSock API, and for this reason can only be run when TCP/IP or IPX/SPX is used as a network protocol. You can start the Windows 95 SNMP agent from a startup script or a command line by entering the command snmp.

Although most Windows 95 systems won't use SNMP much, it will eventually become an integral part in a Microsoft product called the Systems Management Server (SMS), which will let system administrators perform even more functions than SNMP currently does.

System Policies

Windows 95 lets you administer the way users work on a network through a System Policy Editor. The System Policy Editor is located in the Applications folder, in a folder called Administrative Tools. This folder is usually available only to the network administrator. The System Policy Editor window is shown in Figure 27.3.

FIGURE 27.3.

The System Policy Editor window lets you set up a default configuration for all users on the system who share that policy. From this window, you can set up any number of policy files.

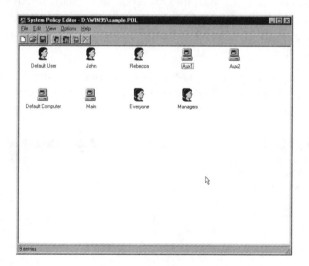

The System Policy Editor is responsible for creating configuration templates for Windows 95 users and entire workgroups. It lets the network administrator specify the type of desktop users will see, restrict applications, and control access. There can be many different policy files, with each one applicable to different users depending on their needs. You could, for example, have an administrator's policy file for all users who need access to the System Policy Editor. All other users could be restricted from starting the Editor.

The key aspect of the System Policy Editor is the creation of User Policy Files, which create system-wide policies. Through the User Policy File, you can specify such items as which wallpaper will be used on each user's desktop and which printers can be accessed, and you can limit file sharing and place other restrictions on a user's access.

> **NOTE**
>
> Imposing policies on what users of a network can do should be used only when there is a very strong case for not allowing users the freedom to share files, share printers, and create their own desktops. Restrictions on users tend to cause dissatisfaction.

System policies might not be needed on most local area networks or for many users. It is much easier to allow users on a small LAN to do whatever they want with their system. However, in some cases, it might be necessary to impose restrictions of some sort to prevent unauthorized access or misuse of network resources.

Setting Up a New System Policy File

You use the System Policy Editor to set up system policy files that can apply to a number of users. The default template for system policies is maintained in a file called ADMINCFG.ADM. Access to the file, and permission to make changes through the Policy Editor, is usually restricted to the system administrator. You can use the ADMINCFG.ADM file to create other policy files.

To create a new policy, choose the New File option under the File pull-down menu. Two icons appear in the window, as shown in Figure 27.4. These icons are labeled Default User and Default Computer.

FIGURE 27.4.

The first step in creating a new policy file is to select New File under the File menu. This adds two icons to the Policy window.

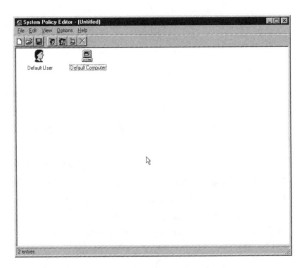

The Default User icon will apply to everyone on the system unless they are specifically excluded. Similarly, the Default Computer icon applies to all machines that do not have a specific policy created for them. Most small networks will have only the two Default icons in their policy file, which means that any policies apply to all users or machines. However, you might want to make specific policies for some users, a group of users, or a specific machine. To do that, you must add the user, group, or machine to the policy file.

To add users to the list that the new policy file applies to, use the Edit pull-down menu's Add User option. This displays the Add User window shown in Figure 27.5. In the entry field, enter the user's name. The name should be the same as the user's login so that the policy entry and the login match. Otherwise, the policy file will not apply to that user.

FIGURE 27.5.

The Add User dialog lets you enter the names of the users the policy file applies to. The user name should correspond to the user's login.

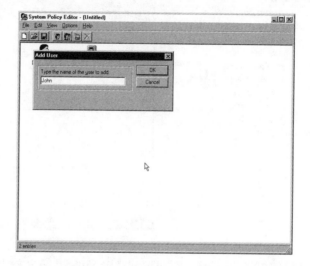

Figure 27.6 shows the new policy file after several users have been added. An icon appears in the main Editor window for each user added.

FIGURE 27.6.

Each user that is added to the Policy appears as an icon in the main window. You can have as many (or as few) users for each policy as you like.

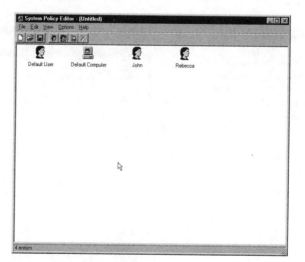

To make setting policies for large numbers of users a little easier, you can set policies based on a group name. Any user who belongs to that group will be affected by the policy file. To add a group, use the Add Group entry under the Edit pull-down menu. A dialog similar to the Add User dialog will appear. Entering the name of the group adds an icon to the Policy Editor window. Figure 27.7 shows two groups added. The icon for a group is very similar to that for a single user, except that a second head profile appears behind the first.

FIGURE 27.7.

If all the users you want to affect with a policy belong to a group, you can add the group using the Add Group option. All members of the group will use the same policy file. The group icon looks very much like the user icon, except for the second head profile.

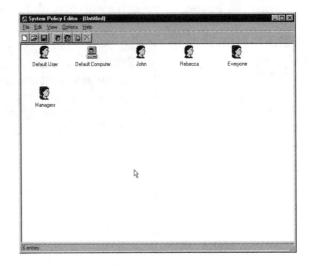

You can also specify particular machines that the policy file will apply to, regardless of which user is logged into that machine. To add a machine, choose the Add Computer option under the Edit menu. This displays an Add Computer dialog similar to the Add User and Add Group dialogs. Figure 27.8 shows the Policy Editor with three computers added.

FIGURE 27.8.

If you add a specific computer to the policy file, all users who log in to that computer will be affected by the policy file. This is a good method of ensuring that access privileges are restricted on general-access computers.

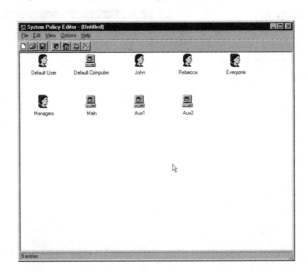

If you want to remove a user, group, or computer, you can highlight the item to be removed with a single mouse click and select Remove from the Edit menu. There are icons for all three Add functions and the Remove function too.

You should save your policy file to make sure you don't lose any entries. Your changes to the policies can then be aborted by canceling your changes and restoring the previous saved file.

You can make policies that apply to all users or to a single user, a single group, or a single computer. The approach is similar for each process. Let's begin by looking at setting a policy for an individual entity.

Setting Policies for a User, Group, or Computer

If you have created individual users, groups, or computers in your Policy file, you can set individual policies for them. To set the policies, select the icon that represents the user, group, or computer you want to work with. Highlight the icon by single-clicking on it, and then choose the Properties option under the Edit menu. Alternatively, double-click on the icon. The window that appears next depends on the type of icon you selected. Let's start with a computer icon. The window that appears is shown in Figure 27.9.

FIGURE 27.9.

The Properties sheet for a computer in the Policy Editor lets you select specific policies to enforce. Book icons can be expanded by clicking on them. A check indicates that the item is selected.

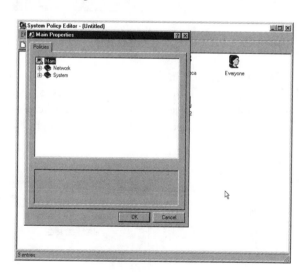

The Properties window uses a hierarchical structure to display all possible policy settings. If a checkmark appears next to an entry, it means the policy is in effect. A book icon means there are more entries underneath that entry. Clicking on the book expands the entry to show the next level of detail. There can be many levels of entries, each of which must be expanded by clicking on the book icon.

To illustrate the process, click on the Network Options icon. Next, click on the box next to Access Control. In the example window shown in Figure 27.10, there are two items underneath this option. (Depending on the type of system and network you have installed, you might see a different number of items under some of the entries used in these screen captures.) The two items are both not selected, as shown by the grayed out box next to them. When not selected, they are ignored by Windows 95. Ignored items are not processed when a user logs in, which saves time.

FIGURE 27.10.

Expanding the policy options by clicking on the box icons leads down the tree. In this case, the Network Access Control options are shown. Both options are grayed out, which means that they are ignored by Windows 95.

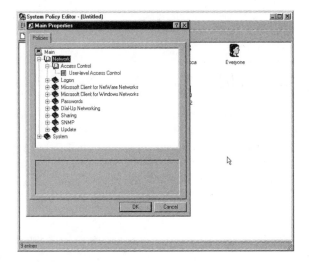

To set a Security type, click on the box next to the entry. It changes to a box with a check in it, and the lower part of the Properties window changes to show a prompt with a scroll list. This is shown in Figure 27.11. Select the type of Security Access you want to apply from the scroll list. Some items will not have scroll lists, but they might have different check boxes or entry fields.

FIGURE 27.11.

This window lets you select the Security type that applies to the policy user. Select the desired entry from the scroll list.

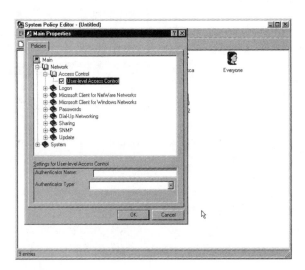

You can continue this process to select all the policies that you want to enforce for the user, group, or computer selected. Note that each icon must be treated separately, so care should be taken in setting up groups to minimize the amount of time you spend with the Policy Editor.

Setting Up a Default User Policy File

The User Policy File is set by default to no policy, meaning no restrictions on users. If you want to enforce user policies, you must manually change the settings. If you want to apply a default value for user or computer, you use the Default User or Default Computer icon. Note that if you have created specific users, groups, or machines, these are not affected by the Default values you set in the Policy Editor. This lets you set up specific privileges for some people or machines, while the rest are affected by the Default settings.

To change default policies, double-click on the Default User or Default Computer icon (or highlight it with a single-click and use the Properties option under the Edit pull-down menu). This displays the Properties for Default Computer sheet, shown in Figure 27.12.

FIGURE 27.12.

The Properties for Default Computer sheet lets you specify policies that affect all computers on the local area network that do not have specific policies created.

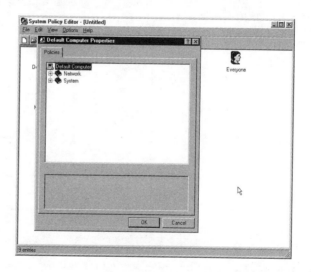

When this sheet is changed from no policy, the policy will apply to all computers on the network. The same applies to the Properties for Default Users sheet as well. From the Properties for Default Users sheet, you can set the wallpaper type, as well as disable file sharing and print sharing. Passwords, remote access, access to the Microsoft Network, and Client software can also be controlled.

The Properties for Default Users sheet shows all the attributes that can be controlled by the network administrator. A check box next to an item indicates its current status. If the box is filled with a checkered pattern, it indicates that no policy is set for that item. You could, for example, establish policies for sharing printers, but leave the users free to choose their own wallpaper, by leaving the Wallpaper item set to a checkered box.

When you have edited the Properties for Default Users sheet to suit your network's requirements, you must establish the policy to make it effective. This is done through the Control Panel's Password icon. From the Password window, you can enter the Update page, which allows you to specify that the policy file is updated every time a Windows 95 machine starts its networking services. The path (which is in UNC format) to the shared user policy file must be specified.

Desktops

You can specify that all users have the same desktop through the Properties for Security window's Profile page. This is shown in Figure 27.13. There are two options available, one to force all users to share the same desktop settings and the other to allow users to customize their desktop.

FIGURE 27.13.

The Properties for Security Profile page lets you specify restrictions on user desktops.

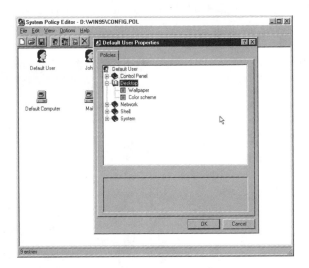

Restrictions on a user's desktop might cause a considerable degree of dissatisfaction. Unless there is a valid reason for imposing restrictions, it is best to let users customize their machines and desktops however they want.

Establishing Remote Administration

Normally, a single PC is designated as the network administrator's console for changing network configurations. If you want to be able to change network and user parameters from anywhere on the network, however, you can assign remote administration privileges. This is accomplished through the Properties for Security window Remote Administration page, as shown in Figure 27.14.

FIGURE 27.14.

The Properties for Security Remote Administration page lets you make changes to network administration configurations from other machines on the LAN.

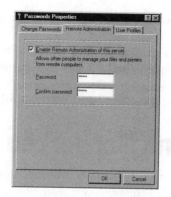

To establish remote administration, check the box next to the enable line and supply a password. This lets you jump into network administration mode from another Windows 95 machine by supplying the network administrator's password.

The Policy Editor and Network Connections

You can use the Policy Editor to tell a Windows 95 machine to download automatically from Windows NT or Novell NetWare servers. To set up automatic downloading, use the Open Registry option under the Policy Editor's File menu. When the policy editor main screen appears, double-click on the Local Computer icon.

When the Properties sheet appears, click on the plus sign next to the Network entry. Click the plus sign next to Microsoft Client for Windows Networks (for Windows NT servers) or Microsoft Client for NetWare (for Novell NetWare servers). This displays one or more choices. To enable the automatic login process, click the box next to Log On To Windows NT (for Windows NT servers) or Log On To NetWare (for Novell NetWare servers).

An entry field appears in the lower part of the Properties screen asking for the domain name of the server (Windows NT) or preferred server (Novell NetWare). Enter the domain name or server name as appropriate.

To complete the process, on the Windows NT server, create a folder called Netlogin and make it shared. Save your automatic login policy file in this folder, making sure it has a .POL extension. For a NetWare server, save the policy file with a .POL extension in a shared directory under the server's preferred directory (such as \\preferred\sys\public).

The Registry

The Windows 95 Registry is the central repository of configuration information. Some of the configuration is related to the network and network permissions. The Registry was examined in an earlier chapter.

For networked machines, the Registry allows a network administrator to manage an entire network's user privileges through a single file that is read by every machine. This file, called POLICY.POL, allows all networked Windows 95 policies to be the same. Alternatively, separate policy files can be created for each user, as mentioned earlier in this section. The Registry Editor can be used to edit the Registry information. If a primary network Registry file is used, it can be imported through the Connect Network Registry option of the Registry Editor.

Managing Networked Windows 95 PCs

When you have a network installed and functioning, there is the inevitable problem of managing it effectively. Although network management isn't very important for a network of two or three Windows 95 machines that simply share an occasional file, it becomes much more important when you have dozens of machines sharing the same network.

What can go wrong with a network? Network traffic can bog the whole system down to a crawl. An incorrect configuration or protocol on one machine attached to the network can cause the entire network to halt effective processing of packets of data. Nonstandard software can corrupt network packets so that the network can't handle the information properly. Simple utilities that are fine on a stand-alone machine can tie up network drives, effectively taking servers and other clients off the network. The list goes on.

Network management tries to solve these problems through a series of steps to optimize the network usage, standardize software, and monitor network conditions. Windows 95 has several utilities included with the network software that helps you manage and maintain an effective network.

Using NetWatcher

The System Administration folder contains a few utilities that help you watch networks and begin to diagnose problems. One of the basic tools is NetWatcher. NetWatcher lets you do a few things:

■ It shows the status of sharing on clients and servers.

■ It lets you create shared resources.

■ It lets you disable access to a shared resource.

By default, when it is launched, NetWatcher displays the status of shared resources on your local machine. Three icons at the end of the toolbar adjust the display to show users, shared folders, and shared files. The NetWatcher display changes depending on which icon is active.

When the Show Users icon (the one with two heads on it) is active, the display shows all the users that are attached to your machine's resources. This is shown in Figure 27.15, which indicates that only one remote machine is currently attached to the local Windows 95 machine.

The remote machine has three drives or folders open, as shown by the list on the right side of the NetWatcher window. The second icon from the left of the toolbar, showing a head with an X behind it, enables you to disconnect whichever user is currently highlighted in the window.

FIGURE 27.15.

NetWatcher shows you the status of sharing on your local machine when first launched. This display shows the users that are currently connected to your machine.

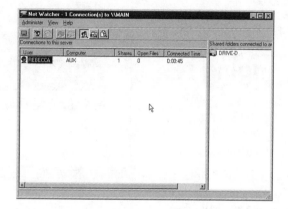

The shared folders icon lists all folders that are currently shared by your local machine. This window is shown in Figure 27.16, which shows that four different folders are currently being shared.

FIGURE 27.16.

In this window, NetWatcher shows you the status of two different folders that are currently being shared.

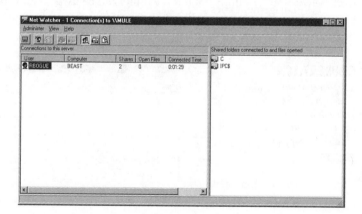

The two icons in the middle of the toolbar that show shared folders (a hand under the folder) enable you to activate and disable sharing by clicking on the icon. Whichever folder is highlighted in the window will be affected. This lets you switch off sharing from within NetWatcher if necessary.

You can select the server to administer if remote administration is on. The Administer pull-down menu has the Select Server option, which enables you to enter the name of the remote machine you want NetWatcher to reflect. This window is shown in Figure 27.17. The Browse button displays the network layout (similar to the Network Neighborhood windows), enabling you to select the remote machine with a mouse click.

FIGURE 27.17.

If Remote Administration is active on your network, you can have NetWatcher reflect another machine's status by entering its name in this dialog.

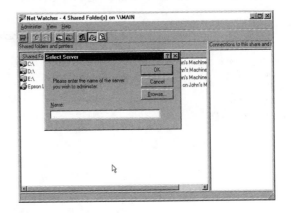

System Monitor

Windows 95 includes a utility called the System Monitor, which lets you observe a wide range of different system behavior. Much of the System Monitor's functions do not reflect the network behavior of Windows 95, but the utility can be used to show potential and actual problems with your local machine. Figure 27.18 shows the System Monitor as it appears when it first starts up, showing CPU usage.

FIGURE 27.18.

The System Monitor can show several different usage graphs. It can be used to show where bottlenecks occur on heavily shared machines.

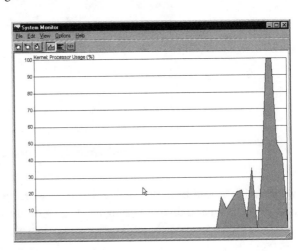

To display parameters of more interest to Windows 95 networking, use the Edit pull-down menu and select Add Item. This displays a dialog that has a list of general parameters in the left side of the window, and more detailed selections for some of the items in the right side. This window is shown in Figure 27.19.

FIGURE 27.19.

You can display selected items in the System Monitor window by choosing them in the Add Item window.

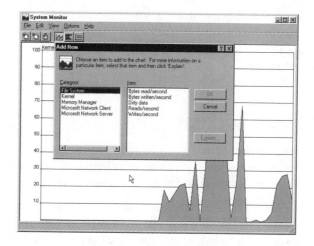

Of interest to the network user are the items that reflect the protocol and driver (such as the IPX/SPX compatible protocol listed in the window in Figure 27.10), as well as the behavior of the client and server machines, which let you select disk read and writes. You can add as many items to the System Monitor display as you want, because the System Monitor will adjust the display to show the proper number of graphs. You can also change the graph style to bars and numbers.

Figure 27.20 shows the System Monitor set to show a number of server functions. This would show the amount of traffic coming in to the local machine from remote Windows 95 users and the number of disk operations, packets, and errors that occur because of the local machine's server role. If your local system is slow and the sharing is very high, you should consider reducing the number of remote users on your machine.

FIGURE 27.20.

Monitoring the client or server behavior of your local machine through the System Monitor lets you find out how efficiently your machine can handle other users.

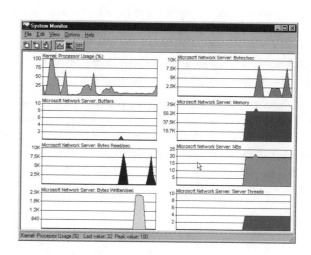

The System Monitor can also watch your memory usage, disk access, and various other parameters that let you know how busy your Windows 95 system is. The System Monitor's network displays are useful for quick checks of the load that your system is under because of the network. However, remember that the System Monitor itself imposes a load and should not be left on all the time unless the updating frequency is a reasonably lengthy amount of time.

Network Backups

One of the useful features of a local area network is the capability to back up one machine to a network resource such as a high-capacity tape drive. Network backups are an efficient method of performing regular backups to high-capacity drives.

To use network backups, you must install the backup software. One product is included with the Windows 95 software, available under the Add Services option of the Network Configuration window. The window in Figure 27.21 shows Arcada's Backup Exec Agent. This can be installed in the same manner as any other Service.

FIGURE 27.21.

Use the Add Services option in the Network Configuration window to add a network backup program.

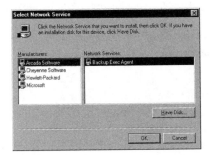

After the network backup software is installed, it will appear on the Network configuration window, as shown in Figure 27.22. The actual name of the product might be different, depending on the software you installed. (Some network backup products do not appear as a network service but as an application folder. Check the documentation supplied with your network backup software for more information.)

To set the network backup software's parameters, use the Properties button after you have highlighted the backup name in the Network list. This will show the Properties dialog with two pages: General and Protocol. The General page, shown in Figure 27.23, lets you enable and disable the network backup routine. If the backup is enabled, you must indicate on which machine the backup device (such as a tape drive, CD-R drive, or optical drive) is located. A password can be supplied to access the device.

FIGURE 27.22.

Network backup software should appear on the Network list when it has been successfully installed. The name that appears on the list depends on the product. This shows the Windows 95 supplied Arcada Backup Exec Agent.

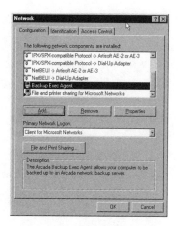

FIGURE 27.23.

The General page of the Network Backup Exec Agent's Properties window lets you enable and disable network backups, as well as supply machine name and passwords for the network backup device.

The Protocol page of the Backup Service lets you select the protocol used to communicate with the backup devices. Usually it will be the same protocol used by your network, but some devices use different protocols for speed or compatibility reasons. This page, shown in Figure 27.24, supports both IPX/SPX and TCP/IP. If the latter is used, the address of the device must be supplied.

To use the network backup software, you must launch a backup application (usually not the Backup software supplied with Windows 95). The process will differ considerably, depending on the network backup software, so you should check your documentation.

698

FIGURE 27.24.

*The Protocol page lets you
indicate which protocol is
used to communicate with
the backup device.*

Security

Windows 95 has several levels of password-based security and password control. It starts with a network login to the Windows 95 program itself, which requires a valid user name and a password. The exact login box displayed by Windows 95 depends on the type of network used. Avoiding a correct login is possible, but the network resources are not available unless security is set for no password.

> **WARNING**
>
> Note that a login prompt does not secure the Windows 95 PC from intrusion. A boot floppy can still gain access to the hard drive, so do not trust the login as the sole security measure.

Setting User Passwords

The Password icon available in the Control Panel is where you can set user-level passwords. This window, shown in Figure 27.25, enables you to change your standard Windows 95 login password (Windows Password) or access other passwords that might be in place for local or network resources.

To change your login password, click the Change Windows Password button. The window shown in Figure 27.26 appears, in which you enter your old password (to verify that you are allowed to change the password) and the new password. The new password is asked for twice to ensure that typographical errors are avoided. If you don't know the old password, you can't change it, which prevents others from changing your password if they get on your machine.

FIGURE 27.25.

The Change Passwords page of the Password window lets you change your login password, as well as access other passwords you own.

FIGURE 27.26.

Changing your Windows password requires the old password. You must enter the new password twice to verify it.

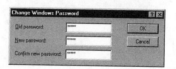

The Other Passwords section of the Password window lets you change passwords that are required for network login, printer access, and so on. Some users like to set the same password for all the password-accessed features, but this allows someone who knows your password to have complete access. Providing several different passwords makes it more unlikely that someone else can have complete access. Of course, it also makes it more difficult to remember all the passwords!

The other password page in the Passwords window that applies to networking is to enable remote administration. As seen earlier in this chapter, you can set a password that enables you to administer the network from any machine attached to the LAN.

Password List Editor

The Password List Editor (PWLEDIT) lets you remove passwords and accounts from a system's password list. This is usually useful only for servers, but any user can access the tool if it has been installed. The Password List Editor displays a window with a list of all accounts that have been created.

When it is started, the Password List Editor displays a list of all accounts and the resources they use. To remove an entry, highlight it with a mouse click and click on the Remove button. The account entry is removed immediately.

Automating Installation from a Server

Windows 95 lets you automate the installation process from a central server. This is only of use to larger networks, but it is a good feature for saving time. The procedure can be used for a first-time installation, as well as for upgrades.

The automatic installation is handled by a utility called NetSetup. When it is launched, NetSetup opens the main Server Based Setup window shown in Figure 27.27. This simple window lets you enter the installation location for all Windows 95 machines on the network.

FIGURE 27.27.

NetSetup lets you install Windows 95 from a main server to any other machine on the network. This single window controls the network setup routines. Most of the window is grayed out until a path to the Windows 95 installation machine is provided.

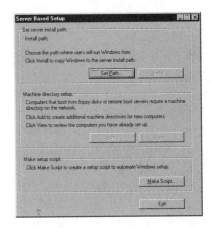

To enable network setup, click on the Set Path button on the Server Based Setup window. A dialog appears asking for the location of the Windows files. (See Figure 27.28.) You can enter a directory on the current machine or on any other machine on the network using UNC. When a path has been entered, the rest of the Server Based Setup window becomes active.

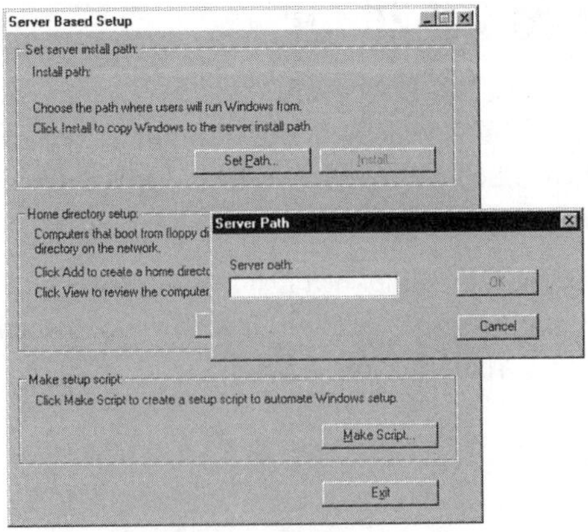

FIGURE 27.28.

From this dialog, enter the path to the Windows 95 primary installation. You can use UNC to simplify remote machine names. This path will be used to install Windows 95 every time.

If Windows 95 is not currently installed in the target directory, you should install a master copy. Click on the Install button at the top of the screen. NetSetup checks for a copy of Windows 95. If one exists, a dialog pops up asking whether you want to overwrite the existing copy. If Windows 95 is not installed in the directory, you will see the Source Path window shown in Figure 27.29.

FIGURE 27.29.

The Source Path window lets you install Windows 95 into the server directory. You can upgrade an existing version with the same dialog.

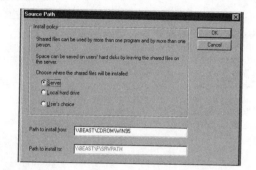

The Source Path window has the option of letting you determine where shared files are kept. By default, they reside on the server, although you can change this by clicking on any of the buttons in the bottom part of the window. When you have completed the window and clicked on OK, Windows 95 installs a master version in the directory specified. This version can be used to install any other machine on the network.

The middle section of the Server Based Setup window lets you create a home directory for remote machines that do not have hard disks. This is useful for terminals or machines that do not have a DOS-format drive.

The Make Script button at the bottom of the Server Based Setup window lets you create an automatic script to install Windows 95. This removes the need for you to answer questions during the installation process. If you want to create a script, click on the Make Script button and a dialog appears asking for a filename. This window is shown in Figure 27.30. The script filename should have a .inf extension.

FIGURE 27.30.

To create a script file for automatic installation, use the Make Script button on the NetSetup window. Supply a filename with a .inf extension.

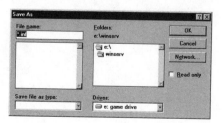

The Policy Editor's Default Properties window appears, which enables you to enter all the default values you want for the remote installations. The process is the same as that explained in the section "The Policy Editor and Network Connections," earlier in this chapter. Figure 27.31 shows a sample Default Properties window that is ready for the generation of the installation script. Clicking on the OK button at the bottom of the Default Properties window starts the script generation.

FIGURE 27.31.

To create a script file for automatic installation, you must provide all the values you would normally be prompted for during an installation. The Default Properties window of the Policy Editor lets you supply these values.

If you want to make changes to the script, you should use the NetSetup process again, instead of editing the .inf file with an editor.

Summary

We've looked at a few basics of network administration and the tools that are available to help you manage and use your local area network in the best manner. There are many commercially available tools that expand on the administration and management tasks, but these are seldom necessary for small- to medium-sized local area networks with a single network protocol. Large networks with many different types of machines will probably need extra utilities, because Windows 95's simple NetWatcher utility can't handle heterogeneous environments.

VII

PART

Overview of
Windows
Programming Issues

Who Programs?

There are two types of people who use small computers. The first, the larger group, views computers as tools to increase productivity, simplify lives, or as a necessary evil integral to their jobs. The second group sees computers as all these, but also as a venue for self-expression. These people are not only curious about what a computer can do, but what it might do. The people in the second category are computer programmers, or at least potential computer programmers.

What Is Programming?

Programming a computer means creating a set of instructions for a computer to follow. In a very elaborate sense it might mean creating a commercial program such as Microsoft Excel or Novell's WordPerfect. However, programs such as these aren't really done by individuals anymore, but rather by highly trained teams building on previously laid foundations.

It's true that once, not that long ago, individuals created major application packages the equal of commercial products. Products such as the shareware PC-Write successfully competed with the much higher-priced MultiMate, Word, WordPerfect and DisplayWrite of that time. Although PC-Write was mostly the creation of one man, Bob Wallace, the commercial packages were the results of large corporate teams.

However, today PC-Write and its contemporaries are no more. The complexity of Windows programming and consumer-demanded feature sets sealed their fate. Even though the maker of PC-Write, Quicksoft, took on more people, it resisted the move to Windows and then decided not to fight any more—and instead folded its tent. Much the same happened to other small shops.

Today it is barely possible for an individual to create a program of the complexity of, say WordPerfect, but there's no incentive to do so. Most people pay less than $100 for major programs, less if bought in suites, so the financial payback for such an effort on the part of an individual just isn't there. Then there's the problem of marketing. A brilliant programmer might create a competitive product, but how will he get it to market? If he does get shelf space at Egghead, why would people switch from their word processors to his? The days of the individual competing with majors on the majors' turf seem numbered.

This doesn't mean there's no purpose in becoming a citizen programmer. Here are some of the reasons to learn programming:

- You want to increase your influence in your company.
- You want to increase your marketability for a new employer.

- You want to create programs for yourself or your company in categories or niches that are ignored or poorly served by the majors.
- You want to make money marketing your programs to niche markets.
- You feel a need for self-expression.

Many people might be taken aback by self-expression. Programming is this in every sort of way that painting or sculpture is for those with that talent.

Is Programming a Fine Art?

Programming is an art just like painting or playing a musical instrument. Just as in any art form you need:

- To have skill
- To know the media
- To be able to manipulate the media in such a way to communicate your vision to laypeople

Also, and perhaps most importantly, great artists in any field create in such a way that appears effortless and, in retrospect, obvious to lesser practitioners or to the public.

In a real sense, programming is more a rigorous art form than most any other. If you are a photography fan, answer this: Who is the better photographer, Ansel Adams or Minor White? However you answer, others will disagree. The same dispute rages in most art fields. What's in today is out tomorrow. Dada is hot one minute, cold the next. The same goes for other art schools and artists.

There is much less dispute about programming art. For example, more than 20 years ago, early MIT computer enthusiasts (artists if you will), engaged in a fierce competition to create a method to convert binary numbers to decimal on an early military computer called the TX-0. Doing this was simple, but the goal was to do accomplish the task in as few machine language steps as possible; that was the art.

For quite a while, people strove to break the 50-step barrier but failed at it. Many felt that this was an unbreakable barrier just as a generation earlier when people thought the four-minute mile was unbreakable. However, just as Roger Bannister proved the doubters wrong, a quiet programmer named Jenson came up with an entirely new algorithm to solve this decimal problem. His successful program took 46 steps. All involved agreed that Jenson's solution was the highest artistic expression possible for that problem.

Today's computer programmers can look at Jenson's solution and still agree that his is the best expression of the decimal problem on a TX-0. Can today's painters agree on which painting is the highest expression of their art form? Hardly.

Practicality and Big Bucks

Many can practice programming, but few are Jensons. That doesn't mean even the most prosaic practitioners can't make real money at it. Programming pays well.

It pays well if you're a professional programmer or if programming is only part of your job. But be practical. Spending your evenings trying to beat Jenson's 46-step TX-0 algorithm might make you a great artist, but does it make a practical contribution to your employment situation? If your goal is increased pay or a better job, first learn what type of programming is in demand and then gain familiarity with that field.

Right now, there's a huge surplus of COBOL programmers. People are moving away from the older systems that relied on droves of COBOL drones filling out forms and typing verbose code lines. Training yourself to be adept in COBOL was the way to a good job 25 years ago. Today it's the way to the unemployment office.

The hot stuff today is C, C++, client/server, and most databases. This will not be true tomorrow, but it's impossible to predict what tomorrow will bring. The only truth about programming is that it will change. You can either change with it or be left behind.

When a business converts from its legacy systems to a modern one, the systems people either have made themselves ready for the change or find themselves on the street with a resume listing obsolete, even quaint, job skills. Being sharp or on the cutting edge today isn't all it takes. You've got to stay there. To do this, you must devote a significant amount of time to continuing education.

On Your Own

You can make money being an independent programmer. Many companies can't justify keeping specialized programmers on staff but have a need for those people from time to time. These *hired guns* are in business for themselves moving from company to company as the need arises.

Not On Your Own

There's also the possibility of working inside a specialty programming company such as Microsoft or Lotus. These companies hire only the top in the field, so don't expect to take six months worth of courses at your local VoTech and get a good paying job at, say, Microsoft. Still, there are smaller companies that have entry-level jobs. These companies can be better places to work for many or can lead to good jobs at the larger places.

Where to Start

You can start either by having a goal of being an independent programmer, or just start hacking around with computers on your own, without a specific, stated end. Get a feel for what programming is either on your own or by taking a course or two. It won't be long before you know if programming is for you. It'll either grab you or repulse you in short order.

What's Coming

The next several chapters form a very concise introduction to programming. They include customizing or macro programming for commercial packages such as Word and Excel. There isn't room here, nor is it the purpose of this book to give a comprehensive overview of programming, especially its advanced aspects such as C++.

You'll get the most from these chapters if you can follow along using either the illustrated programs or their close counterparts; but even glancing through them should give you an idea if programming is something you wish to pursue or avoid.

The Consumer's Guide To Custom Software

by Paul Cassel

28

The Need To Customize

There are a lot of commercial software applications available to perform a broad range of tasks that computer users do every day. There are even more narrow-purpose application programs, called vertical market software, which serve single industries. Most identifiable small business industries such as TV and stereo repair shops, vacation property rental companies, medical offices, and so on, usually have one or two programs that are specifically written to accommodate the special needs of that single industry or occupation. These programs can be purchased from small software companies that specialize in filling the needs of their industry.

The most varied software category of all, however, is known as custom software. Custom software is created to serve the individual needs of a single company or person.

Unless you are very lucky or your computer use is narrowly limited to broad generic tasks such as word processing, at some time your software needs are likely to reach beyond those applications that are commercially available.

As an example, imagine that you work for a company that sells gears. In the beginning, the company sold only three kinds of gears and had only 10 customers, and a simple spreadsheet was all that was needed to create invoices. Soon business was booming, the 10 original clients became 100, and one of the accounting people created a macro for the spreadsheet to enable untrained persons to create invoices. Later, the 100 clients turned into a 1,000 customers, so the company bought an accounting program that had an invoice module.

Business is so good that your gears are now advertised in trade publications worldwide, the customers number in the tens of thousands, and the gear business is getting more complicated because your customers aren't the expert few from the good old days. Nowadays the folks who take phone orders need to be able to tell customers which gear sets are compatible with other gears you sell. You're taking credit card orders, providing customer service, accepting purchase orders, tracking receivables, tracking inventory, and your invoice module in the accounting program is woefully inadequate. To top it all off, IBM has just offered to solve your problems for a little under $600,000.

One morning, your boss walks in the door and says, "You know more about computers than anyone else around here. You know what we need. Find out how much it's really going to cost, and get back to me with your recommendations ASAP."

What Are You Going To Do?

There are three basic levels of dealing with the problem of creating custom software. You can create macros to customize an application such as WordPerfect or Lotus 1-2-3. You can evaluate and purchase vertical market programs to see whether one exists that will solve your current problems. Or you can hire an individual or company to create the software you need for a fee. If you have the inclination and the desire to have total control of creating the application within the organization, you might even learn to write programs and do it yourself. This chapter provides you with the information you need in order to pursue each of these options. The chapters that follow show you some of the most commonly used tools for creating custom software so that you can get an idea about what application development tools might be right for your needs.

TIP

Developing custom software isn't cheap. Large software companies can afford to sell copies of their products inexpensively because they are selling to thousands or even millions of people.

Vertical market applications that serve specific industries and custom-developed applications often cost thousands of dollars. The reason is simple. Fewer customers have an interest in these programs, so each customer must pay a greater share of the costs of creating the program. A small software company with 20 employees just can't survive selling its program to 20 customers a week at $199 a copy.

Simply stated, the more specialized an application is, the fewer the number of potential customers. You just don't get the economy of scale that enables you to buy word processing software for $99.

Modify Commercial Software

If your needs are relatively simple, using a macro language to customize the working of a commercial software package is the easiest, but probably the most limited, solution. Still an impressive degree of customization can be gained from quality commercial packages.

Most commercial software existing today has spread horizontally from its beginnings, and with the adoption of OLE, the border between software categories has become blurred. Spreadsheets have extensions that allow them to spell check, do data management, and create applications that interact with users. Word processors can sort lists, do lookups in full-featured databases, and incorporate tables that (due to OLE technology) act like the underlying spreadsheet server program. Databases do more than just store and lookup data. Today they are, in many cases, full-blown business analysis tools. Even some communications packages, thanks to their built-in languages, can double as fairly capable program generators.

Surely you've heard that the vast majority of people use only 20 percent of their software's capacity. This is true, but each person uses a different 20 percent, so the implication that software is underutilized isn't strictly correct. However, it is accurate to say that few people realize the full potential of the programs they own and use. By familiarizing yourself with your software's full potential, when the need for custom software crops up you will know whether you can use something you already know and own.

Chapter 30, "Visual Basic the Easy Way," shows how you can use macro language-like tools such as Visual Basic to create simple in-house custom software solutions to your needs.

Investigating Vertical Market Applications

Vertical market software is a type of custom software directed at a particular industry. Here are some of the markets targeted by vertical software vendors:

- Chiropractors
- Medical practitioners
- Dentists
- Restaurateurs
- Automotive supply stores
- Real estate brokers
- Light Industry manufacturers

Often this software stems from the industry itself. Let's imagine that a dentist sees a need to automate his busy office. At night and over weekends, he works to develop software that he believes is perfect for his business. After putting it into use for a while and getting the bugs out of it, he realizes that what he developed for himself can also be used by other dentists. At this point, he widens the scope of the software a little and then trial markets it to some other dentists in his area or circle.

If it's successful, he then might try to market it to dentists on a wider scale. To do so, he might advertise in dental trade magazines, attend trade shows, or even hire a sales force.

The Advantage of Vertical Market Software

The clear advantage that vertical market software has for consumers is that it usually has its roots in the target industry rather than in the computer industry (as in the preceding example). A dentist-developed software package will surely address the specific needs of the dental profession. Software developed by professional software developers who might not be familiar with the practice of dentistry might be more sophisticated, but it might not be right on target for the needs of the dental practice.

Computer people know computers. Practitioners know their trade or profession. Many feel that it's easier to teach practitioners enough programming to create a software application than it is to teach computer nerds enough about an industry to make on-target software.

How Do You Find Vertical Market Programs

There are five basic resources available to you for finding vertical market software.

1. Trade or professional shows and conventions: This is the logical place for ambitious or well-to-do vertical market vendors to show their wares. Often they'll have a booth with their software running so that you can give the programs an actual test drive. This is far superior to making a buying decision based on a salesman's assurances or pretty brochures. Another advantage of shopping trade shows is that you can discuss products with practitioners who are in the same line as yourself.

2. Trade or professional magazines for your industry: Like trade shows, targeted publications are logical advertising venues for vertical market software vendors. Frequently, you'll find better representation of vendors in publication advertisements than at trade shows, because it's simpler to place an ad than to attend a show with a display.

   Don't take the lack of trade show presence as an indication of vendor weakness. It might be just the opposite. A vendor who chooses to invest in technical and support assets rather than a trade show booth and high profile sales staff might be what you're looking for.

3. Application publications for specific software products: There are many vertical market programs covering many fields, but there aren't too many software development platforms. Programs such as Clipper, Visual Basic, Access, and FoxPro are the basis of tens of thousands of applications.

   Trade publications devoted to these programs are good places to locate both vertical market software and the people who can generate vertical software to your specification. Generally, the ads for applications in these publications are slightly broader, or more horizontal, than in professional or trade magazines. For example, a quick look through several magazines dedicated to Visual Basic and Access revealed about a dozen customizable accounting packages, each of which could be used by a specific profession but was not exclusive to that profession.

   If your needs can be met by software that is broader in scope than that targeted for your profession, this is a good resource. Accounting is a good illustration. Most businesses have an accounting need, but few have specific accounting requirements that set them apart from other businesses. An accounts receivable tracker will track amounts owed, whether they are owed to a chiropractor, a podiatrist, or an auto parts store.

4. Word of mouth: People love to talk. One of the things people like to talk about the most is a recent purchase they have made. These people, if they're your fellow practitioners, can be a great source of information about software and vendors. Word of mouth works both ways. You can learn not only about what is working for others in your situation, but you can also learn what to watch out for from those who have been burned. Often, the best value you can get from word of mouth is learning what to watch out for or avoid rather than what to buy.

THE PORSCHE SYNDROME OR COGNITIVE DISSONANCE

People will often use others to justify their poor or ill-conceived purchases. Before Porsche automobiles achieved the sophistication they have today, they were overpriced, uncomfortable, and dangerous to drive due to their weight shift during acceleration vector changes and horrid brakes.

People who bought Porsches soon learned of their mistake. In truth, they had paid a lot of money to drive an uncomfortable car that was actually scary to drive slowly and impossible to drive in a sporting manner. These people became Porsche's greatest advertisements. Rather than admit they made a foolish mistake in their purchase, these people often convinced others to make the same mistake, thereby justifying the recommender's purchase.

The new buyers, in turn, raved about the wonders of their cars rather than admit they had been duped. So the great game of "pass it on" was perpetuated through the years. This pattern sold a lot of Porsches, but eventually caught up with the company when people refused to be burned a second time. The company today makes terrific cars that live up to the reputation they falsely gained during the early days when Porsche drivers participated en masse in a huge put-on that was reminiscent of *The Emperor Has No Clothes*.

When listening to software recommendations from your fellow practitioners, keep in mind the lesson of the Porsche Syndrome (sometimes referred to as Cognitive Dissonance in psychological circles).

5. Direct sales: Sometimes you don't need to do anything but sit there to learn about vertical market software. Many vendors have commissioned sales forces that will seek you out wherever you are in hopes of signing you up for their brand of merchandise.

   Any decent salesman will have you feeling like a king or queen when making his presentation. He'll also imply that his software is clearly the best (if not the only) software for you. This might be true, but it doesn't have to be. The trick to ending up with a satisfactory bargain when dealing with direct salespeople is to garner recommendations and, if possible, to get competing bids.

How Much Should It Cost?

The cost of software must be weighed in terms of payback. You should save operational costs, enhance your management control, or both after adopting a new system. You should also create a budget projecting your payback time. After the purchase, you should track your actual costs to see how closely they adhere to your budget. Even if you find you made a mistake in budgeting, learning the cause or causes of your variance will make you a better shopper the next time around.

Make sure that you understand the total cost of your proposed system. Tread carefully when dealing with salespeople. Make sure you know exactly what you are buying and what it will cost not only initially but over time. Here are some of the costs of vertical market software:

1. Initial license fees for software
2. Required hardware
3. Additional software licenses in the event your business grows
4. Software support
5. Software maintenance and bug fixes
6. Software upgrades
7. Hardware maintenance
8. Training

And that's just a partial list. Some software categories extend well beyond that list.

All too often, people just look at initial costs rather than at the entire cost over the projected life of the purchase. Because many vendors target initial pricing to be very low and make it up on support or ongoing services, not factoring these things into your consideration can be a terrible mistake. Remember the shaving company that gave away razors so that it could sell blades? Many software vendors adhere to this marketing concept. If you as a razor user only figure in the cost of the razor, you'll pay for the blades in deep regret.

How Do You Tell Whether The Program Will Suit Your Needs?

The best way to tell whether the software will meet your needs is to give it a trial run. This might not be practical if the software takes extensive setup or requires much specialized training.

The bottom line is that you are the party responsible to determine the practicality of any software. You can try to abdicate your responsibility to the vendor, but ask yourself who will be hurt if the software fails to live up to your expectations. You will be, not the vendor, who at worst will lose some ongoing support revenue.

The best way to assure yourself that the software will suit your needs is for you to create a list of what you need. Give the list to your proposed vendors and let them demonstrate to you how their product satisfies your business requirements.

This puts the onus on the vendors. You can call them in, put pressure on them, and play one off against the others. This gives you purchase leverage as the vendors vie for your order. Don't be shy about letting each vendor know he's only one of a bevy of suitors for your purchase dollar. It's your money, and before the purchase you are the one in the catbird seat. Make the most of it.

Questions To Ask The Vendor

These questions depend upon your business. Here are some sample general-purpose questions:

1. How long have you been in business?
2. How many customers do you have?
3. How many customers that meet my business profile do you have?
4. Do you have a background in my line of business?
5. Is your system open or closed? That is, is your file format one I can access using off the shelf software, or do I need your proprietary program to access it?
6. In the event that you go out of business, have you arranged to escrow your source code so that I can hire others to maintain this software?
7. Does your program require special hardware?
8. If networked, does it run on only one network operating system (NOS)?
9. Must I buy my hardware from you, or can I use off-the-shelf computers and printers?

Is There a Guarantee?

Software warranties and guarantees vary wildly. It would be extremely unusual for a vendor to guarantee that his software will do any more than he claims for it. Don't expect a vendor to guarantee your outcome after purchase. That's not only beyond what you'll get from any honest vendor, but it is also unfair to him. A vendor can sell you software, but he can't force you to use it correctly or have an effect on how you manage your business.

The Uniform Commercial Code has, with all purchases, the implied warranty of merchantability. This merely means that the item purchased must ostensibly be suited for the intended purpose. You can easily apply this warranty to everyday purchases such as a hammer, but it can get dicey with software.

What if you buy software that can do the job, but the training required to use it turns out to be well beyond what your budget can stand? In this case, can you call on the implied warranty? Maybe, but you'll probably have to do it through the courts.

Many software purchase disputes are settled in the courts. Most of them end up with both sides feeling that they lost. Remember, your goal isn't to win a lawsuit but to enhance your management systems. Rather than relying on courts or guarantees, do your work ahead of time to make sure what you buy will satisfy your needs. A little time invested on the planning front can avoid a lot of ache in the implementation.

Do You Have a List of References of Companies Using Your Product?

As shown earlier in the questions to vendors list and the Porsche Syndrome sidebar, you can learn a lot from other users of software. Keep in mind that references aren't necessarily any better at judging the value of software than you are and none of them knows your business as well as you do.

Even if you can't fully rely on recommendations for a purchase decision, they can help. The most important thing to garner from past customers is an opinion of whether the company is pleasant to deal with after the sale. You should be the one to decide whether the software suits your business.

Also keep in mind that the list of customers your vendor supplies are the ones that he hopes and has reason to believe will give him a glowing recommendation. Don't stray far from your skepticism when listening to comments spouted by vendor-supplied recommendations.

What Kind of Support is Offered?

You need to decide ahead of time how much and what sort of support you'll need after the sale. Some vendors force bundled support on you. If this is the case, proceed warily. Do you really think you'll benefit from the price of this forced support?

Essentially, you have to strike a balance between what you need, what you can pay for, and what the vendor will supply. Much of your decision hangs on the capabilities of yourself or your staff. The ideal is to have people in-house who are capable of all support, and also have a vendor available for hire in case your support-capable people leave or hit a problem beyond their abilities.

You would be awfully lucky to hit a perfect balance. Here are a few general questions to ask a vendor about support:

1. Is there a required retainer fee for support?
2. Can I get support on demand?
3. What support is bundled with the purchase? Can I unbundle it?
4. Do you, the vendor, regard bug fixes as support? Do you charge for these fixes? What is a bug?
5. What is your guaranteed response time for support?
6. If you go out of business, how will support be handled?

Creating Custom Software

You have two choices when the decision is made to create custom software: do it in-house, or hire someone on the outside to come in and create the program for you. Which choice fits your situation depends on the resources that your organization possesses. Do any of the folks that work for the company have the skills to create software? Unfortunately, most small companies simply don't have an Information Services department so that they can call and unload the problem on someone else. If there is someone on staff who can do the work, will assigning them the task create some other problem? You certainly don't want your top salesperson to take off three months to write software.

Hiring Outside Help

Your custom software needs often extend beyond what can reasonably be done by modifying existing software applications. You then are forced to examine a solution that is from scratch or almost from scratch. Depending upon your inclinations, talents, and demands on your time, you might choose to do this yourself or assemble a team from within your organization to create the application.

The two most important elements to consider are which development software to use, and your (or your team's) ability to use it. This sounds almost facile when stated: "Use the best tool and use it well." However, like most truisms, this is basically true. Many projects fail, run over time and over budget, or give unsatisfactory results due to people choosing the wrong tool for the job. Even if you choose the right tool, you must be able use it well enough or your project will be in danger of failure.

Pick The Right Tool

You might have heard the Japanese saying, "To a worker with only a hammer, every problem looks like a nail." This holds true with computer programmers to an even greater extent than it does with Japanese workers.

Sadly, many computer people learn a program and then try to apply it to any situation that crops up. Spreadsheet jockeys are especially guilty of trying to adapt their favorite numerical analysis tool into everything from a relational database to a word processor.

Speaking very generally about computer programming, the more flexible a computer tool is, the more difficult it is to use. The same used to be said about power, but today there are very powerful specialized tools that are quite easy to use. Again speaking very generally, you should use the least flexible (which is to say the most specific) tool available that will get the job done efficiently.

When making the right tool decisions, there will always be tradeoffs and toss-up types of choices. This isn't hard science. Despite this, by careful analysis, you can usually come up with one or more best choice tools.

Take a look at Figure 28.1. This is a general scale to show where the programs discussed in Chapters 29, 30, and 31 fit along the scale of ease of use versus flexibility. Don't take this scale as the absolute arbiter of where each particular software program lies. Most of these, as well as other programs, have their specialties. For example, if you want a word processor, the only real choice here is Word. Although CA-Visual Objects is shown to be more flexible than Word, it is an application specifically aimed at data management. It will not make a more flexible word processor than Word.

FIGURE 28.1.

Where programs fall along the scale.

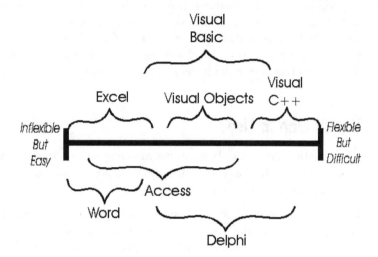

Purists might jump in here and say that you can use the flexible tools such as Visual Basic, Delphi, Microsoft Visual C++, or CA-Visual Objects to make a custom word processor that can be more than Word. But, in reality, few people have the time, inclination, or ability to do this.

Knowing How to Use the Tool

Even if there was a perfect routine for choosing a tool, you need to consider not only what the ideal tool is, but your or your team's ability to use it. Take a look at the following list of languages included in the programs discussed in this section.

1. WordBasic
2. Visual Basic
3. Visual Basic for Applications (VBA) in Excel
4. Visual Basic as used in Visual Basic or Access when you use the Windows API or other .DLL calls
5. xBASE as used in CA-Visual Objects, dBASE 5.0 for Windows, and FoxPro for Windows

6. Object Pascal as used in Delphi

7. C as used in Visual C++

8. C++ as used in Visual C++

9. C++ as used in Visual C++ with Microsoft Foundation Classes

This list is in an arbitrary order of the difficulty of the various languages. The list is not only arbitrary, but it's also neutral regarding experience or background. A seasoned C++ programmer will be at home with numbers 8 and 9 but will be lost using the Pascal dialect used by Borland at number 6 on the list. Similarly, many people are quite at home using the xBASE family of languages made famous by the dBASE and Clipper lines of products. These people might be utterly at sea when faced with the event-driven Basics, which are shown as easier than their chosen language, or with Pascal, which is shown as just a little harder than their chosen language.

Which One to Use?

Choosing the right tool or language has two components, as stated earlier. The first consideration is how apt the tool is to your project; the second consideration is how familiar you or your team are with the tool's use.

Let's look at a concrete example. Visual Basic started life as a forms animator aimed at being a Windows version of the GW Basic or PC Basic that used to be standard issue with all PCs. GW Basic worked acceptably for DOS applications, but as the world moved from DOS to Windows, it grew into an obsolete relic.

Although user-generated custom software isn't as important to those of the Windows generation as it was to early DOS adopters, the urge to create (if not play) remains in the heart of many computer users. This urge fueled sales of Visual Basic sufficiently to make it a success.

At the insistence of none other than Bill Gates, Visual Basic had the capability to use custom controls, which are collectively known as VBXs. These controls, which were made using assembly or other low-level languages such as C, greatly enhanced Visual Basic's capabilities to do anything possible in those low-level languages. So although making a communications package, for example, was clearly beyond what was practical using native Visual Basic, making a communications package using a communications VBX and Visual Basic became fairly straightforward. In other words, Visual Basic itself is quite limited in scope; Visual Basic with VBXs added to it has no horizons.

One area in which VBX and other add-ons really spurred Visual Basic sales was database manipulation. A fairly considerable industry sprang up to supply the tools Visual Basic needed to create the client side of client/server applications.

> **NOTE**
>
> The term *client/server*, or just C/S, came into vogue as LANs (Local Area Networks) started supplanting mainframe computers in corporations. Although there's no exact definition of what this means, essentially the client/server model means one or more specialized servers with a permanent or temporary set of clients.
>
> From a hardware view, a server is usually a PC specially designed for greater throughput and integrity. From a software view, a server application is usually a database program that's much more powerful and robust than the type used for typical PC or Mac desktop applications. Some examples of server software are Oracle, Microsoft SQL Server, and IBM's DB2.
>
> The client side of C/S is usually regular PCs that are able to access the server through the network. Typically, they run front end software to make data manipulation and retrieval much easier than it would be using the native server database.
>
> Another area in which you'll hear the term client/server is in discussions of the Internet. The IP or Internet address `jdoe@dragon.farleft.edu` means that there's a client `jdoe` on the `dragon` server. However, in the programming sections of this book, the term client/server only refers to the database model over the LAN—the non-Internet definition.

The move to make Visual Basic into a client maker for C/S applications reached such a frenzy that at one point, a large software supply house catering to the programming community stated that for every copy of Visual Basic sold, it also sold a VBX-based C/S add-on.

Microsoft has never been accused of failing to follow up on a trend, and Visual Basic's transformation into a C/S tool was a trend it latched onto quickly. The next version of Visual Basic that Microsoft brought out had a professional edition, which came with database extensions. Soon Microsoft was implying that Visual Basic's transmogrification from a forms automator to a popular C/S tool was part of the company's grand plan.

The success of Visual Basic wasn't lost on the folks down in Scotts Valley, California—the folks of Borland International. Building on the robust engine of Object Pascal, Borland introduced Delphi in the winter of 1995, calling it VBK for Visual Basic Killer. Delphi has much of what's good in Visual Basic, plus it ups the ante in several very important categories.

Delphi uses Object Pascal as its underlying language, rather than Visual Basic's BASIC. Some consider that a good thing, others don't. Delphi adheres much more closely to the object-oriented programming (OOP) method. That's something a few people will greatly care about, some will ignore, and others will openly scoff; but it's there.

Delphi has three aspects in which it clearly exceeds Visual Basic. It can make real Windows native executable files, while Visual Basic only compiles to pseudocode and needs a runtime library to execute. Delphi also can make .DLLs or dynamic link libraries for use in its programs as well as other programs. This makes it the envy of the Visual Basic crowd who have been lobbying Microsoft for years for such capability. The only response Microsoft made was the rather smug remark that its Visual C++ was the tool for .DLLs. Lastly, Delphi was conceived almost from the beginning as a C/S tool, while Visual Basic grew into being one by default. Thus, Delphi has had the successes and failures of Visual Basic to learn from.

There's much more to the comparison than there is room for here. But you might get the idea that, viewed equally, Delphi is the program of choice for C/S programming. If you conclude this, you won't be alone. Delphi is also a top choice to complete Visual Basic's original mission—being an easy to use forms automator for user-created Windows programs. Does that mean you should always choose Delphi over Visual Basic? No it doesn't. There's much more to the choice than arbitrary level playing field evaluations.

For the sake of argument, let's say that if all things are equal, Delphi Version 1 is a better C/S tool than Visual Basic 3 Professional Version. Many will disagree, but let's accept that for now. Still, most people will be better off using Visual Basic for the following reasons:

Visual Basic's Language Is Basic

This is a language that most people find intuitive because it's very close to plain English and specifically tailored to the needs of nonprofessional, as well as professional, programmers. Delphi uses a language derived from Pascal, which was invented as an academic exercise to teach good programming practices (so it is a student language). Although Borland has done wonders in extending Pascal from its academic roots, many still find Pascal to be excessively verbose, unclear, and unnecessarily difficult for some tasks that other languages take in stride.

Visual Basic and Object-Oriented Programming (OOP)

Many promote OOP as a coming thing for professional programming. But to use it, you need to spend a lot of time learning the theory and practice behind it, and then spend more time to implement it. Rather than just complete a project, you must create objects and then derive your project from those objects. These steps and methods, which are greatly oversimplified here, might make sense for a well-oiled professional team, but nonprofessional ad hoc programming people or teams will only be confused by OOP. Someone who is less than a full-time professional or nonprofessional won't see any productivity gains from OOP until OOP grows significantly less complex.

Although you can use or ignore OOP with Delphi, the nature of Delphi forces you to have some exposure to this. Borland touts this as a boon to the professional programmer, and it might be. It also will be a bane to the part-timer or nonprofessional.

Look at Figure 28.2. This shows Delphi responding to a button click with a simple message box that shows the familiar Hello World message.

FIGURE 28.2.

A simple message box in Delphi.

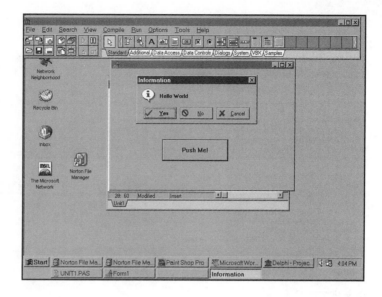

Here's the code behind that message box:

```
unit Unit1;

interface

uses
  SysUtils, WinTypes, WinProcs, Messages, Classes, Graphics, Controls,
  Forms, Dialogs, StdCtrls;

type
  TForm1 = class(TForm)
    Button1: TButton;
    procedure Button1Click(Sender: TObject);
  private
    { Private declarations }
  public
    { Public declarations }
  end;

var
  Form1: TForm1;

implementation

{$R *.DFM}

procedure TForm1.Button1Click(Sender: TObject);
begin
MessageDlg('Hello World', mtInformation,mbYesNoCancel , 0);
end;

end.
```

Now look at Figure 28.3. Here's a similar message box displayed in Visual Basic.

FIGURE 28.3.

The Hello World message box in Visual Basic.

Following is the code behind the Visual Basic message box:

```
Sub Command1_Click()
MsgBox "Hello World!", 3, "Hi There"
End Sub
```

There is quite a difference, right? This comparison is unfair to Delphi. When coding these two applications, the programmer must only enter

```
MessageDlg('Hello World', mtInformation,mbYesNoCancel , 0);
```

in Delphi, and

```
MsgBox "Hello World!", 3, "Hi There"
```

in Visual Basic. The programs themselves generate the rest of the code. Still, this illustrates the general verbosity of Object Pascal compared to Visual Basic for Applications. You might not need to know why all the rest of the code is there in order to do something like this simple message box in Delphi, but at some point you'll need to know what all the rest of that stuff is.

Visual Basic Has a Wider Variety of Controls

Borland has promised that later versions of Delphi will be able to use the same kinds of controls (VBXs) as Visual Basic. However, until that occurs, Visual Basic is clearly the leader here. Delphi will only use Version 1 VBXs. Your project might not need custom controls, but most do.

The new OCX control also has the advantage of being useful within Access, where no VBX can go. Thus, if you buy an OCX control, you'll be able to use it in Access and several other programs.

The worst possible scenario occurs when you get well into a project and learn that you need a custom control or that using one will shorten your job. Then you find out that, due to your host application's limitation, you can't use what you need. This might occur under Delphi, but it is much less likely under Visual Basic.

Now Which Tool?

Delphi initially seemed to have a significant advantage over Visual Basic, but there are many other factors to consider. In many instances, the small factors (such as Basic's ease of learning), in the aggregate, tilt the balance in favor of a tool that at first glance isn't as suitable as the others.

This comparison is only by way of example. Don't take it to mean that Visual Basic is better than Delphi for all projects. The comparison is only to demonstrate that you need to delve further than the sales brochures when deciding what tool to use.

This little study had a fatal flaw. To keep it reasonably simple, it only considered two of many possible tools. If the project in question has a database at its foundation, you also need to evaluate both Access and CA-Visual Objects from those products discussed in this book. If the project is a nondatabase stand-alone application, you need to figure in Visual C++ instead.

In-House or Outsource

In the final analysis, you'll likely decide to keep a custom application in-house if you have the time for it and if you or a home team have the knowledge to succeed (or the desire to acquire that knowledge). The four biggest advantages of keeping any project in-house are as follows:

- You maintain control of the project flow.
- The programming personnel know the business, its personnel, and its corporate culture.
- You maintain control of the project personnel.
- Any knowledge gained from the project remains in-house and becomes an asset to the firm.

Don't discount that last item because it alone can outweigh many other considerations. The money spent on a project is deductible, but the asset gained through acquired knowledge isn't taxable.

The following are five pressing reasons not to do a project in-house:

- Unless you have a dedicated programming team, you divert personnel from their regular tasks.
- Unless you have programming talent on board, your team will be less adept than professional hired "gunslingers."
- The politics of project implementation might disrupt the organization. This might have impact well beyond the project.
- Many people have a fascination with small computers and programming. If these people become part of the project, they might lose interest in their jobs when the project concludes.
- The acquired skills from a project make your employees more employable and less tied to a particular company.

As you can see, there are many considerations to a project. In the end, they come down to two major questions:

- Do you want to keep this project in-house, or do you want to outsource it?
- If you keep it in-house, what tool should you use?

Outsourcing a Project

Outsourcing a project might seem to be a simpler solution to the in-house decision, with the only tradeoff being the loss of the expertise gained by keeping things internal. This isn't true. An outsourced project can be even more difficult to manage than an in-house one, but the challenges are different.

Unless you're willing to throw yourself on the mercy of your contractor, which is the equivalent of casting your fate to the wind, you have a considerable management job with an outsourced job. This takes two forms. You first must decide on a contractor and then manage whomever you've decided to hire.

Choosing a Contractor

Oddly enough, you not only need to know how to hire any outside contractor, but you also need a full familiarity with the programming tools he proposes. You need to know about the tools used for a project kept in-house or outsourced.

This isn't the place to discuss the general steps to take or the legal concerns when hiring a contractor. That's more a general business topic. Suffice it to say that you must be very careful to negotiate terms very specifically, and you should get your agreement in writing. The latter condition isn't a comment on the honesty of computer contractors, but rather a recognition that they often speak a different language than you do. Terms such as *user friendly, attractive interface,* and *ease of use* might mean something particular to you but something quite different to the cyberdweeb you hire.

When evaluating a contractor, you should evaluate him based on his proposal. That sounds simple doesn't it? However, you can't evaluate well unless you understand what's in the proposal. The tools that your prospective contractor suggests, combined with your assessment of the contractor and any recommendations you can garner, are all part of the proposal. Without a knowledge of the tools, you can't do a good evaluation because you'll only be evaluating part of your contractor's proposal.

Consider the following situation: Your sales department wants a sales tracking and analysis tool to track yearly volumes of $3 million to $4 million occurring through roughly 8,000 transactions per year at one location. One person will do the data entry, but a workgroup of 20 (two or three at any one time) will need to see the data. Three contractors bid on the job.

- Contractor 1 proposes using Turbo Pascal Version 4 to run under Novell NetWare 4.1.
- Contractor 2 proposes using Access and Excel to run under Windows.
- Contractor 3 proposes doing the entire project in C++ to run under VINES.

OK, this was a setup. The only reasonable proposal here is the second one—the one with Access and Excel. That was easy because the differentiation is so wide. You probably won't have such obvious choices, but you will have choices.

DO YOU WANT TO SPEND $21,000 OR $800?

A major university had a credit program at its extension facility. This facility couldn't be hooked to the computer system of the main campus for a reasonable cost, so the university sought alternative methods to track the student credits earned at the extension facility.

The university solicited a bid from a source it had done business with before and with whom it had participated in several successful projects. The contractor bid the job using a Pascal language compiler and a database library. The cost came to a total of $21,000, or $7,000 per workstation on the network.

The university was slightly taken aback at this price but accepted it because the personnel at the extension university were used to budgeting for mainframe type projects. However, the rules of bidding required this bid be reviewed by a third party. The university called in an expert.

The expert agreed that the bid was fair if you accepted the bidder's tools and licensing fees. At the end of the report, the consulting expert mentioned that the chosen tool was "less than optimal." The head of the extension university read the report and called the expert in and asked him to elaborate on the "less than optimal" comment.

The expert explained that this was a database project, so it wasn't an ideal project for a programming language, whether it was Pascal or another. He contrasted this bid with the way he would tackle the job.

Because the university already had licensed copies of Paradox on each of the workstations, he proposed using that as a data manager. He estimated that he could program and debug the university's application in about two days, or 15 hours, using Paradox. At his usual rate of $55.00 per hour that amounted to about $800.

The important lesson here is that the initial bidder wasn't being dishonest or padding his fees. A $21,000 fee was reasonable given the tool he chose. The problem wasn't in his integrity, it was in his choice of tools. Had the university not called in a second expert, it would have ended up paying $21,000 for an $800 job.

The more you know about the tools your contractor proposes to use, the better you can evaluate the bid. Trusting a contractor to use the optimal tools for every job is a path that wanders well beyond folly.

Certifications

There are several certifications for programmers and consultants. Probably the most well known is the Novell offered CNE, which stands for Certified NetWare Engineer. Lately, some people have gained certfications from Microsoft such as the MCP, for Microsoft Certified Professional. Microsoft has also been awarding the MVP, or Microsoft Valued Professional for demonstrated professional ability in one or more fields.

Microsoft awards MVP without testing for demonstrated performance and competence. The MCP and CNE are among those given for passing one or more tests. There's a great deal of debate in the industry as to the value of these tested certifications.

For many years, holding a CNE was a key to steady employment—and for a good reason. Those holding the certification surely knew what they were talking about when it came to Novell networks. However, today there are many schools that offer first a cram course and then an immediate test to force the CNE certification. Many feel that the CNEs yielded by this method aren't nearly as adept as those from the early days. Yet both hold an identical certification.

Microsoft's certifications are much newer, and the value of the MCP is even more a matter of debate than the CNE. Microsoft is trying to certify in a wider arena than Novell and faces serious challenges as to what it should be testing.

What should you test for to certify a professional? Look at Access. Do you test for

- Relational theory
- Screen design and ergonomics
- Structured Query Language
- Client presentation
- Client training
- Access Basic Coding
- The Access macro language
- Client relations
- Legal issues related to consulting
- Client/server architecture
- The Windows API

Or, do you test for other things? Each of those categories and more are part of what an Access programmer or consultant needs to know. A test covering it all would take days to administer, exhaust the takers, and even then the debate would remain as to what questions to ask for each category.

When a consultant presents you with a credential of some sort, take it as a positive point but not as a be-all and end-all. By all means don't assume the noncertified person is less adept than the certified one.

LOOK MOM, I IS A CERTIFIED RITER!

Certification only means that someone passed an arbitrary test—nothing more. Unless you know that you require the type of expertise tested for, certification isn't any guarantee that the person is any better for you than someone without certification.

Who Owns the Project?

Here's a surprise for you. Many consultants will write a custom program for you, but insist that they still own it. You need to be very specific when hiring an outside person as to where the title, or copyright, of the work resides after completion.

Many programmers won't give you full rights to the code you've hired them to write. Before you get upset at that prospect, keep in mind that in many jobs, a programmer will include algorithms (recipes or stock routines for getting things done in software) that he has developed before your project and intends to reuse for future projects. If he grants you exclusive rights to those algorithms, he won't be able to do this.

The important thing to keep in mind when negotiating this part of the contract is to be very specific. Are you hiring a programmer to

- Create and then license the program to you for a specific number of workstations?
- Create and then license the program to you for an unlimited number of workstations?
- Create a program that you wholly own and can resell?
- Create a program that you wholly own and can't resell?
- Create a program that you wholly own and can't resell, but the programmer can resell?
- Create a program you own except for certain parts, for which the rights remain with the programmer?

Those are only a few variations on the theme of who owns what in software development. Be absolutely sure that you know where you stand on this issue, or you might be in for a bitter fight.

> **NOTE**
>
> Many software developers won't let you have title to the source code they used to create your program. That's just fine as long as you don't mind dealing with that vendor indefinitely, but what happens if the vendor goes out of business or moves away? The next person you hire to maintain your software needs that source code or he will have to redo your project from scratch.
>
> One answer to this dilemma is the escrow account. The programmer places the source code in escrow, and upon certain agreed upon conditions (such as his death), the escrow agent releases the source to you.
>
> It's reasonable for a consultant not to want to reveal his source code under normal business conditions. After all, his algorithms and techniques are his intellectual property. It's not reasonable for him to want to conceal them in the event of his incapacity or under other conditions in which he's unable to maintain the software he's vended to you.
>
> Not having rights to source code leaves you at the mercy of the vendor. Not having rights to source code in the event that the vendor can no longer deliver code mainte-nance is the sign of a poorly negotiated contract.

Managing the Project

When you've settled on a contractor and the terms, you have to oversee the project. The best way to do this is to see frequent builds of the program as it progresses. This will give an early warning if your idea of where the program should go and your contractor's idea of what he's doing diverge.

The worst possible strategy is to come to terms, and then watch your contractor ride off into the sunset only to return after some period of time with a finished product. The chances of the product being what you want, despite any contractual agreement, are slight. Keep in mind that a good contract, backed up by expensive lawyers and a glacial judicial system, might make you financially whole in the event that what you get isn't what you expected to get from your contractor. However, the game isn't to sue successfully, make mischief for a contractor, or provide another case to clog the courts; it is to succeed in your project. The best way to do this, given that all your eggs are in one basket held by a contractor, is to watch that basket carefully.

A Type of Conclusion

When the need for custom software pops up in your life, you have a fairly obvious decision tree to follow. The tree's branches might be readily apparent, but deciding which branches to take can be quite difficult. Each branch has dependencies on other branches—sometimes branches that ostensibly lie ahead of where you are.

For example, the first decision most people want to make is whether to do the project in-house or outsource it. However, before that decision can be made, you need to decide what are the appropriate tools for the project and whether anybody inside your organization can use those tools. Then you have to decide the impact on your organization if that person suspends his usual tasks temporarily for the project. Mixed in with all this, you have to decide how much weight to give to keeping the project in-house. The two most common factors causing people to decide to keep a project in-house are to create expertise in-house or because the information the programmer needs to see is especially sensitive. You might end up deciding that the entire mix is impossible to do in-house but extremely undesirable to do outsourced. In that case, you must decide whether to drop the entire matter or hire new personnel to increase your in-house capacity.

The In-House Project

The two biggest advantages of the in-house project are that you maintain absolute control of the project and there's no issue as to where the expertise gained from performing the project resides. Some also find it important that there's no question as to where the title of the program lies.

Identifying People For Your Project

Instead of their current employment, many people dream of a career in programming or using small computers. These are the people who are the natural fit for including as a taskforce for your project. In many cases, you'll find these enthusiasts are more capable than their jobs imply. These people tend to buy computers for their homes and use them extensively for various work- and nonwork-related projects.

Don't be discouraged if these people don't have any formal knowledge of programming. Naturally, the more they know the better. But today's visual programming tools such as Visual Basic or Delphi make programming much easier and faster to learn than old tools.

The best people to use for an in-house taskforce are people who are interested in computers and computing generally and who will be using the product they help create. Be sure not to include any people who feel, rightly or wrongly, that the project underway will reduce their importance at your company. Your in-house project will be challenging enough without sabotage.

Macros, Programming, or Point and Shoot

These are the three basic categories of programming today, but the classifications are somewhat blurry around the edges. Most programming jobs will emphasize one of these techniques, but most will also incorporate at least one other technique.

Macros

Classically speaking, macros are recordings of keystrokes that can be played back to automate repetitive tasks. Take a look at Figure 28.4. This is a simple Excel spreadsheet showing sales for three cities in three categories.

FIGURE 28.4.

A simple spreadsheet.

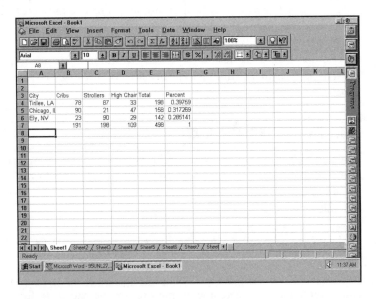

Figure 28.4 shows all the information for the cities and sales, but loses a lot due to a rather listless presentation. You surely wouldn't want to show this spreadsheet to your boss or to a board of directors without spiffing it up some.

Imagine that you have to create this table every month but also want to format it more attractively. You could do it manually or turn on Excel's macro recorder, do your formatting keystrokes, and then each month just play the macro back to reproduce your original formatting. Figure 28.5 shows the start of a new macro recording.

FIGURE 28.5.

Starting a new macro.

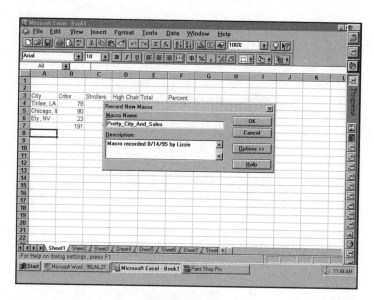

Figure 28.6 shows the formatted spreadsheet and Figure 28.7 shows the macro automatically recorded by Excel that can be played back any time a table, such as that shown in Figure 28.4, needs to be formatted.

FIGURE 28.6.

The formatted spreadsheet.

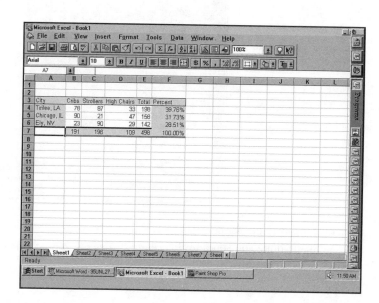

FIGURE 28.7.

The macro Excel automatically recorded.

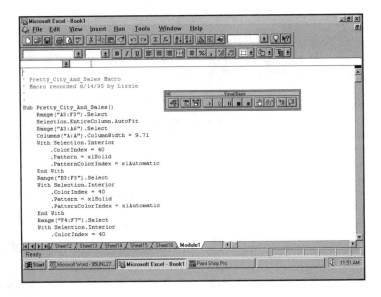

Figure 28.7 only shows part of the macro Excel recorded. To play that macro back again within the same workbook, you only need to choose the menu selections Tools | Macro and select the right macro name as shown in Figure 28.8.

FIGURE 28.8.

Running the macro.

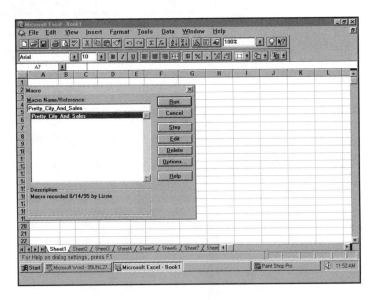

Don't be concerned if this example went too fast to follow or if the recorded macro isn't clear to you. The next chapter goes into Excel and its macros in much greater detail and at a slower pace.

Programming

Manual programming used to be the only way you could give operational instructions to a computer. The procedure differed only slightly between low-level languages such as assembler, in which you write code very close to machine language; C, in which you write something akin to human language; and Basic, in which you write code very similar to English.

In each case, you need to use a special language to tell the computer what to do in great detail. Look at Figure 28.9. This shows part of a program written in Basic. The programmer had to enter each word, each line number, and each punctuation mark perfectly for this program to operate properly.

FIGURE 28.9.

A Basic handwritten program.

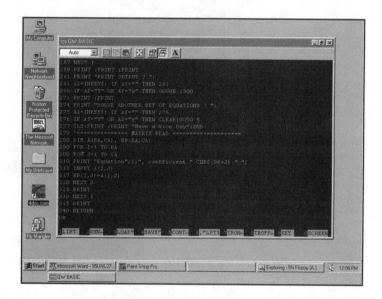

This particular program solves simultaneous equations using a matrix.

Handwriting programs is both tedious and challenging. If you make any typo, you end up with either a program that won't run or one that gives wrong answers.

Hand coding such programs, as shown in Figure 28.9, was somewhat reasonable in the world of MS-DOS; but, due to Windows, the work required simply to tell the computer how and where to paint the screens became incredibly bothersome. Point and click programming came to the rescue.

Point and Click

Point and click programming, also known as visual programming, is some combination of manual programming and macro programming. To create a program using the point and click (or visual) technique, you first tell the computer what tool or element to use, and then what to do with it.

Like macro recording, you show the computer what to use rather than hand coding the instructions. Figures 28.10 through 28.13 show a very quick example of how this works using Visual Basic as a programming tool.

Figure 28.10 shows the blank Visual Basic workspace with a new project loaded.

FIGURE 28.10.

Ready to go in Visual Basic.

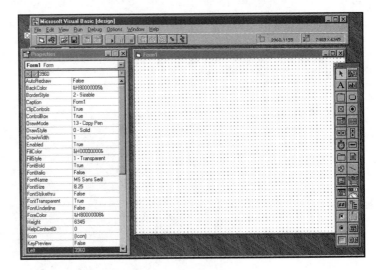

When loaded, this program shows a simple message saying `Hello Windows 95!`. The first thing to do is to create a space on the blank form to show the message. Figure 28.11 shows how this is done.

The programmer clicked on the button with the capital A on it from the button selection on the right of the screen in Figure 28.10. He then moved his mouse to the center of the form area, and clicked and dragged to get the resulting box you see in Figure 28.11. The next thing to do is tell Windows 95 to show the message in the boxed area. Figure 28.12 illustrates this message and the box resized so that it looks proportional.

To get the message `Hello Windows 95!` in the box, the programmer only had to tell Visual Basic to change the caption of the box to read this. Take another look at Figure 28.12 and note that the box at the left of the screen has an entry called Caption. Next to that entry, the programmer has entered the text `Hello Windows 95!`. That's all it took to get this message in the box. Figure 28.13 shows the completed program running under Windows 95.

FIGURE 28.11.

A place for a message.

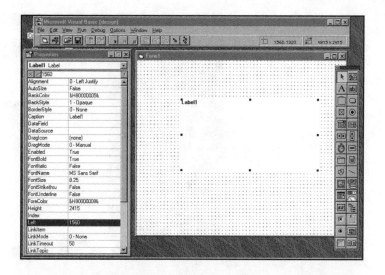

FIGURE 28.12.

The message in the box.

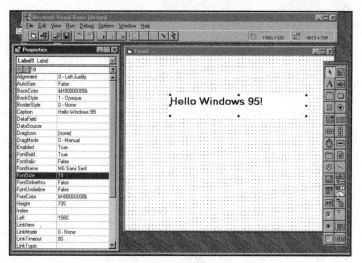

Naturally, most of your programs will perform more complex tasks than the one shown in Figure 28.13. Also, don't be concerned that the example went a little fast for you. You'll get a good starting tutorial on Visual Basic in Chapter 30.

FIGURE 28.13.

The completed program.

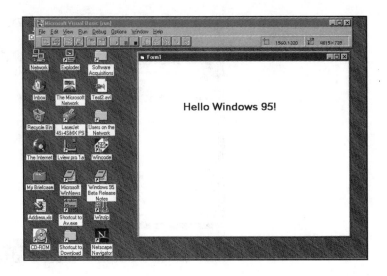

Getting Started

Programmers like to puff themselves up a bit by claiming that programming is an iterative process. This is just a fancy term for trial and error. All programmers—from those just starting out to those who make the tools mere mortals use to program computers—make false starts, hit dead ends, and get thrown for losses. The difference between those who succeed in programming and those who don't is basically the difference between those who accept these setbacks while learning from them and those who feel discouraged because of the inevitable. If you program computers, you will

- Get discouraged occasionally
- Hit walls and wonder how to proceed
- Confront topics that seem, at first glance, to be impenetrable
- Wonder from time to time if the whole thing's a good idea

On the other hand, you will also

- Feel tremendous satisfaction for being a problem solver
- Get enormous gratification from doing what others cannot do
- Learn that you are among the intellectual elite of the world
- Be in command of your computer rather than it being in command of you

To Begin

You begin programming by simply beginning to program. There are no preliminaries. Look over the next several chapters to get an idea of what different tools can do and how they're used. Decide which of these or similar tools suit your needs, ability, and personality. Go get the tool. Run through the tutorials that come with the tool of your choice. Go out and get a few books written about your chosen programming language or environment. These books will take you further than the manuals that come with your software.

Now launch either your project or a pilot project. Does it seem to be going well? If so, you likely have chosen wisely. If you get a bad feeling from the start, examine your choices. This is the time to change course. The further you are committed to a project, the more difficult it will be to switch programming options.

When You're Stuck

You will get stuck. You will wonder how to proceed. You will encounter things you not only don't know how to handle but don't even know if your programming tool can handle. Now what? Here are some resources with which you can help yourself out of almost any tight spot.

1. **Publisher's support:** All software publishers such as Borland International or Microsoft Corporation have various levels of consumer support. Some minor support comes bundled with your software, but you can purchase a much higher level of support at a reasonable price. Considering that, at the higher levels, this support amounts to top experts that will actually solve your problem for you, paid technical support can be the best buy you will make.

2. **Online services:** All the major online services have areas where vendors and other experts in various programming disciplines hang out. CompuServe is surely the major player for commercial software with just about every vendor represented. By posting your questions online, you expose your problem to thousands of people, one of whom will surely have the answer you seek. The only caution is to make sure you pose your question correctly. A poorly asked question will elicit a poor answer or none at all.

3. **News or Usenet groups:** The Internet teems with groups dedicated to discussions and problem solving on any imaginable programming topic. Few of these groups are attended by vendors, so the support tends to be spotty. You'll even get some wrong answers by people with more enthusiasm than knowledge, but at these prices who can complain?

4. **Special interest publications:** Every program has at least one magazine that is either dedicated or pertinent to it. Then there are magazines that specialize in general topics that apply to your projects. Most corporate projects incorporate a database component so that information published both as part of a database specialty magazine and a magazine dedicated to your particular program can help you down the path toward enlightenment.

5. **Books, books, and more books:** Every programmer worth his salt reads as much as he can about programming. A serious component to being a programmer is continuing education for continuing improvement. Programming books are expensive compared to, say, mystery novels. However, if a programming book that costs you $30 saves you two hours of work—something it can't help but do—it's right up there with the sale of the century. If that $30 book saves your project, which it can easily do, it approaches being priceless.

Doing It

To summarize, here's how you can start programming:

1. Read the following chapters to get an idea of what kind of programming tool you need and want to use.
2. Buy it.
3. Run the tutorials that come with your program. Study the examples that came with it.
4. Get some third party manuals to gain even more familiarity with your chosen programming tool.
5. Launch your project or a pilot one. Move along in it.
6. Get stuck.
7. Unstick yourself using the various resources available to you, some of which are listed earlier.
8. Read, study, and read some more about programming. You will never know it all.

What *Windows 95 Unleashed* Can Do

Many personnel and security questions that need to be addressed when doing custom software in-house or outsourced aren't those that a book like this can address. This is a computer book after all. However, the majority of the bothersome questions you face when confronted with the need for custom software are related to what tools to use and how. This book can help you in this regard, whether you do projects internally or hire external personnel.

The next three chapters step you through the several programs you can use to solve your custom programming needs under Windows 95 or Windows NT. The programs you'll see in action are as follows:

- Microsoft Word for Windows 6
- Microsoft Excel 5
- Baler Software's Visual Baler
- Borland International Delphi

■ Microsoft Visual Basic 3 Professional Version

■ Microsoft Visual C++ 2.1

These tools aren't by any means a comprehensive list of appropriate tools for use under Windows, but they each represent a product class. For example, seeing what you can do with Word for Windows will give you a good idea of what WordPerfect for Windows can do. Likewise, if you have an idea of what Visual C++ does and where its foundation classes (MFC) fit in, you also have a good feeling for what Borland C++ and its framework, OWL, can do. The inclusion of one particular product in a category isn't an endorsement of that product over its competition. There are many good products in each category.

All of these programs will get at least one section in following chapters devoted to them. Each section will step you through the process of writing at least one sample application using each product. If you own any of these programs, you can follow the book step by step. Even if you don't own or have access to a particular product, the walkthrough of it should give you an idea of

■ The product's strong points

■ The product's weak points

■ The product's range of application

■ The difficulty of implementation with the product

■ The background one needs to use the product successfully

Now let's move on to learn what each of these products can do to make your life simpler and easier. After all, isn't that what computers are supposed to do?

Summary

There are many reasons you might want to embark on custom programming either yourself, as part of a company team, or by hiring a consultant. Your needs might be a modest tweaking of off-the-shelf software or the creation of a full-featured vertical program.

Whichever, your decision matrix remains the same. Do you do the project in-house or out source it? In either case, you need to have an idea of what you are doing. Supervising or participating in an in-house project where the wrong tools have been chosen is a quick road to failure. Similarly buying the services of an outside expert who uses the wrong tools will, at the best, assure you of an overly expensive purchase. At the worst, the project will fail.

Don't think you can substitute an iron-clad contract for your expertise when hiring outside help. The point isn't to have a good court case but to get the job done. You need to be an intelligent consumer if the project is given to an outside source. You need to be more than that to keep the project in-house.

Tens of thousands, maybe millions, of people have learned how to program computers. Most of these people aren't as smart as you are. If they learned enough to get by, you can, too, if you truly want to. Here are a few tricks:

- Take it slow.
- Programming is easier learned while doing. Dive in without spending too long worrying about how to approach it.
- Accept that you will make several false starts. Don't become discouraged.
- Accept that you will make many errors no matter your level of expertise. Learn from them.
- Read everything you can about programming. This includes not only books and articles about your area of programming, but peripheral stuff. You never know when that odd piece of information will save your bacon.
- Chat it up. Join and participate in various open forums such as those on CompuServe and Usenet groups. Jump in and try to offer help yourself. The best way to learn is to teach.
- *Never* cease your journey of discovery.

Microsoft Office and More

29

by Paul Cassel

You might have heard that most people use only roughly 20 percent of the capacity of their programs. This is a rather debatable number, but accept it for the sake of argument.

There are two reasons why people fail to utilize their software to the fullest. The first, and for now unavoidable, reason for some of this is that most programs today suffer from feature bloat to some extent. *Feature bloat* is a term that describes features in a program you don't need. For example, the engineering functions in Excel don't have any use for a financial analyst, but then again the financial functions probably don't interest the engineer much. The penalty that general-purpose programs exact is that you get more than you need or want with them.

The other reason people don't fully use all their programs' power is that they don't know their programs' capacities. This chapter and the next one show you how you can extend the power of your everyday programs beyond what they can obviously do.

Anybody can see that a word processor such as Microsoft Word can create documents, but did you know that it also can create forms useful to a variety of businesses? If you knew that Word had this power you could likely read up about it in the documentation or the online help system, but how can you look up what you don't know exists? That's where this chapter and the following one will lead you.

Oh, No! Not Programming!

Technically, this and the following chapters concern some aspect of programming. If you have had some programming experience in the past, either in school or on the job, and found it boring or intimidating, don't worry. There isn't a smidgen of regular programming in any of the next two chapters. Here's what you won't find:

1. Interminable entry of source code hand-entered line-by-line.
2. Baffling and confusing keywords.
3. Bizarre syntax.
4. Frustration due to hours of coding only to find it won't run.

Here's what you will find:

1. Ways to greatly extend the power of your software.
2. Things you only suspected your software could do.
3. Learning how you can make the computer program itself.
4. How to make yourself more effective on the job.

YOUR PROGRAM IS THE RIGHT ONE

The following sections of this chapter cover the Microsoft Office products Word, Excel, and Baler Software's Visual Baler. If you have these products you can follow along step-by-step with the instructions, but that's not necessary to learn from the following chapters.

All of the major Windows products mirror each other's capabilities. If, for example, you prefer to use Lotus' WordPro, Novell's Quattro Pro, and Borland's Paradox for Windows instead of the programs shown here, don't feel these chapters hold nothing for you. The specific ways to accomplish the ends shown here vary from program to program, but they all arrive at just about the same place.

Once you see how Excel handles keystroke macros, you can easily translate that knowledge into how you can do exactly the same thing in Quattro Pro or, for that matter, in Lotus 1-2-3 for Windows.

Think about the following chapters in car terms. If this book uses a Chevy as a demo car, surely the knowledge gained applies quite easily to Fords or Chryslers. Similarly, the demos using Word also transfer quite easily to WordPro or WordPerfect and other similar programs.

Something Different: Visual Baler

The easiest, and arguably the most powerful, tool for corporate number crunching is the spreadsheet. The personal computer and the automated spreadsheet have fundamentally changed modern business practice. First accountants, and then salespeople, and today almost everybody use spreadsheets for all sorts of tasks from budgeting to personnel management.

Not long after personal computers got spreadsheet programs to run, people began creating templates for them. A spreadsheet template is a formatted spreadsheet with blank cells available for variable entry. Figure 29.1 shows a very simple template for Gil's Sporting Goods chain.

Each week the branch store managers for the Gil's Sporting Goods stores fill out a sales report based on the Excel template. After it is filled out, the spreadsheet looks like Figure 29.2.

After filling out the template, the store managers save it with a unique name and send it to Gil's headquarters where it and other branch reports are collated into a corporate report. This system has been working well, but needs each branch of Gil's to have a working copy of Excel.

Gil's controller wants to expand a modified version of the system to his traveling sales reps for their daily reports, but doesn't want to buy an Excel license for each of the representatives, nor does he want to buy Excel-capable laptops for these field reps.

FIGURE 29.1.

A simple spreadsheet template.

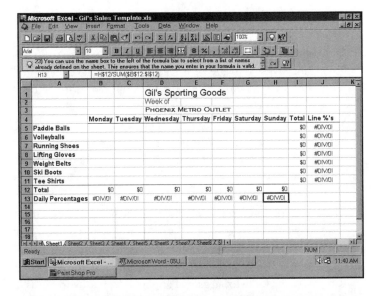

FIGURE 29.2.

The filled-out template.

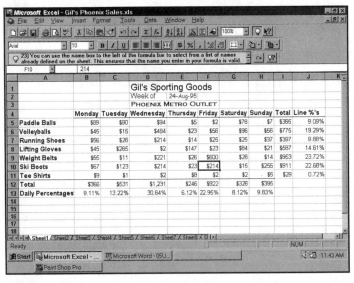

One solution is to use a product called Visual Baler. This product takes a spreadsheet like the one shown in Figure 29.1 and turns it into a Windows executable file. One copy of Visual Baler can make an infinite number of applications, none of which require further license fees. Also, the resource requirements for a Visual Baler-made program are a fraction of what's needed to run Windows 95 and Excel well.

The following are the steps to making a Windows 95 executable file using Visual Baler:

1. Make the application using a spreadsheet or Visual Baler itself.

2. If you used a nonstandard (by Baler definition) program you'll have to translate into the .WK3 or .WK1 format used by Lotus products. The Baler programs were initially designed for Lotus 1-2-3 spreadsheets and require this file format.

3. Make a help file if you want a help facility with your program.

4. Fire up Visual Baler if necessary.

5. Set security and lock number.

6. Direct Visual Baler what range to use for the program.

7. Give Visual Baler the go-ahead to make the program.

8. Test and debug the program.

As with so many visual tools, this is easier to do than to imagine from reading a list. The following demonstration shows what it takes to move Gil's filled template, an Excel-only application, to a Windows executable file that's fully distributable without further fees.

Visual Baler in Action

To show how Visual Baler might help you in your business, the following example shows how the controller of Gil's can convert the Excel spreadsheet into a stand-alone Windows 95 application for his sales force to use in the field.

Figure 29.3 shows the exportation of the Excel spreadsheet to a Lotus 1-2-3 .WK1 file format so Visual Baler can read it. Visual Baler is a fairly full-featured spreadsheet itself, and as an option the controller could have reproduced the entire template in Visual Baler.

FIGURE 29.3.

Exporting an Excel spreadsheet.

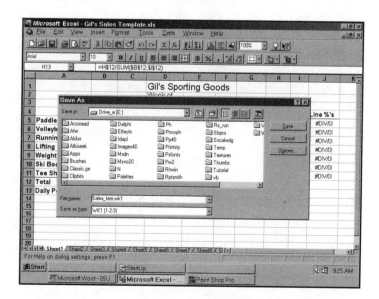

748

Figure 29.4 shows the same spreadsheet template opened in Visual Baler.

FIGURE 29.4.

The template opened in Visual Baler.

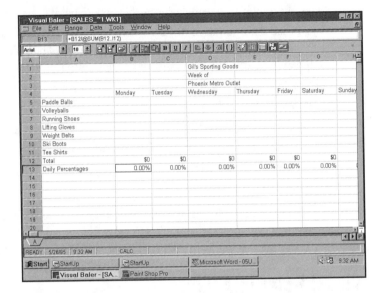

Take a look at the formula bar in Visual Baler. The Excel export routine has converted Excel's functions to Lotus 1-2-3 ones. Also, the file has lost much of its formatting during the conversion procedure.

BALING FROM SCRATCH

If you are creating a new application using Visual Baler, you're probably better off creating the application directly in Baler rather than doing it in Excel and then exporting it. This way you can be sure you won't create something in Excel that's unsupported in Baler.

The only reasons to use Excel and export are if you have an existing template you want to use or feel uncomfortable with the formulas Lotus 1-2-3 and Visual Baler use.

One of the most important aspects of a template is preventing your users from changing cells that must remain standard. At this point the entire worksheet has write protection; that is, when the worksheet is converted to a program, none of the cells will accept editing. There are some cells that need to be user editable, however. To remove the protection from those cells, first highlight their area (or range) and then remove protection, as shown in Figure 29.5.

FIGURE 29.5.

Removing write protection from a cell range.

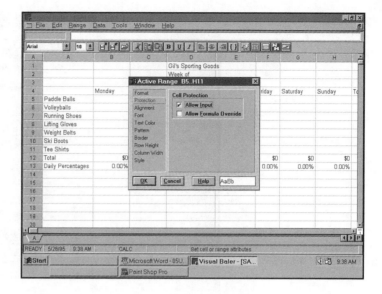

Visual Baler gives you a veritable blizzard of options. You can, among other things, do the following:

- Show only a part of your worksheet
- Hide or expose formulas
- Set cell and range characteristics
- Suppress or show zeros
- Password-protect your work
- Set startup defaults
- Show or hide the grid
- Name the tabs
- Set cell colors and patterns

Figure 29.6 shows the same template, but with its tab already named and some formatting added back to the label cells.

The next step, assuming you don't want to add any more fancy formatting, is to bind the built-in security to the spreadsheet. This is as simple as making the menu selections, Tools | Security, or right-clicking the caption bar and then filling in the dialog box. Figure 29.7 shows this step.

FIGURE 29.6.

Formatting in Visual Baler.

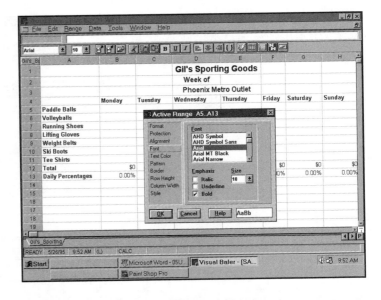

FIGURE 29.7.

Binding the spreadsheet.

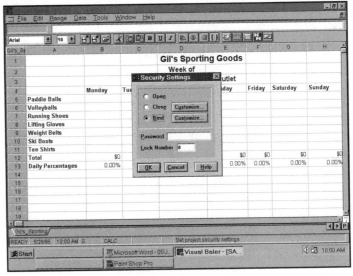

You must go through the binding step even if you don't want to set any specific security measures. Figure 29.7 doesn't set either a password or a lock number to this template, but still needs to go through the binding step.

The last pre-Bale step this demonstration will take is the optional setting of the Viewport. This is the area or range of the spreadsheet users will be able to see. Figure 29.8 shows how this option is set using the Tools | Workbook | Viewport menu selections.

FIGURE 29.8.

Setting the view range.

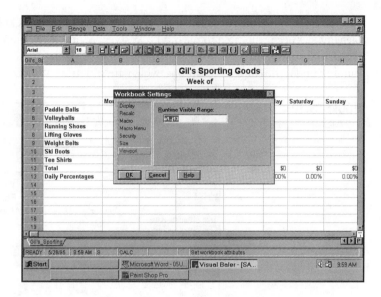

The only thing left to do is to tell Visual Baler to generate the program. Do this by choosing Tools | Bale from the menu. This will bring up a multipart dialog box, as shown in Figure 29.9.

FIGURE 29.9.

Visual Baler's compile dialog box.

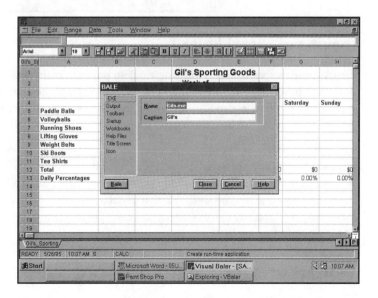

Figure 29.10 shows the compiled application running on one of Gil's laptops. Note that the filename has been truncated to the old DOS style because the version of Visual Baler used for this demonstration isn't enabled for Windows 95's long filenames (LFN). Also, this demo is running under the company's laptops, which are still using Windows 3.11.

FIGURE 29.10.

The finished, fully compiled template running on a laptop.

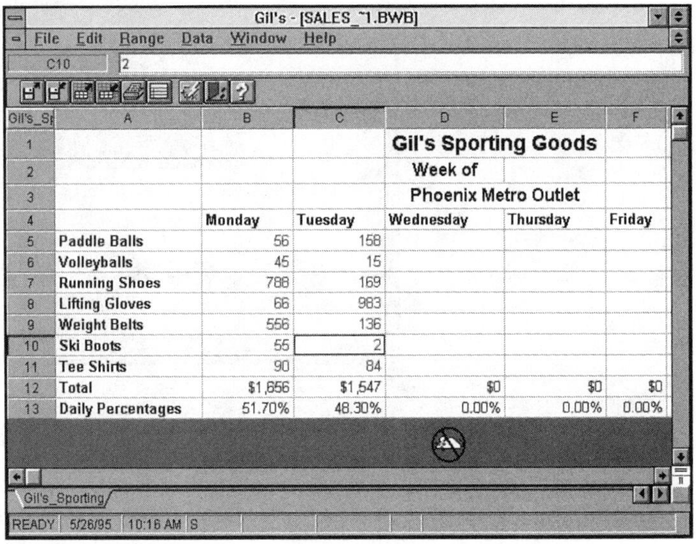

Looking at Visual Baler

Programming a spreadsheet is the easiest way to program many financial and numeric applications. The problem with distributing such programs is that the user needs to own a copy of the spreadsheet to run these applications. This can be costly, especially if the user doesn't need a general-purpose spreadsheet for regular use.

Visual Baler addresses not only this issue, but the growing resource requirements demanded by modern full-purpose spreadsheets. Using Visual Baler, it's only a matter of seconds before you turn a *dumb* template into a fully compiled, stand-alone application. Also, Visual Baler has several runtime options available that regular spreadsheet programs do not. These view, formatting, and security options might make the difference between distributing your applications in comfort or not.

Word Processors: Microsoft Word

The following short section shows some of the more useful, but less well-known, capabilities of word processors. Although the example uses Microsoft Word version 6 as the illustrated program, other major Windows word processors such as WordPerfect or WordPro have similar capabilities.

Simple Macros

Many programs can record keystrokes for later playback. This is a handy feature for automating repetitive operations. Here's how you can automate the creation of a simple memo header without any programming at all. You can use this technique to automate other undertakings. If you have Word for Windows 6 you can follow along step-by-step. If you have another word processor you can also probably follow along well enough from the text, although the screens you see will differ from the ones shown.

Starting a Macro

The trick to creating no-programming automator macros is to tell Word to remember your keystrokes for later playback. The following are the steps you take to create a playback macro:

1. Choose Tools | Macro from the menu.
2. Fill out the dialog boxes and name the macro.
3. Click OK to start the macro recorder.
4. Create your macro by doing the keystrokes.
5. Click the Stop button to end the recorder.
6. Edit the macro (optional).

To start this process, choose the menu choices, Tools | Macro. Word will respond with the dialog box shown in Figure 29.11.

FIGURE 29.11.

The Macro dialog box.

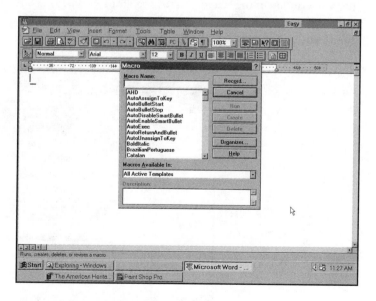

Each macro needs a name. This example will use the name SimpleMemo, as shown in Figure 29.12.

FIGURE 29.12.

Giving the macro a name.

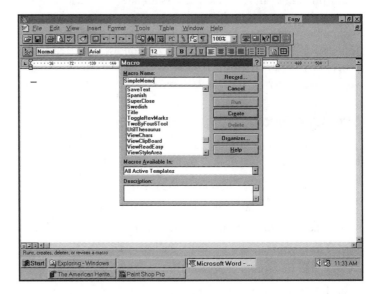

Click Record to tell Word you want it to go into keystroke record mode. Word will respond with another dialog box, as shown in Figure 29.13. At this point, you have the chance also to give a description of the macro, but to assign it to a keystroke combination, a menu choice, or a toolbar button. This example doesn't assign a macro to any of these, but later on you'll see how to do the toolbar assignment step manually.

FIGURE 29.13.

The assignment dialog box.

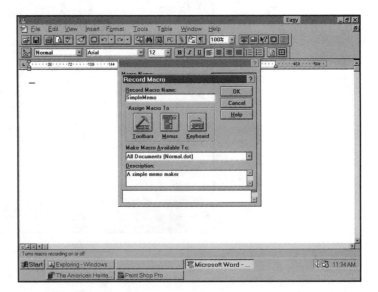

After clicking the OK button in the dialog box shown in Figure 29.13, Word's macro recorder will drop into the background. The two visual hints you have that the recorder is going are the cassette tape-like icon attached to the mouse cursor and the tiny toolbar with a stop and a pause button.

Enter the keystrokes you want recorded and click the Stop button after you're finished. Figure 29.14 shows the results of typing in the two memo header lines the user wants the macro to be able to play back.

FIGURE 29.14.

The memo header.

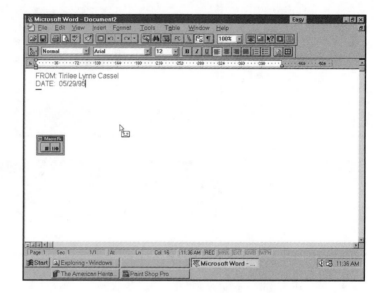

Note that the user didn't type the date, but instead chose the menu selections Insert | Field | Date so this macro will insert the current system date in subsequent memos.

That's it. To play back this macro, all you need to do is choose the menu selections Tools | Macro, and then locate the SimpleMemo macro and click the Run button. The macro run dialog is shown in Figure 29.15.

If you want to edit the macro, or just see what Word recorded, click the Edit button in the dialog box shown in Figure 29.15. Word will then reveal the code behind the recorded macro, as shown in Figure 29.16.

The edit macro window seen in Figure 29.16 is where you can correct faulty macros (such as a misspelling) or add custom features.

FIGURE 29.15.

Running the macro.

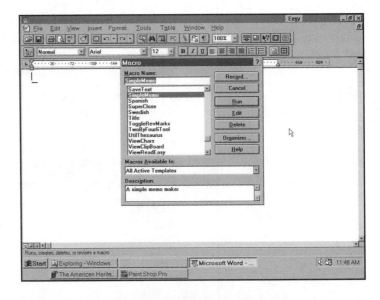

FIGURE 29.16.

The code behind the macro.

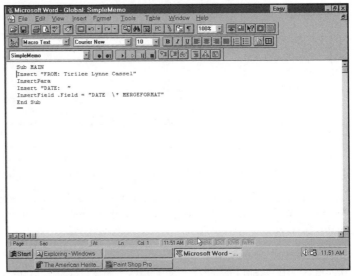

Changing Your Profile

The macro as shown in the previous section plays back all right, but the date comes out in the rather informal dd/mm/yy format. Word will use the date format as specified in the Winword6.ini file unless overridden by the `SetPrivateProfileString` function. If there is no DateFormat entry in the .ini file, Word will default to the short date format, as shown in the SimpleMemo example.

To change the way Word displays dates, change or add the DateFormat line to Winword6.ini, as shown in Figure 29.17.

FIGURE 29.17.

Changing the profile string in Winword6.ini.

After making the changes to DateFormat, Word will insert the data fields in the more acceptable mmmm d, yyyy format from now on. Figure 29.18 shows the same macro after being played back, but with the DateFormat change from Figure 29.17 done in this computer's Winword6.ini.

FIGURE 29.18.

The effect of changing the DateFormat entry.

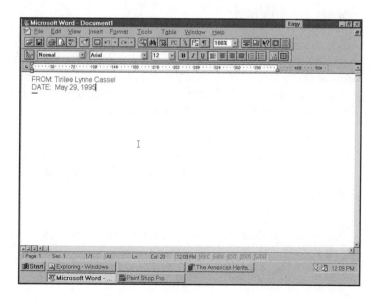

CHANGING ON THE FLY—AN ADVANCED TOPIC

If you want to change your DateFormat profile during a Word session, you'll have to use the `SetPrivateProfileString` function. The template for doing this is

```
...
SetPrivateProfileString "Microsoft Word", "DateFormat", \
"MMMM D, YYYY", "Winword6.ini"
...
```

Note the ellipsis before and after the code fragment mean that this code has been snipped from a larger code block.

This will set the DateFormat to the MMMM D, YYYY format. Insert whatever format you want for this string. The backslash (\) tells Word that the line is continued on the next line. Usually, a line break will signal the end of a command.

If you want to preserve the default `PrivateProfileString` so you can return to it later, use the `GetPrivateProfileString` function like this,

```
...
MyFormat$ = GetPrivateProfileString "Microsoft Word", "DateFormat", \
"Winword6.ini"
...
```

and return to it with the following line:

```
...
SetPrivateProfileString "Microsoft Word", "DateFormat", \
MyFormat$, "Winword6.ini"
...
```

Forms and Word

When most people think of forms, they usually think of paper forms such as insurance applications, or electronic forms such as those used by database programs like Access. Less well-known is Word's rather robust forms capacity. You can use Word's forms facility to create boilerplate documents or to take information, just like you would use a paper form. The steps to create a form with fields vary, but the following is one approach:

1. Create a boilerplate text.
2. Choose the menu Insert | Form Field | Show Toolbar to bring up the form toolbar. Alternatively, you can right-click any toolbar and choose the Forms entry.
3. Insert the fields.
4. Add entries to the fields if necessary.
5. Protect the form that starts it running and functioning as a form.

The following example is admittedly rather silly, but it will give you an idea of what a word processor form is and what it can do.

Making the Form

Figure 29.19 shows the memo from the earlier example with a recipient and some boilerplate text added. The user has also right-clicked a toolbar and selected the Forms toolbar shown floating in the middle of the document.

FIGURE 29.19.

Boilerplate text and the Forms toolbar.

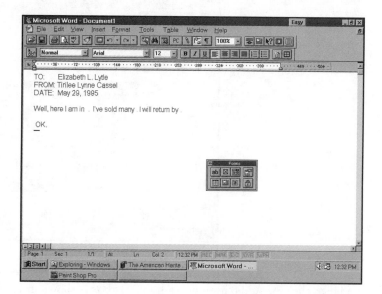

To insert a drop-down box, or combo box, click where you want to insert the box, and then click the combo box button in the Forms toolbar. Figure 29.20 shows the first combo box inserted in memo form.

FIGURE 29.20.

Inserting a combo box.

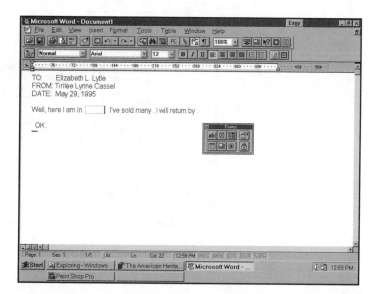

To add selections to this combo box, double-click it. This will bring up the dialog shown in Figure 29.21.

FIGURE 29.21.

The adding choices dialog box.

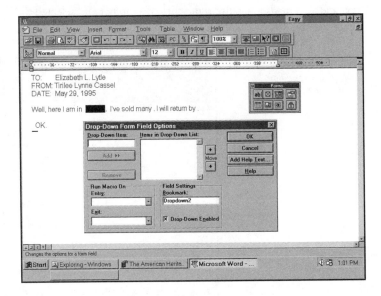

To add choices to the pull-down list, add the entries in the text box in the upper-left corner, and then click the Add button beneath the text box as shown in Figure 29.22.

FIGURE 29.22.

Adding entries to a combo box.

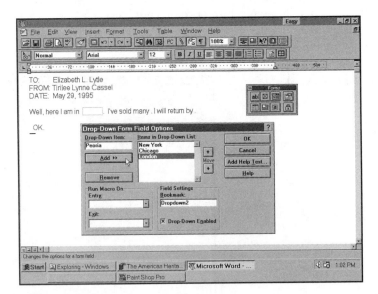

Figure 29.23 shows several other combo boxes added to this form using the same method as shown in Figures 29.20 through 29.22.

FIGURE 29.23.

The form with all combo boxes.

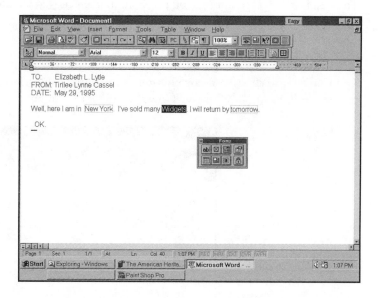

The last form item to add is a checkbox Elizabeth can check upon receipt of this memo. Adding a checkbox is the same as adding other form objects. Figure 29.24 shows Tirilee adding a checkbox to her form.

FIGURE 29.24.

Adding a checkbox to the form.

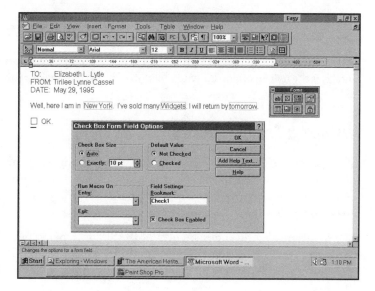

Note that there are many options to a checkbox, as shown in the dialog box. The most interesting option is the capability to trigger the running of a macro when the checkbox is clicked. This is quite handy if your form requires a conditionally triggered subform. That's it. The form is finished.

Running Forms

To run the form, click the Protect button in the Forms toolbar. That's the button with the padlock on it. Figure 29.25 shows Tirilee's memo form running.

FIGURE 29.25.

Running the memo form.

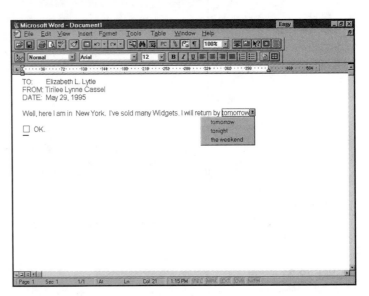

When the cursor is in the field with the pull-down box, Word shows that this is a combo box, and gives the user an opportunity to pull down the list and make a choice from it. The checkbox works just like any Windows 95 checkbox.

Writing a Custom WordBASIC Routine

To write custom WordBASIC routines, about the only things you need to know are what functions you have available to you and their proper syntax. You can also use WordBASIC to call on the Windows API (Applications Programming Interface), which makes any and all of the power of Windows itself available to you.

You can learn what functions are in WordBASIC by looking in the online help text or purchasing a manual such as Microsoft's Word Developer's Kit. Two of the following examples show how to make a custom program using WordBASIC functions. The third example shows how to use the Windows API to make a custom program. To get to the macro edit screens shown in the following three examples, choose the menu selections Tools | Macro, and then give the macro a name and click the Create button.

Figure 29.26 shows a macro that will cut the current sentence to the clipboard.

FIGURE 29.26.

A custom macro.

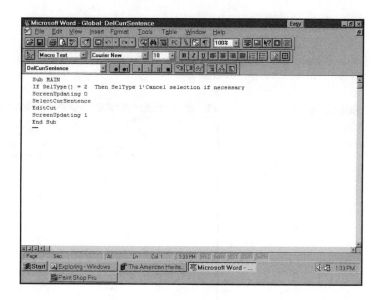

The operation of the macro is self-explanatory. However, in order to operate the macro, you need to know about the EditCut and SelectCurSentence functions built into Word. The two ScreenUpdating functions just prevent some "flash and boom" when the macro runs, and aren't part of the macro's function.

Essentially, this macro does the following:

1. Cleans up the insertion point choice.
2. Stops screen updating.
3. Selects the current sentence.
4. Cuts the selection to the clipboard.
5. Resumes screen updating.

The user has assigned this macro to the keyboard selection Ctrl+S. Whenever the user of this copy of Word presses Ctrl+S, the current sentence is cut to the clipboard.

Old WordStar hands might miss the old Ctrl sequences. The user of this copy of Word is one of them. The following code shows a macro that will delete one word to the right of the cursor:

```
Sub MAIN
DeleteWord
End Sub
```

Assign this macro to the key sequence Ctrl+T and every time the user presses Ctrl+T, Word will cut the word to the right of the cursor. Assigning a macro to a key sequence is as easy as choosing the menu selections Tools | Customize, and then clicking the Keyboard tab and filling in the dialog. Programming can be quite easy when you know what the keywords and tricks are.

Figure 29.27 shows a rather complex macro that will call upon the Windows API to change the text of the title bar in Word. This is a complex macro because it first registers some functions in the USER library (part of the Windows operating system) for its own use, and then calls on those functions to do the work.

FIGURE 29.27.

Calling on the Windows API.

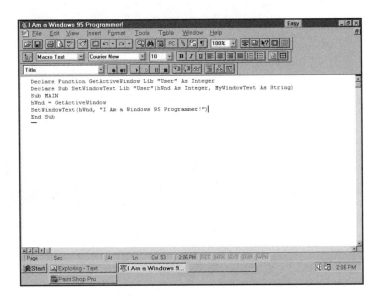

When run, this macro changes the title bar of Word to read I am a Windows 95 Programmer! Like the SetPrivateProfileString function illustrated earlier, you might want to preserve as a variable the current title bar text before running a macro like this so you can restore it.

Don't be discouraged if the macro in Figure 29.27 isn't perfectly clear to you. This book hasn't taken the time to fully explain all that's behind it. If you wish to pursue Windows programming in WordBASIC, there are many good books covering the topic in depth.

Assigning Macros to a Toolbar Button

Up to now in this chapter, the only way to play back a macro was to either use a keystroke sequence, such as Ctrl+T, or to go through the tedious menu and dialog box selection routine.

You can easily assign a macro to a toolbar button for macros that you want to be readily on hand. To do this, do the following:

1. Choose Tools | Customize from the menu.
2. Click the Toolbar tab.
3. Tell Word you want to assign a macro to a toolbar.
4. Choose one of the macros.
5. Bind the macro to a button by dragging the macro name to the toolbar.
6. Assign an icon to the new button.

Again, this is much easier to do than to imagine. The next example assigns a macro called SimpleMemo to a button on the standard Word toolbar.

If you don't have a macro named SimpleMemo, and want to follow along, you can create a short macro yourself or use one of the sample ones Microsoft bundled with Word and substitute either for the macro shown.

Choose Tools | Customize from the menu. Click the Toolbar tab. Scroll down the list on the left until you have Macro highlighted. Scroll down the list on the right until you find the SimpleMemo macro that you did in the first exercise in the Word section. Figure 29.28 shows this.

FIGURE 29.28.

Selecting a macro.

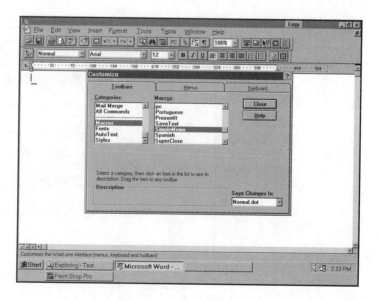

Drag the SimpleMacro macro name to any toolbar. When you release the cursor, Word changes the dialog box to one with a button selection, as shown in Figure 29.29.

FIGURE 29.29.

Dragging the macro to the toolbar.

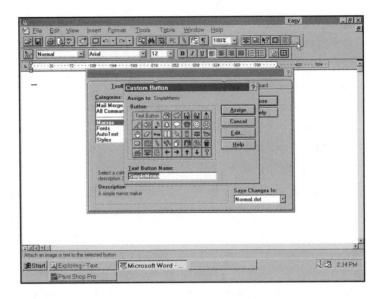

This example uses the happy face as a button face. Click that and click the Close button. Word assigns the happy face icon to the SimpleMemo toolbar button. Figure 29.30 shows the operation just before closing the dialog box.

FIGURE 29.30.

Finishing up the new toolbar button.

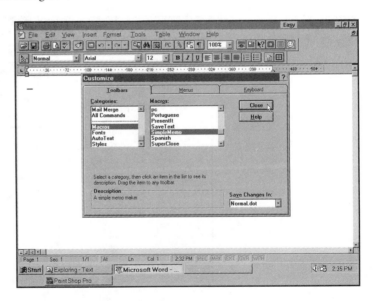

Now, whenever the user clicks the happy face button in the standard toolbar, the SimpleMemo macro will run.

Word Programming

There are hundreds of little things such as the SimpleMemo macro or the one to delete the word to the right of the cursor that can make your life with your word processor much easier. Similarly, there are functions such as form making, list sorting, and simple math that your word processor can do, but that you might not be aware of.

Although using WordBASIC to call on the Windows API is more than most people care to tackle, there are many keystroke recording tasks or simple custom programs you can make that are easily within the scope of even those who adamantly don't want to program. The trick to programming in WordBASIC is to know what's there. Once you know that the keyword `DeleteWord` will delete the word to the right of the cursor, making the macro is as easy as entering that one word to Word's predefined macro structure.

Very little learning effort on your part can reap enormous rewards by enabling you to customize your word processor to be just what you want it to be.

Spreadsheets: Microsoft Excel

This section, like the preceding one, is a very short glance at some of the less often-used, but simple to implement and quite useful aspects of spreadsheets. The examples use Microsoft Excel Version 5, but the same facilities exist in other Windows spreadsheets.

Subtotaling, Filtering, and Forms

Look at Figure 29.31. This is a fragment of a fictional salary worksheet used for budgeting in a large corporation.

FIGURE 29.31.

A salary worksheet.

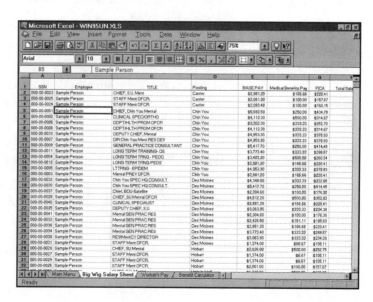

There's nothing wrong with this worksheet other than it's a little hard to get information about specific postings or departments. You could use the SUMIF() function and supply different criteria to, say, learn about the totals for each posting, but that would be tedious and you'd only see the results for one posting at a time.

Subtotals

Excel and other spreadsheets have an easy subtotal facility. In Excel, adding subtotals is as easy as

1. Either creating a name range for the data you want to subtotal or highlighting it by dragging the mouse.
2. Sorting the range on the fields for which you want subtotals.
3. Choosing the menu selections Data | Subtotals.
4. Filling in the form.

> **NOTE**
>
> The salary worksheet has the entire salary range named Database. The full name of this range is Big Wig Salary Sheet!Database. The first part of the name refers to the title of the worksheet (on the tab), and the second part refers to the user-given name. The name Database has special meaning to Excel for data entry forms.
>
> You can't have more than one range with the same whole name in any workbook, but you can have more than one range with the same partial name. Therefore, you can't have more than one range named just Database, but you can have one range named Big Wig Salary!Database and another named Workers!Database.

To enter subtotals into this salary worksheet, just choose the menu selections Data | Subtotals. Excel will return with a dialog box shown in Figure 29.32.

This application requires subtotaling on each posting, or department, with a sum for each. The dialog box reflects this. After you click the OK button in the Subtotals dialog box, Excel rearranges the spreadsheet. You can see the results of the subtotals command in Figure 29.33.

> **NOTE**
>
> Be sure to sort your range on the field you want to subtotal before activating the subtotals dialog box. Look at Figure 29.32 carefully and note that Excel will add a subtotal at each change of the Posting field. If this list wasn't sorted first on Posting, Excel would generate many spurious subtotals, one for each change in Posting.

FIGURE 29.32.

The Subtotal dialog box.

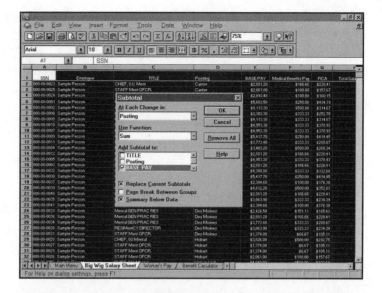

FIGURE 29.33.

The subtotaled spreadsheet.

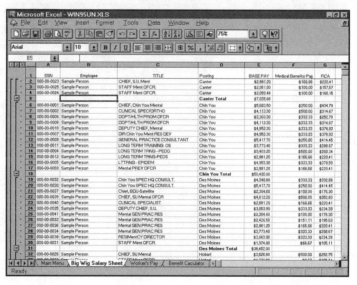

The result of the subtotal command is an improvement. A manager can see at a glance the totals for each Posting, or department, for this company. Still, a manager must scroll through the subtotaled list in this worksheet until he finds the Posting in which he's interested. There must be a better way.

> **NOTE**
>
> You can have more than one subtotal for a range. For example, you could add a count subtotal to the sum one shown in Figure 29.33. When adding additional subtotals, make sure you uncheck the Replace Current Subtotals checkbox in the Subtotals dialog box.

Filters

Filters only pass specified information. Think of them as a strainer or sieve that will only allow particles of a certain size through. The salary sheet used in this example now shows all postings. It would be useful if it could use a filter to specify only one posting at a time.

To add such a filter, choose the menu choices Data | Filter | AutoFilter. Excel will add pull-down, or combo boxes, to the top row of the Database named range, as shown in Figure 29.34.

FIGURE 29.34.

Adding a filter.

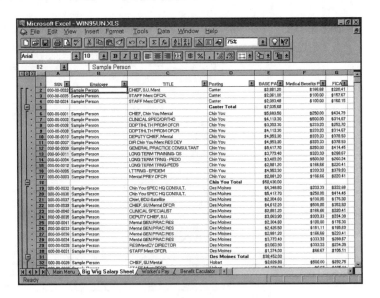

Now all a manager has to do to restrict the display to one or more filter criteria is to pull down a combo box and make a choice, as shown in Figure 29.35 and Figure 29.36.

This particular example added a filter, so now it shows only those employees posted at the Ship Wreck Posting. Removing a filter is as easy as pulling down the combo box and choosing All from the list. You can also add more than one filter to a spreadsheet. If you wanted to see only those employees of a certain title at a particular posting, you would need to make two choices, one from two pull-down lists.

FIGURE 29.35.

Choosing a criteria.

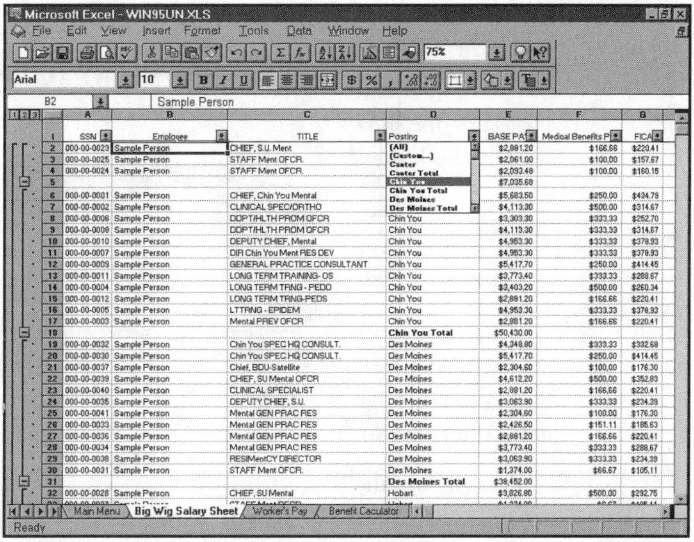

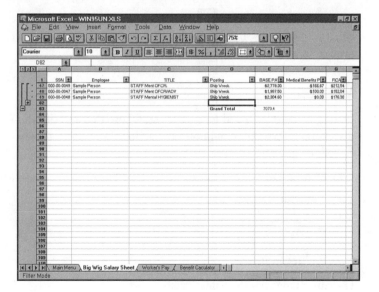

FIGURE 29.36.

The results of adding a filter criteria.

Forms

Many people prefer entering data using a form rather than the standard spreadsheet grid. To do this in Excel after you've named a range database, choose Data | Form from the menu. Figure 29.37 shows the results of this menu choice.

FIGURE 29.37.

A data form.

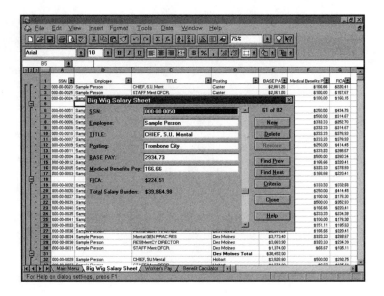

The same data form is useful for finding a particular record. All you do is enter the field on which you want to search, and then enter a criteria in the Criteria text box. Next, tell Excel to go ahead and find your record.

Macros

Excel can record keyboard macros. If you followed along with the Word example in the previous section, you pretty well know how to do this. Making a keyboard macro in Excel requires the following steps:

1. Choose Tools | Record Macro | Record New Macro from the menu.
2. Name the macro.
3. Add a description (optional).
4. Record the macro.
5. End recording.

The entire range has the name Database.

The next example creates a macro that will change the view from a spreadsheet to a form. Choose the menu selections Tools | Record Macro | Record New Macro and fill in the dialog box as shown in Figure 29.38.

Click OK and Excel will return to normal except for a small toolbar with a VCR-style stop button on it. Click the menu choices Data | Form to bring up the form. Click Close to close the form view, and then click the VCR stop button in the floating toolbar.

FIGURE 29.38.

The Record Macro dialog box.

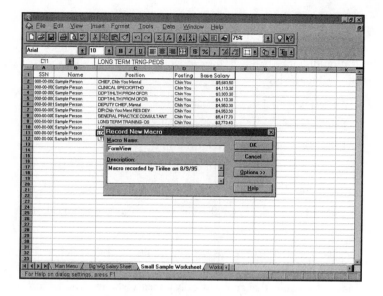

That's it. You've recorded an Excel macro. To play it back, choose the menu selections Tools | Macro, and then find your macro, click it, and click the Run button.

Unfortunately, that's more effort than just clicking the Data | Form menu choices, but there's more coming. Also, remember that this macro is a very short one. In practice, there's no limit to how long your keyboard macros can be. If you want to see your macro, scroll to the last worksheet in your workbook. It will be called Module 1 unless you have other modules already created for the current workbook. Click the tab and see how Excel recorded your macro. Figure 29.39 shows this example's Module 1 worksheet.

FIGURE 29.39.

An Excel module.

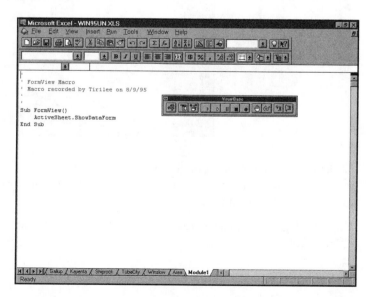

Adding a Macro Button

This macro isn't terribly handy because you have to navigate a forest of menu choices to get to it. Wouldn't it be handy if, instead, you could call up your macros at the push of a button? You can, and here's how.

1. Activate the Drawing toolbar.
2. Click the command button toolbar button.
3. Draw your command button on the worksheet.
4. Fill in the Assign Macro dialog box.
5. Change the caption of the command button (optional).

As usual, this is easier to see than imagine. Watch or follow along as the FormView macro gets its own command button.

First, you need to activate the Drawing toolbar by right-clicking a toolbar and choosing it. Figure 29.40 shows the activated Forms toolbar, the newly added command button, and the Assign Macro dialog box that automatically appears when you add a command button to a worksheet.

FIGURE 29.40.

Adding a command button to a worksheet.

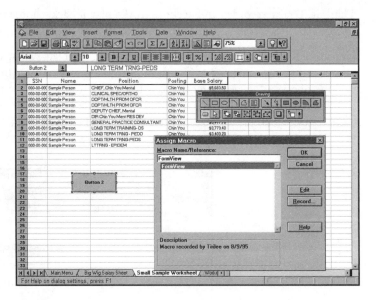

Click the selection tool in the toolbar. Click the button, which will cause the button's caption to enter edit mode. Change the caption to Form View. Click the selection button in the Forms toolbar to unselect it, and you're done.

Now, clicking the command button on this worksheet activates the FormView macro, as shown in Figure 29.41.

FIGURE 29.41.

The command button in action.

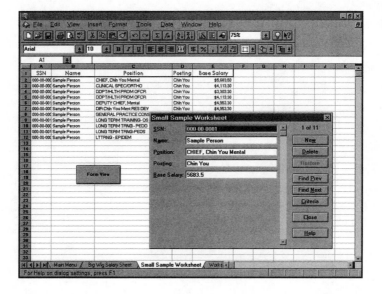

Looking at Excel

Most people use Excel and other modern Windows spreadsheets just like they did their old DOS counterparts such as Lotus 1-2-3 version 2.01. There's nothing wrong with this, but there are many more things today's spreadsheets can do to make your life easier.

This chapter didn't have the space to give Excel, or any other program, a good workout, but it did show you some of the more subtle things modern spreadsheets can do.

Programming Excel, like Word, can be utterly painless. Learning VBA, the command language of Excel, can be daunting, but anybody can create keystroke macros perfectly from the first try. Attaching these macros to command buttons, graphics, or toolbars is fairly straightforward. This chapter showed how simple this is with command buttons.

Summary

If this chapter has given you a taste for painless point-and-click programming, there are many books that go into this topic in greater detail. Given the vast amount you can accomplish with almost no effort, there's really no reason to avoid pointing and clicking your way to programming success.

Visual Basic the Easy Way

by Paul Cassel

30

Pointing and Clicking

Creating your own programs from scratch is the height of computer power. If you can do this, there's no limit to what you can harness your computer to do for you and your business. To put it another way, programming is the brass ring on the computer merry-go-round. Today's programming techniques are a far cry from the grunt labor of just a few years ago. What once took years to learn and misery to implement is easily within reach of all who choose to try.

The Old Way

Traditional programming is a laborious, and to many, tedious, process. Here are the steps involved:

1. Enter source code by hand in a somewhat English-like language. The amount of detail you need to enter depends on the language and the operating system. Essentially, the more power your language has over your computer, the more laborious your job. The following lines are a tiny fragment from a program written in C++. Every word and every sign, including punctuation, must be exact for this program to work.

```
#include "hostenv.h"
#include "cenumpt.h"


CEnumPoint::CEnumPoint()
{
    m_refs = 0;

    m_psa = NULL;
    m_celts = 0;
    m_iCurrent = 0;
}
```

2. Compile your program. This means running your code through a translating program to change the English-like statements into a code that tells the computer how to operate. Often, this won't go smoothly due to typos or other source code errors, and you'll have to edit your original source to make it work.

3. Link your program. *Linking* is combining your source code with standard routines called libraries. Again, this usually won't go smoothly and you'll have to edit and debug to get your link.

4. Test, debug, test, debug, and test again. Even a program that compiles and links perfectly can have logic bugs that will trip up users down the line. Debugging often takes longer than creation.

Different programming languages have different steps, but the preceding steps give you the general idea. If it looks difficult, it is. It is so difficult and tedious that few enjoy traditional programming.

That routine was bad enough in DOS. Add the complexity of Windows, and even hardened programmers have opted for retirement rather than make the transition. Fortunately, as Windows has developed over the years, so have the tools used to create programs. In the last couple of years a whole new way to program a computer has emerged. Creating Windows programs is now actually easier than creating programs for DOS. It is so easy and fun that just about anybody can do it. This new way of programming is what this chapter is all about.

The New Visual Basic Way

Visual programming is an amazingly enjoyable way to use your computer. The steps to creating a computer program using the visual, or point-and-click, method are

1. Decide what you want.
2. Design your screens using point and click. This is similar to painting with a program like PaintBrush.
3. Set the properties, such as color, for the different parts of your screens.
4. Tell the program how to react to user actions.
5. Instruct Visual Basic to convert steps 1–4 into a Windows 95 program. This is as simple as making one menu selection.

That's it! It's every bit as painless as it seems. If you have Visual Basic, you might enjoy working along with the examples that come after the short introduction that follows this section. Even if you don't have Visual Basic, you should have no trouble following and even understanding the steps shown.

Introducing Visual Basic

As tempting as it is to just leap into the first Visual Basic program, it's a good idea to pause for a few moments to learn about the Visual Basic environment and to get acquainted with a little jargon.

> **NOTE**
>
> Every specialty has its load of jargon, but to many the specialized words computer folk use is especially annoying. However, anything new needs a new set of nouns and verbs by virtue of being new. This isn't limited to computers.
>
> Consider this sentence: "I drove my automobile down the interstate and got off at the Peoria cloverleaf." What would a nineteenth-century person make of that? He'd understand something about Peoria, but *automobile*, *interstate*, and this use of *cloverleaf*? Even the word *drove* might to him imply something like driving cattle.
>
> Just as the automobile forced some new jargon on us, so too does the computer.

The Visual Basic Environment

Figure 30.1 shows the Visual Basic environment's four most important parts.

FIGURE 30.1.

The Visual Basic environment.

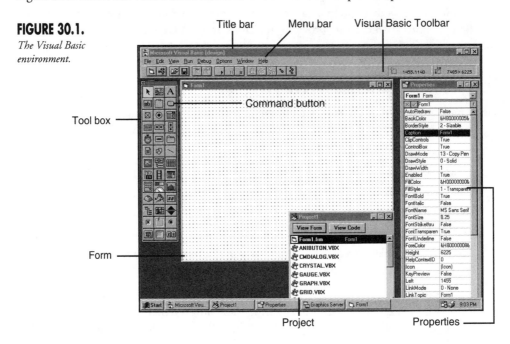

The rectangle with all the buttons on the far left of Figure 30.1 is the toolbox. Each button in the toolbox represents one type of tool you can use to build your program.

The rectangle in the middle of the screen, the one that has Form1 in the title bar, is a blank form where you place controls using the tools from the toolbox. Think of the form as the canvas where you will use tools to paint your program. When your program is run, forms are windows the user sees. Controls are things like textboxes, buttons, radio buttons, and all the other screen elements you have become familiar with when using Windows.

The rectangle on the far right of Figure 30.1 is the Properties list box. Controls and forms in a Visual Basic program have properties, such as color, that you can set during the design of a program or, in some cases, that can change in response to conditions while the program runs.

The floating bars at the top of the screen are the familiar Microsoft Windows three bars. At the top is the title bar, which gives information about the document (or project, in the case of Visual Basic) and the program. Second is the menubar with the usual array of pull-down and fly-out choices. The last bar is the general-purpose Visual Basic toolbar. Each of these three standard bars works the same in Visual Basic as in other Microsoft Windows programs.

Now for the Jargon

The following are terms used in Visual Basic and visual programming generally. If these are unfamiliar terms to you, don't try to memorize them. Look them over now to get a feel for what's here and then refer back to this list if you encounter one of these words later on in the chapter.

- **Control:** Textboxes, pushbuttons, labels, and other items on your form you use to display information to receive input from your users. The tools in the toolbox are called controls after you place them on a form.

- **Event:** An occurrence. Examples are a keypress, a mouse click, and data entry. Events can come from the user, the computer, or from other sections of the program, even other programs.

- **Event Handler:** How the program responds to an event. For example, say you can tell the program to change the color of a control when the user clicks a button. To rephrase in jargon, you've handled the click event of the button by changing the setting of a control's color property.

- **Properties:** Characteristics of controls. Each property has a setting. For example, the setting Blue for the property BackColor tells Visual Basic to set the background color of a control to blue.

Now that that's out of the way, the playing field is clear to move on to the first programming example.

Example One: A Simple Run Around the Bases

This first example is short and simple but demonstrates the essentials of programming in Visual Basic. It shows how to create a Visual Basic project, how to add controls to a form, and how to set control properties both at design time and as the program runs. The graphics and the program itself, both as a project and a ready-to-run program, are part of the sample data included with this book.

Designing the Form

This example has several graphics—a car, a question mark, and an airplane—designed ahead of time. If you're following along, you can either use the supplied bitmap images or design your own using PaintBrush or a similar program such as Paint Shop Pro, a shareware bitmap editor included on the CD-ROM that comes with this book.

This form will have three controls: a rectangle to display the images and two buttons to select which image to display in the rectangle. If you're following along, open Visual Basic, or if it's open, choose the menu choices File | New Project. Your screen will resemble Figure 30.2.

FIGURE 30.2.

A new project.

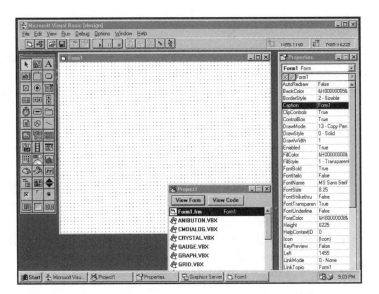

Locate the Command button tool in the toolbox, which is the button that looks like a standard pushbutton.

FIGURE 30.3.

The Command button.

Command button ——

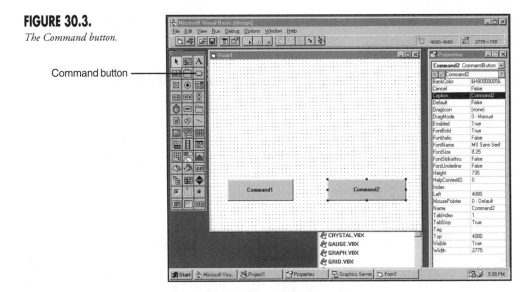

Click the Command button. Move your mouse to the bottom of the form, and click and drag to form a reasonably sized push button. Do this again, placing the second button alongside the first. Your screen should resemble Figure 30.4.

FIGURE 30.4.

Adding command buttons.

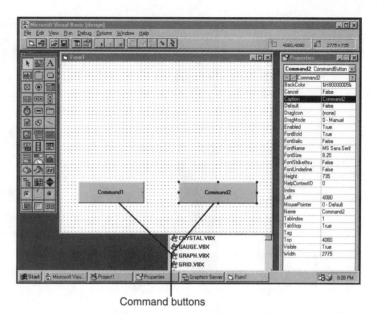

Command buttons

The last element or control for this application is a rectangle to display the various images, or bitmaps. There are several ways to display a bitmap in Visual Basic. This example will use a PictureBox control. This is the button in the toolbox with a little picture that looks like a scenery painting. Figure 30.5 shows the cursor over the PictureBox control.

FIGURE 30.5.

The PictureBox control.

PictureBox control ─

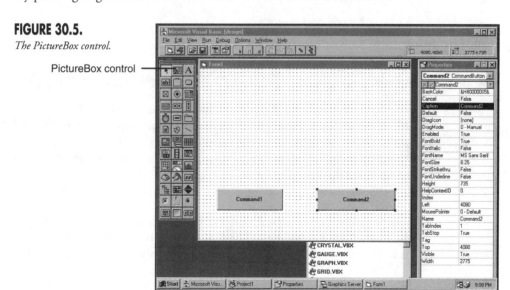

If you're following along, click the PictureBox control, move your cursor to the form, and click and drag a rectangle so your form looks similar to the one shown in Figure 30.6.

FIGURE 30.6.

The form with all controls.

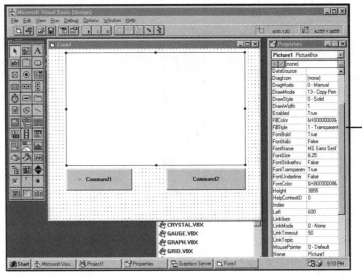

Properties ──────

Setting the Properties

Now that the form is completed, the next step is to set the design time properties for this program. The three properties to set are

- The caption for the title bar of the form
- The captions for the command buttons
- The initial picture for the PictureBox

> **TIP**
>
> In a more complex project, you would also assign your own names to the various controls rather than accept Visual Basic's default ones. When you have lots of forms and controls in a program, the default names can become confusing because of their similarity. Giving controls names of your own choosing enables you to give them names that remind you of their purpose.

You set properties at design time by changing entries in the Properties list box. If this list box is not already visible, make it so by pressing F4. The Properties list box is on the right in Figure 30.6. Clicking a control or the form itself invokes the list of the properties for that control or the overall form.

The PictureBox has the focus, or the highlight, in Figure 30.6; therefore, the Properties list box shows the properties for that control. Figure 30.7 is the same as Figure 30.6, but the programmer has clicked the left command button and the Properties list box now shows the properties associated with that control.

FIGURE 30.7.

The Properties for a command button.

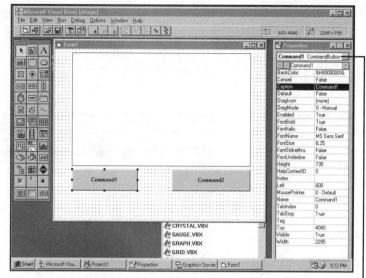

Properties of Command Button ——

After you click the control, move to the Properties list box, locate the property you want to set, and make the changes you wish. If you haven't already, click the command button on the left, locate the Caption property in the list box, and change it from Command1 to Car. In the same manner, click the right command button, locate the Caption property, and change that from Command2 to Plane. Figure 30.8 shows the program after the Caption property for the right button has been changed.

FIGURE 30.8.

Setting the properties.

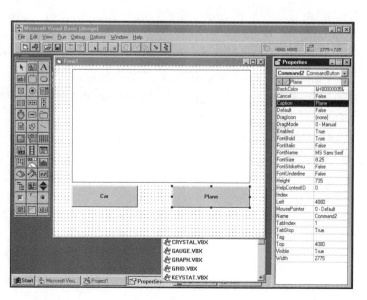

In a similar manner, click any blank spot in the form that is anywhere off a control to make the form have focus, and locate the Caption property and set it to read Picture Gallery—a rather grand name for this modest program.

Now for a slightly complex property setting. Click the PictureBox control and locate the Picture property. Figure 30.9 shows the Browse button.

FIGURE 30.9.

The browse button in the Properties list box.

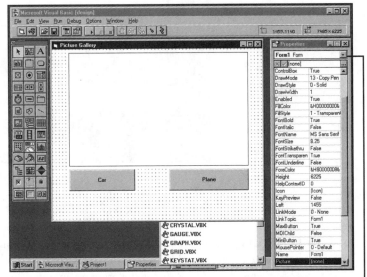

Browse Button

Click this button and you'll open a file browsing utility. Locate the file you want to set as the one initially displayed when this application launches. This example uses the file question.bmp, which is part of the sample data. Figure 30.10 shows the browse utility locating this file.

After finding the file you want, click the poorly named Open button and Windows 95 will insert this file in your Properties list box but will just call it a bitmap. If you use the sample data, your screen will resemble Figure 30.11.

That's it for setting design-time properties.

FIGURE 30.10.

Browsing for files in Windows 95.

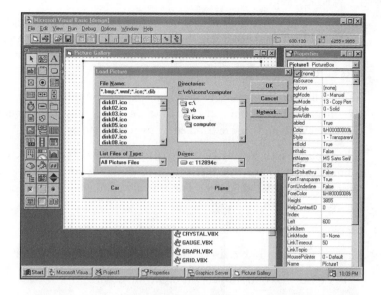

FIGURE 30.11.

The bitmap displayed as part of the application.

Writing the Event Handlers

Now you're at a part of writing a Visual Basic program that somewhat resembles computer programming. In Visual Basic, the only code you have to write is the instructions that the program should follow when an event occurs. The amount of code you need to supply will depend on the complexity of the action your program must perform.

Actually, if you've been following along with this example, you've been programming like crazy, but Visual Basic has been doing all the grunt work for you. Now it's time to dig in a little and hit the keyboard. This, for the simplified example at hand, will amount to adding two short lines of text.

This application is supposed to switch the picture from the question mark to the car when the user clicks the Car button, and switch to the plane when the Plane button is clicked. These clicks are events and they're handled by switching the picture.

When a button is clicked, that is the signal for Visual Basic to load a new picture in the PictureBox control. So you need a way to refer to the PictureBox control, the Picture property, and what setting the property should have. The general way you tell Visual Basic which property of which control you want it to change is

```
Control.Property = Property Setting
```

Here are the steps for creating a simple event handler for a control:

1. Locate the control where the event will occur.
2. Double-click it to change to the Code window.
3. Locate the particular event you want to handle.
4. Write the event handler.

This sounds much more complex than it really is. Taken one step at a time, you'll see how easy it really is.

First, create an event handler for the Car command button, the one on the left. First, locate this command button then double-click it. Your screen will resemble Figure 30.12.

FIGURE 30.12.

The Code window.

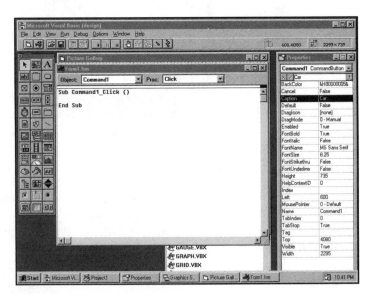

The click event is the event you want to handle for this button. It so happens that this is the event that's up when the button is double-clicked, so you're right where you need to be. If you wanted to set another event for this command button, you would pull down the combo box on the right in the Toolbar section of the Code window, locate the event in which you're interested, and click it.

In this case, you're all ready to go because you're at the click event by default. Enter

```
Picture1.Picture = LoadPicture ("f:\car.bmp")
```

between the two lines shown in Figure 30.12. Your screen should resemble Figure 30.13. This line tells Visual Basic to respond to a click on the Car command button by loading the car.bmp file (a picture) and placing it as the Picture property of the Picture1 control. Picture1 is the name Visual Basic assigned to the PictureBox when you added it to the form. You can optionally change control names to ones adhering to a naming convention of your own or a naming convention already in existence. In even slightly complex projects, it's a very good idea to name your controls according to an identifying convention.

FIGURE 30.13.

The event handler.

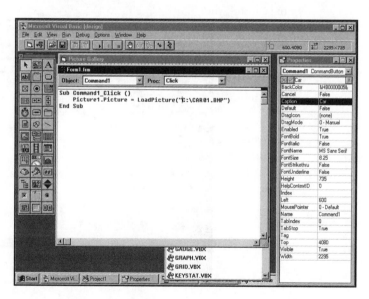

Naming Names

Naming conventions for visual programming usually rely on a two part scheme. The first part of an object's name is a mnemonic to describe the type of object being named and the second part its use. For example, most conventions prefix Text boxes 'txt'. So a Text box control that accepts input that will become the numerator of a fraction might have the convention name 'txtNumerator'. Similarly a command button (cmd) that exits a program will have the convention name 'cmdExit'.

Some projects will require longer or more complex naming conventions. One example is the multi-programmer project where a supervisor might want to include a programmer's signature on each object or variable. In a scheme such as this, a programmer named Tirilee Lynne Cassel might create a command button with an exit function and give it the name cmdTiriExit.

The visual programming field rages with debates about the pros and cons of different naming conventions and even approaches. You can find several white papers posted in the various online forums where authors promote their own schemes. Choose one or make your own. Make sure to be consistent throughout a project and you'll likely be all right.

Be sure to specify the correct path for whatever bitmap you use. This example has the bitmaps located on drive F: in the root directory. Yours will likely vary.

You could exit the Code window, double-click the Plane command button, and repeat the preceding steps to create an event handler for the Plane command button. However, there's a shortcut. Pull down the left combo box on the toolbar of the Code window, locate the control named Command2, and click it. Figure 30.14 shows this process.

FIGURE 30.14.

Navigating in the Code window.

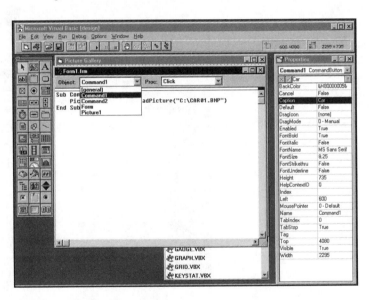

This brings up the click event for the second Command button, the one on the right. This button has the caption, or label, Plane, but its name is Command2—the one Visual Basic assigned it when you added it to the form. Again, it's a good idea to name your own controls rather than rely on Visual Basic to do so, but for the sake of simplicity, this example omits this step.

Add the line

```
Picture1.Picture = LoadPicture("f:\plane.bmp")
```

Again, make sure your path is right for your computer.

That finishes this project. At this point, it's a good idea to save your work in case something goes awry. Click the File menu in Visual Basic, locate the Save Project, click it, and give discrete names to both the form and the overall project. If you have the sample data, this project is called 30-1.mak.

Up and Running

To run your project, press F5 or choose the menu selections Run | Start. Your screen will resemble Figure 30.15.

FIGURE 30.15.

The finished project.

Now to test the program. Click the Car button. The image should switch to the car.bmp file, and your screen should look like Figure 30.16. For a final test, click the Plane button. Your screen should switch to look like Figure 30.17.

Click the stop button in the Visual Basic toolbar, the one that looks like a VCR stop button, when you want to halt the program. Alternatively, you can halt the program by clicking the Windows 95 X button at the extreme upper-right of the Picture Gallery form. If you've used Visual Basic to make this program, you can optionally compile it to an application you can distribute to users as a stand-alone application by choosing the menu options File | Make EXE File. Keep in mind that for this application to run correctly, it needs to be able to find the car.bmp and plane.bmp files in the root of drive F:. If you choose to compile, adjust your application accordingly.

FIGURE 30.16.
The car image.

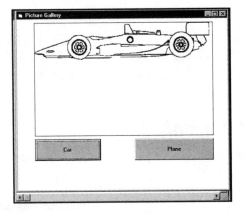

FIGURE 30.17.
The plane image loaded.

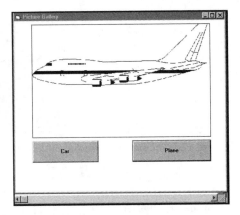

Logic and the Computer

Computers are logical devices. Programs follow logical courses or paths. The preceding application had no programmer-supplied logical choices. It loaded an image upon startup (question.bmp) and one of two other bitmaps as a response to a button click (plane.bmp or car.bmp).

Programs can branch, or seem to intelligently decide what to do in response to certain conditions. This is called *branching* because the entire logic path might seem complex, but each step remains, essentially, a choice of two outcomes.

Rather than step through another example, take a look at Figure 30.18, which shows a variation of the first project at design time.

FIGURE 30.18.

The switching project.

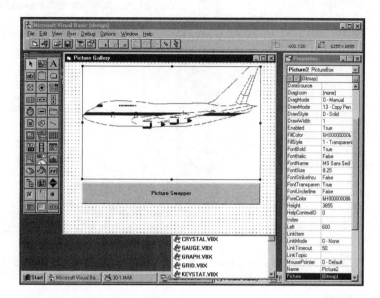

The differences between this project and the first, both of which you'll find as part of the sample, include the following:

- There's only one command button. This will, through programming logic, act as a picture toggle for two loaded bitmaps.

- There are two PictureBox controls on this form. They overlap each other in the actual application. Figure 30.19 shows the two PictureBox controls shifted slightly so you can see both of them.

- At startup, the Visible property of the PictureBox with plane.bmp is set to False, making it invisible. So when the application starts, the user will see only the PictureBox with the car.bmp image.

- The click event for the single command button first tests the Visible properties and takes action (branches) according to what it finds.

All other elements of this application are the same as in 30-1.mak.

FIGURE 30.19.

Showing the two PictureBox controls.

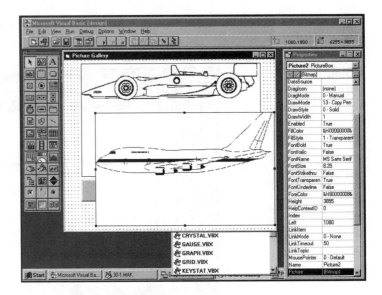

The secret to this application is in the click event for the single button. Take a look at Figure 30.20, which shows the Code window containing the event handler for the click event of this button.

FIGURE 30.20.

The logical event handler.

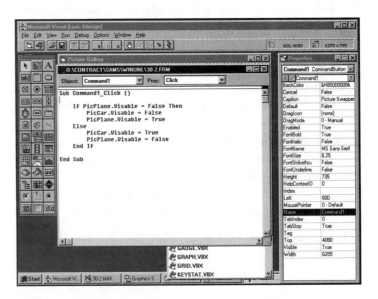

If you find the Visible property for the PictureBox control called picPlane set to False, and then first set the Visible property of the PictureBox called picCar to False, making picCar invisible. Then, set the Visible property of the picPlane PictureBox to True to make picPlane visible.

The next part, which starts after the keyword ElseIf, says that if the picPlane PictureBox's Visible property is True, then set it to False and set the picCar PictureBox's Visible property to True, making the plane invisible and the car visible.

When the program launches, the Visible property for picPlane is False because the programmer set it that way during the design phase. Refer back to Figure 30.19 and examine the Visible property in the Properties list box to confirm this for yourself.

So, when the program launches and the user clicks the command button, the first part of the If statement is true and the lines that change the picPlane's PictureBox Visible property to True and the picCar's PictureBox Visible property to False are executed.

The second time the button is clicked, the first part of the If statement isn't true anymore. The picPlane's PictureBox property isn't set to False any longer, so the computer skips down (branches) to the next test. This second test is right after the ElseIf statement.

The second test proves to be true. The program does find that the condition stated here is met because the picPlane's PictureBox Visible property is set to True. As a result, the program executes the second part of the event handler. This second part resets the Visible properties of the two PictureBox controls back to their initial settings.

Following programming logic isn't at all easy or self-evident when you're confronted with it like this. If you have access to Visual Basic, fire up or duplicate project 30-2.mak and run over it yourself. If you don't, you can always fire up the Windows 95 executable file, 30-2.exe, to see the logic switch in action. If nothing else, running down the code lines shown in Figure 30.20 should make things clear to you even if you have to go over it two or three times.

Learning programming logic and branching is like riding a bicycle. Once you get the hang of it, it'll be with you forever.

That's It? I'm Now a Visual Basic Expert?

If only that were so. There's quite a bit more to programming in Visual Basic than has been covered so far, but this is fundamentally how it's done. The big three of learning Visual Basic are

- Learning what controls you have available to you
- Learning the properties for those controls
- Learning the events possible for those controls

There are many controls, all with many properties and many events. All Visual Basic programmers, advanced as well as beginners, rely heavily on online help for a reference. Nobody should bother to memorize all the properties, all the events, and the correct syntax for each. Lean on the online help and the excellent search facility for help files supplied with Windows 95 and you'll make your life much simpler.

Custom Controls

No discussion of Visual Basic would be complete unless custom controls are mentioned. These are add-in controls that make up for what Microsoft left out of Visual Basic.

It's not an exaggeration to say that custom controls have made Visual Basic the success it is today. It is simply not possible for any programming tool to include everything that a programmer might need. The ability to add custom controls to your programs gives you a lot more power and flexibility to add useful features to programs. Custom controls come in all sizes, flavors, and prices from free to those costing several hundreds of dollars. There are controls for spinner buttons, scrollbars, calendars, image processors, fax systems, scanning application, and grids so powerful they rival full-powered spreadsheets such as Quattro Pro. That's only a tiny sampling of what's out there.

After you add custom controls, you use them just like you use regular controls in your project. Drag the control onto a form, set some properties, and write a little (or a lot) of code to handle events.

Take a look at Figure 30.21. It shows a simple Visual Basic application with a calendar and an appointments list—sort of a very simple Personal Information Manager (PIM). This entire semifunctional application took one minute to make using a set of custom controls called Calendar Widgets from Sheridan Software.

FIGURE 30.21.

A PIM application done in one minute using Visual Basic.

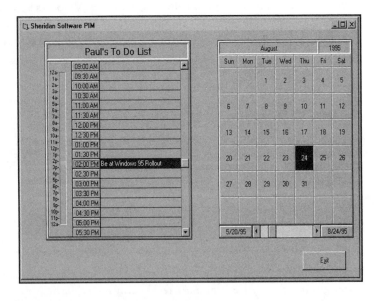

Consider for a minute how much time and effort it would have taken you to hand code all that in Visual Basic—or any other application.

> **NOTE**
>
> The correct way to use Visual Basic is to use it as little as possible. Before you start on a project, gather up as many custom controls as might be applicable and use them together; they can save you effort on the project. Most custom controls on the market are of very high quality. The more you add, the less you do and the better your project will turn out.
>
> Rumor has it that at least one major commercial program had its beginnings through the custom control route. A group of people bought up all the major custom controls they could find. They then spent a few weeks seeing how they could string them together into various application programs. This process was like stringing together pearls to make chains of various lengths and configurations.
>
> When the group decided on a good target application, they took the applicable custom controls, mixed them to the project, glued them all together using Visual Basic, and went commercial. Reportedly they did very well financially.

Database Applications

This chapter is supposed to be a very short introduction on the possibilities open to you through the use of Visual Basic. It has only scratched the surface in describing the capabilities you gain when you use this program. It is impossible to list in just one chapter all that you can do with Visual Basic. However, in recognition that most business applications have a database component, before leaving this subject, take a look at how you can use Visual Basic to make a database-type application.

The following example is a quick survey. If you have Visual Basic and an existing database file of a compatible type, you can follow along, but be forewarned: this exercise moves rather quickly. This example uses the Northwind database, NWIND.MDB, that's part of the sample data supplied with Microsoft Access. As of this writing, Visual Basic supported the following file formats. More are being added all the time.

- Access
- dBASE III
- dBASE IV
- Paradox 3.x
- Paradox 4.x
- Btrieve
- FoxPro 2.0
- FoxPro 2.5

- Excel 3.0 after translation
- Excel 4.0 after translation
- Excel 5.0 after translation
- Excel 7.0 after translation
- ODBC

The Elements

Making a simple browse application using an existing database with Visual Basic requires the following steps:

1. Start a new project.
2. Add a Data control to a form.
3. Set the properties for the Data control to bind it to an existing database.
4. Add an unbound text box control to the form.
5. Set the properties for the text box control to bind it to the Data control.

The Data Control

Fire up Visual Basic or start a new project if necessary. Locate the Data control in the toolbox, click it, move to the form, and click and drag to add the control to the form. Figure 30.22 shows how this is done.

FIGURE 30.22.

Adding a Data control.

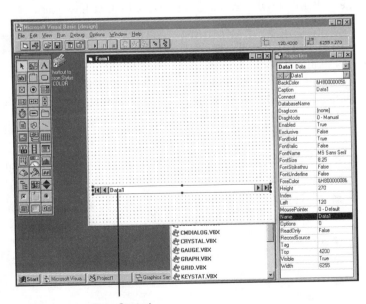

Data Control

Note that you can make the data control any size you wish. The Properties list box isn't visible because it is behind the main form. If you find yourself missing the Properties list box, you can open it or bring it to the foreground by pressing F4.

Locate the Properties list box and set the Connect property to the type of database you'll connect to. Click the DatabaseName property for the Data control and either enter or browse for the existing database to which you'll be connecting. Set the RecordSource property for the table you want to display in the form. In this example set the Connect property to Access, DatabaseName property is set to NWIND.MDB, and the RecordSource property to Employees (see Figure 30.23).

FIGURE 30.23.

Binding the Data control to a database.

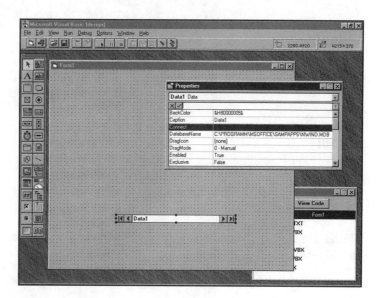

An Unbound Text Box Control

You've started a new project, added a Data control, and set its properties. You're now on step 4 from the previous list. It's time to add the unbound text box control to the project. The text box control is one of Visual Basic's standard entries in the toolbox. Visual Basic adds custom controls to a project at startup according to the contents of the Autoload.mak file. You are free to edit your Autoload.mak file to change the defualts for a project startup. If you accumulate many often used custom controls, you'll likely want to modify Autoload.mak to show these controls at startup.

Add a text box control to the form by locating it in the toolbox, clicking on it, and dragging it to the form in the usual way. Set the DataSource property to Data1—the name of the Data control added in the previous section. Set the DataField property to the LastName field. Figure 29.24 shows this done for the example project.

FIGURE 30.24.

The text box bound to the data control.

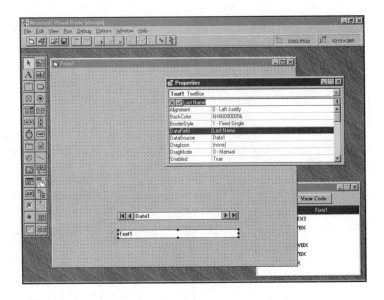

Done!

That's it! If you've been following along, save your project and form by choosing File | Save Project As from the menu, and then press F5 to launch your creation. Figure 30.25 shows the sample project running.

FIGURE 30.25.

The finished data browse project.

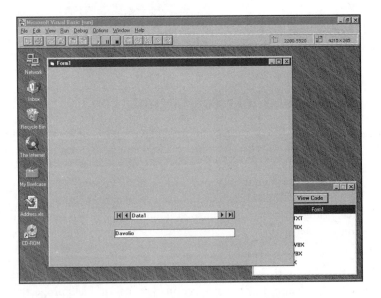

At this point, you can browse through the Employees table, edit it, or make additions just as you could using Access itself. You can set the properties for the various controls and/or add event handling code to restrict rights to this table or the entire application. Of course, if this had been a real project, such properties as the captions for the Data control and form itself would have been changed from Visual Basic's defaults. To see more fields on the form, just add more text boxes.

Visual Basic in Perspective

This chapter has given you a quick glimpse of Visual Basic, which is surely one of the most flexible programming tools available to the Windows 95 programmer or to the Windows 95 user who needs to occasionally make some custom software.

Visual Basic is a beguiling program. As you've seen here, it's so easy to create simple applications that people underestimate how much effort it takes to tackle the really complex ones. Without a doubt, Visual Basic makes even the most complex projects as easy as they can be, but that doesn't make everything you try with it a half-day project, as the examples in this chapter might imply.

Keep in mind that the best way to use Visual Basic is to do as little as possible with it. Use custom controls whenever possible. Like the custom control calendar shown earlier in this chapter, there are add-ons you can buy for Visual Basic that cost from nothing to a few hundred dollars. These add-ons—VBXs technically—are polished applications that would take you weeks to duplicate in Visual Basic if you could do them at all. Because they are written in lower-level languages, they also can run faster than something written in Visual Basic.

If you choose to become a Visual Basic programmer, or just a dabbler, keep one thing in mind: programming in Visual Basic is supposed to be enjoyable. If it grows so it isn't, take a break and come back to it.

The Visual Basic Language

Language variants, or dialects, are an issue for human and computer languages. Programmers often hit serious snags when moving from one manufacturer's version of a language to another. A prime example is Pascal. The language as conceived by its inventor, Wirth, has little relation (other than structure) to the working versions of Turbo or Object Pascal issued by Borland and others.

The situation with Basic and Microsoft was even more confusing. Not only did various Basics differ between manufacturers, but they did so even within the Microsoft family of products. Just a short while ago Excel had its own Basic-like macro language, Word had WordBasic, Visual Basic has, well, the Visual Basic language, and Access had Access Basic Code (ABC).

Microsoft has announced that soon all its products will use one language: Visual Basic for Applications (VBA).

The convergence of languages into VBA has been hailed by many as a panacea compared to the babel of the past, but it might not be. While the core of VBA will remain constant, specific usage varies from product to product. Learning VBA in Access won't make you an expert using VBA for Excel, but it's surely better than having to start all over again using a language with little in common to the language you know.

Some have requested that Microsoft open up VBA so it becomes an open scripting language available to all Windows programs and within Windows itself. As of this writing, Microsoft hasn't committed to doing this.

Microsoft Visual C++ and Borland's Delphi

by Paul Cassel

IN THIS CHAPTER

Hard-Core Programming

You can tackle many, but not all, Windows 95 programming tasks with tools such as Baler, Microsoft Office, Access, and Visual Basic. Although many people who should know better tend to dismiss user-friendly programming solutions as the lightweights of the programming world, these tools do have limits. If your programming needs exceed the limits of point and click programming languages, you'll need to explore the world of hard-core programming.

Oddly enough, even the hardest core tends to be moving toward the point-and-click programming paradigm. Today's Delphi has its roots in Pascal, a text-type programming language. However, Delphi looks and feels quite a bit l ike Visual Basic but extends the scope of Microsoft's offering significantly. Despite its benefits, it is a less friendly language and is significantly more complex.

Visual C++ has its roots in C, the language originally used to program the operating system UNIX. There isn't anything more hard core than C, aside from assembler or machine language. It's the real thing. In this case as well, when you look at the current offering from Microsoft, Visual C++ 2.1, you almost think you're looking at a variant of Visual Basic or Access. However as soon as you get into the nuts and bolts of actual programming, the difficulties of using C++, or even Visual C++, will rear up at you. These difficulties appear because despite its initially friendly appearance, Visual C++ still requires a significant amount of hand coding.

This doesn't mean Visual Basic, Access, or Delphi— some of the most popular point-and-click programming tools—won't even require hand coding. You can, however, get away with less using these tools than you can with Visual C++.

Upside and Downside

You might be tempted to jump right into programming using a program such as Visual C++ on the theory that you'll never run out of power when using it. You would be right about the power side, but that thinking can get you into trouble. Any C, including the extension of C called C++ (or C with classes), is difficult to learn—and all that power can get you into trouble.

C THE TROUBLE IF YOU CAN

For several months, a company called Nu-Mega ran ads in various professional C journals. The ads were for a bug catcher marketed by the company. They showed from three to six lines of C code and challenged the readers to find the bug that, presumably, Nu-Mega's bug catcher would catch. The ads were a big hit with C programmers who enjoyed getting together to see who would be the first to spot the problem in the short code fragments.

> Imagine how complex C must be if Nu-Mega could, month after month, list a short code fragment and challenge professional C programmers to find the problem. Is this a challenge you want to face in your projects?

The language of Delphi, Object Pascal, is easier for some to learn than C. It's harder for others. Some find it maddening and frustrating. Object Pascal stems from the Wirth-developed language Pascal, which was conceived as a teaching tool to inculcate Wirth's programming theories into his students. The original Pascal had few practical uses aside from teaching Wirth's theories to programming students.

Borland has done a wonderful job of extending the Pascal language from a sleepy university exercise into a real-world powerhouse. Today's commercial Pascals rival any language in power, but still carry some of the baggage of their parent scholastic-only prototype. That baggage manifests itself in Object Pascal's stilted style, forced structures, and extreme verbosity. Behind each line of Object Pascal's code lies a teacher with a ruler ready to hit you over the knuckles if you leave out one semicolon or vary from strict Wirth orthodoxy.

Pascal fans say this orthodoxy is an advantage, not a burden. Those who like the programming equivalent of "whatever isn't forbidden is mandatory" love Pascal. For those who like the wild and woolly style of doing things their way, C or Basic are good choices. To the Pascal martinets, the worlds of C and Basic are anarchies full of out of control programmers wantonly doing forbidden things.

Pick your style, and pick your language.

Borland's Delphi

You would be hard pressed to find a programming tool with more scope than Delphi. You can use it as a standard Pascal to make Windows-like programs that run like DOS programs, but under Windows. You can use it to make client applications for client/server applications. You can use it just like Visual Basic to create stand-alone programs. You can make dynamic link libraries (DLLs), which act as server libraries for other applications such as Word, Excel, or Visual Basic—although the structure of Pascal makes that a bit tricky. In short, if you were to choose one tool that could do the most things with the least amount of work, Delphi would be it. What it can't do, as of this writing, is create native Windows 95 applications, but Borland has promised a release that will meet this specification very soon.

Looking at Delphi

Borland learned the well lessons of visual, or point-and-click, programming when it designed Delphi. Take a look at Figure 31.1, which shows the Delphi programming environment.

FIGURE 31.1.

Borland's Delphi.

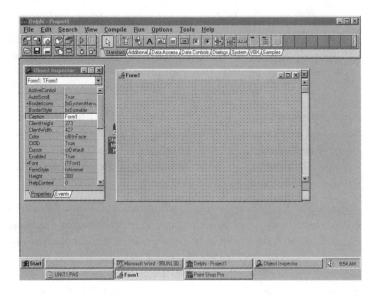

If you read Chapter 30, "Visual Basic the Easy Way," you should find yourself in familiar territory. Borland uses slightly different terminology than Microsoft when naming the parts of its programs, but usage remains the same.

In the middle of the screen, you see a blank form with Form1 in the title bar. That's the blank form in which you paint your application, just as in Visual Basic. To the left, there's a list box with Object Inspector in its title bar. That is where you set the properties for the controls you paint into the form. It's pretty much the same as the Properties list box in Visual Basic.

Across the top of the screen, just under the menubar, sits Delphi's Speedbar. This is a tabbed version of the Toolbox in Visual Basic. Delphi sports a truly excellent user interface, with the Speedbar being a good example of how improved it is over competing products. Clicking on the tabs in the Speedbar brings up different categories of controls. The Toolbox in Visual Basic just lumps all controls into one button collection.

Delphi gives you more access to the nuts and bolts of your application than does Visual Basic. If you look closely, you see another window peeking from behind the blank form in Figure 31.1. This is a code window, or a Unit as Borland refers to parts of Object Pascal code. Figure 31.2 shows this code window in the foreground. It also shows the Speedbar tab Data Controls as current, rather than the Standard Speedbar tab as shown in the Figure 31.1.

The code in the Unit window shows the code that is automatically generated by Delphi to start a new project. For the most part, the code in this window is general statements needed by all (or at least most) Delphi projects, along with some placeholders for programmers to insert their own project-wide declarations.

FIGURE 31.2.

The Unit or code window.

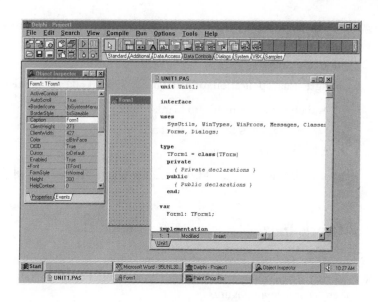

Using Delphi is similar to using Visual Basic when you're asking each to do the same tasks. Take a look at Figure 31.3. Note that the programmer has changed the Caption property in the Object Inspector to Delphi Rules!, and the title bar of the form has likewise changed to Delphi Rules!.

FIGURE 31.3.

Changing properties in Delphi.

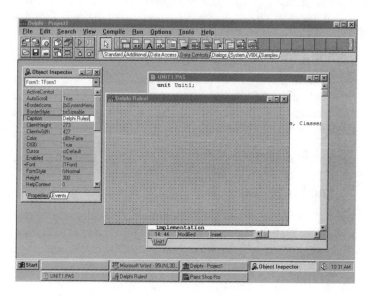

Changing the Caption property in the Object Inspector had an identical effect to the effect that a change in the Caption property in the Properties list box of Visual Basic would have in that programming environment. Captions are captions.

Creating a visual application, or program, in Delphi takes three steps:

1. Add objects, or controls, to blank forms.

2. Set the properties for these objects.

3. Add code to handle events.

If that sounds familiar, it should. Those are the same steps you use when programming in Visual Basic.

A Quick Tour

The following simple program shows how Delphi works. If you have Delphi, you might enjoy following along; but even if you don't, you should be able to follow along because every step has an accompanying figure.

This example will ask for input from the user when a button is clicked, and then take that input and paste it into the title bar of the form. It shows the three steps of Delphi programming: painting the form, setting properties, and entering code to handle events.

Remember that Delphi's code is a variant of Pascal and isn't as obvious as the Basic used in Visual Basic. You'll see some explanation where the code isn't self-explanatory.

Painting the Form

When starting with a new project, add a single button to the form. Do this by clicking on the Standard tab in the Speedbar. Then locate the button object, click on it, move to the form, and click anywhere to place the button. Figure 31.4 shows the cursor over the button object in the Speedbar, and Figure 31.5 shows the button object placed on the form.

That's it for this stage of the project. Your form's done.

Setting Properties

Keep in mind that setting properties in Delphi is almost identical to setting properties in Visual Basic. To bring up the Object Inspector for any object, click on that object. In this case, the button object is highlighted so that the Object Inspector for the button is current.

FIGURE 31.4.

The standard Speedbar.

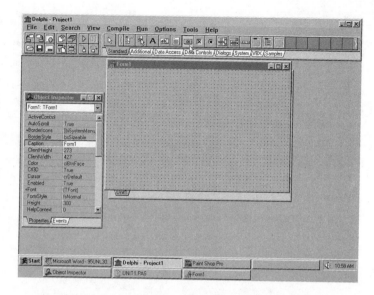

FIGURE 31.5.

Placing a button object on a form.

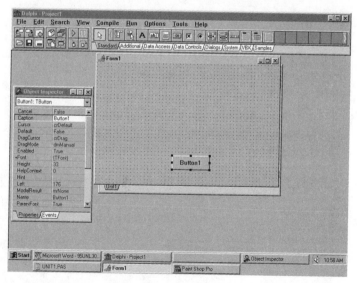

Locate the Caption property for the button object and edit the settings area to read Title Change, as shown in Figure 31.6.

That's it for this stage of the project. You have set all the properties you need to at design time. Steps one and two are done. Now, onward to step three.

FIGURE 31.6.

Changing properties in the Object Inspector.

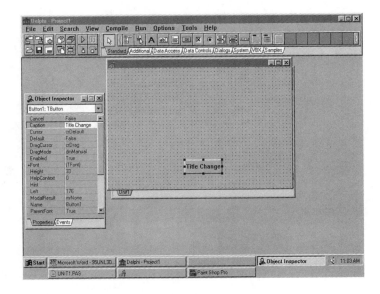

Adding Code

This is getting too easy. The next step will add enough complexity to make up for some of the easy going in steps one and two. The programmer-added code will first respond to a button click by bringing up a dialog box that prompts the user for an entry, and then change the form's title bar to the user's entry.

The code will fire, or run, in response to a button click or a button click event. Click the Events tab at the bottom of the Object Inspector to bring up the events possible for a button. You can see this phase of the Object Inspector in Figure 31.7.

FIGURE 31.7.

The Events section of the Object Inspector.

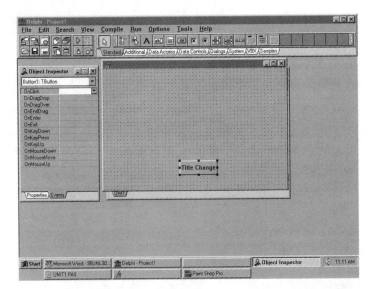

The event that this project needs to handle is the click event. To get to the place where you can enter code, double-click next to the click entry and your screen will change to resemble Figure 31.8.

FIGURE 31.8.

The click event.

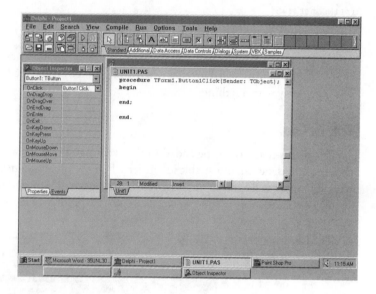

A Side Trip to Identifying Variables

Object Pascal is a strongly typed language, which means that you need to declare what a program should expect in the way of variables. Basic can handle variables on the fly; Pascal can't. The following Basic code is perfectly legal:

```
...
FirstNumber=5
SecondNumber=7
Sum = FirstNumber + SecondNumber
...
```

It's legal because Basic types (or classifies) the variables `FirstNumber`, `SecondNumber`, and `Sum` as integers on the fly when you assign quantities to them in the middle of the code.

Pascal, and other typed languages, insist that you first declare the type of variables before you use them. That same code fragment would choke any Pascal, unless it was preceded by a type declaration such as the following:

```
...
var
FirstNumber, SecondNumber, Sum: Integer;
begin
FirstNumber :=5;
SecondNumber :=7;
Sum := FirstNumber + SecondNumber;
end.
```

Note the usage changes between Pascal and the more intuitive Basic. There are no = operators in that fragment. Instead, the Pascals use the := operator, which should be read "becomes." The line

```
FirstNumber :=5;
```

reads "FirstNumber becomes 5." Pascal reserves the word "equals" for tests of equality.

Also, you must tell Pascal when the declarations are over and the action begins by using the keyword Begin. You also need to tell it where things end by using the keyword End. Pascal won't let you get away with anything.

Back to Coding

The first things that have to be added to the event handler framework shown in Figure 31.8 are the type declarations or variable identifiers. This event handler needs only one variable: the text that the user will enter in response to the dialog box. The programmer chose to name this variable NewTitleBarText. You can see the type declaration in Figure 31.9.

FIGURE 31.9.

Declaring variables in Delphi.

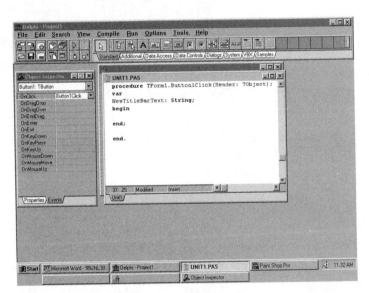

Here are the steps to declare variables in Delphi:

1. Add the keyword Var above the Begin keyword.
2. Add the names of all like variables separated by commas.
3. Add a colon to the end of the list of variable names.
4. Add the keyword for the type of variable you're declaring.
5. End the line with a semicolon (;).

The type of variable that NewTitleBarText will be in this program is a string. *Strings* are alphanumerics and certain characters up to a length of 255 bytes. Other types of Delphi variables include, but are not limited to, the following:

- Integers: signed whole numbers
- Real: numbers with a decimal component
- Word: unsigned whole numbers
- String: characters
- Pointer: pointers to a memory address

A full discussion of Delphi variable types would take up more room than this entire chapter. If you want to see a good discussion of this topic, search Delphi's online help on the keyword Type.

Now that the type declaration is out of the way, it's time to add some code to display the dialog box asking for user input. Figure 31.10 shows this code added to the event handler.

FIGURE 31.10.

Displaying an Inputbox.

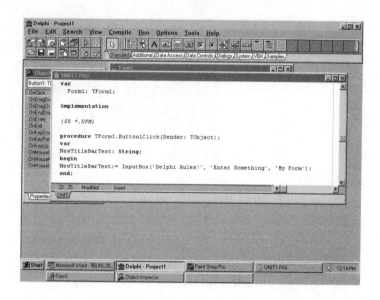

The code window in Figure 31.10 has been slightly enlarged to show the entire code line for the dialog box statement. A dialog box that gets input from a user is called an Inputbox in Delphi. Let's pause for a second and examine the line of code that creates that Inputbox:

```
NewTitleBarText:= InputBox('Delphi Rules!', 'Enter Something', 'My Form');
```

The first part of the line is the variable declared earlier in the Var section of this event handler. The second part is the "becomes" symbol, :=. This assigns the value of the entry of the Inputbox to the variable NewTitleBarText when the user clicks the OK button in the Inputbox.

The third part of the line defines the Inputbox. The first part of that section tells Delphi to show an Inputbox object. The second part is the title of the Inputbox, which in this case is Delphi Rules!. The third part of the Inputbox is the prompt for the user, Enter Something. The last part is the default entry, My Form.

If you're following along, this is a good place to save your project and give it a test drive. After saving, launch your project by clicking the green arrow that faces right in the Speedbar. Figure 31.11 shows the project running after the programmer-added command button has been clicked.

FIGURE 31.11.

The partly finished project.

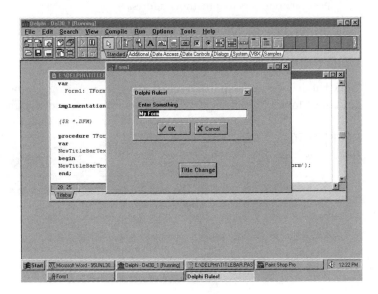

Note that Figure 31.11 shows how each part of the InputBox statement fits into the actual Inputbox.

The last part of this demonstration takes the user input from the Inputbox and places it as the Caption for the form's title bar. Figure 31.12 shows how this is done.

This line is much simpler than the first one:

```
Form1.Caption := NewTitleBarText;
```

Form1 is the name of the form. It's the name Delphi assigned to the form by default. As in Visual Basic, if you were making a real-world application, you would name all your objects using a naming convention of your choice. These steps have been omitted from this demonstration for the sake of clarity and to save space.

FIGURE 31.12.

Changing the title bar caption.

The second part of the line names the particular property of the object in which we're interested. In this case, it's the `Caption` property for the form. Delphi uses the

```
Object.Property := Setting;
```

format to refer to objects, their properties, and their settings. Again, this is very similar to Visual Basic. So the `Form1.Caption` part of this line tells Delphi that this line refers to the `Caption` property for the object named `Form1`.

The third part of the line is the familiar "becomes" symbol, `:=`. The last part is the variable `NewTitleBarText` that was set to the user input by the first statement after the `Begin` keyword.

This line says to Delphi, "Take the value now stored in the variable `NewTitleBarText` and assign it to the `Caption` property of the form named `Form1`."

Figure 31.13 shows the program running with a new entry in the Inputbox.

Figure 31.14 shows the program after the OK button in the Inputbox has been clicked. Note that the string that was in the Inputbox in Figure 31.13 is now the caption for the title bar.

Each time the user clicks the Title Change button, he gets an Inputbox prompting for an entry; each time he clicks the OK button in the Inputbox, the contents of the box become the caption of the form's title bar.

FIGURE 31.13.

The Inputbox with new input.

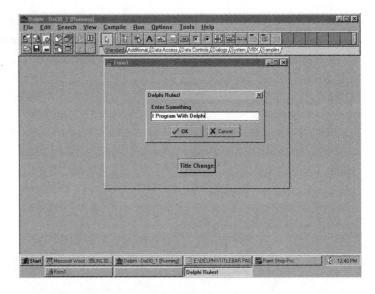

FIGURE 31.14.

The new title bar caption.

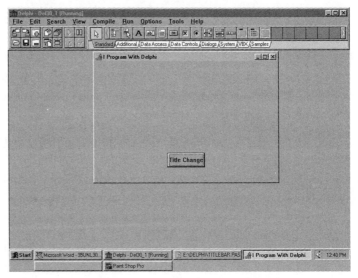

A Little Logic

Delphi, like Visual Basic and all computer languages, relies heavily on logic and branching. Look at Figure 31.15, which shows the event handler from Figure 31.12 altered two ways.

First, the default entry in the Inputbox has been altered from My Form to ' ', which is the Pascal way of saying it contains nothing. The second part of the changes has Delphi evaluating the value of the variable NewTitleBarText. If the variable is null, or if the user has entered nothing,

Delphi flashes a different kind of dialog box: a Message Box complaining about the situation. If the user enters something in the Inputbox, Delphi puts that entry in the title bar of the form.

FIGURE 31.15.

The branching event handler.

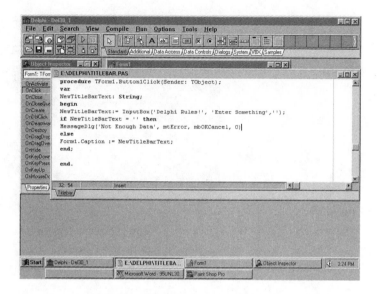

Figure 31.16 shows the results of running this program with the new event handler when the user doesn't enter anything in the Inputbox.

FIGURE 31.16.

The Error dialog box.

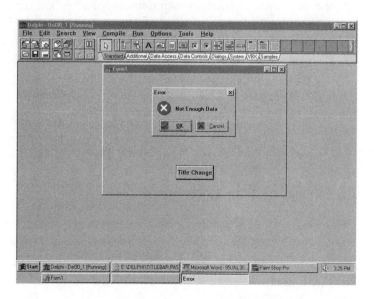

Figure 31.17 shows the same program running; but this time, the user entered I Use Delphi Daily in the Inputbox and clicked OK.

FIGURE 31.17.

The altered title bar.

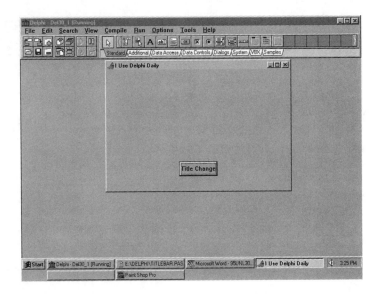

Delphi and Databases

The vast majority of corporate custom software has a database component, and making database applications is where Delphi really shines. Borland promotes Delphi heavily in this area hoping to attract corporate customers for its flagship product.

Doing simple database applications such as the table browser/editor done in Visual Basic for Chapter 30 is almost too easy using Delphi. The following example shows just how well Delphi handles this task.

As with the previous demonstration, if you have Delphi you can work along with these steps. If you don't have Delphi or choose not to follow along, you shouldn't have any trouble getting a feel for how the program works because there are plenty of figures to accompany the example.

An Expert at Your Command

You can manually create a simple table browser as shown next, but there's no reason to bother because Delphi includes an expert to guide you through the process. At the end of the expert, we'll pause to see what the expert did and how it did it.

To start the database expert, fire up Delphi or start a new project if it's running. Click the menu selections Help|Database form expert as shown in Figure 31.18.

FIGURE 31.18.

Starting the database expert.

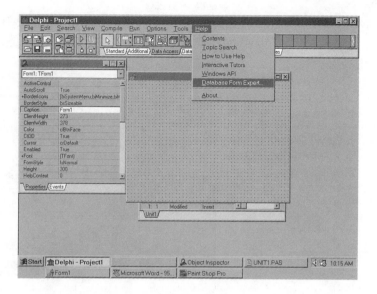

Because this project will be a simple form based on a table object, accept the defaults as shown in Figure 31.19 and click the Next button in the lower-right corner of the expert.

FIGURE 31.19.

Choosing the type of form.

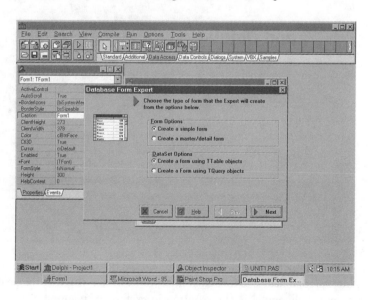

The next thing to tell the expert is what table to use for your program. This example will use the biolife.db table. This table is part of both Paradox for Windows and Delphi's sample data.

Choose whichever table you want for this step if you're following along. In the next step, you tell Delphi which fields from the table you want to include in your application. Click the Next button to move on.

FIGURE 31.20.

Binding a table to the program.

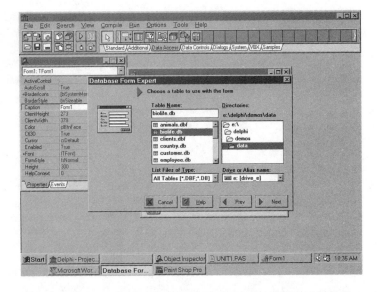

FIGURE 31.21.

Deciding which fields to include.

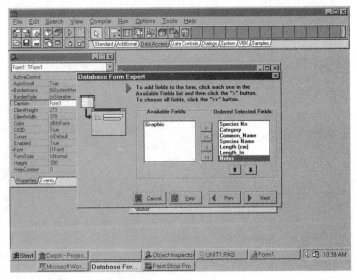

This example will use all the fields except the picture of the fish. The easiest way to include all but that one field is to first click the >> button to include all the fields, and then highlight the graphic field and click the < button to exclude it. Figure 31.21 shows the screen after these steps. Click the Next button. The final step is to tell Delphi what orientation to use for your form. This application uses the default horizontal option. Figure 31.22 shows this part of the expert.

FIGURE 31.22.

Choosing the form's orientation.

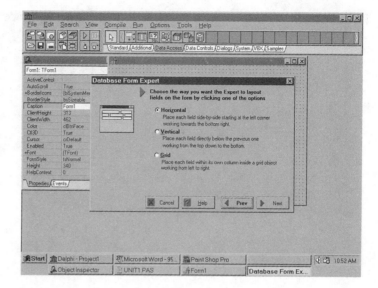

The only thing left is to click the lightning button shown in Figure 31.23 to tell Delphi you're done and ask it to start generating the program.

FIGURE 31.23.

Go ahead, Delphi! Make my program.

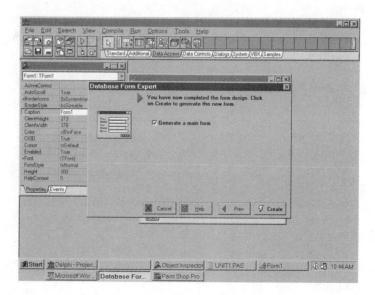

Figure 31.24 shows the finished application in design mode. Note that Delphi has not only placed all the needed controls on the form, but also database browser buttons of the type common to all applications of this sort.

822

FIGURE 31.24.

The finished program in design mode.

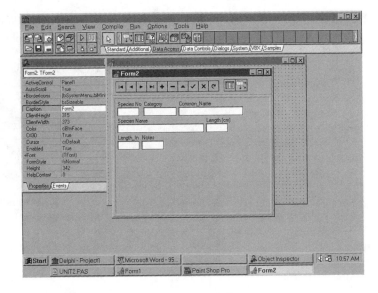

Figure 31.25 shows the finished application running with the user browsing through the biolife database.

FIGURE 31.25.

The finished database application.

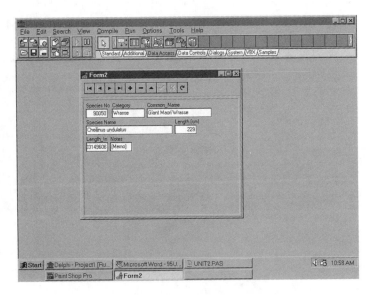

How Did It Do That?

Delphi's actual operation isn't too different from that of Visual Basic, but the expert disguised that fact. Figure 31.26 shows the program back in design mode with one of the two data objects that are hidden at runtime highlighted. Look at the Object Inspector and see that this object has the path to the biolife.db table set as the property settings for the DatabaseName and TableName properties, respectively. Also note that the name of this object is Table1.

FIGURE 31.26.

How Delphi binds the right table.

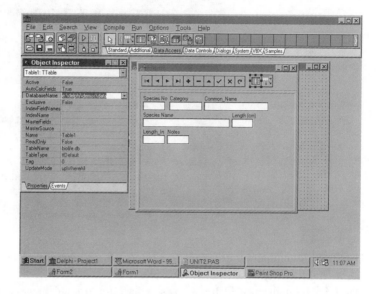

The second hidden object at runtime is the DataSource object, which is pointed to Table1, the first hidden object.

FIGURE 31.27.

The DataSource object.

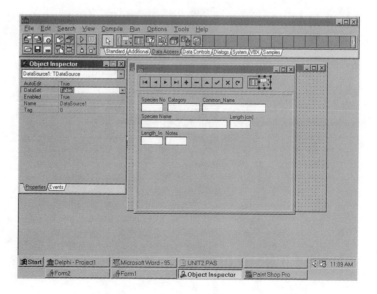

Figure 31.28 shows the demonstration program, which is modified to include the graphics of the fishes in the biolife.db table. It makes for a pretty database application.

FIGURE 31.28.

Adding a graphic.

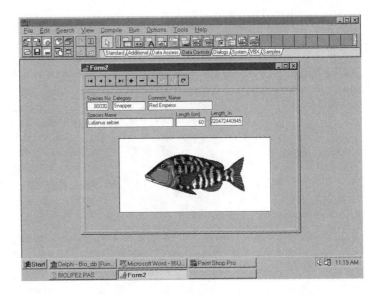

Adding this graphic was as simple as adding a DBImage object found on the Speedbar to the form, and then telling Delphi to look in the DataSource1 object for the Graphic field. After getting that intelligence, Delphi knows to place appropriate images in the object frame. Figure 31.29 shows the form of Figure 31.28 in design mode with the relevant properties in the Object Inspector set correctly.

FIGURE 31.29.

The nuts and bolts of a database graphic.

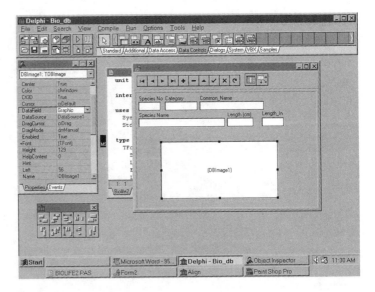

Naturally, every database project won't be as simple as these demonstrations, but they aren't nearly as difficult as they were before we had visual programming tools such as Delphi. Delphi comes with an excellent manual that includes step-through tutorials. With a little bit of time and effort, almost anybody can learn to use Delphi as a first-class database application maker.

Delphi in Summary

This chapter has only scratched the surface of Delphi. There are worlds of things Delphi can do that haven't even been discussed here. Considered as a whole, Delphi is a powerful and difficult package to master, but that's mostly due to its scope. If you have a need for a database front-end maker only, you can learn to use Delphi for this purpose within a reasonable period of time.

The danger in Delphi is getting distracted by it. You can lose weeks, or even months, delving into esoteric subjects that have no bearing on your job or the task at hand. The trick to using Delphi is to keep a narrow focus. Yes, it's true that Delphi has as much power as anybody can use, but do you have the time to harness that power? If you do, you're luckier or smarter than most of us.

Microsoft Visual C++

C++ is a derivative of C, which today is a hard-core language for uncompromising programmers. C and C++ programmers surely win the bragging rights contest among Windows programmers, but just how productive they are compared to the visual programmers is a matter of great debate.

C, C++, and OOP

C was developed as a language to create the UNIX operating system. Over the 20 odd years since then, it has grown into a full-blown language for general-purpose programming. It's latest incarnation, C++, is a dialect of C based on an elegant concept. That concept is object-oriented programming or OOP.

To put it very concisely, OOP is a hierarchical system in which most parts of a program are derived from previously defined code objects. The theoretical result is a very orderly and easy to maintain source code. C++ brings to C what standardized parts brought to the assembly line process.

Unfortunately for the OOP theorists, the practice doesn't seem to be working out as elegantly as the idea. For reasons that are still unclear, C++ projects tend to be more chaotic than they are supposed to be. The OOP lovers say it's only a matter of time until the programming world gets a handle on OOP, and as soon as it does, productivity will grow enormously. Some others say the promise of OOP is a false promise.

The C Language and You

The trouble with any C is size. There's just a tremendous amount to learn before you can get productive with it. A full semester of C in a college-level course will give you only a glance at all there is to learn. Although the basic syntax is standard, each type and use of C has its own conventions, much like those used in the card game Bridge. Just as in Bridge, if you don't know the conventions, you don't know the game.

The main reason to use C or C++ is to be able to manipulate Windows or other operating systems down at low levels. To do this, you not only need to know how to use the language, but you also need a good understanding of the operating system. Most of what you need to know is the API, or Application Programming Interface. These are the hooks you use to get to the operating system.

Take a look at Figure 31.30. This is a short fragment of an API list for the Telephony extensions to Windows 95.

FIGURE 31.30.

A small fragment of one API.

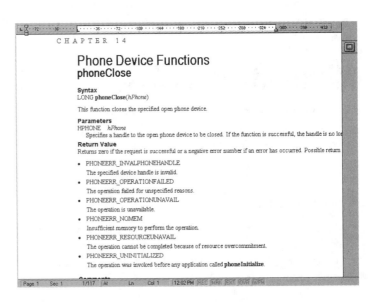

Each entry in Figure 31.30 represents one API call. There are thousands of API calls in a complex operating system such as Windows 95. Although nobody needs to know them all, you do need to know the ones that are applicable to your project, and you also need to know of at least the existence of each group of API calls. For example, if you plan on doing some telephony programming in Windows 95, not knowing of the existence of the calls shown on Figure 31.30 will render your efforts futile.

> **NOTE**
>
> Serious programming in Windows 95 will force you to use some API calls not only in C but in any language. There's only so far you can go in your programs without asking the operating system for some support.
>
> Visual Basic, Delphi, Excel, and Word for Windows programmers call on the Windows API from time to time, but not nearly as often as do C programmers working at lower levels.

Microsoft Visual C++

Microsoft's entry into C++ compilers is Visual C++. The *Visual* part of the name might lead you to believe that this is a Visual Basic with C++ as a language. Although the products superficially look alike, they really are quite different.

Visual C++ comes with Microsoft Foundation Classes or MFC, which are base classes that you use to derive your own C++ objects. The advantages to using MFCs are as follows:

- They are less work, because they are already done.
- MFCs are done by real pros who did a great job making clean code.
- MFCs are documented better than most people would bother doing.
- MFCs are standardized so that others will have a good idea of where you started from.
- Why reinvent anything?

A Very Short Look At Visual C++

This book isn't appropriate for more than a tiny glimpse of Visual C++. Figures 31.31 and 31.32 show a Microsoft wizard in action within Visual C++.

After you're done with the wizard, you end up with a whole lot of code and program parts as shown in Figure 31.33.

Each file has a part in making the shell for your program. The files with the .cpp extension are C++ code. Part of the file that defines the main form, mainfrm.cpp, is shown in Figure 31.34.

Note that the first line of this code is a comment saying that the code is a derivation class CMainFrame, which means that the basic idea of this code comes from CMainFrame. At this point, you can run the generated code, but you won't have much to show for it. Figure 31.35 shows this project as it is up and running under Windows 95.

FIGURE 31.31.

A Visual C++ wizard finding a database.

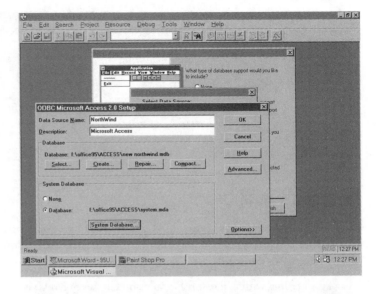

FIGURE 31.32.

Finishing up with the wizard.

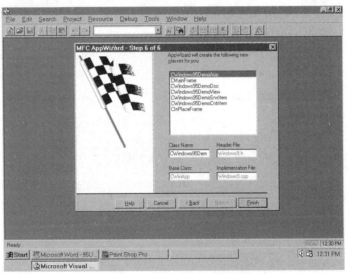

FIGURE 31.33.

The result of the wizard.

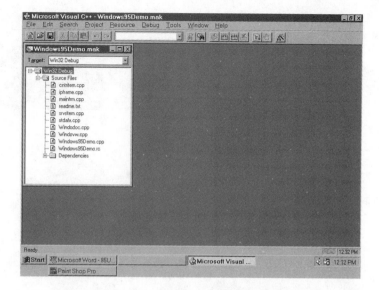

FIGURE 31.34.

One part of a .cpp file.

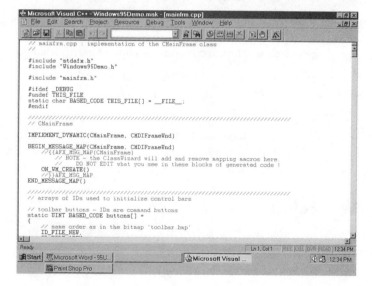

FIGURE 31.35.

The compiled and linked project.

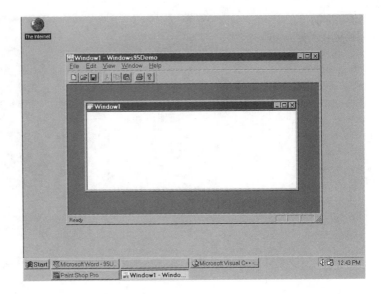

To make this project into anything but a simple framework takes a great deal of effort for the casual user. There are many wizards included in Visual C++, but there is no way to fully point and click yourself to a finished product as you can with Visual Basic or Delphi.

You can, for example, paint a form for a database application. But instead of setting properties in an Object Inspector, as you can with Delphi, you must manually tie each form field to the correct field in your database.

Visual C++ is a great labor saver compared to manually coding an entire application, but it's not a stroll in the park even if you know C and C++ well. If you first need to learn C or C++, you have a long stretch until you'll be productive using this tool or one like it.

Why Bother?

Applications made with Visual C++ are tight, small, and fast. These are the holy grails for programmers and are reason enough for many people to take the time and put in the effort to make their applications with this tool.

Summary

Someday we'll have programming tools as easy as Visual Basic, but they will turn out results with the quality of Visual C++. Borland argues that this day is here with Delphi. As you've seen, aside from using Pascal instead of Basic, it's as easy as with Visual Basic to point and click your way to finished applications. Its output is fast and feels as tight, although it isn't nearly as small as most of what comes out of the C++ compilers, visual or not.

Delphi is a good compromise between the truly massive investment in time and effort you need to put into learning C++ and the ease of Visual Basic. Many find its underlying language, Object Pascal, to be an exercise in frustration, but others have climbed the Pascal mountain and you can too. The advantage of using Pascal is linked to why it's so frustrating. It forces you to program in proper style. The cowboy in you will find that encumbering, but you can't argue against the simple fact that it makes for less buggy and more easily maintained programs.

If you have no investment in any language and you want to get on the fastest programming track, Visual Basic is your obvious choice. If you want to create the highest quality programs and have the time to invest in your education, Visual C++ is the right tool. If you want something in between, if you just like the idea of using Object Pascal, or if you want the most versatile tool so that you're ready for anything life throws at you, Delphi's your obvious choice.

VIII

PART

by
Robert Griswold

Troubleshooting

Troubleshooting is at times an art and magic; other times it is simply repetitive task execution. Whatever troubleshooting is to you, the chapters in this section should provide you with a firm understanding of general troubleshooting techniques, Windows 95 specific techniques, and insight into why Windows 95 fails. Section VIII contains the following chapters:

- Chapter 32: "Troubleshooting Windows 95 Installation." This chapter focuses on why installation can go wrong and how you can resolve some common, and uncommon, problems.

- Chapter 33: "Troubleshooting Applications." Application execution in Windows 95 is not always as smooth as expected. This chapter covers problems with Win16 (Windows 16-bit), DOS, and Win32 (Windows-95-ready) applications.

- Chapter 34: "Multimedia Troubleshooting."This chapter helps the user get those all-important sound and video peripherals working. When multimedia is not working, the world is not a pretty place.

- Chapter 35: "Troubleshooting Communications and Networking." Network troubleshooting shares some basic troubleshooting techniques with other topics and has a whole set specific to networking. Windows 95 changes the network world. This chapter covers those changes.

Troubleshooting Windows 95

Because troubleshooting Windows 95 could be the main reason you bought Windows 95 Unleashed, effort has been put into making sure these chapters are useful. Troubleshooting the unknown really must take some definite steps for success. Senior-level technical support and troubleshooting specialists will tell you that in order to diagnose the problem you must first know what works, rather than what does not work. Since it is very easy to observe what is not functioning, the challenge becomes determining what functions.

Microsoft has started including what will probably be in every CD-ROM copy of Windows 95: the Windows 95 Resource Kit. The Resource Kit directory on the CD-ROM contains three directories, the most important of which is the HELPFILE directory. This is where the Windows 95 Resource Kit Help file lives. This help file might become the most referenced piece of documentation in technical support departments, for Windows 95. This help file has information on troubleshooting techniques, specific device configuration problems, and application support.

When appropriate, these chapters reference the Windows 95 Resource kit. The Windows 95 Resource Kit gives the steps for fixing problems. These chapters also give the reader the understanding to bypass the failure or issue in the future.

The major troubleshooting points that the Windows 95 Resource kit tries to get across are these:

- Has the failure or error condition been sufficiently categorized to eliminate common problems outlined in the first pass troubleshooting documentation?

- Has the error condition been isolated to the point that the problem is reproducible with the known hardware? If not, what is suspected of being the involved hardware? Have the hardware and software revisions involved been identified?

- Has the problem or error condition kept the entire machine from allowing Windows 95 to set up? Run in Normal Mode? Run in Safe Mode?

- Can the problem be reproduced on another machine, if available?

- Have non-Windows 95 drivers or TSRs been eliminated, and if so, does the loading sequence of software influence the way the error condition occurs?

The following troubleshooting points also need consideration with Windows 95:

- Did the hardware and associated software run prior to the installation of Windows 95? Did DOS and Windows 3.1 work with this hardware setup?

- If the problem is with non-Windows 95 drivers and TSRs, can a MultiBoot machine satisfy the requirements? If so, refer to Chapters 4 and 32.

Troubleshooting really does take the Windows 95 user out of the realm of theory and into that of deduction. The user with a machine that does not work takes on the role of a detective. Trying to determine what the next step should be and how the machine will behave on a certain path can be overwhelming for some. Certainly the casual user of PCs and the Windows 95 operating system would become very frustrated with the tedious work involved in trying to get an errant machine to run.

For the experienced user, and those familiar with troubleshooting computers, the ultimate reward is the final resolution, and a running machine. It is difficult to convince a user of how great Windows 95 is while the machine just sits there. OS/2 users will most likely be the hardest converts. They will argue that they have been using a 32-bit operating system for quite a while now, and have no need to switch. Unfortunately for them, most applications running on OS/2 these days are Windows-based, and OS/2 will not be supporting the Win32 API. So let the OS/2 user laugh while you struggle to set up your Windows 95 machine, and see who laughs last.

Figure P8.1 illustrates the Windows 95 Resource Kit and a small sampling of the topics covered by that document. These chapters, along with the Windows 95 Resource Kit, will provide the novice and expert users full understanding of troubleshooting in Windows 95.

FIGURE P8.1

*The Windows 95
Resource Kit and
some available
topics.*

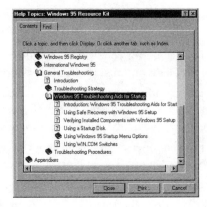

If troubleshooting is new to you, without a doubt you have come to the right place. Troubleshooting does require an ability to put theory into practice, so some thinking on your toes helps. In the spirit of completeness, the following two pages of this introduction will present outlines for troubleshooting.

Outline 1

Outline 1 presents a plan of attack for troubleshooting most issues under Windows 95. These procedures are tried and true, drawing mainly from the authors' own experience. Outline 2 focuses on the problems associated with Windows 95 installation. The most important thing to remember when troubleshooting Windows 95 is that a functioning Windows 95 machine is the goal. This may seem trivial, but it is all too easy to become wrapped up in the diagnosis and the frustration that comes with that, and forget why you are doing this. Computers are tools and should be enjoyable, or at least tolerable, to use. Do not overcomplicate the process, and try to have fun.

1. Can the machine be booted in Normal Mode?

   Yes. Move to step 3.

   No. Attempt to boot the machine by using the WIN.COM command-line switches from Command prompt only mode. See Chapter 32, section 5. If this fails, move to step 2.

2. Can the machine be booted in Safe Mode?

   Yes. Move to step 3.

No. Attempt to boot the machine in step-by-step mode, verifying the loading of all startup files. Choose the creation of a BOOTLOG.TXT file at this point. Search BOOTLOG.TXT for the words `fail` and `error`. Remove or change the entry in the corresponding file that causes the failure, if found. If this fails, boot the machine with a Windows 95 startup disk or the previous version of MS-DOS to verify basic machine functionality. Remove any recently installed hardware to simplify the process and return to step 1. If the machine refuses to reboot in any form of Windows 95, re-installation may be necessary. Refer to Chapter 32, section 3 and 5.

3. Does recently installed hardware, or hardware that used to function, not function?

   Yes. Move to step 5.

   No. Continue to step 4.

4. Does recently installed software, or software that used to function, not function?

   Yes. Is the software dependent on specialized hardware like a SCSI or MPEG board? If yes, and the hardware is known good, move to step 5. Did the software operate under Windows 3.1x and is this machine upgraded from Windows 3.1x? If yes, and you did not specify to upgrade into the existing Windows directory, you will need to re-install the software. If the software is DOS-based, open a full-screen DOS session and attempt running full screen. See Chapter 32, section 3 "Working with Multiple Boot Scenarios," or Chapter 33, section 2 "DOS Applications."

   No. Continue to step 6.

5. From the Start Menu, choose Settings and then Control Panel, and run the System applet. Choose Device Manager and look for any devices displaying a yellow exclamation icon, or a red x-out. These devices are not functioning. Conflicts with other devices, boot session enabling, drivers not being loaded, or just plain hardware failures are the causes. The first property page associated with a failing device will give information in the Device Status field for that device. Be sure to check the box with the word (Current) by it, because this enables this device for the current boot session. If the suspect device is not reporting an error or is reporting an error with the driver, reinstallation of the driver is needed. Reinstall the driver either by running the Add New Hardware applet or by running the manufacturer-supplied installation disk. Hardware that continues to fail might be damaged or might not be supported under Windows 95. Refer to Chapter 32 or contact the hardware vendor.

   If you are here, your machine is working.

Outline 2

This troubleshooting outline focuses on the installation of Windows 95. This outline is a small part of what is in Chapter 32, "Troubleshooting Windows 95 Installation." Refer there when you run out of options here.

Outline 2. Troubleshooting Windows 95 Installation

1. Did the Windows 95 Setup finish completely?

    Yes. See the previous troubleshooting outline.

    No. Windows 95 has four phases of installation, Startup and Information Gathering, Hardware Detection, File Copy, and Final System Configuration. Of these, only Hardware Detection and Final System Configuration can be significantly dangerous. If the installation halted in Hardware Detection, go to step 2, else move to step 3.

2. Did the Installation Wizard stop while analyzing your computer? (See Figure 32.3.)

    Yes. This indicates an issue with the detection routines in Windows 95 and your machine. After starting a reinstallation, the Installation Wizard will attempt to bypass the area that failed, after choosing Safe Recovery. If the installation continues to hang, reinstall without choosing Safe Recovery. Instead, choose your hardware from the list given, rather than allowing Windows 95 to analyze your computer. If this fails, copy the installation files for Windows 95 to the hard disk being used to boot; then reboot with only the DOS drivers loaded that are needed for the hard drive. No drivers is optimal. Finally, reduce the machine to the lowest bootable configuration before trying installation again.

    No. Move to step 4.

3. Does the Installation Wizard fail immediately after the first reboot, or report missing or damaged files.

    Yes. If the setup halted after the first reboot (after all the files had copied), then turn the system off and try rebooting. If the machine does reboot with the "Starting Windows 95..." screen, but continues to hang, there may be problems with ISA devices. Verify that all devices with driver statements in the CONFIG.SYS and AUTOEXEC.BAT files are up and running before setup continues. Evaluate these files and attempt reinstallation, verifying that all devices are up and running in DOS before installation starts. If missing files are reported, verify their existence. If the main VxD (VMM32.VXD) is missing, reinstall Windows 95.

    No. Continue to step 4.

4. Does access to the setup disk or disks fail?

   Yes. The solution is to copy all the installation files to your setup hard drive. This is cumbersome for floppy users, but essential for network installations. Simply set up a separate directory for the 30 MB of installation files, and begin installation from there.

   No. Continue to step 5.

5. Does the Installation fail to start, report memory or disk partition errors, or report the wrong version of DOS or DOS-extender errors.

   Yes. These errors indicate that your machine is on the edge of DOS functionality. Free up some memory by paring down to the essential files, free up some hard drive space, remove EMM386, and upgrade to a DOS version greater than MS-DOS 3.1.

   No. If your installation continues to fail from here, try reinstalling your previous versions of DOS and Windows from backup (you do have a backup), or install Windows 95 to a blank disk. If you purchased an upgrade version of Windows 95, you need a copy of Windows 3.x or greater on your machine.

Troubleshooting Windows 95 Installation

32

by Robert Griswold

IN THIS CHAPTER

Welcome to Windows 95 installation. If you are in the majority, your installation went fairly flawlessly, and all your resources that had such trouble existing together in DOS are working fine now. For those of you who had problems during installation, configuration, or use, these next few sections are for you.

Windows 95 is without a doubt the most publicized, debated, previewed, beta-tested, and anticipated operating system in the short history of personal computers. When Windows 95 is running smoothly, it does seem to be an improvement over DOS and Enhanced Mode Windows. An improvement to the point that most new users swear that their applications, even Win16 (Windows 16-bit or Windows legacy) applications, run faster. This not only seems true; it is true. Most of the underlying code that supports these pure Win16 applications has been re-written to be 32-bit clean.

Many people have decried the loss (and some say good riddance) of DOS with Windows 95. This simply is not the case. Not only does DOS live, it is an even better DOS—one that runs in protected mode and supports filenames that are longer than eight dot three. This DOS is capable of running at almost any point of the Windows 95 load or execution process. It can be full-featured or trimmed. One of my greatest finds of Windows 95 is the new EDIT.COM program—no more QBASIC to make the editor run. The EDIT.COM program is even suitable for use on older DOS machines and used there. DOS lives and is a great troubleshooting tool for Windows 95.

Failed installations of Windows 95 can ruin hard drives, wipe out applications, obliterate Program Manager groups, or run like a champ. Each installation can bring new variables into the processes that throw off what you know to be true. At least one common thread exists for all Windows 95 installations at this point: only Intel x86-based processors are supported. Because of this, a lot of the tools built in the past for DOS and Windows exist for your use in Windows 95.

Windows 95 relies heavily on Plug and Play to load the correct drivers and install the correct support, but most hardware is not yet compatible with Plug and Play. To resolve this, Windows 95 has a large set of detection code and macros that it must process to find non-Plug and Play devices. This code is called mainly from a file called MSDET.INF located in the WINDOWS\INF directory. This Device Information file (.INF) in turn calls other .INF files to process detection code for non-Plug and Play peripherals. The procedure for detecting Plug and Play devices is similar but involves the Configuration Manager.

Windows 95 goes through many different phases as the installation takes place. First, in the Startup and Information Gathering phase, the setup utility will detect if Windows 3.1x already exists on the machine. If Windows 3.1x does exist, Windows 95 will recommend that the setup be run from the File Manager. This is to enable the previous version of DOS to load the HIMEM.SYS driver. If Windows 3.1x cannot be found, then Windows 95 setup will load a high-memory manager and begin to copy temporary files needed for installation. After a barrage of questions comes the Hardware Detection phase, then the File Copy phase, where

Windows 95 files are copied into the selected directory. Finally, the reboot cycle begins. The machine will reboot a minimum of one time in the Final System Configuration phase but could reboot up to three times. This depends on the detection routine used to find the device, and whether drivers exist in the standard installation disks.

For most users who have had problems with Windows 95, the installation has been the worst part of it. As Windows 95 has matured, so have the detection routines, the Plug and Play modules, and the installation interface. The option currently presented during custom install, when you can choose different pieces of the operating system to install, is a feature that was added well into the development of Windows 95. Figure 32.1 is an example of the choices presented during Custom Install.

FIGURE 32.1.

Select Components screen from Windows 95 Install Wizard.

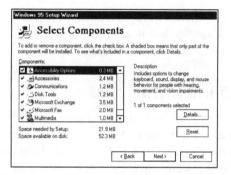

After copying files, Windows 95 will reboot the machine and continue to build the user interface. Windows 95 builds the interface by converting Windows 3.1x Program Manager groups to shortcuts for the taskbar, setting the time zone, and installing printers. If you choose to install the Microsoft Fax or Microsoft Network, then the Microsoft Exchange Wizard will begin to set up Microsoft Exchange. You can run the Microsoft Exchange Wizard later if you wish.

Finally, you need to verify the attachment and operation of all of the required peripherals. For instance, if the machine has a PCMCIA adapter and no Card and Socket services, or card drivers loaded during the installation, then you need to run the PCMCIA wizard from the Control Panel. Also, some sound cards are not easily detected, so you need to add them from the Control Panel using the Install New Device Wizard.

If your Windows 95 installations fail consistently, the problem can usually be traced to the following culprits:

■ The connected network is not functioning correctly, or the drivers for the network are too old for upgrading to Windows 95. This is due to the fact that drivers are loading in the CONFIG.SYS or AUTOEXEC.BAT files that interferes with the Windows 95 network setup. Disable the network by removing the drivers, and then attempt installation again.

- The installation hard drive has integrity problems not fixed by SCANDISK. SCANDISK does not automatically do a surface scan, and your disk may have problems. If setup continues to fail without an obvious error, try to execute a surface scan from SCANDISK.

- CMOS password protection or viruses are causing problems. CMOS password protection will sometimes keep Windows 95 from starting. Scan for viruses on a machine that refuses installation, and then disable all CMOS-based password protection during installation.

Installation Gotchas

Many operating systems have the reputation of being hard to install, configure, or customize. Overall, Windows 95 does not fall into any of those categories, but there is a distinct set of issues that need addressing before installation.

Copying the Install Files

Probably the best installation and troubleshooting advice you can get is to copy the entire installation directory from the CD to the hard drive being upgraded to Windows 95. When you install from the Windows 95 CD-ROM to the boot drive, it is imperative that the CD-ROM drive remains accessible. Anybody who has ever used a CD-ROM drive, SCSI or not, knows that sometimes things do not go right, and the CD-ROM can become inaccessible. When access to the installation source stops, installation becomes very difficult. Installing from CD-ROM is the right way to do installation of Windows 95; the copying the installation files gives the user access to the files when nothing is going right.

Figure 32.2 shows what Windows 95 presents when you install a new driver and it does not exist in the installation path. To avoid this problem, no matter the state of the device used for installation, create the full set of installation disks from the Windows 95 CD-ROM. Use the TRANSFER.BAT file from the Windows 95 install directory to create the disks. To create the disks, you must use 24 blank, 1.44MB floppies. This set of disks can now be used for emergency purposes.

FIGURE 32.2.

Insert Disk dialog box for new network card install.

Option Selection

Figure 32.1 shows the option selection dialog box as presented by the Windows 95 Install Wizard when choosing Custom Install. You need to look at each item and consider its functionality, whether you actually need the item, and whether you will use Microsoft Exchange. Windows

95 setup will install Microsoft Exchange for Microsoft Network and Microsoft Fax. If you choose all of the Multimedia selection, then 9 MB of sound and video files are copied to the hard drive.

The Accessories selection does not default to some of the better options. One selection from Accessories not copied is the Mouse Pointers. Also, Games, the On-line Users Guide (a necessity for the novice), and Character Map are not default selections. These selections to add some additional disk space requirements, especially the Users Guide, but these selections are invaluable. If you want these options but you skip them during installation, you can add them later by selecting the Add/Remove Software applet from the Control Panel.

Hardware Detection

As mentioned earlier, Microsoft has put a lot of work into developing the detection software used during installation. Yet it is far from perfect. The detection process for legacy devices can hit other devices that are not being installed. For instance, if the detection process is going through network cards and a SCSI card is installed and not detected, the SCSI card may fail. This is due to the fact that Windows 95 does some of its detection by reading I/O ports usually associated with known hardware.

Before performing this I/O port "walk," Windows 95 will execute many detection routines that are not as prone to failure. The program first looks for device driver lines in the CONFIG.SYS file that it recognizes. The detection software will also search standard ROM BIOS memory areas for BIOS signatures. Windows 95 also searches for standard motherboard resources, using the Plug and Play BIOS interface to help do the detection. All of these "safer" methods execute before any reading of I/O ports take place.

Microsoft is aware that detection routines may cause the machine to quit working. Figure 32.3 shows the verbiage that is on the Analyzing Your Computer dialog box of the Install wizard. If the machine does quit responding, Windows 95 directs the installer to choose Safe Recovery when the machine restarts. This is similar to the Failed Installation Detected warning displayed by Window for Workgroups if its install routine fails.

FIGURE 32.3.

Analyzing Your Computer progress dialog box.

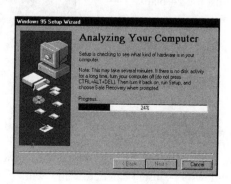

Hardware detection, as part of the Windows 95 setup, adds to the clutter of your hard drive. DETLOG.TXT, a hidden file, is one of the many files copied to the hard drive during the install process. The intermediate user can review this file to get some background on when Windows 95 does detection, and how it does it. This file, along with SETUPLOG.TXT, completely defines how the install proceeded. The following is a portion of the DETLOG.TXT file, showing the results of the detection process.

```
 [System Detection: 05/03/95 - 08:16:38]
Parameters "", Flags=01004233
SDMVer=0400.347, WinVer=0700030a, Build=00.00.0, WinFlags=00000419
LogCrash: crash log not found or invalid
DetectClass: skip class NET
DetectClass: skip class ADAPTER
Checking for: System Board
Detected: *PNP0C01\0000 = [1] System board
Checking for: System Bus
CheckInt86xCrash: int 1a,AX=b101,rc=0
Detected: *PNP0C00\0000 = [2] Plug and Play BIOS
Checking for: Advanced Power Management Support
Detected: *PNP0C05\0000 = [3] Advanced Power Management support
VerifyHW: manual device Net\0000: Dial-Up Adapter
Devices verified: 3
Checking for: Manual Devices
Checking for: Programmable Interrupt Controller
QueryIOMem: Caller=DETECTPIC, rcQuery=0
IO=20-21,a0-a1
```

The third line of the code has the entry SDMVer=0400.347. This indicates that the build of Windows 95 (Windows 4.0) is 347, or Beta 3. Pay particular attention to the fifth and sixth lines. These two lines indicate that this setup did not make the detection code search for Network or CD-ROM (non-SCSI) adapters. Make this choice by not checking the radio buttons presented in Figure 32.4.

FIGURE 32.4.

Analyzing Your Computer pre-analysis radio buttons.

The presentation of these radio buttons at this point depends on how the machine is running before the installation starts. If the network adapter had been up and running before this install started, the selection for the Network Adapter would not have been presented. This is because Windows 95's install can detect a network that is up and running, along with SCSI interfaces and non-SCSI CD-ROM drives. The safe detection routines provide this capability.

When you do not ask Windows 95 to detect any non-SCSI CD-ROM drives or Network Adapters, you avoid the problem of having the detection routine slam into the Adaptec APA-1460 SCSI host adapter. When the detection routine does go wrong and you cannot find the problem, the Windows 95 Resource Kit provides a nice way to diagnose what happened.

Figure 32.5 shows the Windows 95 Resource Kit suggestion for searching the files SETUPLOG.TXT, DETLOG.TXT, and BOOTLOG.TXT. This script provides a quick solution that provides important information.

FIGURE 32.5.

Windows 95 troubleshooting aids for startup log script example.

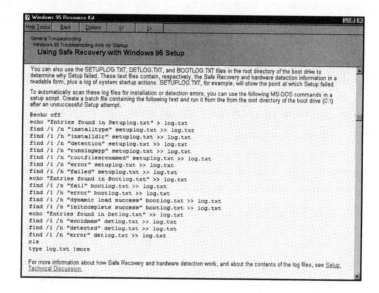

Hard Drive Problems

Windows 95 will do some checking of the hard drive before Setup starts the real installation. Execute Scandisk from the install directory of the Windows 95 installation CD-ROM, or off the first install disk. If Scandisk finds problems, then it will attempt to fix the problem before it continues. If you know your disk is good, because you can run your trusted third-party disk analysis tool, but Scandisk keeps reporting errors, you can tell Setup to run without Scandisk by executing the Setup command with an /is switch. Microsoft suggests that you do not use this switch. Type setup /? from the install directory for the full list of setup switch options.

Furthermore, the Windows 95 Resource Kit suggests that you back up all key system files before installation. The caveat here is to do this only with upgrade installations; new installs do not require this. The Resource Kit lists the following as key files:

- All initialization (.INI) files in the Windows directory
- All registry data (.DAT) files in the Windows directory
- All password (.PWL) files in the Windows directory

- All critical real-mode drivers specified in CONFIG.SYS and AUTOEXEC.BAT in the root of the C drive
- Proprietary network configuration files and login scripts
- All Program Manager Group (.GRP) files in the Windows directory

Choosing The Install Method

When choosing the installation method, the user needs to consider the defaults of each. The differences between each are laid out in the Windows 95 Resource Kit nicely, and presented here also.

Typical Setup: This is the recommended option for most users. This installation method is the least interactive. It concentrates on where you want to install Windows 95, what you name is, and if you would like to create a startup diskette. The target audience is desktop computer users. If the first pass of this install seems too light, try Custom Install.

Portable Setup: This option is the recommended choice for mobile installations. It is also the only default installation where Power Management gets installed. This installation also defaults to installing My Briefcase, and the remote access networking features. Once again, if you want some, but not others, Custom Install is for you.

Compact Setup: This option is for those situations where space is at a premium. The issue here is that the even with Compact, Windows 95 still copies 19 MB worth of files, and still asks you to decide on Microsoft Network. There are lots of files that still copied that are not needed here. Compact setup will come after installation, when removal of files that are not needed, like fonts, text, and DOS command files, can take place.

Custom Setup: The target audience of this style of installation is experienced users who wish to customize the machine during installation. This is the only selection to make for full control. With Custom, any, some, or none of the optional software can be installed. The drawback here is that there are a lot of questions to answer.

Correct Installation Preparation

Windows 95 installation can be difficult, but as long as you follow certain guidelines the procedure can go smoothly. Windows 95 does some of the work during installation by running Scandisk for error checking, and by suggesting that you perform a backup on the machine being upgraded. Other than this, the preparation of the machine is the responsibility of the installer.

To prepare for the installation of Windows 95, pay attention to the CONFIG.SYS and AUTOEXEC.BAT files and find out whether or not all the resources are present. When you have many installations of Windows 95 to do, the first few will set the tone and procedure for the rest. For instance, do not have Windows 95 create a startup disk. Startup disk creation can come at a later time by using the Add/Remove Software wizard located in the Control Panel.

Are Resources Enabled?

The resources needed to run with Windows 95 should all be up and running before the install starts. This is why Windows 95 searches for Windows 3.1x before the install starts. If your machine is up and running under Windows 3.1x, then all of the functions and peripherals of the machine should operate. This reduces the time for install and the chances that hardware detection may hang your machine.

If your machine has PCMCIA support, then install the cards desired and verify the card's functionality. For instance, if you have a PCMCIA Network and Modem multifunction card, install the Card and Socket services, along with the drivers needed to support the attached network. If you have a PCMCIA hard drive or memory card installed, then install the Card services for the ATA or standard services. If you have a PCMCIA SCSI controller installed, the DOS ASPI or CAM driver needs enabling so Windows 95 can detect attached SCSI devices.

If a network adapter is present and connected to a Novell server, then enable all the IPX/NETX protocol drivers. If Windows 95 detects this support before the System Analysis dialog box appears, there is less chance that the system will hang during hardware detection.

Multifunction sound boards are extremely cumbersome to set up in DOS and Windows 3.1x, but a correctly set up and running card is extremely useful for Windows 95. You may have some significant issues with getting multifunction sound boards running that were not enabled when the Windows 95 installation started. If Windows 95 is to detect the sound board during installation, any DOS based setup software must be used to initialize the sound settings. This would include the running of any SoundBlaster setting software, or any Wave Table initialization software. Furthermore, if Windows 95 does not detect these resources during initial system investigation, then Figure 32.4 will have another radio button that says Sound Board.

Are Multiple-Boot Scenarios Needed?

The Windows 95 Setup program assumes that when you are installing, it is to replace the existing copy of DOS and Windows 3.1x found, and make Windows 95 the primary operating system. The author has installed Windows 95 with OS/2 2.x and Warp, Windows NT, and Novell 3.11. The problem installing with these other types of operating systems is knowing how to prepare them for Windows 95. The Windows 95 Resource Kit is full of tips and suggestions for installing on these types of multiple boot machines. This section presents some alternatives for installing onto these machines, while retaining the capability of using other operating systems.

Windows 95, much like DOS, needs the booting partition to exist on the only primary partition on the first drive registered through the POST BIOS interface. OS/2 and Windows NT are a bit more respectful of other operating system boot scenarios. It is possible to have DOS/Windows 3.1x, Windows 95, OS/2 Warp, and NT all on the same machine, but not without a lot of work.

You must remember to first install the operating system that is the most flexible in booting and locating its system files. Windows 95 will inform Installations with OS/2 2.1x or Warp that the BootManager (if present) is not compatible with Windows 95. Windows 95 will disable the BootManager at this point. What actually happens is that Windows 95 sets the BootManager partition to not-Active, and then sets the primary Windows 95 partition to Active. Refer to the section Working with Multiple Boot Scenarios for detailed multiple-boot setup.

Are CONFIG.SYS and AUTOEXEC.BAT Okay?

The problem with the CONFIG.SYS and AUTOEXEC.BAT files of some machines is that they load and execute programs or TSRs that are not very friendly to Windows 95 installation. This can be virus software, disk compression software, network detection software, or password protection software. Many programs and drivers that are compatible with DOS and Windows 3.1x are also compatible with Windows 95. They just need to be disabled during installation. Refer to the SETUP.TXT file from Windows 95 for the latest list of programs that interfere with Windows 95 installation. The section Safe Mode versus Normal Booting later in this chapter outlines CONFIG.SYS and AUTOEXEC.BAT file manipulation.

Working with Multiple Boot Scenarios

When installing Windows 95, the unknowing DOS and Windows 3.1x users may be startled to discover that Windows 95 will overwrite their old versions of both DOS and Windows. The dialog box that reports this does not tell you that it is possible to keep the functionality of your old machine and get Windows 95 also. Windows 95 will also tell the unsuspecting OS/2 user that his or her OS/2 files will be unusable, and Windows 95 is disabling the BootManager. This is completely false. In fact, as mentioned earlier, it is completely possible to have a Windows 95 installation that works with many other operating systems.

Windows 95 and DOS/Windows 3.1x

The most common multiple-boot scenario will be the simple Windows 95 and DOS/Windows 3.1x setup. This is also the simplest set up for a multiple boot scenario. Because both of these operating systems require booting from the active primary partition of the first IPL installed hard drive, they usually will exist in the same partition. Functionality is the main reason for setting up a multiple-boot configuration.

If the machine is already up and running with DOS and Windows 3.1x, you need to make a choice about program access before installing Windows 95. If your applications are up and running fine under Windows 3.1x and you need to keep this functionality, install Windows 95 into that directory. As Windows 95 points out, simply copying group (.GRP) or initialization (.INI) files is not sufficient. This will eliminate the capability to run Windows 3.1x, but all of your program groups will remain, and applications like Microsoft Word will run in Windows 95. An installation of Windows 3.1x is possible after installing Windows 95, if required.

When Windows 95 enters the Final System Configuration phase, it executes a program called GRPCONV.EXE. This program will convert all of the .GRP files in the Windows 95 directory to Start menu items under the Programs listing. You can run GRPCONV.EXE interactively to convert group files by executing GRPCONV /M from the RUN selection of the Start menu. Alternatively, double-clicking the group file directly will run GRPCONV.EXE and convert that .GRP file to the Start menu. This trick really helps when problems have occurred with Start menu items.

If the target machine does not have Windows 3.1x installed yet, or re-installing your applications is not a big deal, then install Windows 95 into a directory other than the one being used by Windows 3.1x. Figure 32.6 shows the dialog box in which you can select the installation directory.

FIGURE 32.6.

Choose Directory selection dialog box.

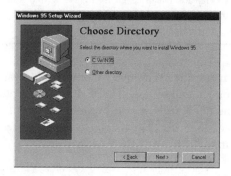

Table 32.1 cross-references the installation of Windows 95 with DOS and Windows 3.1x. The purpose of the table is to clarify how the machine will behave after installing Windows 95 into a new directory, or the old Windows 3.1x directory. This should give the installer some help in deciding how to handle the DOS and Windows 95 multiple-boot machine.

Table 32.1. Multiple-boot DOS and Windows 95 decisions.

| | Windows 95 was installed in: | |
| | Existing Windows 3.1x | A New |
What behavior is expected?	Directory	Directory
Are current Windows 3.1x programs and groups accessible?	Yes.	No. Programs must be re-installed.
Can DOS still be booted?	Yes.	Yes.

continues

Table 32.1. continued

What behavior is expected?	Windows 95 was installed in: Existing Windows 3.1x Directory	A New Directory
Can Windows 3.1x be re-installed?	Yes.	Not necessary.
Can Windows 3.1x still be run?	No, not without re-installing.	Yes.
Is the old DOS still complete?	No. Many files have been removed.	Yes.*

†Windows 95 replaces DblSpace, DrvSpace, Defrag, and Scandisk with batch files that point to the corresponding Windows 95 applications. These batch files keep the old DOS versions from running, since they cause problems on Windows 95 drives.

After some users install Windows 95 for multiple-boot capabilities, they find that they cannot actually boot their old version of DOS. If this is the case, then the installer needs to verify that he or she did not install over the previous version of Windows. After installing for multiple boot, the file MSDOS.SYS (a hidden, read-only system file in the root directory) has the following setting added:

```
[Options]
BootMulti=1
```

You can add this setting to an installation that installed over the previous version of Windows. However, some of the DOS files will be removed. Figure 32.7 shows what appears when you press F8 immediately following the machine's power-on self test (POST) beep.

FIGURE 32.7.

An example of the Windows 95 BootMulti screen.

Chapter 4, "Installing Windows 95," contains information about the settings found in MSDOS.SYS. Chapter 4 also has instructions for setting up a multiboot situation with previous versions of DOS, even when the files for DOS were deleted during Windows 95 setup.

Windows 95 makes decisions on the fly as to what files it should use while booting. In a multiple-boot scenario that includes DOS/Windows 3.1x, Windows 95 actually keeps two sets of the CONFIG.SYS and AUTOEXEC.BAT files around. One set is for Windows 95, and one is for the previous version of DOS. Table 32.2 indicates how Windows 95 renames files during different booting options.

Table 32.2. Multiple-boot file manipulation.

	Windows 95's files	*DOS's files*
Booting Windows 95	CONFIG.SYS, AUTOEXEC.BAT, COMMAND.COM	CONFIG.DOS, AUTOEXEC.DOS, COMMAND.DOS
Booting DOS	CONFIG.W40, AUTOEXEC.W40, COMMAND.W40	CONFIG.SYS, AUTOEXEC.BAT, COMMAND.COM

Windows 95, OS/2, and DOS/Windows 3.1x

When you need the functionality of multiple operating systems on the same machine, there should be no compromise. Installing Windows 95 for booting with other operating systems can be trial and error, but it will get easier. Planning and procedure are absolutely imperative. Follow the steps you set.

Follow these steps to install Windows 95 into a multiple-boot machine where OS/2 is the controlling BootManager. If you follow these steps, you should use a shared partition scheme so that OS/2 and Windows 95 can share applications and files.

1. Configure the machine's Initial Program Load (IPL) hard drive to hold the BootManager and a primary partition for DOS and Windows 95. If the same drive is large enough, configure an extended partition for the installation of OS/2. It is best to use the OS/2 FDISK utility for partitioning (from the second OS/2 installation disk), because it is more robust and it installs the code for the BootManager to work. Table 32.3 recommends a good partitioning scheme if you are going to do a one-hard disk installation.

2. With the BootManager installed, finish installing OS/2. This is the easiest way to proceed because the installation of the BootManager defines an installable partition. OS/2 wants to finish this installation.

3. After installing OS/2, reboot the machine. Boot from the DOS/Windows partition. This will error out with a Non-System disk error, and then boot from the DOS Setup disk. Follow standard DOS and Windows 3.1x installation. When rebooting during this process, always choose to boot from the DOS/Windows partition. Continue to install DOS and Windows 3.1x.

4. After installing DOS and Windows 3.1x, and while Windows is running from this partition, run the Windows 95 setup from CD-ROM or floppy. One of the first things Windows 95 will tell you is that it detected OS/2, and that the files and BootManager will not be usable with Windows 95. In the sense that you cannot run OS/2 executables from Windows 95, this is true, but you can see the partition (assuming it is FAT and not HPFS) and use BootManager. Windows 95 will make the DOS/Windows primary partition the active partition. Complete the Windows 95 installation.

5. When Windows 95 reboots to build the Hardware Registry and customization, it will bypass the BootManager. Finish Windows 95 customization, and verify that Windows 95 is running correctly.

6. To reactivate the BootManager partition, run FDISK from a DOS session in Windows 95. Choose Set Active Partition and then choose the BootManager partition. You will see the BootManager partition listed as partition 1. After setting the BootManager partition to active, reboot the machine.

Table 32.3. OS/2 BootManager partitioning scheme.

Partition	Type	Use	Size
1: Active	Primary	BootManager	1 MB
2: Set as C:	Primary	DOS/Windows 3.1x and Windows 95	User-defined; at least 100 MB
3: Set Installable for OS/2 Defined	Extended	OS/2 2.1x or Warp	User
4: E:	Extended	Shared Usage	User-defined

This procedure will produce a triple operating-system machine. You can use a similar scheme to set up a DOS/Windows, Windows 95, Windows NT machine.

The easiest way to install DOS/Windows 3.1x, Windows 95, and Windows NT on one machine is to start with DOS/Windows and then install Windows NT as a dual-boot machine. After installing NT completely, reboot to DOS/Windows 3.1x and execute Windows 95 setup from Windows 3.1x. The machine should optimally have three Windows directories: one for Windows NT, one for Windows 3.1x, and one for Windows 95. To boot Windows NT, simply choose that selection from the dual-boot selection. To boot Windows 95 or DOS/Windows 3.1x, choose the DOS boot option from Windows NT. Windows 95 will then begin booting. By pressing F8 at this point you can choose to boot from the old version of DOS. Figure 32.8 shows the Windows 95 Resource Kit discussion of running a dual-boot NT machine.

FIGURE 32.8.

Windows NT dual-boot discussion in the Windows 95 Resource Kit.

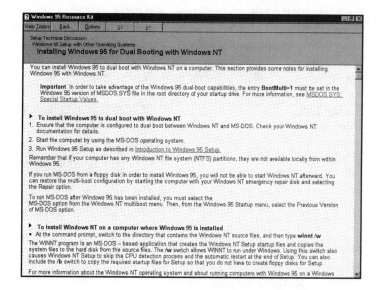

Probably one of the biggest headaches for installations like these are application support. All three of the installed operating systems can run most applications currently written for Win16, so you need to know where to install an application. You can use a common shared partition and install into one partition, and not have to have multiple copies of the same software. This does not, however, mean that you do not have to install the same software three times, because you do.

Software such as Microsoft Office or Adobe Pagemaker needs application support software to exist in the WINDOWS or WINDOWS\SYSTEM directory. At this point, you need to decide if you will use only one operating system for frequent application access. If all three operating systems must get to Windows applications, be prepared to install the software from each operating system. The applications can be installed into the same directory on the shared partition. This will reduce the number of copies of the same software.

Safe-Mode Versus Normal Booting

To the initiated Windows 95 beta tester, Safe-mode booting is well known. This mode of operation is to Windows 95 what Standard mode was to Windows 3.1. Like the Windows 3.1 Standard mode, Safe mode is not very useful unless you are in trouble. This Windows 95 mode of operation is intended solely for troubleshooting. Figure 32.7 lists a couple of selections for Safe-mode booting; but when should the user choose this kind of booting? When it is time to run Safe mode, you will know it.

Windows 95 installation has a unique way of making you think all is well, even after the last installation-triggered reboot has occurred. When the DOS screen that indicates Windows 95 is booting for the first time comes up and never goes away, then you learn about Safe mode. Safe mode presents itself to the user as Figure 32.7, but with a warning that indicates choosing Safe mode is for the best. Windows 95 expects the user will choose Safe mode, and then execute some kind of troubleshooting to resolve the problem. Figure 32.9 shows how the Windows 95 desktop looks when Safe mode is first entered.

FIGURE 32.9.

Windows 95 in Safe mode warning.

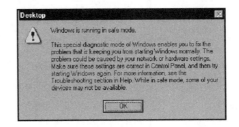

Safe mode, thankfully, runs for the benefit of debugging purposes. During the boot process, Windows 95 builds a log of what is happening. This allows Windows 95 to know if the process has stopped. Windows 95 will reboot into Normal mode after shutting down the machine from Safe mode. Windows 95 attempts to fix the previous boot problem by changing the legacy detection execution, how the Configuration Manager gives out resources, and device enabling. Usually, Windows 95 fixes the problem after an unsuccessful boot, then a Safe mode boot, and then a Normal reboot; but not always.

How to Stay Out of Safe Mode

Building a bootable machine that does not require Safe mode is not too difficult. There are some things you can do that will greatly increase your chances of never having to use Safe mode.

■ A working Windows 95 machine will have little to nothing in the CONFIG.SYS file. This is because the operating system prefers to load drivers for peripherals in protected mode, and not real mode. In most cases, the simple renaming of the CONFIG.SYS to C.SYS will suffice. Before installing Windows 95 on this machine, this is what the CONFIG.SYS looked like:

```
REM Xircom CreditCard Adapter — Do Not Change Lines Below (MENU)
[menu]
menuitem=Xir_enet+modem, Load Xircom CreditCard Ethernet+Modem Drivers For
Network Access
menuitem=Xircom_modem, Load Xircom Modem Drivers Only
menuitem=Nonet, Do Not Load Any Xircom Drivers
```

```
menucolor=15,0
[Xir_enet+modem]
[Xircom_modem]
[Nonet]
[common]
REM Xircom CreditCard Adapter — Do Not Change Lines Above

DEVICE=C:\DOS\HIMEM.SYS

REM Xircom CreditCard Adapter — Do Not Change Lines Below (EMM)
DEVICE=C:\DOS\EMM386.EXE NOEMS HIGHSCAN  X=C800-C8FF X=D200-D3FF
REM DEVICE=C:\DOS\EMM386.EXE NOEMS HIGHSCAN  X=C800-C8FF
REM Xircom CreditCard Adapter — Do Not Change Lines Above

REM BY PCM+  X=C800-C8FF
BUFFERS=20
FILES=30
DOS=UMB
LASTDRIVE=M
FCBS=4,0
DOS=HIGH

device=c:\conf_wss\conf_wss.exe /i=7

rem DEVICEHIGH=C:\DOS\SETVER.EXE
rem DEVICEHIGH=C:\DOS\POWER.EXE
DEVICEHIGH=C:\WINDOWS\IFSHLP.SYS
STACKS=9,256
DEVICE=C:\PCMPLUS3\CNFIGNAM.EXE /DEFAULT
DEVICEHIGH=C:\PCMPLUS3\PCMSS.EXE
DEVICEHIGH=C:\PCMPLUS3\PCMCS.EXE
DEVICEHIGH=C:\PCMPLUS3\PCMRMAN.SYS
DEVICE=c:\xircom\cem2\odi\cxcfg.exe
DEVICEHIGH=C:\PCMPLUS3\PCMSCD.EXE
DEVICE=C:\SCSI\ASPI2DOS.SYS /D /PCMCIA /Z
DEVICE=C:\SCSI\ASPICD.SYS /D:ASPICD0
```

This is what the CONFIG.SYS file looked like after it was modified for running Windows 95:

```
device=c:\conf_wss\conf_wss.exe /i=7
```

Windows 95 Setup takes very little out of the CONFIG.SYS, and the documentation is not clear on the fact that these files need modification. What this means is that Windows 95 leaves the CONFIG.SYS file alone for the Windows 95 installation; it remains virtually the same as in the DOS installation. This is without a doubt one of the most important points of a successful Windows 95 installation. Chapter 4 outlines the default CONFIG.SYS settings prepared on the fly by the file IO.SYS.

■ A correctly configured Windows 95 will also have a light AUTOEXEC.BAT. This file is a little more lenient than the CONFIG.SYS but could still run some very nasty programs. The AUTOEXEC.BAT usually loads the TSRs, and a lot of these attempt to make direct access to the hardware, a real no-no in Windows 95. Before installing Windows 95 on this machine, this is what the AUTOEXEC.BAT looked like:

```
C:\SCSI\MSCDEX.EXE /D:ASPICD0 /M:12
@ECHO OFF
PROMPT $p$g
PATH C:\WINDOWS;C:\DOS;C:\BALLPT;C:\PCMPLUS3
PATH C:\NU;%PATH%
SET SYMANTEC=C:\SYMANTEC
SET NU=C:\NU
SET TEMP=C:\DOS
SET MOUSE=C:\BALLPT
C:\BALLPT\MOUSE.EXE /Q
LH C:\DOS\STRETCH.EXE
C:\NU\NDD C:/Q
C:\NU\IMAGE C:
LH C:\DOS\SMARTDRV.EXE /X
LH C:\DOS\DOSKEY.COM

REM Xircom CreditCard Adapter — Do Not Change Lines Below
@echo off
cls
goto %config%
:Xir_enet+modem
c:
cd c:\xircom\cem2\odi
CXCFG DRIVER=ODI
LSL
CEM2ODI
IPXODI
NETX
F:
login
c:
cd \
goto common
:Xircom_modem
c:
cd c:\xircom\cem2\odi
CXCFG
CM2DRIVE COM3 INTERRUPT=5 IOADDRESS=300 MEM=D2000
c:
cd \
goto common
:Nonet
:common
REM Xircom CreditCard Adapter — Do Not Change Lines Above
REM Xircom CreditCard Adapter — Do Not Change Lines Below (PATH)
PATH=%PATH%;c:\xircom\cem2\odi
REM Xircom CreditCard Adapter — Do Not Change Lines Above
```

This is what the AUTOEXEC.BAT file looked like after it was modified to run Windows 95:

```
@ECHO OFF
PROMPT $p$g
PATH C:\WIN95;C:\WIN95\COMMAND;C:\DOS;C:\BALLPT;C:\PCMPLUS3
PATH C:\WIN95;C:\WIN95\COMMAND;C:\NU;%PATH%
PATH=C:\WIN95;C:\WIN95\COMMAND;C:\BC45\BIN;%PATH%
SET SYMANTEC=C:\SYMANTEC
SET NU=C:\NU
SET TEMP=C:\DOS
```

```
SET MOUSE=C:\BALLPT
LH C:\DOS\STRETCH.EXE
LH C:\WIN95\COMMAND\DOSKEY.COM
```

This is a very well-behaved AUTOEXEC.BAT. This file provides functionality for the machine by setting some global environment strings, but it does not break the operating system. In the previous AUTOEXEC.BAT, there were a lot of network drivers loading. Not only would this have prevented much of the Windows 95 network drivers from working, but it would have probably hung the machine. Remember, Protected mode drivers whenever and wherever possible.

When to Run Safe Mode

Sometimes, knowing when to run Safe mode is not very clear. Safe mode is valuable for resetting values that have gone out of scope, or for checking the setting of devices that are intermittent. You do not need to wait until the machine dies before you use Safe mode.

If the machine is a laptop and is being used as a desktop machine with a larger resolution monitor, you can use Safe mode to reset the resolution to 640×480. If the machine was moved before changing the resolution, the laptop's screen probably will not work. The machine will boot, but the display will not be readable. To fix this, reboot the machine and press F8 when you see "Starting Windows 95." This will bring up the selections similar to Figure 32.7 and enable Safe mode booting. Safe mode booting always comes up 640×480, so the display settings are available for changing.

The Windows 95 Resource Kit tabulates the benefits of the different safe modes nicely. Table 32.4 shows the characteristics of the different booting choices.

Table 32.4. Safe mode boot loading characteristics.

Boot Actions	Normal Mode	Safe Mode	Safe Mode Command prompt only	MS-DOS 7.0 only (Ctrl+F5 or Shift+F5)	Safe Mode with Network
CONFIG.SYS and AUTOEXEC.BAT processed	No Yes	No	No	No	
HIMEM.SYS and IFSHLP.SYS loaded by IO.SYS	Yes	Yes	No	No	Yes
System Registry processed by the Configuration Manager	Yes	No	No	No	Yes

continues

Table 32.4. continued

Boot Actions	Normal Mode	Safe Mode	Safe Mode Command prompt only	MS-DOS 7.0 only (Ctrl+F5 or Shift+F5)	Safe Mode with Network
COMMAND.COM loaded to process DOS executables	Yes	No	Yes	Yes	Yes
Microsoft Disk Compression support loaded	Yes	Yes	Yes	No	Yes
WIN.COM is executed	Yes	Yes	No	No	Yes
All Windows 95 drivers are loaded	Yes	No	No	No	No
Windows 95 Network drivers are loaded	Yes	No	No	No	Yes
NETSTART.BAT is run (like Windows 3.11)	No	No	No	No	Yes

Safe mode can also get you out of annoying situations in which your multimedia devices are misbehaving. Installing a SoundBlaster and forcing an IRQ conflict can cause one of those annoying situations. Rebooting into Safe mode will eliminate the loading of those drives and enable you to resolve the issue. The resolution of the issue will usually involve the use of the Device Manager.

The Device Manager is part of the applet called System from the Control Panel. This is where an end user can turn when things are not going right. A machine where all is well will have a Device Manager listing that looks similar to Figure 32.10. All the device topics appear rolled up, and the machine is functional.

Figure 32.11 represents the Device Manager when things are not going well. Devices with the yellow exclamation point over them need attention. At this point the problem could be drivers, device settings, or resource conflicts. The Device Manager will be a great help to technical support personnel. With its capability to diagnose problems and conflicts, the Device Manager becomes another member of the troubleshooting team.

FIGURE 32.10.

A well-behaved machine's Device Manager.

FIGURE 32.11.

A misbehaving machine's Device Manager.

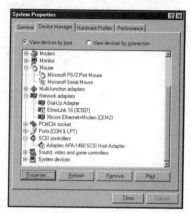

To begin conflict resolution, select a device in need of attention (one that has a yellow exclamation point over it) and then choose Properties. The properties dialog box of the device will display tabs along the top referencing General, Drivers, and Resources. When you choose the Resources property page, you simply need to read the status and choose an appropriate setting to resolve the conflict. Figure 32.12 shows a device in conflict and the resource that is creating that conflict. Notice the listed conflict near the bottom of the dialog box.

To resolve a conflict, an end user may also turn to the Help section of the Start menu. Figure 32.13 shows what the Help Topics selection box looks like. From here, you can choose Troubleshooting, if you are having problems, and the online help will walk you through the basics of resolving hardware conflicts, fixing printing problems, or how to boot in Safe mode. Taking this path in Troubleshooting is easy, because Windows 95 will walk you through the procedure one step at a time. This help is in addition to the Windows 95 Resource Kit help file.

FIGURE 32.12.

A device in conflict.

FIGURE 32.13.

Help Topics top-level display box.

Be aware that if you must use Safe mode, some things are going to change. If you are having problems with your video, and you cannot see your desktop, then Safe mode is the only real way back to the machine. Once Safe mode is running, some of the customizations to the desktop will change. For instance, if you have chosen to customize your Taskbar by placing it in a different location and adding the Auto hide feature and small icons, these settings will all be reset after running Safe mode.

Windows 95 DOS-Mode Troubleshooting

You may be wondering where and when you need to concern yourself with DOS. Even though you are now using Windows 95, DOS is still present, and it still plays an important role in the operation and troubleshooting of the machine. Without DOS mode, or even the capability to boot to the previous version of DOS, rudimentary problem resolution would be much more difficult than it is.

Before you go any further, read a few words of caution about DOS-based utility programs and Windows 95. Windows 95, by default, installs long filename support. Discussed earlier in this book, long filenames enable FAT table-based files to be longer than eight dot three in length. Not all DOS utility programs, especially those products released before Windows 95, are compatible.

Norton Utilities has been a mainstay of the computing establishment for years, but parts of it do not get along with long filenames. If you decide that you need to run Directory Sort from Norton 8.0 or earlier, then be prepared to lose all of your shortcuts. Shortcuts are the equivalent of Program Groups and Program Items from Windows 3.1x, but they can live anywhere. This is not Norton Utilities' fault; it is just a byproduct of long filenames.

Norton Disk Doctor (NDD) will also give you some real headaches when you use it on a drive with long filenames. This is unfortunate, because the default Norton Utilities 8.0 installation runs NDD from the AUTOEXEC.BAT file. NDD will report that it found FAT problems. Do not ask NDD to fix it. In Windows 95, for the time being, run SCANDISK from the Start menu. SCANDISK will not kill your long filenames. Figure 32.14 show what happens to shortcut names after deleting the long filenames.

FIGURE 32.14.

Start Menu selection with shortcut names truncated.

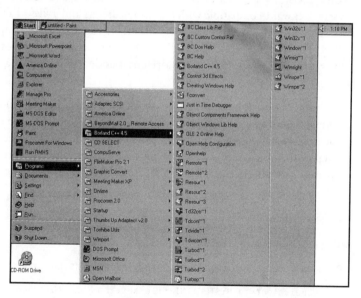

Just recently, Symantec began shipping a beta Windows 95 version of Norton Utilities. In initial use it seems well behaved, and certainly has no problems with long filenames.

Booting for Troubleshooting

Windows 95's DOS is a full-featured DOS. It behaves so much like DOS, that you can actually run Windows for Workgroups 3.11 faster than DOS 6.x does.

When Windows 95 refuses to boot, hangs at the startup screen, or errors out with a "Windows Protection Fault, Please reboot your computer," the Command prompt only boot is a lifesaver. It is hard to find a newer DOS-based program that will not run in Windows 95 Command prompt interface. This is beneficial, because now you have pre-GUI access to all the files that influence the way Windows 95 boots. The following files have a direct bearing, or are generated by Windows 95 and its boot process:

CONFIG.SYS	AUTOEXEC.BAT	SYSTEM.INI
DETLOG.TXT	BOOTLOG.TXT	WIN.INI
USER.EXE	SYSTEM.DAT	NETLOG.TXT
MSDOS.SYS	IO.SYS	SETUPLOG.TXT

The files that are important to the Windows 95 DOS troubleshooter are CONFIG.SYS, AUTOEXEC.BAT, BOOTLOG.TXT, SYSTEM.INI, and WIN.INI. Windows 95 is designed to stay backward-compatible with real-mode drivers and TSRs (Table 32.1 not withstanding). Real-mode installation files are critical. Earlier, you learned the importance of having a clean CONFIG.SYS and AUTOEXEC.BAT file. This remains true. These two files can wreak more havoc than most protected-mode drivers. Besides, there is not a need for most real-mode drivers.

One great aspect about keeping the step-by-step and Command prompt-only booting is that booting these ways does not preclude the loading of the GUI side of Windows 95. After you boot to Command prompt only, you can type WIN to start Windows 95. For the most part, though, when you are troubleshooting it is important to stop before the GUI. The following is displayed by typing the command WIN /? from the Windows 95 command prompt.

```
C:\WIN95>win /?

Starts Windows.

WIN [/D:[F][M][S][V][X]]

/D   Used for troubleshooting when Windows does not start correctly.
  :F  Turns off 32-bit disk access.
      Equivalent to SYSTEM.INI file setting: 32BitDiskAccess=FALSE.
  :M  Enables Safe mode.
      This is automatically enabled during Safe start (function key F5).
  :N  Enables Safe mode with networking.
      This is automatically enabled during Safe start (function key F6).
  :S  Specifies that Windows should not use ROM address space between
      F000:0000 and 1 MB for a break point.
      Equivalent to SYSTEM.INI file setting: SystemROMBreakPoint=FALSE.
```

```
:V  Specifies that the ROM routine will handle interrupts from the hard
    disk controller.
    Equivalent to SYSTEM.INI file setting: VirtualHDIRQ=FALSE.
:X  Excludes all of the adapter area from the range of memory that Windows
    scans to find unused space.
    Equivalent to SYSTEM.INI file setting: EMMExclude=A000-FFFF.


C:\WIN95>
```

Look familiar? It looks just like the WIN /? display from Windows 3.11. This is not just a co-incidence. There was a lot of leverage work done from Windows for Workgroups and Windows 95. Even though the selection WIN /B is not there, a BOOTLOG file is still created by using this switch.

The BOOTLOG.TXT file is very informative once you know what sections of the boot cycle are being reported. A portion of the top of a BOOTLOG.TXT file might look like this:

```
[000458AC] Loading Device = C:\WIN95\HIMEM.SYS    ; Needed For Safe mode
[00045962] LoadSuccess    = C:\WIN95\HIMEM.SYS
[00045963] Loading Device = C:\WIN95\DBLBUFF.SYS
[00045967] LoadSuccess    = C:\WIN95\DBLBUFF.SYS
[00045968] Loading Device = C:\WIN95\IFSHLP.SYS   ; Installable File
[0004596B] LoadSuccess    = C:\WIN95\IFSHLP.SYS   ; System, just like WFW
[0004596E] (Safe boot)
[0004599D] Loading Vxd = VMM                      ; Virtual Machine Manager
[000459A1] LoadSuccess = VMM                      ; This IS Windows 95
[000459A2] Loading Vxd = vmouse
[000459A4] LoadSuccess = vmouse
[000459A5] Loading Vxd = configmg                 ; Configuration Manager
[000459A7] LoadSuccess = configmg                 ; Plug and Play Boss!
.
.
.
[000459E6] LoadSuccess = VDMAD
[000459E7] Loading Vxd = VTD
```

This goes on and on. What the troubleshooter is looking for is an entry similar to this:

```
[000459EA] Loading Vxd = V86MMGR
[000459EC] LoadFailed = V86MMGR Failure code is 0001
```

Although this failure entry is not very informative by itself, it does give a clue to the VMM.VXD file. This file contains many of the base VxDs needed to run Windows 95, and because there is no V86MMGR.VXD entry in the WINDOWS\SYSTEM directory, V86MMGR.VXD is probably an embedded VxD from VMM.VXD. This trick, using virtual device drivers to load different parts of code, is not new, but it does make it difficult to find out why the machine does not boot.

Another interesting point of the BOOTLOG.TXT file is the IOS section. IOS is the I/O System of Windows 95. All access to lower-level devices such as floppies, SCSI devices, ATAPI CD-ROMS, and IDE hard drives occur through the IOS VxD. Once the IOS VxD receives its DEVICEINIT message, it begins the process of dynamic device loading for I/O devices.

This is all based on the Plug and Play interface for Windows 95 and the concept of dynamic drivers. The loading or unloading of these drivers occurs when the need arises, thereby gaining the name "dynamic." The following shows the BOOTLOG entries for the beginning of IOS driver loading:

```
[00045A83] DEVICEINIT   = IOS
[00045A97] Dynamic load device  C:\WIN95\system\IOSUBSYS\apix.vxd
[00045A9C] Dynamic load success C:\WIN95\system\IOSUBSYS\apix.vxd
[00045A9D] Dynamic load device  C:\WIN95\system\IOSUBSYS\cdfs.vxd
[00045AA2] Dynamic load success C:\WIN95\system\IOSUBSYS\cdfs.vxd
[00045AA3] Dynamic load device  C:\WIN95\system\IOSUBSYS\cdtsd.vxd
  .
  .
```

Finally, the part most Windows 3.1x users will recognize the most. If you have ever run Windows 3.1x with the /B option, you have seen the BOOTLOG.TXT file created in the Windows directory. These entries are created when the SYSTEM.INI is processed, and although the loading may be a classic style, it does not make the drivers un-Windows 95. The following portion comes from the bottom of the BOOTLOG.TXT, where it logs the SYSTEM.INI.

```
LoadStart = SYSTEM.DRV
LoadSuccess = SYSTEM.DRV
LoadStart = KEYBOARD.DRV
LoadSuccess = KEYBOARD.DRV
LoadStart = MOUSE.DRV
LoadSuccess = MOUSE.DRV
LoadStart = VGA.DRV
LoadSuccess = VGA.DRV
LoadStart = MMSOUND.DRV
```

The BOOTLOG.TXT and DETLOG.TXT files are critical for troubleshooting a failing installation. Figure 32.5 gave the Windows 95 Resource Kit way of building a script file used to pull the failing portions out of the files. Actually, scanning those files in a DOS editor for the words "fail" and "error" is much easier. For instance, if the entries

```
 [0006E1D7] Loading VxD = msmouse.vxd
[0006E1DD] LoadFailed  = msmouse.vxd
```

were seen in the BOOTLOG.TXT, it would tell the troubleshooter that the MS Mouse driver specified in the Registry did not load. If Windows 95 does not boot because it reports no XMS memory is available, then BOOTLOG.TXT will contain the following error:

```
LoadFailed = C:\WINDOWS\HIMEM.SYS
```

This would indicate that the file HIMEM.SYS is missing or has been corrupted.

Windows 95 DOS troubleshooting is very useful, but sometimes the only way to correct a problem is to strip the machine down or reinstall the program. Stripping Windows 95 of all of the drivers associated with hardware can be too difficult to do. If you suspect a particular driver, the easiest thing to do is to remove the device from the Device Manager. Figure 32.11, earlier in the chapter, shows a Device Manager with devices that are not responding. If these devices are suspect, remove them, and the drivers will no longer load. You must reinstall the devices in order to use them again. This will keep the driver from loading, and you can try rebooting without the offensive device.

An unruly Windows 95 installation needs serious attention. If the machine is a production machine and is having problems that require troubleshooting on a daily or more frequent basis, then the easiest solution is to reinstall. If you have followed the suggestions in Installation Gotchas and have copied the install files to your hard drive, reinstallation takes about 10 minutes. Experience shows that this procedure will sometimes make the most nasty Windows 95 machines run like a top.

Summary

Windows 95 installation is not like anything an experienced DOS or Windows user has seen before. Installing Windows 95 requires the understanding of what happens during the four phases of installation. Installation will get easier over time. Save yourself some time by starting with good install habits. Make sure all devices are up and running under DOS or Windows before you begin. Copy the install directory or files to the hard drive where installation is taking place. Verify network functionality before beginning. Be conscientious of multiple-boot requirements before starting the installation.

The installation of Windows 95 over networks provides enough information for another complete chapter. Installation of Windows 95 over networks can use script files to automate TSR removal, option installation and default machine configurations. The Windows 95 Resource Kit goes through topics such as Automated Installations, Push Installations, and Custom Network installations.

When things go wrong, start at the beginning. Verify Safe mode functionality and use the Device Manager for all it is worth. A new installation might require a step-by-step boot to overcome a misbehaving legacy device, but this is easier than fighting with Normal to Safe mode booting. Paying attention to the CONFIG.SYS and AUTOEXEC.BAT could be the best precautions for bypassing a problematic installation. Using DOS to troubleshoot alleviates the problem of loading all the GUI stuff; so use it. Do not give up. Windows 95 is like OS/2 2.x was in its infancy—a little hyper, but well worth the time.

Finally, use the Windows 95 Resource Kit as much as possible. It is free and contains loads of specific information for the trouble you could be seeing right now.

Troubleshooting Applications

33

by Robert Griswold

After installing the operating system, its purpose comes to life: to use applications under Windows 95. There are really two parts to application troubleshooting: installation and setup, and running the application. In contrast to Windows 95 itself, the end user will experience fewer problems with the installation and setup of applications than with the running of applications. However, the chances that any particular application will have a problem in Windows 95 are fairly low. Windows 95 has demonstrated that it is at least as stable as Windows 3.1x when running most Win16 applications.

When you are deciding what applications to run with Windows 95, you only need to consider what the functionality of the machine is. If you are setting up a desktop machine, you will usually select a word processor, spreadsheet, database, and financial software. If you are setting up a desktop publishing machine, you will need to decide on page layout, art and illustration, and word processing. All of these decisions are influenced by how well the selected programs ran for you in Windows 3.1x, and whether you want Win32 applications. Most first-time users of Windows 95 will select applications that are familiar and reliable.

Windows 95 promises 32-bit application support. The problem for the current beta testers and the first-round Windows 95 recruits is that 32-bit applications are scarce. These applications are in the works, and many will begin shipping right after the release of Windows 95. The moving target of the release date has sent many developers reeling, and some are waiting feverishly for its release. 32-bit applications are coming, and a few small applications have arrived with Windows 95. Microsoft has packaged a few small applications to get the user acquainted with the look of the 32-bit interface. You will look at these applications later in this chapter.

Both Windows applications and DOS application will run under Windows 95. Beta testers and experts on Windows 95 have found that DOS and Windows applications all run faster under Windows 95. Assembly code using MASM 6.11 compiles faster; even DOS-based games like DOOM II run great. What is equally impressive is that any DOS box can have over 600 KB of free lower memory, no matter how many DOS boxes you run. Microsoft did not kill DOS. They have made it even better and easier to use. Some people just cannot give up the idea of running Procomm shareware for all their BBS activities. Old habits die hard.

Windows 95 gives the users of Win16 and DOS applications finer control over how those applications run. For Win16 and DOS applications that need special parameters to run, Windows 95 provides a special place to set those parameters. Maybe you used to have a separate boot session under DOS to support certain applications. With the APPS.INF file, located in the WINDOWS\INF directory, you can add your own settings if they do not exist. Memory support is better for Win16 and DOS applications. Win16 applications take advantage of the resources available to Win32 applications inside their own memory space, while each DOS application gets its own virtual machine with 4 GB of theoretical memory.

Windows 95 has improved over the old Ctrl+Alt+Delete response from inside Windows. This used to produce the infamous white-on-blue "The system is busy…," or if you were lucky, "Close the application…" screens. The three-finger salute will usually provide a response that can actually help the machine regain its composure, as that pictured in Figure 33.1. The Local Reboot dialog box tells you what the currently running programs are, while also indicating some parts of the operating system. Sometimes Windows 95 will also give the dreaded white-on-blue screens, and most of the time recovery is not possible. Windows 95 is a bit more gracious in some of the Windows Protection Fault (WPF) errors it returns, because it will tell you the offending application, dynamic link library (DLL), or virtual device driver (VxD). If the name of the offending VxD is VMM, forget recovery; just reboot.

FIGURE 33.1.

The Ctrl+Atl+Delete dialog box (Local Reboot) from Windows 95.

Win16 or Win32 Applications?

First-time users of Windows 95 and new recruits to Windows will not have an easy time deciding whether or not to use Win16 versus Win32 applications. You have heard a lot about how the Win32 applications have access to preemptive multitasking, long filenames, and memory protection, and are probably excited. The most evident problem is the lack of availability of Win32 API-enhanced applications. Never fear, Microsoft has brought many applications right to you with Windows 95 (much to the chagrin of developers).

Win32 API-based applications will be here soon, and will be incorporating features such as multiple threads, new buttons and interface controls, and toolbars for any application. These features are nice, but they do not make the application. Sticking to the tried and true, those old faithful programs from Windows 3.1x, for right now, is not a bad decision. If you make the decision to stay with a Win16 application, you need to understand how it works with Windows 95. Long filenames are one area that requires understanding. Figures 33.2 and 33.3 show a standard open dialog from a Win16 and Win32 application, respectively. Notice how the directories and filenames are difficult to read in the Win16 application.

FIGURE 33.2.

The Open dialog from Microsoft Word 6.0.

FIGURE 33.3.

The Open dialog from WordPad 4.00.347.

The two figures indicate one of the small differences between Win16 and Win32 applications. This difference is not dramatic unless you are creating a lot of documents with a Win32 application and are then attempting to use them in a Win16 application. Although documents created using long filenames are convenient, you may forget that you have customers and associates who are stuck in Win16 for a while. A list of long filename saved files can create a real headache for a Win16 user. Consider this list of perfectly legal long filenames.

Status Report for Jane 3-16-95
Consensus of titles
Expenses for Japan Trip
Expenses for Havana Trip
conceptual form 5-23-95
Status' of Department meetings

In a Win16 application, these filenames would appear as seen in Figure 33.2. Because of this, the document creator needs to understand naming conventions for documents that are being shared. Documents with long filenames copied to DOS floppies will have the long filename copied with them, but they will be unusable on a Win16 machine.

Message Queues

One of the biggest features touted by Microsoft for Windows 95 is the use of the separate message queue. The *messaging queue* is where the system talks to the applications that are running on it. It is also the main reason why when an application in Windows 3.1*x* stopped responding, so did the rest of the system. Windows 95-based applications promise to take advantage of the separate message queue for each Win32 application. When a misbehaving Win32 application stops responding, the machine will continue to run because the other applications have access to their own message queue. Separate message queues are only a luxury for Win32 applications, however.

The lowly Win16 application uses a shared message queue. This provides backward compatibility but makes Win16 applications more destructive to the entire machine. The problem is that when you convert your machine to Windows 95 and are using all Win16 applications, one errant Win16 application can still bring the system to a halt. In theory, if the queue for the Win16 applications comes to a halt, the rest of the machine is still accessible. This may be true, but usually once the machine's entire Win16 structure has come to a halt, so has all your work. This is another good argument for using Win32 applications.

Windows 95 machines can, and do, crash with General Protection Faults (GPFs), and it is not unusual for Win16 applications to cause the crash. Machines connected to Novell Netware servers in Windows 3.1*x* with NETX support are famous for stopping the system cold when the server drops. Users of Windows 95 machines, though, are fortunate that Microsoft and others have worked to create the 32-bit network support that resolves this. In Windows 95, even a machine that has its physical connection to the network broken will continue to work. The machine will resolve the loss of resources by alerting the user to the missing server, and marking the resources as unusable. Figure 33.4 shows a My Computer window with terminated server access.

FIGURE 33.4.

*My Computer showing
network drives as
unavailable.*

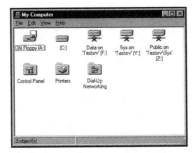

What about Win16 applications that rely on the server to be there? Many e-mail and meeting packages require the use of the server for incoming queues and time-managed broadcasts. Some of these applications do not manage the loss of the server gracefully and will hang the machine. At this point, even if your Win16 application is in the background, when it is brought into focus and polls the server, the machine may hang. Because this is the Win16 shared message queue, a hanging program can (and usually does) bring down the rest of the machine. Until reliance on Win16 applications begins to diminish, machines crashing because of these applications will be common.

Local Rebooting

Figure 33.1 demonstrated the Local Reboot dialog box. When you see this dialog box (not IF you see it), it will most likely be telling you which applications are errant. One problem with this method of identifying which application is to blame is that it may be reporting the messenger, and not the criminal. There are some applications listed in the box that are not applications at all and may actually be the culprit. The following list of VxDs and executables will probably bring the entire machine down if they are categorized as "Not Responding" in the Local Reboot dialog box. Rebooting the machine is the only alternative.

> KERNEL32 or KERNEL or KERNEL386
> USER
> MSGSRV32
> EXPLORER
> VMM32, usually only white-on-blue DOS screen
> WINOLDAP

As you grow more comfortable with the system, you will learn the things from which you can locally reboot, and those from which you cannot. To see what applications Windows 95 believes to be open, save all your work and press Ctrl+Alt+Delete. The results might surprise you.

Observed Problems and Resolutions

Table 33.1 lists problems the author has observed from his own experience with Windows 95, and the associated Windows applications. This is not a full list by any means, and is not intended to be slanderous or malicious.

Table 33.1. Specific Win16 application problems.

Program	Problem	Resolution
Adaptec's EZ-SCSI v3.x Windows programs	Some of these applications report "Unable to initialize ASPI for Windows"	In Windows 3.1x, even without devices attached, ASPI for Windows was loaded. If no devices are attached that need to use WinASPI in Windows 95, then WinASPI is not loaded, and these applications will not function.
Beyond's Beyond Mail 2.0	Will not find the user's inbox, or cannot successfully retrieve incoming mail	This problem was originally seen on some early beta versions of Windows 95. To resolve this issue, users simply reinstalled Windows 95 after Beyond Mail had been installed.
Avantos' Manage Pro v2.1 or v3.0	Text items in goal or project input boxes are displayed with a font that does not space correctly	It appears that the font that is being displayed is set to bold, yet the one being handled by the application is not bold. This results in entry of text that is hard to read. To maneuver around this, choose the zoom in icon for the text boxes, and enter text there, when possible.

continues

Table 33.1. continued

Program	Problem	Resolution
Microsoft's Word 6.0a	Using the Tools menu will occasionally bring up the dreaded General Protection Fault error	This failure seems to be related to the sequence in which Word or Microsoft Office is installed. The secret here is to choose Ignore, rather than Close. Clicking Ignore repeatedly makes the GPF go away. Once you are back in Word, save the document and exit the application.

Table 33.1 is a very small example of the Win16 applications that the author has tried with Windows 95. Windows 95 will surely see its share of odd applications running with it when it comes out, so do not be surprised at the behavior you may see. Using the Ignore button in a GPF dialog box has significantly more advantages in Windows 95 than it did in Windows 3.1*x*. When a Win16 application is going down in flames and a GPF occurs, always try the Ignore button first. Repetitively hitting the Ignore button may force the errant program over the section of failing code. Always, though, save your data and reboot as soon as possible, because all is not well after a GPF occurs.

Office Suite Packages and Windows 95

For many years now, numerous software vendors have shipped full software packages aimed at gearing an entire office toward one standard. These vendors have included Novell, Lotus, and Microsoft. Microsoft Office is probably the best-selling bundled package of all time, and has the biggest exposure to failing with Windows 95. This is because many people have written to the interface that lives inside the Microsoft Office package. This internal Office API, promoted by Microsoft in Visual Basic and WordBasic, has many applications written to it.

The problem arises when people convert their Microsoft Office applications to the Windows 95 version and do not upgrade their Office tools. Most of these tools exist as icons that call DLLs or EXEs from inside Word, Excel, or PowerPoint. Once Word is 32-bit, calling a 16-bit tool from inside it will no longer work, and that Office enhancement will be unusable. The same is probably true for the office solutions from Novell or Lotus.

To solve this, end users need to be in contact with their solution providers, who may be in-house. The programmer who has written to the provided API needs to rewrite the code to call the correct 32-bit functions. Alternatively, the programmer could thunk (a term that means taking the shortest path, in this case changing 16-bit code to 32-bit code on the fly) the 16-bit code with some sort of execution engine. Both of these alternatives, and others, are in the Microsoft Developers Forum. Choose GO MICROSOFT on CompuServe for access to the Developer's or other Microsoft forums.

Basic Win16 Troubleshooting

To help in the day-to-day execution of Win16 applications, check out the following examples. Win16 application support under Windows 95 is actually easier than with Windows 3.1x, and should provide the user with faster response times. These troubleshooting points come from the author's own experience and the Windows 95 Resource Kit.

■ **When I try to run a Windows 95-included Win16 program or utility, I get a "Cannot find the file..." error.** This could indicate a deleted program or one that never got installed (though this is unlikely). Your choices are to run the Add/Remove Programs applet from the Control Panel or remove the application yourself from the cabinet (.CAB) files you copied to your hard drive (or on the CD). The problem with running the Add/Remove Programs applet is that it is only going to enable the addition of the most common applications and accessories. You cannot use the Add/Remove applet to install great programs like GRPCONV.EXE and WINFILE.EXE. These files need to be extracted. To see how to use the EXTRACT.EXE program that comes with the .CAB files, refer to the "DOS Applications" section later in this chapter.

■ **My Win16 application does not install, reporting "Wrong Windows version."** The problem here is that the setup or install program for the Win16 application is expecting Windows 3.10, and does not like Windows 95. First, select the setup icon, click the right mouse button, and choose Quick View. This will indicate the program's (module) name, probably SETUP. After verifying the name, add the following to the [Compatibility] (not [Compatibility32]) section of the WIN.INI file:

SETUP=0x00200000

This will tell any Win16 program called SETUP that the version of Windows on which it is executing is 3.10. This procedure is useful for any program expecting a certain version of Windows. Be sure to remove the SETUP line when you are finished.

■ **My Win16 application reported a "Missing DLL" error right after I installed it.** Some Win16 programs actually ship with DLLs and virtual device drivers that replace Windows 3.1x components. This is acceptable, because the different files usually just provide additional functionality. If the Win16 program you are installing overwrites a Windows 95 system file, then Windows 95 will replace that system file with one from the hidden SYSBACK directory. This will be a problem for some programs. If the DLL or virtual device driver needs to be in the system, then copy it to the WINDOWS\SYSTEM\VMM32 directory. If the program does not run, contact the manufacturer about a Windows 95 version.

■ **A stable program under Windows 3.1x continually gives General Protection Faults under Windows 95.** This may not be caused by the program at all but by the other programs running with it. A lot of things are running in a Windows 95 machine, including Windows-specific Win16 applications. If the GPF for this application is immediately followed by another with a name you have never seen, then it could very well be that a background Win16 task is trampling over this application. Clean the system up by rebooting, and then run the application by itself and view the results. If the offending application becomes apparent, contact the manufacturer.

■ **Your favorite Win16-based disk utility will no longer run.** This is correct. Because most Win16-based applications for disk management made calls right to the hardware, they will fail in Windows 95. Because the program is Win16-based, locking the disk is not going to be something the program would do, because this API structure only came with Windows 95. As a rule of thumb, do not use any disk diagnostic, disk editor, disk defragmenter, or disk utility not written for Windows 95.

DOS Applications

Running Win16 application in Windows 95 really is not that difficult. If the application is a stand-alone application that does not depend on any other functioning Win16 applications, running it is fairly flawless. This is a huge benefit to Windows 95, but not such a huge feat. Windows 95 and all its APIs and DLLs naturally follow what Microsoft has been doing with Windows for a long time. It only makes sense that these older, well-behaved programs should work.

But what about DOS programs? DOS programs do not usually run flawlessly under Windows, especially the older programs. DOS 5.0 and later had knowledge of Windows, and even provided a way for programmers to interface with Windows. Programs written to stay backward compatible with DOS 3.3 may not take advantage of that interface, so it may take some tweaking of the system to make it work.

To run well-behaved MS-DOS applications from an MS-DOS virtual machine, simply execute the application. MS-DOS virtual machines have a significant advantage over Win16 applications, because each DOS virtual machine shares no memory resources with another. Each MS-DOS program has its very own virtual machine, except with the MS-DOS Only boot.

Long filename support built into DOS boxes makes using some of the MS-DOS-based console programs provided with Windows 95 much nicer. Figure 33.5 shows the MS-DOS editor displaying long filenames.

FIGURE 33.5.

The MS-DOS Editor with long filenames.

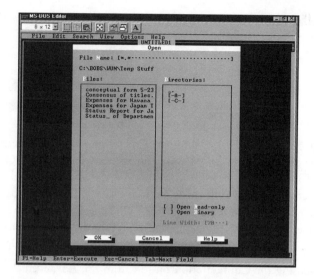

Running Windows 3.1x, the Ultimate DOS Application

Chapter 32 alluded to the fact that Windows 3.1x can execute on top of the Windows 95 environment, so give it a try.

When you first encounter the Windows 95 MultiBoot function and choose Command prompt, you should ask yourself, "Why do I want to run Windows 3.1x?" Is it because you need a certain application that refuses to run under Windows 95? Is it because you really like the Program Manager and File Manager? Maybe you miss the Terminal program.

If you want to run Windows 3.1x because you need a program that will not run under Windows 95, then you have the right reason. All other reasons are really only for the cool factor involved in getting Windows 3.1x to run on top of MS-DOS 7.0.

NOTE

MS-DOS 7.0 will be reported by Windows 95 to DOS or Win16 applications, such as Microsoft's MSINFO.EXE that comes with Microsoft Office 4.2, when these programs ask what DOS version is running.

When the BootMulti option is installed (see Chapter 32), the Shut Down menu will have the choices available for shutdown, as seen in Figure 33.6. After you make the choice to shut down to DOS, Windows 3.1x can start.

FIGURE 33.6.

The Shut Down Windows dialog selections.

You can run MS-DOS 7.0 in two ways: by choosing the Command prompt only boot, or the Shut down into MS-DOS mode. Either choice has an MS-DOS configuration associated with it. To see the associated configuration for the Shut Down selection, go into the Windows 95 directory and find a file called "Exit to DOS." This is a shortcut that has a special DOS-only mode of booting associated with it. Select the icon with the right mouse button, and choose Properties. Once the property page for this shortcut is up, choose Program, and then Advanced. This is where the nitty-gritty of shutting down into MS-DOS takes place.

Choosing the Configuration button from the Advanced Program property page results in the Configuration dialog, which enables you to select different MS-DOS options to support your applications.

How you want Windows 3.1x to run dictates how you set the configuration. If you find yourself having to use this style of running Windows 3.1x, make sure it is only for the occasional program. Going back to Windows 3.1x this way is a real pain after you have committed to using Windows 95.

Beauty in MS-DOS?

Windows 95 is being ballyhooed as the graphical user interface of the future, as the best thing since sliced bread. What has not had a lot of praise is the new way MS-DOS utilizes the machine for performance and functionality. MS-DOS programs that had a problem running under Windows 3.1x will find that the environment is a bit more suitable under Windows 95, that is, MS-DOS 7.0. Microsoft has included support in DOS for long filenames, better DOS window execution, toolbar access in DOS, and scaleable DOS windows with TrueType fonts. The biggest boon is to those memory-hungry DOS programs that would not run under Windows 3.1x.

The first time an end user runs a program from inside a DOS box that used to bark at even the best setup in Windows 3.1x, they know something has changed. Because each MS-DOS box has its own address space and virtual machine, and because very little of the conventional memory is being used, each MS-DOS box gets gobs of memory. Figure 33.7 shows a Windows 95 machine with four DOS boxes, all reporting 600 KB of free memory. This is unbelievable, unless of course you have used OS/2 2.1x or later, then you have seen this before.

FIGURE 33.7.

Windows 95 with four MS-DOS virtual machines running.

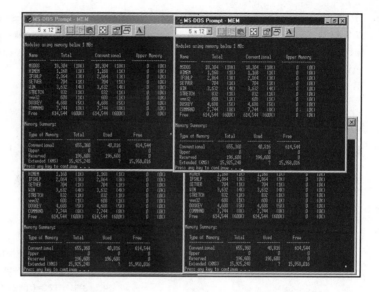

Windows 95 and DOS are not all peaches and cream at this point, though. Some MS-DOS applications still will require some fine tuning if they are extremely hard to manage. Maybe your MS-DOS application does not like being run in its own virtual machine and requires some access to low-level hardware usually not allowed in this protected mode. To give a particular MS-DOS application full access to the machine, you need to prepare it as if you are going to run Windows 3.1x, as shown earlier.

DOS Execution Example

One area that is extremely cumbersome to work with is the area of real mode drivers. A common situation is one in which a piece of hardware needs access to the network or file system before Windows 95 loads protected mode drivers for these services. The real problem is that this piece of hardware does not have Windows 95 protected mode drivers yet, and you cannot use it without the old real mode drivers. If running Windows 95 is not as important as access to the device, and you must run a real-mode driver, you need to do a separate MS-DOS only boot.

What comes to mind is access software for a bank of networked CD-ROMs or networked modems. These types of devices usually needed you to load device drivers after the network access software had been loaded, like IPX protocol drivers. The problem that you encounter with Windows 95 and these types of real-mode drivers is that the network is not available until after the machine is in protected mode. Also, most of these drivers will not execute correctly inside a DOS box in Windows 95. Therefore, look at how to set up a DOS-only boot to support a bank of networked fax modems.

The first step in setting up this fax solution is to create the CONFIG.FAX and AUTOEXEC.FAX files for the boot session. The luxury of the MS-DOS only boot shortcut, or any other MS-DOS shortcut, is that you can have separate CONFIG.SYS and AUTOEXEC.BAT files for it. To create the shortcut, open the Windows 95 directory. With the right mouse button (assuming you have a right-handed mouse), drag a copy of the COMMAND shortcut to your desktop. Because this solution is being created for a machine that probably had fax software running before, refer to the CONFIG.SYS and AUTOEXEC.BAT files used when the fax software ran under DOS. The following list outlines what the CONFIG.FAX and AUTOEXEC.FAX might look like.

CONFIG.FAX	*AUTOEXEC.FAX*
DEVICE=C:\WIN95\HIMEM.SYS	@ECHO OFF
DOS=HIGH,UMB	PROMPT pg
DEVICE=C:\WIN95\EMM386.EXE NOEMS	
	PATH=C:\WIN95;C:\WIN95\COMMAND;C:\I;
BUFFERS=20	C:\BALLPT;C:\PCMPLUS3
FILES=30	SET SYMANTEC=C:\SYMANTEC
LASTDRIVE=E	SET NU=C:\NU
FCBS=4,0	SET TEMP=C:\DOS
DEVICEHIGH=C:\WIN95\SETVER.EXE	SET MOUSE=C:\BALLPT
DEVICEHIGH=C:\WIN95\IFSHLP.SYS	LH
	C:\WIN95\COMMAND\DOSKEY.COM
STACKS=9,256	LH C:\NET\LSL.COM
DEVICE=C:\SCSI\ASPI2DOS.SYS /D	LH C:\NET\NE2000.COM
DEVICE=C:\SCSI\ASPIDISK.SYS /D	LH C:\NET\IPXODI.COM
	LH C:\NET\NETX.EXE
	; Add Login Script Here
	; Add Fax Software Loading here

After you create the CONFIG.FAX and AUTOEXEC.FAX, transfer each file into the appropriate sections of the shortcut. By following the procedure outlined here, select the property page for this shortcut, and paste in the CONFIG.FAX and AUTOEXEC.FAX files. To paste easily, open these files with the Notepad application, and then select each section and paste it into the appropriate area. Figure 33.8 shows the created shortcut's Program Advanced Property page and the pasted files.

FIGURE 33.8.

Setting the CONFIG.SYS and AUTOEXEC.BAT section of an MS-DOS shortcut.

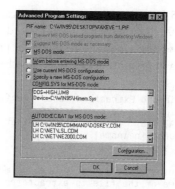

After you prepare the shortcut, you can fax the documents. To do this, set up the shortcut to execute a batch file once the CONFIG.SYS and AUTOEXEC.BAT portions finish running. Figure 33.9 shows the location of the batch file, C:\FAXABIL\FAXALL.BAT. Now that the fax solution is set up, the last thing you need to do is double-click the icon and debug the shortcut.

FIGURE 33.9.

Telling the shortcut what batch file to process.

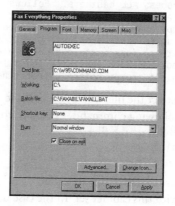

Creation of DOS-only sessions are never straightforward and will always require some debugging. Fortunately, pressing F8 when the shortcut starts loading MS-DOS 7.0 (Windows 95) will enable you to step through the specified CONFIG.SYS and AUTOEXEC.BAT files.

Running the Extract Program

Windows 95 comes packaged on CD-ROM with installation files called cabinets. These files are a Microsoft-specific disk image. These .CAB files contain all the Windows 95 files, including some of the DOS and Windows-based utility programs. The DOS editor is in these files, as is the Registry Editor. The Extract program is perfect for those times when you need a file or program from the installation disks, but you do not want to have to reinstall Windows 95.

The Windows 95 Resource Kit recommends against using the Extract program to restore a failing Windows 95 machine. This is a wise word of warning, but the occasional removal of a file will not hurt, so take a look at how to use the program. Extract displays the following at an MS-DOS command prompt, with no line switches:

```
C:\WIN95>extract /?
Microsoft (R) Diamond Extraction Tool - Version (16) 1.00.0530 (04/3/95)
Copyright (c) Microsoft Corp 1994-1995. All rights reserved.
EXTRACT [/Y] [/A] [/D ¦ /E] [/L dir] cabinet [filename ...]
EXTRACT [/Y] source [newname]
EXTRACT [/Y] /C source destination

  cabinet   - Cabinet file (contains two or more files).
   filename - Name of the file to extract from the cabinet.
              Wild cards and multiple filenames (separated by
              blanks) may be used.

  source    - Compressed file (a cabinet with only one file).
  newname   - New filename to give the extracted file.
              If not supplied, the original name is used.

  /A          Process ALL cabinets.  Follows cabinet chain
              starting in first cabinet mentioned.
  /C          Copy source file to destination (to copy from DMF disks).
  /D          Display cabinet directory (use with filename to avoid extract).
  /E          Extract (use instead of *.* to extract all files).
  /L dir      Location to place extracted files (default is current directory).
  /Y          Do not prompt before overwriting an existing file.
```

If you want to extract the file WINFILE.EXE, for example, and you do not know what .CAB file it is in, the following command, executed from the directory to which the .CAB file had been copied, will extract the file:

```
extract /A /L . win95_02.cab winfile.exe
```

The command breaks down like this. The /A switch will tell Extract to process all the cabinet files associated with this cabinet set. In the case of Windows 95, this processes all the cabinets from 02 to 17. The /L switch is not needed because Extract will default to the current directory. The trailing dot (not period) that comes after the /L switch tells the extraction to take place on the current directory. WIN95_02.CAB is the first cabinet file to process. Finally, WINFILE.EXE is the program that was extracted from the cabinet file. In this case, the file came out of cabinet file number 10.

To get a full listing of files from the set of Windows 95 cabinet files, use this command:

```
extract /A win95_02.cab > filelist.txt
```

Just print filelist.txt with Notepad or WordPad for a complete listing.

Basic DOS Troubleshooting

Although the examples given in this DOS section do lay down some of the principles used in troubleshooting DOS programs with Windows 95, they do not give specifics. These DOS troubleshooting gems come from the author's own experience, and are sure to help in times of trouble.

■ **The DOS box in which I run my program looks very bad, as if the font does not work.** This problem is associated with using TrueType fonts in scaleable DOS boxes. Some programs will not behave correctly with TrueType fonts in DOS boxes, so either run them full-screen or use one of the many system fonts. The 8×12 DOS font works well for 800×600 dpi display settings.

■ **When I run my application, I get a "No EMS Memory error."** As stated in Chapter 32, Windows 95 does not (fully) change the CONFIG.SYS file upon installation. Many DOS-based machines, since the advent of Memmaker, have the switch NOEMS on the device=EMM386.EXE line of the CONFIG.SYS. This driver line switch is put there by Memmaker. If this line remains intact after the upgrade to Windows 95, DOS boxes will have no expanded memory, only XMS or extended memory. The Windows 95 Resource Kit has a full explanation of memory and the allocation of it to DOS-based program. This is a valuable reference.

■ **When running my DOS shell program, it is forced into read-only mode, because it always knows I am in Windows.** The problem here is Windows 95 IS the operating system, or so they say. For those DOS programs that just cannot stand to run in Windows, simply check the "Prevent MS-DOS based programs from detecting Windows" radio button. This selection is in the Advanced MS-DOS property page for any MS-DOS application. Refer to the top of the property page shown in Figure 33.8. Set the grayed-out selection at the top for MS-DOS-based applications that run under Windows 95 and need to be lied to about running under Windows. For DOS programs that execute in MS-DOS only mode, there is not change required.

■ **I have just added a SCSI-removable media drive, and the included DOS drivers see the device, but Windows 95 will not give me a drive letter.** Although the drive is identified by the SCSI drivers in DOS, it has no disk partition. The problem has two solutions. You can use the manufacturer-supplied DOS programs to access the drive and set a partition, or use the Windows 95's FDISK program. Even if the device is not controlled by an installed SCSI BIOS, FDISK will see it. If FDISK does not detect the drive immediately, use the Device Manager to set the device to an Int 13 unit. Open the Device Manager from the System applet, and choose View devices by connection. Select the SCSI controller, and expand the view one level. Select the attached drive and verify that it has the Int 13 unit button checked. Figure 33.10 shows this setting in the Device Manager. Once FDISK can see the device, install a partition, reboot, and format the partition. It's that easy.

FIGURE 33.10.

The Int 13 unit radio button.

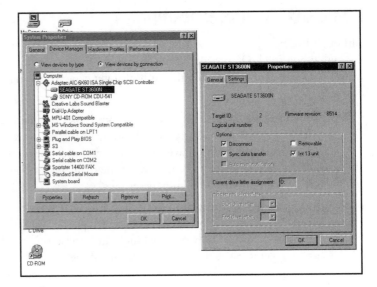

Games

Now you get to the real reason for buying this book: getting your games to work. This is not as difficult as it may seem. Running games under Windows 95 may not be that big of a deal, except for some real hair-pullers. Windows-based games will behave well under Windows 95 and may actually look a little better because of the improvements in the graphics interface. DOS-based games that have multimedia support will require some special handling but should still run fine.

Without a doubt, the biggest hit games this past year have been the DOS smash hits DOOM and DOOM II. DOOM was the original shareware version, and is still available. DOOM II is the full-featured DOS version that has all the features of a full war game. This adventure game has proven itself in the market, and many Windows 95 users will want to run DOOM II with Windows 95. There are not many tricks to doing it.

DOOM and DOOM II

The lowest performance machine on which the author ever installed DOOM, or even Windows 95, is a 386SX/25 with 8 MB of memory. DOOM seemed to run fine as long as the machine had been booted to a DOS prompt and Windows 95 had not been loaded first. If you run Windows 95 on a machine with that speed, you are overtaxing the machine's capabilities. DOOM is very comfortable on 486SX/33 with 8 MB of memory or higher, and runs in a DOS session but only full-screen.

The installation of DOOM goes flawlessly under Windows 95, from floppy or CD-ROM. If you have a Windows Sound System-compatible sound device or real SoundBlaster, all will work well, just make sure that you consult the Device Manager for the settings before you configure DOOM. Figure 33.11 indicates the settings for the Windows Sound System SoundBlaster Emulation.

FIGURE 33.11.

Checking the SoundBlaster settings.

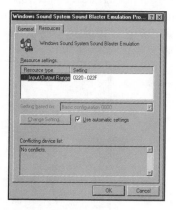

DOOM's setup program is very adept at detecting the correct settings for your SoundBlaster emulation, so it usually presents the correct choices. Running DOOM is just about as straightforward as it can be. Microsoft did reveal that the folks at id software had ported DOOM to the WinG (Win GEE, for Games) interface, and was going to be releasing it sometime last year. That never happened, and development may still be underway. With the changes in the WinG interface, and Microsoft's first Game Developers Conference in San Jose in early 1995, Windows-based games should be coming soon.

You can run DOOM II simply by opening up the standard MS-DOS prompt from the Start menu, changing directories to that directory, and running DOOM2. You can start up DOOM II in a DOS box. It is rather impressive to watch all those resources allocated with no problem. To run DOOM II from a DOS-only machine, you sometimes must remove a lot of driver software. Figure 33.12 shows the progress of the loading of DOOM II.

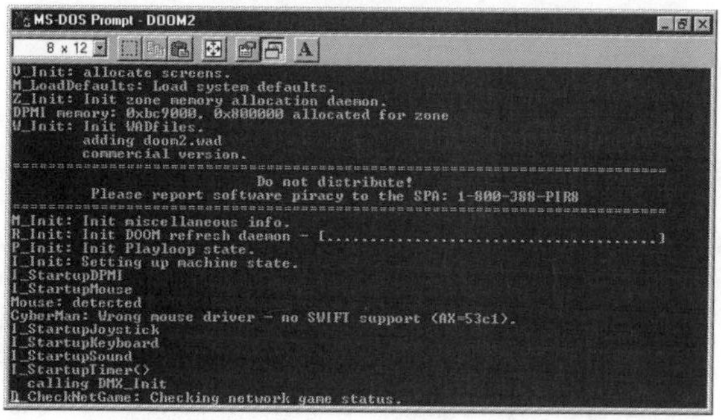

FIGURE 33.12.

DOOM II loading from a DOS box.

You cannot run DOOM in a window, as some have indicated in other Windows 95 publications. The current implementation of DOOM and DOOM II require direct access to the video frame buffers associated with the video card in your system. This access is available to DOS-based applications, but not in a box. Figure 33.13 is what you will see when you press Alt+Enter from the full-screen DOOM II session. This is not discouraging at all, because while playing DOOM, you really need to dedicate your full attention to this game.

FIGURE 33.13.

DOOM II trying to execute in a DOS box.

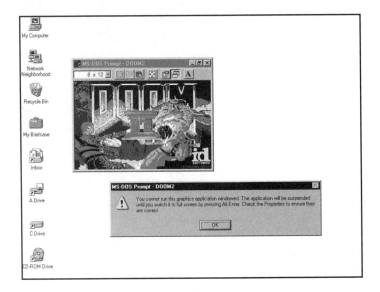

The last really cool thing that you can do with this DOS box and DOOM is capture any screens you like. The screen shots for this book were taken in 16 colors, for publishing purposes. To use screen shots on your desktop, 256 colors is much better. If you are playing DOOM II and you see a really cool screen that you like and want to capture it, all you have to do is press Alt+Enter. (See Figure 33.14.) This will put the screen in a DOS box and enable you to screen shot it. With Microsoft's Paint program that comes with Windows 95, you can copy portions of the screen and manipulate them for use on the desktop. Figure 33.14 shows the desktop with the DOOM II opening screen used as wallpaper.

Chess Maniac 5 Billion and 1

This game is a real hoot. The action that the chess pieces get into when the game is going is hysterical, and the sidebar commentary from the opponent is great. Trying to get this to work with SoundBlaster emulation while using a Window Sound System, though, is not easy. The root of the problem is the fact that the settings for the SoundBlaster are too limited in the SDNSETUP application that comes with this game. This is one of those games set up by using a separate MS-DOS session. This way, full access to SoundBlaster is available, thereby providing the great audio of this game. (See Figure 33.15.)

FIGURE 33.14.

DOOM II wallpaper.

Figure 33.15 shows how DOS-based applications can make Windows 95 report the application requirements of an MS-DOS only session. This dialog is common with the installation of DOS programs, due to the access of low-level hardware. In most circumstances, ignoring this dialog is the right thing to do. In all the applications installed by this Windows 95 user, this dialog box has never presented a problem.

FIGURE 33.15.

Installing Chess Maniac 5 Billion and 1.

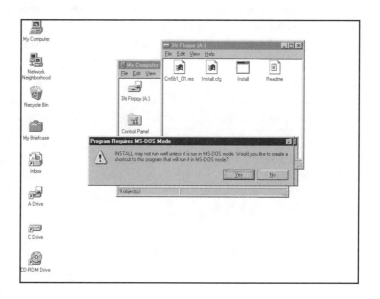

The author was successful in getting CM5 to run in a DOS box, albeit rather slowly. Once again, this is not one of those games where you want distractions while running.

Older DOS Games

Everyone has the horror story of how he or she installed a DOS game before Windows 95 and could not get his or her sound or video to work correctly with it. Windows 95 will do little to solve those problems. Windows 95 does have Plug and Play, but that does not fix code written to only one type of sound card, only one sound card port, or only one type of video resolution.

The devout DOS game player usually has a multiple-boot DOS machine that will enable the loading of different drivers, memory allocation, or video capabilities for particular games. If this is the case, then continue. Because Windows 95 still supports the MultiConfig statements from the CONFIG.SYS that started in MS-DOS, you can retain your CONFIG statement. Remember, running these games under MS-DOS 7.0 is usually not a problem unless your game does DOS version checking and chokes on 7.0. If this is the case, put C:\WIN95\COMMAND\SETVER.EXE in your CONFIG.SYS, and enter the correct value for this game into the SETVER table. After you reboot, the game should run fine.

Windows Games

Of course, Windows 95 will run virtually any Windows-based game—all of the Microsoft Game Packs and most Windows-based shareware games. Windows 95 comes with all the favorite Windows standards, including Minesweeper, Hearts, and Solitaire. For a while, Windows 95 did not ship with Solitaire, but with a game called Freecell. Some people may remember Freecell as the first Win32 app to be seen with the Win32s extensions under Windows 3.11.

The Solitaire that ships with Windows 95 looks and runs just like the old version, and it probably is just recompiled from the Win16 version. Figure 33.16 shows the subtle differences between Solitaire from Windows 3.11 and Windows 95. The Solitaire session in the back is from Windows 3.11. Notice the 3-D style deck of the Windows 95 session. Also, the help menus are different.

Playing games under Windows 95 is not rocket science. Most of these games will run without a hitch. Do not over-complicate the process. When you need full access to DOS, and settings do not work in Windows 95, follow the examples given in the "DOS Applications" section of this chapter. Good luck gaming!

FIGURE 33.16.

Solitaire from Windows 3.11 and Windows 95.

TSRs, Utilities, and Windows 95

Although most of the items covered in the "DOS Applications" section of this chapter are applicable to TSRs and utility programs, this genre needs special attention. To quote Microsoft, from the *Chicago Reviewers Guide*:

"Existing disk management utilities that manipulate the FAT *(File Allocation Table)*, including disk defragmenters, disk bit editors, and some tape backup software, may not recognize long filenames as used by Chicago and may destroy the long filename entries in the FAT. However, the corresponding system-defined 8.3 filename will be preserved so there is no loss of data if the long filename entry is destroyed."

Back in Chapter 31, Figure 31.17 shows what can happen to Start menu items after a DOS-based disk utility destroys the long filenames. After long filenames are corrupted, it is true that the data is still there and executables still work, but the Start menu and Desktop have lost all their shortcuts. This process takes quite a long time to repair; most of the time it is easier to reinstall Windows 95. Hopefully, one of the utility companies will come out with a utility to capture all your current shortcuts for restoration in just such an emergency.

To get an idea of how the FAT is written with long filenames, look at how Norton Disk Editor from Norton Utilities 8.0 sees the FAT on this disk. Figure 33.17 shows the entries from the example of long filenames in Chapter 31.

As you can see, Norton Disk Editor sees the entries in the FAT that hold the long filename as invalid FAT entries. These same entries are reported as lost allocation sectors by Norton Disk Doctor, Microsoft's Scandisk from DOS 6.x and earlier, PC Tools, and most shareware defragmenting programs. Also, directory sorting programs will obliterate these long filenames.

FIGURE 33.17.

Norton Disk Editor looking at long filenames.

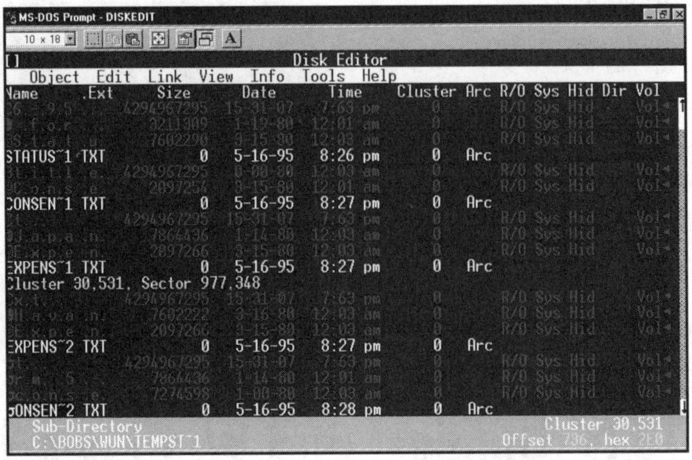

TSRs in Windows 95

Terminate and Stay Resident programs were the boon of the DOS world when they first appeared around the time of DOS 2.x. New TSRs included schedulers, calculators, and even small word processors. As Windows became more entrenched, these TSRs fell out of favor and became simply the underpinnings for hardware setup. Some still exist, and continue to give functionality inside DOS boxes, most notably DOSKEY.COM, a command-line editor that came with MS-DOS 5.x and later. How does DOSKEY work in Windows 95?

DOSKEY loads from the AUTOEXEC.BAT file, in Windows 95, and asks for memory in which to execute. Code is declared as global memory, while the history buffer is declared as instance data memory. Instance data memory is used by applications for holding values appropriate with that running session of the program. DOSKEY uses the history buffer to keep track of the commands that are issued. If DOSKEY were to keep only one history area, each DOS box would have the same history. This is not very useful. To overcome this, DOSKEY declares the area for history as instance data, which instructs Windows 95 to duplicate this area for each DOS virtual machine. In this way, the TSR has functionality across the platform.

The problem with TSRs is knowing how to manage and allocate the memory that they use. Although the author has some experience with TSRs, most of it has been bad concerning Windows 95. For the most part, if there is functionality that you really cannot live without, then contact the manufacturer of the TSR to find out the plans for Windows 95.

One of the things that TSRs did well was monitor DOS interrupts in order to hook themselves into the system's operation. The problem with this under Windows 95 is that some of these DOS interrupts are not being issued. When a TSR loads and tries to hook DOS interrupts, the interrupts will start being issued. This can be a serious hit to system performance, and may actually prevent you from loading Windows 95 successfully. When choosing TSRs to use with Windows 95, avoid those that must have full machine access when their hot key is used.

Summary

Troubleshooting applications and software under Windows 95 is a learned process. DOS programs require focus on the low-level access they might need, while Windows programs require attention in settings and performance. If you are a service professional, allow yourself the time to research the huge amounts of data Microsoft will ship with Windows 95. Get to know the Device Manager, the Add/Remove Wizards, and how the property pages work.

This troubleshooting chapter attempted to give you an understanding of how the machine operates, and also gave you some useful tidbits of information. No one troubleshooting chapter on Windows 95 can cover all the expected scenarios. The ultimate resource for problematic hardware and software is the vendor of these items. Because of how intricate Windows 95 is, no one vendor could possibly answer all of your questions, not even Microsoft itself. Become your own best source of information for your Windows 95 installations.

Multimedia Troubleshooting

34

by Van Thurston, Jr.

Improvements to Multimedia Troubleshooting

Troubleshooting multimedia moves a quantum leap forward with Windows 95. The problems that confounded and befuddled even experienced Windows 3.x users have been addressed. Microsoft took a long look at what was perhaps the strongest argument for "going Mac" in this time when multimedia is spreading like wildfire. Although the blemishes on the past generation of sound, video, and capture cards must still be addressed, the new Plug and Play devices should totally remove those all-night head-shaking and swearing sessions. Microsoft developers have applied the Wizard | Help Engine | Property Sheet solution to this area to resolve problems on your old-style manually configured boards.

Undoubtedly, there will still be conflicts that must be resolved. This chapter deals with the general steps to resolve conflicts between devices and troubleshoot multimedia-related problems.

Using the System Properties Applet in the Control Panel

As you already know, the Windows 95 Control Panel holds many familiar tools that were brought forward from the Windows series. Some new and powerful applets have been added to enhance your ability to configure and control. The System applet is your main tool for multimedia hardware and software conflict resolution. It is designed to aid in configuring system devices and maintaining optimum system performance. This applet can also be started by right-clicking on the My Computer icon and then selecting Properties.

Opening this applet and choosing the Device Manager property sheet brings you to a tree of devices. Figure 34.1 shows the System Properties | Device Manager Sheet.

FIGURE 34.1.

Problem Central. The Device Manager Property Sheet is the main tool for multimedia troubleshooting.

A double-click on any given device, such as a sound card, brings about the display of another form that is device-specific. The title bar reveals the name of the specific device, which should avoid any confusion as to where you actually are in the ladder of forms and sheets.

On the front sheet of this device-specific form (the general property sheet), you find the bold truth. It tells in plain English (or another localized language, for that matter) whether the operating system thinks the device is working. Figure 34.2 shows a specific multimedia device's General Property Sheet. In this case, a sound card is shown to be working properly. If you have a device such as a sound card or capture card that is not working, this Device Manager Sheet and its associated sheets and dialogs are clearly the best place to begin your troubleshooting work.

FIGURE 34.2.

The Device status shows us that the system believes the device is working properly.

The system might not detect any conflicts with other device properties such as DMA or IRQ settings in the case of the old-style boards. If the board's hard settings (the ones physically on the board) are different from the settings that Windows 95 chose when it found the device, the device will not work even when there is no conflict.

If there is a problem with a device, or if the device has been disabled by the user, the tree will be extended and the offending device will be flagged with a marker across its icon. Figure 34.3 shows an extended tree with a disabled or malfunctioning device.

If you wish to select a configurable setting such as an interrupt, you deselect the Use Automatic Settings checkbox.

You can examine the device's low-level settings here. The DMA, IRQ interrupts, and reserved memory locations are clearly shown. As long as the Use Automatic Settings checkbox remains selected, the operating system manages the device properties. Deselecting this box enables you to manage these settings manually. A double-click on a setting that allows change will present the Edit Resource Request Dialog Sheet, where you can scroll through available values. Here, you find the down-and-dirty, back-to-the-basics, fix-it shop.

FIGURE 34.3.

A disabled or malfunction-ing device will be flagged by the system.

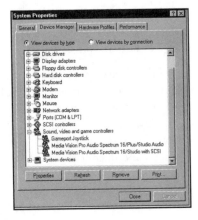

Until old-style (non-Plug and Play) multimedia boards find their way into museums and off of motherboards, you might find yourself on this sheet more often than you like!

As you scroll through new values—whether they are an interrupt request (IRQ) or any other device-specific setting—Windows will not allow you to see (or set) a conflicting setting. In Figure 34.4, you see this Edit Request Sheet.

FIGURE 34.4.

The Edit Resource Request Sheet, where new values can be selected.

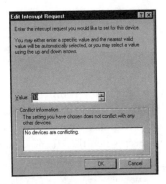

TIP

It's better to configure your old-style manually set board to match the settings that Windows 95 chooses automatically, instead of the other way around. Let Windows choose. Then pull the hardware and configure the hard switch setting to match those Windows has selected.

In the Driver's Seat

Switching to the Drivers Sheet, you find a list of drivers that are installed for use by this device. A single-click on each driver's name displays the version number of the file. In the case of Microsoft-provided drivers, this number should be greater than 4.00. If it is not, start hunting for a new driver. Figure 34.5 shows this sheet and the location where the driver version number is displayed.

Driver numbering should become more standardized and easier to verify in the near future, but use it as an informational resource for now. This driver version number will be very handy when speaking to a hardware support person. Do not waste your time trying to troubleshoot old real-mode drivers if you have any choice.

FIGURE 34.5.

Driver version features allow a quick check of version number.

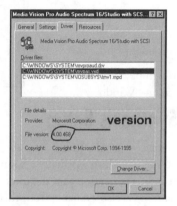

The Multimedia Applet

The multimedia applet is the place for you to put a sharp edge on your multimedia devices. After a multimedia device is properly installed, its management should take place here. Controls are provided to enable and disable these devices as well as to adjust various device-specific controls. The applet contains several subsheets to control the most common device types (audio, CD audio, and MIDI) and an Advanced sheet in which specific driver information and management takes place.

Audio

The general settings for the audio on your computer are located on the Audio Sheet and should be reviewed for correctness. When multiple playback devices are installed on the computer, this sheet provides for selecting a preferred device. Figure 34.6 shows the Audio properties sheet in the Multimedia applet.

Recording quality settings are also available. If you are having a problem with tin can sound when recording to disk in waveform, you should verify that the sound quality setting is as high as possible. CD quality is considered the highest quality with 44.1 kHz, Stereo, and 16-bit specifications. Additional recording performance device settings are configured here.

FIGURE 34.6.

*The Multimedia Applet |
Properties Sheet with Audio
settings displayed.*

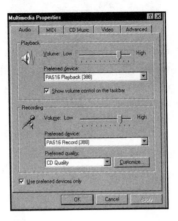

MIDI and Synthesis Setup

The MIDI sheet replaces all MIDI setup applets from Windows 3.x and should be consulted after verifying that the base device (usually a sound card) is correctly installed. The big ticket item on this sheet is the verification that the internal synthesizer has been selected. Additional MIDI channel mapping is also available from this sheet.

CD Music

There isn't that much available to the troubleshooter when it comes to CD music, other than headset volume to adjust. Be sure that the drive letter here does in fact match the CD-ROM drive in which you will play the CD. Any problems in this area will most likely be related to CD-ROM subsystem performance and, even more specifically, to drivers. Try the Systems Applet | Device Manager | Specific CD controller | Drivers address for troubleshooting this area. A correctly configured CD music subsystem will append a music note icon to any displayed shortcut icon for the CD audio drive when a music CD is placed in the drive.

Video Controls

There isn't much in this sheet either; the only control available is for the size of the default video window. This does not mean that an application can't choose what size to play video. It simply exists for the default player to read and size the default play-window accordingly and is best described as a holdover from Windows 3.x days.

The Media Player that comes with Windows 95 uses this size to initially display your digital video.

Using the Advanced Sheet to Enable/Disable and Configure

Consider the Advanced Sheet to be the software drivers (as opposed to hardware drivers) sheet. (See Figure 34.7.) Although there is a small amount of inconsistency in this regard due to the fact that hardware appears in the Advanced Sheet device tree, this thinking will tend to place you in the right spot when deciding where to troubleshoot. If you have a multimedia software driver installed and it can be configured in some way, this is your spot.

If the settings button for a particular device is enabled, try it out. Some software settings that interface a driver have been designed for configuration at this location. More than one manufacturer has used this Settings spot to add an About Box to display the company colors.

A double-click on a particular driver provides a location to disable the device.

FIGURE 34.7.

Drivers from the Multimedia Sheet's advanced perspective.

Specific Troubleshooting Ideas

The troubleshooting of Windows 95 waveaudio problems will probably be the most common process. In addition, Digital Video audio is in fact configured and used as standard waveaudio; problems with this system will be explored in the same manner.

As you use these applets, you will become more comfortable with the *top-down* paradigm. The most general information will be on the top sheet and, as you descend through the tabs, a greater level of complexity and a lower level of system interaction is available. This means that you will have greater access to the actual device settings at the most fundamental level, such as a system interrupt.

The first and most obvious place to begin any audio problem solving is with the output layer. The speaker connections and volume should be checked first! Then check the Multimedia applet | Audio Sheet to see whether Show Volume Control on the taskbar is checked (if not, select it now). Figure 34.8 shows the location of this checkbox.

FIGURE 34.8.

The Volume control is exposed on the taskbar using this checkbox.

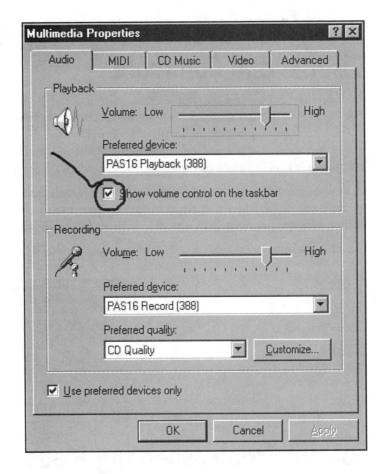

This should make the little speaker visible on the start bar (next to the current time). Double-click this speaker icon to bring up the system mixer. Verify the master and waveform volumes are up to higher levels while playing the waveaudio device. If you still cannot hear a playing audio file, the multimedia device is not enabled or not working.

In the System applet, go to the specific sound card and double-click. See whether the General Sheet says "The Device is Working Properly." Remember, this indicates that the operating system senses no conflicts and not that the device is, in fact, working correctly.

Check the Resources sheet to see whether the DMA and IRQ settings that Windows 95 chose are the same as the hard settings on the board. If the answer is yes, you are getting near the end of your rope and must begin to explore those canned technical support phrases such as "Is the board properly seated in the motherboard?" As a last resort, begin disabling other devices to see whether you can identify the source of the conflict.

If you experience difficulty when recording, the problem-solving method outlined earlier should be reviewed. If the sound has a tinny tone or if the tone modulates high to low over and over again, the Windows 95 multimedia settings do not match the settings that are set with the board's switches.

Jerky Video Playback Problems

If your system suffers from anemic motion-video playback—specifically jerky play or skipped frames—a quick tour down this troubleshooting road is in order.

Problems might arise in two basic areas. The first is the actual throughput of the media across the computer bus. Although Windows 95 (with its 32-bit disk access) has made dramatic improvements in this process, allowing users to play larger video at faster speeds, you still might be using older processors, single-speed CD-ROM players, slow 8-bit video cards, and so on. Let's look at the video display area and the delivery subsystems such as hard disk or CD-ROM.

> **TIP**
>
> You can never play back video at color resolutions, speeds, or sizes beyond those of the original compression scheme without some visual or performance degradation. Even shrinking an AVI will impute some measure of performance penalty as system time is devoted to casting out pixels.

If you find that the digital media plays smoothly off the hard disk and jerkily off the CD, your problem probably lies with the CD-ROM configuration. If this is the problem, you might also notice slow disk reads or transfers of other binary data from this disk drive. Start by verifying that the Windows 95 CD-ROM File System (CDFS) drivers are being used rather than the real-mode driver MSCDEX. Use an ASCII text editor to comment out or remove the line that loads MSCDEX from the AUTOEXEC.BAT, and hard boot Windows 95 to reset the SCSI bus. The operating system should detect the device and attempt to configure the CD-ROM VXD (virtual drivers) and enable the CDFS.

If the problem occurs in MS-DOS applications, check and maximize available XMS memory in the DOS Virtual Machine (VM) on the Properties sheet (under Memory) for your MS-DOS application.

Using Add New Hardware in the Control Panel enables you to verify that the appropriate video driver is installed for the video card you are using.

CD Audio Isn't Working

Does the CD drive work at all? The solution is similar to that for jerky CD AVI playback and probably indicates a bottleneck in the delivery of the media to the operating system.

For best media throughput, it is important that the Windows 95 CD-ROM File System (CDFS) drivers are being used rather than the real-mode driver MSCDEX. Using an ASCII text editor, comment out or remove the line that loads MSCDEX from the AUTOEXEC.BAT and hard boot Windows 95 to reset the SCSI bus. The operating system should detect the device and attempt to configure the CD-ROM VXD (virtual drivers) and enable the CDFS.

After checking the most obvious path to success, the Volume setting, try a full hard boot to reset the SCSI bus. This will fix lots of CD-ROM problems. If you are trying to use headphones right off the hardware, check the Multimedia Applet | CD-ROM Sheet where a volume control is located.

Poor or No MIDI Playback

MIDI music problems are usually related to the incorrect selection of an external device as the default MIDI output. Check to verify that an internal MIDI output is selected. Figure 34.9 shows the MIDI Sheet with the FM synthesizer selected. Try that pesky old audio volume control again. Many hours of troubleshooting have been spent only to find the volume turned down.

FIGURE 34.9.

A MIDI setup with FM synthesizer selected.

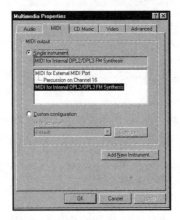

Flashing Colors as Windows Are Selected

If you are experiencing odd psychedelic color flashes as the focus changes between open Windows displaying graphic images, a quick lesson on palettes is in order.

It's time to face the fact that you are behind the times if your video card monitor handles only 256 colors (8-bit). Windows 95 manages palettes better than the 3.x products, but your card is at the bottom of the equipment food chain and will have limitations. Without getting too technical, if you are in 256-color mode, Windows can only display 236 plus 20 System colors. The application that has focus (the active application) gets to control the palette. Windows then manages and maps the colors required in the other applications that need to display palletized

(256-color, 8-bit) images. Sometimes the colors requested are not available and the operating system attempts to dither and match as closely as possible. During this transition time, flashes will occur.

Solutions include operating your video card in a high-color mode (which has 65,000 colors available) or a true-color mode (which has 6.7 million colors available). Both of these modes do not use palettes. You might also remove other palettized (256-color) images from the screen if they are not needed.

Thoughts on Troubleshooting Under Windows 95

Individual devices will have peculiarities with reference to the way they interact with the multimedia layers of Windows 95. Although this chapter does not address specific problems with specific cards or devices, the troubleshooting logic will be the same for almost every situation you encounter. Remember to start at the level that the system presents first (the top property sheet) and work down through the sheets to greater levels of control. Try not to forget those obvious mistakes such as volume. Good luck!

Troubleshooting Communications and Networking

35

by Tim Parker

One of the most discouraging aspects of using any computer system is to go to the trouble of installing a network only to find that it doesn't work. Sometimes error messages help you figure out the problem, but usually there's no clue as to where the problem lies—especially to someone who isn't familiar with networks.

Before blaming the network for problems, though, you should first make sure the applications that are failing to behave properly are not at fault. In some cases, software products require specific protocols (they may not work with IPX/SPX, for example), or must be configured themselves to use the protocols. Although Windows applications are supposed to be transparent to the network, there are a few that cause problems because of the application design, and not the network. Verify that the problem is the network by trying simple file transfers using the Network Neighborhood, and watching for error messages when Windows 95 boots.

Windows 95 solves many potential network problems with its configuration routines, but there are still a few problems that can occur. This chapter looks at the most common problems and how you can solve them. Essentially, network problems can be traced to one of three sources: network card, protocol stack, or client software.

Network Problems During Upgrading

Some network configuration problems can occur during the Windows 95 upgrade installation process (moving from an earlier version of Windows). This is especially true if your system uses a network protocol for which Microsoft doesn't have a driver, or if your machine is configured in a dual-boot arrangement.

The best way to avoid any configuration problems with a machine that is being upgraded is to record a set of important information.

- Make a list of all non-Plug-and-Play cards installed in your machine (network and otherwise) with a list of their IRQs, DMAs, I/O addresses, and memory addresses (if applicable). This list will help you detect and avoid conflicts. Although primarily useful for ISA machines, those with EISA and other architectures can make use of such a list. You can get IRQ, DMA, and memory address information from a diagnostic such as MSD, or from Windows configuration files like PROTOCOL.INI.

- Record the manufacturer and model number of your network interface card. If the card is an off-brand model that emulates another card, make a list of all emulations the card is supposed to perform.

- If you use two or more network interface cards (to connect to two networks, for example), you should decide whether you will stay with that number or simply use one with multiple protocol support. Check for conflicts between the cards.

- Record your machine's name and workgroup. If you are using a dual-boot configuration for Windows 95, the installation may not detect and record your machine's name and workgroup properly.

If you are upgrading an existing Windows system, you should make sure the network is running before the upgrade. Windows 95 is supposed to detect network software based on the configuration files only, but running the software ensures it is detected properly.

Network Interface Card

There are only a couple of potential problems with the network interface card (also called the network adapter): either Windows 95 can't find it, or it doesn't function properly with the protocols you are using. Both problems are easy to diagnose and solve.

Before proceeding with the following solutions, follow this quick checklist of common problems with the NIC:

■ Ensure the NIC is properly seated in the PC's expansion slots. Often, a card can be partially inserted and not make proper electrical contact, or it can be sitting next to the expansion slot with no contact at all. Examine the card to make sure it is lined up with the expansion slot, and then push the card down into the slot to properly seat it. It is good practice to use the retaining screws to fasten the card into the chassis and prevent movement.

■ Check the network connection. Some network cards will report problems if they are not physically connected to the network. Ethernet systems are particularly vulnerable to this type of problem. If you are not able to physically connect to the network, add a shorting resistor so the card has electrical termination. Some networks, such as NetBEUI and NetBIOS, are not particular about the network connection for the protocol to load properly.

■ Make sure the network system in use is compatible with your NIC. Some network adapter cards cannot support some protocols. Most cards will be clearly labeled as Novell NetWare compatible, for example. If you are not sure whether the protocol is supported, call the manufacturer or your dealer. Note that some "compatible" cards really are not, and can cause problems when used.

■ Check other network interface cards that may reside in the same machine. Some users will want to have more than one adapter card present (for connecting to two or more different networks). If an NIC is giving you problems, remove the other network cards to ensure there is not a conflict between the network cards.

■ Record the configuration information. You should know the IRQ and memory address of each network card in your machine before you install it. Many cards use DIPs or jumpers to set the IRQ and memory address. These should be set to ensure no conflict with other cards in your system. If your card is configured by software, Windows 95 can usually reprogram it, although if the card is being reconfigured from a previous installation, Windows 95 may not be able to access the proper settings. Many reprogrammable NICs include a manufacturer's diskette with a configuration routine on it. Use it to set default values for IRQ and memory address, or use non-conflicting values if the defaults cause a problem.

- Verify that the network interface card's vendor and model number match those used within Windows 95. A simple change of model number can cause the NIC to not respond to Windows 95's queries. If you are not sure of the network adapter's manufacturer and model number, remove the card and examine the silk-screening for the name and model number. If neither are available but you know the card is compatible with another manufacturer's adapter card (such as Novell's NE2000), use those settings.

- Verify that there is no conflict with sound cards and other peripherals with the NIC's IRQ and memory address. The primary reason for NIC failure is conflicting IRQ and memory addresses. You may not be aware of the problem if your system has a sound card, SCSI adapter, or dedicated tape drive adapter card in your system. Check each card for conflicts, or use a diagnostic utility such as MSD to display IRQs and memory addresses.

After you have performed these steps and made sure none of them were the cause of the problem, you can proceed to isolate the problem in a little more detail.

Network Adapter Not Found

The most common problem with the network interface card is that Windows 95 doesn't recognize it. This is easy to detect because Windows 95 will display an error dialog when it starts up telling you that the network adapter doesn't respond to the operating system's queries. In this case, the network card's parameters are almost always at fault.

- Use the Network dialog from the Control Panel to display the adapter's properties. Make sure your adapter is displayed in the list, as shown in Figure 35.1. If the name of the adapter card does not appear, it must be installed again using the Add button. See Chapter 22 for more information about installing network interface cards.

FIGURE 35.1.

The Network window, accessed from the Control Panel, should show your network adapter card's name in the list of installed components.

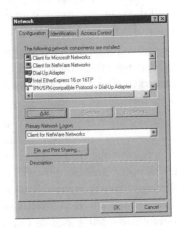

■ From the Network window, highlight the adapter name in the dialog, and then click the Properties button below the list. A window with four page tabs across the top will appear. These contain all the configuration information about the network adapter.

■ Click the Resources page tab at the top of the screen. The window shown in Figure 35.2 will appear, showing you Windows 95's settings for the adapter card.

FIGURE 35.2.

The Properties window for the network adapter card shows the current settings for the NIC. These must coincide with the card's settings for the network card to be recognized by Windows 95.

■ Record the values shown for the network adapter card's IRQ and memory address. If you have a network card that sets the IRQ and memory address using DIPs or jumpers, shut down Windows 95 and open the case. Verify that the settings on the NIC match Windows 95's settings. If they do not match, either change the NIC's settings or start Windows 95 and adjust the settings on the Resources screen. Windows 95 will inform you of potential conflicts with other cards.

■ If your network card is software programmed and the card is not responding properly, change the IRQ and memory address values, reboot Windows 95, and then return the settings back to the original values. During this process, Windows 95 may start the NIC reprogramming process.

■ If the network adapter card does not respond to changes in DIPs, jumpers, or Windows 95 configuration settings, remove the card from the Network installed components list completely, reboot Windows 95, and add the card again. This will usually reprogram software-programmable cards.

■ As a final step if the network adapter is still not functioning, check that the card is active by either installing it in another machine, using another network card in yours, or trying another operating system that may reside on your system. Network interface cards do not fail often, but it does happen.

Network Adapter Found but Not Working Properly

If Windows 95 doesn't report any problems with the network interface card when it boots, it doesn't mean the network is trouble-free. It simply indicates that a query from the Windows 95 operating system was properly answered. If you are having problems with the network and the card is not reported as a problem, chances are the NIC is not responsible. More likely it is a protocol or service problem, so these should be checked first. Assuming you have isolated the problem to the NIC, or you want to thoroughly check the NIC first, follow these steps:

- Verify the network adapter's IRQ and memory address are correct. Even if Windows 95 doesn't report a problem, it could be another card that answers the IRQ and memory address query. If your network card uses DIPs or jumpers, physically verify that the settings match those in the Resources screen in the adapter card's Properties window. If your adapter card is software programmed, change the settings, reboot Windows 95, and then change them back.

- Make sure the protocol and the network card match. An Ethernet card cannot always function in an IPX/SPX network, for example. If you have recently changed network protocols and reconfigured the change within Windows 95, the card may not report a problem with the new network protocol.

- Check the network connections. A network adapter card can respond to Windows 95 properly, but if the network itself is not functioning, it may appear as a problem with the NIC. Ensure that there are no breaks in the connections, and that the cable is properly terminated (if applicable). Ensure that other machines on the network are functioning properly.

- If the network interface card is still not functioning properly (and it is not a service or protocol problem), you probably have a defective network card. Contact the manufacturer or dealer for further information on replacements or testing.

Network Protocols

The most common problem with a failed network connection is with a protocol mismatch. There are several places within Windows 95 that should be checked to ensure that the configuration information is correct. Follow this checklist to verify your settings. (Note that your information and Windows screens may differ from those shown in this section, depending on the network protocol, service, and adapter cards in use.)

- Determine the network protocol that you should be using on your network. Do not assume that because you are on a Novell NetWare network, for example, that you should be using IPX/SPX. Check with other users or the system administrator to determine the protocol.

■ Check the Network window (accessible from the Control Panel) for the protocol drivers. Figure 35.3, for example, shows that three protocol drivers are loaded: IPX/SPX, NetBEUI, and TCP/IP. Although all three protocols can be in use, you should check only one protocol at a time, starting with the primary protocol.

FIGURE 35.3.

Use the Network window to find out which network protocols are in use. This window shows that three protocols are loaded but doesn't show which is the default.

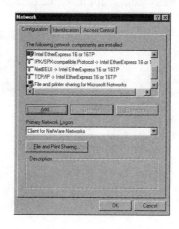

NetBEUI

■ If you are using a NetBEUI protocol, highlight the NetBEUI line in the Network window and click the Properties button. A window with two pages should be displayed. The first page, shown in Figure 35.4, shows the binding to the NetBEUI protocol. At least the Client for Microsoft Networks button should be checked. If file and printer sharing is used on your NetBEUI network, that option should also be checked. If neither of these options are checked, Windows 95 won't use the NetBEUI client software to connect to the NetBEUI network.

FIGURE 35.4.

Make sure that the NetBEUI protocols are bound to the client software by checking it on this Properties window. If you are using file and printer sharing on your network, that option should also be checked.

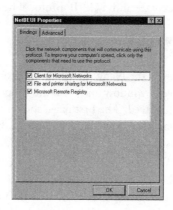

■ Check the Advanced page of the NetBEUI Properties window. This shows a set of configuration parameters and a selection box at the bottom of the screen to choose NetBEUI as the default protocol, as shown in Figure 35.5. The default protocol box must be checked to use NetBEUI as the network default protocol. Don't change any of the parameter values, but leave the default values as they are.

FIGURE 35.5.

To use NetBEUI as the default network protocol, the default button at the bottom of this Advanced page of the NetBEUI Properties screen must be selected.

■ If you did not use the Windows 95-supplied NetBEUI protocol drivers (you may have used a third-party driver) or you are not sure which driver is loaded, try removing the driver and reloading it with the default Windows 95 NetBEUI protocol. This step will not solve the problem with some third-party networks that require a special driver. Contact the manufacturer of the local area network to obtain a Windows-compatible driver. Windows 16-bit drivers can be used instead of Win32 protected-mode drivers, although they will consume conventional memory.

■ If the information in the Properties window is correct, then the protocol is properly loaded and bound to the client. The problem must lie elsewhere. Check the sections after the NetWare and TCP/IP protocol headings for more steps.

NetWare IPX/SPX

■ If you are using the NetWare IPX/SPX protocol, highlight the IPX/SPX protocol line in the Network window and click the Properties button. A window with two pages should be displayed. The first page, shown in Figure 35.6, shows the bindings. At least the Client for Microsoft NetWare button should be checked. If file and printer sharing is used on your NetWare network, that option should also be checked.

■ Check the Advanced page of the IPX/SPX Properties window. This shows a set of configuration parameters and a selection box at the bottom of the screen to choose NetBEUI as the default protocol. The default protocol box must be checked to use IPX/SPX as the network default protocol. Don't change any of the parameter values, but leave the default values as they are.

FIGURE 35.6.

Make sure that IPX/SPX protocols are bound to the network clients. The Client for NetWare Networks must be checked if you are attaching to an IPX/SPX network.

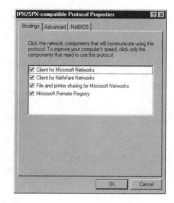

- If you did not use the Windows 95-supplied IPX/SPX protocol drivers (you may have used a third-party driver) or you are not sure which driver is loaded, try removing the driver and reloading it with the default Windows 95 NetBEUI protocol. If you are using Novell's drivers, you should try to obtain a 32-bit protected-mode VxD version, because it is much more efficient. Microsoft's drivers are (at least at the moment) better than Novell's for IPX/SPX.

TCP/IP

A common problem with TCP/IP is that two machines will be configured with TCP/IP drivers, and then connected by a cable. Users expect to be able to transfer files back and forth. That seldom works properly, because TCP/IP is designed to use a gateway or server for all requests. A peer-to-peer TCP/IP network is possible, of course, but needs the IP addresses to be set properly.

Most problems with TCP/IP and Windows 95 occur when you add a machine to an existing network. TCP/IP requires much more configuration information for its protocol driver than NetBEUI or IPX/SPX. You should know your machine's IP address (or the IP address of a machine that supports DHCP or BOOTP), and the IP address of a gateway (if one is used).

- If you are using the Microsoft TCP/IP protocol, highlight the TCP/IP protocol name in the Networks window and click the Properties button. A window with six pages should be displayed. The first page, shown in Figure 35.7, shows the IP address for the machine. You must supply an IP address for your machine to work with a TCP/IP network. If your network uses DHCP (Dynamic Host Configuration Protocol) you will have to supply the IP address of the server. You must also supply a subnet mask. If you are not sure how to determine this, see Chapter 23.

FIGURE 35.7.

The TCP/IP Properties window has six pages. The first page is the IP address setting, and one must be supplied for Windows 95 to function on the network properly (unless DHCP is used).

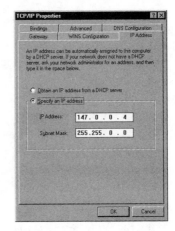

■ Check with your system administrator to find out if you need to set Windows Internet Naming Service (WINS) on your machine. WINS enables NetBIOS-based programs to run over TCP/IP, if WINS is required, it may be the cause of network problems. If WINS is needed, add the WINS server IP addresses to the WINS Configuration screen, as shown in Figure 35.8. This page is required only if you need WINS, which most installations won't use.

FIGURE 35.8.

If NetBIOS is supported over TCP/IP through WINS, you must specify the IP address of the WINS server. If this is not in place, the network will not work properly.

■ If your machine needs to communicate with a gateway to send data packets, you must supply the gateway IP address on the Gateway page. This is shown in Figure 35.9. Not all TCP/IP networks need a gateway address. Check with your system administrator.

FIGURE 35.9.

The gateway IP address must be supplied if your machine must send data through the gateway. Not all networks need a gateway.

■ If your machine doesn't seem to be sending information properly, it may need the Domain Naming Server (DNS). Again, your system administrator will be able to tell you if DNS is used. (DNS provides a translation between IP address and common name, but it must be handled through a server.) If DNS is used on your network, provide the DNS server IP addresses on the DNS page, as shown in Figure 35.10.

FIGURE 35.10.

The IP addresses of the DNS servers must be specified if your network or applications are set to use DNS.

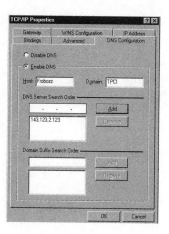

■ If TCP/IP is the default protocol on your machine, the box on the Advanced page should be checked. This ensures Windows 95 uses TCP/IP when there is a choice of protocols. The Advanced page of the TCP/IP Properties window is shown in Figure 35.11.

FIGURE 35.11.

Check the default protocol box on the Advanced page if TCP/IP is the default protocol for your network. When checked, Windows 95 will use TCP/IP when assembling data unless overridden by an application.

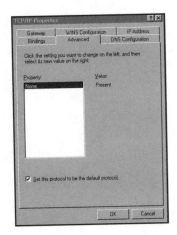

■ Check the Bindings page of the Properties window. Regardless of whether DHCP, WINS, and gateways are used, the binding for TCP/IP to the client software drivers must be in place. This window is shown in Figure 35.12. In this case, TCP/IP is bound to more than one client. At the very least, it should be bound to the Client for Microsoft Networks.

FIGURE 35.12.

Check the bindings to ensure the Client software is bound to TCP/IP. If not, select it. The other bindings shown on this window are not necessary for TCP/IP to function.

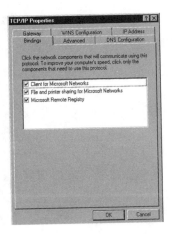

Besides checking the configuration information in the Properties pages, also check your applications. Some applications need you to specifically identify the protocol to be used to communicate over a network, whereas others will not support all protocols. Verify that all the software is properly set.

Client Drivers

The client drivers provided by Windows 95 include the client software to connect to remote servers. Each has a properties sheet that indicates the servers and behavior the client should perform when connecting. Check these pages to make sure the client software is connecting to the server properly.

There is little else to worry about with the client software, assuming you have installed it and bound it properly. The following is a quick check-list of client troubleshooting steps:

- Ensure that the client is loaded properly (check the Network window to see which clients are loaded). Make sure the proper client is active. For example, the Client for Microsoft Networks will not work with a NetWare IPX/SPX network.

- Check the protocol bindings to ensure the protocol and the client are coupled. This is checked through the Bindings page in the protocol's Properties page (see the troubleshooting steps explained in the section titled "Network Protocols," earlier in this chapter) and not through the service itself.

- Check the client's Properties page, accessible through the Networks window, to ensure the server information is accurate. Figure 35.13 shows the Properties page for the Client for Microsoft Networks.

FIGURE 35.13.

The Properties page of the client components asks for information about the behavior of the Windows 95 software when it connects to the server

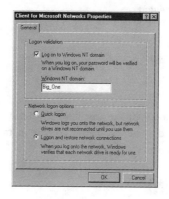

Configuration Files

Windows 95 uses a set of configuration files to control its behavior, and the networking aspect of Windows 95 is no different. Microsoft tends to discourage users from modifying the configuration files (most of which have the extension .INI) because changes can render entire aspects of the Windows 95 system inoperable and require you to reload the software.

Although the configuration files are written by the setup or installation routines, you may occasionally have to edit them to correct a problem that Windows 95 doesn't seem to be able to overcome. However, this is relatively rare. The following sections explain the configuration files you should know about.

NETDET.INI

This file contains the network detection settings—hence its name—used for some less-common network drivers and cards. The file is lengthy and contains a lot of entries that are not used by most installations, including special requirements for some software packages.

There may be an entry for each of the network protocols your system uses. In most cases, though, the NETDET.INI file isn't required if the network drivers you use are standard Windows 95 drivers (as with IPX/SPX, NetBIOS/NetBEUI, and TCP/IP drivers supplied by Microsoft). Each entry in the NETDET.INI file has some information for the network drivers about the manner in which it communicates. For example, the following entries specify any special behavior required for the Novell NetWare IP (not IPX/SPX) driver, and the Cheyenne Arcserve software:

```
;;;;;; Netware/IP ;;;;;;;
[NWIP.EXE]
detection0=mcb
full_install0=prevent
;;;;;;;;;; Cheyenne Arcserve ;;;;;;;;;;;
[WINAGENT]
detection0=mcb
full_install0=remove
[DOSAGENT]
detection0=mcb
full_install0=remove
```

You should not have to make any changes to the information in the NETDET.INI file. If new entries are required by new software you are installing, they should be added automatically by the installation routine.

PROTOCOL.INI

The PROTOCOL.INI file contains information about the network protocols used. This file is the same format as the PROTOCOL.INI file used with Windows for Workgroups. A sample extract from the PROTOCOL.INI file looks like the following:

```
[nwlink$]
DriverName=nwlink$
Frame_Type=4
cachesize=0
Bindings=EXP16$

[NETBEUI$]
DriverName=NETBEUI$
```

```
Lanabase=1
sessions=10
ncbs=12
Bindings=EXP16$

[EXP16$]
DriverName=EXP16$
transceiver=Twisted-Pair (TPE)
iochrdy=Late
irq=5
ioaddress=0x360

[protman$]
priority=ndishlp$
DriverName=protman$

[ndishlp$]
DriverName=ndishlp$
Bindings=EXP16$

[data]
version=v4.00.330
netcards=EXP16$,*PNP812D
```

The entries in your PROTOCOL.INI file may be different, of course. Each section of the file describes the settings for a particular aspect of the protocol. For example, the EXP16 section is specific to the Intel EtherExpress 16 card and sets the driver name for the card, its IRQ, and I/O address. Other entries in the PROTOCOL.INI file point to drivers.

When you are installing new software, changes are usually made to the PROTOCOL.INI file, although some require manual editing. The formatting of the file is rigorous (mistakes in layout can cause severe problems), so make sure you enter any changes properly. If there are errors in your entries, they may not parse properly and will be ignored or generate error messages.

Summary

For the most part, troubleshooting a network problem is a matter of ensuring each component is properly configured, monitoring any error messages on startup, and trying to isolate the problems. The steps mentioned in this chapter should help isolate most of the typical problems, although if problems persist you may want to contact Microsoft or the vendor of your network hardware and software.

IX

PART

Appendixes

Microsoft Technical Support Services

A

Technical Support

Technical support for Windows 95 can be obtained from Microsoft at no charge for the first 90 days you use the product. You pay for the call (in the U.S.) by dialing (206) 637-7098, but the 90-day clock doesn't start ticking until you make your first call. Calls are accepted between 6:00 a.m. and 6:00 p.m. (pacific time on weekdays), except holidays. If you are outside the U.S., contact your local Microsoft office.

After the 90-day free support expires, you can obtain support from Microsoft on a per-incident basis. If you can call the 900 number, the cost is $2 per minute, with a $25 maximum. You are not charged for time spent on hold. Call (900) 555-2000 to pay by the minute. The toll will be billed to your telephone account.

If you prefer, you can call (800) 936-5700 and use a credit card. Microsoft pays for the long distance, and you pay a flat $25 per incident.

There is one small "gotcha." Microsoft does not include support for TCP/IP for Windows 95 through normal support channels. For information on TCP/IP support, call (800) 227-4679.

You can obtain help with your problem via Microsoft-moderated forums on all the major commercial online services. See Appendix B, "Microsoft Information Services," for more information about Microsoft support online.

Support For Users with Special Needs

Hearing-impaired users equipped with a special TT/TDD modem can dial (206) 635-4948 during the normal technical support hours, 6:00 a.m. until 6:00 p.m. (pacific time, Monday through Friday).

Sight-impaired users can use either the online documentation contained on the CD-ROM build of Windows 95 or order documentation for Windows 95 from Recording for the Blind, Inc., by calling (800) 221-4792.

Physically impaired users may want to obtain a copy of the CO-NET CD, published twice yearly by the Trace R&D Center, (608) 263-2309. This CD contains a database of 18,000+ products designed to provide accessibility to computers for persons with special needs.

For more information about accessibility issues, call Microsoft Sales and Service at (800) 426-9400.

Microsoft Information Services

B

IN THIS CHAPTER

Whether you just like to tinker or are the self-reliant type who hates to call tech support lines, there is a wealth of information available to you if you take the time to go looking. This appendix is a rundown of the major technical information resources available.

Microsoft Online

Microsoft maintains a presence on all of the major commercial online services. Microsoft maintains moderated forums (like a BBS) on each of the services. Moderated means that Microsoft support people log in daily to answer questions. Many times, a fellow user of the service will answer your question or provide suggestions before Microsoft personnel even have the chance to read and respond to messages. You can usually get a problem resolved immediately by reading messages from folks who have, or have solved, the same problem. Sometimes getting an answer to your question takes 24 hours, but you may be surprised; there are times when a message gets responded to within minutes on busy services.

On each of the commercial services, the keyword to search to find out what services are available is WinNews. The following is a list of each of the major services and instructions to follow to find WinNews after you are logged into the service:

- **Microsoft Network:** From the menu, select Find and enter the search string WinNews
- **America Online:** Use the keyword WinNews
- **CompuServe:** Go WinNews
- **Prodigy:** Jump WinNews

Microsoft on the Internet

Using a standard text connection, type the command ftp://ftp.microsoft.com/PerOpSys/ Win_News and press Enter.

Using SLIP or PPP to access the World Wide Web, go to http://www.microsoft.com.

Users with e-mail addresses who can be accessed via the Internet can subscribe to the WinNews Electronic Newsletter bimonthly. Subscriptions are free. Just send a message to enews@microsoft.nwnet.com, and include as the only text in the message the words subscribe winnews.

The Microsoft Download Service

The Microsoft Download Service is a DOS (text-based) bulletin board that contains all kinds of support files, including the latest device driver updates, and drivers not included on the Windows 95 disks, that you can download for the price of the phone call.

You need a modem (1200 to 14.4 baud) set to 8 data bits, 1 stop bit, and no parity. Dial (206) 936-6735 to log into the service. As with most bulletin boards, you will need to answer a few questions and register. When you have registered, you can choose your area of interest at the main menu. The Download Service is completely menu-driven, and easy to use.

To obtain drivers when you do not have a modem available, call Microsoft Product Support Services at (206) 637-7098.

The Microsoft Knowledge Base and the Developer's Knowledge Base

The Microsoft Knowledge Base (MSKB) began life as an in-house tool intended for support personnel, but has expanded to be a regularly updated source for a broad range of technical knowledge about Microsoft products. Topics include

- Technical articles
- Answers to frequently asked questions
- Bug lists and known fixes
- Corrections to technical documentation
- Indexes of downloadable files, including device drivers and white papers
- The Microsoft Developer Knowledge Base, which includes programming information

The Knowledge Base is available from a variety of sources. Subscribers to the Microsoft Developer Network CD and the Microsoft TechNet CD products receive periodic updates of the MSKB on disk.

Searchable versions of the Knowledge Base can be found on CompuServe, The Microsoft Download Service, and the Microsoft Network, as well as on the Internet.

Microsoft TechNet

Microsoft TechNet is a CD-ROM subscription service designed for people who support users of Microsoft products, administer networks, and must remain current on technical issues. The TechNet package contains two CDs, updated monthly, that contain the Microsoft Knowledge Base, Resource Kits, up-to-date drivers, and other information. For more information, call (800) 344-2121, weekdays, between 6:30 a.m. and 5:30 p.m. (Pacific time). For queries outside the U.S. and Canada, contact your nearest Microsoft office.

The Microsoft Developer Network

The Microsoft Developer Network is a two-tiered subscription service that is designed for programmers. It includes updates to development tools and programming information on CD-ROM, via a printed newsletter. In short, if you need TechNet on steroids, call (800) 759-5474, 6:30 a.m. to 5:30 p.m. (Pacific time) to subscribe to the Developer Network. For queries outside the U.S. and Canada, contact your nearest Microsoft office.

Command-Line Reference

C

The MS-DOS commands are grouped here in four categories. First, this appendix looks at internal commands, which are part of the command interpreter and therefore always in memory ready for you to use. Next are external commands, individual files that are loaded into memory when you enter the appropriate command.

The third group of commands are used only in batch files, although batch files can also include other internal or external commands. The fourth group includes commands that can only be used in a CONFIG.SYS file. After the list of commands, we'll say our good-byes to those commands that are omitted from Windows 95.

NOTE

Windows 95 leaves untouched the directory on your hard drive containing the files for the version of DOS you were using before installing Windows 95. The native Windows 95 system command files are stored in \WINDOWS\COMMAND. Do not add the COMMAND directory to your path or try to use these files when you boot to DOS using F4, or use Shut Down to restart in MS-DOS mode. Likewise, do not try to use the files in the DOS directory when you are working in a Windows 95 MS-DOS session. All you'll get for your trouble is an incorrect DOS version message.

This discussion of command-line commands includes all the Windows 95 native commands except the networking and TCP/IP commands. The description of each, however, is not a complete discussion of how to use the commands or all the switches available. Refer to your Windows 95 documentation and online support for more information.

TIP

You can enter the command name followed by the /? switch at the command prompt to see a list of the switches the command can use.

Internal Commands

These commands are available at all times as part of the Windows 95 command interpreter, COMMAND.COM.

BREAK: By default, MS-DOS checks for CTRL+C or CTRL+BREAK only while reading from the keyboard or writing to the screen or printer. Set break ON to increase checking frequency or OFF to disable break:

```
BREAK=ON
```

CD (CHDIR), MD (MKDIR), and RD (RMDIR): Change, make, or remove a directory or subdirectory with the name you provide using these commands. Enter CD to display the name of the current directory:

```
MD "WordPerfect Letters"
```

CHCP: Use after invoking country and nlsfunc to display or change the active character set (code page):

```
CHCP 850
```

CLS: Enter CLS to clear the screen:

```
CLS
```

COPY: To copy one or several files to another location, specify the source and the destination, which can be a new filename. Add /Y if you don't want to confirm overwriting existing files or /V to verify files are written correctly. To combine (append) several files into a single destination file, use *file1+file2+file...* for the source:

```
COPY "1995 Budget*.*" A: /V
```

CTTY: You can change the terminal device for the computer to any of the other recognized computer devices such as PRN, LPT1, COM1, or AUX. The default terminal device is CON:

```
CTTY AUX
```

DATE: Enter DATE to see the current date. A prompt is also displayed so you can change the date, if necessary:

```
DATE
```

DEL or ERASE: To delete the files you specify, provide a filename using wildcards or a directory name for multiple files. Use /P if you want to give permission to delete each file. To delete an accumulation of saved searches created by the Find applet, use the following:

```
DEL C:\WINDOWS\DESKTOP\"Files named @.doc*.*"
```

DIR: Use DIR to list the files and subdirectories in the current location or another location you specify. /P displays the files one screen at a time, /A limits the list by file attributes, and /O specifies a sort order:

```
DIR \C:\WINDOWS\DESKTOP\"Files named*.*" /P /OD
```

EXIT: When the command interpreter (COMMAND.COM) is started from another program, enter EXIT to return to the original program:

```
EXIT
```

LOADHIGH (LH): This command runs a program, but loads it in upper memory, if available, rather than conventional memory:

```
LOADHIGH SMARTDRV.EXE 2048
```

MORE: This command is used with other commands to display the command output one screen at a time:

```
TYPE WIN.INI ¦ MORE
```

PATH: A list of directories that you want the operating system to search for executable files that are not stored in the current location. The directories in the list must be separated by semi-colons:

```
PATH=C:\WINDOWS;C:\WINDOWS\COMMAND;C:\"Favorite Utilities"
```

PROMPT: Use PROMPT, particularly in batch files, to control the appearance of the command prompt. Switches for PROMPT are preceded by a $ rather than /:

```
PROMPT=This computer proudly runs Windows95 $_$p$g
```

REN (RENAME): This command changes the name of a file to the name you specify. Use wildcards to rename several files:

```
REN RPT*.DOC "Final Report of *.doc"
```

SET: Use SET to create or remove environment variables. Enter SET at the command prompt to display the current environment variables:

```
SET TMP="Temporary Files Directory"
```

TIME: Enter TIME to see the current time. A prompt is also displayed so you can change the time, if necessary:

```
TIME
```

TYPE: This command prints the contents of a text file on the screen:

```
TYPE AUTOEXEC.BAT
```

VER: Enter at the prompt to display the version number of the operating system:

```
VER
```

VERIFY: This command instructs the operating system to always verify that files are written correctly to disk. Use VERIFY to display the status of verification:

```
VERIFY ON
```

VOL: This command displays the disk label and serial number if the disk has them:

```
VOL A:
```

External Commands

The following commands are called external commands because they are included in the operating system as separate executable files. In other words, they are small programs that must be loaded into memory each time the command is used. When you install Windows 95, \WINDOWS\COMMAND is automatically added to the PATH statement in your AUTOEXEC.BAT file so these commands can be executed without difficulty.

ATTRIB: Use the ATTRIB command to turn the archive, read-only, system, and hidden attributes on (+) or off (-):

```
ATTRIB +R "Form for*.*"
```

TIP

To hide a directory, use ATTRIB +H *directory*.

CHKDSK: The CHKDSK program checks the status of the file allocation table and file system on a disk, and then displays a status report. Use /F if you want errors fixed or /V to list every file checked:

```
CHKDSK A: /F
```

COMMAND: This program starts a new instance of the command interpreter. Use /E: to specify the initial size (in bytes) of the environment, or use /P to prevent the use of EXIT to close the DOS session:

```
COMMAND /E:4096
```

DEBUG: This launches the Debug program, which is used to test, debug, and edit executable files:

```
DEBUG COMMAND.COM
```

DEFRAG: DEFRAG is a Windows utility that can be launched from the command prompt and reorganizes directories and fragmented files to maximize disk performance:

```
DEFRAG /ALL /F
```

DELTREE: This command deletes a directory and all the files and subdirectories that are in it. Use the /Y switch to suppress any confirmation prompts:

```
DELTREE "WordPerfect Correspondence"
```

TIP

DELTREE provides a quick and easy way to delete hidden, read-only, and system files without the need to change the file attributes first. For example, use the command

DELTREE HIDDEN.SYS

to delete the file HIDDEN.SYS if it is flagged as read-only, hidden, or system, or any combination of the three.

DISKCOPY: Use DISKCOPY to make an exact duplicate of a floppy disk to another floppy disk:

```
DISKCOPY A: A:
```

DOSKEY: Loads the DOSKey program into memory. DOSKey recalls command-line commands, enables editing command lines, and runs macros. Overstrike is the default mode; use /INSERT to start DOSKey in Insert mode. Use /BUFSIZE: to increase the size (in bytes) of the buffer used to store macros and command lines:

```
DOSKEY /BUFSIZE:1024 /INSERT
```

DRVSPACE: Compress, reconfigure, or uncompress drives created with DriveSpace or DoubleSpace. Enter DRVSPACE alone at the command prompt to launch the Windows-based DriveSpace utility, or use switches such as /NEW= to assign a drive letter:

```
DRVSPACE /COMPRESS C: /NEW=F:
```

EDIT: This command starts a text editor you can use to create and edit ASCII text files. Edit includes a menu bar with commands for saving and printing files, searching for and editing text, and changing the display:

```
EDIT \AUTOEXEC.BAT
```

EMM386: After EMM386.EXE and HIMEM.SYS are loaded using the DEVICE= command in CONFIG.SYS, use EMM386 to activate or suspend the driver or set it to AUTO to provide expanded memory support if a program calls it:

```
EMM386 AUTO
```

EXPAND: If you have a DOS distribution disk with compressed files, enter EXPAND followed by the filenames and destination (including a correct filename) to decompress the files:

```
EXPAND A:SORT.EX_ C:\DOS\SORT.EXE
```

FC: Use FC to compare ASCII or binary files to one or more other files and display any differences:

```
FC *.doc C:\FILES\"February report.doc"
```

FDISK: The FDISK command configures your hard disk before formatting it for use with Windows 95. Use FDISK with /STATUS to display the current configuration of a hard disk:

```
FDISK
```

FIND: You can search one or more files for specific text using FIND. If the text string is found, the filename and any lines containing the found text are displayed. The /I switch ignores case when searching:

```
FIND "health" "1995 Budget Considerations.doc"
```

FOR: This command enables you to run a command on a set of files instead of entering the command separately for each file. This is most commonly seen in batch files where the syntax is slightly different. The syntax FOR %variable IN (set) DO command %variable is mandatory:

```
FOR %F IN ("1995 Budget*.*") DO FIND /I "health" %F
```

FORMAT: FORMAT divides a disk into a system information area and a files area, and creates the boot sector, root directory, and two copies of the file allocation table. Use the /FS: switch to specify the file system, /S to create a system (self-booting) disk, /V: to provide a volume label (sorry, no long names), and /Q to perform a quick format:

```
FORMAT A: /S /Q /V:MYDISK
```

KEYB: This command configures a keyboard for a specific language or, when used alone, displays the current code page. This example sets the keyboard for German:

```
KEYB GR 850
```

LABEL: This command changes, deletes, or applies a name (label) to a disk:

```
LABEL A:MYDISK
```

LOADFIX: This command launches a program and loads it above the first 64 KB of conventional memory:

```
LOADFIX "My Program"
```

MEM: Use MEM to display information about the amount of used and free memory in a computer. The /CLASSIFY (or /C) switch presents detailed information about each program currently in memory:

```
MEM /C
```

MODE: This command configures a printer, serial port, or display adapter. This example configures the printer for LPT1 with the default number of columns and lines and P to retry until output is accepted:

```
MODE LPT1:,,P
```

MOVE: To move one or several files to another location, specify the source and the destination, which can include a new filename to rename files and directories. Add /Y if you don't want to confirm overwriting existing files:

```
MOVE "1995 Budget*.*" \FILES\"1995 Budget Files"
```

MSD: This command launches the Microsoft Diagnostics program to obtain detailed technical information about your system. Use /F to cause the results to be written to a file:

```
MSD /F"Computer Checkup"
```

NLSFUNC: This command loads into memory the Nlsfunc program, which provides support for switching code pages for language support. Specify the location of the COUNTRY.SYS file if it is not in the root directory:

```
NLSFUNC C:\DOS\COUNTRY.SYS
```

SCANDISK: Use ScanDisk to check the integrity of files and folders, and then search the surface of disks for errors. Use the /ALL switch to check all drives, /FRAGMENT to check for fragmentation, /SURFACE if you want to automatically scan the surface, or /UNDO to undo repairs made previously:

```
SCANDISK A: /SURFACE
```

SMARTDRV: The SMARTDrive program creates a disk cache in extended memory. Use /X to disable write-behind caching:

```
SMARTDRV /X  4096
```

> **CAUTION**
>
> Do not use SMARTDrive with Windows 95, which uses its own method of disk caching. SMARTDrive is retained so you can employ caching when dual booting with your previous version of DOS.

SORT: Sort reads a text file, sorts the lines in the file, and then writes the results. /=N specifies which column to sort by: /+10 would sort by file extension, for example. Use /R for a reverse-order sort:

```
DIR \WINWORD\*.DOC¦SORT>"Word for Windows files"
```

START: Use START to launch a Windows application from the command prompt:

```
START SCANDSKW
```

SUBST: The SUBST command is used to create a drive alias for a directory:

```
SUBST F: C:\WPWIN60\WPDOCS
```

SYS: To make a floppy disk self-booting, use SYS to copy hidden Windows 95 system files and the command interpreter (COMMAND.COM) to the disk:

```
SYS A:
```

XCOPY: This command is a more powerful version of COPY that can copy entire branches of subdirectories and files. New switches make it even more powerful. Use /C to ignore errors, /U to copy only files that exist on the destination, /K to retain the read-only attribute, and /R to copy over read-only files:

```
XCOPY \"Wordperfect Files" A: /S /M
```

> **NOTE**
>
> To copy using long filenames to a destination that requires the 8.3 filename format, use the /N switch.

CONFIG.SYS Commands

The following commands are used to configure various aspects of your system. Each must be included in the CONFIG.SYS file to be effective.

BUFFERS: Information read from or written to disk is also stored in buffers in memory. Use the BUFFERS command to set the number of buffers yourself:

```
BUFFERS=30
```

COUNTRY: Establishes country-specific conventions for date, time, and currency; determining sort order; and which characters can be used in filenames. Provide the country code, code page number, and location of the COUNTRY.SYS file. To set the country to Italy, use the following:

```
COUNTRY=039,850,C:\WINDOWS\COMMAND\COUNTRY.SYS
```

DEVICE: Use DEVICE to load device drivers into memory:

```
DEVICE=C:\DOS\HIMEM.SYS
```

DEVICEHIGH: To load a device driver into upper memory, use the DEVICEHIGH command in the CONFIG.SYS file to load the driver:

```
DEVICEHIGH=C:\DOS\SETVER.EXE
```

DOS: The DOS command is used to cause the operating system to load into the high memory area (HIGH) and to allow memory resident programs to be loaded in upper memory blocks (UMB):

```
DOS=HIGH,UMB
```

DRIVPARM: The DRIVPARM command is used to define parameters for disk and tape drives, a procedure usually handled by the hardware installation program. The following sets the drive as D: (A:=0) and the drive type (/F:) as a 2.88MB super high-density drive:

```
DRIVPARM=/D:3 /F:9
```

FCBS: For programs that use DOS Version 1.0 file control blocks, the FCBS command specifies the maximum number of files that can be open at the same time:

```
FCBS=30
```

FILES: The FILES command establishes the number of file handles to make available for programs to use. Install programs may add this command to the CONFIG.SYS file if needed; some programs check during startup to make sure the number is sufficient:

```
FILES=70
```

INCLUDE: When you create a menu of multiple configurations in a CONFIG.SYS file, configurations can include several of the same commands. You can write those repetitive commands in a named block, and then use INCLUDE to run the commands whenever needed in a configuration block. Create this block:

```
[STANDARD]
BUFFERS=40
LASTDRIVE=F
FILES=70
```

Then use INCLUDE to run the commands in configuration blocks:

```
INCLUDE=STANDARD
```

INSTALL: This command loads memory-resident software in conventional memory:

```
INSTALL=C:\DOS\SHARE.EXE
```

LASTDRIVE: To allow for more than five drive letters, use LASTDRIVE to specify the last drive letter you want to have available.

MENUCOLOR: When you create a menu in the CONFIG.SYS file, set the menu text and background colors in the menu block:

```
[MENU]
MENUITEM=NORMAL,SETUP FOR WINDOWS
MENUITEM=MINIMUM,DOS AND GAMES
MENUCOLOR=14,1              (YELLOW TEXT, BLUE BACKGROUND)
MENUDEFAULT=NORMAL,4
[NORMAL]
ETC.
```

MENUDEFAULT: In a menu block, specify the name of the configuration you want to use as a default and the number of seconds to wait without a choice before using the default menu item. Check the previous example in MENUCOLOR.

MENUITEM: In a menu block, use MENUITEM to name the various configuration choices available and assign each a descriptive name that appears on the menu. Each configuration block must begin with the name in square brackets:

```
[MENU]
MENUITEM=NORMAL,SETUP FOR WINDOWS
[NORMAL]
```

NUMLOCK: If you create multiple configurations, in the menu block you can specify whether NUMLOCK is set to ON or OFF:

```
[MENU]
MENUITEM=NORMAL,SETUP FOR WINDOWS
[NORMAL]
NUMLOCK=ON
```

REM: To add a comment or disable a command in the CONFIG.SYS file, precede it with REM:

```
REM THIS SECTION CREATES A MENU OF CONFIGURATIONS.
```

SETVER: Use SETVER to report an MS-DOS version number to programs or device drivers designed for earlier DOS versions. Used alone, it displays a current table of programs and drivers and the version set for each:

```
DEVICE=C:\WINDOWS\COMMAND\SETVER
```

SHELL: Use SHELL to specify the name and location of the command interpreter you want to use, which is usually COMMAND.COM. You can also specify where to reload the shell, set an environment size, and request the shell be loaded permanently:

```
SHELL=C:\WINDOWS\COMMAND\COMMAND.COM /E:1024 /P
```

STACKS: Stacks are used to store information needed to resume a task when an interrupt demands the computer's services. The STACKS command is used to set the size (in bytes) and number of stacks.

SUBMENU: This command defines an item on a startup menu that, when selected, displays another set of choices. You can use this command only within a menu block in CONFIG.SYS.

SWITCHES: This command specifies special options:

```
STACKS=15,128
```

To include the following device drivers in the CONFIG.SYS file requires a DEVICE= or DEVICEHIGH= statement.

DISPLAY.SYS: Set up the use of international character sets on EGA, VGA, and LCD monitors using display.sys. Provide the type of monitor, code page number, and number of pages to allow space for in memory:

```
DEVICE=C:\DOS\DISPLAY.SYS CON=(VGA,039,2)
```

DRIVER.SYS: This driver creates a logical drive that you can use to refer to a physical floppy disk drive or to configure a floppy disk drive. The following sets the drive as D:(A:=0) and the drive type (/F:) as a 2.88-MB super high-density drive:

```
DEVICE=C:\DOS\DISPLAY.SYS /D:3 /F:9
```

EMM386.EXE: If EMM386.EXE and HIMEM.SYS are loaded with DEVICE= commands, you can load device drivers in the upper memory area. EMM386.EXE can also configure a portion of your extended memory as expanded memory:

```
DEVICE=C:\DOS\EMM386.SYS RAM
```

HIMEM.SYS: Include HIMEM.SYS to manage your computer's extended memory. Place HIMEM.SYS before any commands that start applications or device drivers that use extended memory:

```
DEVICE=C:\DOS\HIMEM.SYS
```

KEYBOARD.SYS: This driver enables the operating system to use a keyboard with other than the standard U.S. QWERTY keyboard layout:

```
DEVICE=C:\DOS\KEYBOARD.SYS
```

MSCDEX.EXE: The MSCDEX.EXE driver configures your computer to provide access to CD-ROM drives:

```
DEVICE=C:\DOS\MSCDEX.EXE
```

Batch File Commands

The following commands are used in batch files, although you can also include virtually all internal and external DOS commands in a batch file.

BREAK: Set break OFF in a batch file to prevent the use of CTRL+C or CTRL+BREAK to interrupt execution of the file, or set it ON to check for a break more frequently:

```
BREAK=OFF
```

CALL: Use CALL to transfer control to another batch program and return to the first batch file when done. The following example can be used to first call a menu program, and then run a batch file to backup your data files before quitting for the day:

```
@ECHO OFF
CALL MENU.BAT
CALL EXIT.BAT
ECHO ***Turn computer off now***
```

CHOICE: This command prompts the user to make a choice while running a batch file. The choice offered is Y or N unless you use the /C: switch to specify other keys. Use /T to specify a default choice and the number of seconds to wait for a response. Put in quotation marks the prompt that you want displayed:

```
CHOICE /T:Y,5 "Do you want to use the mouse?"
IF ERRORLEVEL 2 GOTO CONTINUE
```

ECHO: Use ECHO to display or suppress the display of the text in a batch file. Turn display off in multiple lines using ECHO OFF. @ can be used in place of ECHO and used with ECHO OFF to suppress the display of ECHO OFF:

```
@ECHO OFF
ECHO Insert backup disk in drive A:
PAUSE
COPY \WPDOCS\*.* A:
```

FOR: This command works in a batch file in the same way it does from the command prompt, except it uses %%*variable* instead of %*variable*:

```
FOR %%F IN (\WPDOCS \WINWORD\*.DOC) DO COPY %%F
```

GOTO: This command directs the operating system to a line in a batch program that is marked by a label you specify. You can use this command only in batch programs:

```
CHOICE /T:Y,5 "Do you want to use the mouse?"
IF ERRORLEVEL 2 GOTO CONTINUE
C:\UTILITY\MOUSE.COM
:CONTINUE
```

IF: This command performs a test and then executes the rest of the line if true or continues to the next line in the batch file if false. IF commands can be nested on the same line to run another test if the first one is true. You can test to find out whether conditions exist or whether one string equals another string:

```
IF EXIST C:\WPDOCS\*.WPD COPY C:\WPDOCS\*.WPD A:
```

PAUSE: This command stops the execution of a batch file and displays a message to press any key to continue:

```
@ECHO OFF
ECHO Insert backup disk in drive A:
PAUSE
COPY \WPDOCS\*.* A:
```

REM: To add a comment or disable a command in a batch file, precede it with REM:

```
REM THIS SECTION CREATES A MENU OF CONFIGURATIONS.
```

SHIFT: You can include the replaceable parameters %0–%9 on command lines in batch files. The SHIFT command moves the contents of the replaceable parameters to the left. In this example, you can list several groups of files to move, and SHIFT moves the next file held in the parameter %1 to %0:

```
:REPEAT
MOVE %1 /V
SHIFT
IF NOT "%1" == "" GOTO REPEAT
```

And a Few Farewells

Actually, we have lost more than a few commands, although many of them have actually been gathering dust for years. Missing are the following commands:

append	graftabl	msbackup	smartmon
assign	help	power	tree
backup	interlink	printer.sys	undelete
comp	intersvr	recover	unformat
dosshell	join	replace	vsafe
ega.sys	memcard	ramdrive.sys	
fasthelp	mirror	romdrive.sys	
fastopen	msav	share	

The edlin, graphics, memmaker, print, qbasic, and restore commands are no longer available with the floppy disk version of Windows 95. They are included one more time if you purchase Windows 95 on compact disc.

Glossary

active   Designates an object that is currently operational and ready to accept input.

active window   The window in which the cursor or highlight is located. The active window is usually located in front of all other windows, and its title bar displays a contrasting color.

address class   The categorization of networks by size. The first 8-bit portion of an IP address is a number that indicates the network class. The numbers 1–127 are reserved for Class A networks, which can have more than 16 million hosts; 128–191 indicate Class B networks with up to 65,534 hosts, and 192–223 are Class C networks, which can have no more than 254 hosts per network.

application programming interface (API)   In a graphical interface such as Windows 95, a set of functions and resources used to create features such as pull-down menus, dialog boxes, keyboard commands, and windows.

apply   In many Windows 95 dialog boxes, a button that enables the user to cause any selected options to take effect without closing the dialog box.

arbitrator   In Plug and Play, a device driver that allocates a resource among all drivers that require it. Included with Windows 95 are arbitrators for the standard I/O, memory, hardware interrupt, and DMA channel resources.

ASCII file   A file composed entirely of characters from the ASCII character set. A text file.

associate   To use a file extension to create a link between an application program and the data files created or manipulated by that program. The link also describes the actions that can apply to the associated file. When you open an associated file, for example, the program that created the file opens automatically. Other tasks are also possible. For example, you can associate the extension .ZIP and the file PKUNZIP.EXE so that choosing a ZIP file launches the Pkunzip application, which unzips the chosen file.

authentication   Verification of a user's logon information by a computer running Windows 95.

b-node   A NetBIOS over TCP/IP mode that handles computer name queries by broadcasting the computer name to all computers to elicit a response from the named computer. The computers in the broadcast area are responsible for responding when queried by name.

Basic Input/Output System (BIOS)   Instructions encoded in ROM that handle the computer's POST startup procedure, check for a boot and display device and keyboard, and then make this device information available to Windows 95.

batch program   A text file that contains one or more DOS commands that are executed one line at a time when you load the batch file. A batch program's filename must have a .BAT or .CMD extension.

binding   For a network computer, the process of establishing the communication channel between a transport protocol driver and a network adapter driver.

BIOS   See **Basic Input/Output System**

boot   The startup procedure for a system that clears the memory, loads an operating system, and performs other routines necessary to prepare the system for use. Starting a computer by turning on the power is a cold boot. Using a reset switch or pressing Ctrl+Alt+Del to restart a computer is called a warm boot. A warm boot does not stop and start all of the computer's electronic components, such as the hard drive, making the process less stressful for hardware. However, a cold boot is usually required when you reset hardware, such as a fax/modem.

Bootstrap Protocol (BOOTP)   A proposed industry standard implemented in Windows 95 that enables automatic allocation of IP addresses across internetworks.

branch   A directory and its subdirectories, if any, in the directory tree structure of a drive.

browse   A command used to look through lists of directories and files. On a network, it is also used to look through lists of users, groups, computers, and so on.

buffer   A section of memory used to hold data temporarily, until the data can be transferred to another location, such as a disk drive or elsewhere in memory.

bus enumerator   A bus-specific driver that identifies all the hardware devices and their resource requirements and builds the hardware tree on a Plug and Play system.

button   A graphical element found in toolbars and dialog boxes and used to execute an option or command. Also, one of the several keys on a mouse.

Card Services   A protected-mode VxD that, along with the PCMCIA bus driver, supports and manages the credit card-size interface cards for devices that plug into small portable computers.

cascading menus   A hierarchical menu system in which selecting a menu command causes another menu to appear.

character mode   A display mode in which the computer uses only those characters found in its built-in character set. The standard ASCII character set includes a number of line drawing and shading characters useful for creating simple graphic images such as drop-down menus and dialog boxes. Also called *text mode*.

check box   A standard control that is chosen by the user to toggle an option on (checked) or off (unchecked). When selected, the check box contains a ✓ or ✗.

child menu   A submenu in a cascading menu system.

child window   In a multiple document interface, a document window within a window (called the parent window).

click   To quickly press and release a mouse button while the pointer is over an object.

client   A networked computer that accesses resources located on another computer called a server.

clipboard   The name used by some applications for a storage area where data is placed temporarily after being cut or copied. The Windows 95 Clipboard also includes information about the data type when cutting or copying from OLE-compliant applications.

close   To exit a document or dialog box, thereby removing its window.

component object model   The object-oriented programming model of programming interfaces, data structures, and protocols that are the basis of OLE.

compound document   A document, created using OLE, that contains multiple data types created by different applications and stored by a container application.

compound file   A disk file of OLE objects and associated data. The compound file format supports multiple streams of logically separated objects and a permanent index.

computer name   On a network, a name that identifies a computer to the network. The name must be unique and can have up to 15 characters with spaces not allowed.

Configuration Manager   In the Windows 95 Plug and Play, the component that locates devices, sets up the device nodes in the hardware tree, and runs the resource allocation process. There is a separate Configuration Manager for boot time (BIOS), real mode, and protected mode.

container   An object, such as a window, frame, or picture box, that can hold other objects.

context menu   A menu, activated by clicking the right mouse button on an object, that contains commands specifically applicable to the selected object. Also called a shortcut or pop-up menu.

context-sensitive help   Online documentation that briefly describes the current object, operation, or command and its use. Select an object, and then press F1 to see context-sensitive help.

control menu   A drop-down menu available by clicking the control menu button in the upper-left corner of a window. The control menu button is represented by the icon used to indicate the resource in the window.

cursor   A flashing vertical bar displayed on-screen to indicate the current location of the insertion point.

data type   The middle component of a value entry in the Registry.

datagram   A packet of data and delivery information that is transmitted on a network.

DDE   See **dynamic data exchange**.

default   An operation or value that the system uses automatically, unless the user makes another choice. A user choice may be retained as the default the next time the procedure is used.

default printer   The printer a program automatically uses when the Print command is executed.

demand paging   A method for moving data from physical memory to a temporary paging file (swap file) on disk. Data is moved to disk in pages and then paged back into physical memory when needed.

Desktop   In Windows 95, the display area that fills the screen. Because it is a container, you can customize it by placing objects, such as documents, folders and shortcuts, directly on the Desktop.

destination document   In object linking and embedding (OLE), the document into which a package or object is being inserted. Also referred to as a *container document* when the user is embedding an object.

device   A hardware component or peripheral, such as a serial port, printer, modem, or monitor that can receive or send data.

device contention   The technique that Windows 95 uses to allocate access to devices, such as a printer, when multitasking applications make simultaneous requests to access the same device.

device driver   A program that provides Windows 95 with the information needed for it to recognize and work with a specific hardware device.

device ID   A unique ASCII string created by Windows 95 to identify a hardware device. The device ID is then used for tasks such as installing the device driver, creating a hardware key in the Registry for the device, and identifying Plug and Play devices.

device node   A device's basic data structure built into memory at system startup by Configuration Manager, containing information about the device. See also **hardware tree**.

DHCP   See **Dynamic Host Configuration Protocol**.

dialog box   A secondary window that enables the user to provide additional information. See also **message box** and **palette window**.

dimmed   A very light, indistinct appearance of a control that indicates the control's function is not available.

directory tree   A hierarchical arrangement of directories and subdirectories branching from the root directory.

disk caching   The use of a large area of random-access memory (RAM) to store frequently used data and program instructions. When data is retrieved, a disk cache also reads and stores data from the next few sectors on the disk, anticipating the system's next request. Being able to frequently read and write to memory results in substantially improved performance.

DLL   See **dynamic-link library**.

DMA channel   A channel used to transfer data from memory directly to peripheral devices without involving the microprocessor. Requests for data are handled by a DMA controller chip.

DNS   See **Domain Name System**.

DNS name server   A server that contains part of the DNS database.

dock   To insert a portable computer into a docking station. Also, to move a floating palette window until the toolbar it contains appears at the edge of a window.

docking station   A cabinet designed to house a portable or notebook computer. Docking stations typically provide drive bays, expansion slots, various ports, and AC power, and can include extras such as PCMCIA slots and built-in networking.

document window   A window within an application program that displays the contents of a document that is being created or edited by the user.

domain   A group of computers, identified by a unique name, that share a common database and security policy on a Windows NT Server domain controller. See also **workgroup**.

Domain Name System (DNS)   In TCP/IP, the service that keeps track of IP addresses and domain names, handling the translation from name to address.

double-click   To quickly press a mouse button two times while the pointer is over an object.

down-level file system   An operating system structure for file management that supports the earlier MS-DOS FAT file system.

downloaded fonts   Software fonts sent to a printer before or during a print job and held in printer memory until needed.

drag   To move the mouse while pressing a mouse button.

drag-and-drop   A program feature that enables you to perform operations on an object by dragging it to a new location or another object.

drill down   The process of opening a folder located in a folder through layers of folders until the desired folder is open.

dual boot   The ability to boot up either your old operating system or Windows 95 using the F4 key during the boot process.

dynamic data exchange (DDE)   An interprocess communication channel (IPC) that enables programs to actively exchange information with and control the operation of other programs. Object linking and embedding (OLE) techniques simplify setting up links between programs that support dynamic data exchange.

Dynamic Host Configuration Protocol (DHCP)   A proposed industry standard implemented in Windows 95 for configuration of TCP/IP and IP address allocation and management.

dynamic-link library (DLL)   An application program interface (API) to which an application links at runtime.

EISA   See **Extended Industry Standard Architecture**.

embedded object   An object created in one program that is inserted completely in another program using object linking and embedding (OLE) techniques, yet retains its original functionality.

enumerator   Literally, a census taker; a Plug and Play device driver that detects and identifies devices during startup. Specific enumerators are provided for each component that must be checked, such as a PCMCIA enumerator and a SCSI enumerator.

environment variable   An instruction, such as a path to store temporary files or command prompt format, stored in the DOS environment for use by Windows 95.

event   An action or occurrence, such as a mouse click, key press, or error, that generates a response.

Extended Industry Standard Architecture (EISA)   A 32-bit bus design consortium for x 86-based computers introduced by a consortium of computer companies (AST Research, Compaq, Epson, Hewlett-Packard, NEC, Olivetti, Tandy, Wyse, and Zenith). An expansion of the AT bus, EISA enables more than one processor to share the bus.

extended partition   On a hard disk, a section of disk space that is structured so that it can be sectioned (partitioned) into multiple logical drives.

FAT   See **file allocation table**.

FAT file system   A file system that uses a file allocation table to record whether clusters on a disk are available or contain file data. See also **Virtual File Allocation Table (VFAT)**.

file allocation table (FAT)   A hidden table of all the clusters on a disk, containing information about the status and contents of each cluster.

file association   A relationship established in the Registry between a data file extension, the application used to create the file, and Windows 95 functions such as Open and Print.

file control block (FCB)   A small section of memory that an application uses to hold information about an open file.

file sharing   The capability of a networked computer to share its data on disk with remote computers.

file system   The structure an operating system uses for storing, organizing, and naming files.

file transfer protocol (FTP)   In asynchronous communications, any of several standards used to accomplish error-free bidirectional transfer of binary and ASCII files between local and remote systems. On the Internet, the File Transfer Protocol service, usually referred to as FTP, is the basic file transfer mechanism for transferring files among hosts on the Internet. FTP is also used as a verb, as in "FTP it to ..." In Windows 95, FTP is installed as one of the TCP/IP utilities.

flash ROM   A device hardware feature that enables the device to be configured using software instead of a jumper.

folder   In Windows 95, a container for objects such as applications and files. It usually displays on-screen as a file folder.

font   A set of letters, numbers, punctuation marks, and special characters all in a consistent and identifiable typeface, and having the same weight (roman or bold), posture (upright or italic), and size. Often used to refer only to typeface.

font size   The dimensions of a font, usually stated in points; 72 points is equal to approximately one inch.

font style   The attributes of a font such as normal, bold, italic, and underline.

FTP   See **file transfer protocol**.

fully qualified domain name (FQDN)   In TCP/IP, the complete address of a host computer, usually in the format `computer.organization.type`, although some hosts have only a two-part FQDN (`computer.type`).

gateway   A network device, usually a dedicated computer, that connects local and wide-area networks, as well as other systems such as a minicomputer or mainframe, and is responsible for forwarding packets of data to other gateways for delivery to a specified destination. See also **IP router**.

gesture   In pen computing, lines drawn on the screen that are recognized as a character or command.

glyph   A graphic or pictorial image used instead of or in addition to text on buttons or in a message box. See also **icon**.

h-node   A NetBIOS over TCP/IP mode that resolves computer names as addresses by first using p-node (name query), and then if unsuccessful switches to b-node (broadcast).

handle   In a graphical interface, a display of small black squares surrounding an object. The squares are dragged to move, size, reshape, and otherwise manipulate the object. Also, in programming, a pointer to a resource maintained in a table or other structure.

hardware tree   A record in RAM, created at system startup and modified as the system configuration changes, of the current system configuration based on the configuration information in the Registry.

header   Control information, such as ID number, source and destination addresses, and error-control data, located at the beginning of a packet.

high-performance file system (HPFS)   A file system that supports long filenames but does not provide security features. The file system used by the OS/2 operating system.

home directory   On computers networked to a server, a directory accessible to the user that contains files such as WIN.COM, SYSTEM.DAT, and USER.DAT, the swap file, the spool directory, and programs for use on that computer.

host   A computer that supports other computers on a network. Also, any computer that is connected to the Internet.

host table   On a network, a file (named HOSTS or LMHOST) that lists the IP addresses mapped to host names or NetBIOS computer names.

hot docking   A Plug and Play feature that enables the removal and the insertion of a portable computer from or to its docking station without turning it off. The portable automatically reconfigures itself for the currently available capabilities.

hot swapping   A Plug and Play feature that enables you to remove components from a machine and put the new components in without rebooting the machine.

HPFS   See **high-performance file system**.

icon   A symbol that represents an object. Drawings of a document page, disk, or application logo are icons.

inactive   Designates an object that is currently not operational and cannot accept input from the user.

Industry Standard Architecture (ISA)   The 8-bit bus design of the IBM PC/XT and the later 16-bit version designed for the IBM PC/AT.

.INF file   A device configuration file that provides Windows 95 Setup with the information required to set up the device. .INF files are usually provided by the manufacturer.

inherit   The passing to a specific type of object what its object class knows and can do.

.INI files   Text files containing user information and application configuration startup data for Windows and Windows applications that predate Windows 95. Windows 95 stores this information in the Registry but supports .INI files for applications that require them.

ink   In pen computing, lines drawn on-screen that are not recognized as a command or character.

insertion point   The place where text or graphics will be inserted, usually indicated by a blinking vertical bar.

internal command   A command such as DIR or COPY that's part of the file CMD.EXE, and therefore in memory at all times.

Internet Packet eXchange/Sequence Packet eXchange (IPX/SPX)   A set of transport protocols developed by Novell and used in NetWare networks.

Internet Protocol (IP) A set of rules that govern the actual transportation of packets over networks.

interrupt A signal, usually initiated by I/O devices requiring service from the processor, that interrupts normal processing. The processor branches to a service routine that processes the interrupt, and then returns control to the suspended process.

interrupt request (IRQ) lines The hardware lines over which devices such as a printer or modem can send interrupts to get the attention of the processor when the device is ready to accept or send information.

I/O device Hardware used for sending information to and receiving information from the computer. Printers, monitors, modems, keyboards, and disk drives are examples of I/O (input/output) devices.

IP See **Internet Protocol**.

IP address Equivalent to a FQDN or Internet address, the unique number actually used to identify and specify routing information on an internetwork. An IP address consists of the network ID and a unique host ID assigned by the network administrator.

IP router A network device used to connect TCP/IP networks and route or deliver IP packets between them. Also called a *gateway*.

IRQ See **interrupt request lines**.

ISA See **Industry Standard Architecture**.

kernel The portion of Windows 95's Application Program Interface that manages the processor.

key A topic in the Registry editor, displayed always in the left pane of the Regedit window. The six keys listed initially can be expanded to display subtopics. The value, if one is set, for a selected topic is displayed in the right pane.

landscape An orientation where the width of a rectangular area is greater than its height.

lasso-tap In pen computing, a method for selecting an object on the screen by drawing a circle around the object and tapping in the circle.

link A connection between two objects so that a change in one causes the same change in the other.

linked object A representation of an object that is inserted into a destination document. The appearance and behavior of the linked object depends on how the data was linked when the link was created.

list box In a dialog box, a box with a sorted display of available selections, such as a list of fonts or files. A scrollbar appears if the length of the list exceeds the size of the list box.

local bus   A high-speed data path between the microprocessor and one or more slots on the expansion bus, offering a significant speed improvement for an adapter using a local bus slot.

local printer   A printer connected directly to one of the ports on the computer you're using.

logical drive   A section of an extended partition on a hard disk that is formatted and assigned a drive letter. On a network, a directory that is mapped to a drive letter.

logon script   A series of commands that are run, usually from a batch file, when the user logs on. A logon script can be used to configure the user's environment.

m-node   A NetBIOS over TCP/IP mode that first uses b-node (broadcast) to resolve computer names as addresses, then if unsuccessful switches to p-node (name query).

management information base (MIB)   A set of objects used by a service or protocol to manage devices. The objects represent types of information about a device.

map   To translate or assign one value, such as virtual addresses or network drives, to another.

MAPI   See **messaging application program interface**.

MDI   See **multiple document interface**.

menu   An on-screen list of available commands from which a user can make a choice.

menubar   In an application program window, a horizontal strip below the title bar that contains the names of pull-down menus.

message box   A secondary window that displays information about a particular condition.

messaging application program interface (MAPI)   The Microsoft implementation of an interface that developers can use to establish cross-platform messaging and to make other Windows-based applications mail-aware.

MIB   See **management information base**.

Micro Channel bus   The IBM proprietary 32-bit expansion bus introduced in its high-end PS/2 computers.

mouse pointer   An on-screen arrow or other symbol that is moved around the screen by moving a mouse or other pointing device on a flat surface. The pointer is used in tandem with the mouse buttons to draw pictures and to select commands, buttons, text, or other objects.

MS-DOS-based program   A program that is designed to run with the DOS operating system. Many MS-DOS-based applications run successfully in a Windows 95 window but some can run only at the command prompt. Such programs can be run successfully in MS-DOS mode, where they will have exclusive access to system resources.

multiple document interface (MDI)   An interface in which documents are opened into separate child windows within a single parent window.

Multiuser Dimensions (MUD)   On the Internet, a live version of the highly popular fantasy role-playing adventure game. Enter with care; it's addictive.

My Computer   In the upper-left corner of the default desktop, a Windows 95 object (icon) that represents the user's personal system. Specifically, My Computer includes all the disk drives and the Control Panel and Printer folders that contain the wizards and other tools for configuring every part of the user's system. My Computer is actually Windows Explorer with only the right pane displayed.

name registration   On a network, the procedure used by a computer to provide its unique name to a network name server.

name resolution   A service that maps computer names to IP addresses. The service is provided by either a DNS name server or a NetBIOS name server (NBNS).

named pipe   A mechanism that enables one process to communicate with another local or remote process.

NetBIOS   See **network basic input/output system**.

NetBIOS over TCP/IP   For networks using NetBIOS, an interface that handles computer name-to-IP address mapping for name resolution.

network basic input/output system (NetBIOS)   A transport-level protocol for network communication.

network directory   See **shared directory**.

network-interface printers   Printers with built-in network cards that can be directly connected to a network.

Network Neighborhood   On the left side of the default desktop, a Windows 95 object (icon) that represents the user's access to other computers and networks.

object   An entity in memory that contains data, often expressed as properties, and the code to act on that data. See also **OLE object**.

object linking and embedding (OLE)   Technology that enables the user to share information between applications. OLE is used to create dynamic, automatically updated links between documents created by different applications, and to embed data created by one OLE application into a document created by another OLE application.

OLE   See **object linking and embedding**.

OLE application   A Windows-based application with OLE capabilities. The extent to which data can be shared and manipulated between applications depends on the version of OLE supported by each application.

OLE object   Data, such as a chart, a document or only a paragraph of text, a worksheet or small range of cells, that has been created by an OLE application and has been linked or embedded in a document created by another.

option button   In dialog boxes, a control that enables the user to select one of a group of mutually exclusive choices. Also called *radio buttons*. Compare with **check box**.

p-node   A NetBIOS over TCP/IP mode that resolves computer names as addresses by querying a WINS server for the address of a specific computer. The WINS server must know all computer names and addresses and prevent duplicates.

package   An icon representing an embedded or linked object that is used to play or open the object.

packet   A standard-sized transmission unit of data containing part of a message preceded by a header that has information about the sender, recipient, and error control data.

page   An entry that has been pasted in ClipBook. Also, a fixed-size block in memory.

paging file   A system file that contains the contents of virtual pages that have been paged out of memory by the Virtual Memory Manager. Also called a *swap file*.

palette window   A secondary window that displays graphical choices, such as a toolbar of buttons or a group of line types, colors, or patterns.

pane   Any of the separate sections in a divided window.

partition   A division of a hard disk that functions as though it were a separate disk. See also **system partition**.

password   A string of characters used as a security measure to control access to computers, software or data files. Windows 95 recognizes passwords up to 14 characters, and is case-sensitive.

path   The route to a file on the directory tree.

PCMCIA   See **Personal Computer Memory Card International Association**.

pen   A special stylus that resembles a pen that is used to choose commands and write instructions on the screen of a computer equipped with pattern recognition circuitry.

Peripheral Component Interconnect (PCI)   A local bus design now commonly used in Pentium and PowerPC computers. See also **local bus**.

permission   A rule that grants and regulates access for specified users to objects such as a directory, file, or printer.

Personal Computer Memory Card International Association (PCMCIA)   A trade association standard for a credit-card-sized interface card for devices such as modems and external hard drives that can be plugged into laptop and notebook computers.

ping   A diagnostic tool used to verify Internet (TCP/IP) connections.

plotter font   A vector font, which creates characters by generating dots connected by lines, that is designed for use with plotters.

Plug and Play   A component of Windows 95 that provides for the automatic installation and configuration of devices attached to a computer. Plug and Play-compatible hardware identifies itself during the boot process and maintains contact while active so the system can reconfigure itself dynamically. The system BIOS also participates by helping to recognize which hardware is present and which is not, and communicating with the devices to find out their needs.

point   The act of positioning the pointer over an object or location on the screen. Also, a unit of measurement for fonts where approximately 72 points equal one inch.

Point-to-Point Protocol (PPP)   In Windows 95 Remote Access, an industry standard, presently an RFC, used to ensure interoperability with third-party software.

port   An interface that regulates and synchronizes the flow of data between the processor and an external device, such as a printer, monitor, or modem, and the physical connection or socket used to connect the device to your computer.

portrait   An orientation where the height of a rectangular area is greater than its width.

postoffice   A directory structure on a server that is used to hold mail messages until retrieved by the recipient's workstation.

Power-On Self-Test (POST)   A short program, part of the BIOS chip, that is run at system startup. The POST checks the microprocessor, reads CMOS RAM for valid memory and disk drive information, tests each byte of memory, and initializes all devices including the keyboard, drives, and printer. The BIOS continues hardware testing, and finally searches drive A, then drive C for a bootstrap program provided by the operating system.

PPP   See **Point-to-Point Protocol**.

primary partition   On a hard disk, a section of disk space that is structured for use by an operating system. A primary partition must be formatted by an operating system before it can be used and cannot be partitioned into smaller sections.

print device   In Windows 95, the hardware that provides printed output.

print monitor   A Windows 95 component with printer information that receives print job information from the print spooler and sends it on to the appropriate printer or file.

print provider   On a network, software that supports printing to a device attached to the print server. The print provider also provides information for other printer-related functions, such as installation of new remote printers.

print queue   Print job list in the spooler for later printing. In mobile computing situations, jobs can remain in the spooler until the portable system is reconnected to a printer.

print sharing   The capability, provided in Windows 95, for a computer to share its printer with other computers on a network.

printer   Hardware designed to produce a hard copy of computer-generated text or graphics. In Windows 95, the software interface between applications and a print device. See also **print device**.

printer driver   A file for a specific brand and model of printer that provides information that enables a program to print your work with that printer.

printer fonts   Typefaces in specific sizes or scaleable that are built into a printer. Printer fonts are only accessible to application software if the printer driver is installed in each application.

program file   A file with a .EXE, .PIF, .COM, or .BAT filename extension that starts a program. Note that .PIF files and Windows applications can only operate within Windows.

program information file (PIF)   A file, used to launch DOS-based programs, that provides information about how Windows 95 should launch and run the program.

properties   Configuration options for an object that define the object's behavior, its appearance, and other settings.

protected mode   In 80286 and higher microprocessors, an operating mode that supports virtual memory and enables multitasking. The 32-bit core of the Windows 95 operating system uses protected mode.

protocol   A set of standards for exchanging information between computers across a network or using a modem.

queue   See **print queue**.

quick format   Clears the file allocation table and the first letter of filenames in the root directory of a disk but does not check the disk for bad sectors.

real mode   The operating mode of the 8086 microprocessor in which each program is given direct access to memory and peripheral devices. Although real mode can use up to 1 MB of RAM, it cannot manage more than one program in memory at a time. Protected mode, which addresses this shortcoming, became available beginning with the 80286 microprocessor.

reboot   To restart a computer using a Reset button or pressing Ctrl+Alt+Del. Also called a *warm boot*.

redirector   In Windows 95 networking, file system drivers that accept I/O requests and then redirect them to the appropriate network service on another computer. Redirectors are implemented as file system drivers in Windows 95.

refresh   To update the screen display to reflect current data.

Regedit   See **Registry Editor**.

Registry   A database of configuration information about all system components and applications that know how to store values in the Registry.

Registry Editor   A Windows 95 application used to view and edit data in the Registry.

Remote Access   A service that enables telecommuters and mobile workers to dial in to access the network for services such as file and printer sharing, electronic mail, and database access.

Request for Comments (RFC)   A document promulgated by the Internet Engineering Task Force (IETF) detailing proposed industry standards for TCP/IP protocols.

resource   The keyboard, memory, disk drives, and other parts of a computer or network that are available for use by a process or program.

restart   See **reboot**.

RFC   See **Request for Comments**.

root directory   In a directory tree, the directory from which all other directories branch. The root directory on a disk is created by the operating system when a disk is formatted.

router   In network printing, the component that sends information from the workstation spooler to the spooler on the destination printer. In internetworking, computers that have two or more network adapters connected to different physical networks using the same protocols. Routers can also determine the best route for transmitting data on a packet-switching network.

screen fonts   Bitmapped fonts that mimic on-screen the appearance of printer fonts, used so documents will appear on-screen as they will when printed.

SCSI   See **Small Computer System Interface**.

select   To make one or more objects active.

selection   One or more objects that are currently selected.

Serial Line IP (SLIP)   An industry standard available in Windows 95 Remote Access that is an alternative to PPP for connections to older UNIX networks.

server   On a local area network, a computer equipped with network software that manages access by other computers to the network and its resources. See also **client**.

service   A specific system function, such as card services, that may also include an API that other processes can call.

session The operation of a program from launch to closing. Also, running a program within another program, such as a DOS session running in Windows 95. On a network, an active connection between two applications on different computers. The session layer coordinates communications and maintains security, name recognition, and administrative functions for the session.

share Make resources, such as directories and printers, available to multiple users.

share name The name given to a shared resource.

shared directory A directory accessible to users on the network.

shared resource In Windows 95, a directory, file, printer, or other device made available to network users.

shell The interface supplied by the operating system. Also, a utility program that provides an alternative interface, considered easier-to-use or having different features, for the operating system.

shell extension For an application that provides extended OLE-related functionality, an OLE hook into Windows 95. Applications that support OLE extensions place a ShellX key into the registry.

shortcut menu See **context menu**.

SLIP See **Serial Line IP**.

Small Computer System Interface (SCSI) A device interface equivalent to an expansion bus into which multiple devices, such as hard drives, scanners, and CD-ROMs, can be plugged. Up to seven different SCSI devices can be daisy-chained to a single SCSI port.

socket On a network, a pipe for incoming and outgoing data. In Windows 95, Windows Sockets is the implementation of the University of California at Berkeley Sockets API. Windows Sockets is a protocol-independent networking application program interface tailored for use by programmers using the Windows family of products.

socket services A protected-mode VxD that provides an interface for Card Services by managing the PCMCIA adapter hardware. Each PCMCIA controller requires its own socket services driver.

source directory The directory from which you copy or move a file.

source document The document that was used to create an embedded or linked object.

split bar A graphical device that divides a window in two parts and is used to change the size of each part.

spooler A scheduler for the printing process. It coordinates activity among other components of the print model and schedules all print jobs arriving at the print server.

status bar   A strip, usually located at the bottom of an application window, that displays program information such as the location of the insertion point, the date, font, and operating mode.

string   A group of alphanumeric characters that is treated as a data structure.

subdirectory   A directory structure created in another directory.

swap file   A special file on your hard disk used by Windows 95 to implement virtual memory. Also called a *paging file*. See also **virtual memory**.

syntax   The elements required for a command and the order in which you must type them. The following example illustrates the four possible elements: command name (FORMAT), parameter (A:), switch (/S), and value (1.44).

```
FORMAT A: /S /F:1.44
```

system partition   The volume that contains the files, such as MSDOS.SYS, needed to load Windows 95. See also **partition**.

taskbar   A strip initially located at the bottom of the Windows 95 screen. The Start menu, used to launch applications, is located at the left end of the taskbar. The taskbar serves as a tray for icons representing open programs and other open features such as folders and Help topics.

TCP/IP (Transmission Control Protocol/Internet Protocol)   A large set of protocols used to connect and organize computers and networks. The most important protocols are TCP, which manages the transmission of data on networks, and IP, which actually transmits the data. Windows 95 uses TCP/IP when communicating with networks and UNIX-based services.

Telnet service   A Windows 95 service that provides basic terminal emulation to remote systems configured with TCP/IP and Telnet server software. Telnet enables you to log on to remote computer systems as a guest, and work there as if you were a local user.

text file   A file that contains nothing but characters from the ASCII character set. A text file contains no formatting or control characters.

thread   An object consisting of a unit of code belonging to a single process that can have a time slice from the processor so it can execute concurrently with other threads.

thunking   A translation process provided by the Kernel that transforms 16-bit format into 32-bit format.

time-out   The amount of time the computer waits for a device to perform a task before detecting non-performance as an error.

title bar   A horizontal strip at the top of a window that displays the name of the window. The title bar can be used to drag the window to a new location, and its color indicates whether the window is currently active.

toolbar   A frame for buttons that provide shortcuts to commands. The default location is directly below the menu bar, but toolbars can be dragged to the side or bottom of the window or displayed as a palette window in the middle of the screen.

trust information   A link between two Windows NT domains minimizes the duplication of user account information by enabling them to share the information.

UNC   See **uniform naming convention (UNC) names**.

uniform naming convention (UNC) names   A naming convention for files or other resources on a remote computer. The name must begin with the string \\.

Universal Asynchronous Receiver/Transmitter (UART)   An integrated circuit that transforms the computer's parallel data stream to the serial data stream of asynchronous communications.

user account   A record of the information that defines a user, including the user's name and password, group memberships, and the user's rights and permissions for accessing system resources.

user name   On a network, a name that identifies a user account to the network. The name must be unique, with up to 15 characters with spaces not allowed.

value entry   Data listed under a key or subkey in the Registry. A value entry appears as text with three parts: the name of the value, the data type, and the actual value, separated by periods; for example, *Word.Document.6*.

VCACHE   A disk cache driver for the VFAT and CDFS file system and 32-bit network redirectors that features more intelligent algorithms to improve performance and dynamic sizing of the cache.

VESA local bus (VL)   A local bus standard, created by the Video Electronic Standards Association, for an expansion bus that is connected directly to the computer's central processing unit, enabling high-speed connections to peripherals.

virtual DOS machine (VDM)   A Win32-based application that establishes in memory a complete virtual 80386 or higher computer running MS-DOS. In Windows 95, a VDM is required to run MS-DOS–based or Windows 16-bit applications.

Virtual File Allocation Table (VFAT)   A 32-bit file system that supports long filenames, protected-mode operation, and a 32-bit disk cache.

virtual memory   A technique for increasing the apparent size of random-access memory (RAM) by using space set aside on a hard disk. Virtual addresses are mapped to physical addresses on the disk, and data is moved between RAM and the disk by swapping or paging. With virtual memory, you can run more programs simultaneously at the cost of space on your disk and decreased execution speed during swapping operations. See also **swap file**.

visual editing   The ability to edit the data in an embedded object within the compound document without opening the application used to create the data.

volume   A floppy disk or, on a fixed disk, a partition or collection of partitions formatted for use.

VxD   A virtual device driver, where *x* represents the type of device, which can be anything. In Windows 95, hardware devices are virtualized; that is, software interfaces with the driver as if it were the hardware itself. The driver in turn arbitrates conflicting requests for device services. Protected-mode VxDs are dynamically loaded into memory and unloaded as needed. Real-mode (static) VxDs are loaded into memory when the computer is booted and remain in memory until you shut down the system.

wildcard   Special characters that are used to represent one or more other characters. DOS uses the question mark, which can represent a single character, and the asterisk, which represents one or several characters at the location of the wildcard.

window   A rectangular object in which you can view an application, a document, or other information. A window is a separately controllable area of the screen that typically has a rectangular border.

Windows Internet Name Service   In a routed environment, a name service that resolves computer names to IP addresses. The name registrations, queries, and releases are handled by a WINS server.

WINS   See **Windows Internet Name Service**.

WINS server   A Windows NT Server 3.5 computer with WINS server software installed.

wizard   An interactive dialog box that leads users through the process of choosing all configuration options for a particular task. After all choices have been made, the task is performed without further user actions. Wizards are provided to perform tasks such as installing programs, configuring hardware, and creating charts.

workgroup   Several computers that are grouped together to facilitate sharing resources such as files, a printer, and a scanner. A computer can be connected to a workgroup and a facility or company-wide network.

The Microsoft Network

by Ed Tiley

E

IN THIS CHAPTER

The Microsoft Network, often called MSN, is the newest entry into the world of major online services. In an effort to compete with CompuServe, America Online, and Prodigy, MSN offers a number of features to differentiate it from the competition.

The market for online services is still in its infancy, according to a white paper released by Microsoft under the title *The Microsoft Network, Service Summary*. In this document (reprinted with permission from Microsoft Corporation), Microsoft states the following:

> Microsoft Corporation has long believed in the promise of personal computers to enable new ways of thinking and communicating that are accessible, useful, personal and fun for all computer users. It calls this vision "Information At Your Fingertips." The introduction of The Microsoft™ Network online service represents Microsoft's next step toward the realization of this vision.
>
> While interactive online services are well-publicized throughout the print and broadcast media, today's services are surprisingly less popular with consumers than all the hype might suggest. For example, although 40 percent of users of the Microsoft Windows® operating system have modems, fewer than 10 percent of users of Windows and 4 percent of U.S. households subscribe to any online service.

By including access to MSN as a standard feature of Windows 95 and having the user interface of the service be an extension of the Windows 95 user interface, Microsoft hopes to capture the hearts and minds of a significant portion of the other 96 percent of U.S. households. Of course, the Microsoft Network is available worldwide, so they are trying to capture the hearts and minds of the rest of the world, too.

According to research quoted in the white paper, Microsoft expects the online service market to grow into a two billion dollar a year industry by the end of the century.

NOTE

To be fair both to readers and Microsoft, it must be noted that MSN is itself in its infancy. The material gathered for this chapter was obtained before the final launch of The Microsoft Network.

For this reason the contents of this chapter are long on using the network and short on the content you can expect to find. It is not unreasonable to expect that MSN will take a while to mature, so the things you can access will be changing almost daily as new service providers join the network. During the trial run of the Microsoft Network, literally hundreds of service providers attended training sessions devoted to building online products. By the time you log on for the first time, a wide variety of more than 200 services are scheduled to be up and running.

Gaining Access to MSN

There are four steps that must be taken before you can connect to the Microsoft Network. You must install a modem in your system, install Exchange, install The Microsoft Network, and go through the sign-up process.

Installing the Necessities

Installing MSN is quite simple. If you do not already have a modem installed, use the Add/Remove Hardware dialog in the Control Panel to install one. The basics of modem installation can be found in Chapter 7, "Windows 95 Device Support—Printer, Comm, Fonts, and Video."

After your modem is installed, you might need to install the software for the Microsoft Network if you did not install it when you installed Windows 95 itself. Use the Add/Remove Programs dialog in Control Panel to move the needed software onto your hard disk if MSN isn't already installed.

FIGURE E.1.

When you install MSN, you might also need to install Exchange.

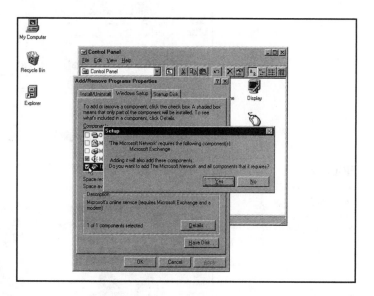

Using the Windows Setup tab shown in Figure E.1, locate the entry for the Microsoft Network and click the checkbox to select it. As you can see in Figure E.1, MSN requires you to install Exchange also. If Exchange is not already installed, you will be prompted to install it.

When you have selected MSN and Exchange, click OK to begin installing the files. All you need to do is follow the prompts for inserting disks. After the files are copied, you will be prompted to restart the system so that the configuration files can be altered to reflect the new additions.

Configuring Exchange

While Exchange is being installed, you are prompted by a Wizard to make changes to the Exchange Profile. If Exchange is already installed, you will need to use the Mail and Fax dialog of Control Panel to make the necessary adjustments. Either way, the process is exactly the same.

Figure E.2 shows the Control Panel access method. Most people will have only a single Exchange profile. Just click the Services tab of the dialog box, click the Add button, and select the Microsoft Network. This reveals the dialog shown in Figure E.3.

FIGURE E.2.

Adding MSN to your Exchange profile is simple. Just launch the Mail and Fax dialog from Control Panel and choose Add.

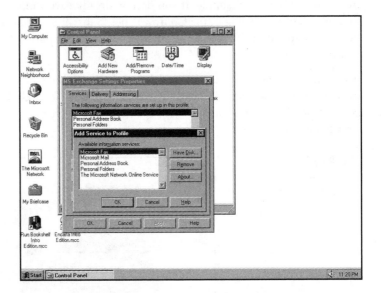

FIGURE E.3.

When you select MSN, this dialog enables you to customize how you want e-mail messages handled.

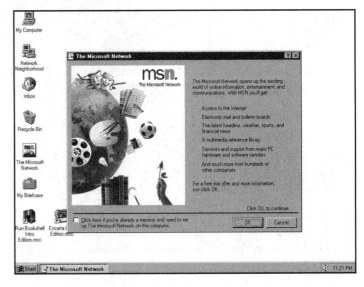

The dialog in Figure E.3 enables you to specify how you want e-mail messages that are received via MSN to be handled. The Transport dialog has three checkboxes that can have a profound effect on the expense of using MSN as an e-mail hub.

The first checkbox, when checked, specifies that your e-mail should be downloaded when you first connect to MSN. If this box is unchecked, you will need to pick up your messages manually.

The second checkbox, which is marked Disconnect After Updating Headers from Remote Preview, tells Exchange to download only the headers of messages, not the full message. Unless you receive a lot of junk e-mail, you should leave this box unchecked so that you get all your mail, not just the name of the sender and a title. Checking this box lets you pick and choose which e-mail messages you want to read and which you want to discard without reading.

The Disconnect After Processing Headers checkbox, when checked, lets you read your e-mail offline in a leisurely fashion. Unless this box is checked, you remain online with the meter running while you process your e-mail, which is seldom a good idea.

The Address Book tab of this dialog lets you select how you want Internet messaging to be handled. Two choices are found on this dialog. Accept Internet Messages with @ Sign specifies that Internet messages should be accepted by your account. Pricing for MSN services was still unpublished as of the writing of this chapter, but presumably Internet communications are received postage due as they are on other online services, which means a small service charge is incurred when you accept messages originating from the Internet.

The second choice, Do Not Connect To Check Addresses, enables you to work offline and not connect to verify addresses for messages sent to Internet addresses.

When these dialogs are filled in, Exchange is configured for MSN and you can move on to the sign-up process.

MSN Settings

On the dialog that appears when you double-click the MSN desktop object, you find a button marked Settings. The dialog associated with this button is shown in Figure E.4. With this dialog, you set up the connection between MSN and your modem.

If everything in your system is properly set up, the settings dialog should be correctly set up, too. However, if you get problems when trying to log onto MSN, open this dialog and make sure your settings are correct. Double-check the modem settings especially.

FIGURE E.4.

The MSN Settings dialog lets you select access numbers, set dialing parameters, and configure your modem settings.

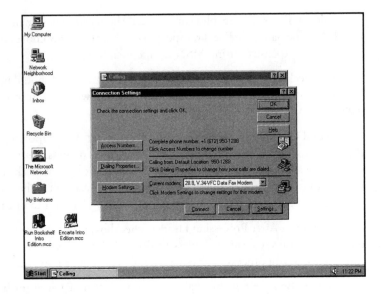

The MSN Sign Up

When you install MSN, an entry is added to your start menu. The first time you click this entry, a dialog appears so that you can begin the sign-up process. The sign-up process involves making a couple of calls to the network. The first call updates your system to the most current version of the MSN access software and sets up your access numbers. Access numbers are the numbers you call to connect to the network. Inside the U.S., the first call is to an 800 toll-free number.

When you connect to MSN, the latest version of the access software is automatically downloaded to you, an MSN icon is placed on your desktop, and you are disconnected. Double-click the icon on your desktop to begin the sign up. A dialog with three buttons guides you through the three steps of the process: entering personal information, entering payment information, and reading the rules. As you complete each section, it is marked with a big checkmark.

First you need to provide your personal information in the dialog shown in Figure E.5. Here you enter your name and address, along with phone information. The checkbox at the bottom left of the dialog, when checked, suppresses messages and mail communications to you about MSN services. If you do not want service providers to e-mail or bulk mail information about MSN to you, check this box.

Next you are asked to provide payment information in the payments dialog. To keep accounting costs at a minimum, MSN is directly billed to your credit-card account. You need to provide this information to set up your MSN account.

FIGURE E.5.

Fill in your personal information in this dialog.

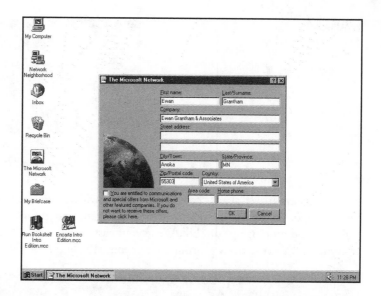

Finally, you are presented with a text box that details the rules and regulations you must adhere to in order to remain a member in good standing. Most of these rules are common sense things, such as not uploading copyrighted software for which you don't own the copyright, and not abusing other members with obscene language or defamatory messages. There is nothing in the rules that is onerous or difficult to comply with.

When you have fulfilled these three steps, you will see three large checkmarks that signal you to complete the process by connecting to MSN for the final part of sign up. When you are online, the dialog presented in Figure E.6 appears, asking you to select your personal user ID and a password.

The member ID is important and permanent. Each member must have a unique ID, which is used throughout the system as your name to other members. When you check into a chat session or send e-mail, you are identified by your member ID. For this reason, you should carefully consider the name you choose. If you only use MSN for recreation, a frivolous name might be appropriate; but if you decide at some time to use it for professional purposes, a name such as Master_Blaster might not be suitable. In any case, choose a name that you wouldn't be embarrassed for your mother to use in sending you e-mail messages.

If another member already has the same ID, you will be prompted to enter a second choice. Remember, also, that you cannot place spaces in the member ID. The best member names are a variation of your real name. However, if you have a common name like Bob Smith, you might need to be early or creative.

FIGURE E.6.

Your member ID will stay with you, so consider carefully before entering one.

When you have arrived at an acceptable name, you will be prompted for a password. Passwords are also important because they keep others from logging onto the network in your name, causing mischief, and running up your bill. Write your password down in a safe, secret place and keep it to yourself. You can freely give out your member ID, but never give someone your password.

> **TIP**
>
> Your member ID is your e-mail address. When you have your member ID registered, you also have an Internet e-mail address that can receive mail from anywhere in the world. Your Internet address is `<memberID>@MSN.COM`. For example, you can send e-mail to your favorite author using the address `EdTiley@MSN.COM`.

Logging On

Now that you have completed the sign-up process and configured Exchange to receive e-mail messages into your inbox, you are ready to log on and go exploring—and *exploring* is just the term. Most of the user interface of the Microsoft Network will be familiar to you because it uses Windows 95's Explorer as its basis.

When you double-click the MSN icon on your desktop or select the Microsoft Network from the Start Menu, the logon dialog shown in Figure E.7 appears. This dialog enables you to enter your member ID and password before clicking the Connect button.

To log onto MSN, just click the Connect button. Your modem is activated, MSN is dialed, and your member ID is presented to the network. If your member ID and password are correct, you are on your way.

When you are connected to MSN, two icons are placed into the Taskbar near the date. The first icon is a modem, complete with flashing lights that show you data transfer activity. Clicking the modem icon shows you the number of bytes of data that have been transferred in each direction.

In addition, a small MSN icon is also placed on the Taskbar. Double-clicking this icon pops up a message box that asks whether you want to disconnect from MSN. Click Yes and your connection is terminated.

Online Activity

When you log into MSN, two windows are opened. The first window is titled MSN Today and shows you a sort of a home page for MSN. In the main area of the screen are topics of interest that you can click to see what they are about. Along the left side of the window are the titles of other topics that you can explore simply by clicking the title. The Calendar of Events, which can be selected from here, enables you to check out scheduled happenings on the network, such as live chat sessions with top Microsoft personnel, sessions with noted Windows authorities, and so on. A sample MSN Today window is shown in Figure E.7.

FIGURE E.7.

The MSN Today window enables you to check out timely events, important articles, and announcements.

FIGURE E.8.

The MSN Central window is your starting point for exploring the many forums and services offered on MSN.

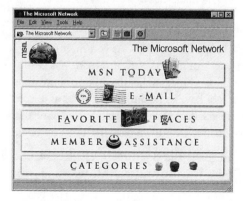

The second window that appears is called MSN Central. (See Figure E.8.) The MSN Central window is the My Computer of MSN in the sense that it is the top level. From MSN Central, you can branch out and explore the many forums and services offered on MSN.

> **TIP**
>
> If you ever close the MSN Today or MSN Central browsing window by accident, it is easy to get it opened up again. From MSN Central, choose MSN Today and the window will reopen. If, from MSN Today, you click on one of the shortcuts, the MSN Central browsing window will reopen, and you can click Favorite Places on the toolbar to get to a familiar jumping-off point.

The MSN Today Window

Although they are not marked as such, the pictures on the main page and the titles in the strip along the left side of the MSN Today window are shortcuts to other places. Think of MSN Today as being like an Internet Web page.

Each day, the MSN Today page is changed to reflect current happenings on MSN, topics of the day, and a convenient jumping-off point to the services offered on the Microsoft Network. Don't forget that the Calendar tab keeps you up-to-date on what is going on around the MSN. Chat sessions with guests in the Babbage Auditorium and other special events are scheduled all the time.

If you see something you like in the MSN Today page, all you have to do is click on the icon that's associated with the text you are reading. From there, everything is arranged in forms or Explorer style hierarchies.

The MSN Central Window

MSN Central is probably a bad name for the window you can use to navigate around MSN, because the title bar changes text every time you change to a new location. There is never a window on the screen marked MSN Central.

Take a look back at Figure E.8. As you might have guessed by now, the Explorer metaphor is a powerful one, and the MSN Central screen is Explorer-based. Each of the objects in the window is an Explorer object. Clicking on one of the objects takes you to the next level. Notice the toolbar. It might have some different icons, but it is still Explorer in the single pane view. There are the familiar Explorer tools at the left edge of the toolbar. The text box lets you navigate quickly and the folder button lets you move up one level with a single click.

Click on Categories and the window changes view to show you something like the view pictured in Figure E.9. As you can see, the window fills with folders that indicate the main headings for locations on MSN where you can find bulletin board systems (BBSs), file libraries for downloading, and chat sessions. Each BBS corresponds to a single topic. For example, if you double-click on the Science and Technology folder, you might see the MSN Central window change to something similar to the one shown in Figure E.10.

FIGURE E.9.

Clicking Categories in the MSN Central window lets you begin exploring the various BBS sections of MSN.

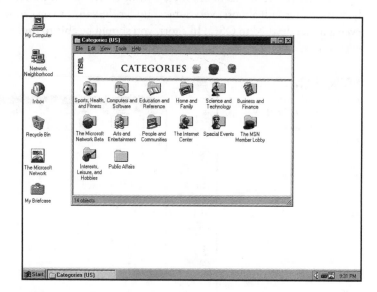

FIGURE E.10.

When you double-click on a topic folder in Categories, you move down a level so that you can see what areas are in that group.

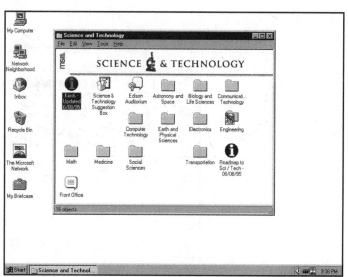

In Figure E.11, you can see that the Science and Technology folder's Electronics folder has been double-clicked to reveal four objects. The kiosk is a text file in RTF format that explains what the Electronics BBS is all about. The BBS is a place where people interested in electronics can share messages, and the Chat object lets you into a live online chat session on the subject of electronics. There is also a BBS for consumer electronics.

By the time you read this book, there will be scores (if not hundreds) of individual bulletin boards dealing with almost every subject under the sun. As you can see in Figure E.12, there is even a folder devoted to OS/2! In short, you should be able to find a location on MSN to deal with almost any topic you find interesting.

FIGURE E.11.

Bulletin boards, and there are many of them on MSN, are devoted to a single narrow topic.

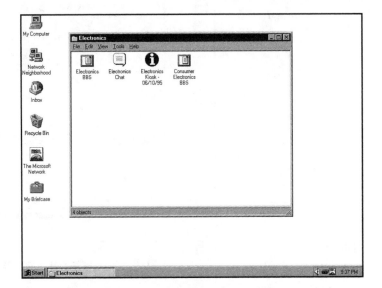

FIGURE E.12.

In the Computers and Software folder you can drill down to a section devoted to OS/2 Warp.

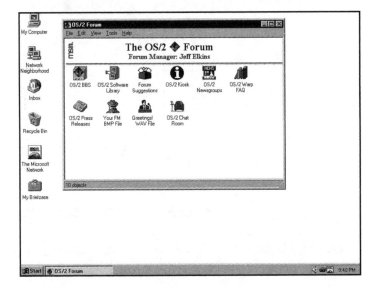

Microsoft Network Messaging

There are two areas where you will send and receive messages to and from other people. MSN's e-mail section provides a place where private messages can be exchanged between MSN members. MSN members can also send e-mail messages to anyone in the world who can be reached via the Internet. The Internet conduit also includes major online services such as CompuServe, Prodigy, America Online, MCI Mail, and any other Internet messaging hub in the world. In effect, you can send electronic mail to any one of the millions of computer users that are wired for e-mail themselves. You can also correspond electronically with other MSN members in the special interest BBS sections.

The main difference between the two methods is that you can use Exchange to provide your e-mail services for MSN and most other e-mail sources you use regularly, while messaging services in the BBSs are provided by MSN in real time without going through Exchange.

MSN E-Mail Using Exchange

Depending on how you have Exchange configured (in the Mail and Fax dialog of Control Panel), you can have Exchange automatically go to MSN and other e-mail sources when you double-click the Inbox object on the desktop. Alternatively, you can wait until you are online in MSN and click the e-mail object in the MSN Central window to collect MSN e-mail messages. Either way, the messages are placed into your Exchange inbox.

Figure E.13 shows a message received via Exchange. As you can see in the figure, Exchange also uses the Explorer metaphor. The Exchange window is divided into two panes. On the left side, various folders can be maintained for sorting and archiving your correspondence. In the right pane, you find all the messages contained in the selected folder. To display a message (as it is seen in Figure E.3), double-click the message in the right pane of Exchange. The message is displayed using a program that looks suspiciously like WordPad.

Take a few minutes to check out the buttons on the toolbar. Of immediate interest is the Reply button, which can be found on the left side of the toolbar next to the Print button. Clicking this button provides you with another message window where you can type your reply to incoming messages. Figure E.14 shows how this works. The same window style is used when you click the New Message button to originate a message to someone.

FIGURE E.13.

The Exchange inbox provides a single location where all your e-mail messages, from whatever source, can be read and responded to.

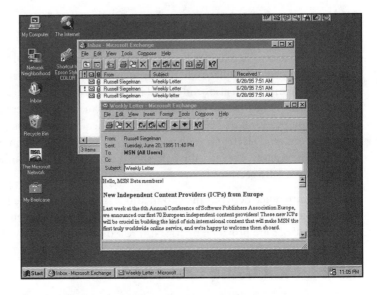

FIGURE E.14.

To reply to an incoming message, click the Reply button and enter your response.

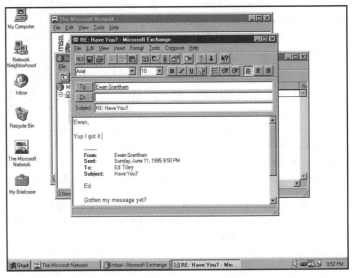

A number of settings can be found in the Microsoft Exchange properties dialog, which can be opened using the Tools | Options command in the Exchange menu. Under the Read tab, one of the checkboxes lets you automatically repeat the sender's message text when replying. This is sometimes helpful in reminding your correspondents of the last communication they sent. Often a reply fails to make the sender remember what he originally said to you. Repeating the original message text can help him to better follow the flow of messages back and forth and also creates a record of those messages.

When you reply to a message, it is automatically sent to the address of the person who sent the message to you. When you originate the message as new, you can select an address from the Exchange address book. When you have finished with your message, click the send button on the toolbar to save your reply or your original message. The text of your message, along with addressing information, is placed in the Outbox folder so that the message can be sent the next time you connect to MSN.

BBS Messaging

Sending and receiving messages in the various BBSs contained in MSN is a slightly different proposition. Figure E.15 shows the layout of messages in an MSN BBS.

FIGURE E.15.

BBS messages are arranged by threads with replies indented from the original message.

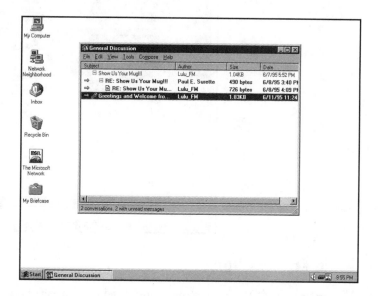

All of the messages currently contained in the BBS are arranged in a window. In the conversation view, those messages you have not read are marked with a red arrow and printed on-screen in bold type. The page icon of a message tells you that there are replies to the message if there is a plus sign in the icon. As you can see, messages are treated just like folders are treated in Explorer in the conversation view. You can also use the View menu of the window to arrange messages in the list view and to see just the files attached to messages.

Original messages and their replies generally deal with a single topic and are called a thread. As more and more replies are posted to the BBS, the thread is indented to the right of the original message.

To read a message, all you have to do is double-click on the message title. Figure E.16 shows the message reader window. The message reader is the same WordPad-style application. The toolbar has been altered to match the usage. Several of the toolbar buttons are worth investigating. The leftmost button enables you to create a new message. The save, print, cut, copy, and paste buttons do exactly what you expect them to do. Then, there is the Reply to BBS button that places your reply back into the BBS. The next group of three buttons takes you quickly to the previous, next, and next unread messages without closing and reopening the reader window. The rightmost group of three buttons takes you to the previous, next, and next unread conversations. In this context, a *conversation* means thread. The button farthest to the right lets you check on the status of downloading that you might be doing in the background.

FIGURE E.16.

The MSN reader for BBS messages is also a WordPad workalike.

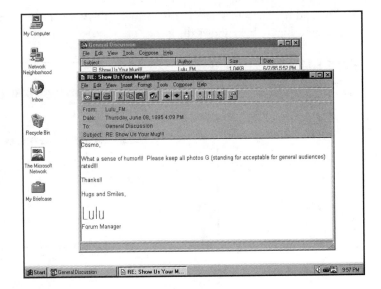

Avoid Ransom Notes

All messages on MSN are stored and transmitted in Rich Text Format. The beauty of RTF is that you can mix type fonts, sizes, and colors to produce visually interesting messages. As with all good things, you should make a couple of considerations before deciding to vary from the standard Arial type font. First, formatting the text can make the message physically much larger, which takes longer to display on the reader's screen. Keep in mind that not all MSN members will have the same high-speed modem you might have installed. Will they sit tight for two minutes waiting to benefit from your wisdom while the message is translated and readied for display?

Worst of all, however, is the fact that messages can end up looking like poor substitutes for ransom notes. See Figure E.17 for an example of what not to do!

Feel free to use color and type style for emphasis. A good rule of thumb is to never use more than two fonts in two sizes, or your messages will end up in the ransom note category.

FIGURE E.17.

Don't create ransom note messages. They only detract from what you are saying.

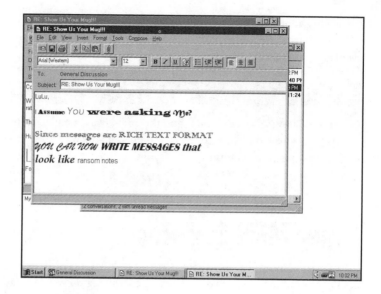

Attaching Files to Messages

If you want to send a binary file to someone as part of your message, it is as easy as sending the message. Like many other actions in Windows 95, there are several ways to attach a file to a message. If you click the paper clip icon in the toolbar, you will get a dialog similar to the one shown in Figure E.18.

FIGURE E.18.

Attaching files to messages is quick, easy, and can be done several ways.

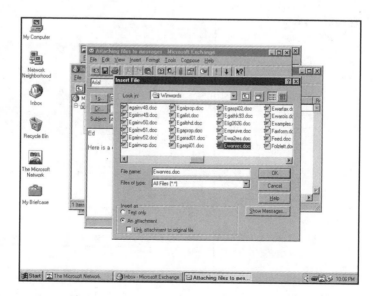

If you click the paper clip, you get a variation of the File Open dialog in which you can select the file to be attached. Alternatively, you can drag a file into the Compose Message window, or even copy and paste as you would when working within Explorer.

> **TIP**
>
> Long files sent as attachments should nearly always be placed into a ZIP file or some other compressed archive format before being attached to the message. It takes less time to upload the compressed file, your recipient will spend less time downloading it, and sending fewer bytes will be less expensive.

Other MSN Services

Please keep in mind that this chapter was written before MSN came online to the general public. Very few of the services you will see when you log on were available when this was written.

Internet Newsgroups

Internet newsgroups are like huge bulletin boards that have worldwide distribution. The Microsoft Network provides access to a number of newsgroups. As you can see in Figure E.19, the presentation is very similar to any other MSN BBS.

FIGURE E.19.

Internet newsgroups provide discussions on almost any topic you can think of.

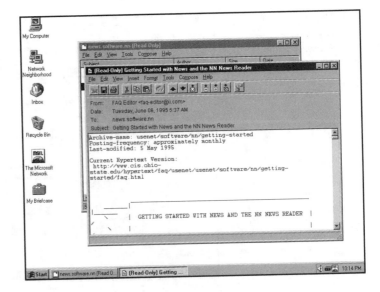

There are newsgroups on the Internet to cover just about any subject you might have an interest in, from help-wanted job postings to current affairs, computer software, and even matters of the heart. When you join a discussion in a newsgroup, unlike on MSN BBSs, you are not limited to only MSN members. Newsgroups are open and available to anyone with an Internet account.

Bookshelf and Encarta

So you have a paper to do on Brazil or the Ukraine, but you don't have an encyclopedia handy. You say it's midnight and you need to know the population of Toronto? No problem. MSN has online readers for the Intro Editions of both Microsoft Bookshelf and Microsoft Encarta. Just check out the Education and Reference folder, and then double-click the Microsoft Home Zone folder. There you will find folders for both Bookshelf and Encarta.

Before you can use either of these products, you must download the online reader files. Just double-click the install icon to begin the process. Figure E.20 shows the download for Bookshelf in progress. Encarta is found in a separate folder.

FIGURE E.20.

It really does take only about five minutes to download the reader software.

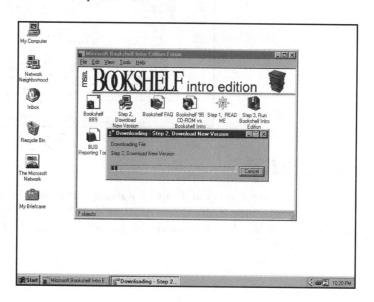

The online reader software for Bookshelf and Encarta is downloaded to your system as a self-extracting archive file that is automatically run and expanded onto your hard disk. When the process is complete—it takes about five minutes at 14,400 baud—you can click the Bookshelf or Encarta icon to begin searching for the information you are looking for. There is even a BBS where you can get together with other MSN members and talk about the best ways to find and use information.

Figure E.21 shows Microsoft Bookshelf in action as it displays a map of Eritrea, a new country in East Africa that was formerly part of Ethiopia. Embedded within the information are icons that let you hear the proper pronunciation of words or listen to the national anthem. Buttons across the top of the window enable you to restrict the search for information to a single book, or to search all the books contained in Bookshelf. To the left of the window is a search tool that lets you specify the information you are looking for. The response time, if you are using a fast modem, is surprisingly good.

FIGURE E.21.

Bookshelf and Encarta are available online 24 hours a day and are always updated to the latest version.

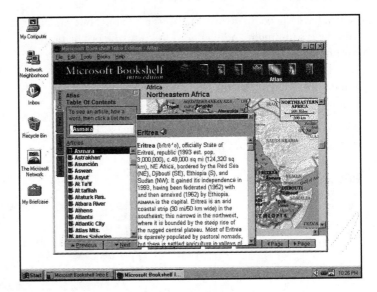

Summary

In this chapter, you have taken the quick walking tour of the Microsoft Network. MSN is a new commercial online service that is based on the Windows 95 Explorer metaphor. If you know how to use Windows 95, you already know how to use MSN.

Epilogue—The Future of Windows

by Ed Tiley

A few weeks before the Windows 95® operating system was released to the world, I had a chance to sit down and chat by telephone with Brad Silverberg of Microsoft. As Senior Vice President of the Personal Systems Division, Brad is in charge of the development of Windows 95 and MS-DOS®. Windows is his baby. He has been there since just after the birth of Windows 3.0, and has had the pleasures and rewards of seeing his vision grow. (Actually, I joined the company shortly after the launch of Windows 3.0. I can't say I was there at the birth.) If anybody has a handle on where Windows is going in the future, Brad does.

In the next few pages, you will find out just what Brad's perspective on Windows 95 and the future of Windows computing is. As you might expect, he is quite upbeat.

Ed: Over the last several months you have had more than half a million people testing Windows 95 to make sure it is solid. Is it ready? What is the reaction from your testers?

Brad: Response from Beta Testing has been fabulous. They've really been enthusiastic and supportive of the product. They are finding just how much more fun the product is to use, how productive they are, and how much more capable they are than they've been with, say, Windows 3.1. So we are very excited about the product. The team has done an incredible job of following through on all the millions and millions of details that's required to get a product like Windows 95 out the door and be successful.

Ed: Literally millions.

Brad: Literally millions, I mean it is a product unlike any other product that's ever been released. We've sold over 85 million copies of Windows 3.*x*; that's a lot of users with millions of configurations. If you look at the path of how PCs get used over the past five years and project forward for the next couple of years, you see a pretty dramatic shift. When we shipped Windows 3.1 on April 6, 1992, there were 10 million Windows users, and now we are up to 85 million.

Look at the different type of customer who is buying PCs and Windows compared to just three years ago. Before it was primarily business-oriented: people running Word, Microsoft Excel, or other productivity applications. While that is still true, the market has expanded in orders of magnitude beyond just the business-oriented productivity users into the home, and into small business. Something like 40 percent of all PCs being sold today are going into the home, and if you look at the growth, the compound annual growth is even higher. That's the fastest growing area in the business.

The focus that we have on making the PCs go from a data-processing device to an information appliance is really the focus of Windows 95. I really look at Windows 95 as a big step forward, a huge step forward compared to existing products on the market like Windows 3.1; but it's just a first step. It's really the first step in a whole new generation of products coming from Microsoft that are really focused on those key themes of a consumer-oriented information appliance and having the PC be fun.

Ed: Things have definitely changed since the days of the first PCs. You had to be a special type of person.

Brad: Yeah, a hacker who loved to tinker with all the low-level aspects of the PC. Today, you walk into a store like Costco or Sams and you see somebody wheeling along their cart, and they pick up, you know, a case of toilet paper, a case of canned corn, and a PC. And people's expectations are so high about what it means to be a consumer appliance. Delivering on that promise is really goal number one for us.

If you talk to everyday users, you find that they have a great sense of frustration that the PC is capable of doing so much more than they are really able to get out of it, and so the goal of Windows 95, and versions of Windows beyond that, is to really make it easy for people to unlock the power of the PC that they have.

Ed: What do you do about those people who are being required as part of their job to use a computer, but they really don't want to?

Brad: A lot of times they don't want to because they haven't really seen all the fun things and productive things that they can get out the PC once they learn how to use it. They have been harder to learn, and harder to use than we would like in the past. We need to make it a lot more accessible to people. Make it a lot more fun. Make it a lot less frustrating through better training materials, better design, and better applications.

Ed: Computers can get under your skin alright.

Brad: Look at people who play Doom. They just get totally enthralled playing some of these video games that are so cool. Other people spend their lives surfing the Internet because of the power of the PC to make their lives more fun and more enriched.

Anybody who has a PC at home with kids sees kids light up when they sit in front of a PC. They figure out how to use it, and they are able to enter a whole new world of education, making learning fun, and they don't possess the same phobias about technology that some adults have. Kids just love this stuff.

Ed: How are the adults taking to Windows 95?

Brad: As we bring people through our usability test and watch people get trained, they just light up, and we can't get it away from them. We are learning in corporation after corporation that they are finding it so much easier to train people on Windows 95 than they had expected. They had been hearing horror stories about how hard it might be with the new user interface and all. We're finding, in fact, that as corporations are beginning to run through their evaluation cycles, and begin to train people they begin to say, "Wow, this is great, this is really easy, we are going to be able to train a lot more people in less time." People are really getting turned on.

For example, we've run some very in-depth usability tests with an outside company called Usability Sciences Corporation. They took a broad range of existing PC users, people who have little experience, intermediate level experience, power user experience, enough people that we could get statistically projectible results. We gave them no formal training on Windows 95 whatsoever. We just set them inside Windows 95 and let them run through the online training materials that we ship with the product and we let them have a play period, then ran them through a set of tasks. Each task takes approximately 20 minutes. The third time they had run through the set of tasks, a total time on Windows 95 of about an hour and a half, they were already twice as productive than they were on Windows 3.1, and the level of satisfaction was something on the order of 95 to 98 percent of the people.

Ed: Well I can tell you from my own personal experience that when I have to go back and use Windows 3.1 on someone else's machine I find it incredibly frustrating; I'm forever right clicking on icons.

Brad: We're finding the exact same thing, Ed. Once someone takes the time to learn Windows 95, they will have found it a lot easier than they expected, and you can't get them to go back.

Ed: A few minutes ago you described Windows 95 as a first step.

Brad: Yeah, I think it's a sign of our commitment to really improving the end user experience when using a personal computer.

Ed: Let me ask a couple of questions in that regard. One of the things that Microsoft is doing is providing that end user experience with a broad range of operating system products. There's good old DOS, Windows 95, Windows NT™ Workstation, and Windows NT Server. There are a lot of the MS-DOS® features of Windows 95 that come from Windows NT, and assumedly a lot of Windows 95 features will end up in Windows NT.

Brad: A lot of stuff comes from Windows NT into Windows 95. They are very complementary systems.

Ed: How do they fit together? How do you differentiate between Windows 95 and Windows NT?

Brad: The best way I find to think about it is to take a step back and look at the missions of the two divisions of Microsoft. Take the mission of the Business Systems Division (BSD), which produces Windows NT Workstation and Windows NT Server, and contrast and compare that with the mission of the group that I'm in charge of, namely the Personal Systems Division (PSD) which developed Windows 95 and MS-DOS.

The BSD mission is focused on the enterprise corporate user, on delivering both the server platform for the enterprise as well as a work station product that is targeted for technical workstation users, for mission critical users, people in a corporate situation who need to run the most demanding type application and who want the most powerful, most secure, most robust system available and are less concerned with other aspects involved with some of the tradeoffs you have to make to achieve that. To them their job is to focus on that large corporate account, and to deliver the product that best meets that customer's needs, and to continue to push technology as far and as fast over time as they can.

The Personal Systems Division mission is focused on individual users (including corporations), home users, small office users, people who use personal computers for productivity applications. We focus on delivering products for the broadest number of users that run on the most mainstream type of hardware.

With Windows 95, our goals are to run fast on more modest hardware, including the installed base. We need to be compatible with people's existing devices, device drivers, and applications, both MS-DOS and Windows. And we are focused on the Intel *X*86 platform.

If you are running a trader's workstation, and you cannot afford for that workstation to go down you'll want Windows NT, but if you are running at home with a 4 or 8 meg system and you want to run games, both MS-DOS games and Windows-based games, and want to run devices that require particular device drivers, or you want to run Microsoft Word or Microsoft Excel, or a standard productivity application for a corporate environment, then Windows 95 is the right choice.

We converged on supporting common APIs, so both Windows NT and Windows 95 support Win16 and the Win32® APIs, so that a typical software developer can just write a single application and have it run on Windows NT as well as Windows 95. So, users who want to run applications don't really have to think about them as being Windows 95-based applications or Windows NT applications. They just think of them as Windows-based applications, and then choose the version of Windows that fits their needs.

Ed: So most people with Intel processors are going to be using Windows 95, which makes it the first mainstream 32-bit operating system. What does that do to software as we know it? Are there any killer apps on the horizon to look out for?

Brad: I think you are going to see a lot of exciting applications.

The first point I want to make about Windows 95 is that, just by itself, it's a great successor to Windows 3.1, Windows for Workgroups, and MS-DOS. If all you want to do is just run the same 16-bit applications that you've been running, Windows 95 is a great product. There is no reason to wait for 32-bit applications, Windows 95 is the best platform available for running those 16-bit applications.

At the same time there are going to be a lot of 32-bit applications coming out. I think Microsoft has already announced that it will be coming out with a version of Microsoft Office that's targeted at Windows 95. It seems every ISV (Independent Software Vendor) in the world is working on Windows 95-based applications so, soon after

Windows 95 comes out, you will see a whole plethora of very cool, new applications that take full advantage of Windows 95. Which ones of those turn out to be the killer app, boy, well if you've got the answer to that one.

Ed: I'd be writing it!

Brad: You'd be writing it, and you'd be looking to go public right now. Killer applications tend to be hard to predict.

Ed: They take the world by surprise.

Brad: They come up with a new paradigm that people hadn't been thinking of. I guess that's what makes them killer applications, because they are a whole new way of doing things that wasn't obvious beforehand. Once they take off, people wonder how they lived without them.

Ed: So if there is a killer app on the horizon, what area of computing would you guess it will come from?

Brad: Things like connectivity-oriented applications. If there is a killer app it will probably come from that area, something like e-mail, or groupware, or online services, integrated fax or telephony applications, something that has to do with connecting people together.

Ed: Another possible area is multimedia.

Brad: There are going to be some really killer multimedia apps when they come out on Windows 95. Whether that's a platform-defining application, I don't know. But because the underlying support of Windows 95 is so much better for multimedia, coupled with Plug and Play, which makes it so much easier for people to use multimedia based PCs, I think you are going to see some really stunning multimedia applications that come out for Windows 95.

We are also developing some new technology that we'll be delivering shortly after Windows 95, for the area of multimedia that I think brings multimedia to a whole new level. You've probably heard our announcement where we acquired RenderMorphics, the company that builds the highest performance 3-D libraries for PCs, so you'll likely be seeing developer kits and seeing us license fantastic 3-D capabilities for Windows. You will see higher quality multimedia titles that are so realistic you get lost in the title. Earlier titles were interesting, but they weren't dynamic and powerful enough so that you really felt like you got lost in the medium. You still felt a little bit of distance from those titles. We're getting to the point now that the quality, performance, and the capabilities of these multimedia titles is so exiting that you really do get lost in them. It's like you're watching a movie in a big-screen theater; you get lost in the medium, rather than thinking you are in a level removed from it. I think you'll see some of that with Windows 95. We make that possible with the power and the quality of what we are doing for multimedia, and I think that will create a whole new class of applications.

As big as multimedia is growing today, I think it's going to get even bigger once Windows 95 comes out.

I've seen some of the applications that some of the third-party companies are doing for Windows 95 that should hit later this year, or early next year, that take full advantage of some of the technologies that we have developed, and are continuing to develop. They are just stunning. The difference between the old days and what you'll be seeing soon in multimedia is like going from character mode to graphics mode.

Ed: Well, along those lines, you've also just recently joined up with the entertainment dream team, haven't you?

Brad: That's right.

Ed: Spielberg, Geffen, and Katzenberg! And they're talking about delivering titles for Christmas of 1996, right?

Brad: That's right. That's coming out of a different division, so I'm not completely up to speed on what's happening there, but, we've shown them all the things that the PC is capable of today with Windows 95, and some of the investments we are continuing to make, and they are really excited. They see how this is going to be a real sea change in how PCs get used that allows traditional content developers, Hollywood-type people who specialize in telling creative stories, to deliver those stories in new and exciting ways.

The power of the PC has gotten to the point where they can deliver that now in 95–96. We at Microsoft are super excited about the opportunity to work with a Steven Spielberg. Boy, that is the opportunity of a lifetime! I was lucky enough to meet him when he was here, and sat down and talked to him for about a half an hour. I was lucky enough to have dinner with Jeffrey (Katzenberg) the night before, and meet with the three of them. They are so creative, they are just coming out with fabulous ideas one after the other. To be able to work with them and see those ideas come true on a PC, we are very lucky and very excited to be able to get into this kind of thing.

Ed: The whole idea of what computers do is changing, isn't it? It seems to me that as video and other forms of multimedia take hold, the general trend moves away from the old text based information, word processing, spreadsheet kinds of things where you are maybe conveying the same information but in entirely different ways.

Brad: We have gone from text mode, basically word processing or spreadsheet applications that have a pretty narrow audience, to graphics mode where things are a lot more visual, making powerful PC's accessible to millions of more customers. With multimedia, I think it's the next level. It really does turn the PC into an experience, an interactive experience, a consumer content device like audio CDs or VCRs.

Ed: How does that change work?

Brad: That's very different from writing a memo, and I think it's a huge transition. Multimedia and the online services are going to change the way people live. They are going to be in every home, in every business, a very high bandwidth interactive multimedia in 3-D with motion. Once they experience it, it will become part of people's everyday lives.

Ed: It used to be that reading was a major form of entertainment in the home. Forty or fifty years ago, practically everyone subscribed to magazines like *Colliers* and the *Saturday Evening Post*. Radio, and especially television, came along and nearly killed reading for pleasure, or so it seems. It has had impacts on society in terms of literacy rates and that sort of thing. What does multimedia computing do in that regard? What I see happening is that we're moving away from the written word as the major form of formal communication?

Brad: I don't know; that may be true for the printed word, but I don't know if that's necessarily true for the written word, because I see my kids just engross themselves in activities on their PC. My six-year-old daughter (she turned six today) is learning to type, and my ten-year old son is a pretty good typist. They are able to explore a visual, multimedia world with a lot of text in it. I see my son soak up new types of information that he never would have done in the past. I see my daughter learning how to do mathematics in ways that really augment what the schools are capable of doing, and I am hopeful that we'll see a renaissance in people's interest in learning, being able to access information and be productive, and have fun too.

Ed: So you think that these new expressions of information actually bode well for literacy.

Brad: I do. I see what has happened to my own kids. To be honest, Ed, five years ago I was a little more skeptical about it, but I see how it's changed my own kids. I see how much they are interested in learning, and how much their thirst for learning revolves around a lot of these edutainment titles. My six-year-old, when she was five, we got a hamster for her, and she told me, "Hey Daddy, did you know that a hamster is a nocturnal animal?" This is out of a five year-old! I said, "I wasn't aware of that. Do you know what a nocturnal animal means?" She goes, "Well, yeah, that means he sleeps a lot during the day and he's active at night." I asked her how she knew that, and she said, "Well, I saw that on Encarta®."

This was something that completely blew me away to have a five-year-old girl tell me about how hamsters are a nocturnal animal. We were reading a book last night, and it had a picture of an elephant, and she said, "I can tell that's an African elephant, not an Indian elephant." "Well how do you know that?" I asked, and she talked about the distinguishing characteristics. This, from a six year old girl, and she gets a lot of this from playing from the PC.

Ed: Hmm, maybe I should be a little less skeptical myself. Well, since Encarta is online on the Microsoft Network, let's switch gears to that topic for a minute. I know MSN is not your baby.

Brad: That's correct.

Ed: Still, how do you see Windows 95 and MSN coming together. After all, MSN seems to be an extension of Windows 95. It's definitely different from my old, familiar CompuServe.

According to a Microsoft white paper, fewer than 10 percent of Windows users and fewer than 4 percent of U.S. households subscribe over all to online services.

Brad: I think that shows that the existing services really haven't tapped into or found the right formula for delivering information in a way that really entices customers to want to use it; it's too hard, and it's not that much fun to use. What we've tried to do is make it as seamless as possible with the environment that the user is used to, to make it as easy as possible to sign up for, and to make it as fun as we can, with a very broad range of content that will provide and build a real sense of community. That's what people are looking for when they go to these online services. Besides just information, they are also looking for a sense of community, people to hang out with, talk to about their various interests, and that is really what we are trying to accomplish with MSN. We believe that if we can deliver an online service that is fun, easy, and provides that sense of community, we think we will do well and help bring people into this new connected environment that's worldwide.

Ed: Well, if you can add the other prong and make it real inexpensive, that will indeed foster the explosion.

Brad: Well, the prices that we have talked about from this end are substantially lower than what the current competitive services are charging today. As you know, it's awful easy to run up a big bill on some of these existing services.

Ed: Yes! My CompuServe bill gets horrendous.

Brad: CompuServe bills can get pretty big, and that's good to a certain extent. It shows that people see that there is a lot of value in the services they provide; but it's always a bear to get it really broad, and we'd like to help to make the service very broadly available for millions of everyday people, to help enrich their lives. Also I think there's lots of opportunity for applications to really take advantage of online services. For instance, you can buy a reference application and get online updates, online extensions to your CD-ROM-based application that you may have purchased to keep things continuously up to date, continually fresh.

Ed: That's kind of happening with both Encarta and Bookshelf® on MSN in online form.

Brad: You could do the same with the Complete Baseball product the consumer division came out with last year. If you wanted to get the up-to-date stats during the season, you could dial up and get all of the information and have it be integrated into the product. I think you will see a lot of applications coming out over the next year or two that are stand-alone applications that have an online component that brings currency to that application. Currency in the sense of being current rather than the monetary.

Ed: Speaking of currency, in both senses, some time back Microsoft announced it was forming strategic alliances with consumer electronics firms. Where does that fit in with Windows 95? Am I going to be able to program a VCR using Windows 95 at some point?

Brad: Well certainly, maybe not Windows 95 in '95, but as we look forward at how we want to evolve Windows, the whole market is really central to who we believe our customer is, and anything that we can do to enhance the experience of PCs in the home environment are things we are looking into.

I think it would be cool to be able to control your microwave oven from a Windows-based PC or a hand-held Windows device. But putting a Windows-based LCD screen on your microwave? I am less confident that you'll see that, because you can do a lot better interface on your Windows-based machine than you can on a microwave, so I think what you will see more often is that people are using their Windows-based PC to control home devices, or have hand-held Windows-based devices that you walk up in front of your television, and be able to control your television, or walk up in front of your VCR and control your VCR with the nice interface that is on your hand-held device or the PC—rather than putting all that cost inside a consumer appliance.

If you had to pay twice as much for a VCR to have a nice display, people might not want to do it, but if you could hook it up to your PC to program it, then it's a different ball game.

I don't know if you've seen these, but to give you an example of what we have done that points toward the future is the watch that we worked on with Timex, the Timex DataLink watch. Have you seen this at all?

Ed: I have not held one in my hands, but I have read a little bit about it.

Brad: It's a watch, like a digital Ironman type of watch from Timex that has a little CPU inside that is able to communicate with the PC. It has the capability of storing a bunch of phone numbers, and appointments, and in fact integrates with your Sched-ule+ calendar that you may keep on your PC. All the capabilities of the watch are accessible through the PC. It comes with a floppy diskette that you install in your PC and you program your watch from your PC. You hit a button on the PC and it transmits the information to the watch.

Now if you've ever had one of these digital watches, trying to figure out how to get all of the features out of them is not always easy…

Ed: Using three little silver buttons?

Brad: Right. Using three little silver buttons and no manual. If you want to set an alarm, you may not be able to figure that out, or you may want to enter phone numbers with a little message, but that is pretty hard to do on these three little buttons, but from a PC it's trivial. You get a nice little menu, fill it out, and do exactly what you want, and you hit OK to transmit. Put your watch in front of it, and it transmits, and it's fabulous. I think that's more the type of model that will be fruitful in the future rather than trying to put all the intelligence in the PC inside a low cost device.

Ed: Makes sense. Lately it seems that every time I turn around some new bit of technology amazes me. Okay, the watch is now, but let me ask you to get out your crystal ball. What kind of a computer do you expect to be using 25 years from now?

Brad: Twenty-five years from now! Boy, you really should talk to Nathan who's our futurist visionary to think 25 years out.

Ed: Well pick a number that's comfortable.

Brad: Well, I'll tell you, Ed, the PC that I'm using today is the same one that I used four years ago, so I tend to be a fairly retro in my choice of PCs. I like to use PCs that are more representative of what our typical user uses today, although the machines I have at home are substantially faster because I want to run all of the cool games for the kids.

I think in the next few years you'll see a lot more computing power that is really dedicated toward these communication aspects I've been talking about, whether it's tying into the Internet, or other online services like the Microsoft Network, telephony applications, data applications, allowing the PC to operate as an unattended appliance at your home while preserving power when they're idle.

I think you'll see Plug and Play telecommunication peripherals, modems that are able to transmit data and voice simultaneously, and really tight integration between the multimedia and communication functions of the PC. I think we went from a text mode device to a graphics mode device that was oriented toward data processing applications, and now the next generation is toward a personal communication information appliance.

Ed: Another information revolution in the making. You guys may not think of yourselves this way, but Microsoft has literally changed the world in the last few years.

Brad: That's always been our mission from the start. The company is 20 years old this year, and our mission has been, from day one, a PC on every desk and in every home. We've believed in the power of the PC to change the way people work and the way they live their daily lives. That's always been our dream, we've been driven by that, we continue to be driven by that. We see it coming true in businesses, we see it coming true now in homes where 40 percent of all new PCs being sold in the US go to the home and 25 percent of all American homes have PCs.

We think by making PCs live up to the promise of being information appliances, by being as easy to use as a color TV, or other electronic devices, that we will be able to put a lot more information in people's hands and allow them to get access to the information that they need, and to have much more control over their lives, to allow them to educate themselves and to educate their children to better their lives.

PCs have become very popular in the schools. We have been very active in the schools, supporting them and donating equipment—we have a number of outreach programs where we go out into the community and train kids, particularly in underprivileged areas to learn how to use these PCs, and they just light up. It's that sense of excitement in learning that is particularly important in those types of underprivileged homes, to get the kids to feel that learning is a great thing, and get turned on to the power of what PCs can do.

I think PCs, particularly with connection to online services and multimedia applications, particularly for edutainment titles, will give people in the future a lot more control and a lot more freedom to run their lives in ways that they are responsible for. So I am very optimistic about how PCs and Microsoft products can help play a role in changing society for the better. You come to Microsoft and you talk to people here, that vision of helping change society for the better everyday is really what fires it up.

Ed: Brad, our time is about up, and I know you need to get back to helping to shape that future. Thanks a million for sharing your thoughts with us today. I really appreciate you taking the time.

Brad: No problem, you're welcome, I'll talk to you later.

Ed: Thanks again, good-bye.

Brad: Good-bye.

So there you have it—Brad Silverberg's look into the future of Windows and the world. Make no mistake about it, Brad's contributions to Windows, and the continuing vision of Microsoft and its people, are helping to shape the world that all of us will be sharing in the coming years. It's going to be an exciting ride.

INDEX

Add to Your Sams Library Today with the Best Books for Programming, Operating Systems, and New Technologies

The easiest way to order is to pick up the phone and call

1-800-428-5331

between 9:00 a.m. and 5:00 p.m. EST.
For faster service please have your credit card available.

ISBN	Quantity	Description of Item	Unit Cost	Total Cost
0-672-30521-3		Teach Yourself Windows 95 Programming in 21 Days, 2E	$35.00	
0-672-30765-0		Navigating the Internet with Windows 95	$25.00	
0-672-30611-5		Your Windows 95 Consultant	$19.99	
0-672-30568-2		Teach Yourself OLE Programming in 21 Days (Book/CD)	$39.99	
0-672-30667-0		Teach Youself Web Publishing with HTML in a Week	$25.00	
0-672-30448-1		Teach Yourself C in 21 Days, Bestseller Edition	$24.95	
0-672-30499-6		Delphi Unleashed (Book/CD)	$45.00	
0-672-30737-5		World Wide Web Unleashed, 2E	$35.00	
0-672-30714-6		Internet Unleashed, 2E	$39.99	
0-672-30520-8		Your Internet Consultant: The FAQs of Online Life	$24.99	
0-672-30459-7		Curious about the Internet?	$14.99	
0-672-30485-6		Navigating the Internet, Deluxe Edition (Book/Disk)	$29.95	
0-672-30595-X		Education on the Internet	$25.00	
0-672-30599-2		Tricks of the Internet Gurus	$35.00	
		Shipping and Handling: See information below.		
		TOTAL		

❑ 3 ½" Disk

❑ 5 ¼" Disk

Shipping and Handling: $4.00 for the first book, and $1.75 for each additional book. Floppy disk: add $1.75 for shipping and handling. If you need to have it NOW, we can ship product to you in 24 hours for an additional charge of approximately $18.00, and you will receive your item overnight or in two days. Overseas shipping and handling adds $2.00 per book and $8.00 for up to three disks. Prices subject to change. Call for availability and pricing information on latest editions.

201 W. 103rd Street, Indianapolis, Indiana 46290

1-800-428-5331 — Orders   1-800-835-3202 — FAX   1-800-858-7674 — Customer Service

Book ISBN 1-672-30474-0

PLUG YOURSELF INTO...

MACMILLAN INFORMATION SUPERLIBRARY™

que · SAMS PUBLISHING · Hayden Books · que COLLEGE · NRP · alpha books · Brady · ADOBE PRESS

THE MACMILLAN INFORMATION SUPERLIBRARY™

Free information and vast computer resources from the world's leading computer book publisher—online!

FIND THE BOOKS THAT ARE RIGHT FOR YOU!

A complete online catalog, plus sample chapters and tables of contents give you an in-depth look at *all* of our books, including hard-to-find titles. It's the best way to find the books you need!

- ● STAY INFORMED with the latest computer industry news through our online newsletter, press releases, and customized Information SuperLibrary Reports.

- ● GET FAST ANSWERS to your questions about MCP books and software.

- ● VISIT our online bookstore for the latest information and editions!

- ● COMMUNICATE with our expert authors through e-mail and conferences.

- ● DOWNLOAD SOFTWARE from the immense MCP library:
  - Source code and files from MCP books
  - The best shareware, freeware, and demos

- ● DISCOVER HOT SPOTS on other parts of the Internet.

- ● WIN BOOKS in ongoing contests and giveaways!

What's on the
CD-ROM

CD-ROM Installation Instructions

The included disc contains new 32-bit Windows 95 applications, best-of-breed 16-bit applications, source code from the book, and much more. The CD-ROM is designed to be explored using a "Guide to the CD-ROM" program (\CDGUIDE\CDGUIDE.EXE).

Instructions for Windows 95 Users:

If Windows 95 is installed on your computer, and you have the AutoPlay feature enabled, the Guide program will start automatically whenever you insert the disc into your CD-ROM drive.

Instructions for Windows 3.x Users:

If you are running Windows 3.1, or have the Windows 95 AutoPlay feature disabled, run INSTALL.EXE from the root directory of the CD-ROM. INSTALL creates a Program Manager group named "Programming Windows 95", and a directory on your hard drive named "\WPU". When INSTALL ends, the "Guide to the CD-ROM" program will start automatically. An icon in the "Programming Windows 95" group allows you to restart the "Guide to the CD-ROM" application without rerunning INSTALL.

NOTE: The "Guide to the CD-ROM" program requires at least 256 colors. For best results, set your monitor to display between 256 and 64,000 colors. A screen resolution of 640 by 480 pixels is also recommended. If necessary, adjust your monitor settings before using the CD-ROM.

To learn how to use the "Guide to the CD-ROM" program, press the Tutorial button which appears on the the first screen, or press F1 from any screen in the program.